Behavior Modification in Applied Settings

Sixth Edition

Alan E. Kazdin

Yale University

WADSWORTH

TM

THOMSON LEARNING

Australia • Canada • Mexico • Singapore • Spain
• United Kingdom • United States

WADSWORTH

THOMSON LEARNING

Psychology Editor: Marianne Taflinger
Publisher: Vicki Knight
Assistant Editor: Jennifer Wilkinson
Editorial Assistant: Suzanne Wood
Marketing Manager: Marc Linsenman
Marketing Assistant: Jenna Burrill
Print Buyer: Karen Hunt
Permissions Editor: Joohee Lee

Production Coordinator: Michael McConnell, Graphic World Publishing Services
Copy Editor: Mamata Reddy
Cover Designer: Cassandra Chu
Cover Image: PhotoDisc
Compositor: Graphic World
Printer: Von Hoffman Press, Inc. / Custom Printing

Printed in the United States of America
1 2 3 4 5 6 7 04 03 02 01 00

Library of Congress Cataloging-in-Publication Data
Kazdin, Alan E.
  Behavior modification in applied settings /
Alan E. Kazdin.—6th ed.
    p. cm
  Includes bibliographical references and index.
  ISBN 0-534-34899-8 (alk. paper)
  1. Behavior modification. 2. Psychology, Applied. I. Title
BF637.B4 K4 2000
153.8'5—dc21   00-032496

Wadsworth/Thomson Learning
10 Davis Drive
Belmont, CA 94002-3098
USA

For more information about our products, contact us:
Thomson Learning Academic Resource Center
1-800-423-0563
http://www.wadsworth.com

International Headquarters
Thomson Learning
International Division
290 Harbor Drive, 2nd Floor
Stamford, CT 06902-7477
USA

UK/Europe/Middle East/South Africa
Thomson Learning
Berkshire House
168-173 High Holborn
London WC1V 7AA
United Kingdom

Asia
Thomson Learning
60 Albert Street, #15-01
Albert Complex
Singapore 189969

Canada
Nelson Thomson Learning
1120 Birchmount Road
Toronto, Ontario M1K 5G4
Canada

To Leon and Harry and their enduring presence

Contents

Preface

The purpose of this book is to provide an introduction to behavior modification techniques in applied settings. The major focus is on the application of operant conditioning principles, implementation of behavior modification techniques, and assessment and evaluation of program effectiveness. The applications cover a variety of settings, such as hospitals, institutions, schools, the home, day-care centers, businesses and industry, and communities, as well as outpatient applications for clients who come for treatment. By emphasizing the application of operant procedures, details are provided that would ordinarily be sacrificed in a cursory review of the entire domain of behavior modification. Yet, the focus is one of emphasis rather than one of exclusion. Because of their increased use in applied settings, procedures that rely on other conceptual views, such as social learning theory and cognitively based interpretations of behavior, are also discussed.

An enormous number of books on behavior modification have appeared. These books include introductory manuals designed for specific audiences, such as parents, teachers, or mental health workers, and scholarly texts that present theoretical issues and review the field generally. There is an obvious hiatus between "how to" manuals and extensive scholarly reviews that de-emphasize applied research in behavior modification. Behavioral techniques in clinical and applied settings have been well studied, and recommendations for treatment can often be derived from research findings. A need exists for a text that integrates research and practice for audiences of diverse disciplines who wish to learn about behavior modification. In this book, I attempt to emphasize applied research and clinical intervention techniques to achieve a balance not usually found in other texts.

Like the previous editions, the sixth edition discusses and illustrates major techniques for altering behavior and the conditions that influence their effectiveness. This edition reflects several developments within the field. First, and perhaps foremost, there has been increased attention to functional analysis, the identification of "causes" of behavior, and use of this information to develop interventions. A new chapter has been added to accord the attention this topic deserves and to convey the interrelations of assessment and intervention. Second, in this edition, more attention is provided to antecedent events and their use and influence on behavior. Here too research has elaborated how these events can be used to develop and alter behavior. Third, the application of any intervention can raise broad social and ethical issues, related to the goals and means to attain them. Because behavior modification has been applied so broadly to improve the functioning of individuals, groups (e.g., in classrooms, hospitals), and society at large, social and ethical issues are given special attention in this revision and elaborated in a separate chapter.

Apart from these specific changes, there are additional changes that are woven throughout in this edition. Applications of behavioral intervention have continued to proliferate and address diverse areas of education, treatment, prevention, rehabilitation, and functioning in everyday life. An effort has been made to illustrate the diversity of applications, for example, as reflected in prevention, treatment, and management of physical diseases such as AIDS, cancer, and diabetes; diverse facets of parenting and child rearing over the course of child development; the care of elderly persons; child abuse and neglect; personal safety and productivity in business and industry; and treatment of social, emotional, and psychiatric problems for which people seek help.

In addition, I have conveyed more clearly than in prior editions how three broad themes characterize behavior modification: assessment, intervention, and evaluation. As behavior modification has developed over the years and has become more popular among parents, teachers, and the public at large, it is critically important to convey what behavior modification is, how it works, and why the evidence has been so favorable. So-called behavior modification programs often consist of superficial efforts to throw rewards at behavior or to use abusive punishment (e.g., hours or days of isolation) under the guise of some principle or technique used in behavior modification (e.g., reinforcement, punishment). The central feature of behavior modification in applied settings is how the task of changing behavior is approached and not a compilation of techniques or a bag of tricks. Consequently, in this edition considerable time is devoted to describing how behavior is analyzed, measured, and evaluated. Behavior modification does include techniques as well and how these ought to be administered to achieve change is detailed and illustrated with many examples from research and from everyday life.

Apart from reflecting new developments of the field and expanded areas of application, this edition provides updated information regarding the techniques and their effects and limitations. This revision has encompassed many different substantive areas. For example, progress has been made in identifying techniques to promote maintenance of behavior change and transfer of change to new settings once behavioral programs have been terminated; in developing self-control and cognitively based techniques for use in applied settings; and in extending interventions to many areas of everyday life. This edition not only provides contemporary examples but presents new techniques, procedural variations, and research findings as well. Advances with many reinforcement and punishment techniques reflect creative practices that were not available, widely used, or carefully evaluated only a few years ago.

Because both research and application are important in this book, several examples are described throughout. The examples draw from classic studies, latest advances from research, and applications from everyday life and experience. Behavior modification techniques are often implemented and evaluated in carefully controlled research. It is important to convey how the techniques can be used in everyday contexts as well. In addition, at the end of each chapter, exercises are provided for students to apply key concepts of the chapter. Thus, students are encouraged to develop their own examples as they apply the techniques or methods discussed in the chapter.

All of the chapters have been extensively revised and new chapters have been added. However, the overall organization of the book is similar to that of the previous editions. Chapters 1 and 2 place the behavioral approach, broadly conceived, in historical context and detail assumptions, characteristics, and principles that underlie applications of behavioral techniques. One of the most distinct characteristics of behavior modification is the careful assessment of behavior and evaluation of treatment techniques. How to define problems, to move from concepts to observable behavior, and methods of assessing these behaviors are detailed (Chapter 3). The move from assessment to intervention is nicely illustrated by methods of identifying what factors may be controlling behavior. Functional analysis (Chapter 4) provides a methodology of identifying possible controlling factors, testing their influence on behavior, and using the resulting information to achieve therapeutic change.

I mentioned the importance of evaluation in behavior modification. Methods of evaluating behavior-change techniques and deciding whether the change is sufficient or important are also detailed (Chapter 5). A major part of the text elaborates positive and negative reinforcement, punishment, and extinction (Chapters 6, 7, and 8). Different technique options, factors that dictate program effectiveness, issues, and limitations are discussed in each chapter. Special technique variations to enhance program effectiveness, self-control techniques, and cognitively based techniques are detailed in separate chapters (Chapters 9, 10, and 11). Chapter 12 covers response maintenance and transfer of training, areas where considerable progress continues to be made. Chapter 13 focuses on the social, ethical, and legal contexts in which behavior modification is conducted. This chapter includes key considerations in the goals and means selected in intervention programs, ethical and legal issues, and professional guidelines for providing interventions. Chapter 14, the final chapter, continues the discussion of these broad issues by conveying challenges that emerge in applying behavioral techniques, limitations of the interventions, and current directions in intervention research more generally.

Several aspects of the text have been designed to aid the instructor and student. Outlines at the beginning of each chapter convey the content, direction, and key points that are to be covered. Examples of principles and techniques are provided throughout the book. More tables are provided than in past editions to summarize key points and concepts and to facilitate mastery of the content. At the end of each chapter exercises are provided to encourage students to apply key concepts to design or evaluate a specific intervention or to solve a problem in repairing a program that is not working very well. Also, key terms are provided at the end of the chapters. Students who complete the exercises and understand the terms will have mastered the core content of the chapters. For students and instructors interested in additional details about contents of the chapters, select references for further or supplementary reading are provided at the end of each chapter. For the student, a glossary is included at the end of the book to help review concepts introduced in the text. For the instructor, a test-item manual is available to develop exams of varied formats.

Many people have contributed significantly to completion of the book. In particular, I am grateful to Professors Nathan Azrin (Nova Southeastern University), Thomas R. Kratochwill (University of Wisconsin), Maura Roberts (Arizona State University), and Roger Harnish (Rochester Institute of Technology), who provided reviews to guide the revision. In addition, scores of students too numerous to name provided recommendations on the content and supporting material. Special appreciation is extended to both my daughters, Nicole and Michelle who have enhanced my comprehension of behavior-change techniques described in this book to alter parental behavior. They have taught a broader lesson and have helped me realize how much of human behavior I cherish but do not understand.

During the period in which this work was completed, my research has been supported by the Leon Lowenstein Foundation, the William T. Grant Foundation, and the National Institute of Mental Health (MH59029). Yale University is a very supportive environment and has provided colleagues—faculty and students—who have greatly influenced my thinking. I am grateful for each of these sources of support.

Alan E. Kazdin

About the Author

Alan E. Kazdin, Ph.D., is the John M. Musser Professor of Psychology at Yale University, Professor in the Child Study Center (Child Psychiatry) and Director of the Yale Child Conduct Clinic, an outpatient treatment service for children and their families. He received his Ph.D. in clinical psychology from Northwestern University (1970). Prior to coming to Yale, he was on the faculty of the Pennsylvania State University and the University of Pittsburgh School of Medicine. He has been a fellow of the Center for Advanced Study in the Behavioral Sciences, President of the Association for the Advancement of Behavior Therapy, recipient of awards from the American Psychological Association and the Association for Advancement, and chairman of the psychology department at Yale. He has been editor of various journals (*Journal of Consulting and Clinical Psychology, Behavior Therapy, Psychological Assessment,* and *Clinical Psychology: Science and Practice*). Currently, he is Editor of the *Current Directions in Psychological Science*. His research focuses treatment for children and adolescents, especially the treatment of aggressive and antisocial behavior, processes involved in behavior change. He has authored or edited over 35 books on treatment, child and adolescent disorders, and methodology and research design. Some of his recent books include:

The Encyclopedia of Psychology

Psychotherapy for Children and Adolescents

Research Design in Clinical Psychology (3rd ed.)

Conduct Disorder in Childhood and Adolescence (2nd ed.)

Methodological Issues and Strategies in Clinical Research (2nd ed.)

Single-Case Research Designs: Methods for Clinical and Applied Settings

Cognitive Behavioral Interventions (with L. Craighead, W.E. Craighead, & M.J. Mahoney)

CHAPTER 1

Introduction

Virtually everyone is interested in changing behavior. As individuals, we may wish to change many facets in ourselves, as illustrated by New Year's resolutions or promises we make to ourselves to eat less; exercise more; spend more time with family and friends; or give more time, money, or thought to charity or those less fortunate. Even though most of these intentions may not materialize, they are genuine efforts to change our ways. Of course, most of us are such wonderful individuals there is not much to work on in ourselves. Consequently, much of the change in which we are interested is in the behaviors of others in our everyday life. Lovers, spouses, parents, teachers, roommates, co-workers, and others invariably wish to change some facet of the behaviors of others with whom they are interacting. For example, parents want to develop scores of habits, skills, interests, talents, and values in their children and these translate to changing or developing behaviors. Apart from changing ourselves or others, change is of interest on a larger scale. At a societal or indeed global level, we would like to decrease violence, aggression, criminal activity, automobile accidents, cruelty to living things and to increase healthy living styles, positive parenting, safety, and conservation.

Of course, it is not too difficult to identify what we want to change or even to come up with a reasonable-sounding way of achieving them. For example, television, magazines, newspapers, and self-help books tell us how to accomplish our goals. If one *really* wants to stop cigarette smoking, get in physical shape, lose 30 pounds, stop drinking, or make a personal fortune, the advertisements say we merely have to take a pill, buy one of the many exercise machines that gives a "complete workout," or listen to a set of tapes that we can buy with one or two easy payments. Obviously, such solutions to key problems are not solutions at all. They mobilize hope briefly, but the hope usually is dashed by the fact that difficult problems usually do not have simple solutions. Alas, behavior modification, the topic of this book, is not another simple solution.

The question of how one changes behavior is important and has extremely broad implications. Behavior modification brings something special to the challenge of changing behavior. Although it is hardly a panacea, behavior modification draws heavily on scientific research to develop and change behavior. Scientific research is drawn on in two ways. First, behavior modification draws on the knowledge developed from animal and human studies about how behavior emerges, develops, and changes and the many factors that can be used to influence behavior. Knowledge is always incomplete, so much of what there is to know is not yet fully known. Nevertheless, the research available has served as a basis for changing behavior in many areas of society. Second, behavior modification draws on scientific methods to evaluate the effects of interventions. Evaluation consists of specifying the goals and the means of achieving these goals, examining whether behavior has changed and whether an intervention really achieved its goals. No intervention is likely to be effective for all persons to whom it is applied, even if this is the most effective medication, surgery, diet, psychotherapy, or behavioral procedure. Evaluation is central to ensuring that the intervention is having the intended effects and if not, changing the intervention.

This chapter provides an overview of behavior modification and its key characteristics. Behavior modification is a broad term that encompasses many different views about behavior and many different intervention techniques. The chapter highlights historical roots and foundations of behavior modification to convey the basis for many of the views and techniques. Also, the historical roots convey the connection between laboratory research and application, as well as science and practice more generally.

BEHAVIOR MODIFICATION AND ITS KEY CHARACTERISTICS

Behavior modification is an approach to the assessment, evaluation, and alteration of behavior. The approach focuses on the development of adaptive, prosocial behavior and the reduction of maladaptive behavior in everyday life. Occasionally, behavior modification is considered to be a specific form of psychotherapy or treatment. In fact, many of the techniques are applied to treat various clinical problems in children, adolescents, and adults such as anxiety, depression, substance abuse, child and spouse abuse, marital discord, and sexual deviance and dysfunction, to mention a few. Yet, the approach embraces a large number of quite different interventions that are applied well beyond the context of psychotherapy. Behavioral interventions also applied to education, child rearing, medicine and health, sports, and rehabilitation. Indeed, behavior modification techniques have been applied in virtually all settings that one can conceive of where humans work, live, and interact. Behavior modification is not a set of techniques or a bag of tricks. Rather, it is better conceived broadly as a scientific approach to understanding and changing human behavior. Four broad characteristics listed in Table 1-1 convey the approach and define the unique features of behavior modification.

Focus on Behavior

Psychology as a scientific discipline seeks to understand feelings and emotions (affect); actions and what people do (behaviors); and thoughts, beliefs, and other mental processes (cognitions). Behavior modification emphasizes actions and performance, that is, what people do in everyday life. Whenever possible, the focus or problem is defined in terms of overt behavior, or behavior one can see, identify, detect, or observe in some way. Human functioning entails more than just what people do. No less important are feelings and thoughts, and these often cannot be reduced to observable behaviors. Any given problem may have behaviors, feelings, and thoughts all rolled into one package. For example, a child who gets into many fights (overt behavior), may feel angry at others (affect) and think (cognitions) that others are trying to pick on him or hurt him. Certainly one might want to address all of these components of the problem and indeed behavioral interventions do just that. Even so, there is a general focus and priority given to overt behavior.

Table 1-1   Key Characteristics of Behavior Modification

Characteristic	Described
Focus on Behavior	Efforts to assess overt behavior directly to identify the problem or focus and to evaluate change; direct assessment of the target problem
Focus on Current Determinants of Behavior	Emphasis on what factors exert influence on current functioning and what factors can be used to alter performance
Focus on Learning	Provide experiences that systematically develop behavior based on learning theory and research
Assessment and Evaluation	Measure the focus of the intervention (what one wishes to change) and evaluate the impact of the intervention (whether the behaviors change and whether the intervention was responsible for the change)
Application	Extend interventions to all facets of everyday life in which maladaptive behaviors are to be decreased and adaptive behaviors are to be increased; intervening in everyday situations where the changes are desired

The focus on behavior does not reflect a lack of interest in other facets of human functioning. Overt behavior is emphasized for three reasons. First, often one can intervene effectively on behavior and influence thoughts and feelings. Second, in everyday situations, overt behavior is often a primary concern that prompts the need to intervene. Third, evaluating the effectiveness of the intervention is facilitated by being able to translate problems into behaviors that reflect key aspects of the problem. For the child who fights, a behavioral approach is likely to begin by focusing on behavior, including the reduction of fighting and the development of prosocial (cooperative) interactions of the child. Very specific procedures can be used to reduce fighting. More so, one can evaluate if, in fact, efforts to help the child are really addressing what was defined as the child's key problem—fighting.

Many psychological problems have, as their key characteristics, thoughts (e.g., obsessive thoughts about something) and feelings (e.g., feelings of sadness or worthlessness as is often the case with depression). An emphasis on behavior does not mean an exclusive focus on merely what people do. Indeed, many people in everyday life are actually "doing" quite well, but they are miserable, feel stagnant, and are unhappy. Often behavior change is an end in itself as in situations where one wants to reduce criminal behavior and increase adaptive functioning. In other situations, behavior change is included in treatment as a means to an end; that is, changing behavior can help change how people feel and how they perceive the environment. For many years a prevailing assumption has been that changing how people feel and what they think and know will change behavior. This may well be true in some circumstances, but the opposite is also true—changing what people do leads to changes in how they feel and what they think. For example, as part of treatment, a depressed person may be encouraged to engage in specific activities involving interactions with others and in setting goals for accomplishing specific tasks at home or at work. Increases in activity and completion of tasks are behaviors that have been found to alter depressive symptoms, including feelings and thoughts.

In some cases where the focus or problem is on emotions rather than overt behavior, it is likely that overt behavior will be included in the evaluation of outcome. For example, an adult or child who is very angry might be treated with techniques that focus on ways to control these feelings. Here, the focus of treatment may be on feelings and internal cues of the individuals (e.g., initial feelings of anger, physiological arousal) rather than on overt behavior. However, to evaluate whether treatment has had impact, overt behavior is likely to be included among the measures. It will be important for this individual to feel differently as a result of treatment (less angry). If there were any overt signs of anger associated with these feelings (e.g., expressing extreme anger to others, fighting), the question is whether the effects of treatment can be seen on these too. The main point to note is an emphasis on overt behavior as part of behavioral interventions and as part of evaluation of the effectiveness of interventions.

Focus on Current Determinants of Behavior

Behavior modification research focuses on efforts to understand the causes of behavior and factors that relate to how individuals function and perform in everyday life. Understanding causes can refer to many different facets of functioning. It is useful to distinguish past from present causes or sources of influence. For example, a 20-year-old college student seeks therapy because she is having problems in relationships with others. The problem may be due in part to how she was treated as a child. Perhaps as a young child she suffered physical abuse or neglect, or simply lived with difficult parents. These problems in childhood may play a role in the current problem. These early problems might be original causes or influences and cannot be neglected. Early causes are clearly important and obviously, to understand the present, one must understand the past. Yet, the guiding question for any form of intervention is, "What can be done now to develop the behaviors of interest and to improve adaptive functioning?" Behavior modification emphasizes current influences on behavior and how they can be mobilized to make changes.

The distinction between early causes and current influences that can be used to make changes is very familiar. For example, lung cancer or heart disease in an individual may be traced to years of cigarette smoking or high blood pressure. Consider these influences as causes of the current problem. The question is, what can be done about these problems now? What changes can be made to ameliorate the problem in someway? The years of factors that influenced the current problem cannot be erased, but something can be done now. Similarly, it is not clear why some parents physically abuse their children, and those reasons are not simple. The belief that they abuse their children because they themselves were abuse is not true and oversimplifies the issue. Many factors influence who abuses a child, and, in fact, most parents who were abused as children do not abuse their own children (Wolfe, 1999). The question for behavior modification is how to change abusive parenting practices, and this requires understanding current influences on the parent and family and what can be done about them to achieve a change.

The focus on current influences and changes does not in any way undermine the importance of understanding how behaviors develop originally. Ideally, research will provide a complete account of how behaviors come about and how they can be changed. When one knows how the problem began, often this knowledge can be used for prevention. For example, cigarette smoking begins during young adolescence for many individuals; if we can prevent smoking, this will reduce the many later diseases that smoking is known to cause. Whether the goal is prevention or treatment, there is an urgent need to understand how to change current behavior. Remarkable progress has been made in understanding influences that can be brought to bear to develop new behaviors and to change patterns that have been maladaptive.

Focus on Learning Experiences to Promote Change

An assumption of behavior modification is that behavior can be altered by providing new learning experiences. Behavioral treatments provide special learning experiences to decrease deviant or maladaptive behavior and to increase adaptive behavior in everyday life. I note "special" learning experiences because learning has to be carefully arranged. After all, learning goes on all the time in everyday life; other people (parents, teachers, and peers) and experiences (reading books, browsing the Internet, watching movies) always "teach" us something. In behavior modification, the learning experiences draw on scientific research on the ways to develop, eliminate, and promote behavior. The learning experiences are much more systematic than what ordinarily takes place in routine everyday life. Clichés of everyday life about learning a skill convey the point. It is not quite true to say that, "practice makes perfect." One can practice endlessly (e.g., playing a musical instrument, learning how to fly a small plane), and there will be little progress for most of us. Merely practicing will not work for the vast majority of people. Practice must be accompanied by other systematic experiences (e.g., instruction, feedback, and gradual progress in developing increasingly complex skills), depending on the skill.

Much has been learned from research about how to develop, change, increase, reduce, and eliminate behavior. Theory and research on different types of learning and the conditions under which learning take place represent rather formal areas of scientific study. Behavior-change programs rely on many learning concepts and findings developed in research. For example, research has established that very specific arrangements may be needed to ensure that learning takes place and that performance is consistent. In later chapters, key concepts on how to apply them effectively are discussed and illustrated to convey more concretely how research translates to application.

To note that many problems and foci of interest can be changed through learning experiences does not necessarily mean that all behaviors are learned and can be changed through learning. Diverse biological, behavioral, social, cultural, and other factors influence the development of behavior and also may be quite relevant to behavior change. The key feature of the behavioral approach is recognition of the plasticity of behavior or the amenability of behavior to change when systematic learning experiences are provided. Providing new learning experiences that effectively alter behavior can be determined only by testing what changes occur. The assumption that learning experiences can alter behavior has proven to be extremely helpful in developing effective treatments.

Assessment and Evaluation

Critical to behavior modification is the careful assessment and evaluation of the interventions. Assessment consists of systematically measuring current functioning or the problem that is to be altered. *Assessment* focuses on what the behavior or problem is and what events might be influencing that behavior. Typically, assessment begins by clarifying the goals of the intervention. Before treatment, the therapist or person overseeing the behavior-change program conducts a careful evaluation to identify what the problem is, how the client and others are affected by it, and the circumstances under which it emerges. The goals are usually expressed in concrete terms or behaviors that can be measured. The measures may include direct observation of how the person performs at school or at work, evaluations by significant others (parents, spouses, peers), and, of course, evaluations by the clients themselves. The assessment is central to identifying the extent and nature of the problem before the intervention begins. As the program is implemented, assessment continues to see whether change is occurring and whether the desired outcomes have been achieved.

For example, parents may want their sixth-grade child to complete homework. Assessment might focus on how many minutes of homework the child is studying each day and also the circumstances such as time of day and what the parents do to foster homework (e.g., nag, sit with the child). The goal of the program may be to improve homework, grades at school, and the child's learning. One or more measures may be used to assess the impact of the program. The overall goal may not be merely to change the number of minutes of studying, although this might be one useful indicator of whether the program is having any impact.

Evaluation acts in concert with but is separate from assessment. *Evaluation* consists of drawing inferences about whether change has occurred and whether the intervention is responsible for change. Assessment is very much like description or seeing what the individual is doing (Is the change enough or important? Does it resolve the problem for which the intervention was sought?); evaluation is more like drawing inferences or making conclusions about the basis of the change and whether the intervention was responsible for the change (Did the person just get better over time? Can we attribute the change to the intervention?).

Behavior modification places major emphasis on measuring outcome and evaluating treatment in controlled studies to decide whether treatments are effective and which ones are more effective than others. Consequently, a great deal of research is conducted on interventions and their effects. This research provides basic findings about what treatments are effective. When treatment or an intervention is applied in everyday situations, the primary goal is to help individual clients. Evaluation is also important in this context to evaluate whether change is important and whether the amount of change is sufficient to make a difference in the person's life. This requires evaluating the magnitude of change in some systematic way such as seeing if the client is functioning as well as others in his or her environment or if others who interact with the client see improvement. Also, sometimes the effects of the program are evaluated to ensure that the intervention and not something else going on in the environment led to the changes.

Evaluation is extremely important in case the intervention is not working or working well enough to make a genuine difference. The person in charge of the program (e.g., therapist, teacher) can use this information to alter treatment and, if necessary, to try different techniques. Assessment and evaluation act in concert with the intervention. The maximum benefits of the intervention can only be achieved when it is clear that change has occurred and is important (makes a difference) and when one knows what produced the change. We shall return to assessment and evaluation later because the success of behavioral interventions owes very much to these components.

Application

Behavior modification focuses on interventions that can be implemented and applied in everyday life and settings (e.g., day-care centers, hospitals, schools, home, and business). Professionals who know about behavior modification obviously play a critical role in designing and implementing interventions. Yet, interventions are often conducted directly in the settings in which behaviors need to be developed. Consequently, persons responsible for the care, management, and education of the clients, such as parents, teachers, relatives, spouses, roommates, peers, supervisors, and colleagues, are often utilized to implement the behavior-change program. These persons are occasionally referred to as *paraprofessionals* because they work along with professionals in achieving therapeutic change. Paraprofessionals are in frequent contact with the client, can observe behaviors in the actual situations in which they are performed, and can then immediately provide consequences intended to develop more adaptive behaviors. In applications with children, for example, parents, teachers, and peers are often trained in behavior-change techniques and can work on changing behaviors of interest (e.g., tantrums, oppositional behavior, and completion of homework).

The scope of applications is quite broad. Table 1-2 samples some of the applications to convey the breadth of behavior modification. In subsequent chapters, examples will be provided in more detail to see what the applications are and how their effects are demonstrated. Even so, it is clear from the samples in the table that behavioral techniques have been applied quite broadly. Indeed, it is safe to say no other psychological intervention or approach has been applied as widely to human behavior.

TWO CASE ILLUSTRATIONS

The characteristics of the behavioral approach described above are somewhat general and hence potentially ambiguous. General characteristics are required to encompass the many techniques that behavior modification embraces and the

Table 1-2 Sample of the Scope of Applications of Behavior Modification

Context/setting	Interventions have been effective in . . .
Therapy/treatment settings	Treating a broad range of psychological problems and psychiatric disorders including anxiety (e.g., fears, obsessive-compulsive disorders, panic attacks), depression, substance use and abuse (e.g., drug, alcohol, cigarettes), conduct problems, hyperactivity, autism, and eating disorders
Education	Improving academic performance; studying; achievement, grades; classroom deportment; creative writing; participation in activities, as relevant to elementary, middle, and high school students
	Mastery of the subject matter at all levels including college students
	Many programs in school settings have focused on behaviors beyond the usual domain of education because schools provide a useful place to deliver the interventions. Thus, behavioral programs have been applied to reduce or prevent cigarette smoking, alcohol and drug use, and unprotected sex among adolescents.
Medicine and health	Teaching individuals to detect early signs of disease (e.g., cancer checks through self-examination), protect against sexually transmitted diseases, reduce pain associated with invasive medical procedures (e.g., lumbar taps) or postoperative recovery, and adhere to medical regimens (e.g., for cancer, diabetes)
Business and industry	Teaching workers to engage in practices that reduce accidents (e.g., when using equipment), improve health or overcome problems that compete with health and work (e.g., alcohol use, cigarette smoking). Helping individuals obtain jobs (e.g., how to seek jobs, interview skills), improve on-the-job performance, reduce absenteeism, tardiness, improve employee-customer interactions, and reduce shoplifting by customers
Sports and athletics	Improving coaching practices, performance of athletes (e.g., in football, gymnastics, tennis, swimming, and track) and stress management among athletes
Everyday life	Training parents to interact with their children, for parents who are in special situations (e.g., handicapped child), for children who are in special situations (e.g., abused, neglected children), and for parents without special difficulties or obstacles. Training children to engage in safe behaviors (e.g., use of seat belts, crossing streets) or ward off dangerous situations (e.g., responding to would-be abductors). Training the elderly in nursing homes to increase physical activity and engage in more social interactions with others. Training individuals to engage in safe-driving practices, conserve energy in homes, and recycle wastes.

many behaviors and clinical problems toward which those techniques are directed. Two illustrations convey more concretely features of the behavioral approach as they are applied in actual practice. Both cases are "real" rather than hypothetical.

Anxiety: The Case of Arlene

Consider the case of Arlene, a 35-year-old woman who suffered from agoraphobia (fear of open spaces). Persons with agoraphobia often remain at home as much as possible. When they leave home, they experience high levels of anxiety, which is reflected in agitation, worry, arousal, sweating, and in general, great discomfort. Anticipation of leaving home and going to public places may increase their anxiety and belief that they will lose control and panic in the presence of others. It is not yet clear how agoraphobia develops, although many theories have been advanced. Fortunately, effective treatments have been identified.

Before treatment began, the therapist interviewed Arlene for approximately two hours to discuss exactly what she considered to be the problem. The therapist asked about the times she felt anxious, the range of the circumstances in which anxiety emerged, and how this anxiety interfered with her everyday life. In addition, Arlene completed a questionnaire to assess a broad range of problems (e.g., other forms of anxiety, depression, sleep disturbance, eating disorders) that she may have experienced. Arlene's problems focused on anxiety when she left her house or thought about doing so. She rigidly structured her daily activities to accommodate her anxiety. For example, to avoid going to a store on her own, she ordered the delivery of groceries or paid a neighbor's teenage boy to pick them up. Also, she arranged for a neighbor to meet her children when they were dropped off by a school bus at the end of the block.

After the evaluation, the therapist explained what the treatment was and how it would be used to overcome anxiety. For Arlene, graduated exposure and relaxation training were used. She was introduced (exposed) to a variety of situations outside her home. The situations were introduced on a graduated basis. At first, situations were introduced that were not too demanding or threatening while the therapist was present. As Arlene progressed, more difficult situations were introduced and the therapist was absent.

Before Arlene began specific tasks, she was trained to engage in deep muscle relaxation. The purpose was to provide her with a technique for remaining relaxed when she felt the onset of any anxiety. Developing the ability to relax deeply usually requires only a few sessions. Relaxation was developed by having Arlene first close her eyes and remain quiet. The therapist then instructed her to focus attention on various groups of muscles (lower arm, upper arm, neck, and shoulders). She alternately tensed and relaxed muscle groups encompassing the major skeletal muscles in response to the therapist's instructions. Arlene learned how to use the release from tensing the muscles as a way of achieving a relaxed state. After a few sessions, she became relaxed relatively quickly with little or no assistance from the therapist.

After Arlene learned how to relax, treatment continued with a series of behavioral tasks that exposed her to various places and situations outside her home. At first, she was required to take a short walk with the therapist near her home, so that the location would be familiar and probably not very anxiety provoking. If she became anxious, the therapist helped her relax. The brevity of the walks, the presence of the therapist, and the use of relaxation decreased the likelihood that high levels of anxiety would emerge. Within two sessions, a significant reduction of anxiety was evident on these brief walks.

In further sessions with the therapist, Arlene was exposed to additional situations, including walking to various stores, driving in a car to a restaurant and a shopping mall, riding a bus, and other tasks related to situations that she found to be anxiety provoking. She was also given "homework" assignments—practice activities to carry out on her own. The first assignment was to visit a friend who lived a few houses away from her. Arlene and her friend spoke on the phone for extended periods each day. The assignment was to visit the friend and talk to her for at least 30 minutes on at least two separate days during the week. The friend, who was well aware of the problem, was eager to help and did so by having Arlene over for coffee. After three visits, Arlene felt better about leaving her home. She was then assigned to go to a store with her friend, to walk to a mailbox (two blocks away from her home) by herself, and to meet her children when they were dropped off by the school bus. After further practice trials with the therapist and further homework assignments, Arlene reported very little anxiety about being out of the house, going out on errands alone, or being in crowds.

Throughout the course of treatment, Arlene kept a daily diary regarding her behavior and anxiety. In it, she recorded each trip she took, how long she was out of the house, and how much anxiety she felt, as rated on a scale from 1 (perfectly relaxed) to 10 (extremely uncomfortable and anxious). At the beginning of treatment, Arlene made few entries in the diary. At that time, she left home only when absolutely necessary—about twice a week. On these occasions, her trips were brief (usually less than 30 minutes) and were rated with very high levels of anxiety (9 or 10 on the rating scale). After many sessions and after homework assignments had been in effect for some time, she left home 15 to 20 times per week (going out to visit a neighbor, walking to a store, driving to a shopping mall). Most of the trips lasted well over an hour. Arlene's anxiety decreased, as reflected in ratings of 3 and 4 on the scale. Eventually, her anxiety for all the outings decreased to 2, 3, or 4 and she stated that being out of the house and in public places did not bother her. Over the course of treatment, the information provided by the diary was useful in deciding when to proceed to more difficult tasks and whether the treatment was achieving its goals.

In Arlene's case, treatment progressed relatively quickly. Within 10 weeks, her ratings indicated that she was not bothered at all by being out of the house. She engaged in more social activities, including going out evenings with her friend and a group of new friends. In addition, within four months after treatment ended, she obtained a full-time job in a department store. Thus, by her own report and information about her activities, therapy apparently achieved its goals.

Sleeping in Mom's Bed: The Case of John

John was a 5-year-old boy whose mother brought him for outpatient treatment because he was, in her words, "extremely difficult to manage at home, had tantrums all the time, and was just out of control." John lived alone with his mother. John's mother and father divorced when John was 1 year old. John's father lived in another state and visited once or twice a year. The mother worked as a secretary at a law office. Her own mother lived nearby and occasionally would assist with babysitting and child care. John had begun kindergarten a few months before coming to the clinic and had been in day care in the two years prior to that.

At the first meeting with the mother, she was interviewed to determine how John was functioning at home, at school, and whether there were outstanding problems that might be overlooked by focusing on his noncompliance. The information suggested that there were no significant social, emotional, or behavioral problems (e.g., anxiety, bed-wetting, sleep disorder) or problems in functioning beyond those related to his stubbornness and oppositionality. The main concern was that John would not comply when asked to get ready for bed, get dressed in the morning, go to the store, wear a coat (in the winter), and so on. Each situation led the mother to argue or force John to carry out the requisite activity. The mother was asked to list what she asked John to do and to keep track each day of whether he did or did not do each one without a tantrum (score yes and no for each one she asked him to do). Over the course of the behavior-change program, the score on this list was used to chart progress. John received stickers for being a good listener, like complying without tantrums. Only one part of the program is highlighted here.

The situation that the mother viewed as most problematic pertained to bedtime. Each night John insisted on sleeping in his mother's bed. If the mother insisted that he sleep in his own room, this led to a tantrum and an extended argument. John often became so upset that he could not get to sleep for a long time. The problem began when John had a nightmare one night about a year earlier and came into the mother's bedroom in the middle of the night and slept in her bed through the night. On the next night, John insisted on sleeping in his mother's bed again. As this went on, the mother began arguing with him about where to sleep. In fact, he had slept in bed with her ever since that initial night. The mother really wanted this to stop.

The intervention was conducted with the mother in which she was trained to interact quite differently with John. Specifically, she was trained to provide clear instructions about what she wanted John to do, to ignore tantrums and not argue, and to provide positive consequences for the behaviors, techniques that will be detailed further in later chapters. A behavior-change program was developed for John and included the following: John was told that he could earn stickers ("smiley faces") on a new chart that was placed on the refrigerator. The stickers would be given for going to bed in his own room. The mother said that he would earn two stickers if they said good night without arguing, two if he went into his bed (lower bunk), and two stickers if he remained in his bed through the night. The plan was to provide stickers for the behaviors, as specified. John did not have to do all three behaviors to get the stickers. If, for example, he completed the first and second behaviors, but in the middle of the night got into his mother's bed, he would still receive four stickers. The stickers would be placed on John's chart on the refrigerator in the morning and could be exchanged for rewards right then or later—depending on the reward. The prizes included small toys (four stickers each), basketball cards (six stickers each), a night of staying up 15 minutes past bedtime (eight stickers), and a trip to a fast-food restaurant for dinner (12 stickers). His stickers could be saved when he did not spend them all.

John had bunk beds in his room. The mother said that for the first few days she would sleep in the top bunk. When John went to bed the first night, he went in his bunk quietly. The mother praised and hugged him enthusiastically for doing this. She reminded him that he would be getting stickers in the morning. The mother had practiced with the therapist to ensure that her comments specified the desired behaviors clearly, were enthusiastic, followed the behavior immediately, and were associated with positive physical contact (hugs, pats, kisses). When John went into his bed (lower bunk), the mother also went to sleep but in the top bunk bed. This was different from previous nights in which she did not go to bed at the same time as John when he merely went to her room. Nevertheless, having the mother present was considered likely to facilitate the initial transition to sleeping in John's room. The plan the first few nights was for the mother to go to bed in the bunk but then leave after John fell asleep. (She actually slept through the night for the first two nights.)

In the morning, the mother mentioned again how well John had done and what a "big boy" he was to sleep in his own bed all night. They went hand in hand to the refrigerator where she placed the stickers on the chart. She explained again how the stickers could be used again and asked if he wanted one of the rewards he had earned (six stickers). He took one of the toys (small truck) and saved two stickers to be spent at another time.

The program continued like this for four nights. Each night, John went to bed without a tantrum and slept through the night. On one of the nights John could not sleep and kept trying to engage the mother in conversation while they were in their respective bunks. She said she could not talk because it was "sleep time" and ended the conversation with more praise about how wonderful he was doing by staying in his own bed. On night 5, the mother asked if he could do the "*real* big boy" bedtime and go into the bunk by himself without her. She asked him to just try it, and she would check on him after a few minutes. He went into his bed and was tucked in and praised for being such a big boy, for going to his room so nicely, and for getting into bed without her doing the same. The mother went in to check and praise him for staying in bed about 10 minutes later, but he had already fallen asleep. This program addition (sleeping in the room alone) continued for another week. No change was made in the sticker program; the addition was just handled by effusive praise on the part of the mother.

After 15 days of this total, the sticker program for bedtime was stopped. The mother said that John could stay up 15 minutes any night he wanted if he had completed all the bedtime behaviors by himself on the previous night. The praise continued but the sticker program was essentially discontinued. Within less than three weeks the bedtime behaviors had changed and no longer were of concern. Six months later, sleeping was no longer an issue. Not mentioned here were other stickers provided for compliance. The program for compliance continued for about 3 weeks and this too had worked well and was maintained by praise. The information that the mother collected at home during the program indicated he complied with her requests and she no longer viewed his behavior as in need of any special program.

General Comments

The two cases convey very different foci of behavior modification, including anxiety of an adult and noncompliance of a child. Perhaps it is difficult to see many commonalities in these cases to view them as a single approach. Actually, several features of the behavioral approach can be seen in both cases of Arlene and John and the programs devised to alter their behaviors. The focus on behavior (i.e., what the person actually does), efforts to provide new learning experiences, execution of treatment in everyday situations, and the involvement of persons other than the therapist in treatment are primary examples. Perhaps less detailed in the examples were the efforts to measure and evaluate progress over the course of treatment. In each case, the behaviors of interest were assessed to examine the extent of the problem and whether the intervention was having any impact. Assessment was continued during treatment and the information was used to decide if the desired changes were occurring and when to stop the intervention.

Another feature worth noting is that change was achieved by focusing on current determinants. In each case, the therapist had no clear idea about how the problem emerged. Even in John's case where the bedtime problem was considered by the mother to be associated with one event (a nightmare), there is no clear idea of why this occurred or how the extensive pattern of noncompliance emerged and became worse. One might speculate and indeed many therapists might make speculations about motivations of the child and mother that are intended to explain John's behavior. For example, some therapists might say that for John sleeping in bed with his mother was filled with psychological significance. Among such interpretations might be that John was taking the place of the father (who had left the home), and this fulfilled both the needs of the mother and boy or that sleeping in the bed served deeply rooted psychosexual fantasies of the child (i.e., Oedipus lives!). Such speculations of course can be listed endlessly. They are wonderfully engaging, mysterious, and even fun but they have absolutely no evidence to support them. If there were support, we still would be required to change the problem (noncompliance, sleeping in his mother's bed) and how to do that would not be immediately clear. In fact, John's behaviors were changed, including the bedtime problem, and there were no reasons to propose that any deeply rooted psychological needs were served by his noncompliance.

We could weave a similar story for Arlene. Perhaps she was afraid of open spaces because of lack of meaning in her life or the "gap" (open space) between her mother and father. A nonscientific exercise would be to continue such wild speculation. Clearly not all behaviors, thoughts, or feelings ought to be taken at their face value, but this is not license to invent interpretations that cannot be tested. More than that, what to do for Arlene? Providing new learning experiences is an option and has evidence on its behalf.

Is it possible that there are underlying psychological processes for behaviors we perform in everyday life? Absolutely. Much of behavior modification focuses on thoughts, beliefs, perceptions, and statements that people tacitly make to themselves (e.g., "I am a worthless person," "I feel horrible"). Changing such cognitions often goes hand in hand with behavior change. Also, many behaviors serve useful functions in everyday life (e.g., they help people attain consequences, develop relations with others, avoid getting asked to do things, or ensure they are asked to do things). It is often useful to know what current functions are served by behavior. More will be said about this later. At this point, the cases are useful to concretely convey key characteristics mentioned earlier.

FOUNDATIONS OF BEHAVIOR MODIFICATION

The two cases suggest how very different the applications of behavior modification can be. It is useful to highlight the foundations of behavior modification to convey how the approach emerged and how proponents of behavior modification conceptualize treatment and other interventions.

Experimental Animal Research

Classical Conditioning. Behavior modification can be traced to animal laboratory research in physiology in the 1800s and 1900s. Among the many influences, the work of the Russian physiologist Ivan P. Pavlov (1849–1936) is particularly significant. Pavlov studied digestion, especially how reflex responses were influenced by substances placed in the digestive system. He stimulated various portions of an animal's digestive system with food or food powder and observed the physiological reactions. As part of his studies, he found that gastric secretions were stimulated when animals—in this case dogs—merely saw the food or heard the food being prepared. This was significant because it suggested that digestive processes could be stimulated even without direct contact with food or direct physical stimulation. Pavlov thought that this resulted from the animal's experience in the laboratory (i.e., learning). He shifted his research to study how connections were made between various environmental stimuli (sights and sounds) and reflex reactions such as salivation in response to food.

The type of learning that Pavlov studied has been referred to as *classical* or *respondent conditioning*. Classical conditioning is concerned with stimuli that evoke responses. Certain stimuli in one's environment (such as noise, shock, light, and the taste of food) elicit reflex responses. These are referred to as *unconditioned stimuli* because the ability of the stimuli to elicit responses is not learned (i.e., not conditioned where "conditioning" refers to "learned" through this pairing process). The responses that are evoked are referred to as *unconditioned responses* or *respondents* because they too are unlearned—they are automatic responses in response to the stimuli. Examples of respondents include a startle reaction in response to loud noise, flexion of a muscle in response to pain, pupil constriction in response to bright light, or salivation in response to the presence of food in one's mouth. The connection between the unconditioned stimulus and the unconditioned response is automatic (i.e., not learned).

Through classical conditioning, a neutral stimulus (i.e., a stimulus that does not elicit a particular reflex) can be made to elicit a reflex response. This stimulus, referred to as a *conditioned stimulus,* at first does not elicit the response but through learning, eventually comes to elicit the response. A color, light, sound, all might not elicit salivation until learning experiences are provided. As shown in Table 1-3, learning occurs when one repeatedly pairs the unconditioned and the conditioned stimuli. Each time this pairing occurs the unconditioned response occurs. Eventually, one can just present the conditioned stimulus. Because it has been paired with the unconditioned stimuli, it eventually elicits a response all by itself. This response

Table 1-3   Classical Conditioning and How Stimuli Come To Elicit Reflexive Responses

Steps	Stimuli presented	Response elicited
1	Unconditioned Stimulus (UCS) (e.g., a loud noise)	Unconditioned Response (UCR) (e.g., startle reaction)
2	Conditioned Stimulus (CS) such as a light paired with the UCS	UCR just like above
3	Conditioned Stimulus (CS) by itself (just the light)	Conditioned Response (CR) (e.g., a startle response that very closely resembles the UCR)

Note: Step 3 occurs after step 2 is repeated several times, that is, after the CS and the UCS are paired.

has been learned in response to the conditioned stimuli and, as you might expect, is referred to as the *conditioned response*. *Classical* or *respondent conditioning* is the process whereby new stimuli gain the power to elicit respondent behavior.

Pavlov's findings suggested one way in which behaviors could be learned. The concepts of conditioning from his laboratory work were extended to explain virtually all learning, including such broad areas as the learning of language, the acquisition of knowledge, and the development of deviant and maladaptive behavior (e.g., alcoholism). It is clear today that the concepts were overextended because they did not give accurate or complete accounts of these areas. Also, more recent research has shown that conditioning itself is more complex than originally thought (e.g., certain kinds of connections are more easily learned than others, and pairing stimuli does not always lead to learning) (Rescorla, 1988). Pavlov's significant contribution was his systematic investigation of learning. His clear demonstration of the process of learning under well-controlled conditions helped foster more elaborate studies of different kinds of learning.

Another significant feature of Pavlov's work was the method of his experiments. Pavlov used precise methods that permitted careful observation and quantification of what he was studying. For example, in some of his studies, drops of saliva were counted to measure the conditioned reflex. His meticulous laboratory notes and his rigorous methods helped greatly to advance a scientific approach toward the study of behavior. Because his methods were described so clearly, they could be used by others. Pavlov's receipt of the Nobel Prize (1904) in physiology for his research on digestion increased the visibility of his work and adoption of his methods.

Operant Conditioning. While Pavlov was conducting his experiments, a type of learning that did not involve reflex responses also was under investigation. Investigators were evaluating the impact of different consequences on the development of new behaviors (Kazdin, 1978). Along these lines, the work of Edward L. Thorndike (1874–1949) is especially noteworthy. Thorndike was concerned with the learning of new behaviors, rather than with establishing new connections of reflex behavior. Among his many animal experiments, the most well known are his puzzle-box experiments with cats.

Thorndike placed a hungry cat in a box and recorded how long it took the cat to escape by moving a barrier. A small piece of food placed outside the box provided the cat with an incentive for learning to escape. The cat immediately attempted to escape by exploring diverse solutions in a trial-and-error fashion. Eventually, the cat removed the barrier and consumed the food. The cat was then placed in the box again and the sequence continued. With repeated trials, Thorndike found that it took less and less time for the cat to escape. Eventually, as soon as the cat was placed in the box, it removed the barrier, escaped, and ate the food. Thorndike showed that with repeated trials less and less time was needed for the animal to escape from the cage. After several trials, the animal escaped the cage immediately after being placed in it. The significance of this demonstration was in showing how learning improves with repeated practice.

From many similar experiments and observations, Thorndike formulated laws or principles of behavior. The most significant of these was the Law of Effect, which stated that consequences that follow behavior help learning. The rewards (e.g., food for the cat after escape) provided consequences that increased learning of the behavior. Thorndike's emphasis on the consequences of behavior was a significant preview of subsequent developments in laboratory and applied research.

B. F. Skinner (1904–1990) was influenced by Pavlov and Thorndike and also conducted a number of animal laboratory studies. Like Thorndike, Skinner explored the impact of various consequences on behavior. He helped clarify learning that resulted from consequences and its differences from the classical conditioning studied by Pavlov. He noted that many behaviors are emitted spontaneously and are controlled primarily by their consequences. He referred to such behaviors as *operants* because they were responses that operated (had some influence) on the environment. Operant behaviors are strengthened (increased) or weakened (decreased) as a function of the events that follow them. Most of the behaviors performed in everyday life are operants. They are not reflex responses (respondents) controlled by eliciting stimuli. Operant behaviors include reading, walking, working, talking, nodding one's head, smiling, and other freely emitted responses. Operants are distinguished by virtue of being controlled (influenced) by their consequences. The process of learning operant behaviors is referred to as *operant conditioning*.

Several types of consequences and principles were developed to explain how operant behaviors could be developed and altered. The major relations that were investigated can be seen in Table 1-4, which summarizes the basic principles of operant conditioning. These principles provide general statements about the relations between behaviors and environmental events. Investigations of these principles began with laboratory animals (e.g., rats, pigeons) engaging in simple responses, such as pressing a lever, under highly controlled conditions. Current applications of the general principles bear very little resemblance to these experimental beginnings.

As with Pavlov's work, the significance of Skinner's work stemmed from the approach toward the study of behavior. Skinner's method included:

- A focus on overt behavior,
- Assessment of the frequency of behavior over time, and
- The study of one or a few organisms at a time.

Table 1-4   Summary of Key Principles of Operant Conditioning

Principle	Characteristic procedure and its effect on behavior
Reinforcement	Presentation or removal of an event after a response that increases the likelihood or probability of the response
Punishment	Presentation or removal of an event after a response that decreases the likelihood or probability of the response
Extinction	No longer presenting a reinforcing event after a response that decreases the likelihood or probability of the previously reinforced response
Stimulus control and discrimination	Reinforcing the response in the presence of one stimulus but not in the presence of another. This procedure increases the likelihood or probability of the response in the presence of the former stimulus and decreases the likelihood or probability of the response in the presence of the latter stimulus

His goal was to identify the variables that influenced behavior by careful and intensive study of one or two subjects. Because of their influence on contemporary behavior modification, we shall return to the principles of operant conditioning and the method of study developed by Skinner.

Development of Behaviorism

The late 1800s and early 1900s reflected a broader orientation of which significant contributors such as Pavlov and Thorndike, and later Skinner, were a part. Increased interest in the scientific method was evident in diverse areas of work that extended beyond a single discipline such as psychology. Sciences in general were emerging with an empirical and experimental focus. The broader context can be seen by noting the work of Charles Darwin (1809–1882), the English naturalist, whose contribution to the understanding of evolution is well known. Darwin's writings on evolution, such as *Origin of Species by Means of Natural Selection* (1859) and *The Descent of Man* (1871) suggested there was a continuity of species. Continuity in this context refers to the view that humans and infrahumans were part of an ongoing evolutionary process, subject to similar influences and principles such as natural selection and survival of the fittest. Of course, the proposed close connections of humans and nonhumans and the view that humans emerged from "lower" forms of life over extended geological periods were those facets that made evolutionary theory the center of social debate about creation and how humans emerged (e.g., evolution vs. biblical views).

The impact of Darwin's writings was enormous. One aspect of this influence germane to the present discussion is the relevance of research on infrahuman species. Given the continuity of species, the study of animal behavior assumed increased importance. Obviously, studying infrahuman species cannot tell us all there is to know about humans. Yet, processes such as learning and principles identified in the laboratory and naturalistic research with infrahumans, apart from interest in their own right, might also shed light on human functioning and adaptation. Research on animal learning became an important line of work that greatly influenced the emergence of behavior modification. Animal research was part of a larger movement toward a more scientific approach to the study of behavior. That approach emphasized investigations in the laboratory, careful control over the experimental situation, documentation and collection of data, and other features we routinely consider to comprise the scientific method. The movement that was evident in Pavlov's work, as an example, but extended beyond a single investigator or country.

In the United States, for example, John B. Watson (1878–1958) crystallized a movement in psychology that is referred to as *behaviorism*. Watson was interested in animal psychology and in applying methods from animal research to the study of human behavior. He criticized psychology because of its use of subjective methods such as introspection (asking people to report on their private experience) to study mental phenomena (thoughts and feelings). This method of study, Watson contended, was neither objective nor scientific. Watson (1919) brought together the concepts and methods of conditioning research developed in Russia and argued for a new behaviorist approach in psychology. He conducted studies advancing his views and greatly influenced psychology. He accorded learning a critical role in many areas. In fact, he suggested that learning could entirely shape human behavior, as illustrated by this now famous quote:

> Give me a dozen healthy infants, well-formed, and my own specified world to bring them up in and I'll guarantee to take any one at random and train him to become any type of specialist I might select—doctor, lawyer, artist, merchant chief and, yes, even beggar-man and thief, regardless of his talents, penchants, tendencies, abilities, vocations, and race of his ancestors. I am going beyond the facts and I admit it, but so have the advocates of the contrary and they have been doing it for many thousands of years. Please note that when this experiment is made I am to be allowed to specify the way the children are to be brought up and the type of world they have to live in (Watson, 1924, p. 104).

Of course, this quote suggests that everyone has the potential to be anything based on training and education. There is *no* support for this level of malleability of human behavior, as this quote suggests. The position was stated extremely and provocatively, and certainly Watson was not the first to take this view (Kazdin, 1978). Nevertheless, the quote is interesting to ponder because we do not know the limits of training, even as we recognize that there are limits. The more important and enduring influence of Watson was his reliance on classical conditioning and learning more generally to explain how behavior was acquired over the course of development. The beginning of movements often are marked by extreme views to help polarize and identify the new position. At the time of Watson's quote and other work, behavior modification had not yet emerged formally. Watson's major contribution was helping to move psychology toward the scientific study of behavior.

Extensions to Clinical Work

Classical and operant conditioning were used increasingly as a basis for conceptualizing personality, psychotherapy, and behavior change. Also, concepts of classical and operant conditioning were used to develop new techniques to treat children and adults for a host of psychological and behavioral problems. A few examples will convey important steps that led to contemporary work.

Classical Conditioning. A historically significant attempt to show the importance of classical conditioning was provided by Watson and Rayner (1920), who conditioned a fear reaction in an 11-month-old boy named Albert. Before the study, the investigators noted that a loud noise (unconditioned stimulus) produced a startle and fear reaction (unconditioned response) in Albert. In contrast, Albert freely played with a white rat without any adverse reaction. The investigators wished to determine whether the startle reaction could be conditioned to the presence of the white rat. To condition the startle reaction, the presence of the white rat (neutral or conditioned stimulus) was immediately followed by the noise (unconditioned stimulus that elicited startle). Whenever Albert reached out and touched the rat, the noise sounded and Albert was startled. Over a period of one week, the presence of the rat and the noise were paired only seven times. Finally, when the rat was presented without the noise, Albert fell over and cried. The conditioned stimulus elicited the fear response (conditioned response). Moreover, the fear generalized to other objects that Albert had not been afraid of previously (e.g., a rabbit, a dog, a Santa Claus mask, a sealskin coat, and cotton wool). This suggested that fears could be acquired through classical conditioning.

The significance of this demonstration stemmed from showing that learning concepts *could* explain behavior outside of the context of laboratory tasks. Providing a learning-based explanation raised the prospect that fears could be developed, studied, treated and conceptualized from the standpoint of psychological processes studied in the laboratory. Currently, human fears and anxiety are not considered to develop in the simple way that conditioning was applied to Albert. Indeed, fears of humans are often acquired for objects such as snakes, heights, trains, and wide open spaces for which the individual has had no direct personal contact.[2] Independent of how fears are actually learned, classical conditioning has been extremely useful in generating effective treatments. Fears can be ameliorated by considering stimuli such as heights, trains, open spaces, and so on as conditioned stimuli and reducing or eliminating their power to evoke anxiety.

One of the most influential extensions of classical conditioning to the development of treatment occurred in the 1950s. Joseph Wolpe (1915–1998) a physician working in South Africa, conducted experiments investigating anxiety and avoidance reactions in laboratory animals (cats). He investigated a phenomenon referred to as *experimental neurosis*—an experimentally induced state in which animals show agitation, disruption of behavior, and other signs that resemble anxiety in humans. Experimental neuroses had been studied for some time, beginning in Pavlov's laboratory. Wolpe's special contribution was to develop a procedure for overcoming anxiety in the cats he studied and then to extend the method to the treatment of humans with anxiety disorders.

After anxiety had been developed, Wolpe gradually exposed the cats to situations that elicited anxiety. When the cats were exposed to the situation (room) in which anxiety had been developed, they showed severe signs of anxiety and would not engage in any other behaviors. Wolpe then exposed the cats to cues (other rooms) that only resembled the original situation. With less avoidance and agitation due to a reduced dose of anxiety-provoking stimuli, he encouraged them to engage in other responses such as eating. He reasoned that exposure to a series of anxiety-provoking situations while engaging in competing responses would gradually overcome the anxiety. Continuation of this procedure eventually eliminated the anxiety of the cats.

A creative step was Wolpe's use of the information he derived from experiments with cats to develop a technique for treating human anxiety. Wolpe developed *systematic desensitization,* a treatment in which humans were exposed in real life or in imagination to situations that provoked anxiety. They were exposed in a graduated series of stimuli. To overcome anxiety, Wolpe trained clients to become deeply relaxed so that exposure to mild representations of the anxiety-provoking situation would cause very little anxiety. Over time, the clients were exposed to real or imagined situations that provoked greater anxiety and relaxation would overcome that anxiety. Eventually, the clients responded without anxiety to the situations that originally provoked anxiety.

The procedure was conceptualized from the standpoint of classical conditioning. Certain cues or stimuli in the environment elicit anxiety or fear. The fear can be altered by conditioning an alternative response (relaxation) that is incompatible with fear. As relaxation becomes associated with the imagined scenes, the capacity of the stimuli to elicit fear is eliminated. Altering the valence of the capacity of stimuli to elicit reactions adheres closely to the classical conditioning paradigm.

Wolpe (1958) reported the use of this technique in various forms with more than 200 patients. He claimed the treatment had been effective. Case studies are not scientifically acceptable because the basis for the change cannot be determined. Yet Wolpe's technique and claims eventually stimulated a great deal of research on the effects of systematic desensitization. Wolpe's work was quickly assimilated because of evidence supporting the effectiveness of desensitization but also because of other influences, such as his reliance on animal laboratory methods, use of learning concepts, and concerns over objective bases of developing treatments.

The few illustrations presented here are among the well-known extensions of classical conditioning to clinical problems. Many other behavioral techniques derived from classical conditioning have been used to alter a variety of behaviors, including enuresis (bedwetting), overeating, alcohol abuse, cigarette smoking, and deviant sexual behavior. Such procedures are designed to alter the valence of events, making them aversive by pairing them with real or imagined stimuli that evoke reactions). Clearly, the most commonly used therapeutic procedures based on classical conditioning are those designed to make events that elicit anxiety no longer do so. This was illustrated previously in the case of Arlene where cues (open spaces) elicited extreme anxiety but no longer did so after treatment based on graduated exposure.

Operant Conditioning. Operant conditioning as applied to behaviors in everyday life often emphasizes role of consequences on behavior. The control that rewarding consequences can exert on behavior is not a new insight identified by operant conditioning. Indeed, throughout recorded history, rewards have been used to promote behaviors that the culture wished to foster. For examples, Ancient Roman and Chinese soldiers and, more recently, Aztec and Plains Indians of the Americas received rewards for bravery and success in battle. Some of the more interesting rewards included permitting heroes to have statues made of themselves or being allowed to relate their experiences in public (Kazdin, 1977c). However, operant conditioning is not merely the application of rewards for behavior. Indeed, behavior modification programs often fail when they are mistakenly construed as merely following behavior with rewards.

Animal laboratory work elaborated the nature of operant conditioning, including the lawful effects of consequences on behavior. Laboratory studies were extended to humans initially as a method of study (e.g., seeing response patterns on laboratory tasks, evaluating similarities or differences in performance compared to the responses of infrahuman species) without considering the implications for treating or helping people change (Lindsley, 1956, 1960). Some of the early laboratory work produced intriguing and unexpected results. For example, laboratory studies were conducted with hospitalized psychotic patients who performed on various apparatus daily to earn small rewards (money, pictures).[3] Performance on the laboratory apparatus was often interrupted by pauses in which psychotic symptoms such as vocal hallucinatory behaviors could be observed. One could see graphically when these pauses took place because responses on the apparatus did not occur. These observations suggested that the operant conditioning methods might be an objective way to study psychotic behaviors, such as when hallucinations occurred and their regularity and patterns. Of greater significance for the present discussion was the unexpected finding that responding to laboratory tasks appeared to result in a reduction of symptoms like staring into space, both in the laboratory and on the hospital ward (King, Armitage, & Tilton, 1960; Lindsley, 1960). This clearly suggested that symptoms may be altered in important ways by increases in operant responding.

Laboratory extensions of operant conditioning were made to study the behavior of many populations such as mentally retarded children and autistic children. At first, the goals were merely to use operant conditioning laboratory methods to investigate how special populations responded. Operant conditioning methods were soon extended to human behavior outside the laboratory and to change behaviors that were more relevant to everyday life. Initial demonstrations were simple merely to see if environmental consequences could influence behavior outside of the context of a laboratory task.

Several demonstrations were completed in the 1960s to examine the extent to which environmental consequences could influence the behavior of hospitalized psychiatric patients. For example, one of these demonstrations involved a depressed patient who complained of sleeping difficulties and reported pains in her back, chest, head, and shoulders (Ayllon & Haughton, 1964). Medical evaluation revealed no physical problems to account for these difficulties. Perhaps these bodily (somatic) complaints were influenced by their consequences such as the reactions of the staff. This is a rather interesting hypothesis, namely, that complaints in this person were operants, or behaviors that operated in the

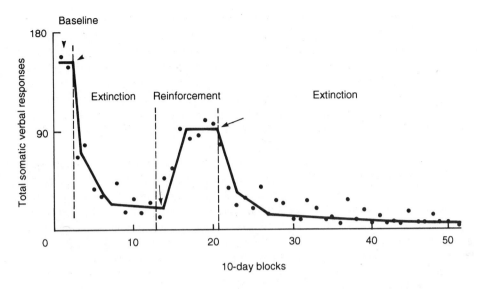

FIGURE 1-1 Frequency of complaints during the baseline, extinction, reinforcement, and extinction phases. During baseline, staff behaved as usual. During the reinforcement phase, they provided attention when the patient complained. During the extinction phases, staff ignored the patient's complaints.

(Source: Ayllon & Haughton, 1964)

environment and were maintained by the consequences. As with any hypothesis, it may well be false.

Observations were made to record the daily frequency of the patient's complaints for several days. After these observations, referred to as *baseline*, the staff was instructed to ignore complaints rather than to provide the usual consolation, sympathy, and attention that they had given. Perhaps attention had served as a reward (reinforcer) for the behavior, leading to its high levels; if so, cessation of the attention would reduce the behavior. Observations of complaints continued. After several days, the staff was told to revert to their previous ways of responding to the patient's complaints. If staff attention was really influencing the complaints, one would expect the complaints to increase again. After several days of this, the staff was finally told to withdraw their attention.

The effects of altering consequences for somatic complaints can be seen in Figure 1-1. The frequency of complaints is evident during baseline (staff behaving as usual), extinction (staff ignoring complaints), positive reinforcement (staff attention for complaints), and extinction (ignoring as before). The frequency of complaints changed dramatically as staff behavior changed. These results suggested that attention and consequences from others can greatly influence patient behavior.

This demonstration and many others like them indicated that human behavior in applied settings can be altered by changing the consequences. These demonstrations were unique because they included extensions of procedures developed in laboratory research, systematically applied consequences to develop behavior, carefully assessed behavior to evaluate the immediate effects of consequences, and demonstrated experimental control of the consequences. By showing that behaviors could be increased and decreased, this established that it really was the environmental manipulations and consequences responsible for change. The early extensions of operant conditioning principles to human behavior began an area of research. The present book illustrates the breadth and range of applications resulting from the extension of operant conditioning principles and approaches.

Modeling and Observational Learning. Classical and operant conditioning have dominated learning theory and research. A third type of learning, referred to as *modeling* or *observational learning,* also has been important in the development of behavior modification. Observational learning occurs when an individual observes another person, referred to as a *model,* engage in a particular behavior. The observer sees the model perform the behavior but does not engage in overt responses or receive any consequences. The observer learns the behavior merely by watching a model.

To clarify modeling effects, it is important to distinguish *learning* from *performance.* Through observation of a model, the observer learns the responses or behaviors. It is assumed that this is accomplished through mental representations or cognitive processes (thoughts, images) that code the observed sequence of behaviors (Bandura, 1977). No overt behavior is required on the part of the recipient of a modeling experience to learn. However, whether a learned response is actually performed may depend on the consequences of the response or on the incentives associated with the response.

The importance of response consequences in dictating performance was demonstrated in a classic laboratory study of modeling (Bandura, 1965). Children observed a film in which an adult modeled aggressive responses (hitting and kicking a large doll). For some children, the model's aggression was rewarded; for others, it was punished; and for still others, it met with no consequences. When the children were given the opportunity to perform the aggressive responses, those who had observed the aggression punished displayed less aggression than did those who had observed the aggression rewarded or ignored. To determine whether all of the children had learned the aggressive responses, an incentive was given to them for performing those responses. With the incentives, all three groups performed the aggressive responses equally. Apparently, all of the groups had *learned* the aggressive responses, but the consequences to the model (on the film) and the observer (the incentive given to the children) determined whether those responses would be *performed.*

Observational learning is an ongoing and ever-present process. Of course, we do not necessarily learn or even notice many of the behaviors around us and consequently much of what we observe is not learned or not learned very well. The extent to which modeling stimuli influence learning and performance also depends on other factors such as the similarity of the model to the observer; the prestige, status, and expertise of the model; and the number of models observed. As a general rule, imitation of a model by an observer is greater when the model is similar to the observer, more prestigious, and higher in status and expertise than the observer and when several models perform the same behavior.

A commonly cited example of modeling in the history of behavior modification was reported by Jones (1924). In this example, a young boy named Peter, who was afraid of a rabbit and several other furry objects (e.g., a fur coat, a feather, cotton wool), was placed in a play situation in which three other children and a rabbit were present. The other children, selected because they did not fear rabbits, interacted with the rabbit in a comfortable fashion. The hope was that through modeling, Peter would learn that there was nothing to fear in the presence of the rabbit. In fact, Peter touched the rabbit immediately after observing others touch it and he overcame the fear. In this case, the precise role of modeling in reducing his fear is uncertain because other procedures were used, as well such as associating the rabbit with the presence of food. The work of Jones was significant because she explored a number of different ways of overcoming anxiety in children, only one of which was modeling. Indeed, her work showed that graduated exposure to anxiety-provoking stimuli was one of the more effective procedures. This work was part of a larger movement of relying on learning-based methods to treat clinical problems.

Modeling has been used in behavior modification but typically is included with other procedures. For example, to reduce fear, therapists often model behaviors (e.g., approaching a feared or anxiety-provoking stimulus or situation) as part of treatment, as was evident in the case study of Arlene at the beginning of the chapter. In other applications, positive reinforcement is often used to develop social behavior of shy or severely withdrawn children and adults. The therapist or trainer often uses modeling as part of the treatment to show precisely what the desired behaviors look like and how the behaviors (verbal statements, gestures, eye contact with the other person) go together as a package. Once the client performs these behaviors, feedback, positive reinforcement, and additional modeling can be used to further develop the behavior.

CONTEMPORARY BEHAVIOR MODIFICATION

Contemporary behavior modification is a heterogeneous area of research and application. Many different treatment techniques can be applied to diverse aspects of human behavior. The characteristics that unite under a single rubric were mentioned earlier in the chapter. In contemporary behavior modification, the breadth of approaches is reflected in different ways that are important to mention.

Social Learning Theory: An Integration of Learning Concepts

Classical conditioning, operant conditioning, and modeling have developed largely on their own with extensive bodies of animal laboratory and human research. Obviously, however, clinical problems that are evident in human behavior represent much more complex phenomena than the behaviors studied in animal research in laboratory settings. Animal research often does not reflect the complexity of processes that appear to be involved in human behavior such as language and thought. For example, the developing fear in Albert demonstration was interesting and influential on views about the impact of learning. Yet, we now know more about fears, how they develop, and how they can be changed. Some of what is known underscores the role of perceptions, thoughts, and language. For example, people often perceive threats where there is no danger; these thoughts foster anxiety and arousal. Alteration of these thoughts and perceptions can reduce or eliminate anxiety.

Several authors have provided theories of behavior that attempt to integrate aspects of different learning paradigms and to take cognitive processes into account (Fishman, Rotgers, & Franks, 1988; Reiss, 1991). For example, Bandura (1977, 1986) proposed a social learning theory that encompasses various types of learning and the wide range of influences that each type entails. Social learning theory integrates events in the environment and cognitive processes (thoughts, beliefs, perceptions) both to explain the development of behavior and interventions that can change behavior. The term *social* in social learning theory underscores the fact that multiple influences on behavior occur in the context of social development and interaction. Indeed, many interventions directly involve changing interpersonal interactions in ways that promote behavior change.

The advantage of a social learning approach is that it can account for a broad range of behaviors to a greater extent than accounts based on simplistic applications of one type of learning. For example, it would be quite simplistic to state that a child despises school because of the repeated association of school with punishment—sort of a loose classical conditioning paradigm where school takes on aversive properties by virtue of association with other aversive stimuli (a screaming teacher, being beaten by peers or a principal). Also, it would be overly simplistic to state that a female adolescent repeatedly induces vomiting to remain thin (symptoms of a psychiatric disorder referred to as *bulimia*) because of the social rewards that follow from being thin. This is sort of a loose operant conditioning paradigm where positive consequences (comments from others) are viewed as the basis of how vomiting is maintained. Additionally, it would be simplistic and maybe even silly to state that an adult male robbed a bank because he observed this on television. This is sort of a loose application of modeling. Although each of these examples is simplistic and misguided as an account for the behaviors, the explanations may be just a little true. This is not a contradiction. The influences of punishment at school, comments from others about being fat or thin, and television can affect behavior, but many other influences are operative, including influences within the individual (e.g., beliefs, thoughts) and the environment (cues, responses of others). The task and challenge of behavior modification is to identify factors that influence behavior and that can be used to change behavior.

Diversity of Behavioral Interventions

Within behavior modification, social learning theory comprises the dominant theoretical approach used to conceptualize the development and treatment of behavior and integrates the varied types of learning. Many different types of interventions are available and used to change behavior. The term *cognitive behavior modification* (or cognitive behavior therapy) is a broad term often used to integrate and encompass the full range of interventions. In an important sense, the term *cognitive behavior modification* serves the same integrative function for intervention techniques as the term *social learning* does for the different types of learning. Cognitive behavior modification underscores the importance of cognitive and behavioral processes and the fact that treatment techniques often focus on both thought processes and behavior.

Techniques within behavior modification vary in the extent to which they rely on cognitive processes, either as an explanation of the clinical problem or as a means of achieving behavior change. In some cases, interventions give little or no attention to cognitive processes. They focus on overt behavior, practice, and efforts to provide new learning experiences without regard to such cognitive processes as thoughts, perceptions, beliefs. In other cases, cognitive processes play a more central role. Finally, many interventions combine cognitive and behavioral components.

An example of a combined focus is illustrated by treatment designed to reduce and eliminate anxiety among children (ages 9 to 13). Anxious children perceive those facets of the environment they fear as dangerous, make implicit comments to themselves that bad things may happen, and have beliefs that foster anxious reactions. Treatment focuses directly on how children think about and perceive situations and the statements they make to themselves (Kendall & Treadwell, 1996). More constructive statements are substituted that help children recognize their initial reactions to anxiety and to say things to themselves to help them cope and deflect anxiety. This is clearly a cognitive focus. In addition, the children repeatedly practice self-statements that help them cope with difficult situations, are assigned to practice at home what they learned in treatment, and are exposed to situations in imagination and everyday life that could provoke anxiety. The practice, role-play, rehearsal, and repeated exposure to situations that provoke anxiety reflect a behavioral focus of treatment.

A major focus of behavior modification is the treatment of clinical problems among children, adolescents, and adults who are referred for or who seek treatment in the context of therapy. Many of the examples already mentioned such as depression, anxiety, stress reactions, marital and other relationship problems are of this type. Cognitive behavior modification is a very useful term to encompass the range of treatments used in such settings and we shall provide many examples of the treatments and the problems. Applications of behavior modification in outpatient and inpatient therapy or psychiatric treatment are very important. Indeed, research suggests that a relatively large proportion (approximately 20%) of the population in everyday life, whether children, adolescents, or adults experience significant psychological problems and meet criteria for a recognized psychiatric disorder (Robins & Regier, 1991; U.S. Congress, 1991). Not all of these individuals seek or receive treatment, but clearly there is a need for effective interventions for those who do.

Treatment in the context of therapy is a small part of the applications of behavior modification. Behavioral interventions are implemented in everyday life and I have used "applied settings" as a generic rubric to encompass the full range of applications. This includes treatment in outpatient therapy but also interventions designed to change behaviors in schools, day-care centers, the home, hospitals, nursing homes, business and industry, the military, and society at large. In applied settings, the primary focus has been the use of operant conditioning principles to alter behavior. The interventions begin with the view that many behaviors people wish to alter in themselves or others can be conceptualized as operants. In other words, the behaviors operate on the environment and have consequences that affect the likelihood that they are performed in the future. Studying, exercising, practicing some skill, socializing, shoplifting, and saying endearing or nasty things to one's peers, friends, spouse, or children, can be conceived as operants. Such behaviors can be altered by applying techniques derived from operant conditioning.

The extension of operant conditioning principles and methods of studying human behavior to clinically and socially important human behaviors has become an area of research within behavior modification. The principles of operant conditioning, noted previously (see Table 1-1), refer to the relations between the environment and changes in behavior. The principles, such as positive reinforcement and extinction, have wide generality in their applicability to behavior. Examples in subsequent chapters will convey the extent to which the principles and procedures of operant conditioning have been used to develop effective interventions for significant clinical and social problems.

The current approach to behavior change in applied settings is more than an extension of specific principles. An area of learning research from which operant conditioning emerged is referred to as the *experimental analysis of behavior*. This work developed in animal laboratory research, particularly the work of Skinner (1938), already mentioned, and includes two components: (1) learning processes based on operant conditioning and (2) a way of studying behavior. The way of studying behavior consists of focusing on one or a few individuals over time and evaluating interventions that influence behavior. Several observations are made of the individual over time, either daily or several times per week, to see how behavior changes as environmental conditions are changed.

The extension of experimental methods beyond the laboratory to applied settings generated a new area of research referred to as *applied behavior analysis* (Baer, Wolf, & Risley, 1968, 1987). The special focus of applied behavior analysis is on clinically or socially relevant behaviors in such areas as psychological and psychiatric disorders, education, rehabilitation, medicine, business, and industry. Applied behavior analysis is a specific area within behavior modification. It has unique characteristics that are highlighted in Table 1-5.

Interventions within applied behavior analysis focus on antecedents and consequences that can be used to alter behavior. Cognitive processes and concepts such as beliefs, perceptions, and thoughts do not usually play a role in the interventions that are used in applied settings. Cognitive processes may be quite important and indeed often serve as antecedents that contribute to problems. For example, what people say to themselves may promote certain kinds of behaviors in themselves or others. Also, cognitive processes may be important consequences,

Table 1-5 Characteristics of Applied Behavior Analysis

1. Focus on overt behaviors
2. Focus on behaviors of applied (social or clinical) significance
3. Assess behavior through direct observation, as in counting the frequency of responses
4. Assess behavior continuously over time (e.g., several days per week) to identify patterns of behavior that occur with and without interventions in place or under various environmental or stimulus conditions (e.g., presence of another person, different situations)
5. Search for marked intervention effects that make a clear difference to the everyday functioning of the individual
6. Focus on one or a small number of individuals over time
7. Use environmental (and observable) events to influence the frequency of behavior
8. Identify, evaluate, and demonstrate the factors (e.g., events) that are responsible for behavior change

that is, what people say to themselves or perceive may influence their own behavior. Interventions based on operant conditioning usually focus directly on overt behavior in settings in everyday life and on the environmental events before, after, and during the behavior that can be used to achieve behavior change.

The present book focuses on behavior modification in applied settings. Although this includes the range of cognitive behavior modification procedures, the emphasis will be on applied behavior analysis. The reason is that the principles of operant conditioning and the techniques derived from them have the widest application of behavior modification procedures.

SUMMARY AND CONCLUSIONS

Behavior modification is an approach toward assessment, evaluation, and behavior change. Among the key characteristics are the focus on behavior and its current determinants, providing learning experiences that change, and assessment and evaluation of intervention effects to ensure that change is taking place. The scope of behavior modification is broad in light of the range of different techniques of achieving behavior change and the range of clients, settings, and behaviors to which the techniques have been applied. Child rearing, education, medicine, business and industry, and psychotherapy, each an area of study in its own right, are a few of the domains encompassed by behavior modification.

The overall challenge of treatment, child rearing, education, rehabilitation, and other areas where change is desired is to identify means of developing and altering behavior. The psychology of learning is a rich area that suggests what experiences ought to be provided and in what ways to optimize learning and behavior change. Classical conditioning, operant conditioning, and modeling highlighted in this chapter provide the underpinnings of many behavior modification techniques.

Among the techniques encompassed by behavior modification, those that derive from operant conditioning have been the most widely applied. Applied behavior analysis is an area within behavior modification in which operant conditioning techniques and methods of assessment and evaluation are applied in everyday settings. The emphasis of this book is on interventions in applied settings and draws most heavily on applied behavior analysis. Subsequent chapters include principles and techniques derived from operant conditioning, illustrate their use and application in many different contexts from treatment and everyday life, and help the reader apply these techniques.

KEY TERMS

Applied behavior analysis	Evaluation	Operant
Assessment	Modeling	Operant conditioning
Classical conditioning		

FOR FURTHER READING

Baer, D.M., Wolf, M.M., & Risley, T.R. (1968). Some current dimensions of applied behavior analysis. *Journal of Applied Behavior Analysis, 1,* 91-97.

Baer, D.M., Wolf, M.M., & Risley, T.R. (1987). Some still-current dimensions of applied behavior analysis. *Journal of Applied Behavior Analysis, 20,* 313-328.

Catania, A.C. (1997). *Learning* (4th ed.). Englewood Cliffs, NJ: Prentice-Hall.

Kazdin, A.E. (1978). *History of behavior modification: Experimental foundations of contemporary research.* Baltimore: University Park Press.

Lattal, K.A. (Guest Ed.) (1992). Special issue: Reflections on B.F. Skinner and psychology. *American Psychologist, 47,* 1269-1533.

Skinner, B.F. (1953). *Science and human behavior.* New York: Free Press.

NOTES

1. The term *client* will be used to refer generally to the person to whom the intervention is provided. The reference is a convenient way to encompass different persons (e.g., psychiatric patients, children and adults in therapy, parents, students, employees in a factory).

2. The demonstration with Little Albert had remarkable influence in suggesting the role of classical (respondent) conditioning in the development of fear and by implication perhaps other behaviors. However, there are problems with the demonstration that relate directly to this book. The original demonstration is not a simply pairing of a neutral stimulus (white rat) with a loud noise to evoke startle, although that is how Watson described this. The demonstration has since been considered to be more appropriately conceived of as operant rather than classical conditioning. In operant conditioning, consequences follow responses, i.e., the individual does something, after which some event follows. In the Watson and Rayner demonstration, Albert reached for or began to touch the rat (Albert's response—an operant), at which point the loud noise sounded (aversive event). This sequence of events more closely follows a punishment paradigm of operant conditioning. In addition to this problem, several attempts were made to repeat the demonstration and these were largely unsuccessful (see Kazdin, 1978). The

significance of the demonstration historically was the boost it provided for conceptualizing the role of learning for important
behaviors and emotions in everyday experience. In the approximately 80 years since
that original demonstration, effective treatments have been developed to treat fears
and anxiety. The Little Albert demonstration
plays some small role in the current successes that are achieved with treatment.

3. *Psychoses* is a broad term that refers to
psychiatric disorders in which patients are
usually quite impaired. Key characteristics of
psychoses are the experience of delusions
(persistent and false beliefs about oneself,
others, or the world such as a belief that

one has been instructed by God to do certain behaviors) and hallucinations (perceptions such as hearing and seeing things,
others, that have are not evident in reality
to others). In psychoses, delusions and hallucinations are part of a range of other symptoms (e.g., staring into space, absence of
social functioning and response to others)
that greatly interfere with the individual's
ability to function.

4. Research in applied behavior analysis is
published in many journals in psychology,
education, rehabilitation, community work
and other areas. The *Journal of Applied Behavior Analysis* is devoted to this type of research.

CHAPTER 2

Principles of Operant Conditioning

Behavior modification programs rely on all three kinds of learning—classical conditioning, operant conditioning, and observational learning—as discussed in the previous chapter. In applied settings such as the classroom, home, hospitals, institutions, and society at large, behavioral programs rely heavily on the principles of operant conditioning. This chapter provides an overview of basic principles.[1] It is important to consider several principles together to convey a way of conceptualizing how to go about intervening to change behavior. In later chapters, principles noted here will be considered in greater detail to convey research findings, applications of the principles, and how to conduct interventions to ensure they are effective.

CONTINGENCIES: THE ABCS OF BEHAVIOR

The *contingencies of reinforcement* refer to the relationships between behaviors and the environmental events that influence behavior. Three components are included in a contingency, namely, antecedents (A), behaviors (B), and consequences (C). The notion of a contingency is important not only for understanding behavior but also for developing programs to change behavior. *Antecedents* refer to stimuli, settings, and contexts that occur before and influence behaviors. Examples include instructions, gestures, or looks from others. *Behaviors* refer to the acts themselves—what individuals do or do not do—that is the focus of the program. *Consequences* refer to events that follow behavior and may include influences that increase, decrease, or have no impact on what the individual does. Table 2-1 illustrates the three components of a contingency with simple examples from everyday life. The examples convey what some of the ABCs are and how they are related. We shall build on this table in this chapter. Even with the simple examples in the table, one can see the interdependence of As, Bs, and Cs.

Consider the first line of the table that includes the behavior "answering the phone." Antecedents are obviously critical and clearly control behavior. For example, the ringing of a telephone usually leads to behavior, namely, going over to and picking up (answering) the phone. Not too many people run to answer the phone when there is no ring (antecedent). Consequences are rather important in this example too. We repeatedly answer ringing telephones because of the consequences that regularly follow our behaviors, namely, that there is almost always someone on the other end of the line to speak with us.

It is useful to convey a simple example here merely to define and identify antecedents, behaviors, and consequences. It is also important to recognize that ABCs are more complex than one antecedent, one behavior, and one consequence. For example, in the phone call example, we may not answer a ringing phone. If we are expecting a call from someone with whom we do not wish to speak or are on our way out, we may not answer. Stated another way, the context or circumstances form part of the antecedent events and may change how we respond—in this case whether we answer.

Developing effective programs depends on understanding the influences of antecedents and consequences and how they can be used to promote, develop, and maintain behavior. A misguided and somewhat superficial view of behavioral in-

**Table 2-1   Three Components of a Contingency
and Illustrations from Everyday Life**

Antecedent	Behavior	Consequence
Telephone rings	Answering the phone	Voice of person at the other end
Wave (greeting) from a friend	Walking over to the friend	Visiting and chatting
Parent instruction to a child to clean the room	Picking up toys	Verbal praise and a pat on the back
Warning not to eat spoiled food	Eating the food	Nausea and vomiting

terventions focuses on consequences alone. Indeed, sometimes merely providing consequences for behavior in a casual way is taken as an application of behavior modification (e.g., "I praise my child when he does what I ask, and he still never listens.") A curse of behavior modification is the view that casual efforts to apply minute aspects of the approach can be effective. Occasionally such efforts might work, just like taking a few days of an antibiotic may make one feel better or even eliminate an infection. However, this is not the approach or the intended intervention. Behavioral interventions can be extremely effective. What is useful about the approach is that many of the conditions that dictate effectiveness have been well studied.

Antecedents, behaviors, and consequences are described in detail to convey and to illustrate key concepts. Although they are distinguished and separated for purposes of presentation, they are quite interrelated. For example, we walk into a room and see an odd facial expression on a person. That facial expression (antecedent to the next behavior) may prompt a behavior from us (e.g., we say, "What happened?" or "Is everything all right?" or "I didn't do it!"). Many antecedent events such as facial expressions can acquire their influence because of their association with certain consequences. We may have learned from frequent pairings of various facial expressions (e.g., from our own direct experience or from movies, books, and cartoons) with various consequences. Also, in any given interchange, ongoing sequences of antecedents, behaviors, and consequences occur. It is useful to dissect the ABCs at this point to convey more clearly what they are.

ANTECEDENTS OF BEHAVIOR

Behavior is influenced greatly by antecedents or what comes before the behavior is performed. Three types of antecedents are distinguished here, including setting events, prompts, and discriminative stimuli. They are easily confused; after all, they all come before behavior. Consequently, several examples are provided.

Setting Events

At the most general level, setting events are antecedent to behavior. *Setting events refer to contextual factors or conditions that influence behavior.* They are broad in scope

Table 2-2   Types of Antecedents and Illustrations

Type of Antecedent	Key Characteristics	Examples
Setting event/establishing operation	Alters value of the reinforcer and increases likelihood of engaging behaviors to obtain the reinforcer	Being deprived of a reinforcer (e.g., food, water, attention); exposure to a pleasant or unpleasant interaction; a success or failure experience
Prompt	Some event or stimulus that directly guides and facilitates performance; directly connected to the behaviors to be performed	Instructions to guide how to hold, play, or use a musical instrument, modeling (showing) how to do something; guiding physically as a child learns how to form letters during a handwriting lesson
Discriminative stimuli (S^D)	A stimulus or event indicating that a particular behavior is likely to be reinforced; the stimuli indicate that the reinforcer is available	The ring of a telephone (signaling that someone is likely to be on the other end of the line), the sound of a timer (indicating the food is ready from the oven); an enticing smile from an attractive person (signaling that approach behavior is likely to be reciprocated)

and set the stage for the behaviors and consequences that follow. Setting events include features of the situation, features of the task or demands presented to the individual, conditions within the individual (e.g., exhaustion, hunger, expectations of what will happen), or behaviors of others. Table 2-2 (top row) provides a few examples. Consider another example in greater detail. A child, getting ready for school, may hear a heated argument or perhaps witness violence between his or her parents right before going to school. That morning at school, the child may be a little more irritable, more reactive, and less attentive to schoolwork than usual. The child's behaviors (e.g., talking to peers, paying attention, completing assignments, provoking arguments) are changed. The changes are not due to consequences or anything different at school but rather to events that altered the child, his motivation, and the set with which he approached school.

Setting event is useful and easy to remember as a term in part because it conveys that some event or factor "sets the stage" and influences behavior. External or environmental events (e.g., the actual setting such as home, school, a restaurant, the behavior of others in the setting), as well as internal states and events (e.g., feeling irritable, having had a wonderful or poor night's sleep, being deprived of food, water, companionship) all qualify as setting events insofar as they can influence subsequent performance. A more precise and specific term is *establishing operation, which refers to an antecedent variable or factor that temporarily alters the effectiveness of some other event or consequence* (Michael, 1993). Motivational states, emotions, and environmental events are establishing operations if they momentarily alter the effectiveness of the consequences that may follow behavior and influence the frequency of some behavior. Two conditions are required to qualify as an establishing operation. First, such operations alter the effectiveness of consequences (reinforcing and punishing events) in the environment. Second, such operations influence the frequency of behaviors that can obtain these consequences.

Consider an example. Assume for a moment that food reinforcement is available for a given response of a laboratory animal or human. Let us say the reinforcement is always available and can be obtained anytime a response is performed. Deprivation or satiation of the individual will influence the likelihood of the response. When the individual is deprived, the effectiveness of food as a reinforcer is much greater than it would otherwise be, and behaviors associated with obtaining food become more probable. In other words, deprivation is an establishing operation, that is, an antecedent condition that influences the effectiveness of food as a reinforcer and increases the likelihood of engaging in responses that obtain food.

This example is good in isolating what is the establishing operation, what is the reinforcer, and what might be the behaviors that are increased as a result. In everyday life, the operations may be complex and more difficult to identify. *Setting events* is used here as a broad term to encompass many such influences that serve as establishing operations, even though the criteria for the two conditions noted above are not always met. For example, how parents interact with their oppositional children appears to be influenced by parent social interaction outside the home (Wahler, 1980); that is, for the parent, social interaction with others serves as an establishing operation for how they interact with their children. When mothers experience positive social contacts outside the home with friends, they show fewer aversive interchanges with their children (commands, reprimands) and as a result, promote less deviant child behavior at home. As assessed on a daily basis, mothers' social interactions seem to provide a setting event that influences subsequent contingencies in the repertoire of the mothers and then their children. Of course, it is not a brilliant insight to say that how things are going in one part of a person's life can influence how things go in another part. Yet, the key insight here is that by understanding these relations more systematically, one can intervene to change behavior.

The world often tinkers with setting events to influence our motivational states and the likelihood of engaging or not engaging in various behaviors. For example, some airlines play music when people are boarding the plane. The music is carefully selected to be familiar and upbeat but not discordant or unpleasant. The goal is to have the stimuli evoke pleasant feelings about travel, the flight that is about to begin, and the experience of the particular airline. Similarly, when people are selling a home, a not-so-old old trick is to make the stimulus conditions of the home appear very "homey" as potential buyers walk through the house. This is accomplished by having cake or bread baking in the oven or by boiling potpourri (flowers, cinnamon) on the top of the stove. The scents are assumed to set the stage for warm, fuzzy, and homelike behaviors, thoughts, and feelings on the part of potential buyers and more importantly, to increase the value of obtaining the "reinforcer" (i.e., purchase of the home).

Setting events are important, which is not the same thing as saying they are completely understood (McGill, 1999; Smith & Iwata, 1997). They are often difficult to identify because they do not necessarily occur immediately before behavior. Having a child, losing a parent, and winning a lottery are broad influences that are not likely to be analyzed in a laboratory but in part, serve as critical influences on subsequent behavior. In everyday life, one can often identify relations between setting events and behavior and use these relations to develop interventions. For example, one can see a parent issue a harsh-sounding command to a child to do something. The child may not comply with the command and may even say "no" in an obstinate fashion. A harsh order or command from a parent sets the stage for noncompliance. This is not a matter of blaming the parent for the child's noncompliance; blame is not relevant. What is relevant is that *how* the request was made, perhaps *when* it was made (e.g., in light of the child doing something else such as watching a favorite TV show), and *what* was in the request (e.g., no choices given, demand for immediate compliance rather than a little warning). That is, the command itself is an establishing operation that could affect the child's motivation and his or her likelihood to respond in one way rather than another. Clearly, an important agenda for research is to understand how such influences take place; an important agenda for intervention is to use setting events to help promote adaptive behavior. From the discussion of setting events, one can see immediately that understanding and changing behavior is more than merely connecting behaviors with consequences. The initial events, stimuli, and states of the individual influence subsequent behavior and hence have to be considered.

Prompts

Prompts refer to specific antecedents that directly facilitate performance of behavior. They are distinguished from setting events, which are more contextual, indirect, and broad influences on behavior. Table 2-2 (middle row) provides some examples of prompts. Other examples include instructions to engage in the behavior ("Please wash up before dinner."), cues (reminders or notes to oneself, lists of things to do), gestures (come in, leave the room), examples and modeling (demonstrations to show how the behavior, task, or skill is done), and physical guidance (guiding a person's hands to show her how to play a musical instrument or how to hit a volley ball).

Prompts serve as antecedent events (instructions, gestures) that help generate or initiate the desired response. They are designed to facilitate the response. When a prompt results in the response, consequences can be provided (positive reinforcement) to increase the likelihood that the response will recur. Without the prompt, the response might occur infrequently or not at all.

Prompts play a major role in developing a behavior. When an individual does not engage in the behavior, prompts can show the person what to do, how to do it, and when to do it. For example, one might want to provide reinforcing consequences to develop a complex set of behaviors (driving a car, completing a term paper) or a simple behavior that never occurs (eating specific foods). If the desired behavior never occurs, it cannot be reinforced. Assisting a person in beginning the response can enable the person to make more rapid approximations of the final response.

When a person has partially mastered the task or skill, prompts can help refine the behavior and help add to the complexity. For example, when teaching a complex ballet or tango dance step, the teacher at first may model (a prompt) basic movements. As the skill is acquired, the teacher may model more subtle little movements of the hands, body, or legs to develop these more specific behaviors.

Several different types of prompts can be used alone or in combination. For example, several prompts were used to teach a job skill to profoundly retarded adult women (Schepis, Reid, & Fitzgerald, 1987). The women could comply only with simple requests and engaged in aggressive and self-injurious behavior. The goal was to train a job skill that consisted of preparing envelopes for mailing, including stamping a return address on the envelopes. To train the task, different kinds of prompts were used. Verbal instructions (verbal prompt) were provided to explain the sequence of behaviors; modeling (visual prompt) was provided if the individual did not show the requisite behaviors; finally, the individual was aided by guiding her through the task with physical assistance (physical prompt). These prompts were designed to increase the likelihood of correct performance of the behaviors, so that the reinforcer (in this case praise) could be provided. While a response is being developed, prompts may be used frequently to facilitate performance of the terminal response.

In most cases, the long-term goal is to develop a behavior so that it is performed without the use of prompts. Although prompts may be required early in training, they can be withdrawn gradually or faded as training progresses. *Fading refers to the gradual removal of a prompt.* If a prompt is removed abruptly early in training, the response may no longer be performed, but if the response is performed consistently with a prompt, the prompt can be progressively reduced and finally omitted. For example, teaching a person how to serve in tennis or how to play the piano may include reminders (prompts) regarding how to hold the racket or how to place one's fingers on the keys. As the person begins to perform these behaviors, the nature of the prompt may change (e.g., from "hold your fingers like this [with the positioned modeled by the teacher]" to "fingers" [without any other verbal statement or modeling]). Prompts are also provided less often. The correct behaviors are reinforced without reminders, and soon these behaviors do not need to be prompted at all or only rarely.

For example, in the study mentioned previously, prompts were used to train a specific set of behaviors with mentally retarded women. Over the course of training and as the behaviors were performed correctly, trainers began to fade the prompts. More intrusive (physical) prompts were decreased and the number of prompts was decreased over time. The goal was to develop the behavior so that it could be performed independently (i.e., without prompts). This goal was facilitated by introducing prompts to develop the behavior, then gradually fading and eliminating the prompts, and finally reinforcing the responses in the absence of prompts. It is not always necessary to remove all prompts. For example, it is important to train individuals to respond in the presence of certain prompts, such as instructions, that exert control over a variety of behaviors in everyday life.

Prompts have uses other than in training new behaviors. For behaviors that are readily available, prompts can play a useful role. For example, getting people to take medication is difficult, even though there may be strong incentives to do so. Many factors are involved, but one of them is that there may be no clear cues to take the medication as prescribed. Prompts can help. For example, many women take oral contraceptives. Of these, almost half forget to take the pill at least once a month. Surveys show that pill users consider remembering to take the pill every day as a disadvantage of this method of birth control. Indeed, approximately one million unintended pregnancies in the United States each year are attributed to misuse, failure, or discontinuation of birth control pills. There are many solutions to this problem, including the use of birth-control methods that do not require engaging in a particular behavior every day. However, prompting might help those who wish to take the pills. To that end, one company that manufactures an oral contraceptive pill, Organon, Inc., has developed a card (size of a credit card) that beeps at the same time every day for 3 months to remind the woman to take the pill (www.organonwomenshealth.com). Hearing the beep each day would be likely to serve as an effective prompt. Of course, ensuring that the card is around, available, and audible is another issue. Even so, the card conveys the use of prompts, namely, to help initiate the behavior.

High-Probability Requests

Making requests is a special type of prompt that warrants separate comment. An antecedent statement is provided to someone to engage in a behavior and, hopefully, initiates the behavior. Precisely how the request is delivered influences greatly the likelihood that there will be compliance. Consider an experience common among parents. Parents often ask young children to do various sorts of mundane tasks (e.g., get ready for dinner, clear the dinner table, start your homework). Based on the child's compliance to many such instructions, the parent is likely to say that the child does or does not comply very well. Certainly individuals differ in the extent to which they respond to instructions, all else being equal. Yet, precisely how instructions and requests are presented (i.e., antecedents) can make a major difference.

Considerable research has been conducted on the presentation of requests and how the presentation influences compliance. Two types of requests have been distinguished, namely, those an individual is very likely to do (called *high-probably requests*) and those an individual is very unlikely to do (*low-probability requests*). The specific requests that fall into these categories vary for individuals. Consider for a moment that a parent wishes the child to comply with several requests that she or he does not do (e.g., do a chore, complete another task). Throughout the day, if the parent asks the child to comply, the low-probability requests are rarely completed. However, if the parent first asks the child to do a few high-probability requests (e.g., "Please see if your sister is upstairs," "Write down 'fruit' on the grocery list," "Watch a little TV before dinner"), the child is much more likely to comply with a low-probability request that follows. Embedding a low-probability request in a sequence of high-probability requests increases the likelihood of compliance with a low-probability request (Ardoin, Martens, & Wolfe, 1999; Mace & Belfiore, 1990).

As an example, two otherwise "normal" 4-year-old girls were identified because they did not comply with several requests (Rortvedt & Miltenberger, 1994).

High- and low-probability requests were identified by testing compliance. Once identified, the intervention began by first making three high-probability requests (e.g., simple commands like "Touch your nose") followed by a low-probability request (e.g., "Put your glass in the sink"). The children greatly increased their compliance with low-probability requests when these requests were preceded by high-probability requests.

Many other such demonstrations have been provided. In one case, compliance with a request to hold still during a complex medical procedure was increased in a 22-month child by first providing high-probability requests (McComas, Wacker, & Cooper, 1998). A sequence of requests such as (1) "Touch your head," (2) "Say 'Mom'," (3) "Blow Mom a kiss," and (4) "Hold still" were provided. In this example, requests 1, 2, and 3 were high-probability requests. The fourth was a low-probability request and was much more likely to lead to compliance when preceded by the first three requests. The demonstration underscores the importance of antecedents in controlling behavior and also the significance of how instructions are provided in addition to what the instructions are.

Discriminative Stimuli and Stimulus Control

Setting events and prompts could be presented without too much discussion of consequences. Stimulus control is not so easy. Stimuli often become associated with various consequences. Once these associations occur, the stimuli themselves exert control over behavior. Thus to understand the influence of the stimuli, antecedents, behaviors, and consequences must be considered together.

In some situations (or in the presence of certain stimuli), a response may be reinforced; in other situations (in the presence of other stimuli), the same response is not reinforced. The concept of differential reinforcement is central to understanding stimulus events and their influences. *Differential reinforcement refers to reinforcing a response in the presence of one stimulus or situation and not reinforcing the same response in the presence of another stimulus or situation.* When a response is consistently reinforced in the presence of a particular stimulus and not reinforced in the presence of another stimulus, each stimulus signals the consequences that are likely to follow. A stimulus whose presence has been associated with reinforcement is referred to as a *discriminative stimulus* (S^D). A stimulus whose presence has been associated with nonreinforcement is referred to as a *nondiscriminative stimulus* (S^Δ or S delta). The effect of differential reinforcement is that eventually the reinforced response is likely to occur in the presence of the S^D but unlikely to occur in the presence of the S^Δ. When responses are differentially controlled by antecedent stimuli, behavior is said to be under *stimulus control*. When there is stimulus control, the presence of a stimulus increases the likelihood of a response. As mentioned previously, the stimulus does not cause response or automatically elicit the response the way reflexes are elicited in classical conditioning. Rather, in operant conditioning, the stimulus (an S^D) increases the probability that a previously reinforced behavior will occur.

Some examples are provided in Table 2-2 (bottom row). Another more detailed example is when a stranger smiles at us on the street, there is an increase in the likelihood that we too will smile and say something friendly. Also, if we smile back, it is very likely the person will say something back to us. Stated a bit more precisely, smiling is a signal (an S^D) that specific behaviors on our part (acts of friendliness) are likely to be reinforced (acknowledged, reciprocated). We do not usually initiate friendly statements to others who present us with a grumpy facial expression. A grumpy facial expression is an S^Δ; it indicates that the reinforcer is not likely to follow. Smiling and grumpy faces of strangers do not *elicit* behavior from us in a reflexive way but rather increase the likelihood of certain behaviors on our part.

Stimulus control is learned, so not everyone responds in a friendly way when confronted with a smiling stranger, that is, what becomes an S^D for each of us may vary, although there are likely to be commonalities in a given culture. For example, when a robber confronts us, this is not an S^D for really friendly, social, back-slapping behavior on our part. The cues that robbers present (weapon, hostile demeanor, outfit, context) suggest that probably only one response will be reinforced (i.e., giving the person the object demanded).

Instances of stimulus control pervade everyday life. For example, the sound of a doorbell signals that a certain behavior (opening the door) is likely to be reinforced (by seeing someone). Specifically, the sound of the bell has often been associated with the presence of visitors at the door (the reinforcer). The ring of the bell (S^D) increases the likelihood that the door will be opened. In the absence of the bell (S^Δ), the probability of opening the door for a visitor is very low. The ring of a doorbell, telephone, alarm, and kitchen timer all serve as discriminative stimuli (S^D) and signal that certain responses are likely to be reinforced. Hence, the probability of the responses is increased.

Stimulus control is pervasive and guides much of our behavior. Consider the selection and consumption of food. For example, the color and smell of foods (such as an orange that has turned green or milk that smells sour) influence the likelihood of eating them. Characteristics of the foods are cues for particular consequences (such as flavor or nausea) and exert stimulus control over our eating. In recognition of the importance of the stimulus, natural foods (fruit) or products (leather) often have artificial colors and fragrances added to increase the likelihood of their purchase. Wedding rings that people wear also exert stimulus control. Wearing a wedding ring is an S^Δ that certain behaviors on the part of others (e.g., flirtation, asking one out for a date) are not likely to be reinforced. Presumably a wedding ring is also an S^Δ to the individual who wears it and decreases the likelihood of engaging in certain behavior (initiating new romantic relationships). Of course, marital behavior is controlled by many more influences within the individual and environment than weddings rings, but stimuli are present that serve as important cues.

People in everyday life are quite familiar with the concepts of differential reinforcement and stimulus control, although these terms, of course, are not used. For example, children behave differently in the presence of their mothers and fathers in part because of the slightly different reinforcement contingencies that operate with each parent. Children often know whom to ask (mother or father) in making specific requests because the likelihood of reinforcement (affirmative answer) differs between parents on various issues. Similarly, at home children often behave quite differently from how they behave at school. The different performances may lead to perplexed parents and teachers who argue that the child is not "really" like that. Yet, the child's behavior may vary considerably as a function of different reinforcement contingencies at home and at school.

The notion of stimulus control is exceedingly important in behavior modification. In many programs, the goal is to alter the relation between behavior and the stimulus conditions in which the behavior occurs. Some behavior problems stem from a failure of certain stimuli to control behavior when such control would be desirable. For example, children who do not follow instructions given by their parents illustrate a lack of stimulus control. The instructions do not exert influence over the children's behavior. The goal of a behavior modification program is to increase responsiveness to instructions.

BEHAVIORS

We have considered the antecedents of the ABCs of contingencies. Behavior change is achieved by identifying the behaviors of interest, that is, the behaviors that one wishes to develop. These are called *target behaviors*. Of course, one does not merely identify behavior but rather plans how to develop them systematically. Two procedures figure prominently in developing behavior—shaping and chaining.

Shaping

The individual may perform target behaviors already and the goal of the intervention may be to increase performance in someway (e.g., more occasions in which the behavior is occurring, longer periods engaging in the behavior, or fostering the behavior in new situations). In these instances, providing antecedents and consequences may be sufficient to increase or extend the behavior. In many other cases, the individual does not have the behavior in his or her repertoire or only has the behavior partially. In these cases one cannot merely wait for the behavior to occur and provide consequences; the response may never occur. The desired behavior may be so complex that the elements making up the response are not in the repertoire of the individual. The behavior can be achieved by reinforcing small steps or approximations toward the final response rather than reinforcing the final response itself.

The reinforcement of successive approximations of the final response is referred to as shaping. Responses are reinforced that either resemble the final response or include components of that response. By reinforcing successive approximations, the final response is gradually achieved. Responses increasingly similar to the final goal are reinforced, and they increase; responses dissimilar to the final goal are not reinforced, and they extinguish. For example, when parents are trying to develop use of the words "mommy" or "daddy" in an infant, they usually reinforce any approximation ("ma" or "da-da") by smiling, hugging, and praising effusively. At the same time, but usually without thinking about it, they do not attend to (or extinguish) sounds that are not close to the words they wish ("goo" or "milk"). Over time, the parents reinforce sounds and syllables that come closer to the words mommy and daddy.

An obvious example of shaping is training animals to perform various tricks. If the animal trainer waited until the tricks were performed (e.g., jumping through a burning hoop) to administer a reinforcer, it is unlikely that reinforcement would ever occur. Animals normally do not perform such behavior. By shaping the response, the trainer can readily achieve the terminal goal. First, food (positive reinforcer) might be delivered for running toward the trainer. As that response becomes consistent, the trainer might reinforce running up to him when he or she is holding a hoop. Other steps closer to the final goal would be reinforced in sequence, including walking through the hoop on the ground, jumping through it when it is partially on fire, and finally, jumping through it when the hoop is completely on fire. Eventually, the terminal response will be performed with a high frequency, whereas the responses or steps developed along the way will have been extinguished.

An example of shaping I recall from my own college years was conducted in class with my peers. This was a psychology class of about 25 students. The professor in class stood in front of a small lectern on a table in the front of the class. He rarely looked at his notes on the lectern but he remained in the center of the class right in front of them all of the time, except when writing on the blackboard immediately behind him. My peers thought how interesting it might be to see if we could shape his behavior. The terminal goal or target behavior was to get the professor to stand and lecture in the corner of the room (to the right of him). Several students met and decided to do this, although the entire class was not involved.

To shape the behavior, one needs a reinforcer. This was not too difficult. Eye contact, attention, mild nods of understanding, and enthusiasm all are likely to be positive reinforcers for poor professors who occasionally stare at a sea of inattentive students who have been up until 3 or 4 AM the night before. (Of course, many professors foster inattentiveness by the content and style of their lectures.) Hence we have the terminal response (lecturing from a specific corner in the room) and a consequence (attentiveness, eye contact, looks of interest) likely to serve as a reinforcer.

Of course, we could never directly reinforce the terminal response of interest. One shapes behavior *because* the final behavior is not present in the repertoire of the individual. The professor never went into the corner or anywhere near it. For shaping, we decided to sit up and look interested, make eye contact, and so on whenever he moved a little bit (one step) forward toward the corner of the room. There is always variability (variation or departures from one's average performance) in behavior, so little changes (movements in one direction or another) occur naturally. On the first day of the intervention, the first time he moved (maybe one-half foot from the center of the lectern), several students in the class leaned forward a bit and looked a little more alert, interested, and attentive than usual. (Yes, it was difficult not to laugh; I readily recall most students in my entire row leaning forward on this occasion.) Thus the initial approximation toward the terminal behavior received attention. This does not necessarily alter all behavior for all time, but it would increase the likelihood of that behavior in the future. He naturally went back to the center of the podium and those same students looked away, that is, they reclined back in their seats and looked down or at their notes. This continued for awhile, whenever he moved to his left, we—I mean, those mischievous other students—leaned forward and looked attentive. He was still about 15 feet from the corner of the room, but shaping was continued. We had time because the course met 3 days per week and was for an entire semester.

Once he was a little away from the center of the room on a regular basis, there would be variation in his performance here too, so naturally, he would move a little more to his left or right. When he moved a little more toward the corner, again the students looked alive. After a few days, the students no longer looked enthusiastic or attentive when the professor was just a little away from the center of the room. We held out for a little more and then a little more. In shaping, one reinforces behaviors that increasingly approximate the final goal and stops reinforcing those early approximations that are well established. After about two weeks of this, the guy was in the corner leaning against the wall lecturing solidly for the entire period. Occasionally he would wander back, peek at his notes but invariably stroll back to the corner. Of course, the class really paid attention all of the time he was in the corner and less so when he wandered back. One day, he raised his foot and placed it on the wastebasket that was also in the corner. My peers spontaneously provided copious attention and leaned forward and thought this would be a great addition to the terminal goal. This behavior increased for a few days too but a few students wanted to stop the program. Clearly the terminal response was achieved, and we had entire lectures delivered from the corner of the room, again barring occasional trips to peek at the notes.

This is almost the end of the shaping example, but not the story. A few students with good values, nice training, and ethics thought that we should return him to where he was before our shaping program began. Also, most of the students involved in the program were pretty tired of sitting up and looking interested, as was needed for 50 minutes three times a week. To begin with, the class did not engender great enthusiasm. Even so, the students agreed to continue the program to reverse the process. Now, attention was provided for staying in the middle of the room and lecturing from there. This was easier to obtain because the professor occasionally left the corner and visited his notes placed on the lectern in the center of the room. Hence, the new terminal behavior (being in the center of the room) was already evident, so we just had to be sure to reinforce this whenever it occurred. This behavior readily developed and the program ended with weeks to spare before the end of the term.

As this example shows, shaping begins by reinforcing behaviors already in the repertoire of the individual that resemble or approximate the final goal. The behaviors already in the repertoire initially were these spontaneous slight movements away from the center of the room and in the direction of the corner. As the initial approximation is performed consistently, the criterion for reinforcement is altered slightly so that the response to be reinforced resembles the final goal more closely than does the previous response. Through reinforcement of responses that approach the final goal and extinction of responses that do not, the terminal response is developed. In shaping the goal is to attain a final behavior, and the behaviors along the way drop out or are replaced by behaviors that are closer and closer to the goal.

Chaining

Most behaviors consist of a sequence of several responses. A sequence of responses is referred to as a *chain*. A chain represents a combination or series of the individual responses performed in a particular order. For example, "getting dressed" is a behavioral chain that includes such behaviors as taking clothes out of the drawer, placing them on a bed, putting on a shirt, and so on for other articles of clothing. Putting on individual articles of clothing also consists of a chain of behaviors. Similarly, completing a term paper or writing a book consists of a sequence of behaviors such as identifying the topic, organizing what will be presented and in what order, obtaining pertinent materials, perhaps reorganizing the material, drafting the paper, and so on. These examples reflect chains of behavior because they comprise many individual responses that are linked together in a specific order.

Most behaviors in everyday life can be conceived of as chains of behaviors. Developing the sequence of behaviors is a process referred to as *chaining*. Chaining occurs by reinforcing completion of the full sequence of behaviors, that is, rather than just developing one behavior, a sequence of multiple behaviors occurs. Reinforcement is provided for completion of the sequence of behaviors. Consider a sequence of behaviors as putting on a shirt, a dressing skill sometimes taught to severely mentally retarded children who cannot dress themselves. Let us assume for the moment that this is a pullover shirt and that the sequence of individual behaviors consists of:

1. Taking the shirt from the drawer
2. Spreading it out on the bed and picking up the shirt
3. Putting one arm through the sleeve
4. Then the other arm through the sleeve
5. Then putting one's head through
6. Finally pulling it down to one's waist

This sequence of behaviors can be developed in different ways, namely, by forward or backward chaining.

Forward Chaining. *Forward chaining consists of developing behaviors in the order in which they are to be performed,* that is, in the above sequence, we begin by first developing step number 1. A child is assisted, with prompts, to take the shirt from the drawer. Perhaps a verbal prompt would begin this way: "Please put on your shirt," followed physical assistance and guidance. Once the first behavior is performed, the reinforcer (praise, hugs) is provided. The shirt goes back in the drawer and this is repeated. After awhile, the second behavior is added, and the child would engage in behaviors 1 and 2 and then receive the reinforcer. This would proceed until the entire sequence is performed.

At first blush, forward chaining may seem to resemble or to be the same as shaping. They are different. Shaping usually is thought of as changing a behavior so it goes from one form to another. That is, the behavior may be changed along quantitative dimensions (maybe studying for 2 minutes) to another form (maybe studying for 20 minutes) or along qualitative dimensions (balancing on a beam first with one's hands stretched out to keep one's balance but eventually balancing without the hands out). Hence, there is *a* behavior that is developed. In shaping, the final behavior replaces all of the steps along the way; one does not see early behaviors that have been trained. They have been replaced.

Forward chaining develops behavior but there are multiple behaviors in a sequence and at the end of training, all of the original behaviors in the sequence are still there. Therefore in the dressing example, all of the behaviors in the sequence are still evident at the end of training; they are just performed in order in a seamless way.

Backward Chaining. Chaining can also be completed in a backward fashion. *Backward chaining consists of starting with the last behavior in the sequence,* that is, one begins by training the last behavior first (step number 6 in the prior example). Thus the training would begin by putting the shirt on the child almost completely with only one step remaining, namely, pulling it down to his or her waist. The child would be prompted to pull it down (maybe verbal prompts and physical prompts). When this behavior was completed, it would be followed by reinforcement. Once this is mastered, perhaps with a few more trials, then the shirt is put on up to the point of pulling the head through. Reinforcement would be provided at the end of completing both behaviors at the end of the sequence. This would continue until the first behavior in the sequence (taking the shirt from the drawer) was finally included.

Why Backward Chaining? Developing a sequence of behavior in a forward fashion seems so straightforward. Indeed, forward chaining makes intuitive sense as one builds additional behaviors after the first behavior is mastered. Why would backward chaining be used? Backward chaining requires an important discussion of how behaviors in a sequence relate to each other and to the consequences that follow at the end of a sequence.

In a sequence or chain of responses, the reinforcer usually comes only at the end, that is, after all the behaviors are completed. For example, dieting, mastering a musical instrument, preparing for athletic competition, studying for an advanced degree, and writing a book all require a series of intermediate responses before the final reinforcing event is achieved. The major question is, what maintains all of the intermediate responses that precede attaining the final goal? The behaviors early in the sequence simply might not be performed because they are so far removed from the final delivery of the reinforcer. The answer requires explaining the factors that link the response components of a chain and in the process why backward chaining makes sense and is effective.

To begin with, it is important to note that an event immediately preceding reinforcement becomes a signal for reinforcement. As mentioned in the discussion of antecedents, an event that signals a behavior will be reinforced is referred to as a discriminative stimulus (S^D). An S^D sets the occasion for behavior; it increases the probability that a previously reinforced behavior will occur. An S^D not only signals reinforcement but also eventually becomes a reinforcer itself. The frequent pairing of an S^D and the reinforcer gives the S^D reinforcing properties of its own. The discriminative stimulus properties of events that precede the reinforcer and the reinforcing properties of these events when they are frequently paired with reinforcers are important in explaining how chains of responses are maintained.

Consider the chain of responses involved in completing a painting. The sequence may include an indefinite number of components, beginning perhaps with purchasing paints and canvases, sketching drafts of the painting on scratch paper, drawing an outline on the canvas itself, actually painting the canvas, and finally seeing the finished product. The first response (purchasing the materials) is quite far removed from completion of the painting. Assume for a moment that seeing the final product (or for those more materially oriented, selling the painting) is the final reinforcer. Only the final response—placing the final strokes of paint—is followed by the reinforcing consequences (seeing the finished product). This final response is directly reinforced with seeing the finished product.

Recall that any event that precedes delivery of the reinforcer becomes an S^D. In this chain of responses, the last response performed (painting the final strokes) becomes an S^D for the reinforcer, since the response signals that the reinforcer will follow. Yet the pairing of an S^D with the reinforcer (seeing the product) eventually results in the S^D becoming a reinforcer, as well as a discriminative stimulus. Hence, the response preceding direct reinforcement has become an S^D for delivery of a subsequent reinforcer and a reinforcer in its own right. It serves as a reinforcer for the previous link in the chain of responses. The response (putting strokes on the canvas) becomes a reinforcer for the previous behavior (sketching the canvas). Since sketching the canvas now precedes the reinforcer, it too becomes an S^D. As with other responses, the pairing of the S^D with the reinforcer results in the S^D becoming a reinforcer. The process continues in a backward direction so that each response in the chain becomes an S^D for the next response in the chain and serves as a reinforcer for the prior response in the chain.

Although the sequence appears to be maintained by a single reinforcer at the end of the chain of responses (seeing the finished product), the links in the chain are assumed to take on conditioned reinforcement value. To accomplish this, building response chains often relies on training from the last response in the sequence that precedes direct reinforcement back to the first response. As noted previously, training the last response first is backward chaining. Because the final response in the sequence is paired immediately and directly with the reinforcer, it is most easily established as a conditioned reinforcer that can maintain other responses. Also, the shorter the delay between a response and the reinforcer, the greater the effect of reinforcement. The last response in the chain is immediately reinforced and is more likely to be performed frequently. Thus one can have the individual complete the final behavior and receive the reinforcing consequence immediately. Then training proceeds to the second to the last behavior, followed by the last behavior, followed by the reinforcer. The assumption is that training will be easier in this fashion because the connection between the final reinforcement and behavior is immediate.

General Comments

In principle, shaping and chaining are both suitable for developing new behaviors. With each technique, prompts such as instructions or gestures and direct reinforcement such as praise may be provided for the desired behavior. The differences between shaping and chaining, as well as the conditions that dictate their use, may be unclear. The major difference is that shaping focuses on developing a specific behavior. Steps along the way toward the final goal are eventually replaced by the final behavior one wishes. In chaining, there is a sequence of behaviors. At the end, the behaviors developed along the way are still evident, that is, they do not drop out as behavior is developed.

In practice, shaping is the procedure used much more often to develop behavior. Sequences of behaviors (chains) can be developed by shaping and using cues and reinforcement for the performance of behaviors in a particular sequence. Thus in many situations either chaining or shaping may be used. For example, toilet training of children consists of a series of responses that follow in sequence: walking to a bathroom, lowering pants, positioning oneself in front of or on the toilet, and so on. After completion of the entire chain, praise for proper elimination can serve as the reinforcer. Both shaping and chaining have been effective in developing this sequence of responses (Azrin & Foxx, 1971; Mahoney, Van Wagenen, & Meyerson, 1971).

Forward and backward chaining can be used to develop sequences and both are effective. Direct comparisons have not established that one is consistently more effective than the other. In applied work, immediate reinforcement is usually provided for the desired response during the course of training. Thus in developing a sequence, one does not only provide the reinforcer when the final behavior at the end of the chain is performed. Usually one praises and prompts along the way. The use of reinforcement along the way in developing sequences of behavior helps both forward and backward chaining work well.

In applied settings, shaping and forward chaining usually are easily understood by those who oversee and implement behavior modification programs. Intuitively, building behavioral units or sequences that are increasingly more complex and that move toward some final goal is consistent with everyday experiences in, for example, child development or mastering a skill, such as music training, where simple responses and smaller units precede more complex responses and larger units of behavior. The notion of chains of behaviors is very important because it alerts us to the fact that our interest is not merely in increasing certain behaviors but rather in building sequences of behaviors. For example, to increase a child's completion of homework, the sequence of behaviors may include bringing home an assignment book and the books needed to do the homework, working on the homework, completing that homework, reviewing or showing this work to a parent, taking it to school the next day or on the due date, and so on. In developing this sequence, it is important to be mindful of the constituent behaviors and the sequence of behaviors. At the inception of the reinforcement program, we may reinforce individual acts; eventually, we wish to reinforce the entire sequence of behaviors.

CONSEQUENCES OF BEHAVIOR

We have now considered antecedents and behaviors of the ABCs. In the process, we have also mentioned consequences that follow behavior. However, let us consider consequences more systematically and the different arrangements of consequences and behavior. The most basic feature of consequences is how they relate to behavior. Specifically, for a consequence to alter a particular behavior, it must be dependent or contingent on the occurrence of that behavior. Stated another way, behavior change occurs when certain consequences are *contingent on performance.* A consequence is contingent when it is delivered only after the target behavior has been performed and is otherwise not available. When a consequence is not contingent on behavior, this means that it is delivered independently or regardless of what the person is doing.

The noncontingent delivery of consequences ordinarily does not result in systematic changes in a target behavior because the consequences do not consistently follow that behavior. For example, elementary school teachers often prefer their students to raise their hands to be called on rather than blurt out the answer or talk or shout when their hands are up. Assume for the moment that teacher attention (calling on the person to answer) is the reinforcer. If the teacher wishes to develop hand raising, the teacher can make "calling on the person" contingent on the desired behavior. However, the teacher must be consistent so that calling on a student only occurs when the behavior is performed. If the teacher calls on students occasionally when hands are not raised or students are not sitting and waiting to be called on, the desired behavior will not develop systematically.

Consequences do not magically alter behavior; they must be delivered in specific ways, and one of these ways is contingent on desired performance. The notion of contingency is important because behavioral techniques alter behavior, in part, by modifying the consequences that follow behavior. In other words, it makes consequences contingent on behavior in ways that promote the desired behavior. The relationship of behavior and consequences are described by the concepts of reinforcement, punishment, and extinction.

Positive Reinforcement

Reinforcement always refers to an increase in the likelihood or probability of a response when that response is immediately followed by consequences. This is important to remember because there are different ways of following behavior with reinforcing consequences. Positive and negative reinforcers constitute the two kinds of events that can be used to increase the probability of a response (Skinner, 1953). *Positive reinforcers* are stimuli or events *presented* after a response has been performed that increase the frequency of the behavior they follow. The word *positive* in this use essentially means something is presented. *Negative reinforcers,* which can also be referred to as *aversive events* or *aversive stimuli,* are events removed after a response has been performed that increase the behavior preceding their removal. Negative in this use essentially means something is removed or withdrawn. Let us consider these in turn.

Positive reinforcement refers to the increase in the likelihood or probability of a response that is followed by a favorable consequence (positive reinforcer). In everyday language, such positive or favorable events are often referred to as *rewards.* However, it is important to distinguish the term positive reinforcer from the term *reward.* A *positive reinforcer* is defined by its effect on behavior. If a consequence follows a behavior and the likelihood of the behavior increases in the future, the consequence is a positive reinforcer. Conversely, any event that does not increase the behavior it follows is not a positive reinforcer. An increase in the frequency or probability of the preceding behavior is the defining characteristic of a positive reinforcer. In contrast, *rewards* are defined merely as something that is given or received in return for doing something. Rewards such as prizes, sums of money, and vacations are usually highly valued and subjectively pleasing. Rewards do not necessarily increase the probability of the behaviors they follow.

In fact, many rewards or events that a person evaluates favorably when queried may serve as reinforcers. For example, people often say that money is a reward (i.e., they like it) and in fact, money, when applied to alter behavior in systematic ways, usually serves as a positive reinforcer. Yet, whether a consequence is a reinforcer cannot be known on the basis of a person's verbal statements alone. A person may be unaware of or may not consider as rewards many events that are reinforcers. For example, verbal reprimands such as "Stop that!" and taking someone out of the room to isolate them occasionally have served as positive reinforcers. It is unlikely that anyone would ever refer to these consequences as rewards. The key point is that a reward is not synonymous with a positive reinforcer. Whether an event is a positive reinforcer has to be determined empirically. Does the likelihood of the behavior to which the consequence was applied increase when the consequence immediately follows the behavior? The consequence is a positive reinforcer only if the behavior increases.

Examples of positive reinforcement in everyday life would seem to be abundant. Strictly speaking, rarely does anyone actually measure whether a favorable event that followed a behavior increases the likelihood of that behavior. Nevertheless, it is useful to mention some everyday situations that probably exemplify positive reinforcement. Winning money at a slot machine usually increases the frequency of putting money into the machine and pulling the lever. Money is a powerful reinforcer that increases performance of a variety of behaviors. As another example, if a child whines or complains before going to bed and is then allowed by his or her parents to stay up longer, the frequency of whining before bedtime may increase. Letting the child stay up is likely to be a positive reinforcer.

Types of Positive Reinforcers. Positive reinforcers include any events or stimuli that, when presented, increase the likelihood of the behavior they follow. The two categories of positive reinforcers are namely *unconditioned* or *primary* reinforcers and *conditioned* or *secondary* reinforcers. Unconditioned reinforcers are reinforcing without requiring special learning or training. Food and water are examples. Primary reinforcers may not be reinforcing all of the time. Food will not serve as a reinforcer to someone who has just finished a large meal. When food does serve as a reinforcer, however, its value is automatic (unlearned) and does not depend on a previous association with any other reinforcers.

However, conditioned reinforcers acquire their reinforcing value through learning. Examples include praise, grades, money, and completion of a goal. Conditioned reinforcers acquire reinforcing properties by being paired with events that are already reinforcing, either primary reinforcers or other conditioned reinforcers. If a neutral stimulus is repeatedly presented before or along with another reinforcing stimulus, the neutral stimulus becomes a reinforcer. For example, praise may not be reinforcing for some individuals. To establish praise as a reinforcer, it can be paired with a consequence that is reinforcing, such as food, money, or physical touch. When a behavior is performed, the individual's behavior is praised and reinforced with food. After several pairings of the food with praise, the praise alone serves as a reinforcer and can be used to increase the frequency of other responses (Lancioni, 1982).

Some conditioned reinforcers are paired with many different reinforcers. When a conditioned reinforcer is paired or associated with many other reinforcers, it is referred to as a *generalized conditioned reinforcer.* Generalized conditioned reinforcers are extremely effective in altering behaviors because they have been paired with a variety of events. Money is an example of a generalized conditioned reinforcer. It is a *conditioned* reinforcer because its reinforcing value is acquired through learning. It is a *generalized* reinforcer because a variety of reinforcing events contribute to its value. Additional examples of generalized conditioned reinforcers include attention, approval, and affection from others. For example, attention from someone may be followed by physical contact, praise, smiles, affection, or delivery of tangible rewards such as food and other events.

In behavior modification programs, generalized reinforcers in the form of *tokens* are often used (Kazdin, 1977c). The tokens may consist of poker chips, coins, tickets, stars, points, or check marks. Tokens serve as generalized reinforcers because, like money, they can be exchanged for many other events that are reinforcing. For example, in an elementary school classroom, tokens may be delivered to students for raising their hands to speak, for completing assignments in class, for attaining correct answers, and for other behaviors. The tokens may be exchanged for special in-class activities such as educational games or movies, extra recess, or free time in class at the end of the day. The potency of tokens derives from the reinforcers that back up their value. The events that tokens can purchase are referred to as *back-up reinforcers.* Generalized conditioned reinforcers, such as money or tokens, are usually more powerful than any single reinforcer because they can purchase many different back-up reinforcers.

In identifying positive reinforcers, it is important to keep two considerations in mind. First, an event (e.g., praise, candy, or a pat on the back) may be a positive reinforcer for one person but not for another. Although some events have wide generality in serving as reinforcers, such as food or money, others may not (e.g., sour candy). Second, an event may be a reinforcer for one person under some but not other circumstances. These considerations require careful evaluation of what is reinforcing for a given individual. Because of common biological background, cultural norms, and experiences, some consequences are likely to be reinforcers for many people (e.g., praise from parents or peers, money). However, there is no guarantee that a particular event will be reinforcing. The critical test is whether the consequence, if contingent on behavior, increases the likelihood of that behavior in the future.

Negative Reinforcement

Negative reinforcement refers to the increase in the likelihood or probability of a response by removing an aversive event immediately after the response has been performed. Removal of an aversive event or a negative reinforcer is contingent on a response. An event is a negative reinforcer only if its removal after a response increases performance of that response (Skinner, 1953). The comments made about the difference between rewards and positive reinforcers hold for negative reinforcers as well. That is, consequences that are subjectively unpleasant or not liked very much may be annoying or otherwise undesirable. They are also likely to be useful as negative reinforcers, but not necessarily so. Whether a consequence really serves as a negative reinforcer can only be determined by seeing if the consequence can change behavior. Other qualifications are also pertinent. An undesirable event may serve as an aversive event for one individual but not for another. Additionally, an event may be a negative reinforcer for an individual at one time but not at another time. A negative reinforcer, like a positive reinforcer, is defined solely by its effect on behavior.

It is important to reiterate that *positive or negative reinforcement always refers to an increase in behavior.* Negative reinforcement requires an ongoing aversive event or stimulus that can be removed or terminated after a specific response has been performed. The aversive event is "just there" or present in the environment. Once this event is present, then some behavior may stop or end it. That behavior is negatively reinforced.

Positive reinforcement is familiar and more easily remembered than negative reinforcement because many examples of unsystematic reinforcement seem evident in everyday life. As a helpful aide, consider the following. In negative reinforcement, the desired behavior *turns off* an aversive event (e.g., stops a noise, stops pain). The behavior may not directly turn off the event like a switch, but has that effect. Performing the behavior results in the immediate termination of an aversive event. Think of situations of escape behavior as instances in which negative reinforcement is operating. Table 2-3 gives some examples to help remember the arrangement of consequences and behavior.

Consider two examples in greater detail. For example, a neighbor may be playing very loud music. This provides an aversive event needed as the first

Table 2-3   Examples of Negative Reinforcement

Aversive stimulus, condition, situation	Behavior that is performed	Immediate effect is to end the aversive condition	Outcome or effect on behavior
Irritability and mild discomfort (from nicotine depletion)	Smoke a cigarette	Terminates the discomfort	Increase the likelihood of smoking in the future
Loud noise from an alarm clock	Throwing the clock across the room	Noise from the alarm ends	Increase the likelihood of throwing the clock
Nagging parent	Leaving the house or the room	Nagging no longer heard	Increase the likelihood of leaving (escape) in the future
Discomfort from extremely cold weather	Entering a building	Terminates the discomfort	Increase the likelihood of escaping cold

condition for negative reinforcement. Any response that terminates this could readily illustrate negative reinforcement. Let us say that someone who finds the music aversive screams, "Stop that music or I will call the police!" Assume for a moment that this behavior (screaming and making a threat) immediately stops the noise. This is precisely the arrangement for negative reinforcement, namely, termination of an aversive event or stimulus contingent on behavior. To qualify as reinforcement, of course, it is assumed that the neighbor is more likely to scream and threaten in the future when such noise occurs.

As another example, consider a person who is addicted to drugs. Depending on the drug, addiction may be partially maintained by negative reinforcement. Perhaps the person has had a dose of the substance. As the effect wears off, very unpleasant bodily sensations, discomfort, and even sickness may occur. This unpleasant state constitutes an ongoing aversive state. Perhaps the person injects or takes another dose of the medication and the aversive condition is terminated. Ingesting drugs is likely to be negatively reinforced by this arrangement.

The examples convey that escape from or terminating an aversive event can negatively reinforce behavior. Avoidance too is involved in negative reinforcement, but this is a bit more subtle. In avoidance, behavior is performed before the negative event even occurs. In the above examples, the negative event (loud music, discomfort as drug wears off) leads to escape. Cues and learned events that precede negative events often take on aversive properties, that is, they too become aversive. Engaging in behavior that terminates these learned aversive events, leads to negative reinforcement. Thus a teenager does not need to hear the nagging parent (aversive event). Escaping from a nagging parent (leaving the room) would be an example of negative reinforcement. A parent who nags a lot might well take on aversive properties and be avoided by the teenager. Thoughts about the parent or seeing the parent can become aversive, and termination of these also negatively reinforces behavior (see Chapter 6 for more on avoidance). However, it is useful here to consider that whenever escape or avoidance behavior occurs, negative reinforcement may be operating.

As with positive reinforcement, the two types of negative reinforcers are unconditioned (primary) and conditioned (secondary). Intense stimuli such as shock, loud noise, or very bright light that impinge on the sensory receptors of an organism serve as unconditioned negative reinforcers. Their aversive properties are not learned. In contrast, conditioned events become aversive by being paired with events that are already aversive. For example, disapproving facial expressions or saying the word *no* can serve as aversive events after being paired with events that are already aversive (Dorsey, Iwata, Ong, & McSween, 1980).

Negative reinforcement requires presenting the individual with some aversive event such as shock, noise, or isolation, that can be removed or reduced immediately after he or she responds. Because of the undesirability of using aversive stimuli, negative reinforcement is used infrequently in programs designed to alter behavior. Several less objectionable and more positive procedures are also readily available.

Although negative reinforcement is not used very often in behavior modification, it does play a role in everyday life. In fact, many interesting combinations of positive and negative reinforcement occur in everyday interactions. Consider two examples from parent-child interactions. A parent is waiting in line at a supermarket to check out groceries. In the checkout line with the parent is a 5-year-old girl. The child sees candy and asks the parent if she can have some. The parent ignores this or says "no." Perhaps the child escalates a little and begins to whine, cry, or tug at the parent's clothing, crying out loudly and persistently, "I want some candy!" The parent (who perhaps has only read up to Chapter 2 of this book) then says, "All right, here's the candy," and hands the child a candy bar from the rack. Where is the positive and negative reinforcement? The child's whining, tugging at the parent, and repeatedly insisting on candy (the behavior) was associated with a positive consequence (candy). That is *positive reinforcement* of the *child's* behavior. The parent giving the candy to the child (the parent's behavior) was associated with the immediate termination of an aversive event (child whining). That is *negative reinforcement* of the *parent's* behavior.

Such combinations of positive and negative reinforcement are common in everyday situations without the mild drama of a grocery store tantrum. Consider parents sitting in the living room chatting and their infant begins to cry loudly from his or her crib. The father goes into the room and picks up the infant. As soon as he does that, the infant stops crying. At this point, the infant, who happens to be unusually bright and amazingly verbal, looks up to his father and says, "Yo, Dad, you picked me up after I cried—that is positive reinforcement because my behavior (crying) was followed by a consequence (being picked up, cuddled, patted, and held). Thanks Dad!" The Dad says, "Mildredsina (daughter's name), no need to thank me. The noise from your crying was, well, pretty aversive for us. When I picked you up, the noise ended right way. That is negative reinforcement because *my* behavior (picking you up) terminated the noise." (Of course, at that point, the mother rushes in and correctly notes, "Remember, both of you, this is not reinforcement unless the likelihood of the behaviors you mentioned increase in the future. Now good night!") This arrangement conveys how both positive and negative reinforcement can be operative in a similar situation but for different people.

In social interaction, the response of one individual is sometimes negatively reinforced because it terminates an aversive behavior initiated by another individual. At the same time, the aversive behavior of the other individual may be positively reinforced. This can be seen in more frightening interactions such as being mugged or robbed. Positive and negative reinforcement occur when the victim of an aggressive act such as physical assault complies with the wishes of the aggressor (giving up his wallet) in order to terminate an aversive situation. Unfortunately, the act of compliance of the victim positively reinforces the aggressor, increasing the probability of future aggression by the aggressor.

Punishment

Punishment is the presentation or removal of a stimulus or event after a response, which decreases the likelihood or probability of that response. This definition is somewhat different from the everyday use of the term. In everyday life, *punishment* refers to a penalty imposed for performing a particular act. For example, misbehaving children are "taught a lesson" by undergoing pain, sacrifice, or loss of some kind (slap, harsh reprimand, loss of a privilege). Criminals may receive penalties (fines, probation, incarceration) based on the acts they have committed. Yet, punishment in the technical sense is defined solely by the effect on behavior. The above examples, although called punishment in everyday life, might not have any effects on the likelihood of future behavior. In behavior modification, punishment is operative only if the likelihood of the response is reduced, that is, a punishing event is defined by its suppressive effect on the behavior that it follows.

In behavior modification, punishment is de-emphasized for a host of reasons discussed in detail later. When punishment is used, it does not necessarily entail any pain, physical coercion, or many of the demeaning, humiliating, and outright nasty consequences provided in everyday life.[2] Indeed, grabbing, hitting, and shaking that parents or teachers may do with young children in everyday life would not be used in behavior modification.

There are two main types of punishment. In the first type, an aversive consequence is *presented after* a response. The numerous everyday examples of this type of punishment include being reprimanded or slapped after engaging in some behavior. (These examples convey the sequence of events: behavior followed by a consequence. However, it is not likely that they actually influence the likelihood of behavior in the future, given the way they are used, as discussed later in the chapter on punishment.) The second type of punishment is the *removal* of a positive event after a response. Examples include losing privileges after staying out late, losing money for misbehaving, being isolated from others, and having one's driver's license revoked. In this type of punishment, some event is taken away after a response has been performed.

Punishment and negative reinforcement are often confused even though they are very different. *The key difference is that reinforcement, whether negative or positive, always refers to procedures that increase behavior, whereas punishment refers to procedures that decrease behavior.* In negative reinforcement, an aversive event is removed after a response; in punishment, an aversive consequence follows a response.

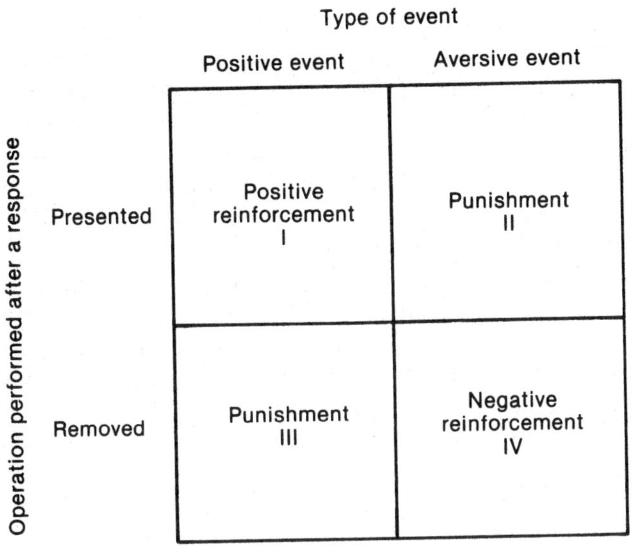

Type of event

	Positive event	Aversive event
Presented	Positive reinforcement I	Punishment II
Removed	Punishment III	Negative reinforcement IV

Operation performed after a response

FIGURE 2-1 Illustration of principles of operant conditioning based on whether positive or aversive stimuli or events are presented or removed after a response has been performed. The figure provides a simple way to convey the major principles of operant conditioning, but the simplicity of the figure has a price. In fact, a more technical discussion of the principles would quickly reveal inaccuracies in the figure. For example, the figure implies that a particular event that can negatively reinforce behavior can also be used to suppress (punish) some other response that it follows. Although this is usually true, many exceptions exist. It is not necessarily the case that the same event whose removal negatively reinforces a behavior will suppress a behavior when it is presented, or vice versa. Hence, in the present text, the term aversive stimulus, or aversive event, will be used to refer to any event that may be negatively reinforcing and/or punishing.

Figure 2-1 provides a simple way of distinguishing the operations involved in reinforcement and punishment, depicting two operations that can occur after a response has been performed. A stimulus or event can be presented to or removed from the client after a response (see left side of the figure). The figure also shows two types of events that may be presented or removed, namely, positive and aversive stimuli or events. The four combinations forming the different cells depict the principles of positive reinforcement (cell I), negative reinforcement (cell IV), and the two types of punishment (cells II and III).[3]

Extinction

Extinction is an important principle of operant conditioning not represented in Figure 2-1. *Extinction refers to the cessation of reinforcement of a response that results in a decrease in the likelihood or probability of the behavior in the future.* As with the other principles, extinction is defined by the relation of a response to consequences and to a change in the likelihood of behavior in the future. No longer reinforcing a response results in the eventual reduction or elimination of the response. It is important to keep this procedure distinct from punishment. In extinction, *a consequence that was previously provided no longer follows the response.* An event or stimulus (money, noise) is neither taken away nor presented. In punishment, some aversive event follows a response (a reprimand) or some positive event (money) is taken away.

In everyday life, extinction often takes the form of ignoring a behavior that was previously reinforced with attention. A parent may ignore a child when the child whines—this is extinction if the parent had been attending to the behavior (the reinforcer) on prior occasions but no longer does so. A teacher may ignore children who talk without raising their hands, assuming they previously were called on when they shouted out. A therapist or counselor may ignore certain self-defeating statements made by the client rather than attending to them. In each of these examples, the reinforcer (attention, approval, or sympathy) previously provided for the response is no longer presented.

In everyday life, extinction may contribute to behavioral problems, as well as ameliorate them. Often, desirable behavior is accidentally extinguished. For example, parents sometimes ignore their children when the children are playing quietly and may provide abundant attention when the children are noisy. This may extinguish quiet play and positively reinforce noisy play. Merely reallocating parental attention so that it follows appropriate play is often sufficient to develop appropriate behavior and to extinguish inappropriate behavior.

Cessation of attention is not the only example of extinction. For example, putting money into vending machines (a response) will cease if the reinforcer (cigarettes, food, or drink) is not forthcoming; turning on a radio will cease if the radio no longer provides sound; and attempting to start a car will cease if the car does not start. In each of these examples, the consequences that maintain the behavior are no longer forthcoming. The absence of reinforcing consequences reduces the behavior.

Extinction can be used as a technique to reduce or eliminate behavior. However, the events that reinforce behavior must be identified so that they can be prevented from occurring after the response. For example, a frustrated elementary school teacher may decide that he or she will no longer look at the class or pay attention to the children when they are talking to each other. The teacher may look down at the floor or turn away from the class with the idea and hope that his or her attention is maintaining the children's disruptive behavior. This is an example of ignoring the behavior. However, this may not be extinction or lead to behavior change. The reason is that much of disruptive behavior in the classroom is maintained by the attention of one's peers (making faces, making comments back to each other, smiling, throwing items). If these are the reinforcers, only *their* cessation would be likely to result in extinction. The key point is two-fold. First, although extinction often includes ignoring, not all ignoring necessarily qualifies as extinction. For extinction to be operative the reinforcer that has previously followed behavior is no longer presented, and the likelihood of the behavior decreases as a result. Second, for extinction to work, one must identify the reinforcer maintaining behavior.

ADDITIONAL PRINCIPLES AND CONCEPTS

The above discussion examined antecedents, behaviors, and consequences. Separating these for discussion is useful for presentation, but of course, they are all combined in programs designed to develop behavior. As reinforcement, punishment, and extinction are elaborated in later chapters, how all of the concepts are combined to change behavior will be illustrated further. There are a few additional concepts that are important to highlight to explain how behavior develops and is maintained.

Discrimination

Discriminative stimuli were mentioned in the discussion of antecedents that control behavior. Stimuli associated with reinforcement, when present, increase the likelihood of the behavior. When behavior is performed in the presence of some stimuli (S^D) but not in the presence of others (S^Δ), the individual is said to have made a discrimination, and behavior is said to be under stimulus control. *Discrimination refers to the fact that the individual responds differently under different stimulus conditions.* Discrimination and stimulus control are almost always operative in behavior modification programs. Programs are conducted in particular settings (e.g., the home) and are administered by particular individuals (e.g., parents). Insofar as certain behaviors are reinforced or punished in the presence of particular individuals or certain environmental cues and not in the presence of other stimuli, the behaviors will be under stimulus control. In the presence of cues associated with the behavior modification program, the client will behave in a particular fashion. In the absence of those cues, behavior is likely to change because the contingencies in new situations are altered.

A familiar example of discrimination and stimulus control that may arise in a behavior modification program pertains to the behavior of students when the teacher is *in* the classroom. As most of us recall from elementary school years, the amount of disruptive behavior often varied depending on whether the teacher was in the room enforcing the rules of the classroom. Once the stimulus (teacher) associated with the reinforcing or punishing consequences was no longer present, behavior often deteriorated. Indeed, the stimulus control that individuals such as parents and teachers exert over behavior often creates a problem in behavior modification. The children may perform the responses in the presence of parents or teachers but not in their absence. Special contingency arrangements are often needed to ensure that the desired behaviors transfer to new people, situations, and places.

The control that different stimuli exert over behavior explains why behavior often is situation-specific. Individuals may behave one way in a given situation or in the presence of a particular person and behave differently in another situation or in the presence of another person. Because different reinforcement contingencies operate in different circumstances, individuals can discriminate among the stimuli that are likely to be followed by reinforcement.

People make discriminations across a variety of situations for most behaviors. For example, eating habits probably vary, depending upon whether one is at home or in a restaurant. At home, it is more likely that people will place crumpled napkins, books, elbows, and feet on the table when they eat meals; these behaviors are much less likely in a restaurant (with the possible exception of a few of my relatives). Similarly, further discriminations are made, depending on whether one is eating in an elegant or a fast-food restaurant. Numerous other variations in behavior are evident because of differences in the situations and the contingencies associated with them.

Generalization

The effect of reinforcement on behavior may either extend beyond the conditions in which training has taken place or extend to behaviors other than those included in the program. The ways in which effects of the program may extend beyond the contingency are referred to as *generalization*.

Stimulus Generalization. *Stimulus generalization refers to the generalization or transfer of a response to situations other than those in which training takes place.* Stimulus generalization occurs if a response reinforced in one situation or setting also increases in other settings (even though it is not reinforced in the other settings). Generalization is the opposite of discrimination. When an individual *discriminates* in the performance of a response, this means that the response fails to generalize across situations. Alternatively, when a response *generalizes* across situations, the individual fails to discriminate in his or her performance of that response. Often when a behavior is reinforced in one situation or in the presence of one set of conditions, it may be performed in new situations that are similar, even if reinforcement is not provided in those situations.

Figure 2-2 illustrates stimulus generalization. S_1 refers to the *stimulus condition* or the situation in which the response is reinforced. R_1 refers to the *response,* or the behavior that is reinforced. The figure shows that the trained response (R_1) is performed across a variety of stimuli or situations (S_2, S_3, S_4, S_5). The degree of stimulus generalization often is a function of the similarity of new stimuli (or situations) to the stimulus under which the response was trained. Of course, over a long period, a response may not generalize across situations because the individual discriminates that the response is reinforced in one situation but not in others.

Examples of stimulus generalization are common in everyday experience. For example, a child may talk about certain topics in the presence of his family because talking about those topics is reinforced (i.e., discussed freely, attended to) among family members. The child may also discuss the same topics in the presence of guests. In that case, the child's behavior (talking about certain topics) has generalized across situations. Parents may show considerable embarrassment when

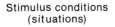

Stimulus conditions
(situations)

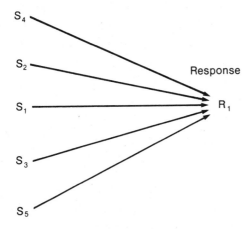

FIGURE 2-2 Stimulus generalization: A response (R_1) reinforced in one situation (S_1) generalizes (carries over) to other situations (S_2, S_3, S_4, S_5).

children freely discuss family secrets or personal topics (e.g., how one's father puts on his toupee or how a parent looks in the shower). Generalization is also readily apparent when a child responds to a teacher in a fashion similar to the fashion in which he or she responds to a parent (in the expression of affection). To the extent that a child sees parents and teachers as similar, the stimulus control exerted by parents will be shared by the teacher. Because the antecedent events (approaches by the adult, expressions of affection) and the consequent events (hugs, kisses) are different for the child in relation to teachers and parents, the child quickly learns a discrimination. Consequently, expressions of affection are more likely in the presence of parents (S^D) than of teachers (S^Δ).

Stimulus generalization represents an exceedingly important issue in behavior modification. Invariably, training takes place in a restricted setting such as a classroom, a home, a hospital ward, or an institution. It is desirable that behaviors developed in these settings generalize or transfer to other settings. There are many procedures to ensure that behaviors transfer from one setting to another, and these are discussed later.

Response Generalization. Another type of generalization involves responses rather than stimulus conditions. *Response generalization refers to the changes in behaviors or responses other than those that have been trained or developed.* Response generalization occurs if a specific response is developed through reinforcement or other procedures and this systematically alters other behaviors that have not been directly trained.

Altering one response can inadvertently influence other responses. For example, if a person is praised for smiling, the frequency not only of smiling but also of laughing and talking might increase. This is referred to as *response generalization*. Response generalization is depicted in Figure 2-3, where S_1 refers to the stimulus condition in which training of a response takes place and R_1 refers to the response that is reinforced. Although only one response is trained in the situation, a variety of other related responses (R_2, R_3, R_4, R_5) may also be performed.

Examples of response generalization are plentiful. For example, according to one report, altering noncompliance (not completing the requests of adults) in four children also decreased such inappropriate behaviors as aggression (pushing, hitting, biting), disruption (whining, crying, screaming), property destruction (pushing, kicking furniture, pounding on or throwing objects), and the placing of inedible objects in their mouths (Parrish, Cataldo, Kolko, Neef, & Egel, 1986). The intervention, based primarily on variations of positive reinforcement, effectively increased compliance among these children. Interestingly, when their compliance increased, their aggression, disruption, and other inappropriate behaviors decreased, even though these latter behaviors were not the focus of the intervention.

The notion of response generalization is often used to explain changes in responses other than the target response. The concept is based on the view that the effects of an intervention will generalize from one response to other responses that are *similar* in some way. Technically, the term response generalization may not be accurate for two reasons. First, responses that are not supposed to be focused on may inadvertently receive reinforcing consequences. For example, a child praised for studying in class may improve in reading, even though reading may not have been the response to which the reinforcing consequences were directed. Although this may be spoken of as generalization, it may reflect the direct operation of reinforcement and not be generalization at all. When a child is praised for paying attention, he or she may be reading on some of the occasions that reinforcement is delivered. Thus it is difficult to speak of response generalization, because the behavior was directly reinforced.

There is a second, slightly more complex reason that response generalization may not accurately account for the many changes that occur with treatment. Response generalization refers to changes in behaviors that are similar to the target behavior. Yet change in one behavior (studying) often is associated with changes in other behaviors (socializing, complying with requests) that appear to have no direct relation or resemblance to the target behavior.

The tendency of responses to change together or as a cluster has been referred to as *response covariation*. This is a descriptive term that merely notes that behaviors change together, that is, they co-vary. Which behaviors change can be predicted by knowing what other behaviors are in the cluster (Wahler, 1975). Response generalization as a concept has emphasized that changes occur in behaviors that are similar to those that are altered directly. Although changes in similar responses may occur, this does not explain the breadth of changes that may result. A key point from the standpoint of behavior modification is to note that changes are likely to go beyond the specific behavior one is focusing on in treatment.

In behavior modification, the concepts of stimulus and response generalization are ordinarily used to denote that changes occur across various stimulus condi-

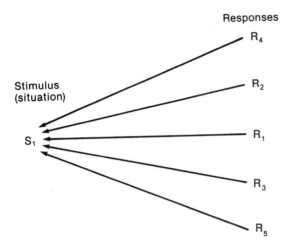

FIGURE 2-3
Response generalization: Reinforcement of one response
(R₁) in a given situation (S₁) may result in an increase of
other responses (R₂, R₂, R₃, R₄)

tions (situations or settings) or across responses. In fact, however, there is rarely any evidence that the spread of treatment effects across stimulus or response dimensions is actually based on the similarity of the stimuli or responses to those used in training. Technically, therefore, the terms stimulus and response generalization are often used incorrectly. Even so, the technical difficulties in using these terms do not detract from the importance of the spread of treatment effects across stimulus conditions or behaviors during the course of treatment.

SUMMARY AND CONCLUSIONS

The principles outlined in this chapter provide the basis for most of the operant conditioning programs in applied settings. The principles describe basic relations between antecedents, behaviors, and consequences and account for diverse treatment interventions. Settings (situations, contexts), prompts (cues or guides that help initiate the response), and discriminative stimuli (S^D) are key antecedents that influence development of behavior. Behaviors that are altered may include a specific response that is developed or a sequences of multiple responses. Shaping was mentioned as a key concept to reinforce approximations to attain terminal behaviors that may not be in the individual's repertoire. Forward and backward chaining were discussed as ways of building sequences of several behaviors.

Consequences for behavior rely heavily on reinforcement, punishment, and extinction. Reinforcement always refers to an increase in the likelihood of the behavior in the future when consequences are contingent on that behavior.

Punishment refers to a decrease in the likelihood of behavior when consequences are contingent. Extinction consists of no longer providing a reinforcer that previously was provided for the response and is also associated with a decrease in behavior.

Discrimination and generalization were also discussed. Discrimination refers to responding differently across different situations or circumstances. Individuals learn to respond differently to various situations through differential consequences such as reinforcement. Behaviors reinforced in one situation but not in another tend to be performed in the former situation but not in the latter. Generalization refers to responding similarly across different situations (stimulus generalization) or changes in many behaviors other than those that are directly focused on in the intervention (response generalization or response covariation).

Many principles were introduced in this chapter. The purpose was to provide an overview of key concepts that form the building blocks of interventions. The concepts, the many procedures that follow from them, and how these are implemented in special ways to be effective are elaborated in later chapters.

KEY TERMS

ABCs

Chaining

Discrimination

Establishing operation

Extinction

Generalization

Negative reinforcement

Positive reinforcement

Prompts

Punishment

Shaping

Stimulus control

APPLYING PRINCIPLES AND TECHNIQUES
TO EVERYDAY LIFE

1. Antecedents, behaviors, and consequences occur as sequences in daily life and social interaction. Consider the behavior of someone in your life (a friend, roommate, peer, partner, relative) that involves social interaction such as talking, dancing, or spending time together. In some part of the interaction, identify what might be an antecedent condition of the other behavior (what he or she says, does, or looks), the behavior on your part that this evokes, and the consequence of your behavior (how the other person responds). Give an example from your experience that reflects such an interaction and note the antecedent, behavior, and consequence.

2. Describe how you might use prompts and shaping to develop a behavior in a friend or relative. Assume that the behavior is engaging in an exercise of some sort. The goal is to achieve 20 minutes of some exercise at least 5 days a week.

Use at least two different types of prompts. How would you prompt, shape, and reinforce behavior? Be as specific and concrete as you can.

3. Describe a situation in which positive and negative reinforcement are evident. Remember the example in the chapter in which the parent attended to a crying infant in which the child's crying was positively reinforced and the parent's picking up of the child was negatively reinforced. Think of another example like that. Identify precisely what behavior is positively reinforced and what behavior is negatively reinforced.

4. An acquaintance or friend is approaching you. Think of two different ways the person looks and describe them. What about the way the person looks is an S^D indicating that your positive comments will be reciprocated (positively reinforced)? What about the person is an S^Δ that would indicate to you that positive comments are not likely to be reciprocated?

5. What would be two examples of extinction of behavior? Consider a behavior in which you engage in every day, such as interactions with others, and another behavior of a friend or acquaintance.

FOR FURTHER READING

Catania, A.C. (1997). *Learning* (4th ed.). Englewood Cliffs, NJ: Prentice-Hall.

McGill, P. (1999). Establishing operations: Implications for the assessment, treatment, and prevention of problem behavior. *Journal of Applied Behavior Analysis, 32,* 393–418.

Nevin, J.A. (1996). The momentum of compliance. *Journal of Applied Behavior Analysis, 29,* 535–547.

Smith, R.G., & Iwata, B. (1997). Antecedent influences on behavior disorders.

Journal of Applied Behavior Analysis, 30, 343–375.

Sulzer-Azaroff, B., & Mayer, G.R. (1991). *Behavior analysis for lasting change* (2nd ed.). Fort Worth, TX: Holt, Rinehart & Winston.

Wahler, R.G., & Fox, J.J. (1981). Setting events in applied behavior analysis: Toward a conceptual and methodological expansion. *Journal of Applied Behavior Analysis, 14,* 327–338.

NOTES

1. Discussion of the principles introduces several new terms. To aid the reader, major terms and their definitions are italicized when they are first introduced. Also, a glossary at the end of the book provides a summary definition of the major terms that arise in this chapter and throughout the text.

2. Pain and punishment are inextricably bound in language and thought, despite their lack of relation in behavior modification. Indeed, the word pain can be traced to Latin and Greek words for punishment and penalty.

3. Occasionally the terms *positive* and *negative punishment* are used to distinguish whether an event is presented (reprimand) or is withdrawn (loud noise) after behavior. This is not a common practice in part because juxtaposing the terms "positive" with "punishment" seems like an oxymoron because of the nontechnical use of the word "positive" as something "good." In behavior modification, positive and negative refer to presentation or withdrawal respectively rather than the subjective value of something.

CHAPTER 3

How to Identify, Define, and Assess Behavior

The principles of reinforcement and the many techniques that derive from them have proven to be quite effective in changing behavior. The success of the intervention is due in part to the techniques themselves. Much is known about the techniques and how they must be implemented to be effective. The success of the interventions also derives from assessment and evaluation practices within behavior modification. Methods of assessing and evaluating intervention effects permit one to see how well a program is working. When interventions are not working or are not working very well, changes can be made to try a different intervention or variation. Assessment and evaluation provide feedback to the persons in charge of the program (e.g., investigator, clinician, parents) regarding the impact of changes and contribute greatly to the success of behavioral interventions. No other psychological approach to treatment has emphasized or developed assessment methods as part of treatment as well as behavior analysis has. This chapter considers basic issues regarding identifying the goals of the program, translating these goals into well-defined behaviors, and strategies and methods for collecting data and actually measuring the behavior. The two chapters that follow consider the ways in which assessment can be used to identify effective interventions and how to evaluate the effects of interventions.

IDENTIFYING THE GOAL
OF THE PROGRAM

Implementing a behavior modification program requires clearly stating the goal and carefully describing the behaviors to be developed. The main goal of a program is to alter or develop a particular behavior—the target behavior. Of course, the goal may be to alter many behaviors, but for simplicity's sake, in describing assessment, a single target behavior is considered. The goal of changing behavior applies to a particular stimulus condition such as the home, classroom, certain times of day, or presence of particular individuals. Even if the goal of the program is eventually to change a particular behavior in all or most settings, it is useful to begin the program with a well-specified setting in which behavior can be observed and consequences can be applied.

Guidelines

Identifying the goal of the program in most cases seems obvious and straightforward because of the direct and immediate implications of the behavior for the adjustment, impairment, and adaptive functioning of the individual in everyday life. For example, many behavioral interventions have decreased behaviors such as self-injury (e.g., headbanging) among autistic children, anxiety and panic attacks, neglectful parenting among adults, and driving under the influence of alcohol. These interventions have increased behaviors such as engaging in practices that promote health (e.g., exercise, consumption of healthful foods) and academic performance among individuals performing poorly at school. In most of the examples throughout this book, the behaviors reflect quite reasonable, if not quite important, goals of the intervention.

Examples are useful but they do not address the broader issues, namely, what makes a behavior worthy or in need of intervention? At least four broad criteria are used by society and these capture most of the foci of psychosocial interventions, whether from a behavioral or other approach. First is *impairment,* or the extent to which an individual's functioning in everyday life is impeded by a particular problem or set of behaviors. Impairment consists of meeting role demands at home, school, and work, interacting socially, adapting with others, and not being restricted in the settings, situations, and experiences in which one can function. Facets of individual functioning (thoughts, feelings, behavior) that lead to or are associated with impairment are likely to warrant intervention. Impairment is a criterion invoked in defining psychiatric disorders such as major depression, schizophrenia, or attention deficit/hyperactivity disorder (American Psychiatric Association, 1994). Individuals with all sorts of problems, perhaps by their own identification or identification of others (e.g., anxiety, alcohol use), do not necessarily meet criteria for psychiatric disorder; multiple symptoms are needed but also evidence that there is impairment.

Second, behaviors that are *illegal* or *rule-breaking* are also brought to treatment. Illegal behaviors would include driving under the influence of alcohol, using illicit drugs, and stealing; rule-breaking that is not illegal might include a child leaving school repeatedly during the middle of the day or not adhering to family imposed curfew. Illegal and rule-breaking behavior may or may not affect functioning in everyday life very much, that is, it may not cause impairment. For example, adolescents and adults who use illicit drugs often function reasonably well in everyday life, so significant impairment or collapse of one's personal life does not occur.

Third, behaviors that are of *concern to individuals themselves or to significant others.* For example, parents also bring their children to treatment for a variety of behaviors that affect daily life. The behaviors may or may not be severe enough to reflect impairment or rule breaking. Examples might include toilet training, school functioning, social interaction, and more mild cases of behaviors that, if severe, might indeed reflect impairment. Behaviors of concern is a broad, catch-all category but is one that is meaningful nonetheless. Of course, just because significant others are concerned about a problem does not make it worthy of intervention. There are occasions in which concerns of significant others are of questionable relevance as targets of treatment. For example, a case at the clinic in which I work entailed a very aggressive and antisocial 8-year-old boy. His behavior was clearly impaired, as was reflected in his multiple and repeated expulsions from school for fighting (physically) with children and teachers. The single parent was extremely concerned about other behaviors that are generally annoying (e.g., he leaves his clothes on the floor, does not always flush the toilet, leaves his shoes outside of the closet, discards candy wrappers on the furniture, and fails to cap the toothpaste). These latter behaviors do not predict long-term child adjustment, criminality, psychiatric disorder, or impairment. The aggressive and antisocial behaviors do predict these outcomes. Concerns of significant others are important and often reflect behaviors that are also associated with impairment, even though it is easy to consider conditions in which concerns may not be important or lack of concern with a problem (e.g., abusive parents) does not mean all is fine.

Fourth, behaviors are focused on *that may prevent problems from developing.* The focus is not on a problem but on behaviors that will avert the likelihood of a problem or minimize the occurrence. Often children or adults at risk for a problem are included in behavioral interventions. Premature babies and children from economically disadvantaged environments are at risk for difficulties in school, and early intervention to develop preacademic behaviors at home are relevant interventions. Also, developing behaviors to promote safety (in business and industry or in the home) or health would qualify.

Behaviors brought to treatment usually involve one or more of the above criteria. For example, individuals with a diagnosis of some medical or psychological condition or dysfunction might reflect impairment. In addition, one may intervene to prevent the situation from becoming worse. Examples would include limitations associated with physical disabilities, disease, or other conditions that interfere with functioning (e.g., chronic pain, insomnia). Psychological problems such as depression, anxiety, and delusions are obviously candidates for intervention.

It is useful to go beyond the above general criteria and to consider more concretely key criteria that influence selecting goals of behavioral interventions (see Hawkins, 1986; Nelson & Hayes, 1986; Weist, Ollendick, & Finney, 1991). These criteria are better conceived of as guidelines derived from an examination of what is, in fact, the focus of many intervention programs. Table 3-1 lists some of the criteria or guidelines that determine the goal of a program and target behaviors that are examples of each criterion. Obviously, a given behavior may meet more than one criterion.

In many cases the goal is to increase positive, prosocial behavior (e.g., increase interactions with peers); in other cases, the goal is to decrease undesirable or inappropriate behavior. In behavioral approaches to treatment, this distinction is often blurred because there is an effort to develop positive, prosocial behaviors in virtually all programs. Even when the goal seems to be to decrease, suppress, or eliminate behaviors, the conceptualization of the problem and the interventions used to change the problem are often based on developing positive, adaptive behaviors.

A useful orienting question in identifying goals of a behavior modification program is to ask, "What behaviors are to be developed?" If the primary goal of the program is conceived as reducing or eliminating behavior (e.g., reducing or eliminating fighting, nagging, social withdrawal), this is often reformulated in terms of behaviors that are positive opposites. *Positive opposites are those adaptive and prosocial behaviors that denote how the individual is to behave instead of engaging in the maladaptive behavior.* The search for positive opposites, whenever possible, is very important because developing positive behavior takes advantages of many potent reinforcement techniques. Also, efforts to suppress and eliminate maladaptive behavior raise several problems that can be greatly reduced by reinforcing prosocial behavior. These problems are made more clear in later chapters devoted to rein-

Table 3-1   Selected Criteria for Identifying Goals of Intervention Programs

Criterion/Guideline	Target Behavior Examples
Behaviors that bring clients to normative levels of functioning in relation to their peers	Interaction with peers; exercise and activity of elderly persons
Behaviors that are dangerous to oneself or others	Self-injurious behaviors; fighting at school; spouse abuse
Behaviors that decrease risk for injury, illness, or physical or psychological dysfunctions	Safe sex practices; not smoking cigarettes; wearing seat belts
Behaviors that affect adaptive functioning	Deficits in social interaction; not attending school or work
Behaviors that can lead to other positive changes	Increasing prosocial speech; taking medicines as prescribed
Behaviors that reduce felt problems of individuals (parents, teachers, colleagues) with whom client is in contact	Tantrums of child; poor marital communication

forcement, punishment, and extinction. However, for now, the key point is to try to reformulate goals so they include behaviors to be developed. For example, if the goal of the program is to reduce tantrums, that usually can be readily achieved. However, it is useful to add to the goal the positive opposite, that is, concrete behaviors the parents wish to see in their place. Non-tantrum behaviors might include walking away from a provoking situation, expressing disagreement to the parent without swearing or throwing things, asking the parent for a compromise, or other behaviors individually suited to the child and parents.

Important Considerations

Although the goal of the program may be to change behavior, the situation, setting, and context in which the behavior occurs are likely to be very important as well. For many behaviors, the definition of the problem includes contextual and stimulus conditions. Many behavioral problems stem from a failure to perform behaviors in the presence of particular antecedent events. Such failures are considered to reflect a lack of appropriate stimulus control. For example, a child may complete schoolwork when he or she should be looking at the board, reciting, or playing at recess. The teacher may constantly remind the child to put his or her materials away or to pay attention. Yet the child's behavior is not controlled by these instructions (antecedent events). Training may focus on instructing the child to engage in some behavior and reinforcing compliance. The target behavior then is to be performed in the classroom (setting) and in response to specific instructions (prompts).

Similarly, parents may wish to train their children not to talk to strangers who offer them candy or ask them to enter their cars. Parents do not want children to act suspiciously toward all new adults they meet (e.g., new teachers at school, distant relatives they have not met previously, parents of the children's friends). The goal requires training children to act cautiously only in special circumstances that may be dangerous. Thus the antecedent events and situational cues become essential for deciding what behaviors are to be performed. For all behavioral programs, a basic question can be asked: Under what circumstances or in the presence of what cues should the target behavior be performed? Ultimately, the program will focus on developing specific behaviors in the presence, and not the absence, of certain cues. In many situations, the goal is to develop a behavior that is performed across many different situations (e.g., in the presence of others, in all public places, etc.). Training may begin with developing the behavior in one or two situations, and so it is still important to specify the contexts for beginning the program.

The focus on selecting target behaviors has been on developing concrete actions. In some cases, the initial goal of the program may be to develop the responsiveness of individuals to certain consequences. These individuals usually do not respond to events that play a major role in social interaction, such as attention, physical contact, praise, or mild disapproval. For example, autistic children who show pervasive deficits in language and social behavior, are often unresponsive to events that are reinforcing for most children (Schreibman, 1988). Similarly, delinquents and children with conduct problems in the home are occasionally unresponsive to praise (Herbert et al., 1973). In such cases, contingencies are devised to alter the value of such stimuli as physical contact or praise from an adult. In these programs, neutral stimuli such as statements of approval are paired with reinforcing events such as food or termination of an aversive event. Eventually, the previously neutral stimuli serve as positive reinforcers. Once the events have been established as reinforcers, they can be used to develop specific behaviors.

Table 3-1 contains criteria regarding the selection of goals and target behaviors. These criteria are helpful for proceeding in a behavioral program; however, they do raise broad issues. First, the target behavior that serves as the focus may be one of a larger set of behaviors the client brings to treatment. The child may have all sorts of problems (academic, social), bringing into question which of these ought to be the main, initial, or sole focus. Second, the behavior may be embedded in a larger context, and perhaps the context ought to be the focus. For example, at the clinic in which I work, aggression and antisocial behavior among the children is severe and clearly warrants intervention. However, the focus may also be on parenting practices because harsh and inconsistent punishment contributes to such behavior (Kazdin, 1995). There is very little evidence to guide the precise focus of treatment and what will maximize the short- and long-term benefits. This has led researchers to suggest that more attention should be given to establishing how the target behavior will affect the individual and relate to broader outcome issues such as adjustment (Weist et al., 1991). Again in most cases, the need to intervene and the focus of the intervention do not raise significant dilemmas. Yet appropriate goals for intervention research are debated within and well beyond behavior modification. Broader issues related to target behaviors and their selection and change are examined in a later chapter. For now, rudimentary information about selecting and assessing target behaviors is the main focus.

DEFINING THE TARGET BEHAVIOR

A behavioral program usually begins with a statement from someone that there is a problem or a need to intervene to address a particular end. Global or general statements of behavioral problems are usually inadequate for actually beginning a behavior modification program. For example, it is insufficient to select as the goal such things as alteration of aggressiveness, learning deficits, speech, social skills, depression, psychotic symptoms, self-esteem, or similar concepts. Traits, summary labels, and personality characteristics are too general to be of much use. Moreover, definitions of the behaviors that make up such general labels may be idiosyncratic among different behavior-change agents (parents, teachers, or hospital staff) and the client. The target behaviors have to be defined explicitly so that they can actually be observed, measured, and agreed on by individuals administering the program.

Operational Definitions

An initial task of scientific research in general is to identify the concept or focus of interest and to translate it into measurable operations. The move from concept (characteristic or idea) to operations (ways in which that concept will be measured) is a critical facet for all of the sciences and permits advances and the accumulation of knowledge. In the case of interventions (e.g., treatment, prevention, education, rehabilitation), it is also critical to move from the general concept to the measure.

For example, we may be interested in changing anxiety in an adult referred for outpatient therapy or in eliminating temper tantrums in a child. Anxiety and tantrums are the concepts of interest and are important initial designations to help direct the focus. Yet the concepts or abstract notions must be translated into operational definitions. *Operational definitions refer to defining a concept on the basis of the specific operations used for assessment.* Paper-and-pencil measures (questionnaires to assess the domain), interviews, reports from others (e.g., parents, spouses) in contact with the client, physiological measures (e.g., measures of arousal, stress), and direct observation are among the most commonly used measures in psychological research to operationally define key concepts. Several measures might be selected in any given intervention program. For example, an operational definition of anxiety might include one or more of the following measures: self-reports of anxiety, physiological measures of arousal, nonverbal facial expressions that suggest the experience of stress, and direct signs of avoidance or turning away from the anxiety-provoking stimuli.

There are many ways to operationally define a response domain of interest. In behavior modification, emphasis is placed on direct observation of overt behavior

because overt behavior is viewed as the most direct measure of the treatment focus. For example, the frequency and severity of tantrums can be assessed by having parents and teachers complete paper-and pencil measures of a child's
disruptive behavior. Parents often report on their child's dysfunction in part
because they are in the best position to see their child. Yet reports *about* tantrums
are a step removed from the tantrums themselves. Moreover, parent report,
although useful, is influenced considerably by the stress and symptoms (e.g., depression) of the parent. The more stressed the parent, the greater the deviance they
report in their children, even when data show that children are not that deviant
(Kazdin, 1994). In any case, if possible and feasible, it is useful to observe the
tantrums directly and to see when they occur, under what circumstances, and
whether they change in response to intervention.

Operational definitions are essential to begin to assess, change, and evaluate interventions. At the same time, it is important to recognize that operational definitions are limited. In defining an abstract concept such as anxiety or tantrums, an
operational definition does not capture the entire domain of interest. Overt behavioral signs of anxiety—or tantrums for that matter—do not capture all there
is about these domains/behaviors. Feelings, thoughts, and associated behaviors are
part of the package encompassed by anxiety. Even so, an operational definition is
a working definition of the concept or problem foci of interest.

The relation of operational definitions to the concept of interest warrants further comment. Consider all of the facets of a given concept as reflecting a large
pie chart. For example, depression as a concept can encompass all sorts of components such as how a person interacts with others; the activities in which he or
she engages; what he or she thinks, feels, and discusses; and even how that person
looks to others (appearance). All of these are in a large circle (pie chart) that is
considered when discussing the concept of depression. Operational definitions are
ways of working with the concept by taking a slice or two to represent critical
components. Usually we are interested in the entire concept and use operational
definitions to represent this. In such cases, we do not merely wish to change the
one measure we assess but hope to change the many components of the larger
concept. In other situations, operational definitions may reflect virtually all or
most of the components of interest. In the case of tantrums, for example, frequency of the tantrums may be the main aspect of interest. In general, when intervening to change a particular problem or behavior, there is usually interest in
more than just the operational definition. When change is achieved on the measure that is used to define the concept, other features of the domain may change
as well.

Different types of measures (e.g., self-report, reports of others, questionnaires,
interviews, physiological measures) of a given abstract notion assess different but
overlapping facets of a concept. One measure does not necessarily replace or ob-
viate another type of measure. Indeed, sometimes, different measures of the same
concept are only moderately related. Conclusions about a relationship can even
vary considerably among different operational definitions of the same concept.
For example, deviant behavior in a child (e.g., tantrums, aggressiveness, shyness)
when measured by child, parent, or teacher report yield somewhat different con-

Table 3-2   Criteria To Be Met When Defining Behaviors for Observation

Criterion	Defined	Example
Objectivity	The measure refers to observable characteristics of the behavior or to events in the environment that can be observed	The number of times that a child engages in tantrums (as an operational definition of tantrums); the number of cigarette butts in the ashtray or cigarettes remaining in the pack (as an operational definition of cigarette smoking)
Clarity	A definition is so unambiguous that it could be read, repeated, and par-aphrased by an observer or someone initially unfamiliar with measure. Little explanation of what is needed to begin actual observations of the behavior.	A tantrum includes anytime the child shouts, whines, stomps feet, throws things, or slams a door in response to a comment from his or her mother or father during the hours of 3:30 PM to 5:30 PM, Monday through Friday, when the child and at least one parent are at home.
Completeness	Delineation of the boundary conditions so that the responses to be included and excluded are enumerated.	Not included in a tantrum is a raised voice that is part of excitement while watching TV or playing a game or an initial expression of disappointment when a request (e.g., staying up later for bedtime) is denied. A statement of disappointment that lasts less than a minute without behaviors noted in the example of clarity (above) is not a tantrum for present purposes.

clusions and can vary as a function of which informant completes the measure (Achenbach, McConaghy, & Howell, 1987; Kazdin, 1994).[2] In most behavioral programs, regardless of whether multiple measures are used, overt behavior is the salient assessment procedure and hence constitutes the focus of this chapter.

Criteria for Defining Behavior

We begin by specifying the general domain (e.g., tantrums) and then by identifying a specific definition that permits assessment. To make this transition, one ought to ask of others (e.g., parents, teachers, clients), precisely what are the desired or undesired behaviors? Also, it is useful to observe the client informally. Descriptive notes of what behaviors occur and which events are associated with their occurrence may be useful in generating specific response definitions. From inquiries and informal observations, one might be able to answer several questions about the target behavior (e.g., when does it occur, what does it look like, under what circumstances does it occur?). From such queries, one moves to an operational definition to specify how the behavior will be assessed for purposes of observation and intervention.

As a general rule, a definition should meet three criteria: *objectivity, clarity,* and *completeness* (Hawkins & Dobes, 1975). These concepts are defined and illustrated in Table 3-2. Developing a complete definition often creates the greatest difficulty because decision rules are needed to specify how behavior should be scored. If the range of responses included in the definition is not described carefully, observers have to infer whether such a response has occurred. For example, a simple greeting response such as waving one's hand to greet someone may serve as the target behavior for a socially withdrawn child. In most instances, when a person's hand is fully extended and moving back and forth, there would be no difficulty in agreeing that the person was waving. However, ambiguous instances may require judgments on the part of observers. A child might move his or her hand once (rather than back and forth) while the arm is not extended, or a child may not move his or her arm at all but simply move all of the fingers on one hand up and down (in the way that infants often learn to say good-bye). These responses are instances of waving in everyday life, because we can often see others reciprocate with similar greetings. For assessment purposes, the response definition must specify how these and related variations of waving should be scored.

Developing clear definitions requires specifying what is and is not to be included in the behavior. For example, in one program, the focus was on reducing the frequency of talking to oneself for a hospitalized schizophrenic patient (Wong et al., 1987). Self-talk was defined as any vocalization not directed at another person but excluding sounds associated with physiological functions such as coughing. This is straightforward. As observations are conducted, examples that are difficult to score may emerge, and these may be used to make more precise what is and is not to be counted. A clear definition does not eliminate judgments but allows a way to codify these judgments so they are made relatively consistently.

Task Analysis

The prior discussion of identifying and defining behavior focused on the case where there may be one or two target behaviors that serve as the intervention focus. In many cases, the goal of the program is to develop a complex set and sequence of behaviors. A process referred to as task analysis facilitates altering more complex sets of behaviors. *Task analysis is a way of proceeding from the general goal of the program to a number of small, trainable, and highly concrete behaviors.* The purpose of task analysis is to identify specific behaviors that are required and to specify the sequence in which these component behaviors are performed.

A task analysis is deceptively simple because the behaviors that eventually are selected may seem obvious and straightforward. The initial challenge of task analysis is to identify the desired behaviors. Evaluating the behavior among persons who are performing well may facilitate this. The guiding question is what does the behavior consist of when it is performed well or appropriately? For example, if one wishes to develop social skills in a withdrawn or rejected child, an initial task is to examine the competent social behavior of peers, children who are functioning well (i.e., those who are accepted or popular). These observations can suggest the target behaviors to focus on for the withdrawn child.

In some cases, soliciting the input of persons with expertise in specific areas identifies the desired behaviors. Such persons are consulted to identify the behaviors to be performed or how they are to be performed. For example, developing a program of behaviors to prevent or to detect a disease early may require soliciting the views of health experts. The behaviors they identify (e.g., how to check oneself for early signs of the disease, in what practices to engage to prevent infection) are translated into concrete behaviors that form the goals of the program. The expertise of those who conduct behavior modification is in the area of intervention and evaluation. The behaviors to which the interventions ought to be applied often require input from those who seek change for themselves (e.g., clients), those who seek change for others under their charge (parents, teachers, administrators on behalf of others), and experts whose knowledge is required to specify precisely what those behaviors may be.

However the behaviors are identified, a critical feature of task analysis is to specify the requisite behaviors in small, trainable units. This aspect of task analysis may be difficult, because there are no firm rules for dividing behaviors or for establishing the units that constitute trainable components. Training may require smaller or larger units of behavior, depending on the initial level of client skill or ability. Along with the identification of specific trainable components, the order or sequence of the behaviors needs to be specified. Training then proceeds to develop each individual component into the larger sequence until the entire set of behaviors is trained.

Task analysis is nicely illustrated in a program for adolescents and adults who suffered brain injuries from vehicle accidents (O'Reilly, Green, & Braunling-McMorrow, 1990). Each individual experienced severe cognitive and behavioral dysfunction due to his or her injury. The purpose of the program was to train individuals to prevent hazards in daily living. Common preventable home hazards that most frequently lead to injury were identified from materials available from the National Safety Council. Task analysis for each hazardous situation was developed by observing how non-handicapped adults remedied unsafe situations. Hazards were identified in separate rooms of an apartment used for training. Behaviors for rectifying hazards in relation to the kitchen, one of four rooms studied, are listed in Table 3-3. As the table shows, very concrete behaviors were identified. Completion of these behaviors would constitute appropriate behaviors to prevent common accidents in the kitchen. The careful specification of behavior in this example illustrates the behavioral approach toward identifying goals of the program, translating these goals to concrete behaviors, and previewing the task of treatment, namely, training the specific behaviors. In the case of this example, safe behaviors were trained by practice, prompts, and reinforcement to develop each of the constituent behaviors in each of the rooms. Task analysis was useful in breaking down the behaviors for shaping, that is, developing successive approximations of the behavior.

In a quite different focus, adult males, ages 25 to 35, were trained to examine themselves for signs of testicular cancer (Friman, Finney, Glasscock, Weigel, & Christophersen, 1986). Such self-examination is important because testicular cancer is one of the leading causes of death in men ages 15 to 40. To teach correct self-examination, it was first critical to identify precisely what behaviors were required. The list of required behaviors was obtained by discussing the task with urologists and by consulting written and video materials about testicular cancer. The specific behaviors that constitute appropriate self-examination are listed in Table 3-4. Again, careful identification of the requisite behaviors greatly facilitated evaluation of the program and effective training. Individuals were successfully trained in self-examination and reported continuing performance of the behaviors up to several months later.

Table 3-3   Task Analysis for Remediating Hazards in the Kitchen

A. Grease on stove top.
   1. Get paper towels and appropriate cleaner from materials box under sink.
   2. With towels and cleaner, wipe grease from stove until no grease can be seen.
   3. Throw paper towels in trash and return cleaner to materials box.
B. Paper napkins on stove top.
   1. Remove paper from stove top.
   2. Place paper in trash.
C. Smoke detector beside stove.
   1. Remove smoke detector from cooking area.
   2. Get paper towel from materials box under sink.
   3. Wipe dust from smoke detector until no dust is visible.
   4. Press test button to make sure smoke detector is working.
   5. Place smoke detector near ceiling at least 15 feet from stove.
D. Trash can beside stove.
   1. Place trash can at least 5 feet away from stove.
E. Drinking glasses at edge of counter.
   1. Place glasses at least 1 foot from edge of counter.
F. Broken glass on floor.
   1. Get broom and dustpan from broom closet.
   2. Sweep glass into dustpan until dustpan is full.
   3. Empty dustpan into trash.
   4. Repeat until no glass can be seen on floor.
G. Cleaner (poison) beside food in cabinet.
   1. Place cleaners at least 5 feet away from food.
   2. Place cleaners that are not in their proper containers in the trash.

(Source: O'Reilly, Green, & Braunling-McMorrow, 1990)

Table 3-4   Task Required for Testicular Self-Examination

1. Gently pulls scrotum so that it hangs freely.
2. Uses fingers and thumbs of both hands to isolate and examine one testicle.
3. Locates the soft tender mass (the epididymis and spermatic cord, on top of and extending behind the testicle.
4. Rotates the entire surface area of the testicle between fingers and thumbs.
5. Uses fingers and thumbs to isolate and examine the other testicle.
6. Locates the soft tender mass on top of and extending behind the testicle.
7. Rotates the entire surface area of the testicle between fingers and thumbs.

(Source: Friman, Finney, Glasscock, Weigel, & Christophersen, 1986)

In many behavioral applications, task analysis has been crucial in breaking down complex behaviors so that they can be assessed and trained. Task analyses have been extremely helpful in training persons in cardiopulmonary resuscitation (CPR) techniques to help revive individuals who have had a heart attack (Seaman, Greene, & Watson-Perczel, 1986), teaching adults with a diagnosis of autism to purchase items in stores (Haring, Kennedy, Adams, & Pitts-Conway, 1987), and training persons with mental retardation to engage in first-aid skills (Marchand-Martella, Martella, Agran, Salzberg, Young, & Morgan, 1992) and prepare food for themselves (Griffen, Wolery, & Schuster, 1992). One can see from these examples, observing the target behaviors in everyday life (e.g., purchasing items in stores) or consulting with experts (e.g., for CPR) help identify the component behaviors to be trained.

A complexity of task analysis has to do with the degree of specificity of the individual behaviors and with the unit or amount of behavior that any one step should include. For some behaviors or clients, many small units of behavior may be grouped into one step in the task analysis; for other behaviors or clients, many more steps may have to be delineated and trained separately. As an example, teaching dressing skills might require multiple steps in a task analysis for children with severe intellectual impairment. Division of the behavior into smaller units might facilitate training with the children functioning at a lower level. There are no firm guidelines for delineating the number of steps, but it is likely that the decision will be based on the complexity of the goal, the initial behaviors (baseline level) of the persons who are to be trained, and the speed with which the behaviors are acquired during training.

Assessment

When behavior has been defined in precise terms, the next step is systematic assessment or measuring the behavior of interest. Assessment of behavior is essential for at least two reasons. First, assessment identifies the extent to which the target behavior is performed. Assessment reflects the frequency of occurrence of the target behavior before the program. The rate of preprogram behavior is referred to as the *baseline* or *operant rate*. Second, assessment is required to reflect behavior change after the program is begun. Because the major purpose of the program is to alter behavior, behavior during the program must be compared with behavior during baseline. Careful assessment throughout the program is essential.

It may be tempting to rely on human judgment or general impressions, rather than on direct measurement to evaluate the extent to which behavior is performed or whether change has occurred with treatment. Yet human judgment may greatly distort the actual rate of behavior. Indeed, the "normal" biases of human judgment have been studied extensively and reveal that systematic patterns are often seen in evaluating characteristics and relations among two or more variables of interest when, in fact, no systematic patterns exist (Dumont, 1993; Nezu & Nezu, 1989; Smith & Dumont, 1997).

In relation to behavioral programs, one might understand why judgment cannot easily identify the scope or frequency of the problems. For example, such behaviors as tantrums may be so intense that parents or teachers may recall them as occurring very often even when they are relatively infrequent. In contrast, some children have so many tantrums that their parents have become accustomed to a high rate and perceive tantrums as being less frequent than they really are. Judgment may also be inadequate to evaluate whether behavior change has occurred. Human judgment often does not correspond to the actual records of overt behavior. Indeed, we have known for some time that parents, teachers, and institutional staff may judge behavior as improving when there is no change or even when the behavior has become worse (Kazdin, 1973; Schnelle, 1974). Judgments about behavior can be influenced by many factors other than the behavior itself. As mentioned previously, in the case of parent evaluations, the psychological state of the parent influences how deviant the child is rated, over and above the actual level of deviance evident in the child (see Kazdin, 1994).

Direct observations are designed to reveal more directly than global impressions or ratings the level or amount of the target behavior and the degree of behavior change. Observing behavior has its own obstacles, sources of bias, and pitfalls. For example, direct observation of behavior is not entirely free from human judgment. Typically, observers or persons within the environment must record (judge) the occurrence of behavior, and extraneous factors can influence the results. Even when judgment seems to be eliminated, as when a response is recorded by some equipment or apparatus, judgment may still play a role. The investigator or the machine defines what response is to be counted as important or significant. Many facets of developing the measure such as task analysis and developing objective, clear, and complete definitions are designed to minimize judgment in the behaviors selected as the focus and in counting whether they have occurred. Overt behaviors are focused on in part because they usually provide a direct measure of how well or poorly a behavior-change program is working, and provide a very useful basis for making decisions about the intervention and about whether changes in the program are needed. However, just because they are overt behaviors and not people's reports about these behaviors does not mean that all judgment or inference is removed.

Strategies of Assessment

Assessment of the target behavior is critical to the behavioral program. Understanding antecedent conditions and consequences in relation to behavior are also very important, and this is further explained in the next chapter. This chapter focuses on the target behavior and how it is assessed. This focus is critical because application of the intervention (e.g., reinforcement, extinction) and evaluation of the program's impact depend on defining and assessing behavior carefully. In most behavior modification programs, behaviors are assessed on the basis of discrete occurrences of the response or on the amount of time that the response occurs. Several variations and different types of measures are available.

Frequency Measures. Frequency counts simply require tallying the number of times the target behavior occurs in a given period. *A frequency measure is particularly useful when the target response is discrete and when it takes a relatively constant amount of time each time it is performed.* A discrete response has a clearly delineated beginning and end so that separate instances of the response can be counted. The performance of the behavior should take a relatively constant amount of time so that the units counted are approximately equal. Discrete behaviors can be readily assessed by just tallying instances in which they occur. Examples include the number of times a person attends an activity, throws an object, turns in homework on time, takes medication, goes to the gym to exercise, and so on. Frequency measures require merely noting the instances in which behavior occurs.

When frequency measures are used, usually there is a requirement that behavior be observed for a constant amount of time. Of course, if behavior is observed for 20 minutes on one day and 30 minutes on another day, the frequencies are not directly comparable. However, the *rate of response* each day can be determined by dividing the frequency of the responses by the number of minutes observed each day. This measure will yield frequency per minute, or response rate, which is comparable even if the behavior is observed for different amounts of time.

As noted already, a frequency measure is well suited to behaviors that have a clear beginning and end and are roughly of equal duration. The measure is less well suited to ongoing behaviors such as smiling, sitting in a seat, lying down, and talking. It is difficult or misleading to record ongoing behaviors simply by counting because each response may occur for a different amount of time. For example, if a person talks to a peer for 15 seconds and to another peer for 30 minutes, these might be counted as two instances of talking. However, a great deal of information is lost by simply counting instances of talking because they differ in duration.

A frequency measure has several desirable features for use in applied settings. First, frequency is relatively simple to score. Keeping a tally of behavior is usually all that is required. Moreover, counting devices are available, such as a golf counter worn as a wristwatch to facilitate recording. Second, frequency measures readily reflect changes over time. The number of times that a response occurs is sensitive to change resulting from alterations in contingencies. Indeed, the principles of operant conditioning refer to changes in the frequency of a response. Consequently, frequency and response rates are direct measures that are most likely to reflect change when using techniques derived from these principles. Third, frequency expresses the amount of behavior performed, which is usually of concern to individuals in applied settings. The goal of most programs is to increase or decrease the number of times that a certain behavior occurs. Frequency provides a direct measure of the amount of behavior.

Discrete Categorization. Often it is very useful to classify responses into discrete categories such as correct/incorrect, performed/not performed, or appropriate/inappropriate. Discrete categorization can be used for behaviors that have a clear beginning, end, and a constant duration, as was the case for frequency measures. However, there are two important differences. With a frequency measure, performances of a particular behavior are tallied. The focus is on a single response. Additionally, the number of times the behavior may occur is theoretically unlimited. For example, one child hitting another may be measured by frequency counts. The number of times the behavior (hitting) may occur has no real limit. *Discrete categorization is especially useful in measuring whether several different behaviors have occurred.* Only a limited number of opportunities to perform the response is available, and one can score whether the response was completed or performed.

For example, discrete categorization might be used to measure the messiness of one's college roommate. A checklist can be devised that lists several behaviors such as putting one's shoes in the closet, removing underwear from the kitchen table, and putting dishes in the sink and food in the refrigerator. Every morning, each behavior on the checklist could be categorized as performed or not performed. Of course, each behavior on the checklist needs to be carefully defined to ensure it is reliably recorded. The total number of behaviors or steps that have been performed correctly constitutes the measure each day that observations are made.

A more interesting example derives from a college senior who conducted a project as part of a behavior modification class. The goal of the project was to increase the type and amount of expressions of affection and caring from her boyfriend. She operationally defined this with several behaviors, including calling her when she did not prompt him to call, saying something affectionate such as how much he loved her or liked being with her, holding her hand or putting his arm around her when they walked together or attended some event (e.g., movie, football game), scheduling time together on the weekend, and leaving her notes expressing love in her dormitory room, and others. Every morning, the presence or absence of each behavior was recorded as having occurred or not occurred in the previous 24 hours. Although not all of these were expected on a daily basis, they constituted multiple behaviors of interest as a way of operationally defining affectionate behavior. Discrete categorization was useful because each could be scored yes or no and because the sum (combining the different behaviors) represented a meaningful definition of the concept of interest.

Discrete categories have been used in many behavior modification programs. For example, in one project, personal appearance was altered among autistic children and adolescents living in community-based group homes (McClannahan, McGee, MacDuff, & Krantz, 1990). Twenty behaviors related to personal appearance (e.g., having a clean face, unstained clothing, shoelaces tied, matching socks, and so on) were included in a checklist and classified as appropriate or not. Changes in the number of discrete behaviors performed were used to evaluate training. As another example, in a camp setting, cabin-cleaning behaviors of emotionally disturbed boys were evaluated using discrete categorization (Peacock, Lyman, & Richard, 1978). To evaluate the effects of the program, such tasks as placing coats on hooks, making beds, having no objects on the beds, and putting tooth brushing materials away were categorized as completed or not.

Discrete categorization is easy to use because it requires listing a number of behaviors and checking off whether they were performed. The behaviors may consist of several steps that all relate to the completion of a task, such as dressing or grooming behaviors in children. Behavior can be evaluated by noting whether or how many steps are performed (e.g., removing a shirt from the drawer, putting one arm through, then the other arm, and pulling it over one's head). On the other hand, the behaviors need not be related to one another so that performance of one behavior may not depend on a prior behavior in any sort of sequence. For example, among the affectionate behaviors noted previously, holding hands and verbally expressing love do not depend on each other.

Discrete categorization is useful because often, concepts of interest to parents and teachers include more than a single behavior. Identifying a small number that can be categorized as having occurred or not occurred can capture many of the behaviors of interest. Each behavior, of course, has to be defined to meet the criteria noted previously. The utility of discrete categorization also derives from convenient summary scores that are provided. The total number of desired behaviors performed or percentage of correct responses can be easily calculated by forming a ratio of occurred or performed responses to total possible responses and multiplying by 100. The student who focused on affectionate behavior simply calculated the percentage of behaviors that had been engaged in the previous 24-hour period, among those she was observing. A more familiar example of the yield from discrete categorization is correct responses on an examination, which can be expressed as either a total number or a percentage. Overall, discrete categorization is a very flexible method of observation that allows assessment of all sorts of behaviors independently of whether they are necessarily related to one another.

Interval Recording. Interval recording is a commonly used strategy for measuring behavior in applied settings. With this method, behavior is observed for *a single block of time,* such as 30 or 60 minutes once per day. A block of time is divided into a series of short intervals (each interval may equal 10 or 15 seconds). During each interval, the target behavior is scored as having occurred or not having occurred. If a discrete behavior such as hitting someone occurs one or more times in a single interval, the response is scored as having occurred. Several response occurrences within an interval are not counted separately. If the behavior is ongoing with an unclear beginning or end such as talking, playing, and sitting or occurs for a long period, it is scored during each of the intervals in which it is occurring.

Behavior modification programs in classroom settings frequently use interval recording to score whether students are paying attention, sitting in their seats, and working quietly. The behavior of an individual student may be observed for 10-second intervals over a 20-minute observational period. For each interval, an observer records whether the child was working quietly in his or her seat. If the child remains seated and works for a long period, many intervals will be scored for attentive behavior. If the child leaves his or her seat (without permission) or stops working, inattentive behavior will be scored. During some intervals, a child may be seated for half of the time and out of the seat for the remaining time. Because the interval has to be scored for *either* attentive or inattentive behavior, a rule for scoring behavior in such instances has to be devised. Often, getting out of the seat is counted as inattentive behavior and nullifies the portion of attentive behavior within the interval.

Interval recording for a single block of time has been used in many programs beyond the classroom setting. For example, one program focused on several inappropriate behaviors that children performed while they accompanied their parents shopping, such as roughhousing, touching objects, or playing with merchandise, (Clark et al., 1977, Exp. 3). Observers followed the family in the store to record whether the inappropriate behaviors occurred during consecutive 15-second intervals. Interval assessment was also used in a program designed to reduce self-injurious behavior (biting one's own hand, arm, or shoulder and scratching oneself) in a way that caused bodily damage to two profoundly retarded adolescents (Pace, Iwata, Edwards, & McCosh, 1986). Observations in the hospital were conducted daily in an individual therapy room and a group therapy

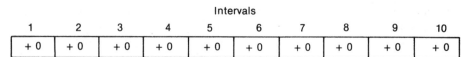

Intervals

1	2	3	4	5	6	7	8	9	10
+ 0	+ 0	+ 0	+ 0	+ 0	+ 0	+ 0	+ 0	+ 0	+ 0

Circle appropriate symbol in each interval.
+ = behavior occurred during interval
0 = behavior did not occur during interval

FIGURE 3-1

Example of Interval Scoring Sheet for One Individual

Intervals

Individuals	1	2	3	4	5	6	7	8	9	10
1	+ 0	+ 0	+ 0	+ 0	+ 0	+ 0	+ 0	+ 0	+ 0	+ 0
2	+ 0	+ 0	+ 0	+ 0	+ 0	+ 0	+ 0	+ 0	+ 0	+ 0
3	+ 0	+ 0	+ 0	+ 0	+ 0	+ 0	+ 0	+ 0	+ 0	+ 0
4	+ 0	+ 0	+ 0	+ 0	+ 0	+ 0	+ 0	+ 0	+ 0	+ 0
5	+ 0	+ 0	+ 0	+ 0	+ 0	+ 0	+ 0	+ 0	+ 0	+ 0
6	+ 0	+ 0	+ 0	+ 0	+ 0	+ 0	+ 0	+ 0	+ 0	+ 0
7	+ 0	+ 0	+ 0	+ 0	+ 0	+ 0	+ 0	+ 0	+ 0	+ 0

FIGURE 3-2

Example of Interval Scoring Sheet for Many Individuals

room. In each setting, an observer recorded whether any self-injurious behavior occurred during each of several 10-second intervals.

Interval scoring of behavior is facilitated by a scoring sheet on which intervals are represented over time. In Figure 3-1, each number across the top denotes a time interval. During each interval, a + or 0 is circled or checked to denote whether the behavior has occurred for the client. The basic sheet can be expanded to include many clients and intervals, as shown in Figure 3-2. For example, each student in a classroom or each patient in a hospital can be observed for a large number of intervals. The first person would be observed for the first interval (e.g., 15 seconds). After that person's behavior has been recorded, the second person would be observed. This would be continued until each person has been observed for one interval (down the left column in Figure 3-2). The order would then be repeated until each person had been observed for another interval and so on for the remaining intervals. Often more than one behavior is scored during an interval so that the presence of several behaviors will be judged during each interval. To accomplish this, a data sheet may include many symbols in each interval block so that various behaviors can be coded. A letter or symbol is checked or circled for the different categories of behavior that occur during the interval.

In using an interval scoring method, an observer looks at the client during the interval. When one interval is over, the observer records whether the behavior occurred. If an observer is recording several behaviors during an interval, a few seconds may be needed to record all of the behaviors that were observed during that interval. If the observer records a behavior as soon as it occurs (before the interval is over), he or she might miss other behaviors that occurred while the first behavior was being scored. Hence, many investigators use interval scoring procedures that allow time for recording after each interval of observation.

A variation of interval recording is referred to as *time sampling*. This variation uses the interval method, but the observations are conducted for brief periods *at different times rather than in a single block of time*. For example, with the time sampling method, a child may be observed for 10-second intervals, but these intervals may be spread out over a full day. As an illustration, psychiatric patients participating in a hospital reinforcement program were evaluated with time-sampling procedures (Paul & Lentz, 1977). Every hour, an observer watched a patient for a 2-second interval. At the end of the interval, the observer recorded the presence or absence of several behaviors related to social interaction, activities, self-care, and other responses. The procedure was continued throughout the day, sampling one interval at a time. The advantage of time sampling is that the observations represent performance over the entire day. Of course, in many settings like the home or the classroom, it is more convenient to complete observations in a single observation session.

Significant features of interval recording make it one of the most widely adopted strategies in research. First, interval assessment can record virtually any behavior. Whether a response is discrete and does not vary in duration or is continuous or sporadic, it can be classified as occurring or not occurring during any period. Second, the observations resulting from interval recording can be easily converted into a percentage. The number of intervals during which the response is scored as having occurred can be divided by the total number of intervals observed. This ratio, multiplied by 100, yields the percentage of intervals in which the response has been performed. For example, if social responses are scored as having occurred in 20 of the 40 intervals observed, the percentage of the intervals of social behavior is 50% ([20/40] × 100). A percentage is easily communicated to others by noting that a certain behavior occurs a specific percentage of the time (intervals). Whenever there is doubt as to what assessment strategy should be adopted, an interval approach is always applicable and can be readily employed.

Amount of Time. The amount of time can be used in different ways to record behavior. The first of these is *duration* and refers to the amount of time that the response is performed. This method is particularly useful for continuous, ongoing responses, rather than for discrete acts or responses of extremely short duration. Programs that attempt to increase or decrease the length of time that a response is performed might profit from a duration method. Examples may include the amount of time that a student takes to complete homework, exercises, or practices a musical instrument; or the amount of time a couple spends together or in enjoyable activities. For someone who fears open spaces or contact with people, duration may serve as a measure of treatment progress; time outside of the home (e.g., at a shopping mall) or with a friend could be increased over the course of treatment.

The amount of time (e.g., number of minutes or other unit) in which an individual engages in a response is often immediately meaningful to parents, teachers, and others to whom the program results may be communicated. Time can also be converted to a percentage as another way to communicate the results. The amount of time in which the behavior was observed, divided by the total time of an observation period and multiplied by 100 yields a percentage. Thus a student who studied for a total of 30 minutes during a 60-minute study period would be counted as studying 50% of the period (30 min/60 min × 100).

Another measure based on the amount of time is *latency* and refers to *how long it takes for the client to begin the response*. Duration focuses on length of the period in which the behavior is performed (e.g., 20 minutes of homework), whereas latency refers to how long it takes before the response begins (e.g., how many minutes after coming home before the student began homework). Latency is the amount of time that elapses between a cue or some beginning point (e.g., arriving to class or at home, sitting down at one's desk, being asked to start some behavior) and the response (e.g., taking out one's class materials, beginning to work, initiating the requested behavior, respectively).

An excellent example where latency is clearly relevant is in the context of insomnia. Insomnia consists of attempting to go to sleep but having a long time elapse before sleep begins. Essentially going to bed is the beginning point for assessment and actually falling to sleep is the end point. Latency has been used to evaluate the effects of treatment. One program assessed adults (ages 60 or older) who have insomnia and who received treatment based on stimulus control procedures (Puder, Lacks, Bertelson, & Storandt, 1983). Treatment consisted of having clients associate drowsiness with going to bed. Sleep-incompatible behaviors such as worrying, eating, or watching TV were to be performed in a room other than the bedroom. Gradually, the consistent association of the bedroom with sleeping helped clients get to sleep better. The effectiveness of treatment was reflected in the reduced latency in going to sleep after going to bed.

Assessment of response duration or latency is a fairly simple matter: one starts and stops a stopwatch or notes the time when the response begins and ends. However, the onset and termination of the response must be carefully defined. Without clear definitions of onset and termination, duration and latency are extremely difficult to employ. For example, duration could readily be used to assess tantrums of a child. Presumably, the goal of the program might be to reduce the tantrums from their average duration of perhaps 10 to 0 minutes. This could readily be assessed, but a tantrum may wax and wane and change in intensity. For example, a child may cry continuously for several minutes, whimper for short periods, stop all noise for a few seconds, and begin intense crying again. In recording the duration of the tantrum, a decision is required to handle changes in the intensity of the behavior (e.g., from crying to whimpering) and pauses such as periods of silence so that these are consistently recorded as part of the response or as a different (e.g., nontantrum) response.

Response duration generally is used in situations in which the length of time a behavior is performed is a major concern. In most behavior modification programs, the goal is to increase or decrease the frequency of a response rather than its duration. There are notable exceptions, of course. For example, it is desirable to increase the length of the time that students study or that persons practice a skill they wish to learn, such as playing an instrument or speaking a foreign language. An advantage of duration and latency measures in applied settings is that they are user-friendly to parents, teachers, and others. The measures require careful definition of behavior, as all of the other measures, but then only use of a clock or watch. In research where special observers are available to record behavior, interval assessment is used more often than duration or latency, in part because of the flexibility of interval assessment and the ability to measure multiple behaviors in an interval. Such resources are not available to parents and teachers and hence time-based measures that use duration or latency may be preferable and more feasible.

Intensity. Intensity refers to the magnitude, strength, amplitude, force, or effort of the response. Examples include volume of one's voice, noise level, and magnitude of a tantrum (e.g., ranging from shouting only to shouting, throwing things, and hitting others). Although programs occasionally focus on intensity of the behavior, this is not often used as a way of assessing the impact of the program. Sometimes intensity can be recorded through automated, mechanical devices. For example, voice volume, physiological arousal and reaction to stress or anxiety-provoking situations, and relaxation states all can be evaluated with various devices to assess amplitude or strength of a response. Without such measures, degrees of intensity may require judgments that are difficult to make or make consistently.

An example conveys how intensity can be useful and important to integrate into a behavioral program. In one program in which I was involved, a 6-year-old boy had very intense tantrums anytime his mother or father did not let him have his way or made a seemingly simple request of him, such as to pick up toys. The goal of the program was to eliminate the tantrums. This was approached first by reducing the intensity of the tantrums. A point system was devised in which he could earn points for speaking nicely or saying nothing in anger when he was told "no." This was practiced at different times throughout the day in simulated situations at home. The mom or dad would go to the child and say (in a playful way), "OK, this is a time to see what you can do," or "Here's a chance to earn points." Then the parent would say one of the common statements used in the house or set up a situation in which the child was asked to do something. The child was prompted further to speak nicely, to say no without hitting or throwing things, or to say yes and agree. Also, during the day, natural occasions arose in which the child could and did have a tantrum and these were included in the point program too. Points were given for nontantrum behavior (speaking nicely or walking away). However, for the first week, a smaller number of points were earned if his tantrum decreased in intensity (included no hitting of the parent or throwing objects against the wall.) After a week of reduced intensity, points were added for not swearing during the tantrum and for talking quietly. In short, more points were earned for less intense tantrums. Within a couple of weeks, intensity of the tantrums decreased (not expressing anger by throwing things, hitting, and swearing) and the frequency of speaking appropriately increased.

Here the program focused on intensity of the response. To make the observations easy for the parent, discrete categorization was used. Whether shouting, throwing an object, hitting, and swearing occurred and whether appropriate taking occurred (five behaviors, each yes or no) were recorded for each tantrum. An intensity rating would have required an evaluation of the intensity of the entire tantrum, and that is a more difficult to obtain.

Number of Persons. Occasionally, the effectiveness of behavioral programs is evaluated on the basis of the number of persons who perform a response. Obviously, the measure is used in group situations such as classrooms, institutional settings (school, hospital), or society at large. In such cases, the purpose is to increase the overall performance of a particular behavior such as completing homework, coming to an activity on time, or driving a car safely. Once the desired behavior has been defined, the observations record how many participants in the group have performed the response. As with frequency and categorization measures, the observations require classifying the response as having occurred or not occurred. However, here the *number of individuals are counted* rather than the number of times an individual performs the response.

Several programs have evaluated the impact of treatment on the number of people who are affected. For example, in one program the investigators were interested in reducing speeding among highway drivers (Van Houten, Nau, & Marini, 1980). To record speeding, a radar unit was placed unobtrusively along the highway. A feedback system visible to drivers was evaluated by measuring the percentage of drivers who exceeded the speed limit. Another program was designed to improve seat belt use among elementary school children (Sowers-Hoag, Thyer, & Bailey, 1987). The effects were evaluated by recording the percentage of children who used their seat belts when their parents picked them up at the end of the day.

Interventions are often conducted on a large scale, and there is keen interest in determining the number or proportion of people who are influenced. The concept of *prevalence* from epidemiology refers to the number of individuals at a given point in time who show a particular problem (e.g., disease, substance use, psychiatric disorder). Large-scale interventions may be implemented in an effort to reduce the number of cases with the problem. For example, in Oregon an effort was made to decrease cigarette smoking throughout the state (Pizacani et al., 1999). The intervention consisted of an increase in the tax on cigarettes (30 cents per pack), as well as educational efforts in the schools and through advertising to increase public awareness of the hazards of smoking. During the 2-year intervention period, there was a 6.4% decrease in the number of cigarette smokers, a seemingly small proportion. However, this translated into 35,000 fewer cigarette smokers.

As the previous example shows, knowing the number of people who perform a response is very useful when the explicit goal of the program is to alter performance in a large group. Consistent with this overall goal is developing behaviors in an institution and even in society at large. Increasing the number of people who exercise, give to charity, eat healthful foods, and seek treatment when in early stages of serious diseases, and decreasing the number of people who smoke, overeat, drive while under the influence of alcohol, and commit crimes are important goals of this kind that behavioral interventions have addressed.

When large-scale interventions are used, the overall rate or average (mean) may be altered, but the identity of the individual is lost. The performance of any particular individual may be sporadic or not well represented by the group average. This does not reflect an inadequacy of the measure of merely counting the number of persons. The information about individual performance may or may not be critical as a measure of intervention effects, depending on the goals of the program.

Other Assessment Strategies. Occasionally, other measures than those already described are used because they provide direct measures of behavior that are of obvious importance. For example, behavior modification programs for obesity or cigarette smoking have evaluated intervention effects by simply recording client weight in kilograms or pounds or the number of cigarettes smoked. In other programs, the specific behavior may lend itself to a measure unique to the investigation. For example, interventions designed to conserve energy can monitor gas or electric meters at home. In applications to medical problems such as hypertension or diabetes, specific measures such as blood pressure or the glucose concentration in the patient's urine have been used to evaluate behavioral treatment programs.

Many readily available measures reflect key indices of interest and can be used as reliable and valid measures in light of considerable research on what they reflect. Measures of blood pressure and blood glucose levels are of this type. However, not all readily available measures may be adequate as primary measures of an intervention effect. For examples, records of crime and teenage drug use are obtained annually and serve as a basis for tracking trends and the effects of policy changes. Among the difficulties in interpreting the information is the fact that the measures are surveys and the surveys themselves have changed over time. Some of the changes, or rather seeming changes, in crime rates and drug use seem to be due to the changes in how crime and drug use have been measured (DiLulio, 1997; Moss, 1996). Available records ought not to be automatically discarded or worshipped and may or may not be useful in any given instance.

Proponents of behavior modification are very concerned about measurement because careful assessment and evaluation are essential conditions for developing effective interventions. As a practical suggestion here, one can use readily available measures as part of intervention studies. Often such measures may need to be supplemented by other measures. For example, in the case of measuring juvenile delinquency, arrest rates are often used as a measure, but they also are supplemented with reports among adolescents about the number and type of specific crimes in which they engage. Self-reports of crime yield much more information than the less sensitive measure of arrest rates (Elliott, Dunford, & Huizinga, 1987).

Selection of an Assessment Strategy. In most situations, investigators use an assessment procedure based on frequency, interval, or one of the other methods mentioned above. Some behaviors such as the number of profane words used, toileting "accidents," or eating responses lend themselves well to frequency counts or categorization because they are discrete; others such as reading, working, or sitting lend themselves well to interval recording; and still others such as time spent studying, crying, or exercising lend themselves well to duration. Target behaviors can usually be assessed in more than one way, so there is no single strategy that must be adopted. For example, an investigator working in an institution for delinquents may wish to record the aggressive behavior of a particular adolescent. Hitting others (e.g., making physical contact with another individual with a closed fist) may be the response of interest. What assessment strategy should be used?

Aggressive behavior might be measured with a *frequency count* by having an observer record how many times the youth hit others during a certain period each day. Each hit would count as one response. The behavior might also be observed using *interval recording*. A block of time such as 30 minutes could be set aside for observation. The 30 minutes could be divided into 1-minute intervals. For each of these intervals, the observer would record whether any hitting had occurred. Perhaps *time sampling* might be used. Each hour during the day, the youth could be observed for a 15-minute period, for which the presence or absence of aggressive behavior would be recorded. This interval method has the advantage of sampling behavior over the entire day.

It may be difficult to time the *duration* of hitting because instances of hitting are too brief to clock unless there is a series of hits (as in a fight). Recording the amount of time from the beginning of each day until the first aggressive response might be easier. This *latency* measure records the time of no hitting. This may seem odd but actually is feasible. For example, a program in which I was involved provided tokens to a boy named Steve who was in the fourth grade, based on the amount of time before his first fight or argument in class, or his latency to respond. The teacher informed Steve when he first entered the room that if he could go for a certain number of minutes with "great behavior" (no arguing with peers, no hitting) he would earn 10 points. Various back-up rewards included longer recess for the whole class, a special game at the end of the day, and others. Presumably, if the program decreased aggressive behavior, the amount of time from the beginning of the day until the first aggressive response would increase. The time interval (latency) was increased over time so that the program eventually provided tokens only when the latency increased to "the whole day." (Chapter 6 elaborates reinforcement schedules in which programs like this can be used.)

Although many different measures can be used in a given program, the measure finally selected may be dictated by the purpose of the program. Different measures sometimes reflect slightly different goals. For example, consider two behavioral programs that focused on increasing tooth brushing, a seemingly simple response that could be assessed in many different ways. One of the programs observed the number of individuals in a boys' summer camp who brushed their teeth (Lattal, 1969). The boys knew how to brush their teeth, and an incentive system increased their performance of the response. In the other program, the clients were residents with mental retardation at a state hospital (Horner & Keilitz, 1975). The residents were unable to brush their teeth at the beginning of the program, so the many behaviors involved in tooth brushing were developed. Discrete categorization was used to assess tooth brushing; each component step of the behavior (wetting the brush, removing the cap, applying the toothpaste, and so on) was scored as performed or not performed. The percentage of steps correctly completed measured the effects of training. Although both of these investigations assessed tooth brushing, the different methods reflect different goals, namely, getting children who can brush to do so or training the response in residents with mental retardation who did not know how to perform it.

CONDUCTING OBSERVATIONS

Decisions in Assessing and Sampling Behavior

Three decisions need to be made regarding the observations. First, the *number of times* that data will be collected must be decided. When possible, it is desirable to observe behavior each day or during each session (e.g., in a classroom) that the target behavior may occur. The frequency of observation depends on such factors as the variation of behavior over time, the availability of observers, and scheduling exigencies in the setting. If the target behavior is very stable from one day to the next, daily assessment becomes less essential than if the target behavior fluctuates radically. As a general rule, behavior should be observed on as many occasions as possible, and preferably daily or multiple occasions per week. Evaluation of the effects of the program, discussed further in Chapter 5, underscores the importance of identifying a pattern or trend in the data, and this requires multiple assessment occasions (e.g., days of observation) whenever possible.

A second decision to be made is the *length of time* set aside for a given observation period. The guiding general rule is that behavior should be observed for a period that will allow the behavior to be displayed and to provide a sufficient sample of the behavior. For some behavioral problems or in some settings, the target behavior may occur only during a specific period of the day. For example, child behaviors at home, such as getting dressed for school, completing chores, or going to bed without a tantrum, all occur at brief and specific times during the day. In such cases, observation periods of the target behavior need not be long. They can focus on the times when occurrences of the behavior are more important or especially relevant, given the goals of the program. For other behavioral problems, the behaviors occur or do not occur only under specific cues or stimulus conditions. For example, completing chores (setting the table, doing dishes, making one's bed) occur throughout the day and cannot be observed at a specific block of time. As a general rule, behavioral programs are concerned with assessing behavior primarily on those occasions in which change is needed or across one or a few time periods (morning, afternoon) or settings (home, school).

A third decision related to the length of the time that behavior is observed is *when the observations are conducted*. Assuming that behavior will be observed for 30 minutes each day, will this all be in one block of time or dispersed over two or more periods that add up to 30 minutes? Observations using frequency, interval, or duration methods can record behavior in a block of time in a single day or at different times throughout the day. The advantage of sampling behavior at various times over the entire day is that the observed behavior is more likely to be representative of behavior over different time periods.

For practical reasons, usually it is not feasible to observe behavior over an extended period or over several shorter periods throughout the day to represent performance across all time and settings. In such instances, behavior might be observed for a single block of time during the period in which behavior change is most obviously required. An initial assessment at different times over a few days can determine which periods require the greatest attention. Subsequently, assessment can focus on those periods.

If interval assessment is used, in addition to the above decisions, the duration of the interval has to be decided. This refers to the individual intervals. For example, if observations may be made for a 30-minute blocks of time each day, how long will the intervals be within that block of time (e.g., 30 seconds, 1 minute)? Several considerations dictate the duration of intervals. First, interval duration should be relatively short (10 or 15 seconds) for behaviors that occur frequently. Longer intervals like 60 seconds would exclude much of the responding, because the interval is recorded for the presence or absence of only one response (occurred vs. not occurred). If the behavior occurs 20 times during one 60-second interval, the interval is scored on the occurrence of the first response and the behavior cannot be scored again until the next interval. Thus a great deal of behavior goes unrecorded. As a result of a behavior modification program, behavior may change from 20 times to 10 times per 60-second interval. However, this change will not be reflected in the data because the interval will continue to be scored merely for the presence or absence of the response.

Second, very short intervals (5 or fewer seconds) are sometimes difficult to score reliably because observers have difficulty in synchronizing observations. The interval is so short that it is not clear in which interval the behavior was performed. Third, the length of the interval may be less important when behavior is continuous, such as reading or watching television, than when it is discrete, because shorter or longer intervals are not likely to exclude "instances" of behavior. Many studies have used 10-second intervals, whereas others have reported intervals of one or a few minutes. Because there are no fixed rules for interval length, a wide range of durations has been employed.

Interval assessment is often used in research. However, as one can see, more decisions are required and this is not the easiest method to use in applied settings. Consequently, with people in everyday life involved in assessment, an effort is made to simplify the observations by using frequency counts, discrete categorization, or some record that is automatically reflected (minutes late on a time card at work, truancy). It is important to understand the diverse options for conducting assessments so that feasible and useful methods can be selected from all of those available.

Conditions Under Which Observations Are Obtained

Observations are usually completed by placing one or more observers in a position to see the client. In research, the observer may be out of sight, such as behind a one-way mirror in an observation booth adjacent to a classroom or a hospital ward. At other times, observations may be taken from videotapes, so the observer is not present in the situation. In most settings however, observers and clients are in the same situation, such as in the home or the classroom.

If the client is aware of the observer's presence, the assessment procedure is said to be *obtrusive*. A potential problem with obtrusive assessment is that the client's behavior may be affected by knowing that observations are being made. Assessment is *reactive* if the observer's presence alters the client's behavior. Obtrusive assessment (procedures in which the client is aware of assessment) is not necessarily reactive (may not change the client's behavior), but the possibility exists that there may be some influence. From the observations, we wish to see behavior as it normally occurs without the assessment procedures influencing the information we obtain. Fortunately, research suggests that even if the presence of an observer alters the behaviors of the persons who are observed, the effects are usually temporary (Haynes & Horn, 1982; Kazdin, 1982a).

When external observers enter a situation to collect observations (e.g., enter a classroom to record child behavior) or where conspicuous observations begin that clearly depart from the usual practice (e.g., parent observes or charts homework each day), reactivity can be minimized by avoiding interactions between the observer and the persons being observed. Thus in the classroom, an observer would avoid behavior that might maintain the children's interest, such as eye contact, smiles, and conversation. To minimize reactivity by helping the clients to adapt to the novelty of the new person, many investigators place the observer into the situation on several occasions before actual assessment begins.

Several considerations in conducting observations pertain to the observers and the manner in which they are trained and supervised (Foster, Bell-Dolan, & Burge, 1988). First, in some cases, two or more observers are used and for practical reasons are alternated according to some schedule. When the observers are first trained to record behavior, they may adhere to the same definition of behavior. Over time and after training is finished, observers may gradually depart from the original definitions of behavior, a phenomenon referred to as *observer drift*. The criteria for scoring behavior (e.g., being out of the seat in class, talking when one should be working) may change slightly and influence the data. To ensure that observers adhere to the definitions, periodic retraining, review of videotapes, and feedback regarding the accuracy of recording during the sessions can help minimize or eliminate drift.

Second, observer expectations may influence their recordings. If observers expect change once they see a program in effect, these expectations may influence their recordings. If the investigator conveys expectations and then unwittingly fosters biased observations by praising data in the expected direction, biased observations are more likely. To reduce the likelihood of biased recording, periodic retraining throughout the project and emphasis on recording accuracy are important. More generally, clarity of the definition, careful training of observers, and monitoring observers over the course of assessment are protections against biased recording.

Reliability of Assessment

Need for Reliability. It is important for individuals who observe the target behavior to agree on the occurrence of the response. Interobserver agreement, often referred to as *reliability of assessment,* is important for three major reasons.[3]

First, assessment is useful to the extent that it can be made with some consistency. For example, if frequency counts differ greatly depending on who is counting, it will be difficult to know what the client's actual performance is. The client may be scored as performing a response frequently on some days and infrequently on other days as a function of who scores behavior, rather than of differences in actual client performance. Inconsistent measurement introduces variation in the data that adds to the variation stemming from normal fluctuations in client performance. If measurement variation is large, there may appear to be no systematic pattern to the behavior. If a behavior modification program is implemented, it may be difficult to determine whether behavior is changing, because the data are highly variable as a function of inconsistent recording. Stable patterns of behavior are required to reflect behavior change. Hence, reliable recording is essential.

Second, assessing agreement is important because it minimizes or circumvents the biases of any individual observer. If a single observer records the target behavior, any recorded change in behavior may result from a change over time in the observer's definition of the target behavior, rather than in the actual behavior of the client. The observer may become lenient or stringent over time. For example, the observer may expect and perceive improvement in the target behavior, even though no improvement actually occurs. If two or more observers are used, one can see whether the pattern in the data varies as a function of who completes the observations. Agreement between observers provides a check on the consistency of their recording of behavior. Finally, assessing agreement is important because agreement reflects whether the target behavior is well defined. If observers readily agree on the occurrence of the behavior, it will be easier for the persons who eventually carry out the program to agree on the behavior and apply the intervention (e.g., reinforcing consequences) contingently.

The need for reliability checks may vary with the assessment method and the behavior of interest. If behavior is at a consistently zero rate, then this may not need to be checked. In most cases, zero rate (e.g., no exercise, no attendance to some activity) is rather clear. Also, measures are more likely to fluctuate because of observer drift or other types of bias due to the boundary conditions. For example, counting the cigarettes remaining in a full pack or the number of items on the floor of a messy roommate may be less likely to vary as a function of observers than observing kind, social, or attentive behavior. Even when the measure seems beyond question (e.g., measure of blood pressure), fluctuations may lead one to check reliability (e.g., blood pressure at the beginning of a doctor's appointment is usually higher than a few minutes later). In general reliability of assessment is needed for the reasons noted above. At the same time, if the reliability information shows that data can be obtained with consistency, the number of reliability checks can be few.

Conducting Checks on Agreement. To ensure that the behavior is agreed on, reliability checks can be made before baseline data are gathered. A few days of practice or pre-baseline observation generally are useful to finalize the rules for observing behavior and to handle instances in which it is not clear whether the target behavior has occurred. Once baseline begins, it is advisable to continue reliability checks intermittently throughout the program to ensure that behavior is consistently observed. If such checks are made only at the inception of the program, over time, observers may become increasingly lax in their scoring or drift away from the definitions that they should be using. Hence, observers may become less reliable over time.

Agreement has to achieve an acceptable level before baseline observations are begun and has to maintain that level throughout the project. No single criterion for acceptable agreement can be set because the rate of behavior and degree of change in the client can influence interpretation of assessment and the need for precise agreement. As a guideline, convention dictates that agreement be between 80% and 100%. An interobserver agreement lower than 80% suggests that a moderate amount of error occurs in recording. Obtaining low agreement before a program is begun is no reason to be discouraged. In many instances, low agreement signals that the response definition should be more carefully specified. It is desirable to find this out early, so that the response definition can be clarified for those who administer the program and observe behavior.

How the reliability checks are conducted may influence the level of interobserver agreement. Hence, in addition to specifying the level of agreement, it is important to ensure that this level is determined under carefully conducted conditions. A major factor that may influence interobserver agreement is whether observers know that their agreement is being checked. When observers know their observations are being checked, they may show higher agreement than when they believe their observations are not being checked (Foster et al., 1988). They may even record behaviors differently (e.g., less disruptive behavior) if they believe their observations are being checked by a supervisor. As a general rule, it is important to make the conditions of assessment similar on both assessed and nonassessed days. It may be useful to convey the impression that all observations are being checked so that the data obtained on checked days will not differ from the data obtained on unchecked days. Because observers tend to be more accurate when they believe that their agreement is being assessed, keeping them aware and informed of frequent reliability checks may be advantageous even on days on which no checks are made.

General guidelines for conducting reliability assessment are as follows:

- Ensure that observers work independently without access to one another's recording sheets.
- Supervise observers carefully during a reliability check.
- Avoid conveying expectations to observers about what the data ought to show and the extent to which incoming data are consistent with these expectations.
- Consider conducting periodic retraining sessions if there are multiple observers, if behavioral codes are complex, and if observations are to be in place for several weeks or months.
- Have people other than observers calculate reliability.

These practices are in response to studies occasionally showing biases introduced by not engaging in careful reliability procedures (Foster et al., 1988; Kazdin, 1977a). Perhaps even more important than the specific practices is conveying to observers that careful and accurate recording and overall integrity of the procedures are the highest priorities.

Estimating Agreement. Interobserver agreement provides an estimate of how consistently behavior is observed and scored. The procedures for estimating agreement differ somewhat depending on the assessment method used. The procedures that estimate agreement for frequency and interval methods are highlighted here because they can be adapted readily to the other assessment procedures.[4]

Agreement for frequency measures requires that two observers simultaneously, but independently, count the target response during the time set aside for observation. At the end of the observation period, the frequencies obtained by the observers are compared. The major interest is whether the observers record the target behavior with equal frequency. A percentage of agreement can be formed to measure the degree to which two observers agree in their final counts.

It is likely that no two observers will agree perfectly in their recorded frequencies. To determine the percentage of agreement, a fraction is formed from the frequency obtained by each observer. *Interobserver agreement is determined by dividing the smaller frequency by the larger frequency and multiplying by 100.* For example, in the home, parents may count the number of times that a child spills food on the floor during a meal. During a reliability check, both parents independently count food spills. By the end of the meal, one parent has counted 20 instances of spilling, whereas the other parent has counted 18 instances. To form a percentage of agreement, the smaller number (18) is divided by the larger number (20) and the quotient is multiplied by 100. Agreement for this observation period was 90% ([18/20] × 100).

Researchers interpret this percentage cautiously. The figure indicates that the observers agree on the total frequency of the behavior with a 10% (100 percent minus 90 percent) margin of error. This does not mean that the observers agree 90% of the time. Although one observer recorded 18 responses and the other recorded 20 responses, there is no way of knowing whether they recorded the *same* responses. In principle, there may have been 38 behaviors, and one parent caught 18 of them while the other parent caught 20 of them. In practice, this is usually not a concern. Reliability reflects agreement on the total number of responses, rather than agreement in any specific instance, and the total is usually of primary interest. At the same time, it is important to mention a potential disadvantage in using a frequency measure is that when the behavior is not carefully defined, a high percentage of agreement for frequency data may still conceal a substantial amount of disagreement.

Calculation of agreement is different when an interval method of assessment is used. Interobserver agreement is usually computed on the basis of the proportion of intervals in which two observers agree on the occurrence of a target response. An agreement is scored if both observers record the occurrence of behavior in the same interval. A disagreement is scored when one observer scores a behavior in an interval and the other does not. For example, in a reliability check made between two observers independently recording the aggressive behavior of a child in an elementary school classroom, both observers are required to observe the child at the same time. Each observer records behaviors for several intervals. During each interval that the child is observed, the observer marks the occurrence or nonoccurrence of aggressive behavior. When the observers finish recording, reliability can be calculated.

Interobserver agreement is determined by dividing the number of intervals in which both observers mark the behavior as occurring (agreements) by the number of agreements plus the number of intervals in which one observer scored the behavior and the other did not (disagreements) and multiplying by 100. For example, if two observers recorded behavior for 50 10-second intervals and both observers agreed on the occurrence of the behavior in 20 intervals and disagreed in 5 intervals, overall agreement would be 20/(20 + 5) × 100, or 80%.

Although the observers recorded behavior for 50 intervals, not all of the intervals are used to calculate reliability. An interval is counted only if at least one observer recorded the occurrence of the target behavior. Excluding intervals in which neither observer recorded the target behavior is based on the following reasoning. If these intervals were counted, they would be considered agreements because both observers agree that the response did not occur. Yet in observing behavior, many intervals may be marked without the occurrence of the target behavior. If these were included as agreements, the reliability estimate would be inflated beyond the level obtained when occurrences alone are counted as agreements. To avoid this increase, most investigators restrict agreements to response occurrence intervals.

The previously noted formula for estimating agreement for interval assessment is very commonly used. Yet many investigators have questioned its adequacy. The main concern is whether agreement should be restricted to intervals for which both observers record an occurrence of the behavior or should also include intervals for which both observers record a nonoccurrence. In one sense, both of these situations indicate that the observers were in agreement for a particular interval. The issue is important because the estimate of reliability depends on the frequency of the client's behavior and on whether occurrence and/or nonoccurrence agreements are included in the formula. If the client performs the target behavior relatively frequently or infrequently, observers are likely to have a high proportion of agreements on occurrences or nonoccurrences, respectively. Hence, the estimate of reliability may differ greatly depending on what is counted as an agreement between observers. Several investigators have discussed the problem of deciding what should be counted as an agreement and have suggested additional formulas for possible ways of using both occurrence and nonoccurrence intervals (see Kazdin, 1982a).

SUMMARY AND CONCLUSIONS

Identifying the goals of a behavior modification program and translating these into concrete, operational terms are critical steps preceding intervention. Most often, goals are designed to improve adaptive functioning at home, school, or work, or in the community, and to reduce risk of injury, maladjustment, or problems experienced in relation to themselves or to others. Once the goal is identified, the constituent behaviors need to be specified in concrete terms. Often the behavior may be defined simply and constitutes a single behavior with a circumscribed set of instances (e.g., noncompliance at home). The behaviors may include multiple acts or a sequence of actions. Specification of such behaviors is often facilitated by task analysis. This procedure identifies specific behaviors that are required and the sequence in which these component behaviors are performed. Whether a single behavior or several different behaviors are identified as the target(s) of the intervention, the definition has to be concrete. The definition should ensure that few inferences need to be made by observers who assess behavior and others who ultimately will be responsible for providing consequences to alter behavior.

Assessment of target behaviors and other events in the situation can be completed in many different ways. Commonly used methods include frequency measures, discrete categorization, and interval recording, but other measures, including amount of time of the response (duration) or between some cue and initiating the behavior (latency), intensity or strength of the behavior, or the number of individuals who perform the response are also used. Selection may be based on goals of the program (e.g., changing one individual or performance of behavior in a large group), characteristics of the responses, or convenience.

Once the assessment strategy is selected, it is important to evaluate the extent to which observers agree when scoring the response. Interobserver agreement or reliability of assessment is evaluated, as observers independently record the response. The exact formula in which reliability is estimated varies depending on the assessment method. Periodic retraining and constant reliability assessment help ensure consistency in observing behavior among observers. In general, assessment plays a central role in behavioral research. Delineation of the target behavior and the conditions with which it is associated provide an important basis from which to launch treatment.

Assessment of the target behavior is rudimentary and a precondition for effective intervention and evaluation of the behavior-change program. However, assessment entails more than evaluation of the target behavior. Assessment extends to antecedents and consequences and how these are related to behavior. The next chapter discusses functional analysis, an assessment approach that examines antecedents, behaviors, and consequences. Functional analysis reflects a progression from measuring behavior, understanding the factors that control behavior, and using this information to alter behavior.

KEY TERMS

Baseline rate

Discrete categorization

Duration

Frequency measure

Interval recording

Latency

Objectivity, clarity, and completeness of observations

Obtrusive assessment

Operational definition

Positive opposites

Rate of response

Reactive assessment

Reliability

Time sampling

APPLYING PRINCIPLES AND TECHNIQUES
TO EVERYDAY LIFE

1. Movement from concepts to operations (measures, definitions) is central to behavior modification and science in general. Develop an operational definition of two concepts: romantic love and aggression. Consider this as a guide. What behaviors or signs would be reasonable instances or examples to define or elaborate these constructs? Stated another way, if one wanted to observe these, what might be included in the behavioral code?

2. It is useful to recast people's thinking in devising behavior modification when the primary goal initially seems to be reduction or elimination of behavior. Specifically, one tries to refocus on positive opposites. What are positive opposites? Give one or more positive opposites to these presenting complaints of people who come to you consultation. The two clients who come to you say:

   A. "My spouse always complains throughout dinner. I want to get rid of the constant complaining."

   B. "My roommate is messy, and by messy, I mean—like, you cannot even see the color of the carpet in the room because so much is on the floor. Actually, I'm not sure there is a carpet, but I am sure that I want to get rid of the messiness."

3. Defining behavior so that it meets the criteria of objectivity, clarity, and completeness is not easy. It is very important to clarify the definition in this way to ensure the desired behavior is developed and observed. Give a definition of smiling. Write out the definition to show how it would meet the three criteria.

4. You want to start taking better care of yourself and to engage in more healthful behaviors. This is too global and covers virtually all aspects of life. Consequently, do a task analysis of one aspect of your life (e.g., eating, exercise) and write out the behaviors and steps that would help define this goal. (If you are already a paragon of health and have your own aerobics TV show, use a friend for the example.)

5. Identify a behavior to be changed and describe how that behavior might be assessed by a frequency measure and discrete categorization.

FOR FURTHER READING

Bellack, A. S., & Hersen, M. (Eds.) (1998) *Behavioral assessment: A practical handbook* (4th ed.). Needham Heights, MA: Allyn & Bacon.

Carr, J. E., Taylor, S. L., & Austin, J. (1995). A classroom demonstration of self-monitoring, reactivity, and interobserver agreement. *Behavior Analyst, 18,* 141–146.

Hartmann, D. P. (Ed.). (1985). Mini-series: Target behavior selection. *Behavioral Assessment, 7,* 1–78.

Mash, E. J., & Terdal, L. G. (Eds.) (1997). *Assessment of childhood disorders* (3rd ed.). New York: Guilford

Weist, M. D., Ollendick, T. H., & Finney, J. W. (1991). Toward the empirical validation of treatment targets in children. *Clinical Psychology Review, 11,* 515–538.

NOTES

1. Occasionally, I shall make reference to a clinic in which I work. This is the Yale Child Conduct Clinic, an outpatient treatment service for children and families. Children seen at the clinic are between the ages 2 and 13 and are referred for oppositional, aggressive, and antisocial behavior. Treatments provided at the clinic include variations of cognitive problem-solving skills training and parent management training (Kazdin, 1996c and http://pantheon.yale.edu/~kazdin/conductclinic.htm).

2. The fact that different measures of the same concept can vary in the conclusions that are reached is not unique to social and behavioral sciences. Consider the concept of safety (accidents, fatality). Airlines operationally define (i.e., select as a measure and definition) safety as the number of accidents that occur divided by number of passenger miles (e.g., number of passengers times miles flown). Using this measure all by itself conveys that flying is the safest way to travel. That is, if one multiplies miles covered times number of passengers, trains, cars, bikes, rickshaws, and perhaps other means of transportation are not as safe as airplanes. However, the measure is a bit arbitrary or at least incomplete. Air accidents have little to do with distance traveled, and the risk of accident is usually associated with take-off and landing, independently of distance. Also, the risk of fatal injury is greater in planes than other means of travel, that is, given an accident, what is the likelihood of a fatal injury? Finally, for distances under about 500 miles, other means of travel (e.g., trains) are safer (see Barnett, 1998). In short, the conclusion that flying is the safest way to travel depends a bit on the operational definition (measure). Other measures or even the same measure at some travel distances yield different conclusions. The point here is that conclusions reached may depend on the specific operational definition that is used.

3. Among terms, *interobserver agreement* more accurately reflects the issue of interest in applied behavior analysis. *Reliability* is a much broader term in psychological assessment and reflects a number of different characteristics of measurement, most of which have been used in the context of developing and evaluating questionnaires and various inventories. However, the term *reliability* continues to be used as interchangeable with the term *interobserver agreement* in published studies of behavioral programs. Hence, the convention is continued here.

4. The methods of estimating agreement between and among observers extend beyond the material provided here. For a more technical discussion of these methods and how they are used, other sources should be consulted (Iwata et al., 1989: Kazdin, 1982b).

CHAPTER 4

Functional Analysis: From Assessment to Intervention

For purposes of presentation, it is very useful to separate the discussion of assessment from that of intervention. In fact, assessment and intervention are obviously different in an important way—assessment focuses on what to measure, and intervention focuses on what to do to change behavior. Yet assessment and intervention are interrelated in two ways. First, the data obtained from assessment provide feedback to convey whether the intervention is working, whether the change is sufficient, and whether another intervention is needed. In this sense, assessment is fundamental to any intervention (e.g., medical or psychological treatment). Once careful assessment is in place, different interventions can be employed to see if they have impact. (Unfortunately, in most forms of psychological treatment no systematic assessment is provided to determine if treatment is actually helping the individual or achieving its goals.) Second, assessment can be used in ways to identify why the problem is occurring and hence what the focus of treatment ought to be. This latter use is the emphasis of this chapter.

Assessment has multiple roles in behavior modification. The initial role is to identify the extent of the problem and whether change is made over the course of treatment. Another role of assessment is to identify factors in the environment that might be controlling behavior. If these factors can be identified and assessed, perhaps they can be altered to change behavior. This chapter focuses on *functional analysis,* which is a way to identify effective interventions. This consists of a methodology of identifying the relation of behavior to antecedents and consequences and using this information to select the intervention. In functional analysis, the overriding question is, "What factors are contributing to or responsible for the target behavior?" Functional analysis is critical in conveying how assessment and intervention are closely related.

CHARACTERISTICS AND ELEMENTS OF FUNCTIONAL ANALYSIS

Overview

It is useful to consider the term for a moment. "Functional" emphasizes identifying the functions of the behavior, that is, the purposes the behavior may serve in the environment. The behaviors may serve to achieve particular outcomes. A colloquial illustration of this, although loose, is that the "child is just doing this for attention." Such a statement suggests a particular behavior of the child is a function of or performed for attention. (This is a very loose illustration to convey the point; functional analysis does not make vacuous claims without support and rarely is the above statement ever shown to have support.) The "analysis" part of functional analysis emphasizes the careful assessment and systematic evaluation to isolate precisely the factors that control behavior. The analysis consists of obtaining data about the supposed purposes and testing whether the hypothesized purposes actually control or influence behavior.

Functional analysis identifies the current causes of behavior or the reasons that the behavior is performed (Iwata et al., 1994). *Cause* in this context refers to iden-

Table 4-1   Hypothetical Examples of the Consequences or Purposes of Behaviors

Behavior	Outcomes that May Maintain that Behavior
Tantrum of a child before going to bed	Attention from a parent, extra time with the parents, reduction of parent's arguing with each other
Arguing or fighting with a spouse/partner	Affection and promises of life-long commitment that result from making up after the fight, time away from the spouse as he or she walks out for a few days
Complaining	Attention and sympathy from others, not hearing the complaints of others, personal relief or stress reduction as a function of expressing unfortunate conditions
Attaining good grades in school	Praise from others, success, reduction in anxiety about failing

NOTE: The functions of a behavior are usually determined on an individual basis, so there is no single function that a particular behavior invariably serves for all or even most individuals. Indeed, different behaviors can serve the same function for two individuals and the same behavior may serve different functions for two individuals.

tifying the current antecedents and consequences that maintain behavior.[1] Understanding the causes can greatly help to develop effective interventions. Of course, change can be achieved without knowing precisely why the problem has come about. For example, many familiar medical treatments (e.g., aspirin, chemotherapy, surgery, and organ transplant) are effective for headache, many cancers, kidney stones, and liver failure, respectively, even though the causes of the disorders are unknown. Similarly, there are now a number of effective behavior therapy techniques for the treatment of various anxiety disorders (fears, phobias, obsessive compulsive disorder, panic attacks), although the causes of these disorders are not known or understood. Although effective treatment can be identified and developed without knowledge of the causes, we are also very familiar with the fact that when the causes are known (e.g., bacterial infections such as pneumonia, syphilis, or rabies), interventions (treatment and prevention) are likely to be much more effective.

In applied behavior analysis, functional analysis reflects a way of understanding behavior and using causal information to identify effective interventions. The goal of functional analysis is to identify the conditions that control the occurrence and maintenance of behavior. Stated another way, what functions or purposes does the behavior serve? In some way, this question is not new at all. Most approaches toward treatment (e.g., psychoanalysis, family therapy) suggest that a given behavior (e.g., child deviance in the home, spousal abuse, insomnia) serves some purpose. What is novel about behavior analysis is a methodology to identify the functions or purposes served by the behavior and translating the information into effective treatment.

To note that functional analysis is concerned with the purposes of behavior is a little ambiguous. Purposes reflect what is achieved or accomplished by the behavior, that is, the consequences. However, the consequences may not be merely the discrete and concrete ones that follow at the moment (e.g., praise or attention by a parent) but, in addition, how the behavior may influence the environment more generally. Table 4-1 provides some examples of behaviors and some of the functions the behaviors may serve. Consider an example in more detail.

A well-established finding is that in adolescence, a number of risky and problem behaviors often emerge or increase in frequency (Ketterlinus & Lamb, 1994). These include use of illicit substances (alcohol, drug, and cigarettes), unprotected sex, delinquent acts (e.g., vandalism), and other risk-taking behaviors. These behaviors tend to go together as a package even though the specific acts themselves obviously bear no clear resemblance to each other. To say that they go together means that the presence of one is usually associated with the others, although this does not mean that if a person engages in one of these, he or she inevitably engages in all of the others. A leading interpretation to explain the emergence and combination of these behaviors pertains to the functions they serve. Specifically, the behaviors serve to achieve independence and autonomy from parents and cohesion with one's peers. In relation to the current discussion, we would say that the behaviors are likely to be maintained and influenced by these larger functions. The individual actions (e.g., substance use, unprotected sex) have other reinforcers that are more concrete and that immediately stem from the behaviors themselves. However, beyond these, broader functions can be identified that may reflect consistent patterns of consequences associated with the behaviors and the contexts or conditions in which they are embedded. Functional analysis focuses on consequences that may be maintaining behavior, including the specific reinforcers that may be operative and the broader purposes that may result from the behavior.

Key Elements

The key elements of functional analyses are assessment, development and evaluation of hypotheses about factors that control behavior, and intervention. It is useful not only to distinguish these for purposes of presentation, but also to note that there is a flow and movement from one to the other in ways that make them continuous rather than discrete steps. Initially, assessment is designed to identify the relations of antecedents and consequences to the behavior of interest and hence the purposes or functions of the behavior. This assessment is likely to suggest patterns of when the target behavior is performed. For example, the behavior may appear to be more frequent at some times of the day rather than others, when some persons are present rather than others, and when certain effects or consequences occur.

The patterns raise hypotheses about what may be maintaining or controlling behavior. If at all possible, the hypotheses are tested directly by assessing the target behavior as various conditions are changed. That is, if one or two conditions are considered to control behavior, the situation is manipulated to see if changing the conditions actually alters the behavior. The conditions in which the hypotheses are tested may be brief and transient merely to see if different conditions systematically influence behavior. This is an experimental phase designed to evaluate if the controlling conditions can be identified. Ideally, assessment will provide evidence that the behavior is in fact influenced (e.g., increased) only when certain conditions are in place. That is, some of the hypotheses of the controlling conditions will have been supported and others will not.

The information gained from manipulating conditions and from assessment under different conditions is used to help the client directly. Specifically, the conditions shown to influence behavior are altered to decrease inappropriate or deviant behavior and to foster appropriate, prosocial behavior. This is the intervention phase of functional analysis. The purpose of this phase is to put into place the condition that controls behavior to achieve a significant therapeutic change. Several examples will illustrate this sequence but first it is important to convey how the critical information for a functional analysis is obtained.

METHODS OF ASSESSMENT

As mentioned earlier, the goal of functional assessment is to identify the relations among antecedents, behaviors, and consequences. There are many different strategies for obtaining the information and identifying the functions that the behavior serves (O'Neill, Horner, Albin, Storey, & Sprague, 1990; Sturmey, 1996). The methods vary in the degree to which they systematically examine functional relations and their ease of use. Two main strategies are highlighted here.

Interviews

One way to conduct a functional analysis is to interview individuals in contact with the client (e.g., parents, teachers, peers, spouses) or the clients themselves. The interview is designed to describe behavior, setting events in which the behavior occurs, and possible functions the behavior may serve. The interview focuses on the context in which the behavior appears and looks for any systematic facets of the context with which the behavior might be associated.

The person who is interviewed is asked about antecedent events that might include the routine of the individual, activities leading up to and immediately before the behavior, who is present in the situation, and any other events. The interview also focuses on the consequences or results that occur when the behavior is performed. Perhaps reinforcers (attention from others) or opportunities for escape (e.g., the person is allowed to leave the situation or escape from some demand) are some of the consequences that follow the behavior. The point here is to seek information about the functions that the behavior might serve.

The interview is useful insofar as it seeks information about the behavior, stimulus events, and consequences. Developing a behavior-change program at the very least begins with this information obtained from the reports of the clients or those with whom the clients interact. The interview is likely to be very helpful in identifying what ought to be assessed. The information, whether obtained from clients, persons in the clients' everyday lives, or professionals is also limited. It is not so much that the client or those who know the client are likely to lie or to withhold information. Rather, a number of "normal" biases of human judgment affect one's ability to describe details accurately and identify relations between events.[2] For example, behaviors that occur infrequently but are dramatic (e.g., outbursts) are often perceived and recalled as being frequent when individuals are interviewed about another person's behavior. Direct observation may reveal that the behavior actually occurs rather infrequently or not at the magnitude or intensity that the interview suggested. Even so, the interview is worthwhile as a basis for identifying leads for treatment.

In relation to functional analysis, the interview generates hypotheses about what might be controlling behavior, and the comments of those exposed to the behavior is a very reasonable basis for developing these hypotheses. Not related to functional analysis but quite important nevertheless is the information yielded from the interview. The interview often conveys the concerns of persons who interact closely with the client, and these concerns are often important in their own right. They reflect the impact that the client may have on the behavior and impressions of others and this is not trivial.

In the vast majority of behavioral research, direct observation, rather than interviews, is used as the basis for assessing functional relations. Direct assessment may not be feasible for many of the settings in which behavioral programs are implemented because of practical constraints. Consequently, interviews may be the only alternative because observers are not readily available and those in the setting (parents, teachers) may not be able to do both behavior-change techniques and observations.

Direct Observation

Direct observation of the target behavior in the situation along with the antecedents and consequences associated with it is another way to obtain the information required for a functional analysis. Many different observational systems have been used and these vary considerably in their structure and how systematically the information is collected (Sturmey, 1996). Two methods of direct observation are highlighted here.

One method is to chart antecedents, behaviors, and consequences in a narrative fashion, that is, by merely noting what has happened, as illustrated in Table 4-2. Consider as an example, a child (Kathy, age 8) who frequently fought (physically) with her younger sister (Mary, age 4). Both children were in the home from late afternoon (after school and day care) and were observed by the mother for several days from the afternoon until the children's bedtime. We asked the mother to chart two related behaviors when the children were together (in the same room). The first was fighting, which included arguing, shouting, and hitting. The second included playing cooperatively or being together in an activity without the above behaviors. These latter behaviors were recorded because developing positive opposite behaviors typically serves as the focus of interventions that are stimulated by interests in decreasing deviant behavior, a theme that will be revisited throughout subsequent chapters. The behaviors were observed using a frequency count as described in the previous chapter. This was a preferred format for the mother. One minute of either behavior was scored as an instance of that behavior.

Table 4-2 Charts to Record Fighting (Chart A) and Playing Cooperatively (Chart B)—Sample entries from the charts

CHART A (EPISODES OF FIGHTING)

Day/Time	Antecedents: Situation/Setting Conditions/Others Present	Consequences
Monday, 3:45 PM	Watching TV, no one else home	Separated children, sent Kathy to her room, read to her for 15 min
Tuesday, 5:00 PM	Playing on the computer	Took Kathy to her room and talked with her about playing better with her sister, talked about what happened at school
Wednesday, 4:10 PM	Playing on the computer	Sent Kathy to her room and she showed me drawings and a poem she made at school.

Note the behavior observed is the fighting of Kathy with her younger sister. Each entry (row) on the chart refers to an interval of time in which an episode of fighting with her younger sister occurred.

CHART B (EPISODES OF PLAYING COOPERATIVELY)

Day/Time	Antecedents: Situation/Setting Conditions/Others Present	Consequences
Monday, 7:00 PM	Watching TV Bill (husband) and I watching with them	None
Tuesday, 4:00 PM	Watching TV Marge (neighbor) in the kitchen with me	None
Thursday, 7:30 PM	Watching TV; no one else present	Watched until bath time and then went to bed

Note the behavior observed was playing cooperatively, i.e., together in the same room and without fighting. Each entry (row) on the chart refers to an interval of time (5 minutes or more) in which the sisters played cooperatively.

Table 4-2 includes two charts the mother was asked to use to track fighting (chart A) and playing cooperatively (chart B). The purpose of using a chart was to identify whether any patterns emerge and suggest the conditions that may contribute to the behavior. The entries in the chart are samples and reflect some of the information collected from the mother. After several days, it appeared (from chart A) that Kathy's fighting with her sister occurred mostly during the following antecedent conditions: after school but before dinner, in the presence of the mother when she was by herself, and when the girls were playing a game or watching television together. The consequences usually consisted of the mother intervening to stop the fight, sending Kathy to her room, and remaining in the room with Kathy until she calmed down. Chart B was also interesting. Playing cooperatively was associated with the following antecedent conditions: the presence of another adult in the home (the father or a neighbor visiting the mother) and time in which one or both parents were also in the room. No consequences systematically followed playing cooperatively. The parents felt that they ought to leave well enough alone—a strategy that is not helpful when one wants to develop specific behaviors. Here the undesired behavior was positively reinforced (with attention, time with mom) and the desired behavior was not.

Using information from the charts, we hypothesized that Kathy's fighting served as an occasion to have private time with the mother. Presumably, time with the mother was possibly a positive reinforcer that inadvertently contributed to or maintained fighting. Kathy's interest in attention from the mother, obviously normal for any child, was heightened according to the mother, because of the strong sibling rivalry she had felt since her younger sister was born. (Older and first-born children commonly experience greater sibling rivalry than their younger siblings. If you [the reader] are the oldest child or first born, you may be able to identify some seeming injustice where your younger sibling was treated better than you. If you are the younger sibling, none of this is likely to have much import to you or you may be aware of speeches from your older sibling about such injustices.) Also of interest were the observations (chart B) that playing cooperatively among the two children was not systematically associated with positive consequences. We shall suspend this example for a few moments to help keep distinct the method of assessment, the current topic, from actually intervening to produce change.

The observation method described in this example was very helpful but also somewhat informal. The method did not provide a precise assessment of ongoing behavior and the specific events with which they are associated. A more demanding, but often more informative, method of direct observation is to have observers monitor ongoing behavior and record multiple events when the behavior occurs. The chart in Figure 4-1 demonstrates this method of observation (O'Neill et al., 1990). The form allows one to enter the behavior(s) of interest, as well as any special setting events, functions, and consequences that might be relevant. Several possible setting events and functions are listed already. The client is observed during various periods (to be written in), and then whatever happens in a given interval is checked off on the form. For example, if the client teased another child in the classroom during transition periods (after a lesson but immediately before recess) and received attention from the teacher, this pattern might emerge over several time periods of observation.

There are other ways of conducting direct observations and some of these are intricate and require multiple observers to record behavior. A few of these will be illustrated as further examples are provided. The key point to note here however is that direct assessment of ongoing behavior in a situation is clearly the preferred method of functional analysis because it provides more precise information about the behavior, setting, and functions. The relations identified by direct observation can lead to data-based hypotheses about what may be maintaining the behavior. Of course, there might be several hypotheses, and any one or none of them might be correct.

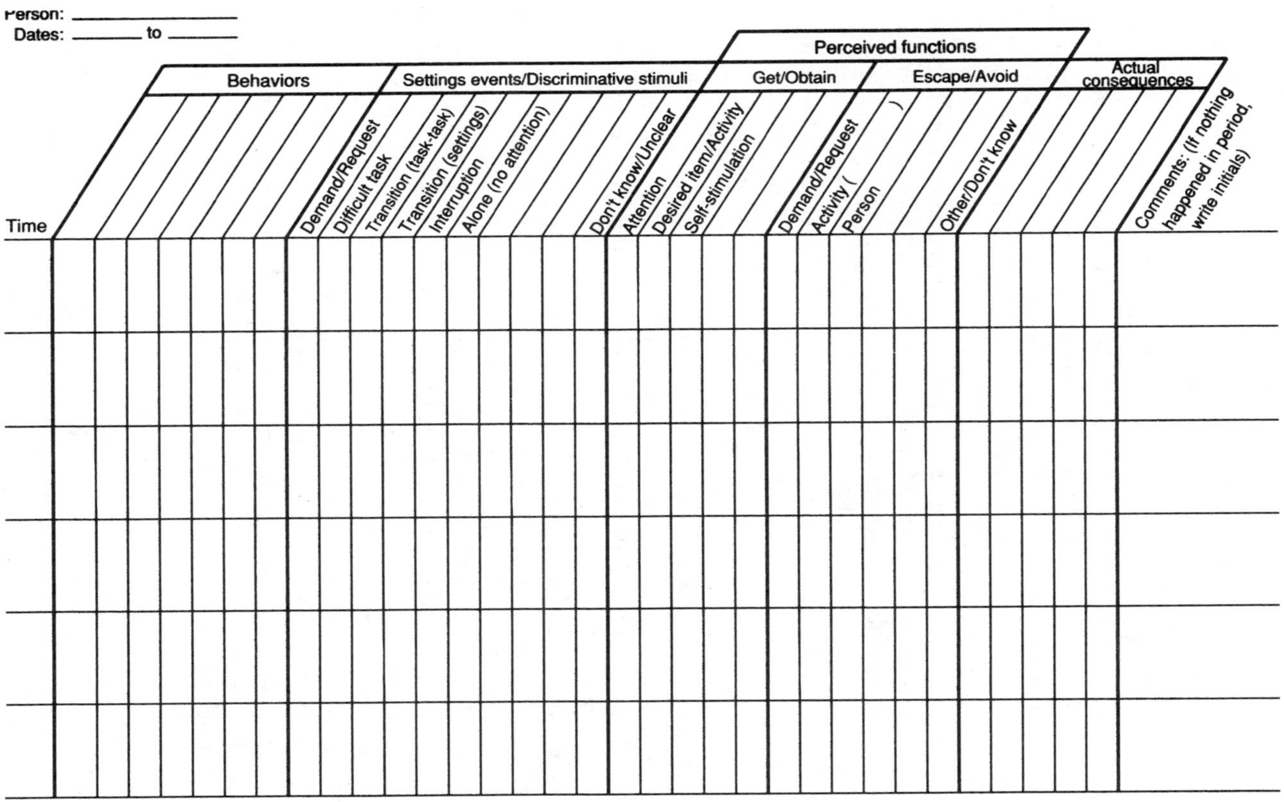

FIGURE 4-1 Functional Analysis Observation Form

(Source: O'Neill, Horner, Albin, Storey, & Sprague, 1990)

HYPOTHESIS TESTING
AND INTERVENTION

The initial assessment suggests patterns between the behavior and other events in the setting. These patterns generate hypotheses about what might be controlling behavior as indicated in the case of Kathy and her sister. Functional analysis includes testing of hypotheses, which consists of experimentally evaluating precisely whether the antecedents and consequences that may control behavior actually do (Iwata et al., 1994). The tests of the hypotheses are important because the naturalistic observations of sequences of antecedents, behaviors, and consequences may have missed critical variables that exert control or are related to other variables that simply were not identified.

Investigators often conduct rather precise experimental tests of the hypotheses by seeing how behavior responds under changing conditions. Each condition reflects a hypothesis about what may be maintaining behavior. The changing conditions are presented to the client in such a way as to demonstrate unequivocally whether the hypothesized influence really controls or maintains behavior. These tests of the hypotheses are intended to identify what is likely to be an effective intervention before actually moving to the intervention phase. In a sense, tests of hypotheses are experiments with miniature doses of an intervention because they can show control over the behavior. Indeed, in some cases, investigators use the initial assessment to generate hypotheses and then move directly to treatment. If the treatment begins to show a strong effect, this provides some support for the hypothesis.

Let us resume the example begun in the previous section in which Kathy was fighting with her younger sister. As mentioned already, after baseline observations of the target behaviors (fighting, playing cooperatively) and the use of the charts, we generated the following simple hypothesis. Kathy's fighting served to provide time alone with her mother. The fighting only occurred when the mother was home without another adult because only on these occasions was the mother likely to provide the private and alone time with Kathy. That is, the mother probably was less likely to leave conversations with the husband or a visiting friend even when Kathy was fighting. We decided to begin directly with a simple intervention, that is, in this example, we moved from assessment to intervention. The intervention tested the hypothesis but as we shall see in another example, hypothesis testing is sometimes a discrete step conducted before actually intervening to change behavior.

The intervention consisted of providing positive reinforcement (time with the mother) for cooperative play and time out from reinforcement (a period when opportunities for reinforcement were removed) for Kathy for fighting. When the girls came home from school or day care, Kathy was told she and the mother could have some play time together if she and her sister played cooperatively for 30 minutes. (Time alone also was provided afterward with the sister.) Briefly, after the time elapsed without fighting, the mother effusively praised the girls and then played with Kathy in her room. If Kathy had a tantrum, she was sent to her room for 10 minutes, and the mother did not remain in the room with her. Requiring longer periods of cooperative play to earn time with the mother and adding father and mother praise for cooperative play essentially eliminated all fighting within the first 5 days of the program. The functional analysis was helpful in conveying the many factors surrounding fighting and suggesting what might be used to increase cooperative play.

In this example, the initial assessment suggested a pattern of factors related to the behavior. The pattern suggested a hypothesis, but this led directly to an intervention. In research, there is a separate step of testing the hypotheses experimentally before moving into the intervention. Usually the tests are conducted in controlled laboratory conditions. The conditions are sometimes referred to as *analogue testing* because a contrived situation is constructed to permit careful control over the conditions presented to the client (Iwata et al., 1994). The conditions only resemble (are roughly analogous to) the interactions or conditions evident in everyday life. Yet, if the laboratory conditions can identify and isolate possible influences (antecedents and consequences), these conditions are likely to exert similar effects in everyday life.

In analogue testing, the client's behavior is likely to be observed in a room with the client and an investigator while various conditions (antecedents and/or consequences) are altered. These conditions reflect the specific hypotheses or possible factors that might be controlling behavior. For example, in one demonstration, self-injurious behavior was evaluated among children and adults diagnosed with autistic disorder (Wacker et al., 1990). This is a psychiatric disorder that emerges in early childhood (before age 3) and consists of impairment and delays in development in several areas of functioning including language, communication, social interaction, and play. The disorder also is associated with repetitive and stereotyped patterns of behavior (e.g., rituals, repeated play with objects), mental retardation (for approximately 75% of the children), and many other symptoms of dysfunction (e.g., hyperactivity, aggressiveness, and self-injury). In this study, assessment was conducted at an outpatient clinic under controlled laboratory conditions. The purpose was to identify factors that might maintain self-injurious behavior.

Consider in detail the case of a 20-year old man named Roy who had a lengthy history of self-injurious behavior (headbanging, arm and hand biting). Self-injurious behavior has been well studied via functional analyses and hence considerable research has identified the likely factors that may be controlling the behavior (Pelios, Morren, Tesch, & Axelrod, 1999). In the case of Roy, the investigators began with three hypotheses about controlling factors. These hypotheses were that the behavior was maintained because of (1) social attention that was provided for self-injurious behavior (i.e., maintained by positive reinforcement); (2) self-injury allowed Roy to escape from the situation to avoid demands that were made of him to perform some task (i.e., maintained by negative reinforcement); or (3) by merely the stimulation resulting from the behavior when he was alone. The stimulation or sensory effects of a behavior warrants comment. In many instances, self-injury (e.g., hitting one's head repeatedly) seems to be reinforced directly by the tactile and sensory effects of the behavior itself. This is sometimes referred to as *automatic reinforcement,* to denote that the behavior appears to have its own reinforcing value without external consequences. The study used this as one hypothesis to explain what might be maintaining behavior.

Assessment of self-injury was conducted while the three conditions were briefly presented (5 to 10 minutes each). Each condition was presented on multiple occasions, in a rotating fashion. This is called an analogue situation because contingencies in everyday interaction are not in a special room, alternated from one condition to the next in brief periods, or in the context of tasks that are devised for purposes of assessment in a laboratory. In any case, the three conditions were presented to simulate the contingencies that might be controlling behavior beyond the analogue situations.

In the *social attention condition,* no tasks or activities were presented. The therapist sat near Roy. When there was self-injury, the therapist provided attention (mild reprimands such as, "Please do not do that.") and a light touch on the shoulder. This condition was designed to simulate situations in which caregivers attend to self-injury and give little or no attention for appropriate (noninjurious) behavior. Perhaps, Roy's self-injurious behavior was maintained by the positive reinforcement unwittingly provided by others. If social attention were maintaining behavior, more frequent self-injury probably would be evident.

In the *escape condition,* Roy was given a task to perform (folding and sorting towels) in the presence of a therapist who provided guidance and assistance. If any self-injury occurred, the behavior was ignored, but the task was removed (terminated). This condition was designed to simulate circumstances in which tasks or activities are terminated when the individual engages in self-injury. Perhaps Roy's behavior was maintained in everyday life by negative reinforcement, that is, escape from unpleasant tasks or activities.

In the *alone condition,* Roy was led to a room and left alone with no tasks or intervention. This condition was designed to simulate everyday life in which he might be left alone. An alone condition is important because self-injurious behavior is sometimes maintained by the stimulation (sensory stimulation) it produces.

Assessment under the varied conditions revealed that Roy's self-injury was much higher (35% of the intervals) in the escape condition than in the alone and social attention conditions (less than 10% of the intervals). In other words, self-injury served the function of allowing Roy to escape from activities. The investigators altered the contingency so that escape followed *appropriate* behavior (non-self-injury). This led to a reduction of self-injurious behavior.

Testing and evaluating hypotheses under analogue conditions in special sessions has been very helpful. Yet, testing hypotheses can be accomplished in everyday settings without all of the opportunities for the meticulous control conditions of the laboratory. As an illustration, consider an example that also focused on self-injurious behavior but this time took place among mentally retarded children in special education classrooms (Repp, Felce, & Barton, 1988). For one of the children, the investigators tested two hypotheses, namely, that the behavior was maintained by positive reinforcement (consequences following the behavior, such as staff approach, eye contact, verbalizations, and touching) or by negative reinforcement (e.g., demands placed on the child that led to the child's deviant behavior, which in turn stopped the demand, or removed the aversive consequence).

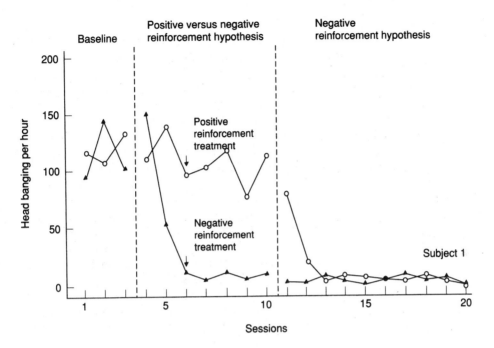

FIGURE 4-2 The number of head-banging responses per hour in two classrooms. After baseline, the negative reinforcement hypothesis was tested in one classroom, and the positive reinforcement hypothesis was tested in the other. In the third phase, the negative reinforcement hypothesis was put into effect in both classrooms.

(Source: Repp, Felce, & Barton, 1988).

During baseline, self-injury and the environmental events associated with the behavior were measured. Baseline observations suggested that negative reinforcement was the critical contingency maintaining behavior. The investigators, however, tested both hypotheses. In one classroom during the day, the negative reinforcement hypothesis was tested by extinction, making sure the behavior no longer resulted in reinforcement. Task demands (responding to simple commands) were made of the child and were not terminated when the child engaged in the undesirable response. If the child responded, positive reinforcers were provided. In short, extinction (no longer terminating commands when the child engaged in self-stimulation) and positive reinforcement for complying with the task were provided. In a second classroom, the positive reinforcement hypothesis was tested. Extinction was used by ensuring that all self-stimulation did not receive staff attention.

Figure 4-2 shows the results of the different treatments implemented in different classes each day. In the second phase, the negative reinforcement hypothesis was tested during one class period; the positive reinforcement hypothesis was implemented in the other class period. The results strongly supported the hypothesis that negative reinforcement was maintaining behavior. Consequently, in the third and final phase, the intervention, based on the negative reinforcement hypothesis, was implemented in both classroom periods. Clearly, this had a strong effect on self-injurious behavior.

Another example shows the use of functional analyses and the movement from hypothesis testing to intervention in an everyday situation. This example included a 4-year old girl, named Vivian, who had a four-month history of repeated coughing (Watson & Sterling, 1998). The coughing began after a respiratory infection but the infection had ended and her pediatrician could not identify any basis for the cough (e.g., no allergies, sinusitis, and other bases). An interview with the parents suggested that coughing was evident primarily during meals. The parents observed and counted coughing under different meal times (breakfast, snack, lunch, and dinner) but also nonmeal times (watching TV, lying in bed, and drawing at a table). As shown in the top portion of Figure 4-3, the behavior clearly was much more frequent during meal times. Thus the setting conditions seem to be identified.

A critical question is whether consequences for coughing might be maintaining the behavior. The parents had suggested in the interview that after coughing at meals Vivian either ate some food or received attention (a comment) from them. To test whether these exerted different effects on behavior, the parents were instructed to administer one of two consequences. The first was to give her a small candy after a cough during a meal (to test the effects of a tangible reinforcer) but not to make a comment or to make a brief comment. The tangible reinforcer tested whether direct reinforcement (food after a cough) maintained behavior. By having the parents control delivery, one could be assured that the behavior was reinforced. (If one depended on Vivian's eating, the reinforcement might be irregular.) The second consequence was to provide social attention (a comment within a few seconds) after the cough occurred. If social attention maintained behavior, one would expect coughing to increase under the social attention condition. Thus two conditions were varied across the different meals. In the bottom portion of Figure 4-3, attention was associated with a much higher rate of coughing than was tangible reinforcement (providing a candy). Attention was designated as the condition that may be maintaining coughing, and the intervention was based on this hypothesis.

During the intervention, attention was withheld when Vivian coughed (extinction) and periods of not coughing were given attention (reinforcement for not engaging in the behavior). Attention was provided first for short periods of not coughing (just a few seconds) and then for longer periods (5 minutes). During the intervention phase (bottom panel of Figure 4-3), coughing decreased to zero. This was checked during mealtime months later after the program had ended, and, as shown in the figure, coughing had been eliminated.

This example shows a relatively straightforward use of functional analyses. Parent interviews about possible controlling factors were followed up with direct observations that the parents conducted. The pattern of situation (mealtime) and consequences (attention) was established and once the controlling feature was identified (attention), this was used to promote the desired behavior (noncoughing). Not all behaviors are likely to be so readily controlled or influenced by a single factor in this way. However, functional analysis conveys that one ought to test controlling influences directly. When controlling influences *can* be identified, this is extremely useful.

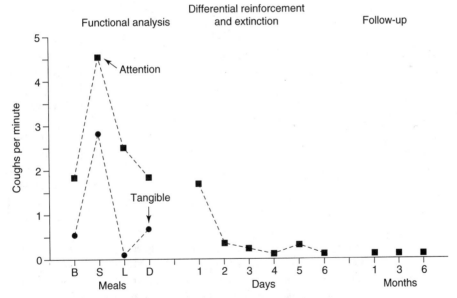

FIGURE 4-3 Data from the descriptive assessment are depicted in the top panel. Data from the functional analysis (lower panel) represent the rate of coughing at breakfast, snack, lunch, and dinner during tangible and social attention conditions. Rate of coughing during treatment is an average across four meals each day. Follow-up observations occurred at 1, 3, and 6 months posttreatment.

(Source: Watson & Sterling, 1998)

The examples illustrate key steps in functional analyses. Self-injurious behaviors were included in more than one example, in part because of the extensive attention that these behaviors have received. Before the development and extensive use of functional analysis, many interventions to eliminate self-injury were based on punishment. Although these often were effective, punishment raises a host of issues (as is later discussed) and is not advisable as a basis of intervention if other options can be identified. Moreover, ethical and legal issues are invariably raised when aversive treatments are used. This is exacerbated when individuals cannot consent on their own behalf (e.g., children, those with serious impairment). Functional analyses provided a methodology to identify factors that control behavior and led to treatments that did not require punishment. This led to extensive research on functional analysis, as well as self-injurious and otherwise dangerous behavior (Pelios et al., 1999; Repp & Singh, 1990). However, functional analysis as an approach has been extended well beyond any particular type of behavior or population.

EVALUATION AND SPECIAL CONSIDERATIONS

Strengths

There are several advantages to conducting a functional analysis. First, the analysis can suggest specific antecedent conditions that promote or give rise to the behavior. In the case of an undesirable behavior, this may mean that reduction of the behavior may require rearranging antecedent conditions. As an example, two children (brother and sister) fight and scream daily over an early evening television show. The antecedent arrangements such as allowing the two children to come to the den, argue each day, and foster the "survival of the fittest" are setting events that in part promote the problem. Rearranging the situation such as the types of behaviors "permitted" by the parents in the den and how choice and program selection are provided can be used to decrease fighting. One advantage of functional analysis is that it sensitizes us to antecedents that might exert influence on the behavior.

Second, functional analysis draws attention to consequences in the situation that may be operating to maintain the behavior and, by implication, what can be changed to intervene effectively. For example, the brother's arguing and fighting with his sister each day may lead to their watching the show of *her* choice. Arguing and fighting may be reinforced by choice of the television show. This contingency could be rearranged so that choice of the TV show follows prosocial and cooperative behavior and not arguing and fighting. A functional analysis in this case suggests where to intervene and how to redeploy the consequences already in the situation to support the behavior of interest.

Third, a functional analysis may suggest the contingencies that are likely to be ineffective. In our present example, praise for cooperative behavior for the brother and sister on days when there is cooperation or low rates of arguing may have some positive effect. Indeed, using praise to reinforce behavior that is incompatible with the undesired response can be extremely effective (see Chapter 6). Yet a functional analysis might suggest that other reinforcers are operative (choice selection, sibling submission to verbally aggressive behavior). Praise alone without rearranging other consequences in the setting may have little or no effect.

Fourth, functional analysis provides a methodology for addressing important complexities of behavior. The first of these is that two (or more) individuals may be performing identical behaviors (e.g., getting into fights at school on the playground, coming late to work or to class, arguing with one's boyfriend or girlfriend), but for quite different reasons. That people engage in similar behaviors for different reasons is not new. What is new is that functional analysis provides a way of identifying the reasons and then using the information to change behavior.

A related complexity of behavior is that two (or more) quite different behaviors may serve the same purpose. For example, one child may have a tantrum at the dinner table every night and also get into trouble at school and be placed on detention. These are quite different behaviors; they bear no obvious resemblance and occur in different settings. It is possible that they serve a similar function. For example, they both bring the mother and father together to discipline the child. A functional analysis provides a methodology for determining the specific controlling factors and can explain diverse behaviors that go together. The analysis also provides an opportunity to identify a single intervention that might have impact on multiple behaviors that are maintained by the same function they serve.

Limitations

A number of limitations or restrictions in using functional analysis are apparent. First, it may be quite difficult to identify the antecedents and consequences that support and maintain the behavior. Indeed, occasionally, careful functional analyses under controlled laboratory conditions have not been able to identify factors that are controlling current behavior (Vollmer, Marcus, & LeBlanc, 1994; Sturmey, 1994). Consider the more general point that makes this quite understandable. A range of factors may influence behavior, both close to and distant from that behavior in time. For example, a child's aggressive behavior is known to be influenced by the history of aggressive behavior of the parents and grandparents, the child's temperament at birth, and the parents' current and past use of harsh physical punishment of the child (Kazdin, 1995). A functional analysis may observe only current antecedents and consequences and of course not provide a complete account of factors leading to aggressive acts. Moreover, as behavior becomes established, it often appears to be less dependent on the factors that initially motivated the behavior. For example, one may begin an exercise regimen to address a particular goal (lose weight, train for a sport) but over a protracted period, the behaviors seem to be performed for less easily identified antecedents and consequences. Social psychologists sometimes speak of behavior maintained in this way as intrinsic reinforcement (e.g., Lepper, Sethi, Dialdin, & Drake, 1997). Personality psychologists sometimes speak of this as functional autonomy, that is, behaviors that are continued but are not connected to the original reasons, purposes, or factors that may have initiated the behavior (Allport, 1937; Freud, 1936). All of this means that it may be difficult to identify current factors that control behavior. However, this is an empirical question. If assessment reveals patterns in the antecedents and consequences associated with behavior, these constitute hypotheses about controlling factors that are tested through a functional analysis. Moreover, a complete explanation of all factors related to the behavior may not be needed to intervene effectively.

Second, even if one has been able to identify controlling influences or the functions of behavior, this does not mean one will be able to alter them. For example, as mentioned previously, in adolescence, a number of "problem behaviors" often emerge or increase in frequency, including use of illicit substance (alcohol, drug, and cigarettes), unprotected sex, and delinquent acts. Assume for a moment that these behaviors serve the function of developing independence and autonomy from the parents (Ketterlinus & Lamb, 1994). This does not immediately suggest viable or practical interventions. It is much easier said than done to intervene so that "super" prosocial behaviors provide the same reinforcers. Parents occasionally joke among themselves that they should tell their adolescents that they *want* them to drink, use drugs, engage in promiscuous and unprotected sex, stay out late with friends, and engage in vandalism. The rationale of the joke is that any prompt from a parent on how to act will automatically evoke the opposite behavior. So if an adolescent seeks autonomy and "rebels" *against* prompts to engage in deviant behavior, the prosocial opposites might occur—not drinking, smoking, using drugs, and so on. The joke is at best mildly humorous to parents of adolescents who understand the frustration that prompts of the usual type are not likely to be effective. However, the point here is that functions, even if identified, are not always controllable for intervention purposes in any easy way. In the case of adolescents, peers play an unusually strong influence in the behaviors related to autonomy (Dishion, McCord, & Poulin, 1999). It is possible to use peer influences to support prosocial behavior through various activities or sports but it is also not easy. Moreover, such prosocial activities do not necessarily provide the reinforcers that drinking, smoking, drugs, and sex provide.

Third, conducting a functional analysis is not always feasible in applied settings. Many analyses have been conducted in well-controlled research where careful observations have been conducted or different stimulus arrangements have been made before intervening. In some cases, investigators have relied on computer technology to record ongoing behavior and antecedent events and to see relations between behavior and these events. Careful control and analyses of stimulus arrangements have greatly helped our understanding of the current causes of behavior. Of course, in many instances in everyday life in settings such as home and school, such detailed analyses and extended observations may not be feasible, either because resources for observation are limited or because of the urgency to intervene (e.g., to stop a child's fighting). Here, too, a functional analysis is still relevant and useful.

On Balance

The value of functional analysis extends beyond whether the assessment or manipulation procedures can be implemented in any particular instance or behavioral program. Functional analysis is not merely a method of assessment and intervening, but also a way of thinking about behavior. The way of thinking includes three features. First, functional analysis alerts us to the context in which behavior is embedded. There are many influences on behavior. Functional analysis prompts consideration of key influences including antecedents, consequences, and other circumstances that can affect performance. This is quite important because when many people think of behavioral approaches they look to consequences (rewarding behavior) (see Smith & Iwata, 1997). To those in the know (which now includes you), this is like trying to fly an airplane and only using half of the instruments. One might be able to fly a bit but not for very long.

Functional analysis draws us to the larger picture. For example, consider developing completion of homework in a 12-year-old. A simplistic way to proceed would be to begin a reinforcement program (e.g., points exchangeable for privileges) for working on homework after school. It is possible and actually quite likely that such a program would increase the time spent on homework and the completion of homework assignments. It is also possible that this is an overly simple analysis and that "throwing consequences" at the behavior, even if contingent, would have little effect. A functional-analytic perspective leads one to consider arranging conditions to promote homework completion. For example, perhaps the program would include a parent sitting with the child when both are not too tired, when there has not been an argument or conflict between them, when the child is not missing an important event (e.g., a party or game) he or she would otherwise prefer, and during other times. Arranging setting events to promote doing homework is important.

Second, as a way of thinking, functional analysis encourages "experimentation" in the sense of proposing and testing hypotheses. These hypotheses are related to significant and applied problems so this is not experimentation for the sake of research. Perhaps your roommate, partner, or spouse engages in a behavior that seems obnoxious or maybe even malicious. Moreover, these behaviors seem to occur just at the time you want sympathy or understanding. Traditional approaches to personality and behavior would make all sorts of attributions about the type of person he or she and you are and how this reflects a personality trait or some set of characteristics of the relationship that "feed" each other. Functional analysis takes a different approach. What might be controlling the behavior?

Consider two or three possibilities and test them with manipulation of the hypothesized antecedents and consequences. This places hypotheses about controlling factors in an empirical arena (i.e., one can actually find out what motivates behavior) and suggests ways of making change. All of this begins with considering hypotheses about the pattern, whether they are derived through careful assessment or informal observation. As a way of thinking, functional analysis fosters an approach that is valuable in its own right.

Finally, functional analysis fosters thinking about the plasticity or malleability of behavior. Plasticity does not mean that all behaviors can be changed, that all behaviors are equally changeable, and that merely tinkering with antecedents, behaviors, and consequences can change any aspect of human performance. Actually, the limits of effective application of learning are not known. However, the thinking shifts the assumptions about behaviors being fixed. The expression that one cannot teach an old dog new tricks is clearly incorrect. All of the permutations are possible (e.g., one can teach an old dog new tricks, a new dog old tricks, and so on!). However, it is one thing to say that behavior can be changed and quite another to provide concrete guidelines on how this might be done. Functional analysis provides a missing step.

Advances resulting from functional analysis will emerge in later chapters. It is important to note that many of the techniques based on reinforcement, punishment, and extinction, as well as other contingency manipulations have proven to be enormously effective in situations in which functional analyses have *not* been done. This is useful to know especially because systematic but simple interventions are often surprisingly effective. Later chapters will convey many of these interventions and the special conditions that require their effective application.

SUMMARY AND CONCLUSIONS

Functional analysis is a method for identifying current causes and conditions that maintain and influence behavior. This is an advance because behavior is examined in the contexts (antecedents and consequences) in which it is embedded. Key elements of functional analysis are assessment, hypothesis testing, and intervention. Assessment consists of identifying possible patterns in behavior, that is, whether the behavior is performed under some conditions more than others (e.g., time of the day, in the presence of some persons, before or after some antecedent condition or setting event). Two general methods for obtaining this information were illustrated and include interviews of the client or those in contact with the client and direct observation. There are many variants of each method (see For Further Reading).

The assessment identifies patterns about what *may* be controlling behavior but one cannot really be sure. The possible influences suggested by the data become hypotheses about controlling factors. These hypotheses can be tested directly be exposing the client to various conditions in which the antecedents or consequences are altered. As observations are obtained under the different conditions, one can see if behavior systematically varies as the conditions are changed. Often stark patterns are identified that show rather clearly that behavior is a function of (i.e., occurs systematically in relation to) a particular set of conditions.

The final component of functional analysis is using the information gained from hypothesis testing to intervene. The environment or contingencies of reinforcement (e.g., interactions with others, antecedents, consequences) are rearranged so the controlling conditions foster positive, prosocial behavior rather than deviant behavior. One has moved from testing what the controlling influences are to deploying them in ways that will achieve the desired behavior changes.

Although functional analysis encompasses several methods for moving from assessment to intervention, it is also a way of thinking about behavior and about interventions. What might be controlling behavior and what functions does the behavior serve? Can these same functions be achieved by prosocial rather than deviant behavior? These are excellent questions for guiding interventions.

Functional analysis represents an important advance. The analysis is not intended to identify all causes of behavior but rather to identify current influences that might be altered to achieve change. Of course, psychological interventions (e.g., psychotherapy, rehabilitation, education, prevention) are interested in achieving change. What is special about functional analysis is a methodology for identifying key influences and using the information to implement effective interventions.

KEY TERMS

Analogue testing   Cause of behavior   Functional analysis

Automatic reinforcement   Function of behavior   Hypothesis testing

APPLYING PRINCIPLES AND TECHNIQUES TO EVERYDAY LIFE

1. A child has a tantrum right before bedtime each night and the parents consult you about what to do. Describe a functional analysis of this behavior. Describe the elements of your analysis:

   A. Assessment of behavior and possible controlling factors

   B. Posing and evaluating the hypotheses about the function of behavior or controlling factors

   C. Developing an intervention

2. You want to do a functional analysis to help out a teacher with a problem (a child who shouts out a lot), but you cannot go to the class to do the observations or do any analogue testing in a laboratory room at the school. You decide to do an interview with the teacher. What are the questions you would ask in this interview?

3. Identify a behavior that might be *automatically reinforced*. What is the behavior? What is the reinforcement?

4. What are two strengths and two limitations of using a functional analysis?

FOR FURTHER READING

Haynes, S. N., & O'Brien, W. H. (1990). Functional analysis in behavior therapy. *Clinical Psychology Review, 10,* 649–668.

Iwata, B.A., Dorsey, M.F., Slifer, K.J., Bauman, K.E., & Richman, G.S. (1994). Toward a functional analysis of self-injury.

Journal of Applied Behavior Analysis, 27, 197–209. (Reprinted from *Analysis and Intervention in Developmental Disabilities,* 1982, 2, 3–20.)

O'Neill, R. E., Corners, R. H., Albin, R. W., Storey, K., & Sprague, J. R. (1990).

Functional analysis of problem behavior: A practical assessment guide. Sycamore, IL: Sycamore.

Pelios, L., Morren, J., Tesch, D., & Axelrod, S. (1999). The impact of functional analysis methodology on treatment choice for self-injurious and aggressive behavior. *Journal of Applied Behavior Analysis, 32,* 185–195.

Sturmey, P. (1996). *Functional analysis in clinical psychology.* Chichester, England: John Wiley & Sons.

NOTES

1. In discussions of functional analysis, investigators sometimes speak of identifying *causes* of behavior. This term is useful to convey the goal and focus of functional analysis—namely, to identify conditions that control the occurrence and maintenance of behavior. If these factors can be identified and then altered, behavior is more easily treated. Yet, the notion of "cause" can have many meanings and can easily imply more than what functional analysis is designed to accomplish (Haynes, 1992). For example, the causes of behavior may include many factors such as early experiences in life and the contingencies of reinforcement operative then, special characteristics of the individual, including temperament, brain development, and others with an endless array of influences, all occurring well before the present. Indeed, many of the influences on behavior are not in the current environment and are no longer operative in the same way in which they may have exerted their influence. Functional analysis focuses on current factors that influence behavior rather than on historical causes or underpinnings of behavior.

2. There are several biases that have been studied and reflect how we organize and process information. They are referred to as *cognitive heuristics* or aids to learning. The heuristics help us negotiate many aspects of everyday experience by grouping people and experiences, categorizing, and solving problems. The heuristics emerge as "bias" when we attempt to draw accurate relations based only on our own thoughts, impressions, and experience. A few examples convey the nature of these processes. The *representative heuristic* consists of drawing connections between events or characteristics based on stereotypes or expected relations. For example, we may believe that a particular ethnic group has certain characteristics. Alternatively, we may believe that a particular practice in which we engage (e.g., eating particular foods) is associated with particular outcomes (e.g., increased energy). In fact, there may be no relation even though we are fairly certain that the relation exists. Our stereotypes and expectations led us to perceive a relation. Part of the explanation comes from another heuristic. The *availability heuristic* refers to a tendency to draw from available information that may be vivid, recent, or salient for some other reason in our own thought processes. There are other such biases (Dumont, 1993; Kazdin, 2000; Smith & Dumont, 1997). They are not academic. For example, in clinical work, we often can change how an aggressive and antisocial child behaves at home and at school. A problem that we have frequently encountered is difficulty in changing how teachers and principals view the child. With strong expectations for deviance and fighting, quite mild instances of oppositional behavior or even being near a fight often leads to the child getting in severe trouble. His or her behavior is just taken as one more instance of the same aggression and antisocial behavior that was evident before treatment. Expectations are not trivial. They do not necessarily lead to deviant behavior of others, but they can make the behaviors of others seem deviant even when they might not be.

CHAPTER 5

How to Evaluate a Behavior Modification Program

Assessment of behavior change is essential in behavior modification. Actually, systematic assessment is essential in any type of treatment or intervention (e.g., medical, educational, psychotherapeutic) in which the goal is to effect a change. Assessment alone is quite valuable merely to identify whether there has been a change. Assessment may reveal that a change has occurred, but it does not show what *caused* the change. Proponents of behavior modification are extremely interested in determining the cause of behavior change. Once the cause is clear, knowledge about the factors that influence behavior is increased. The previous chapter on functional analysis conveys explicitly how assessment can be used to identify factors that control behavior and then how this information is used to develop effective interventions.

Evaluating the basis or reason for change extends beyond functional analysis. Whether or not one conducts a functional analysis, there is an interest in evaluating whether the intervention was responsible for change. The purpose is not knowledge for its own sake. Rather the long-term benefits of interventions for society at large will derive from understanding what produces change, the bases or reasons for the change, and the factors that one might alter to optimize the change.

In many cases, the person who conducts the behavior-change program may be interested only in changing behavior and not in isolating the cause of the change. Yet, even in such cases, it may be important to identify what was responsible for behavior change. For example, a parent may execute a program to reduce the amount of fighting between two children at home. After fighting has been assessed (baseline), a program may be implemented (e.g., praising the children for playing cooperatively). Assessment may reveal that the behavior has changed. Did the praise cause the behavior change? Perhaps the change occurred because one of the children was no longer physically ill when the program began and was therefore less irritable and less likely to get into fights. Perhaps other events (in addition to praising the children) for one or both of the children, such as a new friend in the neighborhood, new after-school activities, or changes in the behavior of the children's peers or parents, contributed to the change. All of these explanations can be ruled out to determine whether delivery of praise was responsible for the change.

The cause of behavior change can be demonstrated in different ways. The program designer usually plans the situation to identify whether the intervention was responsible for behavior change. The plan of the program used to demonstrate the cause of behavior change is referred to as the *experimental design*. The purpose of the experimental design is to identify the variables that influence, control, or are responsible for behavior change. In behavioral research, this is referred to as the demonstration of a *functional relation* between the target behavior and the intervention or other factor. A functional relation is demonstrated when altering the experimental condition or contingency systematically changes behavior. Behavior is shown to be a function of the environmental events that produced change.

Different experimental designs can be used to show that the program, rather than extraneous events, altered behavior. The designs are usually referred to as *single-case experimental designs*. Although such designs can be used with large groups of individuals, their unique characteristic is that they can be used with individual cases (e.g., one patient or student). Commonly used single-case designs are presented next to illustrate both the experimental arrangements themselves, as well as the overall method of evaluating interventions in applied settings.

BASIC CHARACTERISTICS
OF SINGLE-CASE DESIGNS

Continuous Assessment

In single-case research, inferences are usually made about the effects of the intervention by comparing different conditions presented to one or a few individuals over time. The designs share a number of basic requirements that are fundamental to understanding how conclusions are drawn. The most fundamental design characteristic is the reliance on repeated observations of performance over time. The client's performance is observed on several occasions, usually before the intervention is applied and continuously over the period while the intervention is in effect. Typically, observations are conducted on a daily basis or at least on multiple occasions each week. These observations allow the investigator to examine the pattern and stability of performance. The pretreatment information over an extended period provides a picture of what performance is like without the intervention. When the intervention eventually is implemented, the observations are continued and the investigator can examine whether behavior changes coincide with the intervention.

In single-case research, the effects of the intervention are examined by observing the influence of treatment and no treatment on the performance of the same person(s). Continuous assessment provides the several observations over time to allow the comparisons of interest. As discussed later in the chapter, this is in sharp contrast with group research where continuous assessment is not usually used and comparisons are made between individuals, some of whom receive treatment and others who do not.

Baseline Assessment

Single-case designs usually begin with observing behavior for several days before the intervention is implemented. This initial period of observation, referred to as the *baseline phase,* provides information about the level of behavior before the intervention begins. The baseline phase serves two functions. First, data collected during the baseline phase describe the existing level of performance. The *descriptive function* of baseline provides information about the extent of the client's problem. Second, the data serve as the basis for predicting the level of performance for the immediate future if the intervention is not provided. Even though the descriptive function of the baseline phase is important for indicating the extent of the client's problem, from the standpoint of single-case designs, the *predictive function* is central.

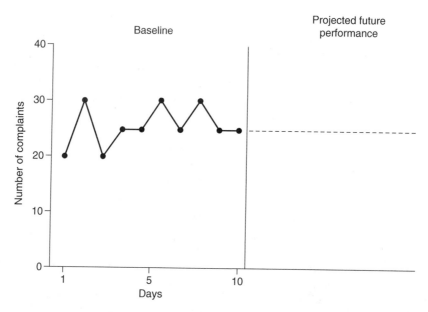

FIGURE 5-1 Hypothetical example of baseline observations of frequency of complaining. Data in baseline (solid line) are used to predict the likely rate of performance in the future (dashed line).

To evaluate the impact of an intervention in single-case research, it is important to have an idea of what performance would be like in the future without the intervention. Of course, a description of present performance does not necessarily provide a statement of what performance would be like in the future. Performance might change even without treatment. The only way to be certain of future performance without the intervention would be to continue baseline observations without implementing the intervention. However, the purpose is to improve the client in some way. Baseline data are gathered to help predict performance in the immediate future before treatment is implemented. Baseline performance is observed for several days to provide a sufficient basis for making a prediction of future performance. The prediction is achieved by projecting or extrapolating into the future a continuation of baseline performance.

A hypothetical example can illustrate how observations during the baseline phase are used to predict future performance and how this prediction is pivotal to drawing inferences about the effects of the intervention. Figure 5-1 illustrates a hypothetical case in which observations were collected on a hypochondriacal patient's frequency of complaining. As evident in the figure, observations during the baseline (pretreatment) phase were obtained for 10 days. The hypothetical baseline data suggest a reasonably consistent pattern of complaints each day in the hospital. The baseline level predicts the likely level of performance in the immediate future if conditions continue as they are. The projected (dashed) line suggests the approximate level of future performance and helps to evaluate whether the intervention leads to change. Presumably, if treatment is effective, performance will differ or depart from the projected (or predicted) level of baseline. For example, if a program is designed to reduce a hypochondriac's complaints and is successful in doing so, the level of complaints should decrease well below the projected level of baseline. In any case, continuous assessment in the beginning of single-case experimental designs consists of observation of baseline or pretreatment performance. As the individual single-case designs are described later, the importance of initial baseline assessment will become especially clear.

Stability of Performance

Since baseline performance is used to predict how the client will behave in the future, it is important that the data are stable. A *stable rate* of performance is characterized by the absence of a trend (or slope) in the data and relatively little variability in performance. The notions of trend and variability raise separate issues, even though they both relate to stability.

Trend in the Data. A *trend* or slope refers to the tendency for performance to decrease or increase systematically or consistently over time. One of three simple data patterns may be evident during baseline observations. First, baseline data may show no trend or slope. In this case, performance is best represented by a horizontal line indicating that it is not increasing or decreasing over time. As a hypothetical example, observations may be obtained on the disruptive and inappropriate classroom behaviors of a hyperactive child. The upper panel of Figure 5-2 shows baseline performance with no trend. The absence of trend in baseline provides a relatively clear basis for evaluating subsequent intervention effects. Improvements in performance are likely to be reflected in a trend that departs from the horizontal line of baseline performance.

If behavior shows a trend during baseline, behavior would be increasing or decreasing over time. The trend during baseline may or may not present problems for evaluating intervention effects, depending on the direction of the trend in relation to the desired change in behavior. Performance may be changing in the direction *opposite* from that which treatment is designed to achieve. For example, a hyperactive child may show an *increase* in disruptive and inappropriate behavior during baseline observations. The middle panel of Figure 5-2 shows how baseline data might appear; over the period of observations the child's behavior is becoming worse or more disruptive. Because the intervention attempts to alter behavior in the opposite direction, this initial trend is not likely to interfere with evaluating intervention effects.

In contrast, the baseline trend may be in the *same direction* that the intervention is likely to produce. Essentially, the baseline phase may show improvement in behavior. For example, the behavior of a hyperactive child may improve over the course of baseline as disruptive and inappropriate behavior decrease, as shown in the lower panel of Figure 5-2. Because the intervention attempts to improve

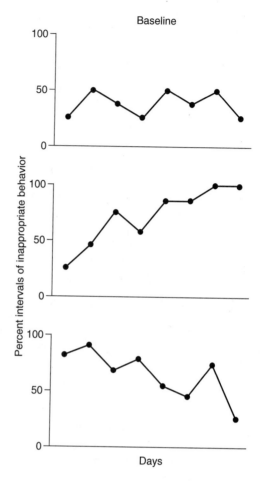

FIGURE 5-2 Hypothetical data for disruptive behavior of a hyperactive child. The upper panel shows a stable rate of performance with no systematic trend over time. The middle panel shows a systematic trend with behavior becoming worse over time. The lower panel shows a systematic trend with behavior becoming better over time. This latter pattern of data (in the lower panel) is the most likely one to interfere with evaluation of interventions because change is in the same direction as change anticipated with treatment.

performance, it may be difficult to evaluate the effect of the subsequent intervention. The projected level of performance for baseline is toward improvement. A very strong intervention effect of treatment would be needed to show clearly that treatment surpassed this projected level from baseline.

If baseline is showing an improvement, the question arises of why an intervention should be provided at all. Yet even when behavior is improving during baseline, it may not be improving quickly enough. For example, crime rate in a city may be declining gradually although no specific intervention is in place (i.e., during baseline). It would still be worthwhile to intervene to decrease the overall rate and to speed the rate (slope). At the level of an individual, the same point applies. For example, an autistic child may show a gradual decrease in head banging during baseline observations. The reduction may be so gradual that serious self-injury might be inflicted unless the behavior is treated quickly. Hence, even though behavior is changing in the desired direction, additional changes may be needed.

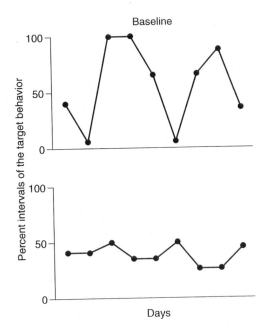

FIGURE 5-3 Baseline data showing relatively large variability (upper panel) and relatively small variability (lower panel). Intervention effects are more readily evaluated with little variability in the data.

In general, the one feature of a stable baseline is little or no trend. The absence of changes during baseline provides a clear basis for evaluating intervention effects. Presumably, when the intervention is implemented, a trend toward improvement in behavior will be evident. This is readily detected with an initial baseline that does not already show a trend toward improvement.

Variability in the Data. In addition to trend, stability of the data refers to the fluctuation or *variability in the subject's performance over time.* Excessive variability in the data during baseline or other phases can interfere with drawing conclusions about treatment. As a general rule, the greater the variability in the data, the more difficult it is to draw conclusions about the effects of the intervention. Excessive variability is relative; whether the variability is excessive and interferes with drawing conclusions about the intervention depends on many factors, such as the initial level of behavior during the baseline phase and the magnitude of behavior change when the intervention is implemented. In the extreme case, baseline performance may fluctuate daily from extremely high to extremely low levels (e.g., 0 to 100%). Such a pattern of performance is illustrated in the upper panel of Figure 5-3, in which hypothetical baseline data are provided. With such extreme fluctuations in performance, it is difficult to predict any particular level of future performance.

Baseline data may show relatively little variability, as represented in the hypothetical data in the lower panel of Figure 5-3. Performance fluctuates, but the extent of the fluctuation is small compared with the upper panel. With relatively slight fluctuations, the projected pattern of future performance is relatively clear and hence intervention effects will be less difficult to evaluate. Ideally, baseline data will show little variability.

SINGLE-CASE EXPERIMENTAL DESIGNS

The characteristics highlighted play a role in each of the single-case designs. The designs provide a range of options for careful evaluation of the individual case and hence contribute in an important way to the science and practice of clinical work. The major designs are presented and illustrated here.[1]

ABAB or Reversal Designs

Description. ABAB designs consist of a family of experimental arrangements in which observations of performance are made over time for a given client (or group of clients). Over the course of the investigation, changes are made in the experimental conditions to which the client is exposed. The ABAB design examines the effects of an intervention by alternating the baseline condition (A phase), when no intervention is in effect, with the intervention condition (B phase). The A and B phases are repeated again to complete the four phases. Because this is a family of designs, one need not be rigid about four phases. Sometimes ABA designs (baseline, intervention, return-to-baseline phases) are used; in other instances many additional phases are added, as discussed below. In all cases, the intervention effects are clear if performance improves during the intervention phase(s) and reverts to or approaches original baseline levels of performance when the intervention is withdrawn.

The design begins by observing behavior under baseline (no treatment or A phase) conditions. When a stable rate of behavior is evident, treatment is implemented (B phase). Assume for the moment that behavior changes when the intervention is introduced. When performance appears stable and consistent, the intervention is temporarily withdrawn. This is equivalent to reinstating the baseline condition (no intervention). The return-to-baseline or A phase sometimes is referred to as a *reversal phase* because the behavior is expected to "reverse," that is, return to or closely to, the level of the original baseline. After behavior reverts to baseline levels, the intervention is reinstated (second B phase).

Figure 5-4 provides a hypothetical example of observations of some desirable behavior plotted over several days. The data suggest that there are rather clear differences in the phases. Each phase shows performance that departs from what would be expected (projected and predicted) from extrapolating the pattern from the prior phase. A dashed line has been added to show an extrapolation of baseline or the predicted level of performance if baseline conditions were to continue. The changes, which occur whenever the intervention is introduced and return to baseline levels whenever the intervention is withdrawn, strongly suggest that the intervention was responsible for change. Other factors than the intervention would be difficult to propose that might plausibly account for this pattern.

The design is referred to as an ABAB design because A and B phases are alternated. The design is also referred to as a reversal design because phases in the design are reversed to demonstrate the effect of the program. If performance changes in the experimental phase relative to baseline, reverts to baseline or near baseline levels during the second baseline phase, and again changes in the final

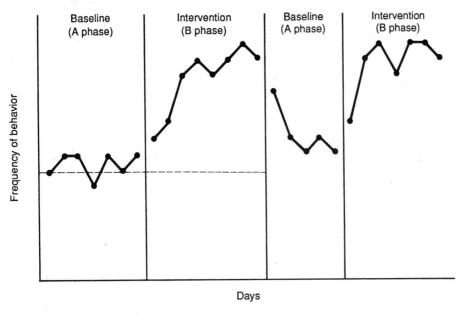

FIGURE 5-4 Hypothetical rate of some behavior plotted over baseline (A) and intervention (B) phases.

experimental phase, this provides a clear demonstration of the effectiveness of the experimental condition.

Examples of reversal designs are abundant. One program clearly illustrating the design focused on the aggressive behavior of elementary school children (Murphy, Hutchison, & Bailey, 1983). The children were 344 first and second graders who played outside before school began. The purpose of the study was to develop and evaluate an intervention to reduce the relatively high rates of aggressive behavior (e.g., striking, slapping, tripping, kicking, pushing, or punching others) on the playground. During baseline, the children were observed for 12 days to assess the number of aggressive behaviors during the 20-minute period before school began. The intervention, which included several components, began after baseline. The major component was organized game activities, including rope jumping and foot races supervised by playground aides. Aides led these activities, which structured the play of the children. Aides were also instructed to praise appropriate play behavior (reinforcement) and to use a mild punishment procedure (placing disruptive children on a bench for two minutes) for particularly unruly behavior. The intervention was discontinued after seven days in a reversal phase to see whether the program was responsible for behavior change. Finally, the intervention was reinstated. The results are presented in Figure 5-5. The figure shows that the number of aggressive incidents during each intervention phase decreased relative to the baseline and reversal phases. From the changes in behavior that occurred when the experimental condition was presented, withdrawn, and represented, it could be concluded that other influences probably did not account for the results.

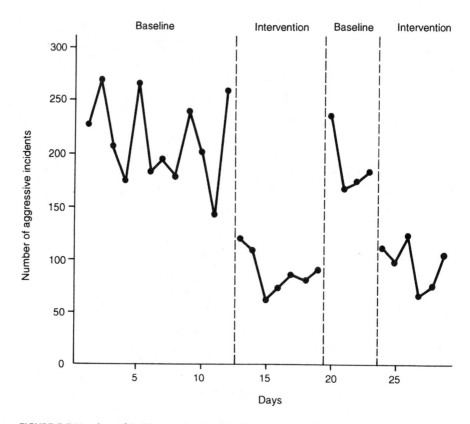

FIGURE 5-5 Number of incidents of aggressive behavior recorded on the playground before school started. Baseline—no intervention. Intervention—organized activities, praise, and time out. Reversal—return-to-baseline conditions. Intervention—return to the activities, praise, and time out.

(Source: Murphy, Hutchison, & Bailey, 1983)

The example is included here to mention another point. Single-case designs can evaluate interventions with individual cases, which is a unique strength of these designs. In the previous example, a large number of individuals were included and the entire group was treated as an individual case. That is, the goal was to reduce aggression in the group, and this was clearly accomplished. The focus also could have been with one or a few cases using the same design.

Design Variations. There are many variations of the design. ABA (three phases) is mentioned as one option that is usually regarded the minimum to provide a strong experimental demonstration. An AB (two-phase) version is usually much weaker because the control exerted by the intervention is not as firmly evident as when changes come and go as intervention and return to baseline alternate.

Variations of the design also include applications of different interventions. The ABAB version includes a single intervention (in the B phase) that is given to the client in two phases. Yet sometimes the intervention is not effective or not sufficiently effective to achieve the intervention goals. A second intervention or variation of the first treatment (B_1 phase) might be added. This might be summarized as $AB_1 B_2A B_2$, in which once an effective intervention is identified (B_2), it is evaluated in the usual way. An important feature of continuous assessment in single-case research is the ability to see whether behavior is changing and is changing sufficiently. If it is not, treatment can be modified (B_2, B_3) as needed to improve the effects achieved for the client.

ABAB designs can also vary by precisely what is implemented in the reversal (second A) phase. The most commonly used procedure is to *withdraw the intervention*. This usually restores the conditions to baseline. Understandably, behavior would likely revert to baseline levels when the intervention is withdrawn.

Another alternative during the reversal phase is *noncontingent delivery of the reinforcer*. Essentially, this refers to delivery of the consequences independent of behavior. This strategy is selected to show that it is not the event per se (e.g., merely providing praise) that results in behavior change but rather the relationship of the event to behavior (praise contingent on performance). For example, to change teasing among two siblings at home, parents may use praise as the reinforcer for cooperative behavior. During the intervention, when the children are playing nicely in the same room, praise is delivered by one of the parents. In other words, praise is contingent on the appropriate behavior. During the reversal phase, praise could be removed (withdrawal of the intervention and return to baseline conditions). Alternatively, praise could be continued but delivered noncontingently. Periodically, the parent might provide praise independent of what the children are doing. It is likely that cooperative behavior would decline because it is not reinforced or not reinforced very consistently. The results would show that it is not delivery of the praise per se that alters behavior but rather the delivery of praise contingent on the desired behavior.

Many other variations of the design can be identified (Barlow & Hersen, 1984: Kazdin, 1982b). In each case, the demonstration is an ABAB design if it meets the basic requirement, namely evaluating the effect of the intervention(s) by implementing a phase that is intended to reverse behavior in the direction of the original baseline.

Strengths and Limitations. ABAB designs nicely illustrate the underlying basis of experimental research by showing how one can draw conclusions by isolating the effect of the intervention. When the changes in behavior follow changes in phases, as illustrated previously, this is a very strong demonstration that the intervention was responsible for change. Several issues emerge in using this design.

The design requires that behavior reverts to or approaches the original baseline level after the intervention is withdrawn or altered (during the second A phase). This requirement restricts use of the design in clinical work. Therapists and clients alike want the benefits of treatment to continue, that is, not revert to baseline levels. Thus from a clinical or applied standpoint, continued performance of the appropriate behavior is important and desirable. Yet from the standpoint of an ABAB design, it could be disappointing if behavior is not made to revert to baseline levels after showing an initial change. Without such a reversal, it is not clear that the intervention was responsible for the change.

Essentially, returning the client to baseline levels of performance amounts to making behavior worse. Of course, treatment can be withdrawn for only a brief period such as one or a few days. In most circumstances, the idea of making a client worse just when treatment may be having an effect is ethically unacceptable. There may be important exceptions if, for example, the required treatment has undesirable side effects and suspension of treatment tests whether the intervention is still needed. Aside from ethical problems, there are also practical problems. It is often difficult to ensure that the client, therapist, or relatives responsible for conducting treatment will actually stop the intervention during the return-to-baseline phase once some success has been achieved. Even if they do stop the intervention, behavior does not always revert to baseline levels.

As a general rule, problems related to reversing behavior make the ABAB design and its variations undesirable in clinical situations. If a reversal does occur, that may be problematic if the behavior is important for the clients or for those in contact with them. If a reversal does not occur, this raises obstacles in concluding that the intervention led to the change. Yet the power of the design in demonstrating control of an intervention over behavior is very compelling. If behavior can, in effect, be "turned on and off" as a function of the intervention, this is a potent demonstration of a causal relation. Other designs can also demonstrate a causal relation without using a reversal of conditions.

Multiple-Baseline Designs

Description. Multiple-baseline designs demonstrate the effect of an intervention by showing that behavior change accompanies introduction of the intervention at different points in time. Once the intervention is presented, it need not be withdrawn or altered to reverse behavior to or near baseline levels. Thus the clinical utility of the design is not limited by the problems of reverting behavior to baseline levels after improvements have been made.

The key feature of the designs is evaluation of change across different baselines. The intervention is introduced to the different baselines at different points in time. Ideally, change occurs when the intervention is introduced in sequence to each of the baselines. The different baselines may, for example, consist of two separate behaviors of a child at home. Each behavior is observed and graphed separately. After baseline observations, the intervention is introduced to *one* of the behaviors. Both behaviors continue to be observed. Later the intervention is also introduced to the other behavior so that both behaviors now are receiving the intervention (e.g., both behaviors earn the reinforcers). The effect of the intervention is demonstrated by showing a pattern of change as the intervention is introduced, that is, each behavior changes when and only when the intervention was introduced.

Design Variations. Multiple-baseline designs vary depending on whether the baselines refer to *different behaviors, different individuals, different situations,* or *time periods.* For example, in the multiple-baseline design across behaviors, a single individual or group of individuals is observed. Data are collected on two or more behaviors, each of which eventually is to be altered. The behaviors are observed daily or at least on several occasions each week. After each of the baselines shows a stable pattern, the intervention is applied to only one of the behaviors. Baseline conditions remain in effect for the other behaviors. The initial behavior to which treatment is applied is expected to change while other behaviors remain at pretreatment levels. When the treated behavior stabilizes, the intervention is applied to the second behavior. Treatment continues for the first two behaviors while baseline continues for all other behaviors. Eventually, each behavior is exposed to treatment but at different points in time. A causal relation between the intervention and behavior is clearly demonstrated if each behavior changes only when the intervention is introduced and not before.

A multiple-baseline design across behaviors was illustrated in a program designed for a 4-year-old girl who had sleep problems (Ronen, 1991). The child would not fall asleep in her bed and would awaken and engage in tantrums throughout the night when placed in her bed. A reinforcement program was developed in consultation with a therapist but was carried out by the child's parents at home. The intervention consisted of reinforcement (praise, attention, candy) for more appropriate sleep behaviors, extinction of tantrums (no longer providing attention), and time out for inappropriate behaviors. Observations by the parents were obtained daily for several behaviors. After baseline information was obtained, the intervention was applied to the separate behaviors in sequence, in accord with the multiple-baseline design. Figure 5-6 illustrates the behaviors, observations, and points in time when the intervention was introduced. The figure shows child performance during baseline before the intervention was implemented (Phase I). The intervention (Phase II) was introduced to each behavior at different points in time. The pattern of change suggests that the intervention was responsible for change. Each behavior changed when the intervention was introduced. The most plausible interpretation of this pattern is that the intervention rather than some other event occurring in time led to change. Assessment continued over a period of weeks to evaluate follow-up (Phase III). The follow-up assessment suggests that the gains were maintained.

The requirements of the multiple-baseline design were clearly met in this report. If all behaviors had changed when only the first one was included into the contingency, it would have been unclear whether the contingency caused the change. In that case, an extraneous event may have influenced all behaviors simultaneously. Yet, the specific effects obtained in this report strongly suggest the influence of training on each behavior.

As another variation, the multiple-baseline design can be conducted across individuals. In the multiple-baseline design across individuals, baseline data are collected for the same behavior across two or more individuals. After the behavior of each individual has reached a stable rate, the experimental condition is implemented for only one of the individuals, while baseline conditions are continued

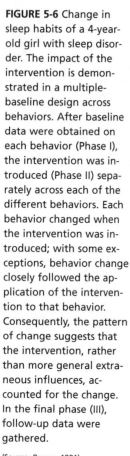

FIGURE 5-6 Change in sleep habits of a 4-year-old girl with sleep disorder. The impact of the intervention is demonstrated in a multiple-baseline design across behaviors. After baseline data were obtained on each behavior (Phase I), the intervention was introduced (Phase II) separately across each of the different behaviors. Each behavior changed when the intervention was introduced; with some exceptions, behavior change closely followed the application of the intervention to that behavior. Consequently, the pattern of change suggests that the intervention, rather than more general extraneous influences, accounted for the change. In the final phase (III), follow-up data were gathered.

(Source: Ronen, 1991)

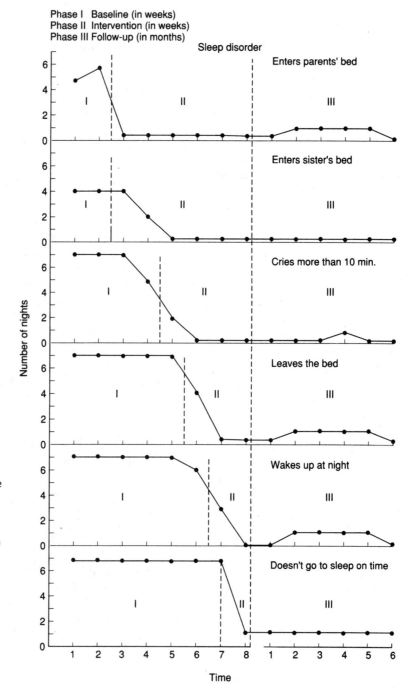

Phase I Baseline (in weeks)
Phase II Intervention (in weeks)
Phase III Follow-up (in months)

Sleep disorder

Enters parents' bed

Enters sister's bed

Cries more than 10 min.

Leaves the bed

Wakes up at night

Doesn't go to sleep on time

Number of nights

Time

for the other(s). The behavior of the person exposed to the experimental condition should change whereas the behavior of the other individual(s) should not. When behavior stabilizes for all individuals, the contingency is extended to another person. This procedure is continued until all individuals for whom baseline data were collected are included in the contingency. As with other multiple-baseline designs, no reversal of the experimental condition (i.e., return to baseline) is required to demonstrate that the contingency was responsible for behavior change. The multiple-baseline design across individuals is useful when a given behavior is to be altered across a number of clients in a group.

A multiple-baseline design across individuals was used in a study designed to increase the extent to which emergency room nurses wore gloves during medical procedures to protect against human immunodeficiency virus (HIV) (DeVries, Burnette, & Redmon, 1991). Hospitals have many procedures and practices to protect health care workers from contact with patients' bodily fluids (e.g., accidental punctures of needles and handling of blood) to prevent infection from HIV. Wearing protective gloves during emergency room procedures is one such procedure. In this hospital, four nurses across different work shifts in at-risk situations for blood exposure participated in a program designed to improve wearing protective gloves. After baseline observations, assessed by other nurses working in the hospital, a feedback program was implemented as the intervention. During the feedback (intervention) phase, each nurse was seen briefly and individually. She was told how many times (in percentage of opportunities) she had worn protective gloves among the at-risk situations, was shown the daily data in graphical form, was informed of the at-risk situations in which gloves were to be worn, was praised for use of the gloves, and was encouraged to increase this frequency. Feedback and praise sessions required five minutes each and were given periodically through the intervention phase.

The intervention was introduced in a multiple-baseline design fashion across four nurses. As shown in Figure 5-7, baseline rates varied for the individuals. Even so, in each case, introduction of the intervention was associated with an increase in the wearing of protective gloves. Other events that might have influenced the behavior, such as repeated observation over time, seeing others wear gloves, or changes in hospital life, could not easily explain the change. The results strongly suggest that the feedback intervention was responsible for changing behavior.

The multiple-baseline designs across behaviors and individuals are the more commonly used variations. There are other variations as well in which baseline data are gathered across several situations (e.g., in class, on the playground), settings (e.g., home, school), or times (e.g., morning, afternoon, evening). The variations are similar in the introduction of the intervention at different points in time. As with other variations, the designs are useful when there is interest in achieving behavior change across different baselines.

Strengths and Limitations. The multiple-baseline designs demonstrate the effect of the intervention without a return-to-baseline condition and a temporary loss of some of the gains achieved. Two major considerations that affect the clarity of the demonstration are the number and the independence of the baselines.

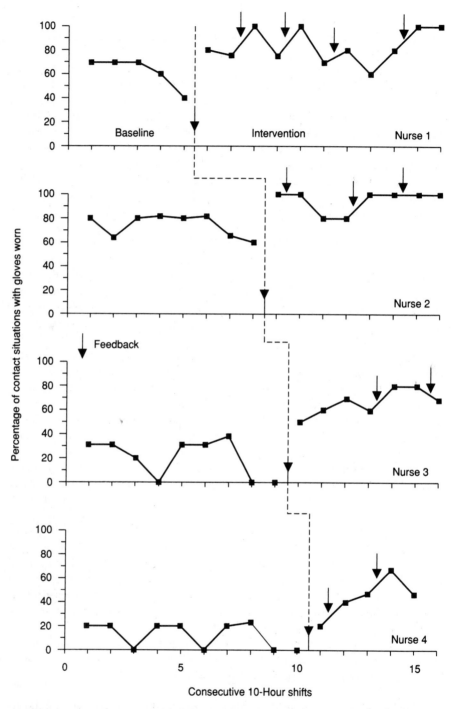

FIGURE 5-7 Percentage of contact (at risk for bodily fluid contact) situations in which protective gloves were worn by four emergency room nurses for consecutive 10-hour work shifts. The intervention (feedback) was introduced in a multiple-baseline design across individuals. Arrows during the intervention phase indicate delivery of feedback.

(Source: De Vries, Burnette, & Redmon, 1991).

The number of baselines adequate for a clear demonstration is difficult to specify. Two baselines are a minimum, but three or more can really strengthen the demonstration. The clarity of the demonstration across a given set of baselines is also influenced by other factors such as the stability of the baseline data (e.g., few or no trends), the rapidity of behavior change after treatment is implemented, and the magnitude of behavior change. Depending on these factors, even two or three baselines can provide a sufficiently convincing demonstration.

The design depends on showing that the behavior changes when and only when the treatment is implemented. Ideally, behaviors still exposed to the baseline condition do not change until the intervention is applied. If they do, it suggests that maybe some factor other than the intervention may have led to the change. Occasionally, an intervention may change other behavior. There are many reasons for this, but one is that two or more behaviors may be interrelated in some way. For example, in a multiple-baseline design across behaviors, teasing and hitting one's sibling may be the two target behaviors. It is possible that for any individual child, changing the former might influence the latter. When changes are not associated specifically with implementation of the intervention, this introduces ambiguity in the conclusion drawn about the effects of treatment. Overall, generalized effects across different baselines appear to be exceptions rather than the rule. When generalized effects are present, features from other single-case designs (e.g., a brief reversal phase) can be added in separate experimental phases to demonstrate a causal relation between treatment and behavior change.

Multiple-baseline designs are user friendly in clinical and other applications because the intervention is applied in a gradual or sequential fashion. The investigator may wish to change many different behaviors of the individual (or different individuals or situations). Rather than introducing the intervention to all of these at once, the program initially focuses on only one of these. If the intervention is effective, then it can be extended to all of the other behaviors for which change is desired. As importantly, if the intervention is not effective or not effective enough to achieve important changes, it can be altered or improved before it is extended.

Changing-Criterion Designs

Description. The changing-criterion designs demonstrate the effect of the intervention by showing that behavior matches a criterion for performance that is set for either reinforcement or punishment. As the criterion is repeatedly changed, behavior increases or decreases to match the criterion. A causal relation between the intervention and behavior is demonstrated if the behavior matches the constantly changing criterion for performance.

The changing-criterion design begins with a baseline period of observation. After baseline, the intervention is introduced so that a certain level of performance is required. For example, the behavior may have to be performed a certain number of times per day to earn the reinforcer. When performance consistently meets or surpasses that criterion over a few days, the criterion is made more stringent. The criterion is repeatedly changed in a gradual fashion until the goal is achieved. The effect of the contingency is demonstrated if the behavior matches the criterion repeatedly as that criterion is changed.

A changing-criterion design was used to evaluate an exercise program for 11-year-old boys, some of whom were obese (DeLuca & Holborn, 1992). In the United States, exercise among children, adolescents, and adults is well below levels recommended for general health. Exercise has widespread benefits on physical and mental health (wide range of diseases and psychiatric disorders) (e.g., Lee, Blair, & Jackson, 1999; Tkachuk & Martin, 1999). In this project, exercise consisted of riding a stationary bicycle during a time of the day at their elementary school. During baseline, each child was told he could exercise as long as he wished. After baseline, the intervention was implemented in which the children had the opportunity to earn points based on the amount of exercise they completed. The points could be traded for different backup reinforcers such as model cars, planes, puzzles, books, handheld games, and other items at the end of the session. The amount of exercise was measured in terms of the number of revolutions (wheel turns) on the bicycle. When a youth was pedaling at the level that would earn points, a bell rang, and a light on the bicycle turned on.

The changing-criterion feature of the design was intended to develop increasingly vigorous exercise. The baseline rate was used to decide the first criterion level that would be used in the intervention phase. When the intervention began, each child was required to increase exercise (revolutions) by 15% over baseline to earn reinforcement. When performance met this criterion, the criterion was shifted to 30% above baseline; when performance met that criterion it was shifted to 45% above the baseline rate. The effects of the program for five of the boys are presented in Figure 5-8. The figure shows that, during the intervention phase, exercise rates shifted to the new criterion that was invoked to earn points. There was a brief return to baseline in the study and then a reinstatement of the highest criterion. (The return to baseline is not needed for the design but further suggests that the intervention was responsible for change.) The results indicated that exercise consistently followed the criterion. Accordingly, it is plausible that the reinforcement program, rather than extraneous influences, accounted for behavior change. As an aside, the boys rated the program very favorably, expressed greater interest in biking in general, and became involved in some athletics at school.

Design Variations. The usual design consists of changing the criteria so that more performance is required to earn the consequences. A variation sometimes used is the one illustrated above in which a brief period is implemented during the intervention in which the criterion is temporarily made *less* stringent. That is, the individual performs better and better and matches the criteria and then a slight lowering of the criterion is implemented. This is not a complete return to baseline but rather return to a prior criterion level. This is done to make even more clear the role of the intervention. If one can show that behavior follows the criterion no matter what direction the criterion is moved (more or less stringent), then this clearly indicates that the intervention is influencing the behavior.

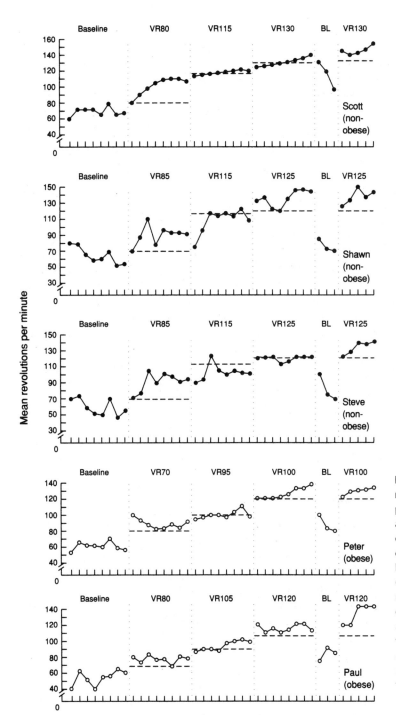

FIGURE 5-8 Mean (average) number of revolutions pedaled per minute during baseline and intervention (15% increase, 30% increase, 45% increase over baseline), return to baseline (BL), and intervention (45% increase) for obese and nonobese boys, age 11. The changing criterion is specified above the phase and reflects a variable ratio schedule (or the average number of revolutions required for reinforcement for that child).

(Source: DeLuca & Holborn, 1992)

Strengths and Limitations. The design is especially well suited to those terminal responses that are arrived at or approximated gradually. Many therapeutic applications focus on gradual development of behavior or skills (e.g., improving marital communication, participation of activities) or reduction of problematic function (e.g., overcoming anxiety). Shaping these behaviors or gradually exposing individuals to anxiety-provoking situations is consistent with gradually increasing a criterion for performance. Consequently, the design is very well suited to many applications in applied settings where progress is likely to be gradual.

Sometimes behavior changes may take large leaps. For example, the program may require the person to decrease cigarette smoking from a baseline rate of 30 per day to 25 (as the first criterion level for reinforcement). When the program is introduced, the person may go to 10 cigarettes per day and remain at that level, for reasons that are not understood. In this example and in general, if change occurs rapidly or in large steps and does not follow the gradual changes in the criterion, the specific effect of the intervention in altering behavior will not be clear. The changes may be influenced by some other factors. This is the reason that a mini-reversal phase (return to a prior criterion level but not back to baseline) is sometimes implemented, as noted previously. Showing that behavior changes in either direction (increase or decrease in performance) as the criterion is changed makes a more powerful experimental demonstration. When there is a temporary lowering of the criterion, this is not a return to baseline and hence objections associated with reversal phases are less likely to apply.

Overall, changing-criterion designs are quite useful. Shaping behavior is important in reinforcement programs under a variety of circumstances (e.g., improving the amount of: homework completed, exercise, practice of some skill). Changing a criterion gradually to achieve a terminal goal can be very useful for developing behavior, as well as for evaluating the impact of an intervention.

Approximations of Experimental Designs

The designs illustrated above are referred to as *true experiments,* which means that they provide a rigorous way of identifying the effect of an intervention. True experiments rule out or make implausible other explanations that might explain the results. For example, in an ABAB design, it is very likely that the effects are due to treatment rather than to many other influences that might lead to behavior change. The repeated pattern of showing that the intervention controls behavior is a very strong demonstration. There is never certainty in science, but a true experiment and the accumulation of many true experiments is how a firm knowledge base is achieved.

The examples convey that the designs in fact are used in behavior modification in applied settings. It is not always the case that the designs can be implemented in applied settings or in clinical work, often for practical reasons or because the priority is unequivocally to achieve change in the client. Sometimes the design requirements may compete with optimizing change (e.g., as in a reversal design); other times, practical obstacles may make it difficult to conduct the design exactly as intended. Evaluation in clinical work remains extremely important, even if the designs themselves cannot be used in their pure form (Kazdin, 1993).

Systematic assessment of changes in the target behavior or domains of functioning that serve as the focus of treatment provide valuable, if not absolutely essential, information. Even if one cannot implement one of the experimental designs mentioned previously, an approximation of these designs still represents an important contribution for understanding treatment and for documenting whether the target behaviors have changed. The key to evaluation is the ongoing assessment of functioning. The situation may permit assessment for only baseline and intervention phases. This is equivalent to an AB design or the first part of the ABAB design noted previously. AB designs often are used in applications of treatment in clinic settings (e.g., Eisen & Silverman, 1991; Erhardt & Baker, 1990). They can still be very persuasive because of the way in which the data are collected and the pattern of the results.

As an example, consider the case of a 49-year-old woman with a long-standing history of obsessional thoughts related to shame and worry about toilet odors and flatulence (Ladouceur et al., 1993). She had a history of intestinal problems and anxiety disorders. The goal of treatment was to reduce intrusive thoughts that usually took the form of internal statements (e.g., "I'm going to fart" and "I'm going to have diarrhea") that occurred several (12-21) times a day. A program was designed to decrease these thoughts by repeated exposure to them via a tape recording. The thoughts were considered to be maintained by the anxiety they elicited. Repeated exposure was attempted to extinguish their anxiety-evoking properties. During treatment, the client listened to the cassette recorder that played a tape she had made that verbalized these thoughts. She was instructed *not* to engage in distracting thoughts because escape can actually maintain anxiety and thwart extinction.

Before treatment, her initial rate of intrusive thoughts was self-monitored. After several days, the program was introduced and thoughts continued to be self-monitored. The results of the program appear in Figure 5-9, which shows her daily rate of intrusive thoughts across baseline and intervention phases. Even though an AB design is much less adequate than an ABA or ABAB, the results suggest that the intervention may have been responsible for change. The inference is aided by continuous assessment over time before and during the intervention phase. The number of intrusive thoughts fluctuated during baseline, but still was relatively stable (i.e., no clear trend). The baseline pattern suggests that no change was likely to occur with continued observations alone. When the intervention was introduced, intrusive thoughts declined and continued to show a decline, which was maintained at a follow-up assessment three weeks after treatment ended. The data pattern suggests that the intervention was probably responsible for the change.

In many instances, one may not be able to infer a causal relation between the intervention and therapeutic change in a way that meets the rigors of experimental research. Even so, as the prior example emphasizes, evaluation is no less important. First, it is important to document change in the client. Without such

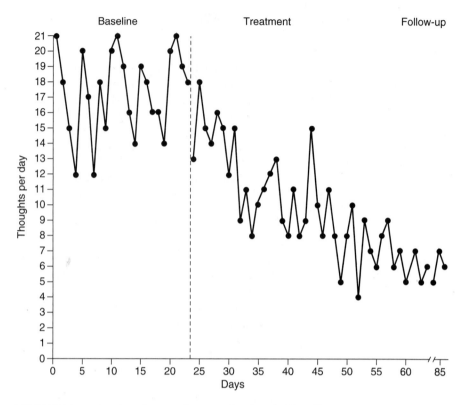

FIGURE 5-9 Intrusive thoughts per day over the course of baseline, treatment, and follow-up (3 weeks after treatment ended).

(Source: Ladouceur, Freeston, Gagnon, Thibodeau, & Dumont, 1993)

documentation, it may not be clear whether the client has improved, remained the same, or become worse in relation to the treatment focus. Assuming the client has improved, assessment is helpful in making judgments about the amount of change and whether that change has been sufficient to have impact on the client's everyday life. Ongoing and continuous assessment provide information about client progress. Second, it is important to use the information from assessment to make decisions about treatment. The data can benefit the client when they are incorporated into decision making. Key decisions usually need to be made about whether more or different interventions are needed, when the goals have been achieved, whether further treatment is needed, and whether it is time to stop treatment. Thus evaluation of behavioral programs is important, even if there are situations in which implementation of a specific experimental design or experimental arrangement is not feasible (see Kazdin, 1993).

General Comments

Single-case research encompasses many different designs, only a few of which could be illustrated here. Most students introduced to research methods are schooled in group research. Single-case designs are just as rigorous and serve the same purposes, namely, to identify a causal relation between some condition (e.g., an intervention) and some outcome (e.g., behavior change).

Single-case designs provide a means to investigate treatments empirically with individual clients. This is very useful in applied settings where the individual (student in a classroom or the home) is studied and where the intervention has to be tested to ensure the desired effects are achieved. Continuous assessment, unique to single-case designs, provides the investigator or clinician with feedback regarding how well the intervention is working. This is perhaps the main applied advantage of single-case designs, namely, the ability to see how or whether treatment is working and making changes as needed while the treatment or intervention is still in effect. Indeed, the success of behavioral approaches using single-case designs not only stems from powerful procedures (e.g., reinforcement), but also from being able to identify mediocre or poor treatment effects early and rectifying them.

Another advantage of single-case designs is that they permit investigation of problems that are not likely to be studied in group research. Many clinical problems are relatively rare, so it would be extraordinarily difficult to recruit subjects for a large-scale treatment evaluation project. Yet single-case designs allow careful investigation of an individual client. Thus the effects of treatment on a wide range of problems can be obtained from experimentation with a single case. This information might not otherwise be available from group studies.

GROUP DESIGNS

Basic Design Features

Group designs represent another way to demonstrate the effect of an intervention. A variety of group designs are suitable for applied settings (Kazdin, 1998). The basic design requires at least two groups: one receives the intervention (the experimental group) and the other does not (the control group). To determine whether the intervention is effective, rates of the target behavior in the experimental and control groups are compared. For example, families might volunteer to participate in a program designed to increase the extent to which their children do homework. Among all parents who volunteer, one half may be assigned to receive a special parent training program in which parents learn how to develop behaviors in their children and the other half may be assigned to a control group. In this instance, let us say the control group received no intervention, but there are many other options available. Immediately before and after the program, the behavior of all children would be assessed (e.g., parent report of amount of time the child engaged in homework in the past week, teacher ratings of homework completion). To determine whether the special parent-training program is effective, the averages in performance for the groups are compared at the end of the program. If the group averages are different, this finding suggests that the program was responsible for the change.

Assessment in group designs usually is made before and after the intervention is delivered. This is distinguished from single-case designs in which observations are continuous before the intervention (baseline) and while the intervention is in effect. Another way to say this is that group designs usually rely on few observations (immediately before and immediately after treatment) of many individuals (subjects), and single-case designs rely on many observations of a few (one or a few) individuals. For applied settings, the benefits of single-case designs derive from the many observations because one can see how the individual is doing while treatment is in place and can make changes as a result (Kazdin, 1993).

In group research, differences between groups at the end of treatment are used to draw conclusions about whether the intervention was effective. To be reasonably sure that any difference between the two groups is the result of the program, the groups must be similar to begin with. Before the program is implemented, the best procedure to control for systematic differences between groups is to assign clients *randomly* to one of the two groups. If subjects are not randomly assigned to groups, the likelihood is greater that the groups may be different in their performance of the target behavior before the program is implemented and may differentially change in the target behavior over time for some reason other than the effect of the program.

Group designs are used in many disciplines and areas of research. When these designs are used to study *treatment,* whether medical or psychological, and subjects are assigned randomly, the studies are commonly referred to as *randomized controlled clinical trials.* For example, treatments to test medication or surgery (e.g., for heart disease, cancer, HIV) or various forms of psychotherapy or behavior therapy (e.g., for anxiety, eating disorders, depression) typically are examined in these trials. In such trials at least two groups are compared, including the group that receives the intervention and the group that receives no intervention or standard (routine) care (e.g., the treatment currently in use for people with the disease, disorder, or problem). Other groups may be included as well (e.g., placebo group, a combination of treatments) (Kazdin, 1998).[2]

The basic feature of group designs is the presentation of different conditions to two or more groups. An illustration of the design can be seen in a program to evaluate interventions for pregnant women who smoked cigarettes (Burling, Bigelow, Robinson, & Mead, 1991). Many of the negative consequences of cigarette smoking to the person who smokes are well known. There are, of course, added consequences for the unborn child and later for the infant if the mother smokes during pregnancy and after giving birth, including reduced birth weight, birth defects, sudden infant death, and childhood psychiatric disorder. The study included 139 pregnant women who were cigarette smokers and who were seen at an obstetrics and gynecology clinic at a large hospital. All women received standard care during their weekly visits, which included information about smoking as provided by a nurse. The information was designed to increase positive health-related behaviors, including the reduction of smoking.

Through random assignment, half of the women received additional information over and above standard care. This additional information consisted of a follow-up letter designed to make the importance of smoking cessation more salient. The letter noted that chronic abnormalities and health problems of the child were increased by cigarette smoke and urged the woman to stop smoking. Further information from the American Cancer Society, including guidelines for

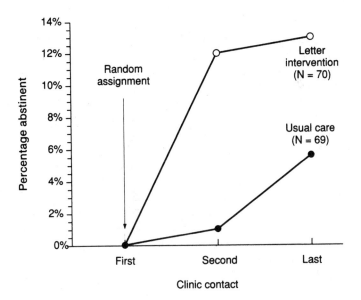

FIGURE 5-10 Percentage of mothers abstinent from smoking in the standard (usual) care program and the standard-care program with the additional information (letter).

(Source: Burling, Bigelow, Robinson, & Mead)

a self-directed smoking cessation program, was also enclosed. Cigarette smoking was measured by self-reports of the women and by taking breath samples to assess blood gasses (carbon monoxide), which measure the level of recent smoking during weekly contacts. Figure 5-10 shows that at the initial assessment, before the intervention, the groups were no different. By the second and final assessment, the percentage of women who had ceased smoking was greater for those who received standard care and the letter/information.

In passing, it is worth noting that interventions based primarily or exclusively on providing information, as this study shows, often are not very potent in the effects they produce. The investigators, well aware of this, noted that such interventions have compensatory advantages, including the ease of dissemination to large numbers of individuals and the low cost relative to most other interventions. Indeed, merely mailing a letter and sending information augmented the standard program at a relatively low cost. Of course, a stronger intervention based on more potent behavior-change techniques would be worthwhile as well, given the serious consequences of adverse health styles during pregnancy. For present purposes, the study shows the use of comparisons between groups as a way of evaluating intervention programs.

Combined Designs

In many instances, group and single-case designs are combined. For example, treatment was evaluated in a combined design for ten individuals (ages 6 to 36) who were diagnosed with Tourette's syndrome (Azrin & Peterson, 1990). The disorder, considered to be neurologically based, consists of multiple motor and vocal tics such as head, neck, and hand twitching, eye rolling, shouting of profane words, grunting, repetitive coughing or throat clearing, or other utterances. The tics, which begin in childhood, usually are quite conspicuous. In this program, features of a control group design and multiple-baseline design were combined. The 10 cases were assigned either to receive treatment or to wait for a three-month period (waiting-list control group). The assignments were made on a random basis. Tics were assessed daily with recordings of tics at home and periodically with videotapes of each person at the clinic. The treatment consisted of habit reversal, which includes several different behavior therapy treatments, such as being made more aware of the behavior, self-monitoring, relaxation training, and practicing a response that competed with the tic (i.e., is incompatible with the tic, such as contracting the muscles in a different way, or breathing in a way that prevents making certain sounds). Also, family members reinforced improved performance at home. Many of the components have been used as separate interventions for various problems, as detailed in subsequent chapters.

The results are shown in Figure 5-11, which graphs the number of tics per hour at home and at the clinic for the treatment group and the waiting-list control group. The baseline phase for the waiting-list group is longer because of the wait period before treatment was given to them. Hence, the continuous observations over baseline and treatment also meet criteria for a multiple-baseline design (across groups). The results indicate that the intervention clearly showed marked impact on tics. This is important because Tourette's syndrome has not been effectively treated with various psychotherapy or pharmacological treatments. The demonstration is persuasive in large part because of the combination of multiple-baseline and group-design strategies, even though either one of these alone would have been sufficient. The control group provided useful information about the likely changes over time without an intervention during the waiting period.

General Comments

Group designs have dominated therapy research, including research on behavior therapy in which interventions are applied to various psychiatric disorders and related problems that bring people to psychotherapy. However, single-case designs have been used extensively to evaluate programs based on reinforcement, punishment, extinction, and other contingency-based interventions in applied settings such as the home, school, hospitals, businesses, and the community at large. Group designs emphasize the behavior of groups and average performance of one group relative to another. Thus the average performance of a group may change, although the program may actually have affected only a few individuals in the group. The focus on averages hides the behavior of individuals. Behavior modification programs in applied settings usually have been concerned with achieving relatively large changes of individual clients. This point is a matter of emphasis rather than of sharp differences. Many applications of reinforcement in commu-

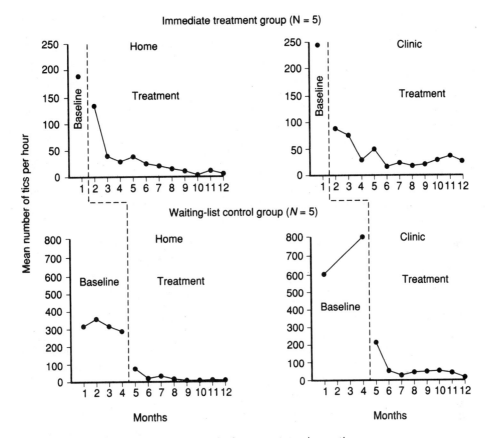

FIGURE 5-11 Monthly mean (average) of Tourette's syndrome tics per hour measured in clinic and home settings for subjects in the immediate treatment (upper panel) and waiting-list (lower panel) groups. The data illustrate the combined multiple-baseline design across two groups: one group that received treatment immediately and one group that waited for the initial period.

(Source: Azrin & Peterson, 1990).

nity settings include several schools or classrooms and hence focus on large groups rather than on individuals. In such instances, group designs alone or combined with single-case designs have been used frequently.

Although different segments of behavior modification tend to emphasize group or single-case experimental designs, this point is not as critical as the overriding issue. One of the salient characteristics of behavior modification is a strong commitment to assessment, experimental design, and evaluation of treatment. Within the overall field of behavior modification, evaluation of behavior-change techniques based on operant conditioning principles have relied more heavily on the single-case designs emphasized in this chapter. Of course, the particular type of design selected depends on many factors, such as the purpose of treatment and the questions of interest to the investigator, rather than on the type of techniques that are used.

For many questions, a control group can provide valuable information that is difficult to obtain with single-case designs (Kazdin, 1998). For example, comparing the effectiveness of different experimental programs is readily accomplished by using different groups of clients who receive the different treatments. Group designs are especially useful for these comparisons. Also, when evaluating different treatments, it is possible and indeed likely that treatments will vary in effectiveness for different types of persons (e.g., younger versus older, men versus women) or for different types of clinical problems (e.g., depression versus aggression, social interaction versus instruction following). Group designs are especially useful because they permit analyses of treatment for different subgroups of persons and for different subject characteristics.

EVALUATING THE DATA

Deciding Whether Behavior Has Reliably Changed

Collecting systematic information on how and whether the client is responding to treatment is obviously useful, but how does one interpret or make use of the information? In research that emphasizes group designs, the results are usually analyzed statistically. Statistical analyses determine whether the differences are reliable, that is, if they are likely to be due to the different conditions that the groups received. Many statistical tests are used to make this determination, a topic well beyond the scope of this book.

In single-case designs, the data are evaluated by comparing performance during baseline with performance during the experimental phase. Statistical evaluation is not usually used with single-case designs. Whether a systematic change is evident is inferred from the design (e.g., ABAB, multiple baseline) and the pattern of the data across phases. For example, in the ABAB design, the experimental condition may be withdrawn, altered, or reinstated at different points based on evidence that behavior has changed or failed to change. The data pattern from the observations over the course of the design help to decide whether the intervention was responsible for change and whether the client has improved sufficiently.

The question is, what criteria are used to decide whether there is a genuine or reliable (systematic) change? In many instances in single-case research, behavior change is dramatic. Indeed, the usual purpose of the intervention is to obtain strong treatment effects. If these are obtained, they are usually quite evident from visual inspection, that is, from merely looking at the graphs to evaluate whether the change was reliable. Three characteristics of the observations or data are used to help decide whether behavior change has occurred. The characteristics are listed and defined in Table 5-1. Assuming an experimental design has been used to evaluate the intervention, these characteristics reflect how the data are to be interpreted. Design and data evaluation together help to assess whether the

Table 5-1   Characteristics of the Data to Decide Whether Behavior Changes are Reliable Based on Graphical Display of the Observations

Criteria	Defined
Changes in means (averages)	The mean rate of the behavior shows a change from phase to phase in the expected direction.
Change in slope (trend)	The direction of the slope changes from phase to phase, as for example, showing no slope (horizontal line) in baseline and an accelerating slope during the intervention phase.
Shift in level	When one phase changes to another, a level refers to the change in behavior from the last day of one phase (e.g., baseline) and the first day of the next phase (e.g., intervention). An abrupt shift facilitates data interpretation.

intervention was likely to be responsible for change. These characteristics are based on evaluating graphs on which performance is plotted across phases.

The first characteristic is to see if there is a *change in means* across phases. Consistent changes in means across phases can serve as a basis for deciding whether the data pattern meets the requirements of the design. A hypothetical example showing changes in means across phases is illustrated in an ABAB design in Figure 5-12 (upper panel). As evident in the figure, performance on the average (horizontal dashed line in each phase) changed in response to the different baseline and intervention phases. Evidence of changes in means by itself may not be persuasive but contributes along with the other characteristics.

The second characteristic is a *change in slope or trend*. Slope refers to the tendency for the data to show a systematic increase or decrease over time. The alteration of phases within the design may show that the direction of behavior changes as the intervention is applied or withdrawn. Figure 5-12 (middle panel) illustrates a hypothetical example in which slopes have changed over the course of the phase in an ABAB design. The initial baseline slope is reversed by the intervention, reinstated when the intervention is withdrawn, and again reversed in the final phase. A change in slope would still be an important criterion even if there was no slope in baseline. A change from no trend (horizontal line) during baseline to a trend (increase or decrease in behavior) during the intervention phase would also constitute a change in slope.

A third characteristic refers to a *shift in level,* which is a little less familiar as a concept than mean and slope. A shift in level refers to a break in the graphical display of the data or a discontinuity of performance from the end of one phase to the beginning of the next phase. A shift in level is independent of the change in mean. When one asks about what happened immediately after the intervention was implemented or withdrawn, the concern is over the level of performance. Figure 5-12 (bottom panel) shows change in level across phases in ABAB design. Whenever the phase was altered, behavior assumed a new rate, that is, it shifted up or down rather quickly. It so happens that a change in level in this latter example would also be accompanied by a change in mean across the phases. However, level and mean changes do not necessarily go together. It is possible that a

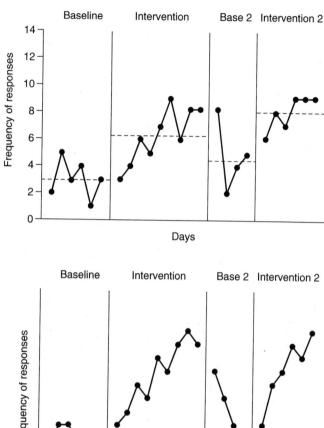

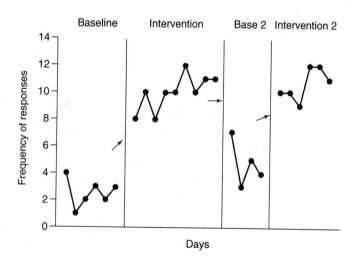

FIGURE 5-12 Data evaluation. Upper panel shows performance in an ABAB design in which there are clear changes in means (dashed lines) across phases. Middle panel shows changes in slope or trend from one phase to the next. Both intervention phases show an accelerating scope; the first and second baseline phases show no trend or a decelerating trend. Bottom panel shows a shift in level. The arrows point to the changes in level or the discontinuities associated with a change from one phase to another.

rapid change in level occurs but that the mean remains the same across phase or that the mean changes but no abrupt shift in level has occurred.

Changes in means, slope, and levels across phases frequently accompany each other. Yet they are separate characteristics of the data and can occur alone or in combination. Judging the extent to which these characteristics are evident across phases and whether the changes are consistent with the requirements of the particular design. When changes in mean, slope, and level go together, conclusions about the impact of the intervention are especially compelling. In such cases, the data across phases may not overlap. *Nonoverlapping data* refer to the pattern in which the values of the data points during the baseline phase do not approach any of the values of the data points attained during the intervention phase. Rather than give examples to apply these data evaluation characteristics, the reader is encouraged to apply these to examples already given in this chapter. The question to use when perusing the graphs for examples is whether you consider the demonstration to show that the intervention was likely to account for the change, based on the characteristics outlined in Table 5-1 and illustrated in this section.

Deciding Whether the Change is Important

The characteristics discussed previously focus on whether the change has occurred and is likely to be due to the intervention. Demonstrating that a reliable or genuine change has occurred by itself does not address the question of whether the change is important or makes a difference in the life of the person or those in contact with the person. For example, an intervention with three obese individuals in a multiple-baseline design might show that each individual lost weight as the intervention was introduced. The data characteristics across phases for each individual (e.g., change in mean, slope, level) might convey that the effects were reliable and due to the intervention. Yet this leaves unanswered a critical question, namely, do the changes make a difference. Suppose each individual was 100 lbs. (45.4 kg) overweight and lost 10 lbs. (4.5 kg) during the intervention. This reduction is not one that might affect the individual's health or make a real difference in everyday life.

A major criterion for evaluating change is the applied or clinical significance of the effects of treatment. *Clinical significance* refers to the practical or applied value or importance of the effect of the intervention. The effects produced by the intervention should be large enough to be of practical value or have impact on the everyday lives of those who receive the intervention, as well as those in contact with them. In the case of obesity, for example, is the reduction in weight sufficient to improve health or to alter how the individuals view themselves?

In some cases, a change that is important might require virtual or complete elimination of the behavior. For example, treatment may reduce the frequency with which an autistic boy hits himself in the head from 100 times per hour to 50 times per hour. Although change has been achieved, a much larger change probably is needed to be of practical value. Self-injurious behavior is maladaptive and potentially dangerous, and it needs to be eliminated. For many other behaviors, smaller changes may be needed. For example, in developing social behavior of withdrawn, shy, or lonely individuals, one need not make a social butterfly but rather increase interactions in such a way that the person or others involved with the person see the change as making a difference.

In general, applied behavior analysis programs seek treatment effects that clearly improve the level of client functioning in everyday situations. Of course, seeking clinically significant effects is a goal of any intervention approach. The special feature of behavioral research is an effort to integrate criteria to evaluate the importance of therapeutic change in the assessment of intervention effects. Several criteria are used to evaluate the clinical significance of change. One criterion, for example, consists of showing that change in behavior places the individual within the normative range of functioning. Before the intervention, the individual may be extreme in level or type of behavior (e.g., aggressive acts, social withdrawal). In many instances, a clinically important change would be evident if the intervention returned the client to the level of functioning of persons in everyday life who have not been identified as in need of treatment.

The criteria for evaluating the clinical significance of change involve several issues related to the social context of behavioral research. The appropriate focus of treatment, the acceptability of the procedures that are used to achieve therapeutic change, and the adequacy or importance of the changes all involve evaluations of the community at large. Clinical significance will be discussed later in the broader social context of evaluating treatment and its effects.

SUMMARY AND CONCLUSIONS

This chapter discussed experimental designs that are used to evaluate the effects of intervention programs. Experimental designs are used to determine whether the intervention was responsible for change. In applied settings in which reinforcement programs are used, single-case designs dominate. A number of the commonly used single-case designs were presented including ABAB or reversal designs, multiple-baseline designs, and changing-criterion designs. Group designs were highlighted because they too are used to evaluate behavioral interventions. The designs and their many variations reflect several ways of demonstrating the relation between the intervention and behavior change.

In some cases, application of one of the experimental designs is not feasible because of the demands of the situation, practical limitations, or immediate priorities regarding implementation of the intervention. Even if one of the specific experimental design strategies cannot be applied, assessment and use of the assessment information to evaluate client progress are critically important. Also, an approximation of the designs, such as evaluating performance over baseline and intervention phases (AB design), can still provide extremely useful information.

The purpose of the intervention is to achieve changes in behavior. Whether change has actually been achieved usually is judged by examining the graphed results to assess whether treatment was consistently associated with changes across phases. Changes in means (average performance), slopes, and abrupt shifts in level of performance across phases are key characteristics of the data that are used to decide whether the changes are systematic. The applied or clinical significance of change is also important to ensure that the intervention has made a difference in the life of the client.

In general, the methods of assessing and evaluating behavior modification programs, as discussed in this and the previous chapter, provide tools that are essential for implementing effective treatments. Identifying techniques to change behavior and obtaining clinically important effects depend on measuring the extent of the client's behavior before intervening, seeing whether or how much change is obtained with the intervention, making adjustments in the intervention accordingly, and determining whether the intervention is responsible for change. Now that these important features have been discussed, we can turn to the many behavioral techniques that have been developed and identified in this fashion.

KEY TERMS

ABAB design	Criteria to evaluate change	Random assignment
Baseline	Multiple-baseline design	Randomized controlled clinical trial
Changing-criterion design	Nonoverlapping data	Reversal phase
Clinical significance		

APPLYING PRINCIPLES AND TECHNIQUES TO EVERYDAY LIFE

1. A teacher wishes to change student behavior (sitting in one's seat, working quietly on the assignment without bothering others) in the classroom. The teacher calls you and wants a program to help. You design a marvelous reinforcement program that is the best ever invented. You convince the teacher that it is important to evaluate the program; however, as soon as you mention "reversal phase" the teacher is shocked at the thought and faints. When the teacher awakens, you have reconsidered your position and propose a multiple-baseline design. Give an example of what that would be (e.g., across times of the day, classrooms).

2. A friend of yours has desserts and candy throughout the day and wishes to change this through some behavior modification program. Using calories, number of sweets consumed each day, or some other measure of your choosing, how would you use a changing-criterion design to evaluate the program?

3. Draw a graph of a hypothetical program evaluated in an ABAB design. Fill in the hypothetical data (lines in each phase). How can you tell if behavior has reliably changed in each B phase? Invoke the criteria discussed in the chapter

and say what the criteria are and whether or not they are met. What are your conclusions about the effects of the program?

4. Clinical significance refers to the practical or applied importance of the change. The goal of course is to achieve a change that makes a difference in the individual's life. What would be the result of some program that seems to make a difference (is clinically significant) and a result of that same program that would not make any difference (is not clinically significant)? Take one behavior (e.g., tantrums, stuttering, room cleaning) and describe two different outcomes.

FOR FURTHER READING

Iwata, B.A., Bailey, J.S., Fuqua, R.W., Neef, N.A., Page, T.J., & Reid, D.H. (Eds.). (1989). *Methodological and conceptual issues in applied behavior analysis.* Lawrence, KS: Society of the Experimental Analysis of Behavior.

Kazdin, A.E. (1998). *Research design in clinical psychology* (3rd ed.). Needham Heights, MA: Allyn & Bacon.

Kazdin, A.E. (1993). Evaluation in clinical practice: Clinically sensitive and systematic methods of treatment delivery. *Behavior Therapy, 24,* 11–45.

Kratochwill, T.R., & Levin, J.R. (Eds.) (1992). *Single-case research design and analysis: New directions for psychology and education.* Mahwah, NJ: Lawrence Erlbaum.

NOTES

1. For a detailed discussion of various single-case designs that are used to evaluate behavioral programs and of the rationale underlying their use, other sources can be consulted (see For Further Reading).

2. Randomized controlled clinical trial, sometimes just referred to as randomized clinical trial, is a useful term and concept to know. When promising treatments are identified in the news but more work is needed, it is often the case that the randomized clinical trials have yet to be completed. A few randomized clinical trials are usually needed to provide evidence for a treatment.

CHAPTER 6

Positive and Negative Reinforcement

The primary task and challenge of behavior modification in applied settings is to develop prosocial and adaptive behaviors. This is evident in many different settings and contexts such as treatment, education, and rehabilitation. Inappropriate, deficient, or maladaptive behaviors in such settings prompt the need for intervention. For example, autistic and mentally retarded children often lack a variety of appropriate personal, social, and communication skills. Delinquent youths engage in aggressive and criminal behavior. Clearly in these instances, adaptive and prosocial behaviors need to be developed. In some instances, the appropriate behaviors may be performed but only in some settings and not others (e.g., child compliance and cooperative behavior at home but not at school). In such instances, reinforcement techniques play a central role and indeed are the mainstay of intervention techniques.

Of course, reinforcement is not just for problematic behavior in special populations. In everyday life and society at large, a number of adaptive behaviors are promoted (i.e., by parents, teachers, medical establishment) such as eating nutritious foods, exercising, driving safely, and working productively at a job. These are not problem behaviors of special populations but behaviors whose increase can improve life. In these cases too, low-frequency behaviors have to be increased, new behaviors have to be established, or behaviors have to be developed in new situations. Because these goals entail developing or increasing behavior, reinforcement techniques are appropriate.

Even in cases where the primary intent is to eliminate undesirable behaviors, reinforcement invariably plays a key role. Merely eliminating an undesirable behavior does not guarantee that prosocial and adaptive behaviors will be evident. Indeed, as discussed at greater length in the chapter on punishment, eliminating behavior does not teach what the desirable behaviors are. For example, eliminating tantrums in a young child or drug use in a young adult does not necessarily result in prosocial and adaptive behaviors. These latter behaviors need to be developed. Reinforcement can develop socially appropriate behaviors that replace the undesirable behaviors. Reduction and elimination of undesirable behavior first comes to mind when people select treatment goals. The challenge is to identify a positive opposite—an alternative behavior that is prosocial and adaptive. This latter behavior is the goal of the program and can be reinforced. Thus when teachers do not want their students to shout out and throw things in class, the task is to identify what behaviors the teachers *do* want (e.g., raising hands, speaking when called on, using materials correctly). Reinforcement can eliminate the undesirable behaviors by being provided for positive opposites. Thus reinforcement plays a critical role in behavior-change programs. This chapter considers positive and negative reinforcement. Greater attention is given to positive reinforcement because it plays a central role in almost all behavioral interventions in applied settings.

POSITIVE REINFORCEMENT

Positive reinforcement refers to an increase in the probability or likelihood of a response following the presentation of a positive reinforcer. Whether a particular event is a positive reinforcer is defined by its effects on behavior. If response frequency increases when followed by the event, that event is a positive reinforcer.

Types of Reinforcers

Several different types of reinforcers are available for use in behavioral interventions. Selection is influenced by characteristics related to their varied effects on behavior and their ease of administration in applied settings.

Food and Other Consumables

Food qualifies as a primary reinforcer because its reinforcing value is unlearned. Because food is a primary reinforcer, it is very powerful. Studies have occasionally used food as a reinforcer, including cereal, candy, cookies, crackers, soft drinks, and ice cream. Nonfood consumables (e.g., chewing gum) have also been used as reinforcers. Because food is a primary reinforcer, its effects should apply widely among different client populations. However, food is not used often in applied settings. The major reason is that food is not ordinarily present in, or a part of, the everyday situations in which behavioral interventions are applied. Introducing food into the situation is not necessary to change behavior, given the availability, effectiveness, and ease of delivering other reinforcers. Food is noted here because it represents an important type (primary) of reinforcer and because it sensitizes us to states of the individual (deprivation, satiation) relevant to reinforcer delivery.

Occasionally, food can be used in some applied settings, particularly, institutional facilities for developmentally disabled individuals, where snacks and food can be used in specific training sessions to develop behavior. For example, an interesting use of food as a reinforcer was reported with hospitalized physically handicapped children 1 to $3\frac{1}{2}$ years of age (Riordan, Iwata, Finney, Wohl, & Stanley, 1984). These children also showed several feeding problems such as not eating enough food, spitting out food fed to them, or eating a limited range of foods that provided an insufficient range of vitamins or minerals. During mealtime, several different foods were fed to the children (presented one bite at a time) to identify the foods that they ate and preferred. The preferred foods were used as a reinforcer for eating a bite of other foods. For example, one of the children preferred dry cereal and graham crackers. These were used as reinforcers. When the child ate a bite of some other food (fruit, vegetable, meat, or starch), the preferred food was immediately delivered. At first, the preferred food was presented with the target food for a few bites; then the preferred food was delivered immediately after a bite of a target food. After several trials, the preferred food (reinforcer) was administered only intermittently. The use of preferred food increased the bites and consumption of a broader range of nutritionally balanced food.

Strengths and Limitations. The effectiveness of food and other consumables depends heavily on the deprivation state of the individual. If the individual is not at least partially deprived, food may be a weak reinforcer. Investigators sometimes use food reinforcement before mealtime or during mealtime itself. A difficulty with food as a reinforcer is that its reinforcement value may decline rather quickly.

Even if the individual is hungry before training, as training proceeds on a given day, hunger and the reinforcing value of food may decline.

The effectiveness of food reinforcement depends on the type of food. Preferences vary for different foods, and hence it is likely that some foods are more reinforcing than others or that some foods are not reinforcing at all unless the individual has been deprived of all food. Specific foods used in a given program may not be reinforcing for particular individuals. For example, although ice cream may serve as a reinforcer for most children, the flavor may influence its reinforcing properties. When a single food or consumable is used, the possibility exists that the event will not be effective with a number of people. Moreover, the preferences of a given individual change from time to time, so a single food or other consumable may have short-lived reinforcing properties.

Administration of food reinforcers can raise problems. The delivery and consumption of food after a response sometimes interrupt ongoing behavior. For example, if a special education classroom teacher distributed candy to her students while they were working attentively on an assignment, they might be distracted momentarily from the task. Also, the consumption of the reinforcer may temporarily distract the students. Typically, one does not want to interrupt ongoing prosocial behavior in any way that competes with performing that behavior.

Delivering reinforcers immediately after behavior is important in developing behavior. Usually, it is difficult to dispense food and other consumables immediately because they are cumbersome to carry or dispense. The setting in which food is used dictates the ease with which a particular type of food can be dispensed. Parents at home and staff in some institutions may be able to dispense food readily, depending on the type of food and ease of carrying a supply (e.g., small candies). In everyday life, parents, teachers, peers, employers, and others cannot easily carry food or other consumables with them all of the time for use as reinforcers.

Many behavior modification programs are administered in group settings. Food is not easily administered to several individuals in a group because administration to several individuals takes some time (e.g., selecting the quantity of food or passing a piece to each individual). Consequently, food is not particularly well suited to group situations in which everyone receives reinforcers. Many programs using food have been conducted on an individual basis rather than in groups.

Finally, ethical and legal concerns restrict the use of food and consumable items. These reinforcers are most effective when clients are deprived. Yet, deprivation of food is ethically unacceptable. Also, such deprivation violates legal rights of clients. Hence, food deprivation is not a viable treatment alternative. When food is used as a reinforcer, clients ought not and cannot be deprived of food they would normally receive. Thus food and consumables are often given over and above the items normally available to clients. Because clients normally have access to food, the extra food used as a reinforcer may be less potent than it would be if they were deprived.

Even if the ethical and legal concerns could be surmounted, people often object to the use of food. Adding food to a setting where it would not otherwise be used, for example, in the classroom or on the playground, has potential health consequences (e.g., increased sugar intake if candy is used) that raise concerns of teachers and parents. For example, parents often object to an elementary school teacher dispensing candies throughout the day for such behaviors as paying attention, working at one's desk, and playing cooperatively. Such an intervention flies in the face of common sense and experience and understandably is objectionable. In light of practical, ethical and legal issues, and other objections, food is not used very often. Also, much of applied research is conducted in community settings, business and industry, and everyday social intercourse. Administering a mouthful of this or that is not feasible or desirable.

Food and other consumables are used in situations where other events such as approval are not effective. For example, in institutions for severely and profoundly mentally retarded persons, food reinforcement is used to develop such behaviors as feeding oneself or using sounds, words, or gestures to communicate. In these applications, other reinforcers often are unavailable or weak in their effects, at least initially. Perhaps as important, food is useful in establishing the reinforcing properties of other events, such as praise, feedback, attention, smiles, and physical contact. Programs using food and other consumables invariably pair the delivery of the reinforcer with praise and other social events, so that these latter events can be used to change behavior. Perhaps the most common use of food is in reinforcement programs where several reinforcers are available and food (e.g., soda, snacks) can be selected as one option, as in a token economy discussed later.

Social Reinforcers

Social reinforcers such as verbal praise, attention, physical contact (including affectionate or approving touches, pats, and handholding), and facial expressions (including smiles, eye contact, nods of approval, and winks) are conditioned reinforcers. Numerous studies have shown that attention or praise from a parent, teacher, or peer exerts considerable control over behavior.

For example, in one program, praise was used to alter the behavior of a 13-year-old boy named Tom in a seventh-grade classroom (Kirby & Shields, 1972). Tom was of average intelligence but was doing poorly on his class assignments, particularly the arithmetic assignments. Also, he rarely paid attention to the lesson and constantly had to be reminded to work. Praise was used to improve his performance on arithmetic assignments. Each day in class, after he completed the arithmetic assignment, he was praised for correct answers on his arithmetic worksheet. At first, every couple of responses were praised, but the number of correct problems required for praise was gradually increased. The praise consisted merely of saying, "Good work" or "Excellent job," and similar comments. Figure 6-1 (upper portion) shows the improvements in Tom's rate of correct answers per minute in the treatment phases of an ABAB design. The lower portion shows that his attentive behavior also improved even though it was not focused on directly.

Many studies have shown that reinforcing academic performance not only improves the specific target behaviors but also increases classroom attentiveness and reduces disruptive behavior (Sulzer-Azaroff et al., 1988). In most classroom studies, teacher attention consists primarily of verbal praise supplemented with

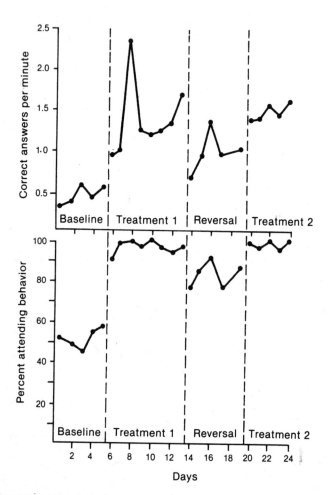

FIGURE 6-1 Number of correct arithmetic answers per minute and percentage of times scored as attending behavior as a function of baseline and treatment conditions.

(Source: Kirby & Shields, 1972)

facial expressions and physical contact. However, nonverbal teacher attention alone (consisting of smiles, physical contact, and approving nods contingent upon appropriate behavior) can also improve classroom deportment.

Social reinforcement can be readily used to change behavior in applied settings. Of course, social reinforcers exert influence in everyday life whether or not they are programmed for behavior change. Occasionally, deviant behavior is reinforced. For example, in late childhood and early adolescence, aggressive and antisocial peers unwittingly provide social reinforcement to maintain deviant behavior. During conversations among peers, comments that reflect rule-breaking behavior are followed by positive social reactions (e.g., attention, laughter) that increase such comments. In contrast, normative topics (non–rule-breaking behavior) are not reacted to positively (Dishion & Patterson, 1997). Interestingly, such interactions predict subsequent delinquent activity and hence may not be merely a matter of talk.

Strengths and Limitations. Social consequences have a variety of advantages as reinforcers. First, they are easily administered in everyday life and in a large number of situations. Providing praise takes little time, so there is no delay in praising a number of individuals immediately. Indeed, praise can be delivered to a group as a whole, as in a classroom. Second, praise need not disrupt the behavior that is reinforced. A person can be praised or receive a pat on the back while continuing to engage in appropriate behavior. Third, praise is a generalized conditioned reinforcer because it has been paired with many reinforcing events. Conditioned reinforcers may be less subject to satiation than food and other consumable items. Fourth, attention and praise are "naturally occurring" reinforcers employed in everyday life. Some reinforcers such as food and other consumables do not normally follow desirable behavior such as paying attention in a classroom, interacting socially with others, or working on a job. In contrast, social reinforcers such as attention from others or credit for a job well done occasionally do follow socially adaptive behaviors. Programming more of these for the purpose of changing behavior is in keeping with existing contingencies. Finally, behaviors developed with social reinforcement may be more easily maintained once the intervention is terminated. Social reinforcers in every day life may continue to follow those behaviors that were developed during treatment, even though they are no longer programmed to do so.

In general, social reinforcers are not objected to and are consistent with what many persons in everyday life believe are acceptable as reinforcers. In addition, although social reinforcers are used in everyday life, they are not delivered that often. During the course of a day, few of us receive or deliver praise contingent on behavior. This quasi-deprivation state may increase the effectiveness of social reinforcement when it is used as part of a behavior-change program (Vollmer & Iwata, 1991).

Before embarking on a program employing social reinforcement, it is important to bear a few considerations in mind. Praise, approval, and physical contact are not reinforcing for everyone. Indeed, for some individuals, praise may even be aversive (Walker, Hops, & Greenwood, 1981). Because social events (praise, approval, and physical contact) are employed in everyday life, it is important to establish them as reinforcers by pairing them with events that are already reinforcers.

Another consideration pertains to the administration of social reinforcers. In principle, it is easy to administer social reinforcers such as praise and attention; however, in practice, this can be difficult. Merely telling parents and teachers to administer praise without providing some aids to help them do that (e.g., feedback or praise for their own performance, systematically tracking how and when they praised) is not likely to increase praise for very long. It is easy to let desirable or good behavior go unnoticed and to attend to disruptive behavior. For example, parents are often instructed to praise their children when they are playing cooperatively rather than to attend (e.g., go in the room, give attention) to arguing, fighting, and tantrums. This is difficult for parents to do. It is sometimes easier to administer tangible rewards (e.g., tokens, stars) because the rewards themselves or the charts that keep track of the tokens serve to prompt parents, teachers, and others to deliver the reinforcers. Praise is more intangible and difficult to monitor and prompt on the part of parents and teachers and hence can go undelivered.

High-Probability Behaviors

The reinforcing events referred to previously include stimuli or specific events such as praise, smiles, food, or stars that are presented after a response. Yet, reinforcers are not limited to the stimuli presented to someone. Allowing an individual to engage in certain *responses* can be used as a reinforcer. When an individual is given the opportunity to select among various responses, behaviors performed with a relatively high frequency can reinforce behaviors performed with a relatively low frequency (Premack, 1965). If the opportunity to perform a more probable response is made contingent on performance of a less probable response, the frequency of the latter should increase. On the basis of laboratory research, the Premack principle has been formulated to reflect this relation: *Of any pair of responses or activities in which an individual engages, the more frequent one will reinforce the less frequent one.* Stated more simply, a higher-probability behavior can reinforce a lower-probability behavior.

To determine what behaviors are high or low in frequency requires observing the behaviors that a person performs when given the opportunity to engage in behavior without restraints, such as what someone does when given free time at home, at school, or on the weekends. A behavior observed to occur more frequently (e.g., playing at the computer, chatting on the telephone) can be used to follow and reinforce a lower-frequency behavior (e.g., studying, engaging in chores). For many children, playing with friends is performed at a higher frequency than is practicing a musical instrument. If the high-frequency behavior (playing with friends) is made contingent on the lower frequency behavior (playing the instrument), the lower-probability behavior will increase. In some ways the principle seems merely to reflect common sense. Yet, it is surprising how commonly the principle is violated every day, as parents say to their children, "Remember, when you get back from [insert a high-probability behavior here], you really have to start working on your [insert low-probability behavior]." Of course, this is not likely to lead to systematic development or performance of the low probability behavior.

For applied purposes, the Premack principle is useful for expanding the range of reinforcers that can be used to alter behavior. Activities selected with a higher frequency can often serve as reinforcers for activities selected with a lower frequency. As a practical guide, allowing persons to engage in preferred activities and to earn various privileges can reinforce behavior. Animal laboratory research has identified high-frequency behaviors by observing performance or by depriving animals of certain sorts of activities, thereby making such activities more likely in the future. In clinical applications, high-probability behaviors are often inferred from the client's expressed verbal preferences or from seeing what the client actually does in his or her free time. Stated preferences are a useful guideline but are never substitutes for direct observation in determining whether something serves as a reinforcer.

High-probability behaviors have been used effectively in several applied programs. For example, one program increased the extent to which mentally retarded adults engaged in daily exercise as part of their rehabilitation program (Allen & Iwata, 1980). During baseline, opportunities and prompts were provided to encourage these clients to exercise (e.g., do knee bends, sit-ups) and to play games involving physical activity (e.g., various ball games). Playing games, the more frequent activity, was used to reinforce exercising. A group contingency was implemented in which everyone had to complete a minimum number of exercises before the games could be played. Exercising (lower-probability behavior) increased in frequency when playing games (higher-probability behavior) was contingent on this behavior.

Strengths and Limitations. High-probability behaviors offer distinct advantages as reinforcers. In most settings, activities or privileges are readily available. For example, in the home, watching television, playing on a computer, interacting with peers, or using the family automobile are likely to be high-probability behaviors, depending on the person's age. At school, engaging in recess or games and reading entertaining materials may serve a similar function. In hospital and rehabilitation facilities, engaging in special recreational events or access to more desirable living quarters can also be used as reinforcers. In short, activities and privileges that can be made contingent on performance are usually available in any setting. Hence, extra reinforcers (e.g., candy or money) need not be introduced into the setting.

There are limitations in using high-probability behaviors as reinforcing events. First, access to an activity cannot always immediately follow low-probability behavior. For example, in a classroom setting, access to recess or games cannot readily be used to reinforce behavior immediately. Such access may need to be delayed so that the reinforcing activity (e.g., games) does not interrupt the task (e.g., writing a story). Immediate rewards such as praise or a token (exchangeable for the activity) can help bridge the delay between behavior and the reinforcing activity, so that some reinforcement is provided immediately. Thus the child can be told by the parent that because a specific behavior (playing cooperatively with a sibling) was "Great!" (praise), he or she can stay up 15 minutes extra at bedtime. The praise is delivered immediately, an important condition for effective reinforcement delivery. The praise may in fact be sufficient to develop the behavior at a high rate. However, the extra bedtime privilege may well add to the effectiveness by introducing an important reinforcer. When behavior is developed, the delay in providing the high-probability behavior may not be problematic, but early in a reinforcement program, the reinforcer ought to be delivered immediately.

Second, providing an activity is sometimes an all-or-none enterprise, so that it is either earned or not earned. This can limit flexibility in administering the reinforcer. For example, activities such as going on a field trip or vacation or to a sleepover, party, baseball game, or special restaurant are reasonable activities to serve as reinforcers. Yet these activities cannot be parceled out so that "portions" of them are earned. They have to be given in their entirety or not at all. If someone's behavior comes very near but does not quite meet the performance criterion for reinforcement, a decision has to be made whether to provide the reinforcer. One solution is to shape behavior by initially setting low criteria for earning the activity. Gradually, the criteria for earning the reinforcer are increased. Another solution is to incorporate many privileges and activities into the reinforcement program. Different behaviors or varying degrees of a given behavior can then be reinforced with different privileges or with a choice among privileges. These are all good solutions but they convey the problem, relying on a single activity, privilege, or high-probability behavior can raise obstacles of administration.

Third, relying on one or two activities as reinforcers runs the risk that some individuals may not find them reinforcing. Since preferences for activities may be idiosyncratic, different activities need to be available. One alternative is to provide free time as the reinforcer, so that individuals can choose from a variety of activities.

A final consideration in using activities and privileges is that in many institutions, activities must be freely available to the clients. Activities that might be made contingent on performance are delivered independently of the client's performance. For example, by law, many activities (e.g., opportunities for exercise, socialization) must be provided noncontingently to ensure that institutionalized persons, such as psychiatric patients, prisoners, delinquents, and mentally retarded children and adults, are not deprived of basic human rights. Hence, the person who develops a behavior-change program must provide special activities over and above those offered as part of routine care. Notwithstanding these considerations, privileges and activities often are incorporated into reinforcement programs. When used as part of a larger reinforcement program with multiple reinforcers, many of the concerns are eliminated.

Feedback

Providing information about how a person has performed can serve as a reinforcer. Feedback is implicit in the delivery of any reinforcer because it indicates which responses those who provide reinforcement regard as appropriate or desirable. Thus when reinforcers such as food, praise, activities, or points are provided, a client receives feedback on how well he or she is doing. However, feedback can be employed independently of explicit approval or other reinforcers. An individual can be informed of his or her behavior or of the extent to which the behavior has changed. *Feedback refers to knowledge of results of one's performance and does not necessarily include additional events that may be reinforcing in their own right.*

Several studies have used feedback as a way of influencing driving, traffic, and car accidents (e.g., Ragnarsson & Bjorgvinsson, 1991; Van Houten, Malenfant, &

Rolider, 1985). In one of the early demonstrations, feedback was used to control the speeding of drivers on a highway entering a residential area (Van Houten et al., 1980). Speeding was measured by a radar unit concealed in a litter can near the highway. After baseline observations, feedback was provided in the form of a conspicuous road sign that indicated the percentage of drivers not speeding on the previous day and the best percentage record obtained to date. Using an ABAB design, feedback was shown to reduce speeding. Moreover, a 57% reduction in the number of accidents was also noted, compared with the 2-year period before feedback had been implemented.

Feedback often is creatively combined with other reinforcers. For example, one program focused on the extent to which individuals were exposed to the sun, a known risk factor for skin cancer. The incidence (number of new cases) of skin cancer is increasing, which is assumed to be the result of a change in lifestyle, increased exposure to the sun, and depletion of the ozone layer. Individuals exposed to the sun rarely engage in sufficiently protective behavior. In this study, an effort was made to increase the extent to which individuals attending two private swimming pools engaged in protective behaviors (Lombard, Neubauer, Canfield, & Winett, 1991). The target behaviors included wearing a shirt to cover the upper body, wearing a hat, using a sunscreen, wearing zinc oxide (covering) on one's face, and other behaviors. An intervention was implemented by providing information posters to convey how to protect oneself, daily feedback posters noting the percentage of adults and children who had performed protective behaviors on the previous day, and a raffle for individuals who completed a form pledging to engage in "safe-sun" practices. The intervention was implemented at two pools at different points in time. As shown in Figure 6-2, the intervention led to increases in the percentage of individuals who engaged in two or more protective behaviors. The results are instructive in showing that relatively simple informational and feedback interventions can lead to change. The magnitude of the results also suggests many individuals did not change and that more potent interventions are needed.

An important area involving feedback is *biofeedback*. Biofeedback consists of providing information to people about various physiological processes such as blood pressure, heart rate, muscle tension, and brain waves. Immediate information is provided to help clients learn to control various bodily processes. Biofeedback represents an important area of research and will be discussed later (see Chapter 10).

Strengths and Limitations. Because of the ease with which feedback can be applied, it has been used with a variety of client populations and in a variety of settings. Feedback can be employed readily when there is an explicit performance criterion, such as academic achievement or work productivity. In other situations, various criteria can be set, such as cigarettes smoked, calories consumed, or days of exercise. Daily feedback can convey how well the client is doing in relation to the criterion. Specifying a criterion for performance is essential so that the desired level of performance is clear.

An extremely important consideration in using feedback is that its effects often are weak and inconsistent. Feedback has been generally effective, but usually

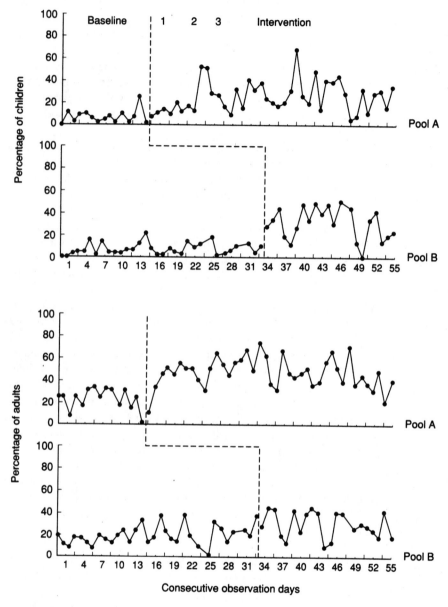

FIGURE 6-2 Percentage of children (upper graph) and adults (lower graph) who showed any two or more protective behaviors on consecutive observation days. The intervention was introduced in stages and in a multiple-baseline design across the two pools.

(Source: Lombard, Neubauer, Canfield, & Winett, 1991)

less effective alone than when combined with other reinforcers such as praise, privileges, or tokens. Hence, feedback is not one of the more potent methods of altering behavior. The moderate effects of feedback are not an argument against its use. In most settings, feedback is not given for performance. When it is given, feedback is often very intermittent or delayed (e.g., periodic work evaluations, end-of-term grades, adherence to safety rules on the job). Feedback might be more routinely provided not merely to gain any benefits it could provide, but also to serve as an occasion to provide more potent reinforcers such as social attention and praise.

Programs based on feedback are often easier to implement than are other reinforcement programs, such as token economies. Also, people who implement a feedback program may be more favorably disposed to delivering feedback alone than to providing extrinsic reinforcers. For these reasons, it may be useful to begin with a program based on feedback, perhaps paired with praise, and then to resort to a more potent source of reinforcement and a more complex program if the desired goals have not been achieved.

Although feedback often is not very potent by itself, an exception would be those situations in which some other reinforcer or consequence is clearly associated with the information. For example, providing time to complete a certain distance for a runner or swimmer constitutes feedback (knowledge of results). Yet other reinforcers are inherent in this situation, including self-praise, praise by a coach, or association of a specific time with another later consequence (e.g., school, city, or world record; Olympic medal).

Systematic and conspicuous feedback is likely to exert impact if it was readily available and if the information could be connected to other consequences. Consider a hypothetical feedback system related to the food we consume on a given day. Suppose a visible mark (e.g., colored strip on the back of our hand) emerged and became longer and brighter in color (pink, to rose, to flaming red) as a function of how much fat or junk food we consumed within the past 24 hours. Suppose as well that some criterion was established so that flaming red would signal that a person was in the danger or risk zone for heart disease, weight gain, or some such other consequence. Immediate and conspicuous feedback when associated with other consequences is likely to exert influence. This is analogous to the feedback provided by many exercise machines that provide ongoing information about distance run, calories spent, and elapsed time. No doubt many would not respond to such ongoing feedback, but many would.

Tokens

Tokens are conditioned reinforcers such as poker chips, coins, tickets, stars, points, or check marks. They are generalized reinforcers because they can be exchanged for a variety of reinforcing events referred to as *backup reinforcers*. The tokens take on value because of the reinforcers with which they are associated. This can occur immediately by merely instructing individuals about what the tokens can be exchanged for or through direct experience of exchanging the tokens for backup reinforcers. In devising a behavior-change program, tokens serve as a way to use many reinforcers and hence overcome the objection or concerns associated with any single type of reinforcer.

A reinforcement system based on tokens is referred to as a *token economy*. In a token economy, tokens function in the same way that money does in national economies. Tokens are earned and then used to purchase backup reinforcers such as food and other consumables, activities, and privileges. The basic requirements of a token economy include specification of (1) target behaviors, (2) number of tokens that can be earned for performance of the behaviors, (3) backup reinforcers that are available, and (4) number of tokens the backup reinforcers cost.

The use of tokens has a history antedating behavior modification in institutional settings such as schools, hospitals, and prisons (Kazdin, 1978). For example, in the 1800s, before token economies were formally developed and evaluated in research, a "mark" system was implemented in a prison in Australia (Maconochie, 1847). A goal was to overcome the punitive and inhumane treatment of prisoners and to foster adaptive behavior. Prisoners could earn marks (tokens) based on their work and good conduct. The marks could be exchanged for essential items such as food, shelter, and clothes, but also early release from prison. The results were reported to be very effective in relation to future crimes and incarceration of those released from the program, although conclusions are precluded by the absence of a careful evaluation. Current applications reflect a greater understanding of how reinforcement operates and how behavior changes are attained and maintained than pioneering efforts like this prison program.

Seminal work leading to current use of tokens as reinforcers can be traced to a token economy begun in a psychiatric hospital in the early 1960s (Ayllon & Azrin, 1968b). Psychiatric patients earned tokens (coins) for a variety of jobs and tasks on the ward, such as assisting with meals, doing chores, leading other patients in activities, and taking care of their own basic needs. The tokens could be exchanged for various privileges (e.g., opportunities for social interaction with staff, movies, trips to the nearby town), improved room facilities, and articles at a store on the ward. This initial program illustrated the feasibility of implementing a system of rewards that encompassed several individuals, behaviors, and backup rewards. The program improved patient behavior. The effects and systematic evaluation of the program greatly stimulated extension of the token economy.

Token economies have been used extensively in psychiatric hospitals. For example, in one of the most carefully evaluated programs, patients received tokens (colored plastic strips) for such behaviors as attending activities on the ward, group meetings, and therapy sessions, as well as for grooming, making one's bed, showering, engaging in appropriate mealtime behaviors, and socially interacting (Paul & Lentz, 1977). Tokens could be exchanged for a variety of backup events such as purchasing cosmetics, candy, cigarettes, and clothing; renting chairs or bedside stands for one's room; ordering items from a mail-order catalog; using a piano, record player, or radio; spending time in a lounge; watching television; or having a private room and sleeping late. As patients improved in the ward, they advanced to higher levels within the program, in which more reinforcers were available and higher criteria were set for performance. Patients could "buy" themselves off the system by doing well, and each carried a "credit card" that allowed free access to all of the available reinforcers as long as personal performance was up to standards. The program was very successful in reducing bizarre behaviors, improving social interaction and communication skills, and developing participation in activities. The gains were reflected in the number of patients discharged and in their assimilation into the community over $1\frac{1}{2}$ to 5 years after the program ended.

The token economy has been extended to many other settings. A particularly influential program was based on a token economy used to rehabilitate delinquent boys who committed various offenses (e.g., thefts, fighting, school truancy, academic failure) (Fixsen, Phillips, Phillips, & Wolf, 1976). The program was conducted at a homestyle cottage setting called Achievement Place and was managed by two houseparents. The boys could earn points for such behaviors as watching the news, reading newspapers, keeping neat and clean, performing chores around the house, and receiving good grades at school. Points could be lost for poor grades, aggressive talk (making threats), disobeying rules, lying, stealing, being late, fighting, and other disruptive behaviors. Points were used to purchase privileges such as staying up late, going downtown, watching television, using tools, riding a bicycle, and receiving an allowance. Interestingly, the boys actively participated in running the program by supervising one another's work, recording their own behavior, and developing and enforcing rules among their peers. The program was effective in altering a variety of behaviors (e.g., social interaction, completion of homework, chores) in the home setting. While the program was in effect, youths participating in the program committed fewer criminal offenses in the community and had fewer contacts with police than did delinquents placed on probation or in other settings where this program was not in effect (Kirigin, Braukmann, Atwater, & Wolf, 1982; Kirigin, Wolf, Braukmann, Fixsen, & Phillips, 1979).

Not all token economies are based on groups or administered on a large scale. Token reinforcement is an effective way to intervene with one or a few individuals. For example, a token system was used to treat patients referred for drug addiction (Budney, Higgins, Delaney, Kent, & Bickel, 1991). Two adult males (Phil, age 28; Mike, age 35) were seen separately for cocaine addiction. Both also used marijuana, which the authors report is the case for 40% to 50% of persons who are addicted to cocaine. Assessment of cocaine and marijuana use was accomplished by urinalyses that detected use within the previous 72 hours. Assessment was conducted four times a week to provide opportunities for earning tokens. Points were provided when the assessment indicated no sign of cocaine use. Bonus points were given for extended periods without a sign of drug use. (Providing reinforcers for consistent performance is an excellent addition to a reinforcement program.) Points could be exchanged for small amounts of money or goods and services, including movie tickets, sporting events, ski-lift tickets, and dinner certificates. The purpose of using these backup rewards was not only to imbue the points with value but also to involve the individuals in prosocial activities and, it was hoped, to develop a reinforcing drug-free lifestyle. After 12 weeks of the program, a maintenance phase was initiated to reduce the frequency of the checks. In the final phase, marijuana use was added to the program. To earn tokens, the tests had to show that the individual did not use cocaine or marijuana.

Figure 6-3 plots the number of negative (no sign of drug use) urine specimens in a cumulative graph for each person.[1] The figure shows that when reinforcement was given for cocaine abstinence, tests for cocaine use were negative. Marijuana continued to be used until the final phase, in which abstinence from both cocaine and marijuana were reinforced. The sequence of interventions across two individuals seen at the clinic and across two drugs follows the criteria of a multiple-baseline design. The pattern suggests that the token reinforcement program was responsible for the change. Follow-up assessment, including reports from others (girlfriend, roommate) and from the clients themselves, indicated no use of cocaine but some occasional use of marijuana.

The adaptability of the token economy can be illustrated by moving from the focus on one or two individuals in the above example, to a larger-scale application in business and industry. In this example, the focus was on worker safety in mining (Fox, Hopkins, & Anger, 1987). The study was conducted at two open-pit mines, one in Wyoming and the other in Arizona. Uranium was extracted and processed at one of the mines; coal was extracted and processed at the other. The two mines used similar equipment (trucks, bulldozers) and procedures (strip mining, crushing, storing materials). The goals of the program were to decrease job-related injuries, days lost from work due to such injuries, and costs (due to medical care, insurance, and equipment damage) among employees in each mine.

An incentive in the form of tokens (trading stamps) was provided at the end of each month to workers who had not been injured or had not required medical care because of an accident. Trading stamps were also given to all members of a group that worked under a particular supervisor if no one in the group had been injured. Bonus stamps were available to workers whose suggestions for improving safety in the facility were adopted. Trading stamps could also be lost (response cost) for missing work due to injury or for causing an accident. The trading stamps could be exchanged at a nearby redemption center that carried hundreds of items, such as small appliances, barbecue grills, spice racks, and clocks. The program was introduced to each mine in a multiple-baseline design and integrated with the mine's routine practices for several years. Figure 6-4 shows a marked reduction in the number of accidents among workers (upper panel) as well as a reduction in monetary costs to the company (lower panel).

Token economies have been used with a variety of populations other than those illustrated here, including persons with mental retardation, alcoholism or drug addiction, prisoners, geriatric or nursing-home residents, and outpatient children and adults (Glynn, 1990; Kazdin, 1982c). Similarly, the various settings in which token economies have been applied include the home, schools, institutions, hospitals, day-care centers, nursing homes, and business and industry. Probably the setting most often used is in the home where parents use points, marks on a chart, or stars on a temporary basis to foster behaviors such as completing chores, homework, taking care of pets, and so on. Simple programs are an excellent way to manage behavior, to move away from nagging, reprimands, and punishment in general. Usually in such applications tokens are not "needed." That is, the behavior could be changed with improved prompts, praise, and shaping. Yet the tokens provide a good way to structure and prompt parent behavior so the consequences are applied systematically.

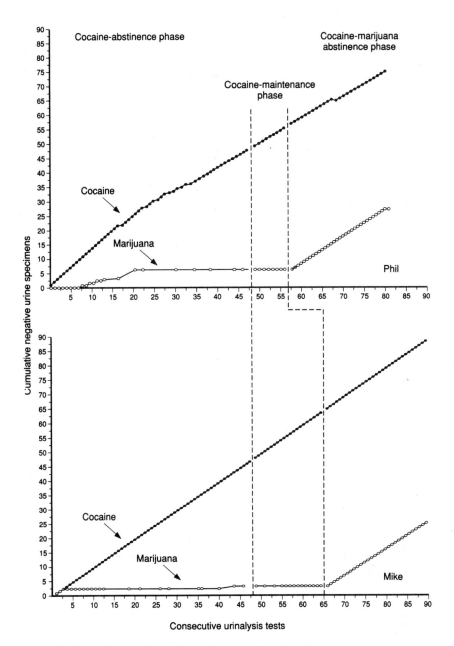

FIGURE 6-3 Cumulative number of negative cocaine and marijuana urinalysis results obtained with Phil and Mike during three phases of treatment as a functions of tests conducted throughout treatment. Cocaine and marijuana test results are presented by closed and open symbols, respectively. Steep slopes in the cumulative record indicate change; horizontal lines indicate no change.

(Source: Budney, Higgins, Delaney, Kent, & Bickel, 1991)

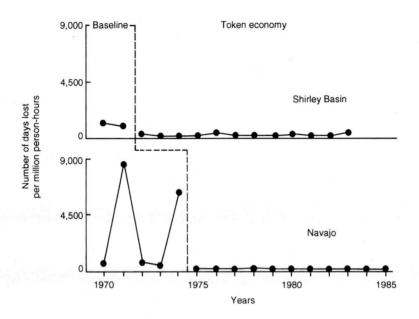

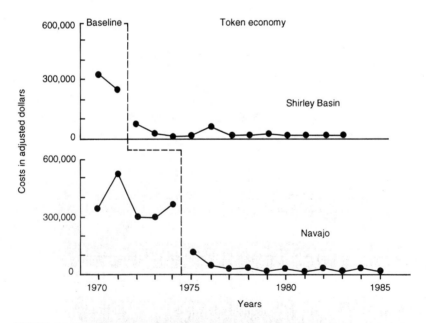

FIGURE 6-4 Yearly number of days lost from work, per million person-hours worked, because of work-related injuries (upper figure) and yearly cost, adjusted for hours worked and inflation, resulting from accidents and injuries (lower figure).

(Source: Fox, Hopkins, & Anger, 1987)

Strengths and Limitations. Tokens offer several advantages. First, they are potent reinforcers and can often develop behaviors at a higher level than those developed by other conditioned reinforcers such as praise, approval, and feedback. Thus it is often useful to begin with a token reinforcement program to obtain high levels of performance. After performance is consistently high, behavior can be maintained with praise or activities that may be more naturally occurring events in the setting. Second, tokens bridge the delay between the target response and backup reinforcement. If a reinforcer other than tokens (e.g., an activity) cannot be delivered immediately after the target response has been performed, tokens can be delivered instead and used to purchase a backup reinforcer later. Third, because tokens are backed up by a variety of reinforcers, they are less subject to satiation than are other reinforcers. If a person is no longer interested in one or two backup reinforcers, usually there are many other reinforcers that are of value. Fourth, tokens can be easily administered without interrupting the target response. Tokens do not require consumption, as with food, or the performance of behaviors that may interrupt the target response, as with participation in a special activity. Fifth, tokens permit administering a single reinforcer (tokens) to individuals who ordinarily have different reinforcer preferences. Those preferences can be exercised in the exchange of backup reinforcers. Hence, with tokens, there is less likelihood that the reinforcers will be of value to only a few of the individuals in the setting. Finally, tokens permit parceling out of other reinforcers such as privileges and activities that have to be earned in an all-or-none fashion. Tokens can be earned toward the purchase of a large or valuable backup reinforcer.

There are potential disadvantages in employing tokens. First, in some programs, backup reinforcers extraneous to the setting are introduced. For example, in a classroom program, tokens may be backed up with food. Food is not normally presented in a class and eventually needs to be eliminated. Of course, in a token economy, backup reinforcers normally unavailable in the setting need not be introduced. Tokens can be used to purchase access to ordinary privileges, activities, and other events available in the setting.

Second, introducing tokens may raise concerns. Tokens constitute an event not present in most settings, with stark exceptions such as money and grades. Parents and teachers often object to introducing tokens and delivering them for behavior, in large part because many children perform the desired behaviors without such inducements. The objection is understandable, but the key point to convey is that the goal to token reinforcement is to develop the behavior. Tokens can be used temporarily to develop behavior in large part because the individual in fact does not consistently perform the behavior and because other interventions that parents and teachers usually use are less likely to be effective.

Third, and related to the previous concern, is the task of removing the token system after behavioral gains have been made. Clients learn that the presence of tokens signals that desirable behavior will be reinforced; the absence of tokens signals that desirable behavior will not be reinforced. Consequently, desirable behavior may decline quickly as soon as token reinforcement is ended. However, specific procedures are available to withdraw token reinforcement programs without a loss of behavioral gains (see Chapter 12).

Another possible disadvantage of tokens is that individuals in token economies may obtain them in unauthorized ways. For example, clients may steal tokens from one another. If tokens can be obtained without performing the target responses, their effect on behavior will diminish. To combat the stealing of tokens, tokens can be individually coded so that they differ for each individual.

General Comments

The variety of reinforcers provides a great deal of flexibility in devising reinforcement programs. At the very minimum, praise, activities, and privileges can be used in virtually any setting. The use of consumables may be limited by restrictions of the setting. For example, food may be too difficult to administer in a large group. Although tokens are usually the most powerful positive reinforcer in applied settings, they may not be needed. Praise, privileges, and feedback may be very effective. A token economy is somewhat more difficult to implement than other reinforcement programs. A token program requires delivering tokens and backup reinforcers, rather than just one reinforcer; keeping track of token earnings and raising the prospect of other problems such as stealing or hoarding tokens; and withdrawing or fading tokens from the setting. These are not insurmountable, and token programs can vary in complexity. Hence, in some applications, tokens may be introduced only if more easily implemented reinforcers have not been effective. On the other hand, token programs are used from the beginning in many cases because they provide a clear way of specifying the relations among several target behaviors and different types of reinforcers. The programs are useful because they help guide behavior of those who administer programs and help make reinforcement delivery more consistent than less structured programs such as those based on social reinforcement.

The discussion of types of reinforcers should not imply that the various types of reinforcers are used independently. A program that incorporates a variety of reinforcers, such as a token economy, is likely to be more effective than one that uses only a few reinforcers. More than one type of reinforcer should be used for an additional reason. Programs using activities, feedback, consumables, or tokens should pair these events with praise and attention. Developing responsiveness to social reinforcers is important because social consequences are likely to be the major source of reinforcement once the client functions outside the treatment setting.

There is a final point to make about the reinforcers that are used to change behavior. It is important that the reinforcer is not objectionable because of the behaviors it is likely to foster. For example, in selecting reinforcers one might use cigarettes or cigars in a program for one's spouse, alcohol (taking a roommate to a happy hour) in a program for a college roommate, or time on the computer to play a violent and aggressive computer game in a program for a child who has problems with aggressive or antisocial behavior. Many potential reinforcers can be used to avoid what may foster maladaptive behavior or may likely have untoward consequences.

As a guideline when selecting reinforcers, it is important to ask, "Does use or consumption of the reinforcer itself foster behaviors that are objectionable to interested parties?" For example, if a person is exercising to get into shape or to maintain and control body weight, use of extra food (e.g., snack foods, desserts) and drinks (e.g., alcohol) as reinforcers might well be counterproductive. Examples about selecting reinforcers that may be inadvisable may not be sufficiently dramatic to make the point. The following is an alternative example: At a clinic for aggressive and antisocial children where I work, one 10-year-old boy really loves guns. Of course he is too young to buy them, but his mother is not. She purchased two handguns for him but did not give him access to the ammunition. Presumably, she could use access to the guns (e.g., time with guns, keeping guns in one's room) as a powerful positive reinforcer. At the clinic, we invariably praise parent creativity in identifying reinforcing consequences. However, in this case of course, the reinforcer fosters behaviors that most would view as horrible, maladaptive, and antisocial. In general consider reinforcers that do not promote maladaptive behavior.

FACTORS THAT INFLUENCE THE EFFECTIVENESS OF REINFORCEMENT

In the development of a reinforcement program, often the primary concern is with the type of reinforcer used. Clearly, the reinforcer is important and some reinforcers (e.g., tokens) tend to be more potent than others (e.g., feedback). Yet the effectiveness of the program depends on how the reinforcer is delivered. Indeed, a program is more likely to succeed or fail based on how reinforcement is delivered rather than which reinforcer among the alternatives is selected.

Contingent Application of Consequences

The most fundamental condition for the effective application of a reinforcer is that the reinforcer is *contingent* (or dependent) on behavior. This means that the reinforcer is provided only if the desired response is performed and otherwise not given. Thus, if one wishes to change, develop, or increase a specific behavior then the reinforcer must be given when that behavior occurs. If the reinforcer is provided regardless of whether the behavior occurs (noncontingently), behavior is not likely to change.

The contingent application of reinforcers is not necessarily an all-or-none matter. That is, in a sloppy program, the reinforcer may be contingent on some occasions but not others. For example, parents, teachers, and others who wish to implement behavioral programs often state that they have already used reinforcement, but with little or no success. Often they are quite correct. However, the reinforcement was usually carried out haphazardly, with slight-to-large violations of the factors on which effective application depends. The most stark violation is delivering reinforcement contingently on some occasions and noncontingently on other occasions.

The differences between contingent and noncontingent reinforcement are dramatic and clear. Contingent reinforcement usually leads to marked behavior change; noncontingent reinforcement leads to little or no change; and reinforcement administered contingently on some occasions but not on others leads to performance somewhere in the middle (Baer & Wolf, 1970; Kazdin, 1973; Redd & Birnbrauer, 1969). One might ask how noncontingent reinforcement can lead to any change in behavior. The reason is that noncontingent reinforcement accidentally follows the desired behavior on some occasions and hence constitutes weak and intermittent reinforcement for the behavior. Nevertheless, when the goal is to change behavior, noncontingent reinforcement should be avoided.

Delay of Reinforcement

The effectiveness of reinforcement depends on the delay between the behavior and the delivery of reinforcing consequences (food, praise, or points). Responses in close proximity to reinforcement are learned better than are responses remote from reinforcement. Thus to maximize the effect of reinforcement, a reinforcer should be delivered immediately after the target response. If this is not done, a response different from the target response may be performed during the intervening period. If that happens, the intervening response will be immediately reinforced, whereas the target response will be reinforced after a delay.

As an example, children are often praised (or punished) for a behavior long after the behavior has been performed. If a child straightens up his or her room, a parent would do well to provide praise immediately. If praise is postponed until the end of the day, it is much too delayed to have strong or perhaps any impact. Moreover, a variety of intervening responses may occur, including, perhaps, messing up the room. Similarly, in classroom settings, children are often told how "good" they are when they are on the verge of becoming restless or disruptive. The teacher may say that the class was well behaved in the morning and that he or she hopes it will remain that way. Such praise will be minimally effective because of the delay after the behavior. The primary task in a reinforcement program is to "catch the person" performing the behavior and to provide immediate reinforcement.

Immediate reinforcement is especially important when the target response is being developed. After a response has been performed consistently, the amount of time between the response and reinforcement can be increased without a decrement in performance. For example, in classroom settings, students sometimes receive points or privileges daily while high rates of academic behavior are developing. After such behavior has stabilized, the reinforcers can be delivered every other day or every few days without a deleterious effect on performance. If a program begins with delayed reinforcement, behavior may not change at all or may change less rapidly than it would if reinforcement were immediate. After a behavior has been well developed, it is desirable to change from immediate to delayed reinforcement so that the behavior is not dependent on immediate consequences. Many consequences in everyday life (accomplishments, wages, grades, and fame) follow long after a series of responses has been completed.

Magnitude or Amount of the Reinforcer

The amount of reinforcement delivered for a response also influences behavior change. The greater the amount of the reinforcer delivered for a response, the more frequent the response will be. The amount of the reinforcer can usually be specified in such terms as quantity of food, number of points, or amount of money.

Although the magnitude of reinforcement is directly related to performance, there is a limit. A reinforcer loses its effect when it is given in excessive amounts. This phenomenon is referred to as *satiation*. Hence, the effect of increasing reinforcement is limited by the point at which the individual becomes satiated. Satiation is especially evident with primary reinforcers such as food, water, and sex. In excessive amounts, each of these reinforcers quickly loses its reinforcing properties and may even become aversive. Of course, satiation of primary reinforcers is temporary; they regain their reinforcing value as deprivation increases. Secondary, or conditioned, reinforcers, such as praise, attention, and tokens, are also subject to satiation, but to a lesser extent than are primary reinforcers.

The effect of the amount of a reinforcer on behavior depends on the satiation and deprivation states of the individual with respect to that reinforcer. An event (e.g., money) is not likely to be very effective as a reinforcer if an individual has unlimited access to it. If an individual is partially deprived of an event, a smaller amount of a reinforcer is needed to change behavior. In most everyday situations, people do not have unlimited access to reinforcing events (e.g., free time in a classroom situation or with friends or children), and thus they normally undergo various mild forms of deprivation. This means that a variety of events can be effective as reinforcers without introducing deprivation.

Occasionally, satiation is used to an advantage. For example, in a day-treatment setting in which I worked, emotionally disturbed and mentally retarded adolescents participated in a sheltered workshop in which they engaged in work (e.g., assembling holiday fruit packages, inserting fliers into envelopes). The goal was to develop interpersonal skills and work behaviors so that youths could be placed in community employment settings. Billy, a 16-year-old male was doing well, but had an odd behavior of picking up pieces of trash (e.g., paper, cigarette butts, and any small items) on the floor and placing them in his pockets. At the end of the day, his pockets were stuffed and bulging. On the next day, he began with empty pockets and the process started over. This had been going on for many years. The staff felt that this behavior alone would hamper his employment. Repeated comments and nagging on the part of the staff to stop picking up trash had a predictable impact (none). Billy's mother was contacted and enthusiastically approved efforts to change the behavior. Apparently, Billy emptied his pockets into the closet of his room each night, which she cleaned out once or twice each week. Satiation was elected as an intervention merely to test whether excessive delivery of small pieces of trash would change their value and lead to behavior change. Baseline data revealed the problem (picking up trash) was quite frequent throughout the day and every day.

When the satiation phase began, the staff gave Billy trash. At the beginning of the day, all staff in contact with him were given several small pieces of trash for their pockets and work aprons. At specified periods (approximately 3 to 5 times/per hour) a staff member went to Billy and said, "Here" or "I found this" (in a friendly manner) and handed him a piece of trash. For the first few days, he said "Thank you," often with enthusiasm, and placed the item in his pocket. After a few days, he was less enthusiastic and began to shake his head no with each of-fer; we observed that he picked up less trash on his own. We continued to make offers. After 4 days of not accepting our trash offers, he ceased completely pick-ing up trash. There were no more bulging pockets nor did he transport trash home. Once his room was emptied of small bits of trash at home, there were no more piles. Satiation guided the program with a goal of reducing the value of trash. Of course, it is not clear how this behavior developed. (Moreover, we never assessed if any of the staff started to collect trash for their pockets!)

Quality or Type of the Reinforcer

The quality of a reinforcer, unlike the amount of a reinforcer, is not usually spec-ified in physical terms. Rather, quality usually is determined by the preference of the client. This has been tested by asking individuals which of two or more rein-forcers are preferred and then testing the reinforcer's value on performance (Green, Reid, Canipe, & Gardner, 1991; Neef, Mace, Shea, & Shade, 1992). In general, highly preferred reinforcers lead to greater performance than do those that are less preferred.

For a given client, it is usually not difficult to specify highly preferred activi-ties. Behaviors frequently engaged in provide a helpful indication of highly pre-ferred reinforcers. Also, a person's stated preference is often quite useful for identifying reinforcers. Yet whether a preferred event will serve as a reinforcer at all or whether one will be better than another is not necessarily related to what one says. The effects of consequences, preferred or otherwise, must be examined directly by observing their impact. Verbal behavior (what people say) is not a sub-stitute for nonverbal behavior (what people do).

Quality of the reinforcer reflects the point that all reinforcers are not equal in their effects. In relation to reinforcers discussed previously, token reinforcement is often more effective than praise in altering behavior, and both of these are usually more effective than feedback. However, there is no need to use only one rein-forcer. Tokens, which include multiple backup reinforcers, and praise are often combined (delivered when the behavior occurs) to maximize the quality of the reinforcer.

Schedule of Reinforcement

Continuous and Intermittent Reinforcement. *Schedule of reinforcement refers to the rule denoting how many or which specific responses will be reinforced.* Reinforcers are always administered according to some schedule. The schedule makes a differ-ence in how effective the reinforcement program will be. In the simplest sched-ule, a response is reinforced each time it occurs. This schedule is referred to as *continuous reinforcement.* For example, to train a child to follow instructions, rein-forcement can be given each time the child responds appropriately. On the other hand, reinforcement may be delivered after only some of the appropriate re-sponses. This is referred to as *intermittent reinforcement.*

There are important differences between continuous and intermittent rein-forcement while the behaviors are being reinforced and after reinforcement has

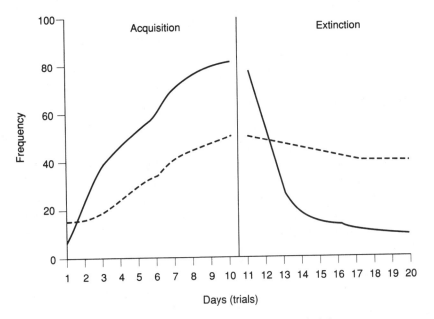

FIGURE 6-5 Effects on behavior of continuous reinforcement (solid line) and intermittent reinforcement (dashed line) while behavior is being reinforced (acquisition or reinforcement phase) and when reinforcement is no longer provided (extinction phase).

been withdrawn (extinction). During the acquisition or reinforcement phase, a behavior developed with continuous reinforcement is performed at a higher rate than is a behavior developed with intermittent reinforcement. Thus while a behavior is developing, a continuous or "generous" schedule of reinforcement should be used. However, the advantage of continuous reinforcement is compensated after the reinforcement ceases. During extinction, behaviors that were continuously reinforced diminish more rapidly than do behaviors that were reinforced intermittently.

Figure 6-5 plots the general relationship between schedules of reinforcement during acquisition (reinforcement phase) and extinction (no further reinforcement). As shown in the figure, the advantage of continuous reinforcement is that performance occurs at a high level while behavior is reinforced. The advantage of intermittent reinforcement is that resistance to extinction is greater when reinforcement is discontinued. Both advantages can be obtained by developing behavior with continuous reinforcement until a high rate of behavior has been well established and then, to foster response maintenance, changing the schedule to intermittent reinforcement and making it increasingly intermittent.

The difference between responses developed with continuous reinforcement and responses developed with intermittent reinforcement is apparent in examples from everyday experience. A familiar response that is reinforced every time is depositing coins in a vending machine and pressing a lever or button. Barring mechanical failure, the response is followed by the reinforcer (e.g., soda, candy) every time, that is, continuous reinforcement. As soon as the reinforcer (i.e., the product) is no longer delivered, extinction is almost immediate. If a vending machine does not deliver the reinforcer, few individuals will continue to put coins and press the lever of the machine unless there is some evidence that the machine has been repaired. In other words, *for behaviors previously developed with continuous reinforcement, extinction is rapid.*

A similar response—putting coins into a machine and pulling a lever—might be maintained by intermittent reinforcement, as in the case of old-fashioned slot machines (before lever pulling was replaced by button pressing). Sometimes putting money into a slot machine is reinforced (with money); other times it is not. If money were no longer delivered (extinction), the response would continue to be performed at a high rate before extinguishing. It is difficult to discriminate when extinction begins on a highly intermittent schedule of reinforcement. The resistance of a response to extinction depends on how intermittent or thin is the reinforcement schedule. *Resistance to extinction is greater if very few responses are reinforced than it is if many responses are reinforced.*

Another advantage of intermittent reinforcement is its efficient use of available reinforcers. Intermittent reinforcement allows delivery of a few reinforcers for a large number of responses. Moreover, if reinforcers are administered only a few times, satiation is less likely to occur. For example, with intermittent food reinforcement, the client is not likely to become full quickly and thus temporarily unresponsive to food. A further advantage of intermittent reinforcement is that it requires less time for administering reinforcers than does continuous reinforcement.

Schedules and Patterns of Responding. The basic distinction between continuous versus intermittent reinforcement conveys how schedules can directly influence performance. The impact of schedules is much broader. The rate of engaging in the target response and the patterns (consistencies over time, pauses) are influenced by reinforcement schedules. This can be seen by highlighting a few basic schedules.

Two simple types of reinforcement schedules can be distinguished. Reinforcement can be contingent on the emission of a certain number of responses. This is referred to as a *ratio schedule,* because the schedule specifies the ratio of the total *number of responses* to the one that is reinforced. An example would be reinforcing every tenth time the response is performed. With a ratio schedule, the behavior of the subject controls the frequency of reinforcement. The more times the subject performs the response, the sooner the reinforcement will be provided. Reinforcement can also be contingent on the *amount of time* that passes. This is referred to as an *interval schedule.* The first response after the interval is up is the one that is reinforced. As an example, the first response that is performed after 10 minutes elapse would be an interval schedule. With an interval schedule, the responses performed before the interval is over (10 minutes in this example), do not have any effect on reinforcement. The frequency of reinforcement is partially determined by the clock.

Table 6-1 Schedules of Reinforcement and Their Effects

Schedule	Defined	Usual Effects	Example
Fixed Ratio (FR)	Reinforcer is delivered after a specific number of responses; the number is always the same	When several responses are required, inconsistent performance and pauses after the reinforcer is delivered	Providing a bonus to a worker for every tenth sale that is completed
Variable Ratio (VR)	Reinforcer is delivered after a specific number of responses but the number changes from one occasion to another	More consistent and higher levels of performance than in an FR schedule; little or no pause after the reinforcer is delivered	Putting money in a slot machine where the response is reinforced after some number of responses but that number varies greatly from one occasion to another
Fixed Interval (FI)	Reinforcer is delivered for the first response that occurs after a specific time period has elapsed; period does not change	Inconsistent performance and a pronounced pause after the reinforcer is delivered	Praise to elementary students every 30 minutes if they are attending at the end of the 30-minute interval
Variable Interval (VI)	Reinforcer is delivered for the first response that occurs after a specific time period has elapsed; period varies	More consistent performance than with FI schedules; little or no pause after the reinforcer is delivered	Praise to elementary students if they are attending at the end of some time interval but that interval changes each time

In both ratio and interval schedules of reinforcement, the requirement for reinforcement can be *fixed,* so that it is the same requirement every time. On the other hand, the requirement can be *variable,* so that it is different from time to time. Four simple schedules of reinforcement will be discussed: fixed ratio (FR), variable ratio (VR), fixed interval (FI), and variable interval (VI). Table 6-1 summarize these schedules.

A *fixed-ratio schedule* requires an unvarying number of responses to be performed before a response is reinforced. The number following FR specifies which response will be reinforced. For example, FR: 1 specifies that only one response is required for the reinforcer to be delivered. (FR: 1 is also called continuous reinforcement, because every response is reinforced.) FR: 10 denotes that every tenth response is reinforced.

Under fixed-ratio schedules there is a temporary pause in responding after reinforcement is delivered. The pause after responding is a function of the ratio, with large ratios (when few responses are reinforced) producing longer pauses. Once the responses resume, reinforcement is maximized by performing all of the responses as quickly as possible. Examples of an FR schedule include any instance in which the reinforcer is delivered for a certain number of responses. For example, the behavior of a salesperson who is paid after he or she has made 20 sales would be on an FR schedule. For every 20th sale, the reinforcer (money) is earned. If several responses are required for reinforcement, there may be a temporary pause (reduced efforts to sell) immediately after reinforcement.

A variable-ratio schedule specifies that reinforcement is to occur after a certain number of responses. That number *varies* unpredictably from occasion to occasion. On the average, a certain number of responses are performed before reinforcement is delivered. The number following VR specifies the average number of responses required for reinforcement. For example, VR: 5 indicates that, on the average, five responses are to be performed before the reinforcer is delivered. The second response may be reinforced on some occasions, whereas the eighth response may be reinforced on other occasions. A different number of responses may be required each time. Across all occasions, however, reinforcement is delivered on the average of the number specified (e.g., five in the VR: 5 schedule). Of course, the number 1 cannot be used in a VR schedule because using that number would be equivalent to reinforcing every response, which is a continuous reinforcement or FR: 1 schedule.

Performance under VR schedules is consistently high. There is no clear pause after reinforcement. The pauses after responding in FR schedules can be virtually eliminated with a VR schedule unless the average ratio is very long. Immediately after a response is reinforced, the subject begins to respond because the next reinforcer may follow only a few responses. Performance continues at a high rate until reinforcement is delivered, and immediately resumes again. Behavior previously maintained under a VR schedule extinguishes more slowly than behavior previously maintained under an FR schedule, particularly if the variable schedule requires many responses for reinforcement. Performance is relatively persistent and consistent following a VR schedule. Thus VR schedules are highly suited to forestalling extinction. Before reinforcement is withdrawn, the ratio can gradually be made very thin by increasing the number of responses required for reinforcement.

Examples of VR schedules are abundant in everyday experience. Slot machines, mentioned earlier, represent a dramatic application of VR schedules. Since any response can be reinforced, the person playing the slot machine usually performs at a consistently high rate. His or her performance is unlikely to extinguish for long periods of time. Unless there is fatigue or bankruptcy, responses can continue without pauses.

A *fixed-interval schedule* requires that an interval of time (usually expressed in minutes) pass before the reinforcer is available. The first response that occurs after the interval passes is reinforced. In such a schedule, of course, the interval is unvarying. For example, in an FI: 1 schedule, the first response after one minute passes is reinforced. An interval schedule requires that only one response be performed after the prescribed interval has elapsed. Although this efficiency in responding rarely occurs, the characteristics of responses to FI: 1 schedules are distinct. Following reinforcement, there is usually a pronounced pause, during which responses are performed. This does not interfere with receiving reinforcement because a response before the appropriate time elapses is never reinforced. Only if the pause is longer than the fixed interval will the subject postpone reinforcement. FI schedules lead to less consistent rates of responding than do FR schedules because nonresponding immediately after reinforcement during an FI schedule does not postpone reinforcement, as it does with an FR schedule.

As an example of an FI schedule, consider reinforcement in an elementary school classroom. Suppose a teacher wishes to increase attentive student behavior and decides to increase the frequency of reinforcement. The teacher may deliver praise every 30 minutes to children who are paying attention (FI: 30 schedule). The teacher may select 30 minutes because this is easy to track on the clock in the room. At the end of 30 minutes, the teacher may praise and mention by name each student who is behaving appropriately. Given the fixed-interval schedule, it is very likely that the desired performance (e.g., sitting, working quietly) will be high near the end of the interval with pauses (lapses in appropriate behavior) immediately after reinforcement. Indeed, I have seen this in a few classrooms. In each instance, the teacher claimed that praise "worked" but did not really have any more than a very temporary effect. Actually, the schedule *fosters* poor performance of the target behavior. The pattern of behavior can be readily changed, as indicated with the next schedule.

A *variable-interval schedule* specifies the average length of the intervals required for reinforcement. For example, a VI: 10 schedule denotes that, on the average, 10 minutes must elapse before a response is reinforced. On any given occasion, the interval may be more or less than 10 minutes. The reinforcer is delivered for the first response after the interval elapses. In general, responding tends to be higher and more consistent under VI schedules than it is under FI schedules. The pauses are reduced or eliminated.

Continue the classroom example mentioned previously with the elementary school teacher who praised on an FI: 30 schedule. A better procedure would be to shift to a VI schedule. This can be accomplished by using a kitchen timer (as used in cooking) that sounds a ring when the timer is up. The teacher can turn the dial to different periods—some short (e.g., 3 to 5 minutes), some long (e.g., 60 minutes), and some in between. When the timer rings on this intermittent schedule, the teacher would praise attentive students. Behavior would be much more consistent over time throughout the day.

General Comments In general, variable schedules promote greater consistency in performance than fixed schedules. Also, ratio schedules tend to produce higher rates of response, because rate of responding influences how soon the reinforcer will be delivered, than do interval schedules. Schedule effects have been well studied in the laboratory, usually in carefully controlled animal studies.

Examples of schedule effects or close approximations of them abound in everyday life. An example of an FI response pattern in everyday experience is looking to see whether one's mail has arrived. For most individuals, mail delivery is once a day, with (fairly) fixed periods (24 hours) between deliveries. (There is excellent stimulus control, however, so that on Sundays and holidays, the response is not likely to be performed.) The response (looking for mail in the mailbox) is reinforced (finding mail) daily. Immediately after reinforcement, there is no longer a response. One does not resume looking for mail again until the next day, when the 24-hour interval is almost complete. Looking for mail then increases until reinforcement is obtained, at which time the pause after reinforcement is again evident. The example conveys how the scheduling of events can contribute to the pattern of performance, even when there are likely to be many influences at play.

In everyday life, schedule effects are not as clear or as precise because many different behaviors are influenced by multiple schedules and under a variety of stimulus conditions. Even so, understanding schedule effects is useful for applied purposes. For example, consider you are an instructor and interested in giving quizzes in class. One way would be to have "pop quizzes" (a more politically correct term may be "mom and pop" quizzes). A pop quiz means that it can be given any day and hence reflects a variable schedule of the event. Another way would be to have a quiz every Friday or only on Friday. This would be a fixed schedule. Events scheduled in these different ways have predictable effects. Studying, reading the material, and related behaviors are more likely to be consistent and at a high rate with the variable schedule. With the fixed schedule, the desired behaviors are more likely to occur at the end of the interval (studying and reading on Thursday night). If an instructor wishes students to keep up on the readings and to study consistently, a variable schedule of quizzes is much more conducive to that pattern. Of course, studying behavior is controlled by many other factors than schedules of reinforcement in a particular class, but the influence is noteworthy and present nevertheless.

As already mentioned, it is desirable to reinforce continuously at the beginning of a behavior-change program. If continuous reinforcement is not feasible (e.g., in a classroom with one teacher, or in the home with a parent away at work), the schedule that provides the most frequent reinforcement of the behavior of interest is preferred. Intermittent reinforcement is useful to maintain the desired behavior once high levels have been achieved. When intermittent reinforcement is used, variable schedules and ratio schedules are preferred.

Meeting the Requirements

The use of rewards or incentives to alter behavior is not new at all in the history of civilization. Behavior modification has advanced well beyond these early applications. Current advances have resulted from years of research elucidating the requirements to achieve behavior change. Now we know many of the circumstances and conditions of administration in which the use of such techniques as positive reinforcement will succeed, produce mediocre effects, or fail. The requirements for administering reinforcement effectively are enormously important. Merely adding an incentive here or there or promising a reward to quickly try in induce behavior are too simplistic to have much impact. Although, the basic requirements of administering reinforcement noted previously exert a remarkable impact, the effectiveness of a program is not guaranteed even if all of the requirements are met. Many other influences might be operative that cannot be controlled. Yet if the requirements are not met or are not met very well, little or no behavior change can be expected.

Parents, teachers, nurses, therapists, and others in applied settings often report that they have tried the use of positive reinforcement and it really does not work. The reports are invariably correct. The usual culprit is in failing to meet basic requirements for effective delivery. That is, reinforcement is too delayed, too intermittent, and even delivered noncontingently. The reason one can note this with some confidence is that the programs, once corrected, often lead to quite different effects on behavior.

Reinforcement Techniques to Reduce
Undesirable Responses

In many situations, the major goal of the program is to reduce undesirable behavior. Because reinforcement is a technique to increase behavior, people often believe that other techniques are required when the goal is to decrease behavior. Hence, punishment and extinction, discussed in the next chapters, are used because they decrease response frequency directly. However, undesirable target responses can be decreased or eliminated by reinforcement (LaVigna & Donnellan, 1986; O'Brien & Repp, 1990). Reinforcement is the obvious intervention of choice when the goal is to increase or decrease behavior.

Reinforcement is designed to develop positive and prosocial behaviors, and this focus is invariably important. Techniques to eliminate behavior such as punishment and extinction, even if effective, do not necessarily lead to the development of desirable, positive, and prosocial behavior. Reinforcement is required to develop these behaviors. Consequently, reinforcement is central to behavior-change programs. This will be elaborated when punishment and extinction are presented in the next two chapters.

Reinforcement of Other Behavior

One way to decrease behavior is to provide reinforcement when the client engages in any behavior other than the undesirable target response. *Differential reinforcement of other behavior* (DRO) consists of providing the reinforcing consequences of all responses except the undesirable behavior of interest. The effect of this schedule is to decrease the target behavior. For example, in a classroom situation, a child might be aggressive or talk out. For a DRO, the teacher could provide praise and an approving pat on the shoulder of the child on occasions that the child is not engaging in either one of these behaviors. That is, all "other" behavior than the undesirable target behavior would be reinforced.

DRO has been effective in reducing the frequency of severe and dangerous behaviors. For example, DRO was used to reduce self-injury (facial hitting, hand biting) in a 16-year-old mentally retarded male named Donald (Iwata, Pace, Kalsher, Cowdery, & Cataldo, 1990). Sips of soda were used to reinforce noninjurious behavior. At the end of 1 minute intervals in which no self-injury had occurred, Donald received a sip of soda. This is a DRO contingency because any behavior that occurred, other than self-injury, earned the reinforcer. The amount of time without self-injury needed to earn the soda was gradually extended (2, 4,

15 minutes). Self-injury declined from approximately 20% of the intervals in base-line to 0% during the DRO phase.

In another example, DRO was used to decrease aggressive behavior (e.g., slap-ping, hitting, biting others), property destruction (e.g., ripping, tearing, or break-ing things), and throwing objects or sweeping them off of a table, desk, or counter (Luiselli, 1996). The case was a 14-year-old adolescent, named Jeff, who was hos-pitalized because of multiple behavior problems. The program took place in a classroom in the hospital. DRO consisted of beginning the day by reminding Jeff that he could earn a treat and a sticker if he did not engage in any of the above behaviors. At the end of each half hour staff praised Jeff if the target behaviors did not occur, allowed him to select an edible treat (gum drop, candy mint), and placed a sticker on his sticker sheet. The stickers accumulated and could be ex-changed for special activities (e.g., playing basketball, listening to a tape). For con-sistent and extended periods of not engaging in the target behavior (e.g. "perfect" mornings and afternoons), additional activities could be earned (e.g., visiting a shopping mall, fast-food lunch). DRO led to marked decreases in the aggressive and destructive target behaviors. The changes were even greater when additional reinforcement was provided for completing tasks and activities during the class.

A DRO schedule provides reinforcement for not engaging in a behavior. The reinforcer is delivered as long as the client is not performing the undesired re-sponse. This schedule is easy to convey to those who administer the reinforcement program because it begins by dividing all behavior into X (the behavior to be de-creased) and non-X (all other behavior). One can convey to those who adminis-ter the program to try to catch the client whenever he or she is engaging in non-X.

Reinforcement of Alternative Behavior

Reinforcement of the nonoccurrence of a response or any other behavior (DRO) is useful when there are very high rates of the undesired target behavior and one wishes to provide reinforcement anytime the response is not evident. In most sit-uations, it is useful to identify specific positive behaviors that can be reinforced. These behaviors are selected because they directly or indirectly interfere with per-formance of the undesired behavior. Usually specific positive behaviors in the set-ting (e.g., working at one's desk at school or completing a chore at home) that the behavior-change agent wishes to develop can be identified.

Often one can identify a behavior that, if performed, would be incompatible with the undesired target behavior. An *incompatible behavior* is any behavior that di-rectly interferes and cannot be performed with the undesired behavior. The in-compatible behavior is often the direct *opposite* of the undesired behavior. Increasing the frequency of an incompatible behavior decreases the undesired be-havior. This procedure, referred to as *differential reinforcement of incompatible behavior* (DRI), focuses on reinforcing behaviors that are incompatible or that compete with the undesired behavior.

Usually, it is quite easy to select an incompatible response that can be rein-forced. For example, if a child fights with siblings at home, reinforcement can be delivered for playing cooperatively. If an institutionalized psychiatric patient has violent outbursts and tantrums, reinforcement can be delivered for talking and sitting quietly and for calmly interacting with peers, which are incompatible with the undesired responses.

The effects of reinforcing a behavior incompatible with the undesired response were demonstrated in a program developed to reduce pica among three institutionalized mentally retarded adults (Donnelly & Olczak, 1990). Pica consists of eating nonfood and nonnutritive objects and can lead to injury, illness, and death. The individuals in this program ate cigarette butts, a form of pica that is particularly bothersome because of the toxicity and addictive properties of nicotine. The intervention was carried out in a room where a fake cigarette butt made of bread was placed in an ashtray and replaced each time it was removed. The fake butt was used to permit careful assessment without jeopardizing the health of the individuals. Each adult, treated individually, was invited to come into a room where the cigarette butt was available. The amount of time (latency) until the butt was eaten was the measure to evaluate the program.

The program consisted of a DRI schedule in which chewing gum was the response identified as incompatible with eating. Chewing gum was given to the individual, and behavior was checked periodically to see if the individual was chewing. An edible reinforcer (sips of decaffeinated and sweetened coffee) was provided if the individual chewed gum over the course of a specific time period. Initially short periods of engaging in the incompatible behavior were reinforced, then longer periods were.

Figure 6-6 illustrates the effects of the program for one of the adults. Baseline shows that this individual immediately consumed cigarette butts when he entered the room and kept doing so as these butts were replaced. With the DRI schedule, behavior changed markedly. In the final phase, the program was extended to the ward by staff. Improvements were maintained, although not to the level in the special sessions in which behavior was monitored and carefully assessed.

It is not always possible or necessary to identify a behavior that is physically incompatible with an undesired behavior that one wishes to decrease. A host of positive behaviors that serve as alternatives to the undesired behavior might be reinforced. These alternatives are behaviors whose performance decreases the likelihood that the undesired behavior will occur. Increasing the frequency of alternative behaviors, regardless of whether they actually are physically incompatible with the undesired behavior, decreases the undesired behavior. This procedure is referred to as *differential reinforcement of alternative behavior* (DRA).

As an illustration, in one program, an adolescent, mentally retarded student spoke out excessively in class (Deitz, Repp, & Deitz, 1976). A DRA schedule was used in which reinforcement was provided for working on academic tasks. This response is not incompatible with talking out because a person can do both. Yet if one is working at a task, the chances are that he or she is not talking. In this program, reinforcement of working at a task decreased talking out.

Similarly, to suppress fighting among siblings, as noted above, playing cooperatively could be reinforced. Playing cooperatively is incompatible with fighting and constitutes a DRI. Yet other alternative behaviors could be reinforced, such as

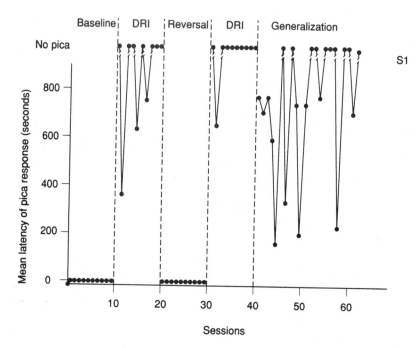

FIGURE 6-6 Mean average latency of pica responses within the session when the child was given the opportunity for baseline, DRI, reversal (return to baseline), DRI, and generalization (on the ward) phases. Low scores mean the individual consumed the fake cigarette butts immediately when the opportunity was provided; high scores mean the individual either had a long latency before consuming the butts or did not consume them at all. (No pica at top of graph.)

(Source: Donnelly & Olczak, 1990)

watching television together or completing a chore together. Neither of these behaviors is necessarily incompatible with fighting, yet their reinforcement is likely to decrease the frequency of fighting. These responses are part of a general class of behaviors that might, in casual terms, be referred to as "getting along." More opportunities for positive reinforcement are made available by identifying many alternative behaviors rather than only the alternative behaviors that are physically incompatible with the undesired response.

DRI and DRA are closely related. Actually, DRA refers to reinforcing any alternative positive responses that decrease the likelihood that the undesired behavior will be performed. DRI is a subtype of DRA in which the alternative behavior is one that is incompatible with the undesired response. In practice and in working with parents, teachers, and others, it is useful to develop a DRA schedule where a few specific alternative behaviors are identified as the target response. In our own work with parents, for example, we ask them to think of a positive opposite whenever there is a behavior they wish to suppress or eliminate.

A positive opposite is a behavior that is an alternative to and preferably incompatible with the undesired behavior. As will become more clear in the discussion of punishment in the next chapter, the suppression of behavior can be greatly enhanced when a reinforcement program is designed to develop a positive, prosocial, opposite behavior.

Reinforcement of incompatible or alternative behaviors has been used effectively in many programs (O'Brien & Repp, 1990). For example, the behaviors of hyperactive children in the classroom and at home have been altered by using reinforcement techniques. Hyperactive behaviors include disturbing others excessively, blurting out statements, being out of one's seat, speaking rapidly, running around the room, not complying with the requests of parents or teachers, and generally engaging in very high levels of inappropriate activity. Rather than punish these behaviors, many programs have been designed to reinforce alternative behaviors. Typically, programs of this kind provide tokens, praise, and consumable rewards (e.g., food) for such behaviors as correct responses on academic tasks, remaining in one's seat to work on specific tasks, and engaging in more restrained and quieter types of activity. Such programs have reduced hyperactive behaviors and increased the performance of on-task and academic behaviors.

Reinforcement of Functionally Equivalent Behavior

Behaviors can be examined from the standpoint of the functions they serve. The functions refer to the broader purposes, goals, and consequences that are achieved, as discussed in the chapter on functional analysis. For example, tantrums might have different (and multiple) functions for different children. Tantrums might divert adult attention from a sibling, stop parents from arguing with each other, or terminate nagging or demands from others. If the undesired, deviant, or inappropriate response is serving some function, perhaps another response can be identified that serves the same function but is more socially appropriate. *Reinforcement of functionally equivalent behavior* refers to reinforcement of a prosocial, acceptable behavior that attains the same goals and consequences as does the problem behavior. The effect of this procedure is to reduce or eliminate the undesirable behavior.

For example, in one demonstration, different conditions that were related to aggression, tantrums, noncompliance, and self-injury were studied in four youths, age 7 to 14, with developmental disabilities (Carr & Durand, 1985). They were individually exposed to different task conditions (easy versus difficult) and to different amounts of adult attention (high versus low). A functional analysis revealed that problem behavior led to different consequences and hence appeared to serve different functions for the children. For some children, problem behaviors were high when they received little adult attention. That is, when attention was high, problem behavior was low. This suggests that problem behavior for these children may function as a way of obtaining adult attention. An appropriate behavior was trained that served the same function for these children. Specifically, the children were trained to ask the teacher, "Am I doing good work?" This prompt by the children led to attention from the teacher and hence the function (attaining attention) would be served. The results showed that identifying the function of problem behavior individually for the children and then training an appropriate behavior to serve that function significantly decreased problem behavior. Other studies have shown that reinforcing functionally equivalent responses can readily reduce problem behaviors such as tantrums, self-injury, and aggression (Carr, Taylor, & Robinson, 1991; Wacker, McMahon, et al., 1990).

Reinforcement of functionally equivalent responses can be regarded as a special case of reinforcing alternative responses. Essentially, the reinforcer that resulted from the undesired behavior is deployed or provided for positive prosocial alternative behavior. The added feature, over and above a DRA, is systematically assessing the consequences of the problem behavior, that is, searching for the function(s) of that behavior, and then selecting a behavior that achieves these consequences. Because this assessment may not be feasible in many applied settings, it is reassuring to note that DRA schedules without this feature have worked well. At the same time, if the function can be identified and served by the new behavior that is developed, the likelihood of achieving the desired changes in behavior may be increased.

In many cases, reinforcement of functionally equivalent behavior has taken the form of training individuals to ask for or prompt access to the reinforcer. This is illustrated in the above example in which the child prompted the teacher for attention. This special case is referred as *functional communication training* (Durand, 1990) and consists of developing communication in the client to obtain the consequences that maintain behavior. For example, some children may engage in tantrums and aggressive behavior. A functional analysis may show that tantrums and aggressive behavior are maintained by escaping from the situation or from attention by a teacher. Functional communication training teaches the client to request assistance with a difficult task (e.g., say, "help me," or "I do not understand.") or to prompt attention (e.g., "Am I doing good work?") (e.g., Durand & Carr, 1991). This has been a very effective variation of reinforcing functionally equivalent responses.

Functional communication training is rather interesting insofar as deviant behavior is often maintained by attention from others. Training the individual to seek attention from others with appropriate verbal behavior in those situations in which deviant behavior would otherwise occur can eliminate the deviant behavior. The effectiveness of the procedure requires a functional analysis insofar as one can be sure the reinforcer maintaining deviant behavior is now provided for the appropriate behavior.

Reinforcement of Low Response Rates

Another reinforcement technique for suppressing behavior is to provide reinforcing consequences for reductions in the frequency of the undesired behavior or for increases in the time intervals in which instances of that behavior do not occur. These procedures, referred to as *differential reinforcement of low rates of responding* (DRL), can effectively suppress behavior.

In one variation of a DRL schedule, the client receives reinforcing consequences for showing *a reduction in the frequency of target behavior.* As an example, a DRL

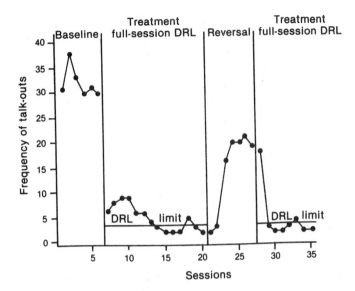

FIGURE 6-7 The frequency of talk-outs per 55-minute session of an educable mentally retarded male. During treatment, if the client emitted three or fewer talk-outs per session, the teacher spent 15 minutes working with him.

(Source: Deitz, 1977)

schedule was used to decrease the inappropriate talking out of an educable mentally retarded male adolescent who attended a special education class (Deitz, 1977, Exp. 2). After baseline observations of talking out, the teacher told the student that if he emitted three or fewer "talk-outs" during a 55-minute period, she would spend extra time working with him. The youth would receive the reinforcing consequence only if he showed a low rate of disruptive behavior. This DRL contingency was evaluated in an ABAB design. The results, shown in Figure 6-7, demonstrate that talking out decreased whenever the DRL contingency was in effect.

The DRL schedule can completely eliminate a behavior by making the requirements for reinforcement increasingly stringent. A client may be allowed a certain number of instances of the undesired behavior (e.g., shouting out, interrupting someone, making an obnoxious comment) within a given period to earn the reinforcer. To eliminate the behavior, this number may be decreased to zero over time. Another way would be to provide reinforcing consequences for going longer and longer periods without performing the undesired behavior. For example, in separate programs, reinforcement has increased the amount of elapsed time between one response and the next to reduce stereotypical behaviors and eating rapidly (Lennox, Miltenberger, & Donnelly, 1987; Singh, Dawson, & Manning, 1981). In other variations, reinforcement for performance of a few or no instances of the response has effectively suppressed behavior (LaVigna & Donnellan, 1986; Repp & Singh, 1990).

Advantages of Using Positive Reinforcement

Reinforcement techniques using the schedules discussed previously have reduced or eliminated a wide range of undesirable and maladaptive behaviors in children and adults. The procedures appear to be at least as effective as various punishment procedures in their capacity to decrease undesirable behaviors. Although punishment and extinction can decrease behavior, these procedures do not train people in socially appropriate alternative behaviors. Even if punishment or extinction is used, effects can be greatly enhanced by incorporating reinforcement for appropriate behavior into the program. Also, many ethical concerns and negative client reactions raised by punishment procedures are largely circumvented if the program is based on positive reinforcement. Given these benefits, reinforcement techniques should be used whenever the goal is to increase or decrease behavior.

A challenge in fostering the use of reinforcement pertains to the orientation and focus many individuals (parents, teachers) bring to treatment. Behaviors one wants to eliminate or reduce immediately bring punishment to mind. After all, so the thinking goes, if the behavior is to be eliminated, the person ought to see that there are immediate and negative consequences for that behavior. In most instances, this orientation as implemented is doomed to failure or mediocre effects, as discussed in the next chapter. The challenge is to reorient thinking. If one wants to suppress behavior, the immediate task is to identify some positive or desirable behavior (other, alternative, incompatible, functionally equivalent behavior) that can be reinforced. In working with parents and teachers, we often provide many practice opportunities and hypothetical scenarios in which an array of deviant behaviors are discussed. The task is to identify two or three different reinforcement programs that might be used to decrease or eliminate an undesired behavior.

NEGATIVE REINFORCEMENT

Negative reinforcement can also be used to develop behavior. A behavior is increased or strengthened through negative reinforcement when it results in *escape* from or *avoidance* of an aversive event. Escape occurs when the individual comes in contact with the aversive event and the behavior eliminates the event. Many behaviors in everyday life are maintained by negative reinforcement through escape. For example, leaving the house to escape an argument with one's roommate or spouse, turning off an alarm to escape from a loud noise, and taking medicine to alleviate pain all represent escape. These behaviors are reinforced by termination of the aversive consequence.

Avoidance behavior allows the individual to prevent or indefinitely postpone contact with an aversive event. As mentioned in Chapter 2, avoidance learning may develop after an individual learns to escape an aversive event. Avoidance involves classical and operant conditioning. Through classical conditioning, a previously neutral event acquires the capacity to elicit escape behavior and hence becomes a conditioned (learned) aversive event. Through operant conditioning, escape from the conditioned aversive event is reinforced by terminating that event. Avoidance refers to escape from a conditioned aversive event, that is, events that have acquired aversive properties or that signal aversive events.

Most avoidance behavior is acquired without direct experience with the aversive event. Verbal cues from other individuals instruct us that certain consequences are to be avoided (e.g., alarm and the smell of smoke in a building or home). The cues are discriminative stimuli indicating that untoward consequences may follow if we behave in a particular way. Examples of avoidance based on verbal cues are present in everyday experience. For example, one can avoid personal harm by responding to the threat of an impending hurricane. Avoidance of the hurricane is escape from the threat. Behavior that reduces the threat is strengthened through negative reinforcement. Other examples of negative reinforcement through avoidance are parking one's car in a particular place to avoid a traffic fine, wearing a coat to avoid a chill, not drinking alcohol to avoid a driving mishap, and leaving a sinking ship to avoid drowning.

Use in Applied Settings

Negative reinforcement, in the form of escape from an aversive event, has not been widely used in applied settings for several reasons. First, negative reinforcement requires an ongoing aversive event (loud noise, pain, some annoying stimulus, nagging) that can be terminated when the desired target behavior occurs. This means that the aversive event must be delivered frequently before reinforcement can occur. The use of aversive events is ethically indefensible if positive events (through positive reinforcement) have not been attempted first. Because there are many types of positive reinforcers and ways in which they can be administered, there is rarely a need to employ negative reinforcement.

Second, the use of aversive events often produces undesirable side effects. Corporal punishment, physical restraint, reprimands, isolation, and other aversive consequences lead the client to escape from the situation, to avoid the persons who administer these events, and even to aggress against them, as elaborated in the next chapter. These side effects can be avoided by relying on positive reinforcement.

Third, negative reinforcement is often difficult to administer. The aversive stimulus must be carefully controlled, so that it can be terminated immediately after the appropriate behavior occurs. Usually this requires carefully monitoring behavior, often with certain apparatus. Also, careful control might require some level of coercion so the individual does not merely avoid the entire situation in which the aversive event is presented. For these reasons, it is no surprise that negative reinforcement has been used quite sparingly.

Notwithstanding the above reasons for not using negative reinforcement, examples can be identified that focus on problems of applied significance. For example, escape was used to alter disruptive child behavior in a dentist's office (Allen, Loiben, Allen, & Stanley, 1992). Approximately 25% of children are behavioral management problems when they undergo dental procedures. When children are uncooperative, dentists usually stop for a moment until they settle down. Yet momentarily stopping could serve as negative reinforcement for the child, namely, termination of the aversive event (the dental procedure itself) contingent on behavior (being disruptive or uncooperative). Essentially, an escape contingency is provided for undesired behavior. In this study, this contingency was altered with four children, aged 3 to 7, who required ongoing dental (restorative) procedures and several visits to the dentist. Disruptive behavior (crying, moaning, complaining, squirming) was observed directly, using interval assessment. Video-tapes were also made for later evaluation. After baseline, the escape procedure was altered. The dentist was trained to make escape contingent on positive (coopera-tive behavior). When the child was cooperative, the dentist told the child that he was so good in lying still that they would take a "little rest break." A brief break was taken. If disruptive behavior occurred during dental work, it was ignored or the child was reminded that there would be a break for lying still.

The negative reinforcement (escape) procedure was evaluated in a multiple-baseline design across the four children. Figure 6-8 shows the average amount of dis-ruptive behavior (solid bars) for each child over consecutive dental visits. The graph also shows the use of contingent escape (open bars), with the average percentage of time the dentist used the escape procedure contingent on cooperative behavior. The escape procedure clearly reduced disruptive behavior. Moreover, two dentists unfa-miliar with the program rated videotapes of baseline and intervention sessions and rated the children as much more cooperative during the intervention phases.

Negative reinforcement requires the presence of an aversive event in the situ-ation that can be terminated quickly and contingently after appropriate behavior. One would not want to introduce a negative event into a situation. The above ex-ample is instructive in this regard. It is often the case that negative events and in-deed negative reinforcement are already present in the situation. In the case of the dental program, negative reinforcement was being used unwittingly in baseline to reinforce uncooperative behavior by providing escape contingent on this behav-ior. If dental work is aversive to a child and momentary rest (escape) periods are to be used, the contingency can be altered so that cooperative rather than dis-ruptive behavior is reinforced.

This example is cited here to illustrate the use of negative reinforcement. Yet it is also useful to draw attention to the behavior. The goal of the program was to reduce disruptive behaviors. To do this, the program was recast as a reinforcement program, namely, reinforcement of positive opposite behaviors and hence differ-ential reinforcement of incompatible behaviors. The goals might have been ac-complished by merely praising these positive behaviors.

Negative reinforcement may be present in many situations and may con-tribute to inappropriate or deviant behavior. In such cases, adding aversive events or introducing negative reinforcement are not at issue. Rather, the relation be-tween aversive stimuli and behavior can be altered to ensure that desired behav-ior is fostered. For example, negative reinforcement has been shown to exacerbate and maintain self-injurious behavior among mentally retarded children and ado-lescents. In one study, tasks and educational activities, such as puzzle completion and stacking or sorting objects, were performed by the client and experimenter (Iwata et al., 1990). When self-injurious behavior (e.g., head banging) occurred, the experimenter terminated the activity, removed the materials, and turned away from the client. Over several trials, the procedure led to an increase in self-injury,

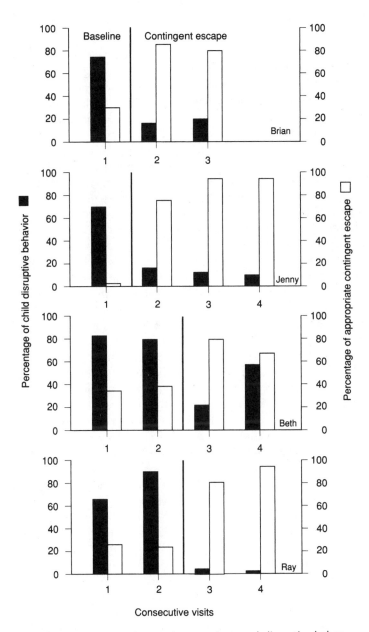

FIGURE 6-8 Percentage changes in mean (average) disruptive behavior of the child and percentage changes in the use of the escape contingency for appropriate behavior on the part of the dentist. The solid bars represent average disruptive child behavior per dental visit; the open bars represent the average use of appropriate contingent escape procedure by the dentist.

(Source Allen, Loiben, Allen, & Stanley, 1992)

compared with other conditions tested (e.g., playing alone, giving reprimands for self-injury). That is, self-injury increased contingent on termination of the task. This information is important to learn because one can then rearrange the contingency so that activity is contingent on periods of not engaging in self-injury, which is an effective away to reduce the undesirable behavior (Steege et al., 1990).

Separate points about reinforcement warrant emphasis. First, whether an event is a positive or negative reinforcer is an empirical matter and cannot always be discerned on intuitive grounds. In the previous example, one would not expect that working on a task is an aversive event and termination could systematically increase self-injury. Second, in some instances the natural reinforcement in the situation (e.g., the dentist terminating the procedure for uncooperative behavior) supports the very behavior one wishes to reduce. In such cases, introducing new aversive procedures is not required; rather, the contingency can be rearranged so that reinforcers in the situation support the desired behaviors.

In the prior examples, it is quite likely that positive reinforcement would have been effective in achieving the desired ends. Positive reinforcement has many variations, and they are usually effective. Consequently, negative reinforcement is a technique that should be employed as a last resort. If negative reinforcement is already part of the situation and altered to support desired behavior, positive reinforcement still can be added to the intervention. For example, another application focused on children who were highly disruptive during their visits to the dentist (Allen & Stokes, 1987). Behaviors such as kicking, screaming, hitting, and noncompliance interfered with restorative dental treatment. It was assumed that the treatment procedure itself (i.e., remaining in the dental chair, having a drill turned on) was aversive. In special practice sessions immediately before dental treatment, the children were individually instructed that they could practice being "big helpers," which meant sitting quietly. The behavior (sitting quietly) was negatively reinforced by terminating the procedure. For example, when the child sat quietly for only three seconds, the aversive event (having the drill on) was quickly terminated. This is an example of negative reinforcement. This response (sitting quietly) was gradually extended (shaping) to 6 minutes. Positive reinforcement was also used; it consisted of praise and stickers for increased cooperative behavior. The effect of the combined negative and positive reinforcement contingency markedly reduced disruptive behavior and permitted completion of the dental session.

Negative reinforcement occasionally has been applied as part of therapy techniques to alter such behaviors as excessive alcohol consumption, overeating, and sexual deviance, including transvestitism and fetishism. For example, one form of treatment for alcoholics that involves punishment and negative reinforcement requires the client to ingest the drug disulfiram (Antabuse). If the client drinks alcohol less than 24 hours after ingesting the drug, intense nausea results. Nausea can be avoided by not consuming alcohol. Of course, the client can also avoid the aversive contingency by failing to take the drug.

Evaluation of Negative Reinforcement

A major restriction in using negative reinforcement is the risk of undesirable side effects. One such side effect is trying to escape or avoid the behavior-change program and those associated with it. It is easy to see how this could happen. If parents, teachers, or supervisors administer aversive events (and not positive ones as well), they become aversive. Escape from such persons by leaving home, exiting the classroom, or changing jobs is negatively reinforced. Programs based on positive reinforcement do not foster this type of escape and avoidance behavior.

From the standpoint of designing a behavior modification program, aversive stimuli should be avoided or minimized. When they are used, emphasis should be placed on positive reinforcement for desirable behavior. In many applications of negative reinforcement, strong aversive stimuli are required because other procedures have failed or because the response (e.g., sexual deviance) is strongly reinforced. In such instances, aversive stimuli, including punishment and/or negative reinforcement, constitute a last resort.

SUMMARY AND CONCLUSIONS

Positive reinforcement represents the core feature of behavior-change programs in applied settings. Several different types of reinforcers have been used effectively, such as food and other consumables, praise and attention, high-probability behaviors, feedback, and token reinforcement. Each reinforcer has its own strengths and limitations such as dependence on deprivation and satiation states, ease of administration, and relative effectiveness. Token economies usually incorporate a variety of backup reinforcers and thus overcome the limitations that accrue to the use of any single reinforcer.

Although different reinforcers can vary in their impact on behavior, the effectiveness of any reinforcer depends heavily on the manner in which it is administered. Program effectiveness depends on the delay of reinforcement, the magnitude or amount of reinforcement, the quality or type of reinforcer, and the schedule of reinforcement. To maximize performance, reinforcement should be delivered contingently (i.e., only when the behavior is performed) and immediately after the behavior. Moreover, a highly preferred reinforcer should be used. During acquisition, continuous reinforcement should be used until the response is well established. Subsequently, intermittent reinforcement can be substituted to maintain behavior. Schedules were discussed to convey that behavior is influenced by how the consequences are administered. Schedules that are unchanging (fixed) often lead to pauses, lapses, and inconsistencies in behavior. Varying the intervals or number of responses required for reinforcement can reduce inconsistencies in behavior.

Positive reinforcement, and indeed reinforcement in general, refers to ways of increasing behavior. Yet, positive reinforcement plays a central role when the goal of a program is to decrease or eliminate undesirable behaviors. Several different ways of using reinforcement to reduce undesirable behaviors were discussed and included differential reinforcement of other behaviors, incompatible or alternate behaviors, functionally equivalent behaviors, or low rates of behavior. The initial task in virtually all behavioral programs is to consider what positive, adaptive, prosocial behavior can be developed. Reinforcing positive behaviors can be effective in its own right as away of reducing or eliminating undesirable behavior.

Even if punishment is used, as discussed in the next chapter, reinforcement of positive behaviors plays a central role.

Negative reinforcement was also discussed and can be used to increase behavior. It has not been used widely as a behavior-change technique in most applied settings. This is largely due to the undesirability of introducing aversive events if alternative procedures based on positive reinforcement can be applied. Interestingly, negative reinforcement contingencies often are already operative in everyday life, as when, for example, escape or avoidance serves to reinforce undesirable behavior (such as self-injury or aggression). In such instances, identifying the negative reinforcement contingency through functional analysis and altering the contingency so that positive, prosocial rather than deviant behavior is reinforced have been used successfully in a number of applications. It is important to be familiar with negative reinforcement and various forms it may take (e.g., escape, avoidance) even if one does not want to implement a program based on negative reinforcement. Signs of escape and avoidance are often useful to recognize because they suggest that some aversive event may be controlling behavior and effective interventions may require altering, eliminating, or changing these events. We shall return to positive and negative reinforcement throughout remaining chapters, given the critical role they play in developing adaptive behavior.

KEY TERMS

Contingent application of a reinforcer

Continuous reinforcement

Feedback

High-probability behavior

Intermittent reinforcement

Negative reinforcement

Positive reinforcement

Reinforcement of alternative behavior

Reinforcement of functionally equivalent behavior

Reinforcement of other behavior

Satiation

Schedule of reinforcement

Social reinforcer

Token economy

APPLYING PRINCIPLES AND TECHNIQUES TO EVERYDAY LIFE

1. In developing a behavior modification, it is important to be able to identify positive, adaptive, and prosocial behaviors whenever the goal is to decrease some undesired behavior. The undesired behavior might well be focused on directly, but invariably, the initial priority is to identify an adaptive behavior that can be increased. What would such positive behaviors be when the goal is to:

   A. Reduce tantrums?

   B. Eliminate interruptions while the parent is on the phone?

2. Describe a behavior-change program based on a DRA or DRI schedule that might be used to reduce A or B in the previous exercise.

3. To make sure that a reinforcement program is likely to achieve change, several characteristics are essential as that program is administered. Design and describe a program. What is the target behavior? What is the reinforcer? How will the reinforcer be administered to optimize the likelihood that the program will be effective?

4. Design a program to change any behavior and in this program, consider antecedents, behaviors, and consequences. Specifically, use two kinds of prompts (antecedents), describe how shaping will be used (behavior), and use two types of reinforcers (consequences).

FOR FURTHER READING

Iwata, B.A. (1987). Negative reinforcement in applied behavior analysis: An emerging technology. *Journal of Applied Behavior Analysis, 20,* 361–378.

Hall, R.V., & Hall, M.L (1998). *How to select reinforcers* (2nd Ed). Austin, TX: Pro-Ed.

Hall, R.V., & Hall, M.L (1998). *How to use systematic attention and approval* (2nd Ed). Austin, TX: Pro-Ed.

Kazdin, A.E. (1982). The token economy: A decade later. *Journal of Applied Behavior Analysis, 15,* 431–445.

O'Brien, S., & Repp, A.C. (1990). Reinforcement-based reductive procedures: A review of 20 years of their use with persons with severe or profound retardation. *Journal of the Association for Persons with Severe Handicaps, 15,* 148–159.

Van Houten, R. (1998). *How to motivate others through feedback* (2nd Ed). Austin, TX: Pro-Ed.

Vollmer, T.R., & Iwata, B.A. (1992). Differential reinforcement as treatment for behavioral disorders: Procedural and functional variations. *Research in Developmental Disabilities, 13,* 393–417.

NOTE

1. In a cumulative graph, the number (e.g., whatever is being counted on any given day) is added to the accumulated number of all of the previous days. Thus the numbers cumulate over time. An increase in behavior is seen in an accelerated slope: the steeper the slope, the faster the behavior change. No change in behavior is shown by a horizontal line because no instances of the behavior are being added to the graph. In a cumulative graph, the slope cannot decelerate (go down).

CHAPTER 7

Punishment

Aversive events play a major role in everyday life. Indeed, aversive techniques are deeply enmeshed in many social institutions, including government and law (fines and imprisonment), education (failing grades, detention, and expulsion), religion (damnation), international relations (military coercion), and normal social intercourse (discrimination, disapproval, and social stigma). Routine contacts and interactions of most individuals with both physical and social environments result in aversive events, including a burn from a hot stove and verbal abuse from a relative. In everyday life, parents and teachers apply aversive events such as reprimands and scoldings of varying intensities in an effort to train young children.

In behavior modification, the types of aversive events used and how they are applied differ greatly from punishment practices in everyday life. Before applications are discussed, a few prefatory comments are in order. To begin with, proponents of behavior modification generally avoid the use of punishment whenever possible. First, alternative procedures can often be used, such as positive reinforcement, as described in the previous chapter. Second, punishment is often associated with undesirable side effects, such as emotional reactions (crying), escape from and avoidance of situations (e.g., staying away from a punitive parent), and aggression (e.g., hitting others). None of these is necessary for behavior to change. Third and related, punishment can foster undesirable associations with regard to various agents (parents, teachers), situations (home, school), and behaviors (doing homework). An important objective in child rearing, education, and socialization in general is to develop positive attitudes and responses toward these agents, situations, and behaviors; their frequent association with punishment may be counterproductive. For example, screaming at a child to practice a musical instrument is not likely to develop a love of music.

Proponents of behavioral techniques are extremely concerned with abuse and misuse of punishment. Such abuse and misuse have been shown to foster serious problems in children and adolescents. For example, use of harsh punishment in the home is related to later deviant and delinquent behavior of the child (Kazdin, 1995; Wolfe, 1999). More frequent punishment is not associated with improved behavior. Both physical and verbal punishment (reprimands) can increase the very behaviors (noncompliance, aggression) that parents, teachers, and others wish to suppress. Unfortunately, the old adage "Spare the rod and spoil the child" still has many adherents. This is unfortunate because a strong case might be made for an opposite contention, "Use the rod and spoil the child" (see Greven, 1992).

To be sure, there are many occasions when mild punishment can be useful as part of a behavior-change program. Additionally, in some cases, people—for example, parents who engage in child abuse to control their children—may need to be trained to administer punishment (and reinforcement) judiciously (Wolfe, 1999). However, the type of punishment procedures, how they are used, and the combination with reinforcement programs make therapeutic applications of punishment very different from applications in everyday life.

Punishment in the technical sense refers solely to the empirical operation (presentation or removal of events) that reduces the probability or likelihood of the response in the future. Punishment does not necessarily involve physical pain.

Indeed, painful events such as spankings may not decrease the responses they are designed to punish and thus may not qualify as punishing events. Alternatively, a variety of punishment techniques do not entail physical discomfort and are not odious to the client.

In behavior modification, several forms of punishment have been developed based on whether aversive events are presented, positive events are withdrawn, or the client's work or effort is required after performance of a particular behavior. Some of the techniques are familiar because they are commonly used in everyday life (e.g., reprimands). However, other techniques such as withdrawing reinforcing events for very brief periods or requiring clients to practice appropriate behavior are probably less familiar. Although many of the techniques may be familiar, the ways in which they are implemented and the features that contribute to their effectiveness are not usually appreciated or practiced in everyday life. This chapter discusses the various types of punishment techniques, their effects and side effects, and their place in a behavior-change program. We shall examine the effectiveness of different techniques and the manner in which those techniques are most effectively administered.

PRESENTATION OF AVERSIVE EVENTS

The most familiar form of punishment is the presentation of an aversive event after a response has been performed. The event or consequence might be a spanking or a reprimand. The two types of aversive events are primary aversive stimuli and secondary, or conditioned, aversive stimuli. *Primary aversive stimuli are inherently aversive events, that is, their aversive properties are unlearned.* Such stimuli as electric shock, intense physical assault, bright lights, and loud noises are primary aversive stimuli. *Secondary, or conditioned, aversive stimuli acquire their aversive properties by being paired with events that are already aversive.* For example, the word "no" serves as a conditioned aversive stimulus for many individuals. The word acquires its aversive value by being paired with such other aversive events as a loud noise (e.g., from shouting and startling someone), physical pain, or loss of privileges. Conditioned aversive stimuli that typically control behavior include gestures, nods, frowns, and traffic tickets.

Stimuli may become aversive even if they are not paired with specific aversive stimuli. A stimulus consistently associated with the absence of reinforcement may become aversive. An event signaling that reinforcement will not be forthcoming, referred to earlier as an S^Δ, may serve as an aversive event. The S^Δ serves as a signal that a period of nonreinforcement is in effect. For example, when a child breaks a valuable object, a parent may make a particular facial expression, become silent, and not respond to the child for awhile. The parent's nonresponsiveness denotes that the child will not receive reinforcement. During parental silence, virtually no behavior receives approval. The signal or cue (e.g., a facial expression) associated with the parent's nonreinforcement (silence) becomes aversive in its own right.

Verbal Statements

Verbal statements in the form of reprimands, warnings, disapproval, saying no, and threats are often used in everyday interactions between teacher and student; parent and child; and among siblings, spouses, friends, and enemies. Occasionally verbal statements have been used to suppress behavior in applied research. For example, reprimands and disapproving statements have been applied in classroom settings to reduce playing during lessons, being out of one's seat, talking without permission, and other disruptive behaviors. Reprimands and disapproval in general have had inconsistent effects. In some cases, for example, disruptive student behavior has been suppressed relatively quickly by saying no after instances of disruptive behavior (Hall et al., 1971). In other cases, reprimands have served as a positive reinforcer rather than as a punisher. In one classroom, the teacher reprimanded the children by saying, "Sit down," when students were out of their seats (Madsen, Becker, Thomas, Koser, & Plager, 1970). Interestingly, the reprimands increased the frequency of standing, serving as a positive reinforcer for the behavior they were designed to suppress.

The manner in which verbal statements are delivered may influence their effectiveness. For example, in classroom applications, reprimands are more effective in suppressing child behavior when they are accompanied by looking directly at and grasping the child and when they are delivered in close proximity to the child (Van Houten, Nau, MacKenzie-Keating, Sameoto, & Colavecchia, 1982). Nonverbal components such as tone of voice, gestures, and staring at the child may exert influence, although these have not been well studied. From what is known, reprimands can be effective, especially when accompanied by gestures and other features that may add to their salience or intensity.

Verbal punishment is likely to lose its effectiveness over time. For example, threats occasionally have been used to suppress behavior. When threats signal that some other aversive consequence will follow, they become conditioned aversive events. Yet some threats are "idle," or not backed by the threatened consequence. Such threats tend to lose their effects quickly. Verbal statements generally are likely to produce temporary effects if they are not followed by other consequences, or they are likely to require increases in intensity to sustain their effects if they are used by themselves.

Strengths and Limitations. Reprimands and threats are easily administered and, hence, from a practical standpoint are readily available for use as a punishment technique. Also, verbal forms of punishment cause no physical discomfort. Receiving a reprimand may be unpleasant, but such unpleasantness is very different from the kind resulting from more extreme procedures such as corporal punishment. Of course, excessive reprimands, belittling of the child, personal verbal attacks, and blaming of the child constitute emotional abuse and can have deleterious effects on the long-term adjustment of the individual (Wolfe, 1999).

It is also possible that reprimands may unwittingly lead to corporal punishment. As parents or teachers become frustrated with the weak effects of reprimands, the next seemingly logical step is to increase the severity of the punishment and to hit the child. Also, as mentioned previously, reprimands have been more effective when a child is grasped while reprimanded. The risk of using this procedure is that, in practice, grasping a child is likely to become more intense and may unnecessarily hurt the child.

The major limitation of verbal statements as punishing events is their inconsistent effects. They often produce little or no behavior change. For most of the behaviors brought to treatment, the weak or inconsistent effects of verbal reprimands are not sufficient to achieve therapeutic change. It is likely that the overuse and misuse in everyday life contributes to their lack of effectiveness. For example, observations of teachers throughout elementary and high school grades have shown relatively high rates of reprimands and low rates of praise in regular classrooms (Thomas, Presland, Grant, & Glynn, 1978; White, 1975). Perhaps the high rates of reprimands attest in part to their likely long-term ineffectiveness.

The excessive use of reprimands raises an obvious question. How come they are used at all if it is true, as noted here, that they do not work very well? It is likely that reprimands immediately suppress behavior (stop the problem behavior at that moment) even though this effect will not alter the likelihood of the behavior over time. Thus the use of reprimands may be negatively reinforced in the behavior of the parent or teacher; as soon as a reprimand is given, the aversive event (child's behavior) stops. The parent's behavior (giving reprimands) is likely to be maintained by immediate negative reinforcement; the long-term ineffectiveness is less likely to influence parent behavior.

The ineffectiveness or weak effects of reprimands in the classroom and other settings is exacerbated by the paucity of reinforcement, because reinforcement for positive behaviors can augment the effectiveness of otherwise weak punishment. To improve teacher effectiveness, one might want to increase the use of positive reinforcement to support positive student behavior. Of course, there are few reinforcement contingencies that support positive teacher behaviors.

An important consideration is that reprimands and verbal admonitions in one form or another comprise a large part of naturally occurring events in everyday life. Hence, in treatment settings, it may be desirable to train clients to respond to disapproval, if they do not already respond to it. Verbal statements can be made to function as aversive events by pairing them with other events such as physical restraint or removal of positive events. Here the purpose of the program is to develop responsiveness to naturally occurring events.

Electric Shock

Shock is another aversive event that can be presented after behavior. Although shock is rarely used, its unique characteristics and effects deserve comment. Most applications of shock have been restricted to persons who engage in behaviors dangerous to themselves or to others and who have not responded to other procedures. When shock has been used in these extraordinary situations, usually it has consisted of a brief shock to the finger or arm. Because shock is a primary aversive event, even its brief application usually produces rapid and marked suppression of behavior.

Shock may be an alternative when rapid suppression of a serious behavior is needed and when other efforts have failed. For example, electric shock was used to eliminate self-injurious behavior among five individuals (ages 11 to 24) residing in an institution (Linscheid, Iwata, Ricketts, Williams, & Griffin, 1990). These individuals showed chronic self-injury involving forceful contact with the head (face and head hitting, head banging) that produced tissue damage, had a history of other treatments that had failed (e.g., medication, overcorrection, physical restraint), and currently engaged in self-injury that required physical restraint or medication. Each individual, studied separately, was fitted with a special device worn over the head (a headband with a small apparatus) that automatically detected blows to the head, recorded these blows, and when programmed, delivered a brief shock to the arm or leg. In carefully evaluated experimental designs for each individual, contingent shock was shown to markedly reduce the behavior. In this study, shock was effective in reducing and in some cases eliminating self-injurious behavior that was dangerous and that did not respond to a number of other treatments.

As another example, shock was used to suppress dangerous and life-threatening behavior of a 9-month-old infant who engaged in ruminative vomiting (consistent vomiting after meals, failure to retain food) (Linscheid & Cunningham, 1977). Vomiting had resulted in severe weight loss, malnutrition, and potentially fatal medical complications. The shock was intense enough to evoke a startle reaction but not intense enough to elicit crying. When shock was applied (to the leg) at the onset of vomiting, vomiting dropped from an average of over 100 instances per day to 1 instance per day after only 3 days of treatment. Follow-up evaluation, nine months after the infant was released from the hospital, revealed that ruminative vomiting no longer occurred and weight gain had increased.

The rapid and often durable effects of shock have led to its occasional use. The uses are restricted to extreme situations in which there is a need to suppress a harmful and dangerous behavior. The rare use of shock is attributed to the fact that many less objectionable but effective procedures are available. Related ethical and legal issues restrict the use of shock. With adults, usually in outpatient treatment, shock has been occasionally used to reduce or eliminate such behaviors as cigarette smoking, overeating, alcohol consumption, and various sexual behaviors such as fetishes (e.g., McConaghy, 1990). Shock has not been particularly effective in these instances, and less objectionable procedures with equal or greater effectiveness are readily available.

Strengths and Limitations. Shock has been used in cases in which dangerous behavior needs to be suppressed rapidly and alternative procedures have not been effective. Because the procedure is painful, it is usually not resorted to unless alternative procedures have been unsuccessful. Indeed, in the examples provided above, shock was used only after several other procedures had failed to change behavior. Major advances have been made in elaborating alternatives to punishment and in understanding the factors that maintain self-injurious and dangerous behavior to which shock and other forms of punishment might be applied. Specifically, through functional analysis, the determinants of self-injury can be identified and then used to reduce or eliminate dangerous behavior (Pelios et al., 1999; Sturmey, 1996). Consequently, change in dangerous behaviors can be achieved without resorting to aversive procedures such as shock. Given the range of effective alternative techniques, based on both punishment and reinforcement, serious ethical and legal objections would be warranted if shock were the first treatment to be considered.

Omitting for a moment the appropriateness and necessity of shock, many other limitations militate against its use in applied settings. To begin with, professionals and clients are likely to view it as unacceptable for treatment purposes (Kazdin, 1980a). Hence, independent of its effectiveness, its use is restricted to very special cases in which extreme procedures appear to be warranted. One would really have to make the case that other less objectionable procedures were unsuccessful. Even if this were surmounted, delivering shock is not straightforward. The administration of shock requires special equipment. Hence, shock has generally been restricted to laboratory or treatment settings where clients are seen individually and are closely supervised. In settings where clients are treated in groups, it is not readily feasible to employ shock. In addition, the person using shock must be well trained so that its intensity is not severe and so that accidents due to misuse of equipment do not occur. The practical issues are moot because of the unacceptability of aversive stimuli in general and shock in particular unless all of the reasonable options have been carefully tried.

Other Aversive Consequences

A variety of other aversive consequences, somewhat less well studied than reprimands and less controversial than shock, have also been used. For example, squirting lemon juice into the client's mouth has been used in a few treatment cases. In one application, lemon juice was used to help suppress biting in a 4-year-old girl who frequently bit other children and her teacher (Matson, Manikam, & Ladatto, 1992). Similarly, in another report, squirting lemon juice from a plastic squirt bottle into the mouth of a severely retarded boy effectively eliminated public masturbation (Cook, Altman, Shaw, & Blaylock, 1978).

Another punishment technique is introducing the smell of aromatic ammonia (smelling salts), contingent on undesirable behavior. For example, in one report, ammonia was used to suppress self-injurious behavior in two children (Altman, Haavik, & Cook, 1978). Severe hair pulling in a 4-year-old girl (who had made herself partially bald) and hand biting in a 3-year-old boy (who had damaged the tissues of his fingers) were suppressed by breaking a capsule of aromatic ammonia and placing it under the child's nose for a few seconds when the self-injurious behaviors were performed.

Other punishment procedures are occasionally used. Two of these procedures are spraying a mist of water in the client's face (water mist) and briefly covering the client's face with a piece of cloth or something else that blocks vision (facial screening). For example, water mist and facial screening have reduced self-injurious behavior (face punching, jaw hitting, self-biting) in mentally retarded adolescents (Singh, Watson, & Winton, 1986). The spray of water (at room temperature) or the brief facial screening (5 seconds) was contingent on instances of self-injurious behavior.

The rationale behind many techniques of this kind has been to develop procedures that provide minimal discomfort but can effectively suppress behavior. The use of lemon juice as an aversive event illustrates this rationale. Although the taste of lemon juice is obviously unattractive to most people, its use as an aversive event is probably more socially acceptable than such other procedures as electric shock. Indeed, in one example above, lemon juice was used to suppress severely dangerous behaviors where shock might have been considered as an alternative.

WITHDRAWAL OF POSITIVE CONSEQUENCES

Punishment often takes the form of withdrawing positive events rather than presenting aversive events after behavior. Familiar examples include the loss of privileges, money, or one's driver's license after behavior. Events that are positively valued and that may even have served as positive reinforcers are taken away as a penalty. The two major techniques, each with several variations, are time out from reinforcement and response cost.

Time Out from Reinforcement

Punishment often takes the form of removing a positive event. One procedure for removing a positive event *is time out from reinforcement (or simply time out), which refers to the removal of a positive reinforcer for a certain period of time.* During the time-out interval, the client does not have access to the positive reinforcers that are normally available in the setting. For example, a child may be isolated from others in class for 10 minutes. During that time, he or she will not have access to peer interaction, activities, privileges, and other reinforcers that are usually available.

The crucial ingredient of time out is delineating a brief period during which reinforcement is unavailable. Ideally, during this period, all sources of reinforcement are withdrawn. This ideal is not always attained. For example, if a child is sent to his or her room as punishment, removal from the existing sources of reinforcement qualifies as time out. However, all reinforcement may not be withheld; the child may engage in a number of reinforcing activities such as playing a computer game, listening to music, or sleeping. Despite these possibilities, time out usually consists of making reinforcing events unavailable to the client for a brief period.

Before illustrating applications of time out, it is useful to distinguish this procedure from extinction with which it is often confused. The defining feature of time out is based on a period of time and the unavailability of reinforcement during that time period. Of course, time out is also a punishment procedure. Something is withdrawn (availability of reinforcers) contingent on behavior. Extinction is not a punishment procedure. In extinction, a response that has been reinforced (e.g., praise for smiling) is no longer reinforced. The key feature of extinction is that a previously reinforced behavior is no longer reinforced. There is no time interval or period involved in extinction. When the response occurs, no consequence follows. In contrast, during time out, when a response to be suppressed occurs, a period is invoked in which no reinforcers can be provided for any behavior.

A variety of time-out procedures have been used effectively in treatment. In many variations, the client is physically isolated or excluded in some way from the situation. The client may be sent to a time-out room or booth, a special place that is partitioned off. For example, noncompliance with requests among mentally retarded residents was suppressed by requiring a child to sit in the corner of the room for 40 seconds for an instance of noncompliance (Doleys, Wells, Hobbs, Roberts, & Cartelli, 1976). Similarly, alcohol consumption among hospitalized chronic alcoholics was suppressed with time out (Bigelow, Liebson, & Griffiths, 1974). The patients were allowed free access to alcoholic beverages on the ward. During time out, they were placed in an isolation booth for 10 to 15 minutes contingent on drinking.

Although many programs using time out have employed isolation (removal from the situation) as the time-out procedure, alternative procedures are available that still meet the definition of time out. One time-out procedure that does not involve removing the individual from the situation was used to suppress disruptive behavior among children (ages 1 to 3 years) who attended a day-care center (Porterfield, Herbert-Jackson, & Risley, 1976). Disruptive behaviors such as hitting or pushing peers, crying and fussing, engaging in tantrums, and breaking toys were punished with time-out procedures while the children engaged in free-play activities. When disruptive behavior occurred, the child was told that the behavior was inappropriate and removed to the periphery of the other children's activity. While away from the center of activity in the room, the child was still allowed to observe the activity and the other children. However, the child was not allowed to play with toys. After a brief period, usually less than 1 minute, the child was allowed to return to his or her activities in the center of the room. Partial removal of children from their activities markedly decreased their disruptive behavior.

Variations of time out have been used in which the client is not even partially removed from the situation. For example, in one program, time out was used as part of a reinforcement program for boys in a special education class for mentally retarded children in a state institution (Foxx & Shapiro, 1978). As part of the reinforcement system, the children received praise and smiles (social reinforcement) for performing their work. Each child in the class was given a ribbon to wear around his neck. The ribbon signified to the child and the teacher that the child could receive social and, occasionally, food reinforcers that were administered while the children worked. When any disruptive behavior was performed, a time-out procedure was used. Time out consisted of removing the child's ribbon for three minutes. Without the ribbon, the child could not receive any of the reinforcers normally administered. This time-out procedure effectively reduced disruptive classroom behavior.

The time-out ribbon is a clever procedure because the ribbon serves as an S^D, that is, a stimulus indicating that reinforcement would follow appropriate

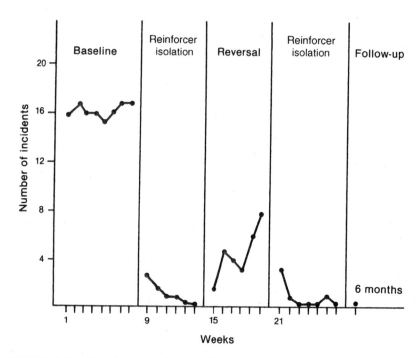

FIGURE 7-1 Number of noncompliant incidents per five-day work-week for each experimental condition.

(Source: Mansdorf, 1977)

behavior. The absence of the ribbon was an S^Δ indicating that reinforcement would not follow appropriate behavior. The presence of the ribbon served as a cue (antecedent event) that increased the likelihood of positive behavior in the children and as a cue to the teacher to praise such behavior. We discussed previously how antecedents can greatly assist in prompting desired behaviors.

Positive reinforcers have been made unavailable in other ways to accomplish time out from reinforcement. For example, time out was applied to an adult with mental retardation who refused to comply with staff requests to take a shower (Mansdorf, 1977). When this resident did not comply, she would simply sit in the dayroom and watch television, listen to music, or go back to bed. Time out was used for noncompliance by removing her opportunities for reinforcement for a brief period. If she did not comply, television or music was turned off, peers were asked to leave the dayroom, and the pillow and bedding were removed. Essentially, the reinforcers she usually used were made temporarily unavailable. If she did comply, these reinforcing events were restored. The procedure was very effective in reducing the number of incidents of noncompliance, as shown in Figure 7-1. The effects were maintained six months after the program had been terminated.

Strengths and Limitations. Time out from reinforcement has been very effective in altering a number of behaviors, including psychotic speech, toileting accidents, thumb sucking, and self-stimulatory and self-injurious behavior (see Hobbs & Forehand, 1977). Usually short time-out durations such as several seconds or a few minutes are effective in suppressing behavior. Longer time-out periods do not necessarily increase the effectiveness of the procedure.

Obvious advantages of time out are that it can be relatively brief and that it does not involve pain. Additional advantages and disadvantages of time out depend on the specific form it takes. Removing individuals from the situation in which deviant behavior occurs (e.g., sending individuals to a time-out room), particularly for extended periods, has potential disadvantages. Removal from the situation reduces opportunities for positive reinforcement of alternative positive behaviors in that situation. Hence, the client cannot learn the desired behaviors and the conditions under which those behaviors are appropriate. Also, in some cases, it may be undesirable to leave the client isolated from others because of the opportunity that isolation provides for engaging in maladaptive behaviors. For example, self-stimulatory behaviors are often maintained by the sensory stimulation they produce (Sprague & Newell, 1996). Thus it is not externally presented reinforcers such as attention that maintain behavior but rather reinforcement that derives from the behavior itself. Understandably, a client in isolation may simply continue to engage in undesired self-stimulatory behavior.

Isolation from others may also be undesirable for clients who are socially withdrawn. Removal from the social situation may further isolate clients who already have only minimal interaction with others. A main goal of treatment is to develop prosocial behaviors in the presence of other individuals rather than to foster any more isolation, whether physical or social, than may already result from the client's interpersonal deficits.

Many of the objections to time out are resolved with variations that do not remove the client from the situation. Leaving the client in the situation (e.g., a classroom) but setting aside brief periods in which reinforcers are not available has many advantages. A client who is allowed to remain in the situation can continue to participate in activities and can perhaps even observe others who receive desirable consequences for appropriate behavior. Of course, an individual's behavior may be so disruptive that he or she has to be removed from the situation so as not to disturb or interfere with the activities of others. To handle this possible problem, some programs have allowed individuals to remain in the situation during time out unless their behavior becomes very disruptive. Using social isolation to back up a less severe form of time out is an excellent strategy because when this strategy is used the client is removed from the situation only if necessary.

The extent to which time out will be effective is likely to depend on the situation from which the client is removed. That ongoing situation, sometimes referred to as *time in,* denotes the situation and reinforcing consequences from which the client is withdrawn. If the environment is highly reinforcing (e.g., frequent praise, earning of points, peer interaction), a brief period of time out is likely to be more effective than it would be if the environment were devoid of reinforcing consequences. In practice, time out does not require that an ongoing reinforcement program or richly rewarding environment is in effect during the time-in period. Yet during any punishment program, some reinforcement should be provided to develop positive and prosocial behavior. Consequently, reinforcement plus time out is likely to be more effective than time out alone (Marlow, Tingstrom, Olmi, & Edwards, 1997; Shriver & Allen, 1996).

In general, time out provides an excellent alternative to many of the forms of punishment used in everyday life, such as reprimands and corporal punishment. Very brief time out, for several seconds or a few minutes, has been effective. Time out has been especially effective when many reinforcers are available in the setting, so that time out from these reinforcing events is especially aversive. Occasionally, time out has been ineffective for some individuals and has even served as a positive reinforcer (Foxx & Azrin, 1972; Plummer, Baer, & LeBlanc, 1977). For example, I worked with a young woman named Delores, who had extreme tantrums and outbursts with the slightest provocation or frustration (e.g., being told no, not getting her way with peers, changing activities). She was in a day-treatment program each day and lived at home. The intervention consisted of providing praise and attention to nontantrum behavior (DRO) and placing her in time out for 2 minutes for each outburst. Time out was in a barren room, with only a table and chair and off from the main activity room of the setting. Time out had little effect. Moreover, Delores eagerly went to time out and kept remarking how much she liked being there. This raised the possibility that time out might serve as a positive reinforcer. We altered the contingency so that nontantrum behavior in response to frustrations and changes could earn immediate access to time out. Also, we placed materials (books, magazines) in the room and allowed her to bring any other materials she wanted. In short, removal from the situation is not always time out. This example illustrates the importance of direct observation of behavior and use of the information to make changes in the intervention.

The example focuses on an exception. Time out usually is effective in suppressing behavior, as attested to by scores of studies using many variations of time out. Also, if time out were a reinforcer, it is not one to be used routinely. Isolation and removal from social influences, for most clinical problems, is a therapeutic move in the wrong direction. Many problems brought to treatment or for intervention reflect problems of adaptation in interpersonal situations or environments with other people. The goal is not only to change behavior but to integrate individuals into normal, everyday, interpersonal situations. Isolation need not be used even if it is reinforcing; other reinforcers can be selected that keep the individual in the situation. In any case, brief time out is an excellent alternative to the presentation of aversive stimuli. As with other punishment, positive reinforcement for prosocial behaviors is essential to use with time out.

Response Cost

Response cost refers to a loss of a positive reinforcer and usually entails a penalty of some sort contingent on behavior. With response cost, there is no period during which positive events are unavailable, as is the case with time out from reinforcement.

Typically, response cost consists of a fine. Examples of response cost in everyday experience include fines for traffic violations or overdue books, fees for late filing of income tax or registering for classes beyond the due date, and charges for checks that "bounce."

Perhaps the most familiar example of response cost is a fine (loss of money) for traffic violations. Indeed, fines are systematically evaluated to identify their effects in this context. For example, controlled studies show that illegal parking (e.g., parking in spaces reserved for people with disabilities) is reduced greatly by giving fines, even small fines (e.g., $2) (e.g., Fletcher, 1995). To note that fines *reduce* illegal parking violations is of course not the same as saying they are effective in eliminating such violations. Fines for traffic violations are a good example of response cost, but fines often are ineffective because of *how* they are administered. They are intermittently delivered so that only some of the behavior is actually fined—parking illegally is not fined most of the time for most people. Intermittent punishment is not optimally effective. Also, there is little enforcement of fines—not paying several parking tickets may not have any other consequences for the person who does not pay. However, we are getting ahead of the discussion at this point, and here it is critical merely to illustrate response cost rather than to discuss optimal ways of administering punishment.

Response cost has variations other than monetary fines. For example, response cost was used to reduce aggressive and disruptive behavior in the classroom of four preschool boys (ages 3 to 5) (Reynolds & Kelley, 1997). The children engaged in such behaviors as throwing things, damaging other children's materials, hitting, and screaming. The response-cost procedure consisted of providing a child with five laminated smiley faces attached to a larger sheet (with Velcro). The chart was labeled Good Behavior Chart and posted in the classroom for all to see. Each time the child engaged in one aggressive behavior, a smiley face was taken away. The teacher stated the reason for the loss of the smiley face and provided a reprimand. If the child retained at least one smiley face at the end of the 40-minute period, he could purchase special rewards (e.g., being the teacher's helper, access to a favorite toy). Consistent performance over at least 4 or 5 days provided additional incentives (a special grab bag). Response cost was introduced as a multiple-baseline design across children. As evident in Figure 7-2, aggressive behavior changed markedly as the intervention was introduced.

Response cost has often been used as part of token economies in which tokens are delivered for some behaviors and taken away for others. For example, in one program with psychiatric patients, fines were levied whenever patients violated a rule of the ward (Upper, 1973). Infractions included such behaviors as getting up late in the morning, undressing or exposing oneself, and shouting. Violations dropped below baseline rates when a fine was subtracted from token earnings. Whether implemented alone or in conjunction with token economies, response cost has altered a wide variety of behaviors such as overeating, disruptive classroom behavior, speech disfluencies, psychotic speech, thumb sucking, and toileting accidents (see Kazdin, 1972).

In everyday life, taking away a privilege is often used as a form of punishment. This is another way in which response cost can be implemented. Taking

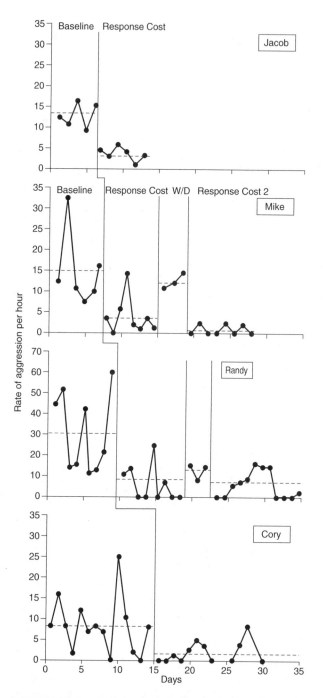

FIGURE 7-2 Rate of aggressive behavior during baseline and treatment conditions across subjects.

(Source: Reynolds & Kelley, 1997)

away a privilege usually consists of a one-shot event (e.g., "Cinderella, you may not go to the ball.") or an activity available daily (e.g., telling a young child that he or she may not use the computer or a bicycle for two days after some undesirable behavior has occurred). Loss of a privilege is not used very much in behavior modification. First, taking away a privilege for one or a few occasions is not likely to be useful because it cannot be applied to a behavior each time it occurs (e.g., Cinderella does not have a ball each week). Also, taking away a single reinforcer (e.g., access to a computer or bicycle) for a particular period is sort of a weak time out (only a single reinforcer is taken away for a *period of time*). Time out or response cost ought to be contingent on behavior and should be provided each time the behavior occurs. In the previous chapter, activities were discussed as a useful type of reinforcer but also limited because it is difficult to deliver an activity contingent on behavior each time behavior occurs and because any single activity may or not be consistently reinforcing. Similarly, removing a privilege also is somewhat more difficult than a brief period of time out or a small fine and may not serve as an aversive event in a consistent fashion. Response cost, when in the form of loss of tokens (a generalized conditioned reinforcer) is likely to be more effective than loss of any particular activity or other single reinforcer that serves as one of the backup reinforcers that can be purchased by tokens.

Strengths and Limitations. Response cost, particularly in the form of withdrawing points or tokens after behavior, is relatively easy to implement. One problem that may arise is that clients who lose many points may soon have no further points to lose. Yet more points or tokens could be earned for positive behaviors to ensure that points can be withdrawn contingent on the undesired behavior.

Providing points raises the clear benefit of response cost in the form of fines. If tokens or points are to be withdrawn, they have to be delivered to the client. Behavior change is likely to be more rapid if the tokens are delivered for behaviors incompatible with the responses that are to be suppressed. Hence, when points or tokens are used, reinforcement and punishment in the form of response cost can easily be implemented as part of a single program. Moreover, token reinforcement and response cost combined are more effective than either procedure alone (Bierman, Miller, & Stabb, 1987; Kelley & McCain, 1995).

PUNISHING CONSEQUENCES
BASED ON EFFORT

As a consequence for undesirable behavior, a client can be required to engage in responses that entail work or effort. This is different from presenting the client with an aversive stimulus (e.g., reprimand) or withdrawing a positive event from the client (e.g., response cost). Here the client is required to engage in effortful behavior.

Overcorrection

With *overcorrection,* the penalty for engaging in an undesirable behavior is performing some other behaviors in the situation. Two components of overcorrection can be distinguished. The first component, referred to as *restitution,* consists of correcting the environmental effects of the inappropriate behavior. Thus if a child throws food at the dinner table, he or she would be required to clean it up completely. The second component, referred to as *positive practice,* consists of repeatedly practicing the appropriate behavior. For example, the child would be required to place food on his or her plate appropriately several times in a row and perhaps to serve others food as well. These responses are some of the "correct" ways of serving and managing food at the table. Restitution and positive practice are sometimes combined and sometimes used alone, depending on the behaviors that are to be suppressed.

In an initial application of the procedure, restitution and positive practice were used with a profoundly retarded 50-year-old female who had been hospitalized for 46 years (Foxx & Azrin, 1972). For several years, this client had engaged in severely disruptive and aggressive behavior, especially throwing things. When she performed a disruptive behavior, such as overturning a bed, she was required to correct the physical effects of her behavior on the environment (i.e., turn the bed to its correct position and straighten the spread and pillows). In addition, she was required to rehearse the correct behavior by straightening all of the other beds on the ward. Thus she had to correct the immediate consequence of whatever inappropriate behavior she performed (restitution) and then to practice repeatedly the correct behavior throughout the ward (positive practice). After 11 weeks of training, she no longer threw objects.

An interesting application of overcorrection was used to eliminate stealing among hospitalized mentally retarded adults (Azrin & Wesolowski, 1974). The residents had a high rate of stealing from one another, especially food during meal and snack times when they purchased items at a commissary (store) in the hospital. A staff member simply required the resident to return the food or the remaining portion if it had been partially consumed. Return of the food did not completely restore the original situation if the food had been partially consumed. With this procedure (called *simple correction*), stealing remained at a high rate. An overcorrection procedure was implemented that required the resident not only to return the food but also to purchase more of that food and give it to the victim. The results, illustrated in Figure 7-3, show that theft was eliminated among the 34 residents within a matter of a few days.

It is not possible to have individuals "correct" the environmental consequences of many behaviors that are to be suppressed. The behaviors may not have altered the environment. For example, if a child whines, hits himself, rocks back and forth, or stutters, there are no clear environmental consequences that can be corrected. For such behaviors, positive practice is often used alone. After the undesired behavior has been performed, the client is required to practice positively an appropriate or incompatible behavior. For example, positive practice was used to alter the classroom behavior of six disruptive boys enrolled in a special summer

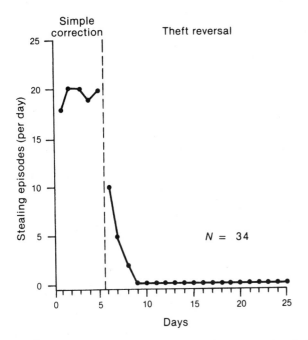

FIGURE 7-3 Number of stealing episodes that occurred each day among 34 mentally retarded adult residents in an institution. During the five days of simple correction, the thief was required to return the stolen item. During the theft-reversal (overcorrection) procedure (subsequent to the vertical dashed line), the thief was required to return the stolen item and to give the victim an additional item identical to the one stolen. The stealing episodes consisted of stealing food items from other mentally retarded residents during commissary periods.

(Source: Azrin & Wesolowski, 1974)

class (Azrin & Powers, 1975). Talking out and being out of one's seat were decreased by having the children who engaged in these behaviors remain inside at recess. During this recess period, a child would practice appropriate classroom behavior by sitting in his seat, raising his hand, being recognized by the teacher, and asking permission to get up. This entire sequence was repeated for approximately five minutes, a procedure that markedly improved classroom performance. Loss of recess without engaging in positive practice did not achieve the marked changes associated with positive practice.

Strengths and Limitations. Overcorrection alone or in combination with other procedures has altered a variety of behaviors such as toileting accidents, aggressive acts, self-stimulatory behaviors, tantrums, nail biting, and table manners (Foxx & Bechtel, 1983). Overcorrection procedures vary widely, depending on the specific behavior that is suppressed and the desired behavior that is developed in its place. The procedures are developed from the general principle of having individuals correct the environmental consequences of their actions, where such consequences exist, and practicing the desired behavior repeatedly after each instance of the undesired behavior. The results of a few minutes of corrective training after the undesired behavior have often led to rapid and long-lasting therapeutic effects.

Certainly, the distinguishing feature of overcorrection, in relation to other punishment techniques, is that it focuses on the appropriate behavior that is incompatible with the undesired response. Most forms of punishment do not convey to the client the behaviors that are appropriate. The positive practice component of overcorrection trains desirable behaviors and thus serves an educative function not included in other aversive techniques. Indeed, research has shown that unlike other punishment procedures, overcorrection not only suppresses inappropriate behavior but also can develop positive appropriate behaviors. There is a related benefit of the procedure. In the usual punishment procedure, parents, teachers, or staff focus their attention on undesirable behaviors that need to be suppressed. Overcorrection shifts attention to desirable behaviors that need to be developed, the priority of any behavior-change program.

For use of overcorrection, one must identify both the behavior that will correct the environment and the appropriate behavior that should be performed. When the undesired behavior is performed, the client is immediately required to engage in the sequence of behaviors that restore and overcorrect the action. If simple instructions to complete the requisite behaviors prove insufficient, the client may need to be physically guided (assisted) by the parent or teacher to go through these behaviors. Guiding the client through requisite behaviors can be problematic if the client resists or becomes aggressive. If physical force is necessary, alternative procedures may need to be used.

Another consideration in using overcorrection is the supervision the procedure often requires. The person in charge of the program must ensure that the client goes through the overcorrection sequence for the allotted time and must provide physical prompts if necessary. In some situations, it may not be feasible to provide one-to-one client supervision to conduct overcorrection. For example, in a classroom situation, overcorrection has on occasion been discontinued in part because of the difficulties in supervising overcorrection while managing the rest of the class (Kelly & Drabman, 1977). On the other hand, applications have shown that in a classroom situation overcorrection can be delayed and conducted at recess time or during free periods, when direct supervision of the client need not detract from others in the room (Azrin & Powers, 1975; Barton & Osborne, 1978).

Overall, the rapid and dramatic effects of overcorrection have made this a viable treatment technique for a variety of problems. In many studies, overcorrection has achieved changes in behaviors where other techniques such as time out, reprimands, reinforcement of other behavior, and physical restraint have not proven effective. Although definitive statements about the relative effectiveness of alternative punishment techniques cannot be made at this time, overcorrection appears to be very effective in its own right. In addition, evidence suggests that parents, teachers, and children view overcorrection as a punishment procedure that is more acceptable than such alternatives as time out (Kazdin, French, & Sherick, 1981).

Other Effort-Based Consequences

The unique feature of overcorrection is that the behaviors that the client must perform as part of restitution and positive practice are directly related to the behavior that is to be suppressed. Behaviors involving effort that bear no logical connection to the target behavior have also been effective. The effectiveness of such applications can be expected, based on a variation of the Premack principle. The principle was discussed previously in the context of positive reinforcement in which high-probability (or highly preferred) behaviors such as playing with friends serve as reinforcers for low-probability (or less preferred) behaviors such as working. The principle also suggests an arrangement of the contingency that can suppress behavior and be used as punishment. Low-probability behaviors can be used as consequences for an undesirable response.

For example, in one program, verbal and physical aggression were suppressed in two emotionally disturbed children in a special education classroom (Luce, Delquadri, & Hall, 1980). One of the children, a 7-year-old boy named Ben, engaged in aggression, severe tantrums, and self-stimulatory behavior. Ben's hitting of other children at school was the target behavior that was to be suppressed. Engaging in exercise was used as the aversive consequence. When Ben hit someone, he was required to stand up and sit down on the floor 10 times, which required less than 30 seconds. Initially, he was physically prompted by the teacher, who helped him up and down. Then, verbal prompts alone were sufficient to ensure that he completed the exercise. The effects of the program, illustrated in Figure 7-4, show that low rates of aggressive behavior were obtained when the exercise contingency was in effect. At a follow-up assessment one and a half years after the program was terminated, Ben's hitting had been completely eliminated.

In a somewhat different procedure, individuals can be required to engage in various aversive chores. For example, excessive swearing of an 11-year-old boy was altered by requiring the boy to wash windows for 10 minutes whenever he swore (Fischer & Nehs, 1978). The procedure effectively suppressed his swearing, and the effect was maintained after the program had been terminated (up to two weeks later).

In another program, two adults were treated for bruxism, which consists of grinding and gnashing of one's teeth (Watson, 1993). Bruxism can result in damage to one's teeth, joints, and muscles, not to mention to relationships with partners and significant others. The spouses of the two individuals in this study were easily enlisted to help with the program. Merely waking up each person when the grinding began was not sufficient to eliminate behavior, although it led to some reduction. Effort-based procedure was used in which the individual was awakened and for 10 minutes engaged in face and hand washing, brushing and flossing teeth, and rinsing of the mouth with water and mouth wash. The procedure eliminated bruxism in both individuals, and effects were maintained for 15 to 18 months after treatment ended.

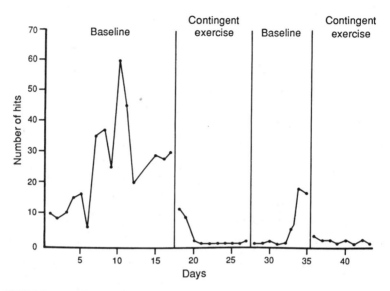

FIGURE 7-4 Number of instances of hitting by Ben while at school. During baseline, the aggressive behavior was ignored and no special program was provided to alter it. During the contingent-exercise phase, Ben was required to stand up and sit down on the floor for instances of hitting.

(Source: Luce, Delquadri, & Hall, 1980)

Strengths and Limitations. The use of effort-based activities as aversive consequences has advantages. The activities (exercises, chores) are quite familiar to parents, teachers, staff, and clients. Consequently, less training is needed in using effort than in using other procedures such as overcorrection, where novel behaviors of the behavior-change agent (e.g., special prompting of the person to engage in activities) and the client (e.g., practicing new behaviors) may need to be trained and closely supervised.

An important consideration with effort-based procedures is whether performing the aversive behavior may interrupt ongoing behavior or be disruptive in the situation. For example, in one study, contingent exercise was used to reduce a boy's inappropriate and bizarre verbalizations in a classroom (Luce & Hall, 1981). Instances of these behaviors were followed by a brief run (20 seconds) around the playground. Although such a procedure suppresses behavior, it may also interrupt sitting at one's desk, remaining in the situation, and possibly receiving reinforcement for remaining at a task. Another potential problem is that engaging in exercise or leaving the situation (going to the playground) may actually serve as a reinforcer (escape from an aversive task or situation) for some children.

Effort-based procedures such as exercise or chores focus on suppressing undesirable behaviors. With such procedures, unlike overcorrection, no attempt is made to teach an appropriate behavior to replace the target response. For example, one does not want a child to exercise in the classroom or to run around the playground in the middle of a lesson. Overcorrection focuses on developing positive alternative behaviors in addition to suppressing the target response. If feasible in the situation, it may be the most preferable of the effort-based procedures.

Selecting Procedures to Suppress Behaviors

The precise punishment procedure selected in any instance may be determined by several considerations, including severity and dangerousness of the behavior, the ease of implementing the procedure in a particular setting, and the training required of the person(s) administering the program. For example, response cost might be relatively easily administered and effective with many behaviors and require less time and supervision than would overcorrection. Overcorrection, if more difficult to implement, might be reserved for cases in which less complex procedures proved ineffective. The punishment procedures selected should be the least restrictive or intrusive among those available. Although shock or physical restraint might be effective in suppressing behavior, the severity of the procedures make them ethically unacceptable unless less restrictive procedures (e.g., reinforcement of functionally equivalent responses, time out, response cost) have failed.

When aversive consequences are used to suppress behavior, special consideration might be given to the specific events used and to the possible long-range consequences of using them. Procedures commonly used in everyday life (but usually not in behavior modification programs) often require individuals to engage in tasks that probably should not be used as aversive events. For example, requiring children to stay in from recess or to remain after school to write "I shall not swear" 500 times on the blackboard, to complete extra homework, or to see the principal when they are disruptive may defeat many of the inherent goals of school. We do not want children to learn that these events are aversive. The fact that behavioral programs have occasionally used escape from the classroom as a reinforcer and completion of academic tasks as a punisher (e.g., Harris & Sherman, 1973; MacPherson, Candee, & Hohman, 1974) suggests that important characteristics associated with school are already imbued with aversive properties. An important goal is to develop positive attitudes and approach responses to these and similar events. To treat various activities (e.g., working on assignments, completing homework, remaining in the classroom interacting with the teacher) as aversive consequences may make school aversive, especially for students who are not obtaining other rewards (e.g., good grades, achievement, peer status and popularity.)

At present, the long-term consequences of using particular aversive events are not known. Hence, considerations about selection of the events need to be based on information about the individual case and about possible consequences that might result. In short, common sense as well as scientific evidence should enter into the selection of specific punishing consequences.

Behavior modification research has developed and evaluated a large number of aversive techniques. This may seem ironic, given the evidence that, if at all possible, punishment should not be used, and then only as a supplement to a reinforcement program. Yet research on punishment in applied settings has several obligations. Not only should such research develop effective procedures, but the procedures should be humane, socially acceptable to clients, relatively easy to implement, and not readily subject to abuse. Also, because punishing consequences are used so often in everyday life, evaluation of the effects and identifying procedures that can replace or supplement punishment contingencies are important topics for research. The development of less objectionable and brief punishment (e.g., time out) has often been based on these considerations.

Advances in functional analysis have helped to reduce the need for and use of punishment in applied settings. As noted and illustrated in a prior chapter, functional analysis can identify factors controlling behavior. Once the controlling factor can be identified, such as inadvertent attention (positive reinforcement) or escape from a task or demand (negative reinforcement), the contingencies can be changed to promote positive prosocial behavior.

The present comments pertain to the selection among alternative punishment techniques. Consideration of alternatives among aversive events is important in the context of punishment techniques used in everyday life. Punishment used in everyday life is often harsh (e.g., hitting or paddling children) and the way punishment is often administered is likely to render the intervention minimally effective. Punishment procedures highlighted in this chapter do not rely on physical punishment and are less severe or harsh than are those used in everyday life. Also, punishment is invariably used in behavior modification with positive reinforcement to develop positive, prosocial, or adaptive behavior. Thus punishment in behavior modification is quite different from applications in everyday life.

FACTORS THAT INFLUENCE THE EFFECTIVENESS OF PUNISHMENT

The prior comments emphasized different types of punishment and might incorrectly suggest that the key in the effective use of these events is selecting the one that will be effective. As with positive reinforcement, some techniques or variations are more effective than others. Yet the effectiveness of punishment, like that of reinforcement, depends on several conditions. Although punishment has been evaluated extensively in the laboratory (Azrin & Holz, 1966, Hutchinson, 1977), most of the laboratory research dealt with the presentation of aversive events. The removal of positive events has been less well studied. Nevertheless, general statements regarding the conditions that maximize the effectiveness of punishment can be extrapolated from laboratory and applied research.

Delay of Punishment

Punishment is more effective when it is delivered immediately after the target response than when it is delayed. If punishment of the undesirable response is delayed, it immediately follows some other behavior that may be desirable. For example, if a parent punishes a child for some behavior performed earlier that day ("Wait until your father [or mother] comes home"), the delayed punishment would have a weak effect on the undesirable behavior. Moreover, a desirable behavior (e.g., helping with chores) may have been performed in close contiguity with that punishment and may thus inadvertently be suppressed by the punishment. Independent of the specific response that occurs during the delay, if punishment is delayed, it is not likely to be associated with the response that is to be suppressed.

In some cases, punishment is delayed because the undesirable response such as theft or lying cannot be detected immediately. The fact that the consequences would be so delayed may raise questions about their likely effects. There are ways to bring the consequences in closer proximity to the undesired behaviors. One method is to reenact portions of the previously performed behaviors that occurred and to apply aversive consequences immediately to the reenactment. Such procedures appear to bring the consequences closer to the behavior and lead to response suppression (Van Houten & Rolider, 1989).

Schedule of Punishment

Punishment is more effective when the punishing consequence occurs every time (continuous punishment), rather than once in a while (intermittent punishment). The greater the proportion of punished responses, the greater the response reduction. However, when punishment is discontinued, recovery of the response is greater with continuous punishment than with intermittent punishment. For example, if time out is to be used in the home, it should be delivered every time the behavior occurs (continuous schedule). Administering time out intermittently, rather than after each occurrence of the response, usually leads to less response suppression (Hobbs & Forehand, 1977). After a response has been effectively suppressed, punishment can be delivered only intermittently to maintain low rates of the behavior (Calhoun & Lima, 1977; Clark, Rowbury, Baer, & Baer, 1973). In some circumstances and in the use of electric shock, the relationship between punishment schedule and response suppression does not hold. There may be no recovery even if punishment was previously delivered on a continuous schedule.

Source of Reinforcement

If a punished response is also positively reinforced, punishment is less effective than if that response is not reinforced. That a punished behavior is performed at all suggests that some reinforcer is maintaining it; otherwise, the behavior would have extinguished. The effect of punishment can be enhanced by removing the source of reinforcement for the punished response. For example, juvenile delinquents frequently provide peer social reinforcement for the commission of deviant acts. Punishment of deviant acts is likely to be less effective when there is such reinforcement.

When punishment is used, potential sources of reinforcement for the punished response should be identified and eliminated if possible. In practice, it is sometimes difficult to identify the source of the reinforcement that is maintaining a deviant behavior. In many instances, social reinforcers are provided for behaviors that one may wish to suppress. For example, in the classroom, peers probably reinforce inappropriate behaviors (e.g., clowning, teasing). Punishing disruptive behavior would be expected to have little effect if peers provide reinforcement for those behaviors.

Timing of Punishment in the Response Sequence

The earlier in the response sequence punishment is delivered, the more effective it tends to be. An undesirable response is not a single behavior but a chain or sequence of behaviors that culminates in an act considered undesirable. For example, a child's "theft" of a cookie before dinner may consist of a series (chain) of behaviors that includes walking into the kitchen, climbing onto a chair, reaching for the cookie jar, opening the jar, taking a cookie, and eating it. Punishment for going into the kitchen or climbing onto a chair will reduce cookie theft to a greater extent than will punishment after the cookie has been taken and eaten.

The importance of the timing of punishment can be readily explained. If the response chain is completed, the terminal behavior (e.g., cookie consumption) is positively reinforced. Punishment imposed at that time is being used to suppress a response that has just been reinforced. This is not likely to be effective. Moreover, if the chain is completed, the reinforcement of the undesirable response is more immediate than is the punishment. As mentioned previously, punishment is more effective when the response to be suppressed is not reinforced than when it is reinforced. Hence, if a response is punished before it is reinforced, punishment should be more effective. Responses early in the chain of behavior may still be reinforced, since behaviors in a chain reinforce prior behaviors in that chain. However the further a behavior is from the terminal reinforcer, the less potent is the reinforcement. Behaviors early in a sequence are further removed from the terminal reinforcer, so their conditioned reinforcing properties are weaker and they are more readily suppressed when punishment is applied. Thus a punishing consequence (reprimand) that might be ineffective at the end of the response sequence might well lead to suppression if administered earlier in the sequence.

A potential problem in applying punishment to initial behaviors in a response chain is that the behaviors at this point in the chain may be part of other response chains that constitute appropriate behavior. To continue our example, punishment of cookie theft might be very effective if it is delivered when the child enters the kitchen. However, entering the kitchen may be a part of appropriate chains such as washing dishes, feeding a pet, washing hands, or hugging parents.

Variation of Punishment

Application of aversive events usually consists of a contingency in which a particular consequence (e.g., reprimand or time out) is applied after the behavior. The effects of punishment can be enhanced by varying the punishers that follow behavior (Charlop, Burgio, Iwata, & Ivancic, 1988). For example, rather than using overcorrection, brief time out, or a reprimand after behavior, the specific consequence can be varied. Thus on some occasions, one of the consequences (time out) may be used, whereas on other occasions another consequence (reprimand) would be used. Variation of the aversive consequence leads to greater suppression of the responses than does use of any of the individual consequences applied to the behavior. Apparently, there is an adaptation to repeated use of the same consequence. This is obviated by variation of the consequence.

The importance of varying the consequences after behavior raises an important point. The effectiveness of mild punishers such as reprimands and time out, can be enhanced by varying the consequences that are presented. Thus less severe punishers can be used to suppress behavior if they are varied. An important caution is in order. Variation of consequences is to be distinguished from the combination of consequences. The findings suggest that application of a consequence after behavior is more effective when that consequence changes; this does not mean in any way that several consequences should be given at the same time after an instance of behavior. The combination of many aversive procedures as a penalty for performance is a misplaced focus and is objectionable for ethical, as well as practical reasons.

Reinforcement of Alternative Behavior

Punishment is most effective when it is accompanied by reinforcement for performing desirable or prosocial behaviors. Aversive events of relatively weak intensity can effectively suppress behavior if reinforcement is also provided for an alternative positive response. Thus intense punishment is not required to suppress behavior. Mildly aversive events (e.g., grimaces, statements of disapproval, or saying no) may only temporarily suppress undesired behavior. However, their suppressive effect will be enhanced if reinforcement is delivered for positive behaviors. For this reason, most applications of punishment in behavior modification include reinforcement for desirable behavior.

For example, in one program, toddlers were required to sit during the activities in a day-care center as a time-out procedure for disruptive behavior (Porterfield et al., 1976). In addition, approval was provided when a child was playing appropriately. In this and other studies, punishment alone might have been used to suppress behavior. Yet, suppressing an undesirable behavior does not guarantee that a desirable behavior will take its place. Punishment usually trains a person in what not to do rather than in what to do. For example, suppression of fighting in a delinquent does not guarantee the appearance of desirable social behavior. Positive prosocial behaviors must be developed and reinforced directly.

Overcorrection, as a punishment technique, includes the practice of appropriate behavior to help make punishment more educative than is ordinarily the case. However, the behaviors that are positively practiced in overcorrection are not always desirable prosocial responses. Rather, they are often behaviors that appear to be incompatible with the response that is to be suppressed. For example, one study reported the use of overcorrection to eliminate self-injurious behavior in a psychotic and severely retarded adult (Azrin, Gottlieb, Hughart, Wesolowski, & Rahn, 1975). The positive practice component of the procedure included engaging in fixed bodily postures (e.g., practice in holding the hands away from the body in a sequence of exercises) that were incompatible with hitting oneself. Since these behaviors were not socially desirable in their own right, separate reinforcement contingencies were included to develop appropriate social behaviors and participation in activities on the ward.

For at least three reasons, it is advisable to use positive reinforcement whenever punishment is employed. First, reinforcement for alternative behavior increases the efficacy of punishment. Second, reinforcement can develop appropriate behaviors to displace the inappropriate behaviors that are to be eliminated. Third, positive reinforcement combined with punishment may eliminate undesirable side effects that might result from the use of punishment alone. As a general rule, whether the goal is to increase or decrease a particular behavior, reinforcement techniques should constitute the primary basis of the behavior-change program. Any of the various punishment techniques may be a valuable adjunct to reinforcement techniques but perhaps should not be used alone.

General Comments

In the discussion of the factors that influence the effectiveness of punishment, one of the more familiar dimensions considered in everyday life, namely, intensity of punishment, was omitted. In everyday applications, such as child rearing, it is often assumed that the greater the intensity of punishment, the greater the suppression of behavior. Thus advocates of "spare the rod and spoil the child" often believe that a "really good" spanking is needed to teach a lesson. In general, however, laboratory and applied evidence does not support the view that increased intensity of punishment results in increased suppression of a response. There is an exception in laboratory research; the presentation of electric shock at higher intensities has suppressed behavior more quickly than presentation at lower intensities (Azrin & Holz, 1966). This relation does not invariably hold for other aversive events in the laboratory (e.g., noise) or for the many events that are studied in applied settings. For example, louder reprimands, shouts, or threats do not show more suppressive effects than do milder forms of these events.

In the withdrawal of positive reinforcers, more-intense punishments are not needed. Even when a reinforcer is withdrawn for a short period (time out), which does not seem to be an "intense" aversive consequence, response suppression may be dramatic. Occasionally, an increase in the duration of time out, up to several minutes, has led to greater suppression of behavior (e.g., Hobbs, Forehand, & Murray, 1978). Similarly, for response cost (loss of tokens), larger fines have occasionally suppressed behavior more effectively than have smaller fines (Kazdin, 1972). However, these findings do not justify long periods of time out or large fines because far milder consequences are quite effective. For example, with time out, extremely brief periods, including periods ranging from 15 to 90 seconds, have been very effective in several studies. This is quite different from sending children to their rooms for 30 to 60 minutes, as parents often do, or for 8 or 9 hours, as abusive parents occasionally do. Such harsh punishments are not only unnecessary but likely to be ineffective for the child and frustrating for the parents. Much milder punishments, included as part of a program that reinforces prosocial or positive behaviors, can accomplish the goals much more effectively.

SIDE EFFECTS OF PUNISHMENT

Types of Effects

An argument against the use of punishment is that it often results in undesirable side effects. Even though punishment may eliminate the target behavior, it may have other consequences that are worse than the original behavior or are at least problematic in their own right. Laboratory research, usually with infrahuman subjects, provides evidence for a variety of undesirable side effects of punishment (Azrin & Holz, 1966; Hutchinson, 1977; Linscheid & Meinhold, 1990). These side effects also arise in applied situations where punishment is used.

Emotional Reactions. Undesirable emotional reactions may result from punishment. These reactions may be temporarily disruptive to the individual. For example, when a child receives a spanking, crying, anger, and similar emotional reactions will probably occur. These reactions are not essential ingredients of punishment but are undesirable concomitant effects. They are undesirable, in part, because they may interfere with new learning. The child may be unresponsive to the social environment until he or she is no longer upset or angry. An additional consideration is that undesirable emotional reactions are frequently paired with cues in the punishment situation. Eventually, the cues themselves (e.g., parent or teacher or a given situation such as the home) may produce similar reactions in the absence of punishment.

Escape and Avoidance. Another side effect of punishment is that it can lead to escape from or avoidance of the punishment situation. If a situation is aversive, an individual can terminate the aversive condition by escaping. Successful escape from the situation is negatively reinforced because it terminates an aversive condition. Even if the punishing event is only mildly aversive and too weak to suppress behavior, it may still lead to escape behavior. Hence, the use of aversive stimuli fosters escape and reinforcement of escape behaviors. For example, reliance on punishment in the home may result in attempts to avoid or escape from the home.

Stimuli associated with an aversive situation may also lead to escape. Recall that any event consistently associated with an aversive event becomes aversive in its own right. If one individual is constantly punishing another individual, the punishing agent will take on properties of a conditioned aversive stimulus. The individual whose behavior is punished will attempt to escape from or avoid the punishing agent because of these properties. This side effect is undesirable because if individuals (e.g., children) escape or avoid punishing agents (e.g., parents and teachers), the punishing agents will be unable to provide reinforcement to train desirable responses.

Aggression. In laboratory work with a variety of species, punishment sometimes results in attacks by one animal on another animal or on the source of punishment (Hutchinson, 1977). In applied programs using punishment, there is the possibility that the punished individual will aggress toward the punishing agent.

Attacking the agent may remove the source of punishment, at least temporarily. Hence, the individual's aggression toward the punishing agent is negatively reinforced by terminating an aversive event. For example, if an adolescent fights back when being severely beaten by a parent, this may terminate the parental assault. Fighting back, if effective, terminates the aversive consequence by the parent and is negatively reinforced. Unfortunately, if fighting back is effective, the adolescent's aggressive behavior is reinforced.

Modeled Punishment. The punishing agent models (or provides an example of) certain behaviors, namely, the use of aversive control techniques that the punished individual may learn. If a parent uses physical punishment with a child, especially harsh punishment, this increases the likelihood that the child will engage in physically aggressive behaviors (Timberlake, 1981). Adults provide models for how to interact with others. Thus in interactions with their peers, children are likely to use behavioral control techniques similar to the techniques their parents use to control them. It is no surprise, then, that children who are referred clinically for severely aggressive behaviors often come from homes where child and spouse abuse have been evident (Kazdin, 1995). Unfortunately, abuse in the home provides effective models that may help train children to become aggressive, apart from other influences operating in the environment. Certainly, caution is required in using aversive techniques—particularly physical punishment— because of the modeling influences of their use.

Perpetuation of Punishment. Another undesirable side effect of punishment is that its use is reinforced in the person who administers it. Punishment usually results in rapid (though temporary) reduction of the target response. If a parent shouts at a child, the child's behavior is usually altered immediately. Thus the parent's behavior (shout) is negatively reinforced (termination of some undesirable child behavior). Because reinforcement is a powerful technique, particularly if it is immediate, the frequency with which the parent delivers punishment is likely to increase. Even though the punishment is not likely to alter the child's behavior for very long, the failure of the punishment is delayed, whereas the short-term effect is immediate. Hence, the parent is likely to rely increasingly on punishment and runs the risk of encountering the side effects discussed above.

Often there is frustration on the part of the punishing agent (parent, teacher) associated with the continued use of punishment. The agent continues to use punishment, no doubt due in part to the fact that use of punishment is immediately reinforced through negative reinforcement. Over time, parents and teachers invariably recognize that the child's behavior is not changing and that punishment, even harsh punishment, is "not working." In a clinic where I work, we have known abusive parents who have escalated to very harsh physical abuse (burning children with cigarettes, hitting them with wooden boards) and unusual procedures they consider to reflect time out (e.g., keeping a young child outside the house for four days while he looked in, asking for food and shelter; locking a child in his room without meals for two days). The parents often state that they increased the amount or intensity of punishment to "teach the child a lesson once and for all." The ineffectiveness of these procedures, recognized by all parties, does not lead to their disuse. The long-term effectiveness of such procedures does not cancel the effects of other contingencies that operate, such as the immediate negative reinforcement that the parent may experience, satisfaction that some effort was made on the part of the parent to teach the child a lesson, and reduction of parent frustration that applying punishment may afford.

The reasons for using punishment in behavior modification are always to suppress behavior and to develop another behavior; the reasons in everyday life are much more complex because they are not necessarily aimed at suppressing behavior (e.g., revenge, expression of frustration) nor are evaluated systematically with that purpose in mind. In everyday life, punishment often reflects expressions of frustration in parents and teachers or efforts to "teach a lesson," "send a message," or "show that a behavior cannot be tolerated" (e.g., so-called "zero tolerance" policies in which no instance of the behavior can be allowed to occur in the setting), rather than effective interventions. It *is* very important to express frustrations, teach lessons, send messages, and convey that some behaviors cannot be tolerated. The frustration of those who study behavior modification is that punishment in everyday life is not likely to teach lessons or suppress intolerable behavior because of the specific punishments that are used and how they are applied.

Illustrations from Applied Settings

Negative Side Effects. Side effects of punishment have been reported in many applications and across a wide range of aversive techniques. For example, in one program, mentally retarded children received verbal reprimands for noncompliance with requests (Doleys et al., 1976). Some of the children showed brief periods of crying and soiling and wetting their pants. Similarly, reports of programs using overcorrection, response cost, time out, and shock have occasionally noted that the crying, tantrums, and emotional outbursts of the clients increased and that the clients were generally upset (Carey & Bucher, 1981; Matson & Ollendick, 1977). These reports clearly suggest that emotional side effects may be associated with punishment.

Studies have also demonstrated that avoidance may be associated with punishment. For example, in two studies, children were exposed to adults who administered different consequences during play activities (Morris & Redd, 1975; Redd, Morris, & Martin, 1975). Subsequently, the children were asked to choose the adults with whom they wished to interact. The adults who had been associated with the delivery of punishment (reprimands) were generally not selected for further interaction, whereas those who had been associated with positive reinforcement (praise) were the most frequently selected for further interaction. This research suggests a clear preference for agents who administer reinforcing consequences rather than punishing consequences. Agents who primarily administer punishment are not sought out when clients are given the opportunity for additional interaction. If these findings extend to education and child rearing, children's avoidance of their teachers or parents may be fostered in part by the types of consequences that teachers or parents administer.

Aggression has also been found to be a side effect of punishment. Applications of overcorrection, reprimands, and brief slaps to the hand have effectively suppressed behavior (e.g., Foxx & Azrin, 1972; Mayhew & Harris, 1978). However, increases in attacks on the trainer (e.g., hitting, pinching, throwing things) have been reported early in training. Occasionally, the aggression associated with punishment has been self-inflicted. For example, applications of overcorrection have been associated with increases in self-injurious behavior in some clients (Azrin et al., 1975; Rollings, Baumeister, & Baumeister, 1977).

The negative side effects obtained in using punishment programs appear to be exceptions rather than the rule. When undesirable side effects appear, they are usually temporary and often subside over the course of treatment. It may be that in most applications in behavior modification, punishment is usually combined with positive reinforcement. Emphasis on positive reinforcement for prosocial behavior is likely to attenuate the negative effects that would result if punishment were used alone.

Positive Side Effects. Occasionally, suppression of behavior leads to positive side effects. For example, mentioned previously was the use of electric shock to reduce chronic self-injury (Linscheid et al., 1990). Shock was extremely effective after a number of other interventions had failed. The target behaviors changed but what about side effects? Actually, positive side effects were evident. Systematic assessment showed reductions in other self-injurious behaviors (e.g., hair pulling, biting, hitting objects) that were not punished. Moreover, vocalizations considered to reflect distress and measures of agitation also decreased systematically. Anecdotal (unsystematic) reports from others in contact with the cases suggested improvements in social interaction, greater compliance with instructions, and more independent self-care behavior (self-feeding) following punishment. These reports suggest that the positive side effects reflected behaviors that improved everyday life and interactions with others.

The positive side effects reported in this example are not restricted to specific forms of punishment such as shock. Social behaviors, including smiling, communication, and laughing with another resident or a staff member, increased as self-injurious behavior was decreased by the contingent application of water mist or facial screening (Singh et al., 1986). Several studies have found that use of punishment techniques such as overcorrection and time out are associated with decreases in such behaviors as aggressiveness, whining, and fussing and with increases in participation in activities, attentiveness to others, and smiling.

The positive side effects of punishment have been less well investigated than have the negative side effects, both in laboratory and applied research. In general, negative side effects appear to be much more likely than positive side effects. The reason has to do with the effects of aversive events on behavior. Negative side effects such as escape and emotional reactions emerge from mild aversive consequences, even when these consequences are ineffective in suppressing behavior.

General Comments

Negative side effects do not necessarily emerge from the use of punishment. However, the side effects have been well documented in animal laboratory research spanning decades of research (Azrin & Holz, 1966; Hutchinson, 1977). Some authors have suggested that special features of the laboratory may maximize the likelihood of negative side effects. For example, aggression as a side effect in animal laboratory research might be due in part to the fact that animals are confined and often in very close proximity to one another and cannot control or escape from the delivery of the aversive event (Linscheid & Meinhold, 1990). These are very different circumstances from applied settings. In applied research, negative side effects may be less frequent. A systematic evaluation of applications of punishment over a period spanning two decades of research has suggested that positive side effects of punishment are reported over ten times more often than are negative side effects (Matson & Taras, 1989). Thus negative side effects may emerge but do not appear to be common.

As mentioned previously, perhaps a major reason that undesirable side effects have been less apparent in applied settings than in laboratory studies is that reinforcement for alternate responses is usually used in conjunction with punishment. For example, if some behavior is reinforced even though others are punished, it is less likely that the situation and punishing agent will be as aversive as the punishment would be if administered by itself. Hence, less escape and avoidance on the part of the client would be evident. In fact, fewer emotional side effects, such as avoidance, emotional reactions, and aggression, are found when punishment is combined with reinforcement for positive behaviors than when punishment is used alone (Carey & Bucher, 1986). Another reason that undesirable side effects have not been widely found may be that mild and brief forms of punishment are usually used in applied settings. Mild forms of punishment are effective in suppressing behavior when reinforcement is delivered for other behaviors. Emotional disruption and aggressive behavior are less likely to result from mild forms of punishment than from intense forms resulting from painful stimuli.

The emergence of side effects, positive or negative, warrants much greater attention in research. Most studies report side effects anecdotally. More systematic assessment would be very important. Also, it is important to study the conditions that lead to the emergence of one type of effect versus another. One study has suggested that positive effects are more likely to occur when deviant behavior is completely, rather then partially, suppressed (Van Houten & Rolider, 1989). This kind of research shows that there are interesting features to be studied. At present, one can only alert individuals to the possibility of side effects during punishment.

CHARACTERISTICS OF THE PUNISHMENT PROCESS

Immediacy of Effects

A reduction in response rate usually occurs immediately following punishment. Using punishment for prolonged periods may result in further suppression. If there is no immediate effect, it is probably not advantageous to continue the aversive contingency. It is difficult to specify precisely how immediate the effect of punishment should be to justify being continued. Laboratory work has shown that some response suppression occurs as soon as the punishing stimulus is delivered a few times (Azrin & Holz, 1966).

In applied settings, the rapidity of punishment effects has been especially evident with shock. In a matter of only a few sessions or even one application of shock, behaviors are reduced and sometimes completely eliminated. The rapid and dramatic effects of shock were illustrated in a 14-year-old boy who had a chronic cough (Creer, Chai, & Hoffman, 1977). The cough did not respond to medical treatment or to attempts to remove attention for coughing and to provide praise for periods of not coughing. The cough was so disruptive and distracting to others that the child was expelled from school until his cough could be controlled. After further medical tests proved negative, a punishment procedure was used. Baseline observations revealed that the boy coughed 22 times in a 1-hour period. Treatment began by applying a mild electric shock (to the forearm) for coughing. Application of one shock after the first cough eliminated the behavior. The boy immediately returned to school, and he did not suffer episodes of coughing for up to two and a half years after treatment. Since shock is rarely used as an aversive event in applied settings, its effects are not a helpful guide in characterizing the effects of punishment. Nevertheless, the general rule about immediacy of effect holds and is applicable to less intense forms of punishment.

Applications of time out, verbal reprimands, overcorrection, lemon juice, and other procedures have shown that reductions in behavior occur after one or a few days of punishment (e.g., Marholin & Townsend, 1978; Singh et al., 1986; Wilson, Robertson, Herlong, & Haynes, 1979). Although exceptions to these results can be found, the general pattern is a reduction in behavior relatively soon after treatment is applied. This does not mean that the behavior will be eliminated or suppressed to the desired level in only a few days, but it does mean that beneficial effects of punishment, when they occur, should be evident in client behavior within a relatively brief period (e.g., a few days). If signs of progress are not evident early in the program, alternative procedures should be attempted. One would not want to continue punishment without clear signs of progress. Consequently, assessment of behavior is essential as part of a punishment program.

Specificity of Effects

Punishment often leads to effects that are specific to the situation in which the response is punished. Punishing a response in one setting or during one period may not carry over to other settings or other periods. For example, punishment effects achieved in special training sessions in a small room off a ward in an institution may not be evident in the same room after the sessions are over (Marholin & Townsend, 1978) or on the ward after the client leaves the sessions (Rollings et al., 1977). Behaviors suppressed in the treatment setting may continue unless punishment is implemented in the new setting.

The specificity of punishment effects has been evident in other ways. The effect of punishment may be restricted to the person who previously administered it. For example, if two individuals are present and only one of them administers punishment (e.g., reprimands), the behavior may decrease only in the presence of that person (e.g., Rolider, Cummings, & Van Houten, 1991). In general, response suppression may be limited to the specific conditions associated with punishment. However, the specificity of punishment effects can be overcome by extending the contingency to other conditions.

Recovery After Punishment Withdrawal

The effects of punishment are often quite rapid, so that the frequency of a behavior is reduced in a short time. However, the effect of punishment may not last; when the punishment contingency is withdrawn, the punished behavior may recover or return to its baseline rate. Recovery is likely to occur when punishment has not completely suppressed the response while the contingency was in effect and when reinforcement has not been used to develop an alternative response. In applied settings, the recovery can lead to efforts to increase the intensity or severity of punishment. For example, parents may mistakenly move from hitting or shaking a child to much more intensive versions of these and eventually to child abuse. The frustration of the parent is evident in such actions. Abuse can be rejected as unacceptable independently of its effects. It is worth underscoring that greater response suppression is not likely to result from escalation of punishment. The behavior is likely to recover with the new level of punishment, apart from additional undesirable outcomes such as further side effects.

Even when punishment is in effect, the individual may adapt to mild punishment and there will be a recovery of the behavior. That is, while the punishment is in effect, it can lose its suppressive effects over time. For example, the more often threats are used, the more they lose their suppressive effects (Phillips, Phillips, Fixsen, & Wolf, 1971). To maximize response suppression with punishment and to minimize recovery, positive reinforcement can be provided for behaviors incompatible with the punished response. When the punishment contingency is removed, the reinforced response will be of a higher relative frequency than the punished response. It will have replaced the previously punished response, and it can be maintained with continued reinforcement.

CONTROVERSY: PUNISHMENT
AND ITS USE

Source of Controversy

The use of punishment in behavior modification has been a major source of controversy and debate (see Repp & Singh, 1990). Much of the debate has emerged in the context of punishment for self-injurious behavior, where there may be severe injury (e.g., permanent physical damage), where painful events (self-injury itself) are already going on, and where the need to intervene is urgent, as illustrated in examples earlier in the chapter. Confronted with a child who is gouging his or her eyes, which is threatening vision, is obviously an urgent situation. Historically, the usual response to such an individual in an institutional setting was to use some form of physical restraint (e.g., a jacket that completely restricts use of hands and arms, or a helmet that does not permit hand contact with the face). Such restraint, of course, is restrictive. A question is whether some behavioral (or any other) procedure might be used to eliminate the behavior and to permit the individual to function more normally and with greater freedom in everyday life. Using punishment in this situation could appear to be quite justified or unjustified to most people, depending on further details of the case, such as the nature of the punishing event and alternatives that had been tried unsuccessfully. The issues raised by punishment are not restricted to self-injurious behavior or any particular treatment population or focus, even though special issues might emerge in each case.

Punishment raises special ethical, legal, humanistic, and value issues because of the aversive nature of the interventions. Questions are raised of whether punishment techniques ought to be used in principle, apart from their effects; whether they are necessary to use, given alternative procedures; and if they are to be used, at what point, when, and with what procedures. It is fairly easy to take an extreme or one-sided view of whether punishment ought to be used to change behavior. Also, case examples are plentiful in which one view (punishment seemed necessary or unnecessary) led to an intervention that reduced significant suffering. The complexities of the issue derive from the manifold definitions of punishment, inconsistencies in society's views and uses of punishment, and incomplete information about the optimal ways of changing behavior. More general ethical and legal issues are raised in Chapter 13. For the present chapter, it is useful to consider punishment as a behavior-change procedure more concretely.

Punishment Redefined

The meaning and use of punishment in everyday life and in behavior modification are different in important ways relevant to the controversy. In everyday life, punishment refers to applying aversive events to behavior. The meaning is complex because it includes a number of notions such as retribution, retaliation, and inflicting pain. Although these are not necessary features of punishment, they are related in everyday use, in the etymology of the word punishment, as noted previously (Chapter 2), and in cultural beliefs. For example, the "an eye for an eye" philosophy of punishment focuses more on the notion of justice and suitable penalties than it does on actually changing behavior. Similarly, "spare the rod and spoil the child" focuses on building character rather than changing the specific behaviors toward which it is directed.

In behavior modification, the definition and focus of punishment are very different from the term and use in everyday life. Punishment refers to a decrease in the likelihood of a behavior when a consequence is provided contingent on that behavior. Punishment includes such procedures as time out and response cost, usually in extremely low magnitudes (e.g., 1 to 5 minutes of time out). These are examples of punishment. One may object in principle to the use of any aversive events especially because positive reinforcement (e.g., differential reinforcement of alternative or functionally equivalent behaviors) is almost always a viable option. At the same time, punishment techniques in behavior modification may not deserve the emotionally laden reactions more appropriately applied to corporal punishment. When the definition refers to a decrease in behavior rather than retaliation, retribution, pain, or providing "justice," what is used as a punishing event can be very different from many of the harsh practices such as corporal punishment and verbal abuse used in everyday life.

Alternatives

There are many alternatives to punishment, although in any instance it is not possible to be certain in advance whether one will be more effective than another or sufficiently effective to achieve the desired change. Thus it is important to keep in mind the portfolio of intervention techniques that can be used. In the present context, consider that we have interest in reducing or eliminating a particular behavior, a situation in which we might first consider one of the many punishment procedures already discussed. There are several alternatives that might be quite effective, without ever considering punishment (see LaVigna & Donnellan, 1986; O'Brien & Repp, 1990). Prominent examples have been described and illustrated previously and hence are mentioned here only in passing.

The identification and modification of setting and stimulus events can suppress behavior. A functional analysis may reveal that events presented in advance of behavior (e.g., comments from a relative, activity in a certain situation) increase the undesired (e.g., aggressive) behavior. The undesired behavior can be reduced and eliminated by altering the situation or antecedents that serve as the occasion for the behavior.

Many positive reinforcement procedures can be used as alternatives to punishment. In the previous chapter, we discussed differential reinforcement of other behavior, incompatible or alternative behavior, functionally equivalent behavior, and low rates of behavior. These methods of providing reinforcement offer multiple options that are often quite effective in reducing behavior and in developing appropriate behavior in its stead.

Negative reinforcement too can be used to reduce undesired behavior. It is possible that the undesired behavior is maintained by an aversive contingency already operative in the situation. Specifically, escape may be contingent on undesired behavior. An example in the previous chapter showed how uncooperative and disruptive behavior of children receiving dental treatment temporarily terminated the treatment (negative reinforcement for disruptive behavior). Negative reinforcement contingencies that support maladaptive behavior are not, of course, restricted to pediatric dentistry. The point is that an undesired behavior can be reduced or eliminated by rearranging the existing events so that they promote desired behavior. No punishment is used in this case; negative reinforcement is used to obtain behaviors that are incompatible with or are an alternative to the undesired behavior.

Extinction, detailed in the next chapter, represents an alternative to punishment as well. During extinction, reinforcers previously provided for the behavior

are no longer given. If the reinforcer(s) that maintains the behavior can be identified and controlled, behavior can be reduced through extinction.

Positive reinforcement, negative reinforcement, and extinction procedures can
be implemented in many ways and in many combinations. Thus one cannot say
there is a fixed number of alternative interventions to punishment. Moreover, our
understanding of factors that control behavior and the reciprocal relations among
motivation, behavior, and consequences is far from complete. Procedures that can
change behavior, options beyond those enumerated here, are likely to develop
even further. However, even at present, there are alternatives to the use of punishment, if one wishes to avoid punishment entirely.

WHEN AND HOW TO USE PUNISHMENT

Punishment is a procedure to be used cautiously for many reasons, ranging from
broad ethical and social issues (e.g., Should it be used? Is the procedure or practice acceptable?) to more concrete caveats such as possibly undesirable side effects.
The evidence simply is not available to argue for a strong position that punishment is absolutely essential to achieve a particular goal in the general case. As a
general rule, other procedures should be employed in advance of punishment. An
initial question that should be asked is whether punishment is needed at all. The
fact that a goal may be to suppress behavior does not necessarily mean that the
program should be based on punishment. Response suppression can be achieved
with many other interventions, as noted previously. In particular, the many reinforcement techniques are especially viable alternatives.

Even though reinforcement techniques present viable alternatives to punishment, several situations are likely to arise in which punishment will be useful, required, and possibly even essential. First and perhaps most obviously, punishment
is a viable alternative when the inappropriate behavior may be physically dangerous to oneself or others. Some immediate intervention is required to suppress responses before the relatively delayed effects of reinforcement and extinction might
operate. Not all professionals would agree that this situation requires the use of
punishment, because evidence indicates that other procedures are effective (Donnellan & LaVigna, 1990). Even so, in some cases, life-threatening behavior (e.g.,
ruminative vomiting in an infant) can be immediately eliminated, and discussions
about alternative procedures seem moot at the level of clinical care.

Second, punishment is useful when reinforcement of a behavior incompatible
with the disruptive behavior cannot be administered easily. For example, if a hyperactive student is literally out of his or her seat all of the time, it may be impossible or not feasible to reinforce in-seat behavior. Punishment (e.g., response
cost along with shaping) may be helpful in initially obtaining the desired response.
Eventually, of course, punishment can be faded or eliminated completely with increased reliance upon shaping with positive reinforcement.

Third, punishment is useful in temporarily suppressing a behavior while another behavior is reinforced. This latter use may be the most common application

of punishment in applied settings. However, it should be remembered that mild forms of punishment (e.g., mild reprimands, brief time-out periods, and small penalties or costs) usually are sufficient to suppress behavior, as long as reinforcement for alternate responses is provided. Indeed, mild punishment can sometimes enhance the effectiveness of reinforcement. In several programs attempts have been made to decrease disruptive child behavior (e.g., noncompliance, aggressiveness) at home or at school by having parents and teachers provide approval, attention, and praise for appropriate behavior (e.g., following instructions, playing cooperatively). Appropriate child behavior may show little or no improvement. When mild punishment is added in the form of a brief time out or response cost, behavior change is often dramatic. The combination of mild punishment and positive reinforcement often is more effective than either procedure used alone (e.g., Bierman et al., 1987; Pfiffner & O'Leary, 1987).

It should be clear that the best use of punishment in applied settings is as an ancillary technique to accompany positive reinforcement. Usually, punishment will suppress undesirable responses but will not train desirable behaviors. Reinforcement is essential to develop appropriate behaviors that replace the suppressed behaviors. This is widely recognized in clinical and applied research, where the vast majority of studies that use punishment also employ positive reinforcement as part of the program (Matson & Taras, 1989).

Several considerations are important to address if aversive techniques are to be used. One way to be alert to these is to ask questions when contemplating the use of punishment. Box 7-1 provides a set of key questions that are intended to guide the person responsible for designing and implementing the behavior-change program. A few of the questions warrant comment. Perhaps foremost, alternative interventions are likely to be available to make the use of punishment unnecessary. Behavior change might be attained with positive reinforcement alone or combined with mild punishment (e.g., response cost). There may be extenuating circumstances such as an urgent need for immediate suppression of a dangerous or life-threatening behavior. Barring these, reliance on aversive techniques may be justifiable only if positive reinforcement procedures have proven unsuccessful. Related, a functional analysis might reveal the controlling factors and direct attention to contingencies that can be changed without relying on punishment. Such an analysis ought to precede moving to a punishment program.

If punishment is to be used, mild punishment and the least restrictive punishment ought to be used and clearly combined with a reinforcement program. Relatively more severe or restrictive events (e.g., shock, physical restraint) can be justified only if aversive events of lesser intensity or severity have been unsuccessful. However the punishment is designed or intended, one must be aware that in the heat of battle (in the home, at school) a parent or teacher might well escalate. For example, it would be unwise to design a program in which a mild slap or gentle shake of the child, delivered by the parent or teacher, serves as the aversive event. Although this aversive event might not pass any of the other questions noted in Box 7-1, it is mentioned here because it is likely that the mild slap or gentle shake would become not so mild and not so gentle as the child becomes very oppositional and as the parent or teacher understandably became frustrated.

BOX 7-1   Key Questions To Ask if Punishment Is To Be Used

Are alternative procedures available that are not aversive and have they been tried?

Are the punishment procedures the least restrictive interventions possible?

Is it possible or likely that the procedures will be abused or escalated?

Can use of the procedures be supervised, monitored, and evaluated?

Will the duration of the program be relatively brief?

When implemented, are there initial signs that behavior is changing?

Beyond these initial signs of progress, are there clear benefits to the client?

As noted previously, punishment effects when evident ought to be reflected in some immediate change. The change may not be sufficient to solve the problem, but on a graph of the data one ought to see some movement that reflects a decrease in behavior. If this is not evident early in the program, punishment ought to be discontinued or modified. Related, as the program continues, there ought to be clear benefits to the clients that result from treatment. If behavior does not change or show a trend in the direction of change, continuation of aversive events is not justified. The above points convey minimal guidelines regarding the use of aversive events; they do not exhaust the issues that need to be addressed. Also important are ethical and legal guidelines as means of protecting client rights; these are highlighted in Chapter 13.

SUMMARY AND CONCLUSIONS

Punishment consists of reducing behavior by presenting aversive events (such as verbal reprimands and disapproval), removing positive events (as in time out or response cost), and requiring effort and alternative behaviors (as in overcorrection or contingent exercise). Several factors influence the effective application of punishment related to the delay of punishment, schedule of administration, sources of reinforcement, timing of punishment in the response sequence, and, most important, reinforcement of alternative behaviors. By reinforcing an alternate response, even mild forms of punishment can change behavior dramatically.

Use of punishment can lead to undesirable side effects such as emotional reactions, escape from and avoidance of the situation or the person who administers punishment, aggression, the use of punishment by the individual who is punished, and overreliance on aversive control procedures. Positive side effects such as increased socialization are more common in applications of punishment in applied settings. Even so, the possibility of adverse side effects makes extensive reliance on aversive procedures somewhat hazardous. Additionally, punishment effects may be very specific, both in the responses that are altered and in the situations in which behavior change occurs.

In general, there is a place for punishment in behavior modification programs, namely, as a supplement to reinforcement programs designed to develop other appropriate behaviors. Emphasis of the present chapter was on the procedures, their effective application, and the characteristics of the punishment process. Controversial issues, highlighted only briefly in the present chapter, will be discussed further in a broader context of guidelines for treatment.

KEY TERMS

Overcorrection

Positive practice

Reinforcement of alternative behavior

Response cost

Restitution

Side effects of punishment

Time out from reinforcement

APPLYING PRINCIPLES AND TECHNIQUES TO EVERYDAY LIFE

1. Develop a time out program at home to reduce the likelihood that a child will make nasty comments to his or her parents. What are two different procedures you might use that would qualify as time out? Give the details of these procedures.

2. You want to make sure the above program is effective. What are three factors that influence the effectiveness of punishment? Describe how the above program would be conducted to ensure that these factors are optimized to make the program effective.

3. Using the concept of negative reinforcement, describe how parents may continue to use a punishment practice (e.g., beating their child, screaming) even though there might be no effect on changing the likelihood of the undesired child behavior.

4. Identify a time when you or a friend received some aversive consequence for something you have done. Did any of the side effects often associated with punishment occur? Which ones?

5. Many behavior-change methods used in everyday life focus on punishment. An important skill and exercise is to be able to reformulate the programs so that they are based on positive reinforcement. The effects and side effects of reinforcement programs, when compared to punishment, are the reasons for this emphasis, as discussed in this chapter. Can you redesign a program to address the following problem? Public libraries lose many books from people failing to return them at all, let alone on time. Indeed, some libraries lose up to 10% of their collections and up to $1 million in stock. Aversive procedures have been employed to get people to return books. One procedure is

to send people with overdue books letters on official stationery from the police department. The letters threaten to charge the individual with a misdemeanor theft, penalized by a fine of up to $500 and 90 days in jail (Lueck, 1999). Other programs threaten to publish the names of offenders in a newspaper ad to embarrass them if they do not return the books by a particular date. Still other programs turn over the library accounts to collection agencies who are known for a series of intense letters and persistent phone calls. Here is the challenge. You are called in by the libraries of an entire state. (The director of libraries learned that you have completed this chapter and are knowledgeable of contingencies of reinforcement, the importance of considering ABCs, the hazards of punishment, etc.) Design a behavior-change program that (1) fosters return of books to the library, (2) emphasizes positive reinforcement instead of or more than punishment, and (3) uses antecedents as well as consequences to promote behavior.

FOR FURTHER READING

Adams, R. (1998). *The abuses of punishment.* New York: St. Martin's Press.

Greven, P. (1992). *Spare the child: The religious roots of punishment and the psychological impact of physical abuse.* New York: Vintage Books.

Hall, R. V., & Hall, M.L (1998). *How to use time out* (2nd ed). Austin, TX: Pro-Ed.

LaVigna, G.W., & Donnellan, A.M. (1986). *Alternatives to punishment: Solving behavior problems with non-aversive strategies.* New York: Irvington.

McCord, J. (Ed). (1998). *Coercion and punishment in long-term perspectives.* Cambridge, England: Cambridge University Press.

Repp, A.E., & Singh, N.N. (Eds.). (1990). *Perspectives on the use of nonaversive and aversive interventions for persons with developmental disabilities.* Sycamore, IL: Sycamore.

Thibadeau, S.F. (1998). *How to use response cost.* Austin, TX: Pro-Ed.

CHAPTER 8

Extinction

In the previous chapter, punishment was discussed as a technique for reducing or eliminating a response. Applying specific punishing consequences can reduce the frequency of behavior, particularly when those consequences are accompanied by a reinforcement program designed to develop positive behaviors. The frequency of behavior can be reduced without presenting punishing consequences. Many maladaptive behaviors are maintained by consequences that follow from them. For example, temper tantrums or interrupting others during conversations are often unwittingly reinforced by the attention they receive. When there is interest in reducing behavior, extinction can be used by eliminating the connection between the behavior and the consequences that follow. *Extinction refers to withholding reinforcement from a previously reinforced response.* A response undergoing extinction eventually decreases in frequency until it returns to its prereinforcement level or is eliminated.

Extinction in applied settings usually is used for behaviors that have been maintained by positive reinforcement. In such cases, eliminating the connection between behavior (e.g., tantrums) and positive reinforcement (e.g., parent attention) can help reduce or eliminate the behavior. Other uses of extinction are for responses that are developed or maintained by negative reinforcement. These latter applications refer to behaviors that are performed to escape or avoid aversive consequences.

EXTINCTION OF POSITIVELY REINFORCED BEHAVIOR

As already mentioned, in applied settings the usual focus of extinction is in relation to behaviors that have been positively reinforced (Lerman & Iwata, 1996). Positive consequences that follow the behavior are no longer forthcoming. There are many examples from everyday life in which extinction of positively reinforced responses occurs. For example, when trying to start a car, the behavior (turning the key, pressing a pedal) is usually followed by the reinforcing consequence (car starting). Extinction would be when the behavior is no longer followed by the consequence. Trying to start a defective automobile ceases (extinguishes) after several unsuccessful attempts. Similarly, we may warmly greet a particular stranger whom we casually pass each day. Our behavior (saying hello, smiling) may be followed by positive reinforcement (acknowledgment and similar behavior on the part of the other person). If the other person's responses no longer were forthcoming, our behavior would be likely to decrease and perhaps cease. Finally, raising one's hand in class (the behavior) usually is followed by a reinforcer (e.g., attention from the teacher). If attention or being called on ceased, it is likely that hand raising would decrease. These are all examples of extinction because the reinforcement that followed the response is no longer forthcoming. This would lead to a decrease in behavior. The examples are simple to convey the concept. In the usual case, the reinforcer does not stop completely (extinction) but follows once in a while or rarely (intermittent reinforcement). For example, we may greet some with a hello and a smile (behavior). It is likely that this behavior is reinforced on some occasions and not others. Behavior may not cease very quickly if it has been maintained by intermittent reinforcement, a reason that extinction is often slow or weak in its effects.

Extinction refers to a specific relation between behavior and the events after the behavior. The principle relates the occurrence of a behavior that has been reinforced in the past and the cessation of reinforcing consequences. Although application of the principle can be used to change behavior, extinction often operates in everyday life to foster problem behaviors. For example, in elementary school classrooms, extinction often operates with reinforcement to sustain inappropriate behavior. As an illustration, raising one's hand to ask a question is often ignored by the teacher. The absence of reinforcement is likely to result in extinction of hand raising. Extinction of this behavior that many teachers like is augmented if the teacher reinforces (provides attention to) children who shout out questions or answers. In fact, it is very easy to reinforce disruptive behavior in a class because it receives teacher and peer attention (social reinforcement). On the other hand, prosocial behaviors, such as hand raising or working quietly, are less conspicuous and hence often ignored. Although quite simple, this example conveys how appropriate or desirable behavior in a setting may be inadvertently extinguished while undesirable behavior may be systematically, albeit unwittingly, reinforced. The present chapter discusses how to utilize extinction as a way of changing behavior in applied settings.

FACTORS THAT INFLUENCE THE EFFECTIVENESS OF EXTINCTION

Extinction of positively reinforced behaviors is almost always used in a behavior modification program. For example, in a reinforcement program, when a target response is reinforced, nontarget responses that are no longer reinforced are implicitly undergoing extinction. Although extinction is an ingredient in most programs, it may be used as the main technique to decrease undesirable behavior. Several factors determine whether or the extent to which extinction will be effective.

Schedule of Reinforcement

The efficacy of extinction and the speed with which the reduction of a response is achieved depend on the schedule of reinforcement that previously maintained the response. A response that has been reinforced every time (continuous reinforcement) rapidly extinguishes when the reinforcer is no longer provided. In contrast, a response that has been reinforced once in a while (intermittent reinforcement) extinguishes less rapidly when the reinforcer is withheld. The more intermittent the schedule (or the less frequent the previous reinforcement), the greater the resistance of the response to extinction.

The relationship between reinforcement schedules and extinction creates a major problem for behavior-change programs that rely exclusively on extinction because many behaviors are maintained by intermittent reinforcement. For example, incoherent verbalizations of psychiatric patients are often attended to by peers and staff but are sometimes ignored. Decreasing the frequency of these behaviors may be difficult because of the intermittent schedule on which they have been maintained. If all the sources of reinforcement were removed from a behavior previously maintained by intermittent reinforcement, the behavior would eventually decrease and perhaps be eliminated. Intermittent reinforcement delays the extinction process, and the delay may be unfortunate. While the long extinction process is under way, it is possible that the response will be accidentally reinforced. The possibility of accidental reinforcement during extinction is always a problem and that problem is exacerbated by a long extinction period.

Other Variables Affecting Extinction

The effects of reinforcement schedules on extinction have been more thoroughly studied than the effects of other variables. Yet general statements can be extrapolated from laboratory research on variables that contribute to resistance to extinction. First, the amount or magnitude of the reinforcement used to develop the response affects extinction. The greater the amount of a particular reinforcer given for a response, the greater the resistance of the response to extinction. Similarly, the longer the response has been reinforced, the greater the resistance to extinction. Finally, the greater the number of times that extinction has been used in the past to reduce the behavior, the more rapid the extinction will be. The individual learns to discriminate periods of reinforcement and extinction more rapidly. If a strong or powerful reinforcer maintained a response and if that response were sustained over a long period, it is likely to be more resistant to extinction than it would be if weak reinforcers had been used and those reinforcers had been delivered over a short period.

Identifying the Reinforcer Maintaining Behavior

Extinction requires that the reinforcer or reinforcers maintaining behavior are identified and that they are withheld when the behavior is performed. Although this appears simple enough in principle, in practice, it may be very difficult to isolate those reinforcers. For example, an emotionally disturbed child's aggressive behavior with peers may be maintained by multiple reinforcers such as the control that aggressive behavior exerts over peers, the submissive response of the victims, admiration from friends, or special attention from a teacher or parent. In such a situation, it is difficult to identify which potential reinforcer or combination of reinforcers is maintaining the aggressive behavior. Removing teacher and parent attention may fail to decrease that behavior because other reinforcers are operative. This was learned early in the application of behavioral techniques. In a classroom program, an attempt was made to extinguish disruptive behavior by withdrawing teacher attention (Madsen, Becker, & Thomas, 1968). However, disruptive behavior increased, apparently because it was maintained by reinforcement resulting from peer attention. Without efforts of the teacher to intervene, peer reinforcement was allowed to operate more freely.

Empirical observation is the only method for determining which reinforcer is maintaining a behavior. If the consequence is withheld and the behavior declines, this suggests that the consequence served as a positive reinforcer and maintained the behavior. A functional analysis and ABAB design could be used to evaluate systematically what reinforces the behavior. The difficulty in using these tools, apart from practical obstacles, is that the reinforcer is not easily identified if it follows the behavior infrequently (intermittently). For example, a child's severely disruptive behavior at school may be maintained by attention from his or her parents. Perhaps both parents provide discipline and attention to the child on these problem occasions and come to the school to meet with teachers. The disruptive behavior may serve multiple functions such as bringing the parents together, providing discipline and structure, and focusing family attention on the child. This might be quite difficult to identify in everyday settings. Also, it is not feasible to bring all such children into the laboratory for a functional analysis. In any case, with multiple consequences and highly intermittent consequences, it may be quite difficult to identify the reinforcer(s) maintaining behavior.

In most instances in which extinction is used in applied settings, attention from adults or peers is assumed to be the reinforcer maintaining behavior. Attention can maintain inappropriate behavior in everyday life. For example, if someone interrupts a conversation, shouts out, or engages in a conspicuous deviant behavior, attention from others invariably is provided. Thus as a general rule, attention is a viable and reasonable initial hypothesis regarding the reinforcer that might be controlling behavior. Yet attention is not necessarily the controlling reinforcer, and withholding it from the behavior may have little or no effect.

The way to evaluate which reinforcer is maintaining behavior is to conduct a functional analysis. As described earlier, a functional analysis is designed to provide data regarding the stimuli and consequences that influence performance of behavior. In the context of the present discussion of extinction, a functional analysis can identify the reinforcer that is maintaining behavior (Richman, Wacker, Asmus, & Casey, 1998). Once identified, the connection between the deviant behavior and the reinforcer can be altered to achieve extinction and to reinforce prosocial behavior.

For example, one study evaluated the aggressive behavior (hitting, kicking, scratching, pushing others) of a 7½-year-old autistic child (named Molly) who was in a special classroom (Sasso et al., 1992). In experimental sessions with an investigator and then later in class with the teacher, a functional analysis was completed to identify the conditions influencing the frequency of aggressive behavior. In one condition, aggressive behavior was ignored. In another condition, attention was given for aggressive behavior by saying such things as, "Please do not do that," or "Stop that; you're hurting me"). In yet another condition, a task was presented to the child. Instances of aggression led to escape (termination) from the task and shift to another activity. Given the frequent use of removing attention (ignoring) in extinction programs, one might expect aggressive behavior to decline during the ignore condition. Yet, ignoring or providing attention did not affect the frequency of aggression in either laboratory sessions or the classroom. However, when termination of the task followed aggressive behavior, this behavior increased. Thus the behavior was maintained (reinforced) by escaping from the task. Treatment was devised for Molly by permitting her to shift to a new task (escape) only for appropriate behavior; aggressive behavior did not lead to escape but to completion of more of the activity. This resulted in a dramatic decrease in aggressive behavior.

The example conveys that attention is not necessarily the reinforcer maintaining behavior in everyday situations. In the example, merely ignoring the behavior would not work as an intervention. This could lead an investigator, therapist, parent, teacher, or other person to say, "Extinction did not work with this child." Yet, extinction is defined as no longer providing the reinforcer; if attention is not the reinforcer, withdrawing attention is not really extinction. The use of functional analysis of deviant behavior has increased in recent years in an effort to establish empirically the events controlling behavior so as to develop optimally effective intervention programs.

Controlling the Source of Reinforcement

Once the reinforcer maintaining an undesirable behavior has been identified, a major problem may be withholding the reinforcer after the behavior. Extinction requires very careful control over reinforcers. Any accidental reinforcement may rapidly reinstate the inappropriate behavior and prolong the extinction process.

An example of accidental reinforcement was reported in one of the earliest documented behavioral applications of extinction in a program designed to eliminate a child's bedtime tantrum behavior (Williams, 1959). When the child's parents followed instructions not to provide attention for this behavior, extinction proceeded uneventfully until tantrums were nearly eliminated within a few days. One night the child fussed when put to bed by his aunt. She provided a great deal of attention to the tantrum by staying with him until he went to sleep. As a result, the tantrums had to be extinguished a second time. After tantrums were eliminated the second time, they did not occur during the following two years. In this illustration, the accidental reinforcement of the behavior by the aunt merely slowed the extinction process. In more complex situations with many more opportunities for accidental reinforcement, such as classrooms where peers may reinforce an inappropriate behavior, extinction may be difficult to apply effectively.

Reinforcement is particularly difficult to control when it is delivered by peers. Parents, teachers, or staff members are often unaware that peers are providing reinforcing consequences for each other's behavior. Clowning in a classroom or stealing among delinquents in the community are examples of peer reinforced behaviors. Constant surveillance would be required to ensure that no such reinforcement occurred. From a practical standpoint, constant surveillance usually is not possible in either applied settings or the community at large. One alternative is to enlist peers so that they ignore (extinguish) the deviant behavior of a particular individual. Peers can receive reinforcing consequences for systematically ignoring certain behaviors. If strong peer incentive for extinguishing a response is provided, it is likely that there will be little or no accidental reinforcement.

It is virtually impossible to control reinforcement for some behaviors. For example, autistic children frequently engage in self-stimulatory behaviors such as repetitively playing with objects or their fingers and rocking back and forth. As already mentioned research has suggested that these behaviors often are maintained in part by the sensory stimuli they generate (e.g., auditory, visual, and tactile stimulation). The behaviors can be extinguished by reducing the stimuli they produce (e.g., by blindfolding the children so that they cannot see what they are doing). However, reducing such stimuli is not feasible or desirable in most settings, so the behavior is likely to be reinforced automatically. Similarly, criminal and aggressive behaviors that one might like to reduce often yield immediate and intermittent reinforcement (e.g., money and material goods resulting from theft, the submission of a victim). When the source of reinforcement is not easily controlled or eliminated, extinction is neither feasible nor likely to be effective.

CHARACTERISTICS OF THE
EXTINCTION PROCESS

Gradual Reduction in Behavior

Although extinction effectively decreases and often eliminates behavior, the process of extinction is usually gradual. Unlike punishment, extinction typically does not result in an immediate response reduction. Rather, several unreinforced responses may occur before behavior begins to decline.

When the undesirable behaviors are dangerous or severely disruptive, the delayed effects of extinction can be deleterious either to the individual or to others. Consider self-injurious behavior among autistic and mentally retarded children. It is possible that attention from others would maintain the behavior. In this case, ignoring the behavior may reduce its frequency. Yet if the extinction process is gradual, significant physical damage may result from self-injury. Indeed, early in the development of behavior modification, extinction was attempted as an intervention for such behaviors and limitations of the procedure were clearly shown. One child who engaged in self-inflicted head banging had multiple scars over his head and face from the injuries (Lovaas & Simmons, 1969). During extinction, the child was taken out of physical restraints and placed in a small room with no adults who could reinforce (attend to) the destructive behavior. The child's behavior, observed through a one-way mirror, eventually extinguished in 10 sessions over a total of 15 hours. However, from the beginning of extinction until the response finally decreased to zero, the child had hit himself almost 9,000 times. Thus a great deal of self-inflicted injury occurred during the course of extinction. Although extinction can reduce behavior, dangerous behavior requires an intervention with more rapid results than extinction usually provides.

The example warrants comment in light of recent advances in behavioral research. Early in the development of behavioral treatment (1960s), there was no consistent attempt to identify which reinforcers were maintaining behavior. Assumptions were made that commonly occurring reinforcers, such as attention, may inadvertently sustain deviant behavior, as in the above example. In fact, attention often maintains deviant behavior, but this cannot be assumed. In contemporary work, functional analyses are completed that are designed to test hypotheses about what is maintaining behavior. As discussed further in this chapter, results typically reveal that attention is not the reinforcer for self-injurious behavior. Even when the reinforcement can be identified and controlled, extinction by itself tends to be gradual in its effects. The effects can be augmented by using other procedures along with extinction (e.g., differential reinforcement procedures).

Extinction Burst

At the beginning of extinction, the frequency of a response may become greater than it was while the response was being reinforced. *Extinction burst refers to an increase in responding at the beginning of the extinction period.* Numerous examples of extinction burst pervade everyday experience. For example, turning on a radio is usually followed by some sound. If the radio no longer works so that no reinforcement (sound) occurs, attempts to turn on the radio will eventually extinguish. However, before this occurs, the response may temporarily increase in frequency (several on/off turns) and in intensity or vigor.

A burst of responses does not always occur at the beginning of extinction, but has been evident in many programs (Lerman, Iwata, & Wallace, 1999). For example, in one report, extinction was used to reduce the frequent asthmatic attacks of a 7-year-old boy (Neisworth & Moore, 1972). The boy's prolonged wheezing, coughing, gasping, and similar responses were usually associated with excessive verbal and physical attention at bedtime. During extinction, his asthmatic attacks when he was put to bed were ignored. When those attacks were shorter than they had been on the previous night, he was rewarded in the morning with lunch money so that he could purchase his lunch at school rather than take his lunch. The results of the program are plotted in Figure 8-1. Of special note is the first phase of extinction (treatment contingencies). At the beginning of extinction, the asthmatic attacks lasted longer than they did during baseline. A similar burst of responses was evident the second time extinction was begun. Eventually, the asthmatic attacks were eliminated but not before temporarily becoming worse.

A burst of responses is especially serious with behaviors that threaten the client's physical well-being. This was clearly illustrated in the case of a 9 month-old girl who constantly engaged in ruminative vomiting (regurgitating food after eating and between meals) (Wright, Brown, & Andrews, 1978). The girl weighed only 8 lbs (3.6 kg) because she received little nourishment from her meals. Her normal weight would have been about 20 lbs (9.1 kg). The girl received excessive staff attention for vomiting. Consequently, an extinction contingency was implemented with the idea that attention was the reinforcer maintaining behavior. Staff

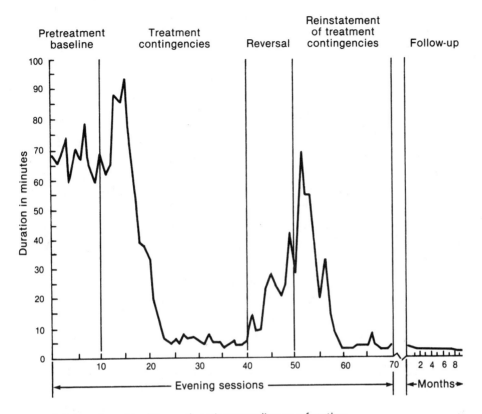

FIGURE 8-1 Duration of bedtime asthmatic responding as a function of contingency changes.

(Source: Neisworth & Moore, 1972)

members were instructed to leave the girl's presence immediately when she began to vomit. When she was not vomiting, staff engaged in normal interaction with her, such as holding and looking at her. At the beginning of extinction, there was a burst of vomiting responses. This was especially unfortunate because it meant even greater food deprivation than the girl experienced during baseline. Fortunately, the burst lasted only two days and was followed by a decrease in vomiting and an increase in weight. The benefits of treatment were evident over a year later, when follow-up data were obtained.

A burst of responses may be undesirable even with behaviors that are not physically dangerous. It may be exceedingly difficult for someone to tolerate the undesirable behavior as it intensifies at the beginning of extinction. Thus during a burst of responses, there is a greater likelihood that these other persons will provide reinforcement for the behavior. For example, a young child may have tantrums when going to bed. Understandably, the parents may attend to the child, to try to have him or her become calm, and even allow the child to stay up a little longer toward this end. Assume that the parents now begin an extinction program and no longer provide attention and other reinforcers to the child. If a child's tantrum becomes worse (extinction burst) when parents systematically ignore the behavior, the parents may give in to the child and provide attention and comfort. Such parental reinforcement will increase the probability of intense tantrums because it is provided when the behavior is worse than usual. To the parents, of course, extinction may appear to be failing because the behavior has become worse. However, the effects of extinction are merely beginning.

It is likely that reinforcement during a burst of responses is a basis for undesirable behaviors often seen in children, such as protracted whining and excessive demands for attention. Parents, teachers, or other persons who may be involved in the extinction program ought to be forewarned of the possibility of a burst of responses so that they do not overreact to a temporary increase in behavior. An initial burst of responses does not always occur. However, when it does occur, the possibility of reinforcement adds to the risk in relying on extinction in the absence of other procedures.

Spontaneous Recovery

After extinction has progressed, a response may temporarily reappear, even though it has not been reinforced. *The temporary recurrence of a nonreinforced response during extinction is referred to as spontaneous recovery.* When a response recovers during extinction, its strength is ordinarily less than it was before extinction. For example, if a child's tantrums are ignored, the frequency of tantrums will probably decrease over time, possibly after an initial burst of responses. However, a tantrum may occur after extinction has progressed for some time. Such a tantrum is likely to be of a lower intensity than that of the tantrums during baseline.

As with extinction burst, a major concern with spontaneous recovery is that the response will be accidentally reinforced. Spontaneous recovery occurs after several responses have not been reinforced. If reinforcement is provided, it follows a long series of nonreinforced responses. This is tantamount to a highly intermittent reinforcement schedule, which may further increase resistance to extinction. If extinction continues and no accidental reinforcement occurs, the frequency and intensity of the spontaneously recovered response decrease. It is important to realize that the spontaneous recurrence of a response during extinction does not necessarily reflect the ineffectiveness of the procedure. Such recurrences often characterize the extinction process.

Possible Side Effects

Another characteristic of extinction is that the cessation of reinforcement may result in "emotional responses" such as agitation, frustration, feelings of failure, rage, and aggression (Lerman et al., 1999). Apparently, the transition from positive reinforcement to extinction is aversive and leads to side effects similar to those evident with punishment. Instances of emotional reactions in response to extinction abound in everyday experience. For example, after individuals place money into a malfunctioning vending machine (reinforcement is no longer delivered), statements of anger, swearing, and aggressive attacks on the machine are common. Individuals who have experienced repeated reinforcement of certain responses may view the cessation of such reinforcement as a failure. When an athlete performs poorly, for example, he or she may swear, express feelings of failure, and throw something (e.g., tennis racquet, hockey stick) to the ground in disgust. The notion of a "poor loser" signifies a person who engages in emotional behavior when his or her responses are not reinforced in a contest—that is, when he or she loses.

In general, adverse side effects of extinction have not been well studied in applied settings. Laboratory evidence and reports from some applications suggest that when side effects occur, they are likely to be temporary and to diminish as the target response extinguishes. It is important to be aware that any situation in which reinforcement is no longer provided may become aversive. An aversive situation may result in escape and avoidance and thus reduce the opportunity for providing the client with positive reinforcement for desirable behavior. To avoid this, reinforcement should be delivered for a response other than the one to be eliminated. Thus there is no net loss in reinforcement for the client. Rather, reinforcement is provided for a new or alternative behavior.

APPLICATIONS OF EXTINCTION

Extinction has been successfully applied to diverse problems. In one of the first demonstrations, extinction was used to reduce the frequency with which a psychiatric patient visited the nurses' office (Ayllon & Michael, 1959). The visits had been going on for two years and interfered with the nurses' work. The nurses usually paid attention to the patient when she visited and often pushed her back into the ward. After baseline observations, the nurses were instructed to no longer provide attention to the patient when she visited. Extinction decreased her visits from 16 times a day during baseline to 2 times a day at the end of 7 weeks.

Extinction was also used to reduce awakening in the middle of the night among infants (France & Hudson, 1990). Nighttime waking, exhibited by 20% to 50% of infants often is noted as a significant problem for parents. Parents may play a role in sustaining night waking by attending to the infant in ways that reinforce the behavior. In this study, parents with infants (8 to 20 months old) participated in an extinction-based program to decrease nighttime awakening. Waking up during the night was defined as a sustained noise (more than 1 minute) of the infant between onset of sleep and an agreed-upon waking time (such as 6:00 a.m.). Over the course of the project, several assessment procedures were used, including parent recording of sleep periods, telephone calls to the parents to check on these reports, and a voice-activated recording device near the child's bed. After baseline observations, parents were instructed to modify the way in which they attended to night wakings. Specifically, parents were told to ignore night wakings. If the parent had a concern about the health or safety of the child, the parent was instructed to enter the room, check the child quietly and in silence with a minimum of light, and leave immediately if there was no problem.

The program was implemented separately for seven infants in a multiple-baseline design. Figure 8-2 shows the frequency of night wakings each week for the children during the baseline and intervention periods; frequency decreased during the intervention period. Follow-up consisted of assessment approximately three months and then two years later, which showed maintenance of the changes. The figure is instructive for other reasons. The gradual nature of extinction and repeated instances of spontaneous recovery are suggested both during the intervention and follow-up phases. The prospect of accidental reinforcement during these periods requires special caution on the part of parents to ensure that the behavior is not reinforced.

A related issue pertains to Child 3 (in Figure 8-2), who did not profit from the program. Parents reported difficulty in distinguishing the usual night wakings from those associated with illness of their child. Additional data revealed that these parents attended relatively frequently to nonillness awakenings during the intervention but improved during the first follow-up phase. The parents cannot be faulted. The pattern of behavior and eventual improvement draw attention to the difficulty in ignoring behavior contingently and discriminating when behavior does and does not warrant attention. In any case, the demonstration is clear in showing that extinction generally was quite effective in decreasing night waking among infants.

Generally, extinction is used in conjunction with other procedures, especially positive reinforcement. For example, in a preschool classroom, extinction and reinforcement were used to alter the aggressive behavior of a 3½-year-old boy named Cain who would choke, push, bite, hit, kick, and poke his peers (Pinkston, Reese, LeBlanc, & Baer, 1973). The teacher usually reprimanded the boy, which seemed to have little effect. An extinction program was initiated whereby the teacher ignored his aggressive behavior. Of course, a problem with doing this was that he might seriously injure the victims of his aggression. To avoid that possibility, the teacher immediately interrupted Cain's aggressive activity by attending to the victim and helping the victim begin another activity away from him. While doing this, she ignored Cain. Thus he did not receive attention from the teacher or submission and adverse reactions from the victim, which also might have helped reinforce his aggressive behavior.

Along with the extinction program, the teacher provided attention (social reinforcement) to Cain whenever he initiated appropriate (nonaggressive) interaction with his peers. The effects of the extinction and reinforcement program appear in Figure 8-3. Extinction reduced Cain's aggressive behavior, as shown in the ABAB design (upper portion of the figure). His aggressive behavior remained low one month after the program (last data point), even though no special procedures remained in effect. The effects of extinction of aggressive behavior were probably enhanced by the reinforcement program (lower portion of the figure), which increased appropriate peer interaction.

Extinction was combined with reinforcement to reduce the delusional speech of four hospitalized psychiatric patients (Liberman, Teigen, Patterson, & Baker, 1973). The delusional speech included comments about being persecuted, being poisoned by the staff, being injected with monkey blood, being James Bond or an agent of the FBI, and so on. In daily individual interviews with the staff,

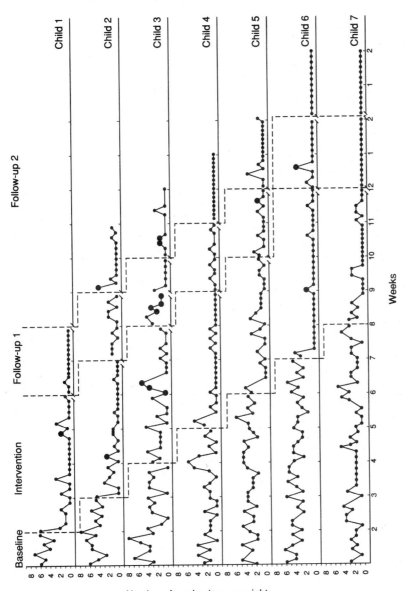

FIGURE 8-2 Frequency of night wakings per week for seven infants treated with extinction. The program was evaluated in a multiple-baseline design across infants. Follow-up 1 and Follow-up 2 represent evaluation at three months and two years after the initial intervention program, respectively. The solid, large dots denote nights in which the infant was ill.

(Source: France & Hudson, 1990)

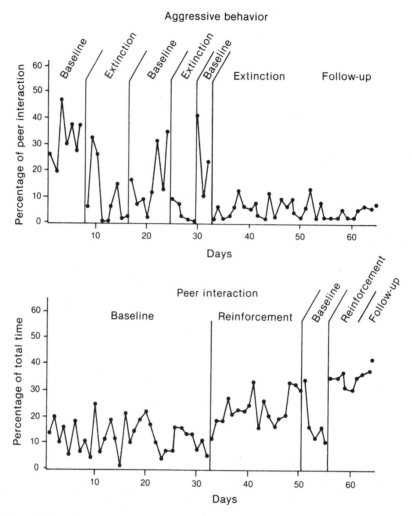

FIGURE 8-3 Subject's daily aggressive behaviors as a percentage of all peer interaction observed (top) and his daily peer interaction as a percentage of time observed (bottom).

(Source: Pinkston, Reese, LeBlanc, & Baer, 1973)

extinction was used by having the staff simply leave the room (no longer pay attention) when delusional speech began. Each patient could also earn reinforcement that involved an evening chat with a therapist. During the chat, the patient and the therapist were in a comfortable room in which snacks were served. The amount of time earned toward the evening chat depended on how much rational (nondelusional) conversation the patient engaged in during interviews earlier that day. The effects of extinguishing irrational speech and rewarding rational speech can be seen in Figure 8-4. In a multiple-baseline design across four

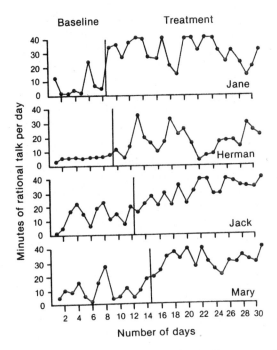

FIGURE 8-4 Duration of rational speech before onset of delusions in daily interviews during baseline and treatment (extinction and reinforcement conditions) in a multiple baseline design across individuals.

(Source: Liberman, Teigen, Patterson, & Baker, 1973)

patients, the effects of treatment appear clear. Rational speech increased when the program was introduced. The example is instructive because delusional speech is a symptom of psychiatric disorder and clearly not begun as a function of social consequences. Even so, the example illustrates that social reinforcement may maintain or exacerbate the behavior.

Many other reports have shown the successful application of extinction alone or in conjunction with other procedures (particularly reinforcement). Hypochondriacal complaints, vomiting, obsessive comments, compulsive rituals, and excessive conversation in the classroom are among the diverse problems that have been treated with extinction and reinforcement. Such applications are particularly noteworthy because they reveal that a number of maladaptive behaviors may be maintained at least in part by their social consequences.

WHEN AND HOW TO USE EXTINCTION

Extinction is useful in situations in which the reinforcer that maintains behavior can be readily identified and controlled. In some situations, it is likely that only one or a few reinforcers maintain behavior. For example, parents may attend to a child's tantrum before the child goes to bed. The reinforcers for tantrums may be attention and food, if a snack is given to placate the child. In this example, the reinforcers maintaining behavior are probably limited to attention and food. Each can readily be withdrawn to test this notion. Of course, if there are other relatives in the house (e.g., siblings and grandparents) who can inadvertently provide reinforcement, identifying and controlling the available reinforcers are more difficult. Another consideration in using extinction is whether the burst that may occur will be harmful to the client or to others. Finally, it is important that the extinction process is tolerable to the persons administering the program. As minor as this may sound, it is critical for effective implementation. For example, if parents are ignoring tantrums of a child, extinction burst may not be tolerable. Parents often note that they feel they are hurting their children by letting them scream or become more upset. If none of these issues is problematic, extinction may be a reasonable approach alone or in combination with reinforcement for positive behavior to eliminate the undesired target behavior.

The effectiveness of extinction is enhanced tremendously when it is combined with positive reinforcement for behavior incompatible with the response to be extinguished. There are many reasons to combine reinforcement with extinction (Lerman, Iwata, & Wallace, 1999; Lerman, Kelley, Van Camp, & Roane, 1999). First, the problems of effectively executing extinction are mitigated. Identifying and controlling reinforcement that maintains the undesirable response are less essential if other reinforcers are provided to develop desirable behavior. Second, the potential undesirable side effects of extinction and the problematic characteristics of the course of extinction are less likely to occur if reinforcement is provided for alternative responses. Providing reinforcement should prevent the side effects that result from reinforcer loss. In addition, a burst of responses and spontaneous recovery may not occur if the reinforced response replaces the extinguished response. Third, extinction may effectively decrease behavior, but it does not ensure that a desirable behavior will replace the eliminated behavior. However, reinforcement can effectively strengthen behavior. If certain undesirable behaviors are extinguished and desirable behaviors are not simultaneously reinforced, extinction may not be very effective. When extinction is terminated, the undesirable behavior is likely to return because no alternative responses have been developed and no alternative means of obtaining reinforcement have been provided. When extinction or punishment is used, reinforcement should be delivered to develop a behavior that will replace the response to be eliminated.

Various reinforcement procedures (e.g., differential reinforcement of other behavior, of functionally equivalent responses, and so on) can be used in conjunction with extinction. In this regard, the reinforcer and the specific contingency used to develop behavior deserve comment. When reinforcement is used along with extinction, it is advisable to provide the same reinforcer to the client but for appropriate rather than for inappropriate behavior. Thus if attention is the reinforcer, then the extinction procedure consists of no longer providing attention for the maladaptive or disruptive behavior. The reinforcer (attention) can still be given, but instead, for appropriate or prosocial behavior. In this way, a new reinforcer (food, tokens) is not introduced; rather, an existing reinforcer can be redeployed to promote prosocial behavior. In other words, maladaptive behavior serves a function for the client, which is to obtain a particular reinforcer, such as attention or escape from an undesirable situation. A behavior that is adaptive or appropriate is more likely to develop if the positive behavior serves the same function and attains the reinforcement (Durand & Carr, 1991; Wacker et al., 1990). Extinction is particularly effective when the reinforcer maintaining behavior is identified, when the connection between the behavior and that reinforcer is terminated, and when that reinforcer is deployed to follow positive, prosocial behavior.

EXTINCTION OF NEGATIVELY REINFORCED BEHAVIOR

Operant Behavior and Escape Extinction

In applied settings, extinction has been used primarily for behaviors that were previously maintained by positive reinforcement. No longer providing positive reinforcement (e.g., parental attention) for behavior (e.g., tantrums) is a common example and useful way to remember the procedure. Extinction also is used for negatively reinforced behavior. These instances refer to behaviors that are maintained because they *escape* or *avoid* an event or consequence. Essentially, the event or consequence serves as an aversive event to the individual. Engaging in some inappropriate behavior is reinforced by terminating the event. For example, a parent may demand that a child complete a chore such as cleaning his or her room. The child may shout back or scream at the parent to leave him or her alone. The aversive stimulus for the child in this example is the parent's demand to perform a task. The child can escape the demand by shouting and getting the parent to stop talking and perhaps to leave the room. Child shouting (behavior) is negatively reinforced (termination of aversive demands of the parent). So far, we have merely described negative reinforcement. Extinction of negatively reinforced behavior means that the behavior occurs (shouting of the child) but does not lead to reinforcement (i.e., the parent does not stop talking or leave, and the demand is not stopped). If the behavior is no longer reinforced, one would expect the behavior (shouting of the child) to decline.

In general, negative reinforcement often is more difficult to remember than positive reinforcement. Extinction of negatively reinforced responses may also seem to be a bit more complex. However, the principle of extinction is the same; no longer providing reinforcement for a response. Consider some examples of extinction of negatively reinforced behavior.

Throughout previous chapters, examples were given of youths who engage in self-injurious behavior, such as hitting themselves or banging their heads. Several studies have conducted functional analyses of these behaviors to identify what is maintaining them (Pelios et al., 1999). For example, in a study of children and adolescents (ages 5 to 16) already mentioned, several developmentally delayed youths engaged in self-injurious behavior (Iwata et al., 1990). Youths were individually exposed to different conditions in brief (15-minute) sessions to see which conditions increased or decreased their self-injurious behavior. In a demand condition, the child worked on educational tasks; the "demand" was for the child to work educational tasks. The experimenter was not literally demanding, nasty, or negative—characteristics that might be connotations of "demand." In fact, praise and pats on the back were given for correct task performance. However, instances of self-injurious behavior were followed by termination of the task. If task termination is a negative reinforcer, then self-injurious behavior would increase.

The results for several children showed that demand conditions in fact increased self-injury and that other conditions generally did not (playing with the child, providing attention for instances of self-injury). Having identified the reinforcer (escape from demand), the authors then used an extinction procedure in which the youths could not escape from demand with self-injurious behavior. When self-injury occurred, the task continued. That is, the reinforcer (removal of task demands) no longer followed the behavior (self-injury). Rather, the experimenter provided guidance (prompts, physical assistance) to continue and complete the task. Self-injurious behavior decreased substantially across youths when extinction was implemented.

The procedure illustrated above is extinction because the reinforcer (escape) did not follow the inappropriate behavior. Sometimes this is referred to as *escape extinction,* and it is a useful way to remember extinction of negatively reinforced operant behavior. The reinforcer (escape) is no longer forthcoming. Several studies of self-injurious, aggressive, and disruptive behavior have shown that escape extinction alone or in combination with prompting (e.g., physical guidance and assistance to complete the tasks) and positive reinforcement techniques can effectively eliminate deviant behavior (e.g., Repp et al., 1988; Sasso et al., 1992).

Anxiety Treatment and Outpatient Therapy

There are other uses of extinction for responses developed or maintained by negative reinforcement. These applications have to do with behaviors performed to avoid anticipated aversive consequences. For example, individuals who have intense fear related to heights (acrophobia) avoid high places in their everyday lives. There is a connection between heights and aversive consequences (perceived danger). Although there may be little or no real danger in many of the situations the individuals fear, certainly the anxiety or panic they experience when they approach heights or are actually in situations involving heights is a deeply felt and genuinely aversive consequence.

It is possible to extinguish responses developed or maintained through negative reinforcement. In such cases, the extinction procedures are generally used in the context of individual therapy for persons who seek treatment rather than in applied settings such as the home, the school, institutions, and the community. Nevertheless, because such procedures are widely practiced in the context of behavior therapy, it is useful to mention techniques in which the extinction of avoidance behavior is considered to be operative.

Everyday experience teaches us that avoidance behaviors such as fears and phobias are difficult to overcome. The resistance of avoidance behaviors to extinction has been demonstrated in laboratory animal research. In classic experiments, dogs were trained to avoid brief electric shocks by responding to a buzzer that preceded a shock (Solomon, Kamin, & Wynne, 1953). A dog could avoid the shock by jumping over a barrier in the middle of the compartment when the buzzer sounded. The avoidance training procedure was repeated in each side of the compartment. At the beginning of training, the dog was shocked and escaped over the barrier. In a short time, it repeatedly jumped back and forth over the barrier in response to the buzzer. Although the shock was eventually withdrawn from the situation, the avoidance response did not extinguish. The dog never remained in the situation long enough to find out that extinction (removal of shock) began.

Anxiety is presumed to play a role in the development and maintenance of avoidance responses. A previously neutral stimulus elicits anxiety and escape through classical conditioning, described earlier. Cues associated with the unconditioned aversive event can elicit the anxiety and escape response. In the case of avoidance in animals, anxiety or fear increases when the buzzer sounds because the buzzer preceded shock. Escape from the buzzer reduces fear. Thus anxiety reduction, by termination of the unconditioned aversive event, negatively reinforces escape. Although the unconditioned aversive event (shock) no longer occurs, successful escape from the anxiety-arousing conditioned aversive event may maintain avoidance behavior.

Fear and anxiety in human behavior have often been conceptualized on the basis of avoidance conditioning studied in laboratory research. With humans, it is not clear how most fears develop, as it is in animal research that specific fear reactions are induced. However, like laboratory-induced fear, human avoidance behavior is highly resistant to extinction. Fearful persons rarely place themselves in the fear-provoking situation. If they did, escape and avoidance behaviors might extinguish, as described below. Anxiety can be reduced by remaining in the provoking situation long enough to allow the conditioned anxiety to extinguish. Most people do not gain the benefit of extinction because they either do not enter into the situation they fear or only remain in it for a brief period. Thus, avoidance of or escape from the situation is reinforced by anxiety reduction.

Several techniques have been effective in extinguishing avoidance responses. One of the more widely practiced techniques is *systematic desensitization,* which was derived from a classical conditioning framework (Wolpe, 1958). As mentioned earlier, desensitization alters the valence of the conditioned stimuli so that they no longer elicit anxiety. Anxiety-eliciting conditioned stimuli are paired with nonanxiety states of the client. To achieve a nonanxiety state, the client is usually trained to relax very deeply. Relaxation is eventually paired with actually being in the anxiety-provoking situation or imagining that one is in that situation. For example, in the more commonly used variation of desensitization, the client imagines approaching only mildly provoking situations while he or she is deeply relaxed. As treatment progresses and the client has successfully associated relaxation with these situations, he or she imagines increasingly arousing situations. Eventually, the client can imagine these situations without anxiety. Stimuli that previously elicited anxiety no longer do so. Moreover, the changes in the client's anxiety responses are not restricted to images or thoughts about the situation but extend to the actual situation.

Another technique often used to extinguish avoidance reactions is *flooding*. Flooding nicely illustrates the rationale for extinguishing anxiety responses because it involves exposing the client to anxiety-eliciting stimuli for prolonged periods. Like desensitization, flooding can be conducted in imagination or in the actual situations themselves. The procedure consists of exposing the client to the fear-provoking stimuli directly. For example, a client who is afraid of heights might imagine being in very high places. When the client first imagines such a situation, intense anxiety is produced. However, as he or she continues to imagine the situation for a prolonged period (several minutes or even an hour or more), anxiety decreases. Repeated presentation of the same situation is likely to evoke much less anxiety. As the situation is repeated and others are presented, anxiety is completely eliminated. The conditioned stimuli have lost their capacity to evoke anxiety.

Systematic desensitization, flooding, and related techniques have been successfully used in many programs to overcome anxiety (Emmelkamp, 1994). Each of these techniques exposes the individual to a situation that usually is avoided and prevents or minimizes the need for an avoidance response. Avoidance behavior extinguishes because no untoward consequences actually occur in the situation, and contact with the feared stimuli is actually encouraged. Extinction of avoidance responses may occur inadvertently in the context of counseling or psychotherapy. In therapy, clients frequently express feelings and thoughts that elicit anxiety and guilt in themselves. These feelings and thoughts may be avoided at the beginning of therapy precisely because they evoke anxiety. Therapists typically respond in a permissive and nonpunitive fashion so that maladaptive emotional responses extinguish. As therapy progresses, self-reported and physiological arousal associated with anxiety-provoking topics such as sex, may decrease over time.

Behavior therapy techniques have been effective in treating a variety of avoidance and anxiety reactions. Phobias in which specific events or situations are avoided (e.g., heights, flying, open spaces), obsessions (repetitive thoughts), and compulsions (repetitive and ritualistic acts) have been successfully treated with behavioral techniques based on imagery or real-life (in vivo) exposure. The techniques merely place persons in the situations that arouse anxiety. The situation is presented in special ways, often in conjunction with the use of other techniques for overcoming anxiety (e.g., relaxation training).

Extinction has been a major explanation or interpretation of how techniques such as desensitization and flooding work. Animal laboratory research has bolstered this interpretation. In controlled settings, animal research has established and eliminated fears and extinction provides a reasonable account. Of course, development anxiety and fear in humans (and in animals that do not live in laboratories) is more complex. Extinction may not be the only explanation of how such fears are eliminated. Perhaps more importantly, by drawing on extinction, particularly extinction of negatively reinforced behaviors, several effective treatments for fears, phobias, and other types of anxiety have been developed.

SUMMARY AND CONCLUSIONS

Extinction often is an effective procedure to eliminate behavior. The effectiveness of withholding reinforcement for a response depends primarily on the schedule of reinforcement that has maintained the response. Behavior maintained with highly intermittent reinforcement is particularly resistant to extinction. In practice, extinction can be difficult to implement because the source of reinforcement maintaining behavior cannot always be readily identified and controlled. Several features of extinction warrant consideration.

First, for behaviors that are dangerous (e.g., self-destructive) or highly disruptive (e.g., shouting and screaming), extinction is not recommended. Even if the precise reinforcer maintaining behavior has been identified (e.g., through functional analysis), extinction alone may not be suitable. Because the decrease in behavior is usually gradual during extinction, a large number of responses may be performed before the undesirable behavior is eliminated. If an immediate intervention is required, extinction may be too slow to produce change.

Second, responses may increase at the beginning of extinction. This is referred to as extinction burst. If behavior is inadvertently reinforced when it becomes worse, increasingly deviant behavior may result.

Third, extinguished behaviors sometimes recover spontaneously, even though responses are not reinforced. Again, a potential problem is that inadvertent reinforcement will reinstate the behavior when spontaneous recovery occurs. Also, reinforcement of behavior during the extinction phase amounts to a highly intermittent reinforcement schedule. Behavior will be much more difficult to eliminate through extinction if reinforced intermittently.

Finally, extinction may be accompanied by undesirable emotional side effects such as anger or frustration. These states are not necessarily inherent in response reduction but are side effects that are likely to occur when alternate means of obtaining reinforcement are not provided. In applied settings, positive side effects have been documented as more frequent than the negative side effects. Yet the specific side effects that emerge are not entirely predictable, and hence the potential for negative side effects raises special cautions.

Although extinction can decrease or eliminate behaviors, it does not develop new prosocial behaviors to replace those responses that have been extinguished. The most effective use of extinction is in combination with reinforcement for behaviors that are incompatible with or that will replace the undesirable behavior. In most cases, positive reinforcement for desired behavior is used. Yet in a number of instances, negative reinforcement already in the situation is responsible for deviant behavior; altering the contingency so that prosocial behavior is reinforced is used to achieve therapeutic change. The use of reinforcement along with extinction is the most frequent use of extinction in behavior modification programs.

Apart from operant extinction, several behavioral techniques are based on extinction of anxiety-based reactions. These reactions are usually conceptualized from a classical conditioning paradigm. Systematic desensitization, flooding, and exposure-based treatments in general have been effective in the treatment of many anxiety disorders. Most of these applications are conducted individually with clients who seek outpatient therapy.

KEY TERMS

Avoidance	Extinction burst	Systematic desensitization
Escape	Flooding	
Extinction	Spontaneous recovery	

APPLYING PRINCIPLES AND TECHNIQUES TO EVERYDAY LIFE

1. What is the difference between extinction and time out from reinforcement?

2. Your consulting business in developing behavior modification programs is doing very well (and you have given yourself a raise and stock options). A parent calls your office and says he wants to stop his child from interrupting him whenever he is on the phone. His 6-year-old daughter makes all sorts of requests and interrupts him as soon as he is on the phone. You do a quick functional analysis and expect that attention, saying yes to requests ("Can [sic—it should be 'may'] I go out and play?" "Can I have a snack?" "Can I watch a violent TV show that may promote my own violent behavior and impede my psychological development?"), and even getting the parent upset are all reinforcing consequences for interrupting. You decide to develop an extinction program. State exactly what you would have the parent do when he is on the phone. Write your description of spontaneous recovery and extinction burst to the parent to prepare him for what may happen while the extinction program is in effect.

3. One of the reasons your consulting business is so successful is that you know never (or almost never) to design a program just to decrease behavior. So in addition to extinction, you come up with a little program to reinforce positive opposites in the child. Briefly describe that program. It would be useful to reinforce functionally equivalent behavior, that is, give the child the desired reinforcers (if they are fine with the parent), but give the reinforcers for prosocial rather than disruptive behavior.

FOR FURTHER READING

Hall, R.V., & Hall, M.L. (1998). *How to use planned ignoring (extinction)* (2nd ed.). Austin, TX: Pro-Ed.

Lerman, D.C., & Iwata, B.A. (1996). Developing a technology for the use of operant extinction in clinical settings: An examination of basic and applied research. *Journal of Applied Behavior Analysis, 29,* 345–382.

Lerman, D.C., Iwata, B.A., Shore, B.A., & Kahng, S. (1996). Responding maintained by intermittent reinforcement: Implications for the use of extinction with problem behavior in clinical settings. *Journal of Applied Behavior Analysis, 29,* 153–171.

Iwata, B.A., Vollmer, T.R., & Zarcone, J.R. (1990). The experimental (functional) analysis of behavior disorders: Methodology, applications, and limitations. In A.C. Repp & N.N. Singh (Eds.), *Perspectives on the use of nonaversive and aversive interventions for persons with developmental disabilities* (pp. 301–330). Sycamore, IL: Sycamore.

CHAPTER 9

Special Technique Variations to Enhance Performance

In previous chapters, reinforcement, punishment, and extinction procedures were discussed. By and large, the applications illustrated individual techniques such as the use of token reinforcement or time out and their many variations. The illustrations showed that relatively simple and straightforward applications of the procedures are often effective in altering behavior. Actually, the procedures can be applied in a very large number of ways alone and in combination.

For several reasons, it is important to examine variations in the ways behavioral programs can be implemented. To begin with, behavioral programs are not invariably effective when they are applied or as effective as one would like them to be. For example, the behavior of an aggressive child may improve with a token reinforcement program, but the improvement may not be great enough to make an important difference to his teachers. Similarly, in a nursing home setting, reinforcement may increase the extent to which many of the residents participate in social activities, yet some of the residents may not have even begun to participate. Or a program may have been designed to change several behaviors but may not have succeeded in changing all of them. In many applications, behavioral programs have not worked well initially. Often, varying the programs, perhaps by altering the magnitude or type of reinforcement or by adding procedures (e.g., response cost), has led to significant increments in client performance (Kazdin, 1983). There is a host of other options for improving client performance. This chapter considers several program variations directed toward improving the effectiveness of the intervention.

Another reason for considering program variations is to convey the range of options available. Different settings have different demands, often practical in nature, that need to be considered when a program is being developed. For example, at home, it may seem reasonable to instruct and train parents to provide reinforcers such as tokens exchangeable for special privileges, for a child who is having special problems. However, the child may have siblings. How should they to be treated, especially if there is no reason to provide special reinforcers for their behaviors? Program variations (e.g., consequence sharing, which is discussed later) permit implementation of effective interventions while considering practical constraints or circumstances of the situation. In large-scale programs, as for example with all people who work in a large corporation, who live in a particular city or neighborhood, or who live in a dormitory, it may not be feasible to provide reinforcers based on the performance of each individual. Difficulties in monitoring individual performance or insufficient resources to administer reinforcers to each individual raise special obstacles. Yet in such circumstances, effective program variations can be used.

This chapter considers a number of technique variations that go beyond the applications discussed previously. These variations can be used to enhance client performance when a behavior modification program is not working well or is not working well enough to meet the goals. Many of the programs also can be adapted to address special characteristics or limitations of various settings.

RECHECKING THE CONTINGENCIES
AND THEIR IMPLEMENTATION

Although behavior modification programs have been effective, occasionally some individuals do not respond to the contingencies or respond only minimally. When a program does not appear to be working or working well, a number of components of the program should be checked. Checking these components is equivalent to seeing if an electrical appliance is plugged in and turned on when the appliance is not functioning. Clearly, these checks are not always the problem, but it is curious how often basic features are relevant. Analogously, in most cases of weak or ineffective programs, the problem stems from how the program is implemented. Features that maximize the effectiveness of a program, such as delivery of reinforcers contingent on behavior, immediately after behavior, and on as continuous a schedule as possible, are not always easy to implement or to implement consistently. Consequently, ensuring that these features are in place may be all that is needed to improve a program. Similarly, punishment programs based on time out or reprimands may not work very well initially but can usually be improved by ensuring that the reinforcement program for desirable behavior also is in effect. Before implementation of the contingencies, a functional analysis can be helpful in identifying factors that might be maintaining behavior. The results of the analysis would also have direct implications for ensuring the program is effective. For example, it is often assumed that ignoring a behavior is equivalent to extinction. Yet ignoring will only be effective if attention in fact was the reinforcer maintaining behavior. Sometimes it is, but often it is not.

Assume for a moment that the initial steps of identifying reinforcers were accomplished, that the program was implemented adequately, and that behavior was changing reasonably well. There may still be a need for further techniques to enhance performance and incorporate into the program. Several such techniques are discussed in the present chapter.

Antecedents

Prompting. If the program is not working or working well, better use of antecedents often makes a large difference in performance. Antecedents refer to stimuli, settings, and contexts that occur before and influence behaviors. It is useful to look more carefully at some of the antecedents and how they can be used to develop behavior. Increasing the use of prompts and efforts to guide behavior can enhance performance. Prompts can include verbal statements, gestures, guided assistance, modeling, or other interventions to help the individual initiate the response. For example, a child may not clean up his or her room even though a reinforcement program has been put into place. Prompts to initiate the behavior might include helping the child clean the room, picking up one or two items to model the desired behavior, gently reminding the child, or keeping the child company while he or she does it. Prompts help the individual begin or complete the response and are especially useful at the beginning of a program. Eventually, the prompts can be faded.

Consider an example where a parent wishes a young child not to have a tantrum and pout every time the parent says no or does not give into a request (e.g., child asks, "May I stay up late tonight, have some candy, have a friend over, have a cell phone, have a car?"). The parent, aided by this book, has learned that praising the child for not having a tantrum is one intervention likely to work. The difficulty is that the child may have a tantrum every time so nontantrum behavior (DRO or DRA schedule) cannot be reinforced. The desired behavior does not occur whenever the parent says no to a request.

There are many options but use of prompts can easily rescue this program. A way to do that would be for the parent to go to the child and say, "In one minute I am going to say 'no' to you—this is just pretend but I am going to say 'No, you cannot stay up late tonight.' If you say back me, 'Why not?' in a calm way and without crying or hitting something, you can earn a token." This is an antecedent event that sets the stage for the desired behavior. Now, the mother says to the child, "No you cannot . . ." and right before she says that or right before the child has a tantrum she whispers to the child, "Remember do these behaviors and you can get a token." If the tokens are tangible items (e.g., a penny, ticket) the mother may even hold this up for the child to see to signal that the reinforcer can be earned. The token displayed before the behavior serves as an S^D and increases the likelihood of the behavior. With this heavy use of antecedent events, the child is very likely not to have a tantrum and will earn the token plus praise. The program would be repeated; the child would have many opportunities. In the clinic where I work, we recommend at least 3 to 5 such prompted trials per day, but there is no research to support any particular number. The general rule is that more practice opportunities and trials in which behavior can occur and be reinforced are better. To return to our hypothetical child, there will be unprompted occasions in which the child does not have a tantrum or has a low-magnitude tantrum (a little whining). These can be reinforced, and perfect behavior that is unprompted of course would be quite heavily reinforced (e.g., maybe 2 to 3 tokens and enthusiastically praised). In this example, prompts were used to virtually ensure that the desired behavior is performed. Also added to this were simulated trials or opportunities for the child to engage in the behavior. Once the behavior is established, the prompts can be readily faded and eliminated.

Parents, teachers, and others often note that they prompt behavior in everyday life and the prompts do not "work." Ineffective use of prompts is fairly common. Familiar examples include nagging children to clean up their rooms or to complete their homework. Prompts of this kind are likely to be ineffective in part because they are not associated with consequences (reinforcing) when the desired behavior occurs. Moreover, the aversiveness of repeated prompts (constant reminders) probably leads to other behaviors (side effects of aversive procedures) such as escape or avoidance, as reflected in not listening, "tuning out," leaving the situation, or staying away from the person who provides the prompts. Nevertheless, prompts can be effective in initiating and occasionally in sustaining behavior. Prompts that are in close proximity to the behavior, provide clear guidance of precisely what is to be done, and under positive setting conditions (a nonstressful situation in the tantrum example) increase the likelihood of the desired behavior.

Instructions. Oral and written instructions are the prompts most often studied in applied settings and used in everyday life and hence warrant special comment. Instructions can help guide performance in different ways. Instructions serve as discriminative stimuli and can tell which behaviors will and will not receive consequences, when to initiate a response, and how to complete the response. Statements about how to perform the behavior can greatly speed development of the behavior and minimize errors. For example, teaching a person to drive a car uses different types of prompts such as modeling (viewing others) and instructions. Instructions are especially useful in directing behavior (e.g., "Release the emergency break," "Gently press your foot to the gas pedal," or "Try not to drive over the curb when you make your next right turn.")

The usual use of instructions and other prompts is to initiate behavior so the behavior can be reinforced. In this use, instructions are a part of the intervention program. Occasionally, instructions have been used in their own right as the primary basis for the intervention. A novel example of the use of instructions in this fashion was to influence cartoonists who drew well-known syndicated comic strips (Mathews & Dix, 1992). The goal was to increase the extent to which cartoonists of different strips portrayed passengers wearing seat belts when passengers were depicted. Comic strips in daily papers were examined. If passengers and cars were depicted, data were recorded regarding whether passengers were shown to be wearing seat belts. After baseline, written prompts were used in an effort to alter cartoonist behavior. The intervention consisted of a letter advocating the use of seat belts in the strips (advocacy letter). The letter was mailed after the appearance of an unbelted passenger in a particular strip, along with a copy of the strip and a statement of the desirability of seat belt use. The letter was sent from the director of a head and spinal cord injury prevention program to help underscore the importance of the issue. Comic strips were subsequently monitored to see whether there was any effect on the behavior of the cartoonists.

The effects of the written instructional prompt can be seen in Figure 9-1. As shown, a multiple-baseline design was used in which the letter was introduced at different points in time among eight cartoonists. Clearly, some of the cartoonists changed their behavior (see *Cathy, Mark Trail,* or *Blondie*). Yet, the effects of written instructions were not uniformly strong or consistent among cartoonists, a point to which we shall return. Prompts without immediate reinforcement for the prompted behavior is not a strong intervention.

Oral and written prompts have been effective in many applications but, as the prior example shows, can be rather inconsistent in their effects. Prompts appear to be more effective when (1) they are delivered immediately before the opportunity to engage in the desired behavior, (2) they specify the precise behaviors that are to be performed, (3) they are provided in a nondemanding and polite fashion, and (4) the prompted behaviors are followed by immediate reinforcement.

An example that illustrates many of these conditions also focuses on the use of seat belts, but in quite a different context (Geller, Bruff, & Nimmer, 1985). In

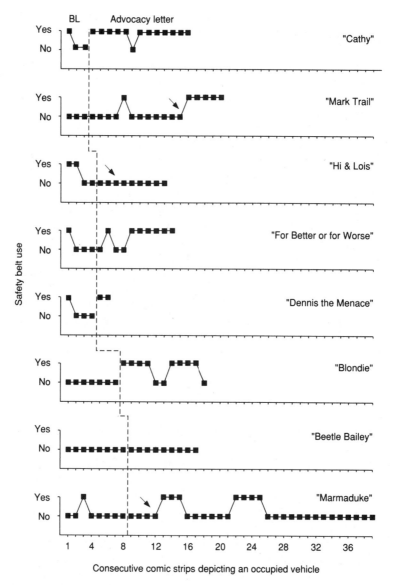

FIGURE 9-1 Seat belt use as depicted in comic strips in which characters occupied motor vehicles. Baseline (BL) included recording how characteristics were depicted before the intervention. During the intervention (advocacy letter), a letter was sent to cartoonists encouraging depiction of passengers using safety belts in future cartoons. Arrows indicate the point at which a second letter was sent. The name of the cartoon is depicted to the right of the individual portions of the figure.

(Source: Mathews & Dix, 1992)

this application, the goal was to change seat belt use among drivers in everyday life and as they were driving. Those who implemented the intervention were driving around in a car. A car passenger, referred to by the investigators as a "flasher," administered the prompts. A prompt was delivered when the flasher's car and an adjacent car pulled up at an intersection, at which both cars were stopped. If the driver of the adjacent car did not have a seat belt on (as evident by an unused shoulder belt in the car), the flasher held up (flashed) a sign (11 × 14 inches) that stated "Please buckle up—I care" and depicted an almost-buckled seat belt.

Conditions designed to maximize the effect of prompts were present in this situation. The prompt was closely associated with the opportunity to engage in the desired behavior (while in one's car), identified and illustrated the desired behavior (with words and a picture), and was delivered in a nondemanding fashion. If the driver buckled up after the prompt, the prompting card was turned over, and the other side stated, "Thank you," to provide social reinforcement. Thus the prompted behavior was immediately reinforced. Data on buckling were gathered by observers in the back seat of the car from which the prompts were delivered. About 21.5% of the prompted drivers buckled their seat belts before leaving the intersection and almost 80% did not. Of course those who were influenced by the prompt did not necessarily maintain the behavior. However, the point is only to note that prompts delivered in special ways can help initiate behavior.

There have been many novel applications of instructions, especially in community settings to increase use of seat belts, conserve energy and water, encourage recycling, and reduce littering (e.g., Geller, Winett, & Everett, 1982). Because prompts by themselves are not strong interventions, they are advocated as an important element of a broader program. Indeed, noted early in the book (Chapter 2) was the importance of addressing antecedents, behaviors, and consequences (ABCs) as part of an intervention program. Antecedents are mentioned here because in a program that is not working or is not working very well, modification of antecedents is a viable strategy to increase program effectiveness.

General Comments. It is important to distinguish the varied uses of prompts in changing behavior. First, prompts such as instructions and other forms of guidance can be used to initiate behavior. In this use, prompts are part of a behavior-change program; other aspects of the program, such as reinforcement of the prompted behavior, play a pivotal role in the program. Second, prompts can be used as the intervention. In this use, the prompt (e.g., instructions, or exposure to a model who performs the behavior) is not necessarily followed by reinforcement of the desired behavior in the client. In everyday life, instructions are often relied on in this latter way, that is, as an intervention in its own right. Commands given to people, such as "Do not smoke, drink, lie, or cheat," "Do your chores," "Do your homework," or "Just say no to drugs," as well as commands codified in religious imperatives (e.g., The Ten Commandments), reflect oral or written instructions. Instructions on what and how to perform often change behavior, as illustrated by prior examples and by our experience in everyday life. Yet, prompts alone as the sole or primary basis of an intervention, without consequences for the prompted behavior, often generate weak, inconsistent, and short-lived effects.

The weak intervention effects of prompts serve as a source of frustration in everyday life. For example, parents in relation to their children or one individual in relation to his or her spouse, partner, or significant other may say such things as, "I told her (him) a thousand times, and it is like talking to a wall," and "S(he) knows what to do but doesn't do it." These expressions and the frustration they reflect derive in part from the fact that instructions, reminders, and explanations by themselves may not be potent. The relative ineffectiveness of such interventions is known. The frustration stems from continued beliefs that telling people what to do by itself is sufficient to change behavior. Sometimes it is; invariably, it is more effective to combine instructions and other antecedents and consequences to develop the behavior.

If behavior is not changing or is not being performed consistently in a behavior modification program, one of the first lines of attack is to examine the use of antecedents that can increase the likelihood of the behavior. In an earlier chapter, setting events and prompts were noted as antecedents. Setting events consist of more contextual influences on behavior that set the stage (e.g., having a child engage in calming behaviors before going to sleep to help set the stage for going to bed calmly). Setting events are less well studied. Prompts were discussed here because much is known about their use and influence and because they directly initiate, mold, and develop the behavior of interest. It is important to ensure that the prompts are provided and that they meet the conditions noted previously. Prompts can usually be altered, expanded on, or provided more consistently to help initiate behavior. At the same time, it is critical to bear their limitations in mind. Prompts are designed to initiate performance. Whether performance is sustained and behavior improves depends on the consequences that follow.

Behaviors

Shaping. Prompting and instructions focus on antecedent events. If a program is not working or is not working well, the next places to look are the behaviors and consequences. Consider the behaviors and how they ought to be examined to improve program effectiveness. One of the initial areas to examine in enhancing the impact of the program is the behavior required for reinforcement. Typically, "too much behavior" or too stringent demands for behavior change are placed on the person at the beginning of a program. For example, consider two college roommates, one of whom does not exercise at all, but wants to. The other roommate, well skilled in behavioral principles and techniques, develops a behavior-change program. The participant (person who wants to exercise) *can* exercise—she used to play tennis or jog five or six days a week. The behavior-change agent (person in charge of the program) reasons that only some incentive is needed because the participant already has the necessary behaviors in her repertoire.

The program begins by informing the participant that in exchange for exercising four days a week, she will be taken out for dinner or a "happy hour" on Saturday. The exercise is monitored daily because of the importance of seeing how the program is working. The two roommates agree to define exercise to be at least

20 consecutive minutes of jogging, playing tennis, or engaging in some similar activity on which both agree. As for the incentives, perhaps several reinforcers are included in a token economy. If the participant exercises four out of seven days, she earns 20 tokens. Any day of exercise beyond the minimum could earn 10 additional points. At the end of the week, the participant can exchange these points for dinner (20 points) or "happy hour" (30 points), or save them toward some event that requires more points than can be accumulated in a week, such as $10 (70 points), a ticket to a live concert (150 points), or services of the behavior-change agent as a servant for 2 to 3 days (175 points).

There are a few problems with this program. The first is the amount of response (exercise) that is being required. If the roommate has not exercised at all during the previous weeks, the first task is to develop *some* exercise. An attempt to develop a lot of exercise could easily fail. Some or a lot is relative but a good place to start is to require a level of the behavior that is only slightly above baseline. As a general rule, a brief or simple response is more likely to occur than a longer or more complex response. Perhaps points should be given for 10 rather than 20 minutes of exercise; a 10-minute response is closer to the baseline level (0 minutes per day) and thus is more likely to be performed.

Although we are not yet discussing ways of altering consequences to improve programs, a conspicuous problem in the way consequences are used is evident in this example. The program requires at least four days of exercise to earn any reinforcers. This means that exercise for one, two, or three days in a given week will not earn points. At the beginning of a program, when the behavior is developing, reinforcers should be provided for any day of exercise. As noted earlier, at the beginning of a program consequences ought to be provided whenever the desired behavior occurs (continuous reinforcement). In this program, allowing the behavior to occur (exercise on a given day) without reinforcement amounts to an intermittent schedule and is not optimal for developing behavior.

The points earned in this program are exchanged for backup events at the end of the week. Although this may be convenient (because the behavior-change agent will not have to go out to dinner in the middle of the week), the consequences are too delayed. Behaviors performed early in the week are not associated with the backup reinforcers. It would be better to include some backup events that can be provided on a daily basis, such as doing the dishes or running errands, in addition to the other reinforcers.[1]

If the program did not increase exercise or had short-lived effects, this would be understandable. The program may need to be revised further so that any short period of exercise is rewarded with points and so that some of the backup rewards can be bought on any given day. The revised program shapes behavior better by making the demands smaller, increasing the likelihood that the behavior will occur, and ensuring that the behavior can be reinforced. After a few days of consistent exercise, longer periods of exercise or more days of exercise could be associated with special bonuses. For example, any exercise period of at least 20 minutes could receive an extra token or any week of four or more exercise days could be followed with a 20-point bonus. In this way, one can move toward the larger sequences of behavior (more exercise). One begins a program by reinforcing behavior close to what the person already does, that is, slightly above baseline levels. Program failures often result from not shaping behavior gradually and from not moving to more stringent demands only after behavior has become consistent at less stringent levels.

In terms of ABCs, this discussion has focused on behaviors and consequences because they are often intertwined. Here, less behavior (B) should be required to earn reinforcers. Also, the reinforcing consequences (C) ought to be provided more often and without delays. It is quite common for parents, teachers, and others to begin programs by asking for big "chucks" or sequences of behavior (e.g., cleaning one's room, completing all of an assignment). A common statement from a parent is that, "I know she can clean her room (set the table, do homework, pick up her clothes) because she does it once in a while." That a person *can* do this large sequence of behavior is only one component of performance. The question is does the person do the behavior consistently? If not, either before or during the program, shaping the behavior and then shaping consistency (repeated performance of the behavior) is usually the place to intervene to improve the behavior.

Response Priming. In many instances, the client readily performs the response and has often done so on recent occasions. In such instances, extensive shaping may not be required. The response merely has to be primed in some way. *Response priming refers to any procedure that initiates early steps in a sequence or chain of responses.* Response priming consists of requiring the client to engage in the initial components of the sequence. Engaging in responses that are early in a sequence increases the probability of performing the final behaviors in the sequence. As noted earlier, any act can be broken down into a sequence or chain of responses. A difficulty with initiating a sequence of responses is that the final reinforcement (at the end of the chain) is remote. For example, a frequent difficulty with completing a term paper, writing a book, or doing a chore is merely beginning the task. Once the task is begun, the prospect of reinforcement is less remote and the sequence of the requisite behaviors is more likely to be performed.[2]

Response priming has been used to initiate responses that otherwise have an exceedingly low frequency. For example, a priming procedure was used to increase the frequency with which residents of a nursing home engaged in various activities (McClannahan & Risley, 1975). Several of the residents were physically disabled and confined to wheelchairs or beds, some were mentally retarded, and most had medical disorders. Typically, residents remained in their rooms, did not engage in many activities, sat around the facility, and avoided social interaction. Activities were increased by making equipment and recreational materials (puzzles and games) available in the lounge. As a resident entered the lounge, he or she was given some materials, even if the materials were not requested. An activity leader demonstrated how to use the materials and provided assistance until the resident began working on them. The priming procedure led to very marked increases in the percentage of residents participating in activities. This procedure illustrates the use of response priming, because residents were encouraged to engage in the initial steps of the response, namely, to take the materials and to begin work with them. Once the behavior was begun, it continued.

Similarly, in another demonstration, the goal was to increase initiation of social interaction among preschool children (ages 2½ to 5) with autism who participated in university preschool program (Zanoli, Daggett, & Adams, 1996). Priming consisted of prompting children to engage in social behaviors such as looking at peers, smiling, and talking to others in a period before activities in which their social interaction was to be changed. These periods of priming social behavior led to increases in spontaneous initiations with peers in activity periods in which the behaviors were not prompted. That is, initiating the behavior led to continuation and extension to periods in which social behaviors were unprompted.

Priming procedures achieve their effects by making the initial responses easier or more likely. In programs in which the target responses are performed infrequently even though they are in the repertoire of the clients, a priming procedure can be used. Even if the responses are not in the clients' repertoire of responses, the priming procedure can initiate early response components and facilitate shaping.

Consequences

Reinforcer Sampling. Usually the first place one looks to improve weak programs is in the consequences and their administration. As already mentioned, the basic parameters of reinforcement (contingency, immediacy, continuous reinforcement) need to be in place. Assuming these are in place, consequences can be altered in other ways to improve program effects.

In reinforcement programs, it is very important that the clients use the available reinforcers. The more often the reinforcers are used, the more likely the clients will engage in the target behaviors required to obtain them. The utilization of a reinforcer can be viewed as a sequence of responses. If the initial responses in the sequence can be primed, the likelihood of completing the sequence is increased. To initiate the sequence, a client can engage in the initial part of, or briefly sample, the reinforcing event. *Reinforcer sampling refers to procedures that provide a brief or small sample of the reinforcing events in order to promote greater utilization of that event.* As a way of remembering this, think of reinforcer sampling as a free sample of some product such as a small bar of soap or toothpaste, as companies provide when they wish to introduce a new product and to get people to buy this product.

Reinforcer sampling is related to response priming discussed previously. In both cases, there is an attempt to encourage engaging in some behavior. Reinforcer sampling is a special case of response priming. The responses primed are those involving the use of a potentially reinforcing event.

Reinforcer sampling has been used relatively infrequently despite the apparently consistent evidence attesting to its effects. In one of the first reports of the procedure, reinforcer sampling was used to increase the frequency with which psychiatric patients engaged in various activities (Ayllon & Azrin, 1968a). The activities were included in a list of backup reinforcers that could be purchased with tokens. The patients were told twice daily that they could go for a walk on the hospital grounds. Payment of tokens was required to engage in the walk. After a few days of baseline, the reinforcer-sampling procedure was implemented. Not only were walks announced but all of the patients were required to assemble outside the ward for a few minutes before deciding whether they would purchase the walk. Essentially, by being required to go outside, the patients *sampled* many of the cues and reinforcers associated with the activity (e.g., outdoor sights, sounds, fresh air). While outside, the patients were asked whether they wished to go for a walk. Those who decided not to go for a walk returned to the ward. The reinforcer sampling procedure increased the utilization of walks. More walks were purchased by patients who had or had not engaged in walks during baseline. During a reversal phase, when the sampling procedure was discontinued, the frequency of walks decreased. Some patients still continued to engage in more walks than they had engaged in during baseline. In other applications, reinforcer sampling was used to increase the use of recreational and social events (Ayllon & Azrin, 1968b). In each instance, a small sample of the event was provided by entering persons in the activity for a brief period before asking them whether they wished to engage in the full activity.

In general, reinforcer sampling appears to initiate performance among individuals who previously did not engage in the event. For these individuals, reinforcer sampling provides familiarity with the reinforcer, which subsequently augments its use. Reinforcer sampling also affects individuals who are already quite familiar with the reinforcer and have utilized it on previous occasions. After reinforcer sampling is terminated, clients may continue to use the reinforcer to a greater extent than they did during baseline. Thus the effects of the sample procedure are maintained.

In any situation in which it is possible to provide a small sample of a reinforcer, the sampling procedure should enhance performance. In using reinforcer sampling, it is usually important to provide only a small sample of the event so as to avoid satiation. If an individual samples a large portion of the event, such as food or an activity, this may amount to noncontingent reinforcement and thus will not increase the behaviors that are required to earn the reinforcer. In applied settings, the effect of a reinforcement program may be relatively weak, in part because the "reinforcers" provide little incentive to engage in the target behaviors. If the activity that is designed to serve as a reinforcer can be made more "valuable" to the client, the likelihood of the client's engaging in the target behaviors to earn that activity is increased.

Vicarious Consequences. Reinforcement and punishment as discussed to this point focus on providing consequences directly to the individual contingent on his or her behavior. In developing, establishing, and maintaining behavior, there is no substitute for repeated opportunities to perform the behavior followed by consequences for that behavior. Interestingly, performance of a client can be altered by having the client observe the consequences that follow the behavior of other individuals. Individuals are more likely to engage in certain behaviors after observing others (models) receive reinforcing consequences for engaging in those behaviors. In contrast, individuals who observe models receive punishing consequences for engaging in certain behaviors are less likely to engage in those behaviors. These two processes are referred to as *vicarious reinforcement* and *vicarious punishment,* respectively.[3]

Vicarious reinforcement is readily familiar in everyday life. For example, as has been mentioned, slot machines utilize intermittent reinforcement to maintain high rates of behavior (depositing coins) with little payoff (reinforcement). In addition, the behavior is cleverly maintained by vicarious reinforcement. When playing the slot machines, one invariably sees and hears other players win, that is, their responses followed by money. Indeed, when someone wins, the slot machine makes loud noises and flashes lights so that the consequences are conspicuous. Similarly, when contests are advertised, reports of happy previous winners are provided to help convey vicarious consequences and optimize their effects.

In behavior modification, vicarious reinforcement has been studied in classrooms, the home, and various rehabilitation settings (see Kazdin, 1979). Investigations have shown that the behavior of one person can be altered by providing reinforcing consequences to others. For example, in a class for behaviorally handicapped children, administering praise to three children for social interaction led to increases in social interaction among children who did not receive praise (Strain, Shores, & Kerr, 1976). Similarly, in the home, praising compliance with parental instructions and imposing time out for noncompliance not only altered the behavior of an uncooperative boy but also improved behaviors of the boy's brother, although these were not directly praised or punished (Resick, Forehand, & McWhorter, 1976).

Although vicarious reinforcement has been demonstrated in several studies, its effects have occasionally been weak or inconsistent. Persons may not respond when they see others receive reinforcing consequences; for those who do respond, the effects of vicarious reinforcement may be quite temporary (Budd & Stokes, 1977; Fantuzzo & Clement, 1981). How reinforcement is administered to the client may influence whether others show vicarious effects. For example, vicarious reinforcement effects are enhanced by delivering reinforcement in a conspicuous fashion and by providing individuals with many opportunities to see others receive reinforcing consequences (Kazdin, Silverman, & Sittler, 1975; Strain et al., 1976).

It is not entirely clear why vicarious reinforcement achieves beneficial effects. The most obvious explanation is that of modeling, in which others see a person receive reinforcing consequences for a particular behavior and then engage in that same behavior to obtain reinforcing consequences. Yet copying a model may not account for all of the findings because the person who is responding vicariously is not always looking at or imitating the person who receives direct consequences (Kazdin, 1977d). It may be that seeing or hearing the delivery of reinforcement (e.g., praise) is a cue to others that the behavior-change agent (parent, teacher) is looking and might also administer reinforcement to them. Praise of one child may serve as a signal (S^D) that other children will be praised if they are behaving appropriately. Hence, children hearing praise may improve their behavior to increase the likelihood that they too will receive praise.

Vicarious reinforcement may also draw attention to the specific behaviors that are desired and serve a prompting function. Delivery of the reinforcing consequences, especially when noting the target behaviors in a conspicuous fashion (e.g., "Look what he did, that's great!"), may help prompt the behavior in persons who do not receive the consequences (Lancioni, 1982). The cueing function of vicarious consequences is suggested by everyday experience. For example, when one is driving on a highway, seeing a police car and another passenger car next to the road serves as a cue to slow down. The cue suggests that one's driving is being monitored and that a similar consequence (presumably a traffic ticket) might be forthcoming.

Vicarious punishment has been less well studied than vicarious reinforcement. Nevertheless, research suggests that when the target behavior of one person is punished, the target behavior may decrease both in that person and in other persons (Van Houten et al., 1982). For example, in one study, the vicarious effects of time out from reinforcement were evaluated in a kindergarten class (Wilson et al., 1979). One boy with a high rate of aggressive behaviors (tripping, kicking, throwing things at others) was placed in time out for instances of these behaviors. His time out consisted of sitting for five minutes in a booth in class from which he could not see his peers. When time out was used, both the boy and his classmates showed a decrease in aggressive acts, even though his classmates never experienced time out for their aggressive behaviors.

In general, the performance of a client may be improved by providing reinforcing and/or punishing consequences to others who are engaging in the target behavior. As noted already, vicarious reinforcement and punishment are not substitutes for providing direct consequences to the client. However, they can serve to prompt behaviors by signaling that these behaviors may be reinforced. Once the client has performed the behaviors, they can be reinforced directly to ensure that they are developed and sustained at high levels.

General Comments. Manipulation of antecedents, behaviors, and consequences to enhance the effectiveness of a program were presented separately to help distinguish the ways in which a program can be modified. For example, prompting and shaping are commonly used together and are quite useful in improving behavior. As a general rule, ABCs are the first place to intervene when a program is not working. Of course, one ought not to wait until a program produces mediocre effects to invoke the options discussed previously. Among the questions to ask oneself when designing a program is precisely how will antecedents, behaviors, and consequences be used to maximize the likelihood that the behavior occurs and develops to the level one wishes?

CONTINGENCY CONTRACTS

Key Characteristics

Many programs are imposed on clients with little or no input by the clients themselves. There are obvious reasons for this. Often clients are not in a position to determine the goals and means through which they can be reached. For ex-

---

BOX 9-1   Key Elements of Contingency Contracts

- State what each party expects to gain
- Specify the behaviors of the client so they are readily observable.
- Specify any sanctions for a failure to meet the terms (e.g., loss of points for the client, extra back-up reinforcers if the person who administers the consequences forgets to do so or engages in behaviors such as nagging that specifically are not allowed).

- Include a bonus clause that reinforces consistent compliance with their terms.
- Monitor execution of the contract including the rate of positive reinforcement given and received
- Specify the means (when, how initiated) for renegotiating the contract conditions

---

ample, in child rearing, all sorts of behaviors might serve as goals for children (e.g., tooth brushing, eating nutritious meals, bathing, completing homework, taking bassoon lessons) without children grasping the short- or long-term benefits. Yet in many instances, including each of the child-rearing examples, the input of the clients can be solicited and the effectiveness of the program may improve as a result.

A common way in which the clients themselves are directly involved is through a *contingency contract*. This is a written agreement between individuals who wish behavior to change (parents, teachers, spouses, hospital staff) and clients whose behavior is to be changed (students, children, partners, patients). An actual contract is signed by both parties indicating that they agree to the terms. The contingency contract specifies the relationship between behaviors and their consequences. Specifically, the contract specifies the reinforcers desired by the client and the behavior desired by the individual who wishes behavior change. This is translated into explicit and precise terms that denote precisely what behavior (how much behavior, when, how often) will earn what consequences (how much, when delivered).

Ideally, contingency contracts usually include several elements, as listed in Box 9-1. First, they detail what each party expects to gain. For example, parents may want a child to complete his or her homework or attend school regularly. The child may want free time with friends, extra allowance, and other reinforcers.

Second, the stipulated behaviors of the client are readily observable. If parents cannot determine whether a responsibility has been met, they cannot grant a privilege. Thus some behaviors may not be readily incorporated into a contingency contract. For example, parents often cannot easily monitor whether an adolescent visits certain friends, so it would not be advisable to include a stipulation regarding such visits in the contract.

Third, contingency contracts provide sanctions for a failure to meet their terms. The aversive consequences for not meeting the contract terms are systematic and planned in advance (agreed to by all parties), not arbitrary and after the fact.

Fourth, contracts often include a bonus clause that reinforces consistent compliance with their terms. Bonuses (extra privilege, activity, or extension of curfew limit) can be used to reinforce consistent performance over an extended period. For someone whose behavior was recently developed, bonuses for consistent performance may be especially important. Reinforcement for longer sequences of performance (e.g., performance for 2 consecutive days or 4 of 5 days) helps to fade or gradually remove the program and to make behavior less dependent on immediate consequences.

Fifth, contingency contracts provide a means of monitoring the rate of positive reinforcement given and received. The records inform each party when reinforcement is to occur and provide constant feedback. Moreover, the records may cue individuals to make favorable comments about desirable behavior when earning of the backup reinforcer is about to occur.

Sixth, contracts provide a means of renegotiating the contract conditions. As the program is implemented, it may become obvious that it is not working or unfair. Each party ought to have the opportunity to initiate a conversation to renegotiate. Also, if the program is working well, as in any behavior-change program, the contract ought to be terminated or move to the next step such as more delayed reinforcement, reinforcement for consistency of the behavior over time, or larger segments of behavior now that early behaviors may have been shaped.

Many elements of a contingency contract are merely elements of good behavior-change programs. The feature of contracting is that these elements are written down and the client plays a clear role in their development and negotiation. Contingency contracts need not be elaborate or complex. A sample contingency contract is illustrated in Figure 9-2. This was a contract used to increase completion of homework of a 9-year-old fourth-grade girl named Ann (Miller & Kelley, 1994). Ann usually completed her work quickly but was inaccurate. She showed other classroom problems as well, including inattention, hyperactivity, and impulsiveness. In this study, four separate families (parent-child dyads) were included; in each case, the focus was on homework. Before the program began, parent, teacher, and child were interviewed to clarify the problem for each child. During the program, problems of completing homework (rated by the parents), accuracy of homework completion, and time spent working on homework were observed.

The parent presented and discussed the contract with the child. The discussion identified what materials would be needed, how and when homework was to be completed, and the reinforcers that could be earned. Goals were set with the parent and child to decide what was reasonable (e.g., how many problems to complete within a given period). Each week, the parent and child renegotiated the contract to specify the goals for that week, the rewards to be used, and sanctions for not completing key terms such as bringing home the necessary materials.

As shown in Figure 9-3, four parent-child homework programs were conducted and evaluated in a multiple-baseline and ABAB design. Considering the overall set of graphs, it is clear that the contracting procedure (goal setting [GS]

The following materials need to be brought home every day: homework pad, workbooks, text books, pencils.

If Ann remembers to bring home all of these materials, then she may choose one of the following rewards: gumballs, 10¢.

However, if Ann forgets to bring home some of her homework materials, then she: does not get a snack before bed.

Ann may choose one of the following rewards if she meets 90% to 100% of her goals: late bedtime (by 20 minutes), 2 stickers or one of these if she meets 75% to 89% of her goals: soda, 1 sticker.

If Ann meets 80% or more of her goals on at least 3 days this week, she may choose one of the following BONUS rewards: renting a videotape, having a friend from school over to play.

_____   _____
Child's signature   Parent's signature

FIGURE 9-2 Sample contingency contract.

(Source: Miller & Kelley, 1994)

and contingency contract [CC] on the graphs) improved performance. Ann (bottom graph) improved in the accuracy of her homework assignments from a mean of 64% during baseline to 88% during the first contracting phase. By the final phase in which contracting was implemented again, she averaged 92% accuracy. The effects were similar for the other children who also improved.

Contingency contracts have been used successfully to alter a variety of problems such as overeating, alcohol and drug abuse, cigarette smoking, problem behaviors of delinquents, academic and disruptive behavior of elementary school children, and studying in college students. Procedures for developing contingency contracts that can be applied to a wide range of problems have been nicely described elsewhere (Hall & Hall, 1998).

Strengths and Limitations

Contingency contracts have several advantages. First, the performance of clients may be better if they are allowed to have some input into designing or implementing a program than it is if a program is imposed on them. Participation of the clients in the design and development of the program is likely to make the program more acceptable to them and foster greater compliance. Second and related, the contingencies specified in a contract are less likely to be aversive to the

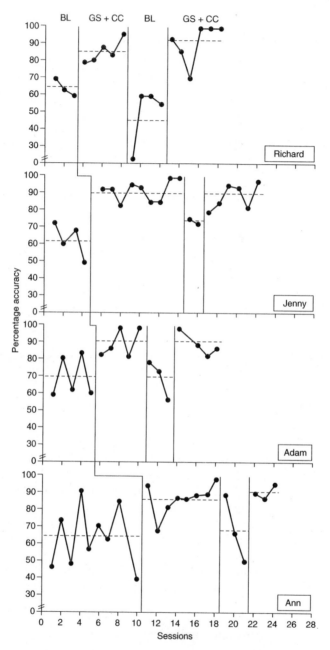

FIGURE 9-3 Percentage of homework completed accurately during baseline and treatment conditions across subjects. Sessions correspond to sequential school days (i.e., Mondays through Thursdays) on which subjects were assigned homework. Data were not collected on days on which homework was not assigned.

(Source: Miller & Kelley, 1994)

client. The client can negotiate the consequences and the requirements for reinforcement. If the system is minimally aversive, the client is less likely to attempt to escape from the contingencies or from those who administer them. Third, contingency contracts are usually flexible in that participants can renegotiate their terms. The reinforcers delivered for particular responses can be adjusted, response requirements can be increased, and so on. Fourth, the contract makes the contingencies explicit. The specification of the contingencies serves as rules or instructions for the client on how to behave and defines the consequences that will follow behavior. Although explicit instructions alone may not produce durable changes in performance, they often increase the effectiveness of reinforcement. Fifth, contingency contracts are particularly useful in structuring the relationship among persons whose interactions may be maladaptive. For example, when compared with the families of "normal" children, the families of delinquent and behavior-problem children engage in a lower rate of positive social exchanges and inadequately reinforce socially appropriate behavior (Patterson, Reid, & Dishion, 1992). Contingency contracts make explicit the requirements for delivering positive consequences and increase the likelihood that reinforcement for the desired behaviors will actually be provided. Putting the contingencies in writing makes it easier to monitor whether they are carried out in the desired fashion.

Contracts, whether they are used in legal matters or in behavior-change programs are not flawless. Making things explicit does not necessarily resolve ambiguities. However, writing programs down into contract form helps minimize misunderstandings. In some situations such as frustrated and angry parent-child relations that might be evident, the contract can help minimize opportunities for misinterpretation of the program.

There are some obvious limits to contingency contracts. For many clients, age (very young children) and serious impairment (severe mental retardation) may preclude the negotiation and discussion process that underlies development of a contract. Also, in many contracts, there is a difference in power and authority between the participants (e.g., parent vs. child), but this is not always the case (e.g., two spouses, partners). When power and authority vary, there is always the possibility that the stronger party will not negotiate or will change conditions and abuse the position. These concerns, while cogent, appear to be exceptions in contingency contracting. In most applications, negotiation and discussion are possible and used.

Contingency contracts have been used frequently. However, extensive research has not been completed to guide many of the specific details to make contracts maximally effective or acceptable to clients. Even so, the use of contracts to structure reinforcement programs, make the requirements explicit to all parties, and encourage negotiation among the parties is to be strongly encouraged. Finally and related, there is not a firm body of evidence to show that programs guided by contingency contracts are more effective than similar contingencies that are imposed without a contract. The benefits of contracting may or may not be evident in behavior change but rather in acceptability and palatability of the program to the persons involved.

GROUP-BASED PROGRAMS

In most of the programs discussed in previous chapters, reinforcing and punishing consequences were applied to individual clients. Even when programs are conducted with groups of individuals, such as a class of students or a sibling in the home, consequences are typically provided to individual clients based on their own performance. Although most programs are individualized in this sense, it is possible and often desirable to administer programs in such a way that the peer group is involved in the contingencies. Programs utilizing the peer group can be implemented in several ways. Three major methods of using the group are group consequences, team competition, and consequence sharing.

Group Contingencies

Group contingencies refer to programs in which the criterion for reinforcement is based on the performance of the group as a whole. The group must perform in a particular way for the reinforcing consequences to be delivered. An interesting application of a group contingency focused on children stealing in three second-grade classrooms (Switzer, Deal, & Bailey, 1977). Students in these classes frequently stole things (money, pens, toys) from one another and from the teacher. The investigators assessed the frequency of theft by placing such items as money, magic markers, and gum around the room each day and monitoring their loss. Before initiating the group contingency, the teacher lectured the students by telling them the virtues of honesty and told them they should be "good boys and girls." Later, when the group contingency was implemented, the teacher told the students that if nothing was missing from the classroom, the class as a whole could have 10 extra minutes of free time. This was a group contingency because the consequences were based on how the class as a group responded. The group contingency was introduced in a multiple-baseline design. As shown in Figure 9-4, the number of items stolen was not affected by the lecture (weak prompts) emphasizing honesty. On the other hand, whenever the group contingency was introduced into one of the classes, marked reductions in theft were evident.

A group contingency was used to reduce the shortage of cash in the register of a family-style restaurant (Marholin & Gray, 1976). Cash register receipts were carefully monitored. At the end of each day, the cash in the register was lower than the amount automatically recorded on an internal record of the register. After a baseline period of recording the shortages, a group response cost contingency was devised. If a cash shortage was equal to or greater than 1% of a day's cash receipts, the shortage was subtracted from the salaries of all the employees who worked at the register that day. The total shortage was simply divided by the number of individuals who worked at the register. Cash shortages were greatly reduced by this procedure, which monitored the performance of all the cashiers as a group and assessed a fine on the basis of the group's performance.

Group contingencies are obviously well suited to situations in which there is a peer group and in which there is interest in fostering similar responses in its members. In large-scale community and work applications, group contingencies

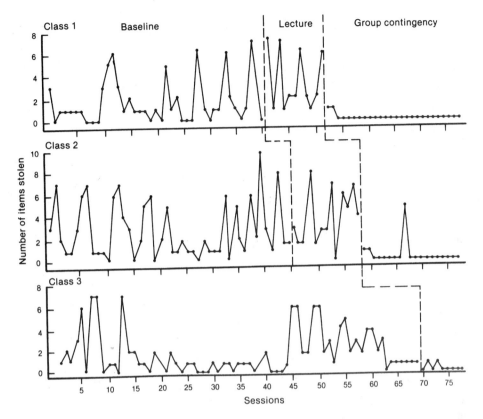

FIGURE 9-4 Number of items stolen per day in each of three second-grade classrooms.

(Source: Switzer, Deal, & Bailey, 1977)

may play an especially important role. For example, in some business organizations, special incentives are provided if a group (e.g., 90 percent of all employees) engages in a behavior of interest (e.g., donates to a charity, participates in an exercise program designed to improve health). In these situations, the interest in developing a particular behavior across many people lends itself well to group contingencies. The effectiveness of such contingencies is evaluated by charting the behavior of the group rather than the performance of one or a few individuals.

Team-Based Contingencies

Team-based contingencies represent a special type of group contingency but are worthy of separate treatment because of their effectiveness. *In a team-based contingency, a group is divided into two or more subgroups (or teams). Each subgroup functions on a separate group contingency.* As with group contingencies, an individual client can earn or lose for the group and the collective behavior of the group determines the consequences the individual receives. However, the subgroups compete

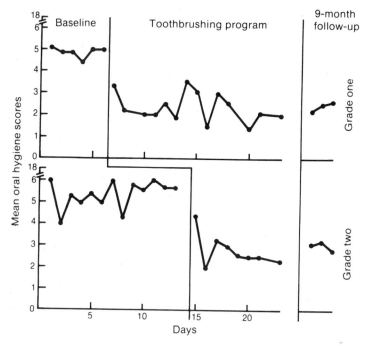

FIGURE 9-5 The effects of a team-based contingency on oral hygiene in which lower scores reflect less dental debris and plaque (i.e., cleaner teeth).

(Source: Swain, Allard, & Hoborn, 1982)

against each other. The consequences are delivered to the subgroup or team with better performance.

A team-based contingency was used to improve dental hygiene among children in first- and second-grade classes (Swain, Allard, & Holborn, 1982). The purpose of the program was to increase the cleanliness of their teeth, which was assessed by standard dental procedures measuring the amount of debris or plaque on the teeth. Before baseline, the children were taught how to brush and were provided with a dental kit (toothbrush, toothpaste, and Redcote tablets that allowed them to detect debris). Teeth were checked daily to assess cleanliness in a random sample of children in each of the two classes. After baseline, a team contingency was introduced by dividing each class into two teams. Each day, the team that had cleaner teeth received praise, posting of its members' names, and stickers. As shown in Figure 9-5, when the team-based contingency was introduced, the average amount of debris and plaque decreased. Moreover, nine months after the program had been terminated, an unannounced check of the children revealed that the gains had been maintained.

In another school application, a team-based contingency was used to improve writing skills in a remedial summer elementary school program (Maloney &

Hopkins, 1973). The students were on one of two teams and received points for writing behaviors that would improve their compositions. The behaviors included increasing the use of different (more varied) adjectives, action verbs, and novel sentence beginnings. The team that earned the higher number of points (by adding the points for each of its individual members) was allowed to go to recess five minutes early and received small pieces of candy. To ensure that excellent performance was reinforced, both teams could win on a given day if their performance met a prespecified high criterion. The team contingency markedly increased the specific writing skills focused on.

The above programs may have been effective independent of the division into teams because group contingencies are generally very effective. However, dividing groups into teams appears to enhance the effectiveness of group contingencies. A nice feature about team-based contingencies is that one team can win but both teams can earn a reinforcer if they exceed a desired criterion level of performance. That is, the teams are informed that if performance surpasses a criterion level, the team will earn this consequence no matter what. In addition, the team that does better also earns some other consequence. This is utilizing a group-based contingency (reward for the group if a criterion is met) and team-based contingency together (the better team receives something special). The advantage is to ensure that the team that does not win the overall competition still receives consequences for the desired behavior.

Consequence Sharing

Another type of contingency that involves the group is consequence sharing. *With consequence sharing, the client's peers share in the reinforcing consequences earned by the client.* The group members earn the reinforcers not for their behavior but for the behavior the client performs. Consequence sharing is particularly useful in situations in which there is a need to focus on the behavior of one or a few persons. A reinforcement system can be developed for one person, but the consequences earned can be provided to the person and his or her peers. When peers share in the consequences, they become involved with the program indirectly and can support and contribute to the client's improvement through encouragement, prompting, and social reinforcement.

As an example, consequence sharing was used to improve the behavior of a 50-year-old female psychiatric patient diagnosed with schizophrenia and brain damage (Feingold & Migler, 1972). The patient participated in a token economy that did not have much impact on her behavior. She engaged in little social interaction, completed her work infrequently, did not keep herself well groomed, and showed inappropriate verbal behavior. To increase her responsiveness to the program, a consequence-sharing contingency was developed in which two other patients on the ward received the same number of tokens as she earned. In an ABA design, the target patient's responsiveness to the contingencies was evaluated when she was in the program in which she earned tokens only for herself and when she was in the program in which she earned tokens for both herself and her peers. As shown in Figure 9-6, the number of tokens she earned, and hence the

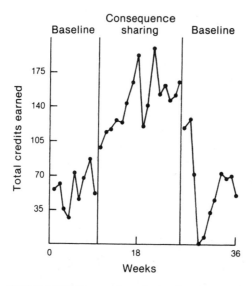

FIGURE 9-6 Token earnings during baseline, consequence sharing, and return-to-baseline phases. During baseline, the patient earned tokens only for herself. During the consequence-sharing phase, she earned tokens for her peers as well as for herself.

(Source: Feingold & Migler, 1972)

extent of her appropriate job and self-care behaviors, greatly increased during the consequence-sharing contingency.

As another example, consequence sharing was used to improve classroom work of two mentally retarded elementary school children in a special education class (Kazdin & Geesey, 1977). Tokens were provided for working on academic tasks and paying attention to the lesson. When a predetermined number of tokens were earned, each of the two children earned a reinforcer selected from a list of reinforcers (such as extra recess) that had been developed in advance of the program. As might be expected, contingent token reinforcement improved appropriate classroom performance. However, the token program proved markedly more effective when the reinforcers earned by the two children were given to everyone in the class (consequence sharing) and not just to them.

Consequence sharing is a convenient way to include persons in a program who might otherwise not be included (e.g., classmates, siblings, other family members). One reason that the contingency may be effective is that it increases the cooperative behavior of group members. Indeed, in a classroom application, cooperative behaviors, such as working with and seeking help from others (friends, teachers) and working as a team, were greater among youths who were involved in a consequence-sharing contingency relative to those who were not (Williamson, Williamson, Watkins, & Hughes, 1992). Thus consequence sharing may be particularly useful when there is interest in mobilizing the group to help develop the target behavior.

Lotteries

Another type of group program involves a lottery. *A lottery is a way of arranging reinforcement contingencies to develop specific behaviors in a group of persons.* It is a token economy in which behaviors earn tokens (tickets) that are exchangeable for backup reinforcers (the prize). In a lottery, there is usually only one backup reinforcer and not everyone earns it. Hence, a lottery is often used to maximize the amount of behavior generated by a small number of rewards. A lottery is usually group-based in the sense that it is applied to large groups of persons. However, in a lottery, unlike the group arrangements discussed previously, each person's behavior is usually unrelated to that of others in the group.

Lotteries are a familiar technique used in everyday life to raise money. In the usual lottery, numerous tickets are sold, after which there is a drawing of one or more tickets. The persons whose tickets are drawn earn money or a prize such as a vacation or a car. In everyday life, "buying a lottery ticket" is the behavior that makes one eligible for the prize. In behavioral programs, engaging in some specific target behavior earns a lottery ticket. Thus a critical difference between lotteries in everyday life and in behavior modification is in the target behavior. In behavior modification, the tickets are contingent on behaviors that are designed to improve the behavioral repertoire of the client (e.g., improve homework, use of seat belts).

A clever use of a lottery to develop behavior was reported in a business setting (manufacturing distribution center) in which there was a high rate of absenteeism (Pedalino & Gamboa, 1974). The intervention consisted of a lottery in which an employee who came to work on time received an opportunity to choose a card from a deck of playing cards. At the end of each week, the employee would, ideally, have five cards, which were used as a poker hand. Several of the employees with the highest poker hands received $20. Stated more as a contingency, the behavior (coming to work) was reinforced with a token (playing card backed up by money). The likelihood of earning the money was increased by coming to work everyday (e.g., and having five cards to form a poker hand). The lottery reduced absenteeism whether it was administered every week or every other week.

Lotteries have been used extensively in community applications of behavioral techniques. Programs concerned with energy conservation, littering, waste recycling, and other community-relevant behaviors have used lottery-based programs. For example, in an effort to reduce the consumption of gasoline, several studies provide lottery tickets to persons who decreased the use of their cars. Reductions in mileage, as measured by odometer readings, are rewarded with tickets that are drawn at the end of the week or month to provide small prizes, money, or, in one study, a free keg of beer (see Geller et al., 1982). There are many behaviors that one wishes to encourage on a community scale such as having children vaccinated before entering school, having pets vaccinated against rabies, having children and adolescents eat nutritious meals at school, and no doubt scores of others. Earning lottery tickets for such behaviors would be an excellent way to increase performance of the overall group.

Lotteries are convenient ways to administer reinforcers in group settings. One advantage of lotteries is their ability to dispense relatively large rewards (e.g., large sums of money, appliances, vacation trips) because few rewards are actually provided. The impact of large rewards is especially evident in lotteries in various cities, states, and countries in which millions of dollars may be provided in a single lottery drawing. That incentive leads to a great deal of behavior of many people. The behavior is "ticket buying" which does not promote prosocial, adaptive, or constructive behaviors (e.g., related to mental or physical health, education, enrichment) of the individuals who partake in the lottery.

A potential problem is that lotteries may not affect the individuals whose behavior is in the need of greatest change. In a behavior-change program, individuals may not enter the lottery, not earn tickets for the drawing, or not receive the rewarding consequences when they do. This is not a disadvantage of lotteries per se. If the goal is to alter the behavior of particular individuals, the better focus is on individual behavior as part of the contingency. The most frequent use of lotteries is in cases where the primary interest is overall group behavior. In such cases, lotteries can be adapted to individuals by combining them with other procedures. For example, individuals could be allowed to earn lottery tickets for themselves and their peers on the basis of their own behavior.

Strengths and Limitations

Group-based contingencies have several advantages. To begin with, they provide an extremely convenient way to implement behavior modification programs. It is easier to administer reinforcing and punishing consequences when the clients are considered as a group than when each client is focused on individually. Indeed, in many of the settings such as school classrooms, hospitals, and businesses, in which behavior modification programs are implemented, few staff are available to conduct individualized programs. Hence, group contingencies often can be implemented more readily than individual programs can. If individualized contingencies are needed to handle special behaviors of a few clients, those contingencies can be added to the overall group program. The ease of administering group contingencies may explain why people who implement contingencies often prefer group over individualized programs.

Another advantage of group-based contingencies is that they help bring to bear peer sources of reinforcement for behavior. Peers often actively support appropriate behavior so that the group or team can earn the reinforcers. Similarly, with consequence sharing, peers may encourage appropriate behavior so that they are more likely to receive the reinforcers (Williamson et al., 1992). Occasionally, peers bring pressure to bear on other group members or clients whose performance determines whether reinforcers are or are not received. For example, peers may make threatening verbalizations or gestures or may reprimand target subjects for not earning the reinforcers. More often, group contingencies have been associated with positive side effects, such as increased prompting among peers and reinforcement of one another for appropriate behavior, verbal and nonverbal gestures of friendship (e.g., back patting), and helping behavior (Greenwood & Hops, 1981; Kohler & Greenwood, 1990).

The interactions resulting from group-based contingencies may depend on how the program is implemented. Aversive peer interactions may be more likely to result if available reinforcers in the setting (e.g., recess) are lost when the group does not meet the criterion for performance. Then it is likely that peers will harass, criticize, or otherwise focus aversive social consequences on the person who seems to be responsible for loss of the reinforcers. Reinforcers normally available in the setting should not depend on group performance because, if they do, individuals may lose events that they would normally receive when their performance is up to standard. Group consequences should include special events or extra privileges (e.g., extra recess) over and above what individuals would normally receive so that reinforcers are not lost because someone else in the group or the target subject did not perform adequately.

Contingencies for the group and individual members are often combined to ensure that individual performance is reinforced and to obtain the added advantages of group incentives. For example, in one program, seventh-grade students received points for participating in a classroom discussion and were given bonus points for especially well-reasoned discussion statements (Smith, Schumaker, Schaeffer, & Sherman, 1982). In addition to this individual contingency, extra tokens could be earned if all of the students in a given row of seats participated in the discussion. The individual contingency increased participation, and this effect was enhanced by the addition of the group contingency.

PEER-ADMINISTERED CONTINGENCIES

Key Characteristics

The use of group-based contingencies illustrates an indirect way in which peers are involved in the behavior modification program. The contingencies structure the situation so as to increase peer investment in appropriate behavior. A more direct way to involve peers in the program is to have them administer reinforcing and punishing consequences (Foot, Morgan, & Shute, 1990; Kohler & Strain, 1990). With peer-administered contingencies, the peers serve as the behavior-change agents and provide direct consequences to the target subjects. This may consist of checking to see if performance criteria have been met and providing prompts and consequences (e.g., praise, tokens) for performance. Of course, the level of peer involvement and control over the program he or she is administering is dictated by the clientele and setting. The central component is that the peer is directly involved in administering consequences. Often someone (e.g., teacher, staff member of the setting) oversees the peer who is administering consequences to monitor peer behavior and to ensure that the program is administered effectively. The peer who administers the program may even receive reinforcing consequences for how well he or she does this job.

BOX 9-2   Key Elements of Peer-Administered Contingencies

- The peer (e.g., child, sibling, spouse) under-goes brief instruction and training to learn how to conduct the program (e.g., administer the task, provide feedback, praise, or points)
- The peer directly administers consequences to the target individual, that is, the person whose behavior is to be changed

- Someone (parent, teacher) provides over-sight and monitors the peer who adminis-ters the consequences
- The peer who administers the program re-ceives consequences for how well he or she does this job

---

Several components of peer-administered programs usually can be distin-guished, as noted in Box 9-2. First, the peer (e.g., child, sibling, spouse) undergoes a brief instruction and training period to learn how to conduct the program (e.g., administer the task, provide feedback, praise, or points). Second, the peer directly administers consequences to the target individual, i.e., person whose behavior is to be changed. Thus the peer becomes the behavior-change agent who prompts, shapes, and reinforces performance. Third, someone (parent, teacher) provides oversight and monitors the peer who administers the consequences. Fourth, the peer who administers the program receives consequences for how well he or she does this job. These last two components ensure that the program is administered correctly by the peer so that the power of providing reinforcing consequences is not abused.

Peers have been used successfully in a variety of programs. Most peer-based programs have been conducted in school settings with elementary school stu-dents. As an example, peers were used to develop social interactions of two so-cially rejected and isolated 5-year-old children. Social rejection is an important focus in part because it is often associated with more serious problems of ad-justment in later childhood and adolescence. Tutors were older children (ages 11, 12) at the same school. The tutors were trained in individual sessions to identify positive social behavior with the tutees and to prompt prosocial behav-ior. Observations on the playground indicated that the positive social interac-tions of the tutees increased, and the effects were maintained when assessed 5 weeks after the program ended (e.g., Gumpel & Frank, 1999). Unlike the tu-tees, the tutors did not show problems in their initial social behaviors before the program began. Even so, the positive social interactions of the tutors also im-proved.

Peer-administered contingencies have been used creatively in a group home setting (Achievement Place) for delinquent youths (Phillips, Phillips, Wolf, & Fixsen, 1973). One of the boys served as a manager of his peers to develop room-cleaning behavior among them. The manager was responsible for ensuring that the room-cleaning behaviors were completed. He assigned the jobs and provided tokens or fines for the performance of the tasks. When the teaching parents checked the room in the facility, he earned or lost tokens based on how well the task had been completed. The peer-manager system of administering consequences was even more effective in obtaining high rates of room cleaning than was the system of having contingencies administered by the teaching parents.

In addition to peers, siblings have been used to alter behavior. For example, in one program, children (ages 6 to 8) were trained to increase the social interactions of their siblings with physical and mental handicaps (James & Egel, 1986). The nonhandicapped siblings were trained, using prompting and modeling, to initiate and reinforce social interactions. The training consisted of brief sessions that totaled about 1 to 1½ hours for each nonhandicapped child. As shown in Figure 9-7, social interaction increased as training was introduced. The multiple-baseline design across different pairs of siblings shows a rather clear effect of the programs administered by the siblings. The final assessment was conducted six months after the program ended and showed that the behaviors were maintained.

Although most peer-based programs are conducted on a small scale where one peer oversees one or a few target clients, this can be extended to encompass many individuals in a group setting. For example, in a school setting, an entire classroom can be used by pairing children to work together (e.g., Kamps, Barbetta, Leonard, & Delquadri, 1994). One student becomes the tutor and the other the learner. The tutor provides feedback (e.g., for reading tasks) and provides points for correct performance (e.g., correctly reading passages) for brief periods (e.g., 10 to 15 minutes). After this, the roles are reversed so that the learner becomes the tutor and the other person becomes the learner. In other instances, peers are individuals who are functioning well or without problems to help those with disabilities (e.g., academic delays, physical disabilities, mental retardation, autism) (e.g., Cushing & Kennedy, 1997). Peer-based tutoring has been effective in increasing academic competence in reading, arithmetic, vocabulary, and spelling among children. Applications usually focus on elementary school students or children in day care or preschool. Students with and without special needs (e.g., autism, retardation) have profited from peer-administered contingencies (Greenwood, Carta, & Kamps, 1990; Odom, McConnell, & McEvoy, 1992).

Strengths and Limitations

Several advantages accrue from having peers administer the contingencies. To begin with, having the opportunity to work with one's peers is often a positive reinforcer. Indeed, peers often work and pay (in tokens) for the opportunity to participate in the training of another client. For example, in one token economy with delinquents, youths would bid for the privilege of serving as a manager in the program (Phillips et al., 1973). The privilege was periodically auctioned to the highest bidder, the person who offered the highest number of tokens to purchase it. Of course, to be in the bidding, the person would need many tokens and earning many tokens means that the desired behaviors must have been performed to a high level.

A second advantage is that peers who serve as trainers often improve the target behaviors they are changing in the trainees. For example, school students who serve as peer trainers and administer a reinforcement program related to academic or social behavior improve in their behavior (Cushing & Kennedy, 1997; Gumpel

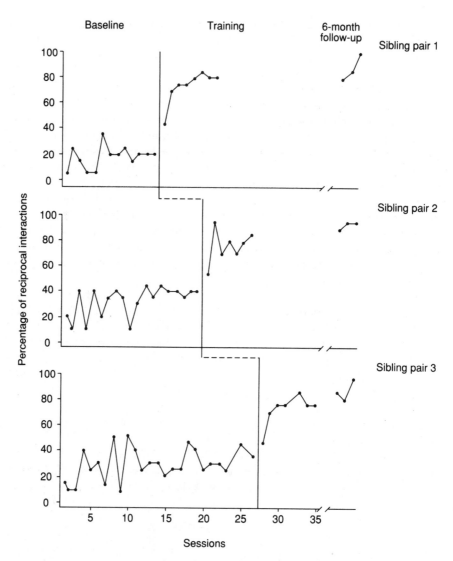

FIGURE 9-7 Positive reciprocal interactions (percentage of intervals of interactions) between handicapped and nonhandicapped siblings over the course of baseline, training, and six-month follow-up.

(Source: James & Egel, 1986)

& Frank, 1999). Thus using peers can serve an important training function for both the trainers and trainees.

A third advantage is the ancillary side effects on social behavior. Occasionally, peer-administered contingencies have improved the social interaction among clients. For example, peers who administer reinforcing consequences or participate in peer tutoring may show an increase in their social interactions even though social behavior is not the focus of the peer-administered contingencies (Kamps et al., 1994; McGee, Almeida, Sulzer-Azaroff, & Feldman, 1992). Also, peers are likely to be evaluated more favorably by others if they are associated with reinforcing consequences. Thus using peers as behavior-change agents can improve aspects of the relationships among peers and target clients.

A fourth advantage is the practical benefits of peer-administered contingencies. Using peers enables clients to receive more individualized attention and training than can be provided by the staff in the setting. For example, in one program, high-school students served as peer trainers to provide driver education to individuals who needed remedial training in mastering information about driving skills (Bell, Young, Salzberg, & West, 1991). The use of peers as a resource permitted more individualized attention and training than would otherwise have been available. In cases where there are limited staff resources as is often the case in regular and special education classroom, peers may be an important resource. Given the other benefits of peer-administered contingencies, peers may be relied on even when the resource question is not at issue.

Finally, peer-administered contingencies may facilitate maintenance and transfer of the behavior. In most programs where peers are not involved, behaviors may come under stimulus control of those who administer the program. Involving peers may broaden the stimulus control and help behaviors spread to settings and occasions beyond those in which parents, teachers, or others are present. Also, peer reinforcement may help sustain behavior because the peers who administer the program may continue to praise or respond favorably to the client after the program has been terminated.

Potential disadvantages are associated with the use of peer-administered contingencies. Peers may not monitor others as well as external agents do (teachers, parents). For example, in one program, children who delivered tokens to their peers occasionally did not withhold tokens as often as they should have when performance did not meet the criteria (Smith & Fowler, 1984). This would constitute reinforcing relatively poor performance or noncontingent reinforcement. In the long run, such contingencies might not produce consistent changes in behavior. However, this problem has been reported infrequently. Moreover, it is likely that all programs are administered less than perfectly. In peer-based programs, feedback and monitoring of peers by an external agent are usually included to ensure that the contingencies are administered as intended. In general, the advantages of peer-based contingencies appear to far outweigh the possible disadvantages. Such contingencies have a variety of side effects that are favorable both to the peers who administer the program and to the recipients of their ministrations.

SUMMARY AND CONCLUSIONS

Numerous technique variations can be derived from the principles of reinforcement, punishment, and extinction. This chapter illustrated several variations. The different variations have special uses such as aiding the program when the initial efforts to change behavior have not been effective or taking advantage of special opportunities to mobilize influences that can enhance the program such as the use of group or peer-based programs.

In many behavior modification programs, a small number of persons may not respond to the contingencies or may respond minimally. Several techniques can be implemented to enhance performance. Before adding a new technique, it is essential to examine how the current contingencies are being implemented and to ensure that basic requirements for effective administration are optimal. For example, the consequences may be too delayed after the behavior is performed or administered intermittently or inconsistently. A small change in these and other characteristics on which effective programs depend, as identified in the chapters on reinforcement, punishment, and extinction, often improves performance.

If there is not a stark flaw in how the program is administered, the next step is to alter the antecedents, behaviors, or consequences (ABCs) to improve the effectiveness of the program. As antecedents, the use of prompts represents an initial line of attack. Prompts are likely to initiate the responses of interest if they clearly specify the desired behavior and are provided in close proximity to opportunities to perform that behavior.

In addition to prompts, it is important to ensure that the demands placed on performance are not too stringent at the beginning of the program. It is critical to consider shaping in developing behavior even if the client has shown on occasion that he or she can perform the terminal behavior. Building small early segments of the behavior and developing these segments so that they are performed consistently are an initial tactic to enhance performance.

Also discussed were response priming (initiating early steps in a response sequence) and reinforcer sampling (providing a sample of the reinforcing event to increase its utilization). Administering positive or negative consequences to others, referred to as vicarious reinforcement and punishment, respectively, can enhance the performance of persons who do not receive the consequences directly.

Contingency contracting was also discussed as a way of integrating the input of the client in the behavior-change program. Each participant in the program negotiates and then formally agrees to the terms of the contract. The reinforcers for performing the target behaviors and penalties for failing to perform the behaviors are made explicit and are agreed on in writing in advance of the program. The primary advantages of a contract arrangement are that clients have an opportunity to be involved in developing the program, in making changes if they wish as the program is implemented, and ensuring that the terms are not coercive.

Other special contingency arrangements can enhance performance and provide many practical advantages. Group contingencies, team-based contingencies, consequence sharing, and lotteries are primary examples of group-based programs. Peers provide a potentially valuable resource for the administration of contingencies. Peers can directly administer reinforcing consequences to alter behavior. A variety of benefits accrue from incorporating peers into the administration of reinforcement. Peer-administered consequences not only improve the behavior of the persons who receive the consequences but also are likely to alter and improve the behavior of the peer who administers the consequences.

KEY TERMS

Reinforcer sampling	Contingency contract	Lottery
Response priming	Group contingencies	Peer-administered
Vicarious reinforcement	Consequence sharing	reinforcement

APPLYING PRINCIPLES AND TECHNIQUES TO EVERYDAY LIFE

1. Alas, one of the clever behavior-change programs you have developed for a teacher is definitely not working. This was a token reinforcement program to increase completion of homework. The teacher assigns homework and the child in question does not do the work. So when he returns to school he cannot receive the tokens. Diagnosing ailing programs is now one of your specialties. What are some (at least 3) things to check to make sure this program is being done in such a way as to maximize performance?

2. In the above program, elaborate one problem in the way the program is being done which may explain why it is not working. Now describe how to fix it, that is, change the program to correct the problem.

3. Give an example of response priming to help someone begin to start a term paper or to apply for a job.

4. Design a program that uses a group contingency for two siblings in the home. Now design a program just for one of the children that uses consequence sharing.

5. You wish to develop a large-scale program for a city or state. How might a lottery be used to support prosocial behavior such as giving to charity, voting, or volunteering to help the elderly?

FOR FURTHER READING

Axelrod, S. (1998) *How to use group contingencies.* Austin, TX: Pro-Ed.

Hall, R.V., & Hall, M.L. (1998). *How to negotiate a behavioral contract* (2nd ed.). Austin, TX: Pro-Ed.

Kohler, F.W., & Strain, P.S. (1990). Peer-assisted interventions: Early promises, notable achievements, and future aspirations. *Clinical Psychology Review, 10,* 441–452.

Masia, C.L., & Chase, P.N. (1997). Vicarious learning revisited: A contemporary behavior analytic interpretation. *Journal of Behavior Therapy and Experimental Psychiatry, 28,* 41–51.

Striefel, S. (1998). *How to teach through modeling and imitation* (2nd ed.). Austin, TX: Pro-Ed.

Van Houten, R. (1998). *How to use prompts to initiate behavior.* Austin, TX: Pro-Ed.

NOTES

1. As discussed in Chapter 6, it is important not to select reinforcers that may be objectionable because of the behaviors they may foster. One of the backup reinforcers in this example is going to a "happy hour," that is, having an opportunity to drink alcoholic beverages, often at highly discounted prices. (In one setting a student of mine mentioned, the price of an alcoholic beverage kept decreasing if an individual kept ordering the same drink—by the fourth drink, the cost was only $.50; this is clever programming of reinforcers but for a highly undesired behavior.) Alcohol consumption (at a "happy hour") may be reinforcing but in a given case (e.g., excess drinking) may be objectionable because of the breadth of potential adverse consequences such as an automobile accident driving home. Also, the exercise program in this example may have been implemented so the person "gets into shape" or maintains a particular body weight. Consumption of alcohol may compete with these broader (less specific) program goals. In general, events used for backup reinforcers ought to be evaluated before their use to ensure they do not unwittingly foster behaviors that are objectionable to interested parties or that undermine the long-term goals of the program.

2. The effectiveness of response priming is based on chaining, as discussed in Chapter 2. In a chain of responses, each behavior further along in the chain is closer to the final reinforcing consequence. Each response in the chain serves to reinforce the previous response and provides an S^D for subsequent responses. Thus once the chain of responses begins, it is more likely to be completed. Response priming attempts to begin the early responses in the chain so as to start the sequence.

3. Strictly speaking, the terms reinforcement and punishment are not appropriate in the context of vicarious learning. The definitions of reinforcement and punishment, as noted in prior chapters, include performing behavior in which consequences follow and behavior changes in a particular way. Because these criteria are not met, the concepts of reinforcement and punishment do not really apply. Also, it is not clear that learning from observing involves the same processes as direct consequences operating on behavior. Nevertheless by convenience and convention vicarious reinforcement and punishment have been the terms used and hence are included here.

CHAPTER 10

Self-Control Techniques

The principles of behavior modification describe lawful relations among various environmental conditions and behaviors. The techniques discussed previously represent instances in which one individual (the behavior-change agent) manages the contingencies to alter the behavior of another individual (the client). The client can apply many of the techniques to control his or her own behavior. When techniques are applied to alter one's own behavior, they are referred to as *self-control or self-management techniques.* The present chapter discusses self-control techniques and how they are applied.

INTEREST IN SELF-CONTROL

There are many reasons for interest in self-control techniques within behavior modification. To begin, self-control techniques can increase the range of applications beyond those available with externally managed procedures. Some of the problems for which people seek therapy are publicly observable in principle but occur in everyday situations that are not readily accessible to the therapist. Examples include overeating, deviant sexual behavior, and arguments with peers; they occur in everyday life and under circumstances in which an external agent cannot easily intervene. In such cases, it may be important to have the client monitor behavior and apply techniques to control behavior in the natural environment.

Another class of problems includes thoughts, images, fantasies, hallucinations, and dreams that are not publicly observable. They are not "observable" by anyone other than the individual to whom they occur. It has been suggested that covert or private events can be viewed as covert operant responses (referred to as *coverants*) (Homme, 1965). Perhaps covert responses, like overt behavior, can be altered by varying the antecedents and consequences. Because the client is the only one who can identify the occurrence of *coverants,* he or she is in the best position to provide contingent consequences for them. Self-control techniques extend behavior modification procedures to events that are not observable (e.g., thoughts) or are not always readily observed (e.g., eating in everyday situations).

Another reason self-control techniques are of interest pertains to the potential limitations and disadvantages of externally administered contingencies. Parents, teachers, and other agents who administer the behavior-change program may inadvertently miss or overlook a great deal of behavior. Monitoring several clients in a group situation (e.g., classroom) or one client whose actions extend across many situations makes it virtually impossible to notice, not to mention reinforce, all instances of a target response. Self-control techniques can extend application of the contingencies to responses and situations that might be otherwise omitted or overlooked. In addition, when contingencies are administered by an external agent in one situation, there is the possibility that behavior will come under stimulus control of that agent and situation. Self-control extends the behaviors and contingencies to all situations, and hence a narrow set of stimuli is less likely to exert control over behavior. Finally, individuals sometimes perform better when, instead of having the contingencies imposed on them, they are allowed to contribute to the planning of the program or to choose the behaviors they are to perform (as in contingency contracting).

A goal of behavior modification is to train individuals to control their own behavior, achieve self-selected goals, and participate adaptively in everyday life without the constraints of an intervention. Thus continuous control over a client by an external agent is not an end in itself. Whenever possible, external control is a means for achieving self-control. Self-control and external control can be viewed as opposite ends of a continuum rather than as discrete procedures. Behavior modification programs vary in the degree to which clients exert control over the contingencies and over the administration of reinforcing or punishing consequences. Self-control techniques attempt to maximize the control that individuals have over the behavior-change program. Of course, external control in some form is essential to initiate the program. Therapists train clients to exert self-control by providing recommendations, advice, systematic praise, and feedback, all of which are external influences on client behavior. It is hoped that after training has been completed, the clients can apply techniques to themselves to alter new behaviors across different situations. When this final stage is reached, self-control has been achieved.

Definition of Self-Control

As a general definition, *self-control usually refers to those behaviors that a person deliberately undertakes to achieve self-selected outcomes.* People exert control over their own everyday behaviors, such as selecting courses of action, abstaining from particular excesses, and adhering to various practices intended to sustain or recover health. Self-control as a concept is often invoked in situations in which it appears that the individual is acting against self-interest or what might seem to be a natural predilection (e.g., acts of heroism, sacrifice that risks danger to oneself). Of course, self-control has many less dramatic instances. In controlling their own behaviors, people use many of the techniques used to control the behaviors of others, that is, they alter the antecedent and consequence conditions.

Table 10-1 presents several ways in which individuals attempt to control their behavior in everyday life. Many of the techniques operate by having individuals perform one behavior (a *controlling* response) to alter the probability of another behavior (a *controlled* response). Thus a person may chew gum (controlling response) to reduce the likelihood of smoking cigarettes (controlled response). Similarly, a person may wear a blindfold (controlling response) in a well-lighted room to increase the likelihood of sleeping (controlled response). In self-control training, the client is taught how to control a response or to apply a particular technique. The client can then extend the procedure as needed to new situations and behaviors.

The term self-control immediately raises an issue. Even if the person selects the goal of the behavior-change program and implements the procedure to achieve the goal, is this self-control? It is easy to argue that a person is never "really" in control of his or her own behavior. When a person appears to be the source of control over a particular behavior, it is possible to explain that behavior

Table 10-1   Examples of Self-Control in Everyday Life

Techniques We Use With Ourselves	Common Examples
Physically restraining oneself	Clasping one's mouth to stifle a laugh, covering one's eyes to avoid seeing something, and clasping one's hands to avoid nail biting
Changing the stimulus conditions (cues)	Listing appointments or important dates on a calendar to increase the probability of engaging in certain behaviors at a later date
Depriving or satiating oneself	Depriving oneself of lunch in anticipation of a special dinner or before participation in an athletic event
Altering emotional reactions	Preventing a laugh by eliciting an incompatible response such as mild pain from biting one's tongue or conjuring up fond memories to evoke pleasant feelings
Using mildly aversive events	Setting an alarm clock ensures that an aversive event (noise) will evoke getting up or making threatening statements to oneself ("If I don't do this, I'll be late.")
Using drugs, alcohol, and stimulants	Altering one's mood, alleviating anxiety, or provoking arousal (e.g., via coffee)
Administering self-reinforcing and punishing statements	Criticizing oneself after failing to achieve a self-goal or praising oneself after accomplishing a feat
Doing something else to avoid aversive consequences	Altering a topic in the middle of a conversation to avoid an argument or whistling a happy tune whenever one feels afraid

These examples are presented and discussed elsewhere (Skinner, 1953).

on the basis of events in the person's past that have perhaps determined his or her current decision. This leads to a discussion of free will versus determinism.

Free will versus determinism is not a key issue for two reasons. First, the dichotomy is false and not a way one usually views behavior from a scientific standpoint. Behaviors are multidetermined (there are many influences), and actions are probabilistic (likely in varying degrees as a function of these influences). Not all of the influences may be understood or identifiable, but it is unlikely that behavior is entirely determined by a volitional act (free will) or by forces over which the individual has absolutely no influence (determined). Second, one cannot usually conceive of an empirical test to refute the proposition that a particular action can be traced to free will or determinism. A difficulty in philosophical or scientific discussions of self-control is in specifying the criteria for what would constitute a "true" instance. This makes self-control not easily measured or operationally defined and hence not testable within the context of a scientific demonstration. If evidence is not relevant or cannot be provided, this leaves the discussion for logic and debate rather than for empirical science.

In behavior modification, self-control is considered to reflect interventions in which the individual plays a central role in overseeing, administering, or implementing the procedures in some way. Self-control is considered to be a matter of degree rather than an all-or-none phenomenon. Behavior-change procedures can readily be distinguished by the extent to which the client is in charge and bears responsibility for carrying out the program. The person can be a complete object of a treatment procedure that others administer (external control), or the person can completely design and implement treatment for himself or herself (self-control). Also, the person or external agents of change may be involved in varying degrees so that self-control and external control both operate. *Self-control procedures in behavior modification refer primarily to techniques in which the client plays an active part and occasionally the sole part in administering behavior-change intervention.*

The notion of self-control usually refers to regulating behaviors that have conflicting consequences, that is, both positive reinforcement and punishment. The reinforcing consequences that follow the behaviors may be immediate and the punishing consequences may be delayed. Behaviors in this category include excessive consumption of food, cigarettes, alcohol, and drugs. For example, excessive eating results in immediate positive reinforcement derived from the taste of food. However, the aversive consequences that follow overeating, such as physical discomfort, weight gain, difficulty in zipping one's pants or skirt without the aid of other people, and the regrettable but real social ostracism pursuant to being overweight, are delayed. There are other behaviors in which the aversive consequences that follow behavior appear to be immediate and any positive consequences, if present at all, are delayed. Behaviors in this category include heroic, altruistic, and charitable acts.

Acts of self-control often appear to forego immediate rewards for the prospect of future rewards. Thus a student may forego the opportunity to attend a party to sacrifice immediate rewards (entertainment, time with friends) for the prospect of future rewards (doing well in courses that will increase the chances of getting into graduate school). Similarly, people often undergo moderate discomfort in the present to avoid potentially greater discomfort in the future. For example, going to the dentist for cleanings, checkups, and occasional fillings may be uncomfortable in the present, but doing this reduces the chances of much greater discomfort in the distant future, when serious dental problems might otherwise warrant attention.

In the context of behavioral interventions, self-control procedures have been applied primarily to behaviors that appear to have immediate positive consequences and delayed aversive consequences. A person performs a response that counteracts or appears to counteract the effects that would be expected from external reinforcers. Thus refusing a rich dessert after a meal appears to run counter to the expected contingencies. Of course, self-control is often invoked when simplistic accounts of behavior are proposed. Behaviors may normally be controlled by a variety of positive and aversive consequences in the present, past, and future (anticipated consequences). Simply refusing dessert may result from all sorts of influences that are not immediately apparent (pain from eating too much, previous experiences of nausea when overeating, allergic reactions to ingredients in the dessert, anticipation of not being able to get into one's clothes). In applications of self-control, the issue is not whether the individual or other events account for certain sorts of responses. Rather, the focus is on helping the individual bring to bear influences to achieve ends that he or she would like to attain and involving the individual directly in administration or oversight of these influences.

Development of Self-Control

Self-control is assumed to reflect behaviors that are learned in much the same way as are other behaviors. In early development, a child's behavior is controlled by external agents such as parents and teachers, who set standards and provide consequences for performance. The standards vary for different behaviors. Some parents set high standards for musical or academic achievement but not for mechanical or social skills or household chores. Indeed, standards may vary for different-sex siblings within the same home. These standards are setting events that convey expected, desired, and acceptable levels of performance. Positive reinforcement is provided when the child achieves the standard, whereas punishment (or lack of reward) is provided for performance below the standard. As training continues, achieving a particular standard may take on reinforcing consequences because achievement in the past was paired with external reinforcement. Conversely, the failure to achieve a standard may become aversive by being paired with punishment or lack of reward. Thus attainment or lack of attainment of an externally or self-imposed standard may contain its own reward or punishment. Through early training, the process of setting standards and providing consequences of achievement eventually becomes independent of external consequences.

The above interpretation of how self-reinforcement and self-punishment patterns of behavior develop has received some support (see Bandura, 1977). Laboratory research has shown that individuals learn to evaluate their own performance based on how others evaluate their performance. Individuals who are rewarded generously by others are more generous in rewarding themselves. Thus one administers reinforcers to oneself consistent with the way in which others have provided reinforcement. Stated more simply, external standards can eventually become self-imposed standards.

Modeling is also extremely important in transmitting self-control patterns. For example, children adopt standards of reinforcement that they observe in someone else (a model). If a child is exposed to a model who sets high or low standards for self-reinforcement, the child adopts similar standards for himself or herself (Bandura, 1977). Individuals exposed to models with low achievement standards tend to reward themselves for relatively mediocre performance. The self-rewarding and self-critical statements made by a model are transmitted to and made by observers when they evaluate themselves.

Self-held standards and self-administered consequences for achievement are also regulated by others in everyday interaction. For example, self-reinforcement for achieving consensually low standards of performance is not viewed favorably. Students rarely flaunt a D grade point average; runners rarely give "high fives" to themselves when placing last or close to last as part of a race. (However, if the race is a marathon, one may well celebrate because finishing is viewed as a major accomplishment in its own right.) Praiseworthy standards of performance are conveyed through explicit statements of expectations, direct reinforcement, modeling, and social control by peers and the culture.

TECHNIQUES OF SELF CONTROL

Several techniques are used within behavior modification to train people to control their own behavior or to play a central part in administering the program directed toward their behavior. Major techniques discussed in this chapter include self-assessment, stimulus control, self-reinforcement and punishment, alternative response training, biofeedback, and self-help resources.

Self-Assessment

Self-control techniques in behavior modification consist primarily of specific intervention techniques designed to alter behavior. However, assessment alone and in combination with interventions also play a role in self-control and some assessment procedures actually blur the distinction between merely measuring a problem and intervening to alter it. Some assessment procedures change behavior, at least temporarily.

Problem Identification and Screening. In light of advances in information technology, individuals have many opportunities to assess their physical and mental health. For example, access to information from the Internet allows individuals to evaluate the extent to which they are experiencing a condition or problem (problem identification) or might be at risk for a problem and warrant further evaluation (screening). This evaluation or assessment online and in the privacy of one's home, constitutes a self-assessment and self-diagnostic method. Self-assessment of current status of a particular condition or problem is included here as a self-control procedure because the assessment is under the person's own control. Although assessment may not change the target behavior of interest (e.g., depression, anxiety disorder), the information that people learn from assessing their own functioning may prompt them to seek professional treatment. Information about health, nutrition, and available treatments may serve this prompting function.

As an example, heart disease is still the number one cause of death in the United States. Individuals are encouraged by the media to have various characteristics assessed that influence the extent to which one is at risk for heart disease. Also, free blood pressure and cholesterol screenings (e.g., at grocery stores, mobile trailer units in the community) are efforts to provide information to individuals that might prompt action on their part if needed. The American Heart Association (www.americanheart.org) provides a quick quiz online that permits a user to evaluate the extent to which he or she is at risk for heart disease or stroke. One can complete the questionnaire and learn the extent to which one is at risk, current findings regarding these risk factors (e.g., cholesterol levels and how to reduce them, role of nutrition), and available treatment options. Self-assessment of risk or problems may alert individuals to seek treatment.

Within the domain of mental health, a number of Web sites provide assessment opportunities (questionnaires, checklists) that permit people to evaluate whether they meet criteria for a particular psychiatric disorder, spanning the full range of disorders related to anxiety, depression, sexual dysfunction, personality style, eating problems, and many others (e.g., www.med.nyu.edu/psych/public.html; www.mentalhealth.com/p71.html; www.mentalhelp.net/guide). Sites sometimes include information about appropriate treatments and where such treatments can be obtained in one's geographical area. The hope is that such information will initiate steps that lead people to treatment (Chase, 1999).

In relation to the present chapter, such assessment opportunities might play a significant role in individuals taking control of their mental and physical health. The information that is provided can serve as a prompting function (antecedent) that leads individuals to seek treatment, if they are in a risk domain and to alter some aspect of their lifestyles. Indeed, some of the Web sites include or are connected to sites that convey information about available treatments, provide chat room opportunities to discuss treatment, and offer self-help materials free or at a cost to treat the conditions.

Information that is on the Internet is not necessarily new (or even accurate). That is, the content is available in many other sources including books and free publications by government agencies and professional societies. However, accessibility to the information and ability to move through multiple sources are new. One can quickly learn what kinds of behaviors, symptoms, problems, thoughts, and feelings, may have what kinds of consequences and what interventions can be applied. To obtain a tentative psychiatric diagnosis, perhaps individuals will not have to go to cocktail parties and ask psychologists, psychiatrists, and social workers about the problems of a hypothetical "friend" they have. Moreover, many individuals are reticent to seek professional advice for medical or psychological conditions, even when there is strong evidence that they have a problem and when friends and relatives recommend seeking help. Access to information may assist such individuals and provide opportunities to move closer to seeking help. As noted in the discussion of response priming, engaging in early behaviors in a larger chain of behaviors increases the likelihood of completing that chain. Perhaps providing assessment information will initiate help-seeking among individuals in need.

A critical issue in relation to self-assessment and Web information more generally is that there is no quality control for the information. Some of the information is provided by individuals interested in selling materials (e.g., subscriptions to self-help magazines, self-help tapes) or in providing services (e.g., individual or group therapy). These motivations do not mean in any way that the information is inaccurate but only that those who provide information may have multiple interests, some of which are aided by promoting the need for the information or services. Consequently, one has to look at the source; professional organizations such as those sampled here are likely to represent the best information, latest findings, and consensus among experts. It is equally important to note that merely because information is obtained in person from a professional rather than from a computer does not automatically make the information more accurate.

Another issue is that self-assessment information can be unnecessarily alarming. The availability of information, even detailed, authoritative, and accurate information, is no substitute for professional consultation. For example, people can identify whether they meet criteria for an anxiety disorder on the various Web sites mentioned previously. At the same time, whether one ought to enter treatment extends beyond meeting diagnostic criteria. Whether the individual is impaired in daily functioning and how the rest of one's life is going are relevant. Self-diagnosis, assessment, and screening can easily be misused.

Information alone and access to diagnostic information are not likely to be very effective interventions. Indeed, merely conveying that one is engaging in maladaptive behavior (high fat diets, not exercising) does not promote positive behaviors among the masses. Even so, such information does promote behavior change among some small proportion of individuals. Moreover, the information may prompt people to seek more formal treatment and that would be a significant contribution. Self-assessment is mentioned here as a self-control technique because it provides individuals with information that they use to initiate behavior change. It is likely that self-assessment will take on a greater role as access to information about a range of disorders and available treatment options becomes available on the Internet and as a greater proportion of individuals world-wide will have access to that information.

Self-Monitoring. Self-assessment as discussed previously refers to a one-shot effort to identify whether or the extent to which an individual may have a problem or be at risk for one. The effects of such procedures on behavior change are not widely studied. In contrast, another assessment procedure has been more systematically studied and included as a self-control technique. *Self-monitoring,* or self-observation, consists of systematically observing one's own behavior over time, that is, on several occasions, in an ongoing fashion (Korotitsch & Nelson-Gray, 1999).

Most people are not entirely aware of the extent to which they engage in various behaviors. Habitual behaviors are automatic. People rarely observe their own behavior in a systematic fashion. However, when people are provided with the opportunity to observe their own behavior carefully, dramatic changes often occur.

The reasons that self-monitoring alters behavior are not completely understood. The information obtained through careful observation may provide important feedback about the person's level of behavior. The information conveys whether the behavior departs from a culturally or self-imposed standard of performance. If behavior departs from an acceptable level, corrective action may be initiated until the level has been met (Kanfer, 1977). For example, weighing oneself may provide information that one is overweight and may initiate other actions (avoiding snacks, exercising) until the desired weight has been achieved. Thus although self-monitoring does not itself alter weight, it initiates other behaviors that do.

Self-monitoring may be effective because the act of observation itself may take on reinforcing or punishing properties. For example, for the individual who records hours of study behavior or miles of jogging, each hour or mile tallied may provide reinforcement. Here the act of self-monitoring may operate by providing reinforcement for the behavior.

The use of self-monitoring was illustrated in a program with a 25-year-old woman who complained of obsessive thoughts about cancer of the breast and stomach (Frederiksen, 1975). She was very upset about these frequent thoughts, which appeared to become worse over a six-year period before treatment. She was instructed to monitor the frequency of the obsessive thoughts while at home. Keeping a daily tally of the thoughts was associated with a rapid reduction in their frequency from a high of 13 per day to about 2 per day. The woman was then instructed to monitor her thoughts in a more detailed fashion by recording the time of the thought, what she was doing at that time, the specific content of each thought, and so on. When this more detailed assessment procedure was used, her obsessive thoughts decreased further. They did not recur up to four months after treatment.

As another example, self-monitoring was used with four learning-disabled children (ages 9 to 10) who were behind in academic areas (Harris, 1986). They participated in a program in which they self-monitored their classroom behavior. In one condition, they monitored whether they were paying attention (by marking yes or no on a sheet) whenever a sound was randomly emitted from a tape recorder. In another condition, they recorded and graphed the number of words they had written at the end of the work period. In general, when one of the behaviors was monitored (i.e., paying attention or words written), on-task behavior and work performance improved.

These examples convey the use of self-monitoring; other applications have focused on cigarette smoking, anxiety disorders, overeating, tics, studying, and nail biting, to mention a few (see Cone, 1999). The examples may misrepresent the effects of self-monitoring. The literature has been reasonably clear that self-monitoring by itself is a weak intervention. Often it does not alter behavior and when it does, the effects are usually transient. This is in keeping with understanding of contingencies of reinforcement, as well as with common sense. Namely, if there are no consequences associated with observed behavior, it is unlikely that there will be consistent and enduring changes. Consequently, self-monitoring is used infrequently as a technique by itself. It is usually combined with other techniques, especially self-reinforcement and self-punishment, as discussed later.

Stimulus Control

Behaviors are performed in the presence of specific stimuli. Eventually, the stimuli regularly associated with a behavior serve as cues (S^D) and increase the probability that the behavior will be performed. Three related types of behavioral problems result from maladaptive stimulus control. First, some behaviors are under the control of stimuli that the client wishes to change. For example, cigarette smoking may be under the control of many stimuli, such as getting up in the morning, drinking coffee, talking with friends, studying, and being alone. It is cued by a variety of situations because it has been repeatedly associated with these situations. Because of these associations, the individual is likely to smoke a cigarette as these situations occur. The therapeutic goal is to eliminate the control that these stimuli exert over smoking.

Second, some behaviors are not controlled by particular stimuli when such control would be desirable. For example, students who have difficulty studying often have no particular setting, time, or cues associated with studying. Their studying is not consistently performed in the presence of any particular stimuli. The problem is experienced as difficulty in studying at one's desk or as being easily distracted wherever one studies. The therapeutic goal is to develop stimulus control over study behavior. Studying is likely to be more easily completed if there are specific cues associated with studying and not with behaviors incompatible with studying.

Third, some behaviors are under the control of inappropriate stimuli. Sexual deviance such as exhibitionism and fetishism is included in this category. With these behaviors, sexual responses are controlled by stimuli that deviate from appropriate stimuli as determined by social standards. The goal of treatment is to alter the control that some stimuli exert over behavior and to the extent possible, establish control of socially appropriate stimuli.

A person who is aware of how certain stimuli control behavior can structure his or her environment to maximize the likelihood that the desired behavior will occur. For example, avoiding a bakery is one illustration of using stimulus control as a self-control technique. When going by a bakery, a person may be unable to "control himself" when observing all the pastries through the window. The connection between the cues and behavior may be rather strong, and hence the individual enters the bakery and purchases pastries. This may not be the place a person can easily intervene to exert self-control, at least at first. However, not walking by the bakery or crossing the street just before approaching the bakery can remove the sight of the tempting stimuli (pastries), so that they cannot exert their influence. That is, early in a sequence of stimuli that may control behavior, a person may more readily intervene to controvert the influences.

Self-control can be attained in the tempting situation by gradually approximating the original controlling stimulus in mild doses. The individual tempted by the bakery window can pass the window when the bakery is closed, walk by the window quickly when the bakery is crowded, walk by the window while looking away, and stop by the window after eating a large meal. If the person does not enter the bakery in the presence of increasingly tempting cues, the bakery may no longer exert its influence over his or her behavior.

The use of stimulus control ordinarily requires that a therapist initially consult with the client to explain how stimulus control operates and to help the client identify events that control or fail to control his or her behavior. Treatment may consist of helping the client perform behavior under a narrow or new set of stimuli to develop stimulus control or of helping the client perform new behaviors under familiar stimuli to eliminate existing sources of control. For example, in early applications of stimulus control in behavioral research, clients who failed to study or who ate excessively were instructed to perform the behavior only under certain stimulus conditions (e.g., studying in a special place and at a certain time of the day or eating only at the table and with a full place setting) (Fox, 1962;

Goldiamond, 1965). Such procedures were designed to bring behavior under the control of specific stimuli to help increase studying when the clients were in certain situations or to decrease eating when the clients were not in specific situations ordinarily associated with eating.

Insomnia has been quite successfully treated using stimulus-control procedures (Bootzin & Rider, 1997). For whatever reason insomnia develops, it follows a familiar pattern. A person may be tired before retiring, but as soon as the person goes to bed, he or she may begin to worry about the day's activities. Thus the stimuli usually associated with sleeping (bed, darkness, and a specific time and place) become associated with behaviors incompatible with sleeping (e.g., eating in bed, watching television, chatting on the phone, obsessing about relationships or activities at work). Many of these activities are cues for arousal. Stimulus control is intended to establish or strengthen associations between the cues more compatible with going to bed and with sleeping.

The procedure was developed in the early 1970s in the case of an adult insomniac who went to bed about midnight but was unable to fall asleep until approximately 3 or 4 AM (Bootzin, 1972). Before sleeping, he would worry about several mundane problems and finally would turn on the television. He would fall asleep while the television was still on. Treatment attempted to bring sleep under control of the stimuli associated with going to bed. The client was told to go to bed when he felt sleepy but not to read or watch television. If unable to sleep, he was to go into another room and stay up as long as he liked. When he again felt sleepy, he was to go back to bed. If he still could not sleep, he was to repeat the procedure. The goal of course was to associate going to and staying in bed with sleep.

For the first few days of treatment, the client got up four or five times each night before going to sleep. Yet after two weeks, he no longer got up at all. When he went to bed, he stayed there and fell asleep. The client reported sleeping much better and getting much more sleep each night. During a follow-up period conducted up to two months after treatment began, the client got up during the night less than once a week. Thus the treatment appeared to work very well.

Although stimulus control requires the therapist to explain the principles, techniques, and recommended applications, the clients themselves apply the procedures in their daily lives. Ideally, the clients can extend the use of stimulus control techniques beyond the area that served as the impetus for seeking treatment. To do that, several rules or instructions are provided to the client. The rules, listed in Table 10-2, are designed to help individuals become more sensitive to internal cues of sleepiness so they are more likely to go to sleep (rule 1), to break up the association of activities with going to sleep (rule 2), to associate the bed with sleep and to disassociate going to bed with frustration and arousal from not being able to go to sleep (rules 3 and 4), to develop more regular sleep schedules and sleep rhythms (biological), to keep patients from disrupting their sleep by irregular napping, and to prevent them from losing the benefits of being tired from not sleeping since the previous night. Several controlled outcome studies have shown stimulus control procedures to be effective as a treatment of insomnia using these rules and procedures (Bootzin & Rider, 1997).

Table 10-2 Stimulus Control Rules for Treating Insomnia

1. Lie down intending to go to sleep only when you are sleepy.
2. Do not use your bed for anything except sleep; that is, do not read, watch television, eat, or worry in bed. Sexual activity is the only exception to this rule. On such occasions, the instructions are to be followed afterward, when you intend to go to sleep.
3. If you find yourself unable to fall asleep, get up and go into another room. Stay up as long as you wish and then return to the bedroom to sleep. Although we do not want you to watch the clock, we want you to get out of bed if you do not fall asleep immediately. Remember the goal is to associate your bed with falling asleep *quickly!* If you are in bed more than about 10 minutes without falling asleep and have not gotten up, you are not following the instruction.
4. If you still cannot fall asleep, repeat Step 3. Do this as often as necessary throughout the night.
5. Set your alarm and get up at the same time every morning irrespective of how much sleep you got during the night. This will help your body to acquire a consistent sleep rhythm.
6. Do not nap during the day.

(Source: Bootzin, Epstein, & Wood, 1991)

Self-Reinforcement and Self-Punishment

Reinforcing and punishing consequences administered to oneself have been used as self-control techniques (Gross & Drabman, 1982). Clients are trained to administer consequences to themselves contingent on behavior rather than receiving consequences from an external agent. Self-reinforcement has received more attention than has self-punishment.[1]

The major requirement of *self-reinforcement* is that the individual is free to reward himself or herself at *any time*, regardless of whether a particular response is performed (Skinner, 1953). The person who self-administers reinforcers must not be constrained by external pressures to perform a response or to deliver or withhold consequences. Although as noted at the outset of the chapter, self-control is a matter of degree, so for self-reinforcement, few or no constraints would qualify. An additional requirement to qualify as reinforcement is that the behavior followed by a self-administered consequence must increase in the likelihood of occurring in the future.

In most applications of self-reinforcement, two procedures can be delineated. First, the client can determine the response requirements needed for a given amount of reinforcement. The client controls when to deliver reinforcement and the amount of reinforcement to be delivered. When the client determines the criteria for reinforcement, this is referred to as *self-determined reinforcement* (Glynn, 1970). Second, the client can dispense reinforcement for achieving a particular criterion, which may or may not be self-determined. When the client administers reinforcers to himself or herself, this is referred to as *self-administered reinforcement*. Who administers the reinforcers (oneself or someone else) may not be crucial. The crucial elements are determining *when* to deliver reinforcement and for *what* behaviors. Yet if a person is not permitted to self-administer reinforcers, there may be external agents who influence the self-reinforcement process.

Self-reinforcement is probably best achieved when the client self-determines and self-administers the reinforcers. Self-reinforcement usually requires the client to observe and record his or her behavior so as to determine whether it has met a criterion. Thus self-monitoring is an ingredient of the procedure.

Self-reinforcement has been used in several classroom programs. For example, self-reinforcement was used to improve story writing of elementary school children (Ballard & Glynn, 1975). The children self-recorded the number of sentences, the number of different descriptive words, and the number of different action words on a special sheet. Self-recording (i.e., self-monitoring) did not alter these behaviors. Self-reinforcement was added in which the children were told to administer one point to themselves for increases in the number of sentences they had written. The points were exchangeable for such activities as free time, access to games, art materials, books, and public display of one's story. The number of sentences increased markedly with self-reinforcement. An extension of the self-reinforcement contingency led to increases in the other writing behaviors. Interestingly, the quality and interest value of the stories were rated as better during the self-reinforcement phases than during baseline by two university faculty in English who were unaware of the program. That is, the specific and concrete behaviors directly affected overall quality of the stories.

In a quite different context, self-reinforcement was used with middle-management men working for large businesses (Nakano, 1990). The focus of the intervention was on Type A behavior, which refers to a behavioral pattern characterized by impatience, competitiveness, time urgency, anger, and hostility. Type A behavior is a significant focus because the pattern has been linked to coronary disease. In this study, assessment began by having individuals monitor several Type A behaviors (e.g., eating fast, not relaxing after a meal, hurrying others to communicate a point when they were speaking). During baseline, the men monitored their behavior (self-monitoring) and were told to set goals for taking more time to eat meals and relax. Spouses of the participants also assessed various behaviors related to impatience to provide a further check on the program. Self-reinforcement programs were introduced in which each individual constructed a reward menu (reinforcers he would like to earn) and set prices for each reward (as in a token economy). As evident in Figure 10-1, the effect of self-reinforcement was examined in a multiple-baseline design across the six men. When the intervention was introduced, the amount of time the men engaged in eating and relaxing (taking more time for each) increased. Measures from the spouses showed similar changes. The results for both sets of data indicated that the positive changes were maintained at the six-week follow-up assessment. Other measures of Type A behavior and of physical health symptoms also improved with treatment.

Self-punishment has been used infrequently. The reasons are similar to those outlined in the chapter on punishment, namely, that reinforcement techniques are usually viable alternatives and are less likely to evoke undesirable side effects. Also mentioned before was the central role of positive reinforcement for appropriate behavior whenever punishment for inappropriate behavior is used. In keeping with this recommendation, self-control programs that use punishment usually incorporate positive reinforcement.

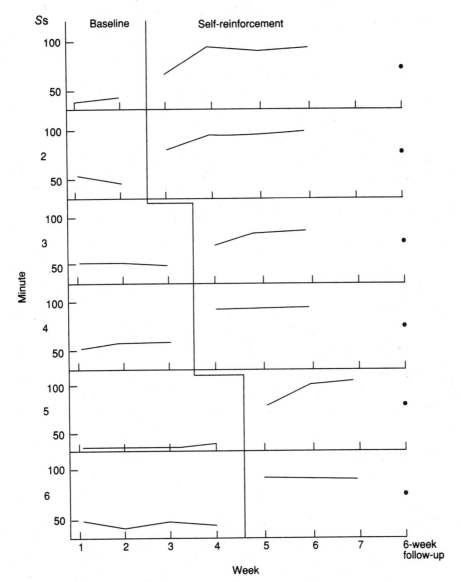

FIGURE 10-1 Amount of time spent eating and relaxing each day (average per week) over the course of baseline (self-monitoring and self-evaluation were included in baseline) and self-reinforcement. The effects are shown in a multiple-baseline design across six subjects (Ss). The final assessment was a six-week follow-up after the program had ended.

(Source: Nakano, 1990)

As an illustration, self-reinforcement and self-punishment were combined to control the cigarette smoking of a 65-year-old male named Joe (Belles & Bradlyn, 1987). Joe lived 200 miles from the clinic, so treatment was planned over the telephone. A self-control program was devised to decrease the number of cigarettes that he smoked. This was corroborated by counts that his wife made unobtrusively. After baseline, Joe rewarded himself for smoking a reduced number of cigarettes. (This follows the differential reinforcement of the low rates schedule noted in Chapter 6.) Specifically, for each day on which he met or fell below the criterion number of cigarettes smoked, he provided $3 to a fund for items that he wished to buy. For each day on which he exceeded the criterion, he agreed to send a personal check for $25 to a charity he disliked. To verify implementation of this latter contingencies, the check was to be mailed to the investigator, who would then forward the contribution to the charity. In short, the program included reinforcement for low rates and response cost for not meeting the criterion.

The program was implemented and evaluated in a changing-criterion design so that in many separate phases the criterion for the number of cigarettes was set progressively lower. As shown in Figure 10-2, the criterion (horizontal line) was closely approximated in each phase (labeled as phases B through U). When Joe reached the criterion of five cigarettes per day, he indicated that he wished to remain at that level. The level was maintained and the program was terminated. Follow-up conducted up to 18 months later indicated that smoking remained at this level, obviously well below and much safer than the rate of 80 to 100 cigarettes each day before the study and baseline (A) phase began.

Self-reinforcement and self-punishment techniques have been applied to a wide range of problems, including craving drugs, deviant sexual behavior, cigarette smoking, and poor dating skills, to mention a few applications. In many applications, clients do not administer an overt consequence, such as money or points. Rather, clients may *imagine* various events or consequences. Imagery-based procedures are addressed later (in the next chapter) because they encompass a variety of techniques in addition to self-reinforcement and self-punishment.

Alternate Response Training

Another self-control technique is training a person to engage in responses that interfere with or replace an undesired response. Essentially, the person is trained to replace one behavior with another. Of course, to accomplish this, the person must have an alternate response in which to engage. For example, people can think pleasant thoughts to control worrying or they can relax to control tension.

The most common focus of *alternate response training* is the control of anxiety. Relaxation has been widely used as a response that is incompatible with, and therefore an alternative to, anxiety. Typically, a client is trained by a therapist to relax deeply. Many methods for achieving relaxation are available (Benson & Klipper, 1990). In behavior therapy, a client is usually trained to tense and relax individual muscle groups. Alternatively tensing and relaxing helps the person discriminate different levels of muscle relaxation. Another relaxation procedure that has been used is to have the client make suggestions to himself or herself of

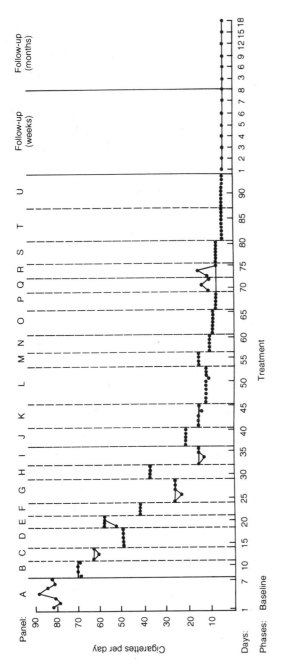

FIGURE 10-2 Number of cigarettes smoked per day from baseline (A phase) through each intervention phase (B-U phases) in which the criterion was altered. The criterion within each phase of the self-reward/self-punishment program is indicated by the horizontal line.

(Source: Belles & Bradlyn, 1987)

feeling warmth and heaviness in the muscles. Various forms of meditation can also be used to develop relaxation skills. Once relaxation has been learned, it can be used as a self-control technique and invoked to overcome anxiety in a variety of situations. Individuals have applied relaxation to themselves to effectively manage anxiety associated with interactions with the opposite sex, natural childbirth, public speaking, interviews, and many other problems.

Relaxation training also has been used effectively to decrease headaches, including those from mild tension to more severe migraine headaches. As an illustration, three adults (ages 24 to 48) were treated with relaxation for headaches (Gutkin, Holborn, Walker, & Anderson, 1992). Their histories of headaches extended from 6 to 23 years. Medical evaluations could not identify any biological condition that might explain or contribute to the headaches. The patients were seen and treated individually at the clinic. Each began by keeping a diary, a commonly used assessment strategy, in which a daily record was made of headache frequency, intensity, and duration. After weeks of baseline observation, each patient was given 10 sessions of relaxation training, which included alternately tensing and contracting individual muscle groups. An audiotape of the instructions was provided to guide practice of relaxation at home. Patients could relax themselves in a very brief period (1 to 2 minutes), and were then instructed to continue the procedure. Each achieved a reduction in the number of weekly headaches and an increase in the number of days free from headaches. Figure 10-3 presents the data for one of the patients. The figure shows improvement during the treatment (when relaxation training was provided) and maintenance phases (when individuals were instructed to continue the program on their own). Moreover, follow-up assessment one year later indicated that the gains had continued.

Relaxation was used in another application to treat three hemophiliac patients who suffered from severe arthritic pain (Varni, 1981).[2] The pain resulted from recurrent internal bleeding that affected the joints and caused cartilage and bone damage. Because of possible drug dependency, long-term use of medication is of limited value in controlling chronic pain. To help control pain, a self-control strategy was developed in which the patients were trained to relax deeply, to engage in deep breathing while saying the word "relax" to themselves, and to imagine themselves in situations previously associated with relief of pain. The patients' reports of pain, illustrated in Figure 10-4, decreased when the self-control training was introduced. The effects were maintained from 7 to 14 months after treatment. Moreover, after treatment, the patients decreased their use of medication to control pain.

Relaxation training is a noteworthy intervention for several reasons. To begin with, various procedures to induce relaxation (e.g., progressive relaxation, exercises, meditation, biofeedback) have been studied in relation to a number of clinical problems and have been shown to produce change. In addition, relaxation is of special interest because of the rather extensive evidence noting the role of stress in placing individuals at risk for physical disease and psychological dysfunction (such as depression). For example, relaxation training as a way of overcoming or coping with stress enhances the strength of the immune system and reduces the biological impact of stressors (see Kiecolt-Glaser & Glaser, 1992). Such findings

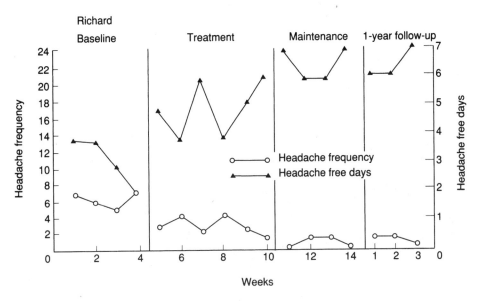

FIGURE 10-3 Headache frequency and number of headache-free days for one case (adult male) during baseline, treatment (relaxation training), maintenance (completion of training but with instructions to continue relaxation at home), and 1-year follow-up. The intervention was evaluated with three cases with staggered baselines, as in a multiple-baseline design across cases, although this figure presents data for only one of the cases.

(Source: Gutkin, Holborn, Walker, & Anderson, 1992)

raise the possibility that relaxation training may bolster bodily defenses against many different types of disease.

Biofeedback

Many physiological processes are directly involved in problems brought for treatment, including hypertension, headaches, epileptic seizures, muscle spasms, cardiac arrhythmias (irregular heartbeats), and anxiety. Management, reduction, and occasionally, elimination of the problem can be aided by control of the processes. Indeed, various medications that are used for treatment control medical problems by interrupting the specific processes (e.g., blocking transmission of neurotransmitters or chemical reactions) that directly contribute to the problem. Nonmedical procedures can also be used to alter, interrupt, or influence physiological processes that influence behavior.

Biofeedback refers to a number of intervention techniques that are designed to alter physiological processes (e.g., heart rate, brainwave activity) through training. Generally, biofeedback consists of providing information to individuals about their ongoing physiological processes. The information is displayed to the client so that

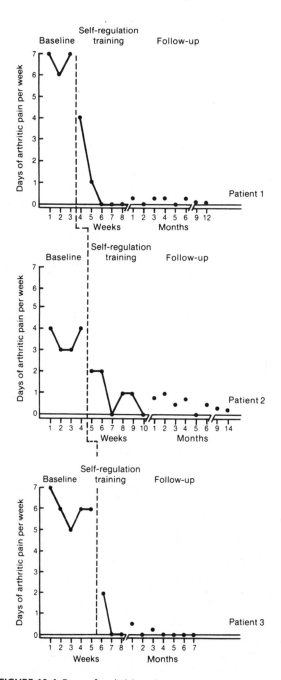

FIGURE 10-4 Days of arthritic pain reported per week during baseline, self-regulation training, and follow-up for each of three patients.

(Source: Varni, 1981)

moment-to-moment changes in these processes can be monitored. The goal is to change these physiological processes and in many cases, the behaviors, thoughts, or feelings with which these are associated. Several different biofeedback procedures can be distinguished, depending precisely on what physiological processes are monitored and how feedback is administered (Schwartz & Andrasik, 1998).

Biofeedback is included here as a self-control procedure because the goal of many biofeedback procedures is to teach clients specific techniques for regulating their own responses in the natural environment (Soroka, 1996). For example, biofeedback may be used to control blood pressure. In treatment sessions, the client may be connected to a device that monitors blood pressure and provides visual feedback (on a television screen or digital counter) or auditory feedback (tone) when the blood pressure is above or below a specified criterion. The client can be instructed to decrease blood pressure and will receive immediate feedback on the extent to which this has been successfully accomplished. Ideally, the client will learn to engage in responses (e.g., pleasant thoughts, relaxation) that are effective in decreasing blood pressure. These responses, it is hoped, will be extended to everyday situations long after biofeedback training has been completed.

For example, biofeedback was used to help train relaxation as a means of managing stress in a 36-year-old woman with insulin-dependent diabetes (McGrady & Gerstenmaier, 1990). Control of blood glucose levels is attained through careful diet, regular exercise, and insulin injections. Diabetic patients monitor their glucose levels daily to ensure that glucose remains within a normative range. In this case, glucose levels were erratic and not completely controlled, even though the patient complied with the prescribed regimen. Several stressors were identified that might be contributing to this because it is known that stress can influence control of glucose in diabetics. Biofeedback and relaxation together were the treatments and were used in conjunction to control stress.

Treatment was provided in sessions over a 10-month period. The client was trained to engage in relaxation. Biofeedback consisted of muscle and temperature feedback while she was relaxed. Biofeedback was used by providing a tone based on muscle tension (forehead and neck) and hand temperature. Reduction of muscle tension and increases in hand temperature were the goals to reach a more relaxed state. Biofeedback was trained in the laboratory. However, as mentioned, a goal is to provide self-control strategies for clients in many applications of biofeedback. In this case, the client was encouraged to practice relaxation at home and to use a portable, hand-held thermometer to monitor her hand temperature. She was encouraged to carry out relaxation sessions whenever she was aware of increased muscle tension or a cooling of her hands. For most people, this might be difficult to detect. Indeed, one of the purposes of biofeedback is to permit improved monitoring of such states. Over the course of treatment, the blood glucose levels were monitored, given that this was the focus of initiating treatment. The results indicated that her blood glucose levels were more controlled and less variable (less frequently outside the desired range). That is, both the mean (average) and variability of blood glucose scores were positively affected. The case illustrates the use of biofeedback in training sessions and the extension of the procedures to manage stress in everyday life.

Applications of biofeedback have focused on a variety of responses, including cardiac arrhythmia, tachycardia (accelerated heart rate), hypertension, muscle paralysis and inactivity, seizure activity, sexual arousal, and anxiety (Schwartz & Andrasik, 1998). To alter these conditions, feedback about biological processes have conveyed level of muscle tension, blood pressure, skin temperature, heart rate, brain waves, blood volume, and galvanic skin responses. Biofeedback has been effective in many studies and reports.

Two concerns are worth noting about biofeedback. First, relaxation training is often just as effective as biofeedback. This is noteworthy because of the many different ways relaxation can be achieved (e.g., relaxation training, meditation) (Benson & Klipper, 1990). Also, relaxation training is more easily implemented because no equipment is required and, hence, also more readily extended to the natural environment. Relaxation training can be more readily applied to a wider range of problems because the technology for assessing many physiological processes is not yet available, especially in relation to measuring clinical problems (e.g., obsessive thoughts) based on private events. One need not pit biofeedback and relaxation against each other; they can be used together, as a previously noted example shows.

Second, biofeedback does not invariably provide a technique that clients can implement on their own. The requirement of special equipment may limit the range of applications. Of course many portable and affordable devices (e.g., to test heart rate, blood pressure, blood glucose levels) are available for the public and can provide the necessary feedback or periodic monitoring to extend biofeedback in everyday life. When the effects cannot be monitored in everyday life, it is not clear whether the effects of the intervention will be maintained. Nevertheless, biofeedback has often been shown to result in sustained treatment effects. A broader issue of self-control methods is the extent to which clients apply the skills they learn in treatment to their everyday lives. This is not a unique issue for biofeedback but is raised by the special needs of equipment with this particular method of self-control and the practical obstacles this requirement might raise.

Self-Help Resources

Many of the self-control techniques discussed to this point develop skills in clients during treatment sessions. After the skills have been developed, the clients can extend these to the environment to control their own behaviors in a variety of situations. Several self-help techniques have been developed that clients implement for themselves with minimal or no therapist assistance. Until relatively recently, the techniques have been referred to as *self-help manuals* or *bibliotherapy* because the procedures are conveyed to potential clients in written form, usually as books and pamphlets that can be purchased in stores or are made available at clinics. A broader term, self-help resources, is used here to encompass written materials but also to include materials available on the Internet.

Self-help resources are available for an extraordinary range of problems, including anxiety, depression, substance use and abuse (e.g., cigarettes, hard drugs, alcohol), eating disorders, dysfunctional relationships, stress, grief-management, sexual dysfunction, perfectionism, low self-confidence, and others (see Pardeck, 1993; Rosen, 1987; www.odos.uiuc.edu/Counseling_Center). The techniques included in these resources encompass a variety of procedures, alone and in combination. The materials describe, in a step-by-step fashion, how the client should proceed to alter his or her problem.

Self-help manuals, that is, the written resources, have been evaluated in many studies. A frequent focus is assisting parents in child rearing. As an example, self-help materials were provided for parents to develop appropriate mealtime behaviors in their children (McMahon & Forehand, 1978). Three "normal" preschool children from different families participated on the basis of their parents' interest in changing such inappropriate behaviors as playing with food, throwing or stealing food, and leaving the table before the end of the meal. An initial consultation in the parents' home explained the procedures. At this point, the parents received a brochure (2 pages), describing how to provide attention and praise for appropriate mealtime behavior and how to use time out from reinforcement (isolating the child in another room) for inappropriate behaviors that the child did not cease to engage in when asked. With only this brief description of reinforcement and time out, the parents implemented training. Observations were made of actual eating behaviors in the home. The program was very effective, as shown in a multiple-baseline design across different children, plotted in Figure 10-5. The effects of the program were maintained at follow-up assessment approximately six weeks after treatment. These results are impressive because of the ability of the parents to administer treatment completely on their own.

Another self-help program was developed for parents who wish to toilet train their children quickly (Azrin & Foxx, 1974). The manual included a series of procedures based on many of the techniques that have been reviewed in prior chapters, including prompting, shaping, positive practice, and reinforcement. Instructions, guidance, edible rewards, praise, feedback, and occasional punishment (positive practice) were intertwined to develop the child's self-initiation of toileting skills. The specific procedures on which the manual is based have been carefully researched in experimental studies in which those procedures have produced rapid results. Indeed, the manual suggested that toilet training can be conducted in "less than a day" (average time about four hours). Parents can indeed toilet train their children with the use of the book.

As prior chapters have emphasized, the effectiveness of behavioral procedures require that they be implemented in special ways (e.g., prompting, shaping, continuous and immediate reinforcement). As might be expected, parents or indeed anyone left to their own devices without training are not likely to invoke the conditions to optimize performance. The book has been found not to be very effective by itself without someone available to provide parents with supervision on how to use the procedures (Matson & Ollendick, 1977). A self-help manual that requires minimal therapist assistance could be very helpful to many children and families.

Self-help resources have proliferated on the Internet. The resources make available various materials, including books, audiotapes, or videotapes that are used for treatment. In addition, the resources provide self-help guidelines directly to over-

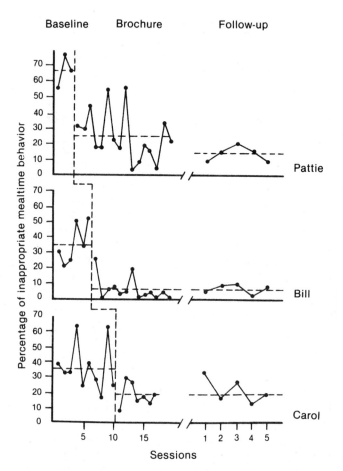

FIGURE 10-5 Percentage of intervals scored as inappropriate mealtime behavior. The broken horizontal line in each phase indicates the mean percentage of intervals scored as inappropriate mealtime behavior across sessions for that phase.

(Source: McMahon & Forehand, 1978)

come a problem. For example, one Web site provides a series of self-help guidelines to address a range of psychological problems, including addictive relationships, coming out, perfectionism, loneliness, depression, grief and loss, eating disorders, and others (www.odos.uiuc.edu/Counseling_Center). As an illustration, treatment recommendations are provided to manage stress (Table 10-3). The information is intended to help, and no claims are made that following these guidelines will ameliorate the problem. Indeed, the Web site provides information about how to obtain treatment at the counseling center, which provides this information.

This Web site illustrates a broader point about self-help resources. It is quite possible that self-help tips and suggestions may be a useful initial point to provide

Table 10-3   Self-Help Recommendations to Manage Stress

How Can I Manage Stress Better?

Identifying unrelieved stress and being aware of its effect on our lives is not sufficient for reducing the harmful effects of stress. Just as there are many sources of stress, there are many possibilities for its management. However, all require effort toward change—changing the source of stress and/or changing your reaction to it. How do you proceed?

1. **Become aware of your stressors and your emotional and physical reactions.**
   - Notice your distress. Do not ignore it. Do not gloss over your problems.
   - Determine what events distress you. What are you telling yourself about the meaning of these events?
   - Determine how your body responds to the stress. Do you become nervous or physically upset? If so, in what specific ways?

2. **Recognize what you can change.**
   - Can you change your stressors by avoiding or eliminating them completely?
   - Can you reduce their intensity (manage them over a period of time instead of on a daily or weekly basis)?
   - Can you shorten your exposure to stress (take a break, leave the physical premises)?
   - Can you devote the time and energy necessary to making a change (goal setting, time-management techniques, and delayed gratification strategies may be helpful here)?

3. **Reduce the intensity of your emotional reactions to stress.**
   - The stress reaction is triggered by your perception of danger—physical and/or emotional danger.
   - Are you viewing your stressors in exaggerated terms and/or taking a difficult situation and making it a disaster?
   - Are you expecting to please everyone?
   - Are you overreacting and viewing things as absolutely critical and urgent? Do you feel you must always prevail in every situation?
   - Work at adopting more moderate views; try to see the stress as something you can cope with rather than something that overpowers you.
   - Try to temper your excess emotions. Put the situation in perspective. Do not labor on the negative aspects and the "what if's."

4. **Learn to moderate your physical reactions to stress.**
   - Slow, deep breathing will bring your heart rate and respiration back to normal.
   - Relaxation techniques can reduce muscle tension.
   - Electronic biofeedback can help you gain voluntary control over such things as muscle tension, heart rate, and blood pressure.
   - Medications, when prescribed by a physician, can help in the short term in moderating your physical reactions. However, they alone are not the answer. Learning to moderate these reactions on your own is a preferable long-term solution.

5. **Build your physical reserves.**
   - Exercise for cardiovascular fitness three to four times a week (moderate, prolonged rhythmic exercise is best, such as walking, swimming, cycling, or jogging).
   - Eat well-balanced, nutritious meals.
   - Maintain your ideal weight.
   - Avoid nicotine, excessive caffeine, and other stimulants.
   - Mix leisure with work. Take breaks and get away when you can.
   - Get enough sleep. Be as consistent with your sleep schedule as possible.

6. **Maintain your emotional reserves.**
   - Develop some mutually supportive friendships/relationships.
   - Pursue realistic goals that are meaningful to you, rather than goals others have for you that you do not share.
   - Expect some frustrations, failures, and sorrows.
   - Always be kind and gentle with yourself—be a friend to yourself.

NOTE: This is an example of information available from the Internet. The information is available from the University of Illinois at Urbana-Champaign and from the Web site (www.odos.uiuc.edu/Counseling_Center).

interventions. The materials can reach a large audience including those who might not otherwise come for treatment. A proportion of such individuals may profit sufficiently without requiring further intervention. Those who do require further information might be directed to treatment. Self-assessment materials usually included in such Web sites may provide guidelines regarding whether treatment is warranted.

Web sites provide other advantages. Information, support, and the ability to "chat" with others about a problem are available 24 hours a day and, hence, are much more available to an individual than other forms of treatment. Also, for many individuals, confiding in others, revealing information, and asking certain questions would be easier from one's own computer or other device that can access the Web than would contacting a professional in person. Information and interventions delivered via the Web are not well regulated and their effects are not well enough evaluated to advocate their use in comparison with more formalized forms of therapy.

Self-help resources have proliferated in recent years. The resources have important advantages. Because they can be widely disseminated, treatment can be provided to many individuals who might not otherwise seek or receive treatment. Also, many clinical problems are so pervasive, that it may be unrealistic to consider therapists as a means of providing individual or indeed even group treatment on a weekly or regular basis. For example, major depression is likely to be experienced by approximately 20 million individuals in the United States during their lifetimes. There are a number of effective forms of treatment, including psychotherapy and medication. Even so, it is difficult to disseminate treatment to ensure that those who are in need of treatment will receive it. Self-help resources are not *the* answer, but they may be *an* answer for some individuals. For example, self-help manuals, based on cognitive-behavioral procedures, usually consist of providing clients with the materials, a meeting with a therapist, and telephone support. Reviews have suggested this is an effective intervention (Cuijpers, 1997). Self-help manuals probably are not a replacement for other forms of treatment, especially for severe cases. Yet many individuals who might not otherwise enter therapy might be amenable to this form of treatment.

The ease, promised simplicity, and ability to disseminate self-help resources also raise a number of caveats about their use. To begin, self-help resources often make exaggerated claims and promise to improve virtually all facets of life that a human may encounter in a 24-hour period (e.g., improved relationships, feelings of confidence, eating, sleeping, sexual functioning, etc.). Because self-help materials are often sold commercially, they are promoted in the usual way one would expect from advertising and marketing. That is, claims are made to boost sales, and there is little or no regulation of the claims. For example, the titles of several manuals include promises for *effective, permanent,* and *rapid* change (see Pardeck, 1993; Rosen, 1987). These claims are equivalent to "get-rich quick" schemes for one's emotional and behavioral problems. Even when there is no commercial interest, for example, as in free self-help information available on the Web, the recommendations and materials usually are untested and have not been shown to achieve the effects they promise.

The problem is not merely that the advice and recommendations might be ineffective or not produce the promised result; in some cases, there might be harm. For example, dieting manuals might lead to temporary weight loss but fail to point out that repeated dieting and weight loss, deprivation or overuse of a particular food, food group, or vitamins may have untoward health consequences. Self-help resources are likely to vary in their effectiveness and to be differentially effective for different individuals and types of problems. Consultation with professionals may be important not only to help implement procedures but to identify procedures that have been shown to be effective.

Occasionally a treatment is very well studied and shown to be effective when administered by therapists. The treatment is then placed into the form of a self-help manual with the implicit assumption that it will be effective in this different form. For example, cognitive therapy for depression and anger management training are procedures with demonstrated effectiveness for adults referred for treatment. Both treatments have been placed in self-help manuals (Gentry, 1999; Greenberger & Padesky, 1995). The treatments have a firm empirical basis when professionally administered. They might also be effective when applied as self-help interventions. Yet careful studies are needed to show that the results obtained in therapist-administered versions can also be achieved with self-help manual versions.

Tests of several manuals have shown that individuals often fail to comply with manuals aimed at overcoming fears, controlling eating, or eliminating sexual dysfunction (Rosen, 1987). That is, the manuals might be effective, but people do not in fact execute the procedures. Some contact with a professional to help guide the use of the self-help manual is likely to be more effective than is use of the manual without such help. Thus some data already suggest that for many problems, manuals are a useful component of treatment but perhaps insufficient by themselves.

STRENGTHS AND LIMITATIONS

Several advantages accrue from the development of self-control procedures. First, such procedures permit various techniques to be more widely extended to the public than would ordinarily be the case with techniques completely carried out by trained professional therapists. Disseminating treatment to the public is very important. Consider some of the barriers of delivering treatment to people in need. First, there is a resource problem; there is not a sufficient number of therapists or treatment services to meet the needs of the public. A surprisingly large proportion of children, adolescents, and adults in everyday life (e.g., 18% to 20% meet criteria for a psychiatric disorder, that is, significant social, emotional, and behavioral problems (Regier et al., 1984; US Congress, 1991).[3] This proportion translates to millions (e.g., more than 50 million) individuals in the United States who might profit from treatment. Many more individuals have conditions that would not be delineated as clear psychiatric disorders but are experiencing problems of living or would profit from some intervention. Traditional methods of delivering treatment for people who come to sessions for various forms of psychotherapy can only reach a minute proportion of persons in need or who could benefit from intervention. Self-control methods might benefit scores of individuals who do not come to treatment or whose problems are bothersome to them or to others but not sufficiently debilitating to bring them to treatment.

Also related is that many individuals in need and with access to treatment do not seek treatment. For many people, there is stigma associated with seeking help; for others, there are cultural impediments (e.g., one does not seek help outside of the family or disclose private family information to strangers). Also, cost of treatment is an impediment. Many in need do not have insurance and cannot pay for treatment. Self-control procedures may bring interventions to those who otherwise would not receive treatment. Such procedures might, for example, be made available at public clinics where individuals could obtain materials and instructions on how to apply them. The cost of self-help treatments is much less than for treatment administered professionally and hence more available to those who might not otherwise afford treatment (Mudde, de Vries, & Strecher, 1996).

In self-control techniques such as stimulus control and alternate response training, clients have initial contact with a therapist but carry out the procedures on their own. The initial contact means that little professional time and client expense are involved in beginning and conducting treatment. With self-help manuals and Internet resources, the potential for widespread dissemination of treatment is even greater than with other self-control techniques. If consumers carry out behavior modification techniques presented through self-help resources, a large number of people might be reached who ordinarily would not even seek treatment.

A second advantage is that clients may prefer self-control procedures over a therapist-administered treatment. People may prefer implementing a treatment on their own because self-administered treatment may be less expensive and more efficient, and because it enables them to play a more direct role in their own treatment. Many clients might be more apt to undergo treatment if they could self-administer the procedures. For example, a Gallup opinion survey indicated that only about 34% of cigarette smokers would come for treatment at a clinic and that most cigarette smokers preferred self-help methods (Glasgow & Rosen, 1984). In general, clients may prefer and find as more acceptable techniques in which they play a role (Kazdin, 1980b). Treatments that are more acceptable are more likely to be sought and adhered to (Reimers, Wacker, Cooper, & DeRaad, 1992).

The application of self-control techniques raises important questions that remain to be resolved. First, self-control procedures have been applied to a variety of problems, including anxiety, depression, sexual dysfunction, overeating, cigarette smoking, alcohol abuse, the management of diseases, and a variety of behaviors in everyday settings (at home and school). There has been very little research to evaluate the types of problems for which self-control treatments are effective and who is likely to respond well to such treatments. It may be that self-help procedures are particularly useful for problems that have not reached a certain level of severity.

The fact that many of the treatments (e.g., self-help manuals) are part of "pop" [popular] psychology and are promoted for sale signal that claims about effectiveness have far outstripped what has been demonstrated in research. Consequently, many people are applying treatments to themselves that do not work and indeed may be harmful. Moreover, if the treatment does not work, this may discourage individuals from seeking other treatments that might well ameliorate their problems.

Another concern raised by self-control techniques pertains to adherence to the procedures. Effective application requires carrying out the procedures in specific ways. If the client is truly in charge of administering the program, will the procedures be delivered as intended? Self-reinforcement and self-punishment techniques have led to problems in adherence. If an individual is completely free to deliver rewarding or punishing consequences for behavior, will those consequences be administered contingently? The natural contingencies (i.e., those normally fostered by the environment) may discourage adherence to self-reinforcement and self-punishment. In fact, if individuals are given control over the administration of reinforcers for their own behavior, they often become more lenient, that is, they deliver the reinforcers to themselves even if the behavior has not been performed or has not met a prespecified criterion (Gross & Drabman, 1982; McReynolds & Church, 1973). In a self-reinforcement program, there is no penalty for merely delivering the reinforcers noncontingently, which is not likely to develop the desired target behavior. Thus noncontingent reinforcement and suspension of the contingencies are probably much more likely in self-control programs than in externally managed programs. Periodically monitoring the delivery of consequences can help ensure that self-reinforcement contingencies are administered properly, although, of course, the extent to which there is external monitoring decreases the degree of *self*-control.

Adherence to treatment has been somewhat of a problem when clients are given self-help resources and left to their own devices to implement treatment. People left entirely on their own to conduct treatment have relatively high rates of attrition (dropping out of treatment), a finding shown in self-help training for such problems as anxiety associated with public speaking, fears, and sexual dysfunction (Marshall, Presse, & Andrews, 1976; Rosen, Glasgow, & Barrera, 1976; Zeiss, 1978). Also, clients who stay in treatment often do not carry out the required procedures when they are left on their own with a self-help manual. For example, investigators have reported that 50% or more of the clients who used a self-help manual for the treatment of anxiety failed to complete the procedures that they were instructed to perform (Marshall et al., 1976; Rosen et al., 1976). In a study on the treatment of problem drinkers, approximately one-third of the clients said that they had not even read the self-help manual that was used to help maintain treatment gains (Miller, 1977).

Adherence is a problem for treatment whenever clients are given control over administration. For example, patients who take cholesterol-lowering medications to reduce their risk of heart attack have high rates of compliance when participating in a research program in which there is monitoring of medication and encouragement of those who administer the medication. Ninety-four percent of patients take their daily medication. Left on their own, compliance decreases to approximately 50% and then to 15% of the patients 1 to 2 years later (Mundell, 1999). Similarly, in applications of self-help manuals, evidence suggests that contact with an external agent (e.g., therapist) may be important to ensure that treatment is conducted properly, to provide encouragement when problems arise or when the client begins to discontinue the procedures, and to help decide when other procedures should be tried.

Although many questions about self-control remain to be resolved, its accomplishments have already been impressive. The available techniques provide clients with a number of means so that they can implement treatment for themselves. Although techniques for controlling one's own behavior have been advocated throughout the history of psychotherapy, only recently have such techniques been evaluated experimentally to establish their effectiveness. The results have demonstrated that for many applications, various procedures can help people gain control over their own behavior.

The key challenges of treatment, whether behavioral or other forms, is ensuring they are effective and can be applied. Applying treatments means that clients and consumers of treatment (e.g., parents, teachers, individuals, couples, families) will seek, carry out, and adhere to the treatment methods. Involving clients in treatment has many benefits related to preferences for, belief in, and adherence to treatment. Interventions might be considered in a continuum of the extent to which the individual has input into treatment, including selection and implementation of the procedures. There are no well-established or well-studied guidelines regarding what is the right mix of external control (parents, therapists) and self-control to optimize the effectiveness of treatment. For adults interested in changing a particular problem behavior or developing more positive prosocial behaviors, self-control procedures (e.g., self-help manuals) may provide an initial avenue to pursue to see if the desired benefits can be achieved. Subsequent treatment might be sought as needed, in which there is more external guidance and oversight of the procedures.

SUMMARY AND CONCLUSIONS

Self-control refers to the behaviors that an individual deliberately undertakes to achieve self-selected outcomes. Self-control procedures in behavior modification refer primarily to techniques in which the client plays an active part and occasionally the sole part in administering the behavior-change intervention. Self-control is a matter of degree. Interventions can be managed and controlled entirely by external agents (e.g., parents, teachers, therapists) or by the client's themselves with little or no input from an external agent. Self-control techniques are efforts to optimize the involvement and control given to the client over the administration of the intervention.

Several self-control techniques were discussed. Self-assessment to obtain information that might prompt seeking treatment was mentioned. Among assessment procedures, self-monitoring has been used as an intervention. Self-monitoring requires that individuals keep a careful record of the target response. Merely observing one's own behavior often leads to a systematic change. Stimulus control allows individuals to control their own behavior by altering environmental and situational events that serve as cues for behavior. Self-reinforcement and self-punishment require that individuals apply certain events to themselves after a specific behavior has occurred. The crucial aspect of self-reinforcement or self-punishment is the freedom to partake of the reinforcer or to not apply the punishing event.

Alternate response training requires that a client engage in a response that interferes with or replaces the response that the client wishes to control. Biofeedback procedures provide information to clients about their physiological processes. Ideally, clients can learn to control the bodily processes related to the problem for which they sought change. Self-help resources comprise a variety of techniques that have in common the manner in which they are presented to clients. Clients receive written material in brochure or book form (self-help manuals) or obtain similar materials on the Internet. The materials convey methods to conduct on oneself to ameliorate the problem with little or no help or contact with a therapist or consultant. In many of the self-control techniques, some preliminary training may be required to convey both the principles behind a technique and the requirements for effective application. Once the basic principle is understood and the initial training has been completed, the client can implement the treatment intervention and determine the range of behaviors or situations to which it will be applied.

Self-control techniques extend treatment to the public in ways that cannot be readily accomplished with traditional therapist-administered treatment. The costs of treatment are minimal, as in the case of self-help manuals. Contact with a therapist, if any, is brief as well. In addition, clients often prefer to have a role in their own treatment; self-control techniques foster direct involvement and application of treatment that may increase adherence to the procedures, as well as their effectiveness. There are no well-researched guidelines regarding when and how to use self-control techniques. The challenge is to balance two major considerations, namely, ensuring that the conditions for effective application are invoked and involving the client to the extent possible in developing and administering the program. Self-control techniques in this chapter and some of the techniques discussed in the prior chapter (contingency contracts, peer-based administration of contingencies) provide different ways of involving clients in their own treatments and to do so in ways that will not sacrifice program effectiveness.

KEY TERMS

Alternate response training

Biofeedback

Self-control

Self-help manuals (or bibliotherapy)

Self-monitoring

Self-reinforcement

Stimulus control

APPLYING PRINCIPLES AND TECHNIQUES
TO EVERYDAY LIFE

1. Describe the stimulus control program for treating insomnia. How might a stimulus control program like this be extended to help someone who cannot study and concentrate in their college dormitory room? Describe your recommendations to the individual to foster study behavior.

2. Design a self-reinforcement program to change a behavior in yourself? What is the behavior? What are the reinforcers? How and when will they be administered? Can you think of anything to add to the program so you are just not giving yourself the reinforcers noncontingently all of the time?

3. Self-help programs are usually more effective when there is some involvement of a therapist or some consultant, even if that involvement is minimal. What might be the reasons for this?

4. What are some advantages and disadvantages of self-administered programs?

FOR FURTHER READING

Bensen, M.D., & Klipper, M.Z. (1990). *The relaxation response.* New York: Avon.

Cone, J.D. (Ed.). (1999). Special section: Clinical assessment applications of self-monitoring. *Psychological Assessment, 11,* 411–497.

Karoly, P., & Kanfer, F.H. (Eds.). (1982). *Self management and behavior change: From theory to practice.* New York: Pergamon Press.

Pardeck, J.T. (1993). *Using bibliotherapy in clinical practice.* Westport, CT: Greenwood.

Schwartz, M.S., & Andrasik, F. (1998). *Biofeedback: A practitioner's guide.* New York: Guilford.

Watson, D.L., & Tharp, R.G. (1992). *Self-directed behavior: Self-modification for personal adjustment* (6th ed.). Pacific Grove, CA: Brooks/Cole.

NOTES

1. The terms self-reinforcement and self-punishment are commonly used, even though they are rather odd. *Reinforcement* refers to consequences contingent on behavior that increase the likelihood of the behavior in the future. Only behaviors are reinforced or punished. Strictly speaking, one cannot reinforce (or punish) a self, whatever that would mean.

2. Hemophilia is an inherited disorder of blood coagulation in which there is frequent and difficult-to-control bleeding.

3. These percentages refer to prevalence rates, that is, the proportion of individuals with a current disorder when sampled at a given point in time. Lifetime rates are much higher. For example, more than 32% of adults can be expected to experience a psychiatric disorder over the course of their lives (Robins & Regier, 1991).

CHAPTER 11

Cognitively Based Treatment

P rior chapters have emphasized behavioral procedures derived from operant conditioning research. These techniques such as reinforcement, punishment, extinction, and the many variations already discussed are the most commonly used behavioral interventions in applied settings such as the home, schools, hospitals, business and industry, and the community at large. Techniques derived from operant conditioning focus primarily on overt behavior (what the individual does) and environmental events (antecedents, consequences) that can influence that behavior.

Within behavioral approaches, another set of treatments focus primarily on cognitive process, that is, perceptions, self-statements, attributions, expectations, beliefs, and images. *Cognitively based techniques* are a family of procedures that adhere to the general notion that behavior change can be achieved by altering cognitive processes. The assumptions underlying cognitively based techniques are that maladaptive cognitive processes lead to maladaptive behaviors and that changing these processes can lead to behavior change. The purpose of this chapter is to describe cognitively based therapy, illustrate current treatments especially as they are used in applied settings, and convey the relation of cognitively based and behaviorally based treatments.[1]

Cognitive process refers to an array of mental events (thoughts, perceptions, beliefs, expectations, attributions). From our own everyday experience, it is clear that such events greatly influence us. How the environment is perceived can greatly influence the impact of environmental events. For example, two people riding a roller coaster may react quite differently, in part because of the different ways in which they *perceive* the experience. For both people, the physical characteristics of the ride itself—the "environmental factors"—are essentially the same. Yet one of them may *believe* that the ride is dangerous and life threatening, and may feel extremely anxious, whereas the other may believe that the ride is safe and may feel excited and exhilarated. During the ride itself, the former may *say to himself or herself* (self-statements) that something horrible might happen any minute, whereas the latter may say to himself or herself that the ride is wonderful and exciting. The ride can have a different impact on the two persons in part because of the differences in their perceptions, beliefs, and self-statements.

Differences in perceptions are not to be regarded lightly. The arousal, stress, anxiety, dread, and other biological and psychological signs of these two people may be dramatically different. Moreover, the events (roller coaster ride and the associated cues) are not just different "in their minds." Their perceptions can have a direct impact on the safety of the experience. The person who views the experience as entirely risk free might become careless and not take advisable safety precautions. This might increase the risk of injury. The person who views the experience as dangerous might consume alcohol or tranquilizers and thus be unresponsive if an untoward eventuality occurred. Perceptions are significant not only in their own right but also through their influence on behavior.[2]

The interrelationships among cognitive processes, environmental events, and behavior are perhaps more clearly conveyed in the context of social behavior. For example, a person who believes that other people are very friendly may initiate social responses (greetings, conversations) with acquaintances and strangers. The belief (cognitive process) leads to greeting and chatting with others (behavior), which in turn generate environmental consequences (attention, praise, and other sources of reinforcement from others). These consequences are likely to affect the person's perceptions and behaviors in the future. Indeed, there is a rather large body of psychological research showing that if a person is led to believe another person has a particular characteristic (e.g., past serious mental illness, great academic skill, physical handicap), he or she perceives the actions of that person differently from someone without that characteristic and acts differently. Clearly, cognitive process (e.g., perceptions, expectations) and environmental events (e.g., behavior of others) mutually influence each other.

BACKGROUND

Historical Overview

As highlighted in Chapter 1, learning research in psychology played a central role in the development of behavior modification. Much of that research focused stimulus-response learning, where stimuli referred to environmental events outside of the individual and responses referred to what the organism (e.g., laboratory animal) actually did in the experiment. That is, in an S-R view, learning takes place by pairing stimuli (e.g., classical conditioning) or various behaviors and consequences (e.g., operant conditioning). S-R research grew out of concern of making psychology a science without relying on seemingly fuzzy mental processes that could not be objectively measured. Moreover, some researchers considered knowledge of stimuli and responses sufficient to give an account of or explain behavior. This view is still evident in many types of research.

While basic human and animal laboratory research demonstrated the importance of S-R learning, researchers became interested in processes within the organism that might be important to understand to explain learning. Other positions emerged that were referred to as S-O-R learning. To the equation of stimulus and response, the O for organism was added. That is, one needs to understand *processes within the organism* to explain how learning takes place. S-O-R researchers were no less scientific or interested in objective methods than researchers who looked only at environmental influences, but rather believed one could explain learning better by considering internal processes.

Two immediate questions emerge: (1) Why does one need to consider internal processes within the organism to explain learning, and (2) what are these processes? The first question was stimulated by many findings in basic animal research. Much of the research showed that an animal could be trained to go to one arm of a maze by directly reinforcing the desired behavior, that is, turning to the right or left side followed by food reinforcement. However, direct connections between stimulus events and behavior (S-R) could not easily explain all of the findings. For example, animals learned a great deal merely by exposure to the maze in advance of direct training. That is, learning which arm of the maze to enter could be greatly improved and sped along if the animal were allowed to explore the maze in advance. In other words, to many theorists learning could not be explained by simple S-R interpretations, that is, reinforcing specific behavior. The animal somehow coded facets of the environment in a way—a sort of cognitive map—that was later drawn on when the learning trials (reinforcing the response of turning down one arm or side of the maze rather than another) (Tolman, 1948). Needless to say, this one illustration does not do justice to a rather large animal research literature that drew on S-O-R theories, but it does illustrate one line of work leading basic researchers to focus on processes within the individual organism.

The second question is raised, namely, what cognitive processes underlie some forms of learning? Over the years, many cognitive concepts have been proposed and evaluated in the context of human and animal learning, child development, and interpersonal influences (e.g., stereotypes, perception of other people more generally). There are many such processes, and they vary in levels of abstraction. Among the terms that cognitive processes encompass are strategies, plans, and schemes. These are overarching concepts that extend beyond specific stimulus-response relations—they are more general and more pervasive in their influence.

Consider language and its development as a useful context in which to underscore the importance of broader learning than simple stimulus-response connections. In learning language, one does not merely acquire connections between words and meaning or between grammar rules in specific situations. Rather quickly, broader strategies are learned, and one can generate novel applications of what has been learned that cannot be easily explained by simple conditioning processes.[3] Hence one can see that rules, structure, and meaning have been learned as well. These rules, structure, and meanings are included among cognitive process.

Mentioned in prior chapters were three types of learning: classical conditioning, operant conditioning, and observational learning (modeling). The role of cognitive processes in each type of learning has been an active topic of theory and research. Pavlov, who elaborated classical conditioning—clearly an S-R type of learning—also was concerned with how language somehow allowed humans to acquire learning without direct contact through stimuli and responses (Pavlov, 1903). This previewed theory development about mental processes and their roles in learning. More than classical conditioning, observational modeling is often viewed as conveying the importance of cognition in learning. As noted previously, one observes without necessarily performing any behaviors and can acquire large units of behavior. Cognitive processes are assumed to explain this, that is, acquisition of broad strategies and coding through images and self-statements regarding what has been observed.

From the early 1900s through the present, there has been an ongoing debate about how learning takes place and the role of processes such as cognition in learning. Of course, there is not merely one type of learning, and so there is no single answer. Cognitive psychology as an area of basic research focuses on perception, learning, and memory in human and animals, the ways in which such processes operate, and the neurological structures and functions that provide the underpinnings of such processes.

Cognitive Processes in Behavior Modification

Interest in cognitive processes as behavior-change procedures can be traced to many additional influences than those mentioned previously. Two such influences are highlighted here. First and most influential were the efforts to extend findings from basic animal learning research to psychotherapy. Examples were mentioned previously such as the work of Watson and Rayner (1920) and Little Albert as an extension of classical conditioning. Extensions that focused on cognitive processes were made as well. Among the extensions were those based on private events such as imagery and self-statements (e.g., Salter, 1949; Wolpe, 1958; Lazarus & Abramovitz, 1962), as elaborated later in the chapter. Efforts to use imagery and self-statements as a way of changing behavior were clear therapeutic applications of cognitive processes. Many of these remain as central to behavior therapy.

Another influence on development of cognitively based treatment pertains to the nature of many clinical problems. Cognitive processes have been shown to relate to or form a central part of a number of clinical disorders, including depression, schizophrenia, anxiety, and others (Stein & Young, 1992). Perhaps more than another disorder, cognitive processes involved in depression have received the greatest attention. Depression is a psychiatric disorder characterized by sadness, lack of interest in activities, and often other symptoms such as disturbances of sleep and eating. Several cognitive processes are associated with depression. Depressed individuals tend to view themselves as failures, see their world as filled with loss, feel pessimistic and hopeless about the future, view themselves negatively, and attribute stressful events and negative occurrences to their own actions (see Clark, Beck, & Alford, 1999). These beliefs are related to the various symptoms of depression, as well as to reduced interactions with others and a lack of interest in activities. Suicidal thoughts or attempts, which are often associated with depression, have been identified with even more specific beliefs. In both children and adults the belief that the future is hopeless, more than other characteristics of depression (e.g., sadness) and the severity of depression, is related to suicide ideation, attempt, and completion (Beck, Kovacs, & Weissman, 1975; Kazdin, French, Unis, Esveldt-Dawson, & Sherick, 1983). Many forms of psychotherapy and medication are available for depressed people. One effective treatment, referred to as *cognitive therapy*, focuses directly on altering the belief system of depressed people (Clark et al., 1999).

Many other clinical problems have important cognitive features that contribute to maladaptive behavior. For example, aggressive children appear to have a predisposition to perceive their interpersonal environment in ways that help promote their aggressive reactions. Such children often perceive ambiguous social behaviors in which the intent of others is not as clear as if they were hostile acts (Dodge & Schwartz, 1997). For example, if an aggressive child or adolescent is accidentally and innocently bumped in the hall while walking to class, he is more likely than a nonaggressive child to perceive this as an act of aggression. Understandably, when such situations are perceived as hostile, the child is more likely to respond aggressively. A number of other cognitive processes have been shown to relate to aggressive behavior, as illustrated in the discussion of specific techniques later in the chapter.

There are many cognitively based treatment techniques. They are distinguished by adherence to one or both of these propositions: (1) maladaptive, distorted, or deficient cognitions underlie the clinical problem that is to be treated; and (2) cognitive processes are central to therapeutic change independently of the underpinnings of the clinical problem. Most cognitively based techniques are applied in the context of psychotherapy sessions in which children, adolescents, or adults are seen individually or in a group by professional therapists on an outpatient basis. However, this chapter will highlight applications of treatment in everyday, applied settings and in situations in which problem behaviors have emerged or are evident.

There is no standard way of classifying the many different cognitively based treatments. To facilitate organization of the material, I have grouped several treatments into two broad categories: (1) treatment of distorted or deficient processes and (2) imagery-based treatments. Examples of techniques within these categories are highlighted to convey key features of cognitively based therapy.

TREATMENT OF DISTORTED OR DEFICIENT THOUGHT PROCESSES

The prototype of a cognitively based treatment is a focus on thought processes that are considered to guide behavior. These processes include perceptions, assumptions, beliefs, attributions, and expectations. These thought processes often reflect implicit assumptions about oneself, one's behavior, and the actions of other people. The task of therapy is to identify and challenge these processes and to substitute more adaptive thoughts in their place. Consider exemplars of this type of therapy.

Rational-Emotive Psychotherapy

Rational-emotive therapy, developed by Albert Ellis, is based on the view that psychological problems arise from faulty or irrational thought patterns (Ellis, 1979, 1999). These patterns are evident in implicit verbalizations that people make, that is, things people say to themselves. These verbalizations arise from assumptions that we make about the world and the events that happen to us. More specifically, some event occurs in our lives and in response to that, we have a series of thoughts. These thoughts or implicit self-statements, lead to a series of emotions (e.g., disappointment, anger, disgust, negative views about oneself) and behaviors (e.g., vengeful acts, suicide attempt). For example, a person might be laid off from a job. Any number of implicit verbalizations may follow this event. The person may say that these are difficult economic times, that things are "tough," and so on. Alternatively, the person may say that this is not really a layoff but a vendetta from the boss who never liked him or her or a reflection of how he or she cannot do anything right. The latter set of implicit verbalizations may lead or contribute to vengeful behavior such as getting back at the company, the boss, and co-workers or depression. In everyday life, the experience of stress and other events are fostered or fueled by the verbalizations we make to ourselves (e.g., we are "no good," "Everything happens to me," "Why can't I ever get a break?"). The purpose of rational-emotive therapy is to examine the implicit self-verbalizations that people make, to challenge them and point to their irrationality, and most importantly, to substitute more adaptive self-verbalizations.

Several irrational beliefs are common to our culture and contribute to emotional and behavioral problems. Examples of common beliefs are as follows:

- It is necessary for an adult to be loved or approved of by virtually every other important person in his or her life.
- An adult must be totally competent, adequate, and efficient to be worthwhile.
- Life is miserable and disastrous when events are not turning out the way one would like.
- Human unhappiness depends on external forces beyond an individual's control.

These beliefs, and others like them, lead to emotions and behaviors that are maladaptive. Therapy challenges these beliefs, substitutes other types of self-statements, and fosters practice of appropriate self-statements in everyday life. As an example, rational-emotive therapy was used with a 17-year-old adolescent girl who chronically engaged in pulling her own hair (referred to as trichotillomania) (Bernard, Kratochwill, & Keefauver, 1983). The behavior had been ongoing since the age of 12 and had led to her wearing a wig to cover bald spots. Initial evaluation revealed that the behavior was not a problem at school but was so at home when she was doing schoolwork alone. At these times, she felt worried, anxious, and depressed. The authors hypothesized that hair pulling was a reaction to stress that itself could be traced to irrational cognitions. Assessment revealed that the girl engaged in various irrational cognitive thought processes (e.g., that she was worthless unless she was competent in school, that she must be approved of by her father for her work, that it was awful when performance at school did not meet her expectations). Rational-emotive therapy was used to dispute the thought processes and to try alternative thought processes instead. The client recorded hair pulling at home (numbers of hairs pulled within a given period) while studying. After baseline assessment, therapy was conducted weekly for 12 weeks.

Figure 11-1 presents the amount of hair pulling on a daily basis. After baseline (A phase), rational-emotive therapy sessions were conducted (B phases) and led to reductions in hair pulling. A suspension of the procedure (return to baseline during week 6) and a return to rational-emotive therapy suggested that the treatment was associated with reductions in behavior. However, during weeks 7 and 8, the behavior still was not eliminated. Another intervention (self-instruction training) was added. This intervention (C) was used with rational-emotive therapy and

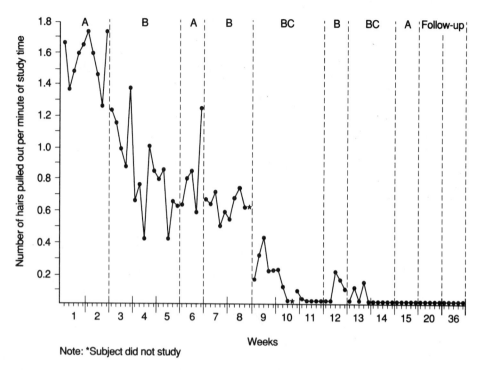

FIGURE 11-1 Number of hairs pulled per minute of study time over baseline (A), treatment (B, BC), and follow-up phases. During B phases, rational-emotive therapy was used. To increase the impact of treatment, self-instruction training (referred to as C in the figure) was added.

(Source: Bernard, Kratochwill, & Keefauver, 1983)

focused on having the client instruct herself to cope with anxiety, focus attention on her work, and provide self-praise for completed work and not engaging in hair pulling. The results indicated that hair pulling was substantially reduced. During session 15, all treatments were ended. Follow-up assessment several weeks later indicated that the behavior had not returned.

Rational-emotive psychotherapy has been applied to a number of clinical problems such as anxiety disorders, depression, alcohol abuse, anger control, and others (Ellis & Dryden, 1998; Lyons & Woods, 1991). These applications are provided primarily in the context of individual psychotherapy. Work in applied settings is less frequent, although as the above example illustrates, treatment can be extended to everyday situations. Rational-emotive therapy and many other treatments discussed in this chapter rely on what individuals say to themselves. The structure and content of these statements can be examined and challenged in the context of treatment sessions. Yet application of the treatment (e.g., substituting more adaptive self-statements) can be carried out in everyday life.

Table 11-1   The Negative Cognitive Triad Associated With Depression

Negative Cognitions Toward . . .	Examples of underlying beliefs and self-statements
Oneself	I am worthless. I can't do anything right. I will never overcome my problems.
The World	The world is a bad place. All sorts of negative things happen.
The Future	Things will not work out in the future for me. The future is grim.

Cognitive Therapy for Depression

One of the most well studied cognitively based treatments is cognitive therapy for depression developed by Aaron Beck .[4] Since the 1960s when the treatment was first developed (Beck, 1967), the theory and research have developed considerably. Many different cognitive processes are considered to underlie depression. These concepts pertain to how individuals who are depressed or who have a predilection toward depression perceive the world, process information, and ascribe meaning to key events they experience (Clark et al., 1999).

Among the concepts is a pervasive negative view of the world that depressed individuals often have. This is reflected in many ways, but three have been especially central to the theory. Three concepts, referred to as the *negative cognitive triad,* consist of negative thoughts toward oneself, the world, and the future. Other terms are sometimes used to capture these, including low self-esteem, pessimism, and hopelessness, respectively. Table 11-1 provides sample statements that reflect the negative triad. Depressed individuals are likely to see the world and to imbue meaning based on these statements. The cognitive processes are pervasive and automatic. That is, they are part of the information-processing structures through which the world is seen. Consequently, it is difficult for any new information or a positive dose of reality to change them. For example, success on an examination or at work will not lead depressed individuals to view themselves positively. Rather, they are likely to discount the event as chance or unrelated to any talent or skill they might have. Over several years of research, a broad range of cognitive processes has been identified, including a tendency to see oneself as helpless and to attribute good events or outcomes to external events (e.g., circumstances outside of the individual's control or to others) and negative events and outcomes to oneself.

Among the key tenets is that negative cognitions critically influence and promote depression and lead to the pervasive behavioral, affective (mood-related), and motivational symptoms (e.g., sad affect, loss of interest in activities). That is, cognitions are not viewed as *the* cause of a depression. Rather, multiple influences (e.g., biological, familial, or environmental stressors). Yet negative cognitive processes contribute to the development of and vulnerability to depression (Clark et al., 1999).

Cognitive therapy focuses on beliefs and negative cognitive processes that promote depression (Beck, Rush, Shaw, & Emery, 1979). Sessions are conducted individually. Most studies have focused on depressed adults although some extensions have applied treatment to children and adolescents. Among the ingredients of treatment are efforts to identify maladaptive cognitive processes. Within the sessions and outside of them as "homework" assignments, the client is encouraged to identify negative thoughts and to record alternative explanations that might be generated in their place. During the treatment sessions, the client is taught to evaluate beliefs and their roles in depression. The client is encouraged to consider key beliefs as hypotheses to be tested, rather than to be taken as givens or necessarily true. The therapist and client together examine these beliefs and point to disconfirming evidence or challenges. For example, extensive self-criticism may be identified as a problem. The therapist will challenge that the individual is responsible for a particular event or that the event reflects on the individual's self-worth. Alternative interpretations are raised, such as the likelihood that the individual played a significant role in the positive outcome.

Although the therapist challenges fundamental negative cognitions, treatment is not merely an attempt to talk the client out of his or her depression. The client is asked to act in new ways outside of the session and to use this information to challenge various cognitive attributions. Behavioral tasks and assignments outside of the treatment session help disconfirm the negative cognitive beliefs. For example, a client who says he or she cannot do something or will be no good at an activity, some hobby, or sport will be given an assignment to engage in the activity. The experience will help the client identify the negative cognition that held him or her back and disconfirm the particular cognition ("I can't do anything," or "It's useless to try anything new."). In other words, assignments to behave in particular ways and to engage in goal-directed activities are central to therapy. The activities are viewed as a way to change cognitions.

As an illustration, cognitive therapy was used to alter the depressive symptoms and delusions of a 31-year-old man who lived at home (Chadwick & Trower, 1996). The client was diagnosed as meeting criteria for schizophrenia, a mental illness that involves many symptoms, including delusions (erroneous beliefs that involve misinterpretations and perceptions of experience [e.g., beliefs that all people in the crowd are staring at or thinking about you or are controlling your mind]) and hallucinations (distorted sensory experiences such as sights and sounds—hearing voices that direct one to engage in actions). Many other symptoms also reflect disorganized thoughts, speech, and behavior (e.g., difficulty in performing daily functioning, social behavior). In this case, the prominent symptoms were paranoid delusions, a belief that people in everyday life were punishing him. He believed others could read this thoughts. Another paranoid delusion was that God was punishing him for blasphemy and for having broken a promise to attend church. In addition, the client had a very negative evaluation of himself as part of a set of depressive symptoms. He felt he was a totally bad and perverted person. The delusions and negative evaluations were major sources of stress.

Individual cognitive therapy sessions were provided in which the key beliefs (e.g., "I am a bad person.") were challenged in the treatment. The lack of evidence for the beliefs was discussed, the inconsistent features of the beliefs were noted, and alternative interpretations were provided. The client was encouraged to think differently about experiences in reality and how they supported nonparanoid interpretations. Treatment was carried out for several weeks and measures were made of the degree of conviction he showed for three irrational beliefs, namely, that he was a bad person, others were reading his mind and conspiring against him, and God was punishing him. The beliefs were addressed one at a time in therapy and evaluated in a multiple-baseline design. Figure 11-2 shows changes in the degree of conviction was altered when the beliefs were systematically challenged. After treatment ended, additional meetings were held with the client to assess whether the changes were maintained. Over the course of these contacts 1, 3, and 6 months later, the treatment gains were maintained. Over baseline and the course of treatment and follow-up, depression was also assessed using a standard measure of depression (Beck Depression Inventory). At the beginning of treatment, the client met criteria for moderate clinical depression. By the follow-up, depression decreased and fell in the range of "no depression."

The above case is useful in showing the effects of treatment. However, it is important to note that the bulk of the evidence has focused on depression and includes a large number of well-controlled group studies (Hollon & Beck, 1994). In light of this rather extensive evidence, cognitive therapy is regarded as an effective treatment for depression. Some other forms of psychological treatment and various medications also have been effective for the treatment of depression. There are many interesting questions that remain to be addressed, such as the components of cognitive therapy that lead to change and the individuals for whom change is most likely to occur. Also, there is agreement that the treatment is effective, but the reasons why it works have not been clearly established. Nevertheless, the treatment is widely recognized to be a viable treatment for clinical depression.

Problem-Solving Skills Training

Cognitively based treatment has been applied extensively to children and adolescents in programs that develop interpersonal problem-solving skills (Durlak, Fuhrman, & Lampman, 1991; Kendall & Braswell, 1993; Shure, 1997). The programs are based on evidence that children and adolescents with adjustment problems have deficits in various cognitive processes that underlie social behavior. Specific problem-solving skills have been well studied (Table 11-2). Deficits in these skills are evident among maladjusted children. These skills are considered the basis for social behaviors that individuals perform in everyday situations. For example, children with adjustment problems often have difficulty in identifying alternative solutions to interpersonal problems (e.g., resolving an argument), the consequences of their behaviors (e.g., the reactions of others), and the steps that need to be taken to achieve a goal (e.g., how to make friends). These and related skills can be developed by training the children to use problem-solving steps and self-statements. Training helps the children to think about the particular task, problem, or situation, the behaviors that need to be

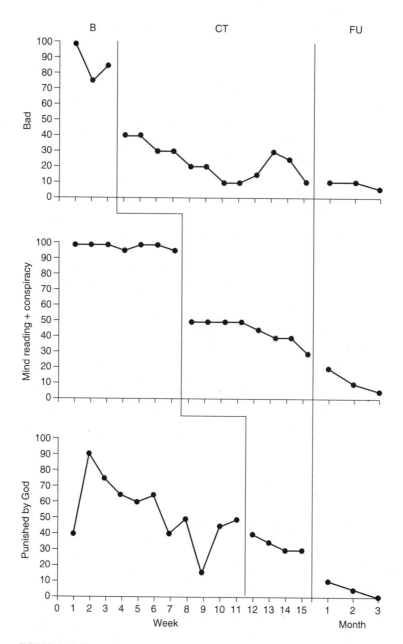

FIGURE 11-2 The client's scores on a measure of degree of conviction of each of three irrational beliefs during baseline (B), cognitive therapy (CT), and follow-up (FU). The intervention was introduced across beliefs in a multiple-baseline fashion. The follow-up included three meetings at 1-, 3-, and 6-month intervals.

(Source: Chadwick & Trower, 1996)

Table 11-2 Problem-Solving Skills That Relate to Adjustment

1. *Alternative solution thinking*—the ability to generate different options (solutions) that can solve problems in interpersonal situations.
2. *Means-end thinking*—awareness of the intermediate steps required to achieve a particular goal.
3. *Consequential thinking*—the ability to identify what might happen as a direct result of acting in a particular way or choosing a particular solution.
4. *Casual thinking*—the ability to relate one event to another over time and to understand why one event led to a particular action of other persons.
5. *Sensitivity to interpersonal problems*—the ability to perceive a problem when it exists and to identify the interpersonal aspects of the confrontation that may emerge.

(Source: Adapted from Spivack, Platt, & Shure, 1976).

performed, and the alternative courses of action that are available, and then selection of a particular solution. The children ask specific questions or make specific self-statements that help themselves develop problem-solving skills (e.g., "What am I supposed to do? What is my plan? How do I do it?"). The questions serve as cues to provide possible solutions, to consider their consequences, and so on. Children are trained to answer these questions in the context of interpersonal situations in which their behavior is problematic and to identify and carry out socially appropriate solutions to problems. The treatment is usually conducted in therapy sessions but children and their parents apply the steps to situations at home in everyday life.

Several studies have shown that problem-solving skills training can decrease disruptive and impulsive behavior and increase peer popularity among children and adolescents (Kazdin, 1996c; Kendall & Braswell, 1993; Spivack & Shure, 1982). In the most well-developed programs of research, problem-solving skills training has been studied for a period spanning 20 years (Shure, 1997, 1999). In one of the reports, training was provided in the classrooms of economically disadvantaged elementary school children. The effects of problem-solving skills training were demonstrated by decreases in disruptive student behavior and increases in positive, prosocial behavior, compared with youths who did not receive the training. Although the effects were evident when training was conducted for one year (kindergarten), the impact was greater when training was continued for two years (kindergarten and first grade). Either way, the benefits of the intervention were still evident at least up to two years after the program ended. The program is noteworthy because it can be implemented on a large scale in the schools and used to improve outcomes of children who are at high risk for academic, social, emotional, and behavioral problems.

Problem-solving skills training has been used extensively in the context of treatment with children and adolescents who show disruptive, aggressive, and delinquent behavior. The benefits have been evident in behavior changes at home, at school, and in the community, and these gains are evident up to one year later (see Durlak et al., 1991; Kendall & Braswell, 1993). For example, in one project, problem-solving skills training was used with children (ages 7 to 13) referred for outpatient treatment because of their severely aggressive and antisocial behavior (e.g., fighting at school, stealing, lying, truancy, cruelty to animals) (Kazdin, Siegel, & Bass, 1992). Children were seen individually on a weekly basis and trained to engage in problem-solving steps in a variety of interpersonal situations such as interactions with parents, teachers, peers, and siblings. Parents were also involved in treatment by learning the problem-solving skills and practicing their application to situations at home and at school. Training children in problem-solving skills led to reductions in aggressive and antisocial behavior at home, at school, and in the community; the effects were maintained up to one year after treatment.

Problem-solving skills training has been applied to many different populations and clinical problems. For example, the approach has been effectively applied with mothers who neglect their children. Parental neglect refers to a chronic failure of parents to meet their children's needs with regard to physical safety, health, nutrition, and emotional development. For legal purposes, neglect is often grouped with physical abuse and sexual abuse; occasionally emotional abuse is included as well. These all reflect extreme, harmful, and maladaptive child-rearing practices. Child neglect is the most prevalent (approximately 30 of 1000 children in the United States); among all reported maltreatment of children, 70% of these are based on neglect (Wolfe, 1999). Why parents neglect their children is no doubt the result of many influences. Among the influences are deficits in judgment and capacity to anticipate the needs of their children and the consequences of their neglect. In this program, problem-solving skills training was applied to mothers whose neglect was brought before the courts (Dawson, deArmas, McGrath, & Kelly, 1986). The project focused on three mothers (ages 20 to 27) who had been identified by child-protective services as neglectful and referred for treatment. Several vignettes related to the care of children were constructed based on past reports and the mothers' descriptions of situations in which they failed to meet their children's needs. Each of the vignettes was read aloud to the parent, who was asked to engage in problem solving to define the problem, consider possible solutions, describe the consequences and obstacles of each solution, and choose the best solution. Here is a sample vignette:

> You and your mother have an argument on the phone. She tells you that you can just forget about bringing your children over tonight for her to babysit while you go out with your boyfriend (husband). It is 5 PM, and you do not have any money to hire a babysitter. The story ends with you and your boyfriend (husband) going out for the evening. (Dawson et al., 1986, p. 213)

During baseline, problem situations were presented to see how each mother managed the care of her children, whether she identified a plan to solve the problem, selected various means or steps toward the goal, and identified obstacles that would interfere with completing appropriate behaviors. The problem-solving skills training approach was then taught individually to each mother, using modeling, shaping, and feedback. The effects of training were evaluated in a multiple-baseline design.

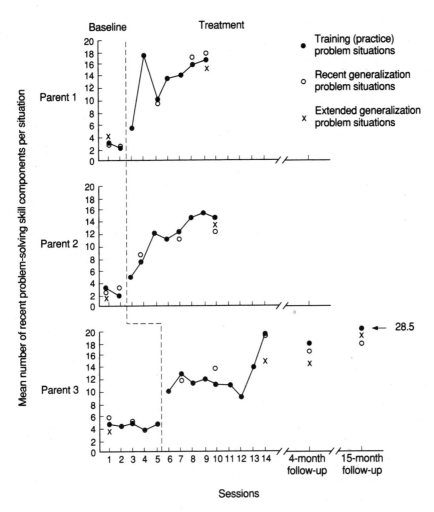

FIGURE 11-3 Mean (average) number of problem-solving skill elements included in responses to problem situations for each parent.

(Source: Dawson, de Armas, McGrath, & Kelly, 1986)

As shown in Figure 11-3, each mother's solutions to the problems (vignettes) included more of the problem-solving skills components than did her baseline performance. Effectiveness ratings were also completed by social workers associated with each case to assess the extent to which the mother improved in her child-rearing practices, as reflected in such activities as providing food, clothing, and child care and solving child-related problems in the home. Effectiveness ratings increased after treatment for each of the mothers. At follow-up 15 months later, only one of the mothers was available for reassessment on the vignettes. She continued to show high levels of problem-solving skills. The other two mothers, who had moved, had had full custody of their children restored by the child welfare department, with no further reports of neglect.

Stress Inoculation Training

Stress inoculation training is designed to help individuals cope with stressful events such as situations in which anxiety, anger, or pain arise (Meichenbaum, 1985). The approach teaches a variety of cognitive and self-control skills to reduce the impact of these events. The medical notion of "inoculation" is used to convey the idea that clients are exposed to small or manageable doses of the stressful event that do not overwhelm their defenses (Novaco, 1979). Through this exposure, the clients build a capacity to cope with the events and new events that otherwise might induce high levels of stress.

Treatment helps clients anticipate and identify stressful events and the cognitions that arise when clients are confronted with these events; evaluate the events differently by applying various coping strategies, including relaxation, imagery, and adaptive self-statements; and practice the coping skills in both treatment sessions and everyday life. Training helps clients replace maladaptive cognitive appraisals (interpretations) of the events with positive evaluations and self-statements. To accomplish this, self-control and cognitive components are included in treatment.

Because of the relevance of stress to several areas of life and the importance of coping skills, stress inoculation has been applied to a broad range of problems, such as controlling anger among hospitalized patients or delinquents and reducing stress among persons whose jobs expose them to frequent crises (e.g., law enforcement officers, probation counselors). Several applications have used stress inoculation training to help individuals cope with stressful medical procedures. For example, the technique has been used effectively for patients (ages 14 to 62) who were undergoing elective surgery (Wells, Howard, Nowlin, & Vargas, 1986). The anxiety and pain associated with surgery make the notion of inoculation against stress particularly relevant. In this project, patients were assigned either to the stress inoculation or to a control condition that was the standard hospital preparation for surgery. Stress inoculation patients were instructed about the stress associated with surgery and taught to identify cognitive and physical cues associated with or leading to stress (e.g., increased heart rate, negative self-statements). They were also instructed in the use of relaxation, deep breathing, pleasant imagery, and coping and positive self-statements. Training was completed before surgery. Assessment revealed that before and after training, but before surgery, the anxiety of the patients in the stress inoculation training group decreased. In contrast, the anxiety of the patients in the control group increased. After surgery, the patients who had received stress inoculation reported less anxiety during their recovery in the hospital and lower pain intensity than did the patients in the control group. The patients who had received stress inoculation training also were rated by nurses as having adjusted better to their hospitalization. Thus the study demonstrated that stress inoculation reduced both preoperative and postoperative distress.

Stress inoculation training has also been applied to children undergoing stressful medical procedures. One program focused on children with leukemia who were being given a special medical test (bone marrow aspiration) to identify whether cancer cells were present (Jay, Elliot, Katz, & Siegel, 1987). The medical test requires the injection of a needle through bone and the suction of bone marrow; this is both stressful and painful, despite the use of local anesthetics. Distress, reports of pain, and blood pressure were significantly lower for the children who received stress inoculation training than for the children who received mild tranquilizers.

Special populations have also received stress inoculation training to help them cope with the complications of physical disease. For example, one program focused on adults who suffered from multiple sclerosis, a physical disease of the central nervous system (Foley, Bedell, LaRocca, Scheinberg, & Reznikoff, 1987). The physical symptoms of this disease include impairment of sensory, motor, visual, bladder, and other functions. Many patients are restricted to wheelchairs or the use of crutches. Apart from the physical symptoms of multiple sclerosis, the psychological complications often include anxiety, depression, poor body image, and low self-esteem. Stress inoculation training was used to increase coping skills and to reduce psychological symptoms. Patients were randomly assigned to stress inoculation training or to routine care, which included various forms of psychotherapy and medication. The stress inoculation patients were trained in muscle relaxation; self-monitoring of stressors, thoughts, feelings, and behavior; the use of imagery and reinterpretation or cognitive reappraisals of the situation; and role-play of these coping strategies. Stress inoculation training led to reductions in anxiety and depression and to improved ability to cope with stressors. These effects were maintained at a six-month follow-up assessment. The patients who had been given routine care did not improve on these measures and hence were eventually given stress inoculation training.

The examples illustrate the key foci of stress inoculation training, namely, identifying the stressor and using strategies to minimize its impact. Self-statements to cope and to invoke self-control strategies such as relaxation are usually part of the procedures. Stress inoculation training includes cognitive interventions (self-statements, appraisals of the situation) but also some of the self-control procedures (alternate response training) mentioned in the prior chapter. The technique is included here as a cognitively based treatment because of the emphasis of using self-statements and appraisals of the situation to guide behavior.

IMAGERY-BASED TREATMENTS

The main focus of cognitively based treatment is on various thought processes, cognitive distortions and deficiencies, and self-statements, as illustrated by the prior techniques. It is also useful to consider among cognitively based techniques, interventions that rely heavily on imagery to alter behavior. This is not a large conceptual leap because imagery is a way of coding information and experience and reflects key topics of cognition such as learning, memory, and thought. Techniques that focus on imagery do not assume that clinical problems stem from distorted or faulty imagery. That is, imagery is not used in treatment because it is considered to be the basis of clinical problems. Rather, imagery is considered as a way to develop new learning and to change people.

Exposure Treatments

Early in the development of behavior modification, systematic desensitization and flooding were procedures developed for the treatment of anxiety. These treatments have been mentioned previously, but it is worthwhile to reintroduce them because variations of the procedures rely on imagery. As mentioned earlier, *systematic desensitization* as a treatment for anxiety consists of training someone to be deeply relaxed and pairing relaxation with exposure to the situations that evoke anxiety (Wolpe, 1958). For example, a person who fears high places (acrophobia) might be exposed to varied situations that evoked anxiety. The situations might include looking up at a skyscraper, climbing stairs, going up in an elevator, looking down from a skyscraper, and so on, each of which is likely to evoke anxiety. The situations can be presented in imagery or the person can approach these with the therapist in real life. The characteristic of desensitization is to approach these anxiety situations gradually, beginning with those that evoke little or no anxiety. As these can be imagined or approached in everyday life, situations that provoke more anxiety are presented. All of the situations are presented (e.g., in imagery) while the person is deeply relaxed. Repeated images of the situations while relaxed reduce and can eventually eliminate the anxiety that the actual "real-life" situations evoke. At the end of treatment, those situations that evoked the greatest anxiety can be approached with little or no anxiety.

In *flooding*, the client also is exposed to those situations that evoke anxiety. However, the individual is not trained to engage in relaxation. Also, only the most anxiety-provoking situations are presented. The idea, as discussed earlier, is to evoke anxiety and to keep the situation present so that the person habituates to it. The situation, when presented repeatedly, eventually loses its ability to evoke anxiety (e.g., as measured by physiological assessments and subjective experience). In our hypothetical example with fear of heights, the client might imagine looking down from a skyscraper or actually do this (in real life) for several minutes or hours until anxiety (physiological arousal, behavioral signs of anxiety, reported distress) subsides. Repeated exposure in this way diminishes and can eventually eliminate anxiety.

In general, desensitization and flooding represent exposure-based treatment methods. They can be conducted by having individuals imagine the anxiety-provoking situations or by exposing individuals to the actual situations themselves. Exposure to the actual situations, referred to as *in vivo* treatment (e.g., in vivo desensitization) tends to be more effective than exposure in imagery. In clinical practice, sometimes imagery is used in the treatment sessions and clients are given practice assignments where they approach actual situations in everyday life. The advantage of imagery is the ease of presenting a wide range of situations and controlling the presentation of these situations.

As an example, an imagery-based flooding procedure was used to treat a 6-year-old boy, named Joseph, who had posttraumatic stress disorder (Saigh, 1986). This disorder is induced by exposure to a major trauma or tragedy (e.g., war, rape, and disaster). The symptoms include persistently reexperiencing the trauma (e.g., in thoughts and dreams); avoidance of stimuli associated with the trauma; numbing of responsiveness; outbursts of anger; difficulty in sleeping; and exaggerated startle responses. Joseph was a Lebanese boy who experienced the disorder after exposure to a bomb blast. His symptoms included trauma-related nightmares, recollections of the trauma, depression, and avoidance behavior.

To treat Joseph, five scenes were developed that evoked anxiety (e.g., seeing injured people and debris, approaching specific shopping areas). He rated his discomfort as each scene was described to him. The scenes were presented to him for extended periods (over 20 minutes). During this exposure period, he was asked to imagine the exact details of the scenes. The five scenes were incorporated into treatment in a multiple-baseline design so that exposure to the scenes occurred in sequence or at different points in time. In each session, Joseph rated his discomfort in response to all of the scenes.

The results are presented in Figure 11-4. As evident, Joseph improved markedly after only 10 sessions (one session of baseline assessment, 10 sessions of treatment). Assessment immediately after treatment and six months later indicated that the scenes no longer caused discomfort. Perhaps more important are the results from other measures. Before and after treatment, Joseph was assessed directly in the marketplace where the bomb blast had occurred. After treatment, he showed less avoidance of the area and remained there longer. Other measures, including assessment of anxiety, depression, and classroom performance at school, also indicated improvement after treatment. Thus, imagery-based treatment appeared to affect several important areas of functioning.

Covert Conditioning

The use and application of imagery in desensitization led to the development of a broader set of imagery-based behavioral techniques. In the 1960s, Joseph Cautela (1927–1999) developed a set of techniques referred to as *covert conditioning*. The treatments were called covert because the client is asked to imagine target behaviors and consequences. They are referred to as conditioning because they draw on learning, including classical conditioning, operant conditioning, and observational learning. The techniques assume that there is an interaction between overt and covert (imagined) behaviors and that changes in one are likely to influence the other.

Table 11-3 lists several of the techniques and what they attempt to accomplish. A few procedures can illustrate how covert conditioning proceeds. In general, clients imagine various events in specific ways that lead to change in their behavior. For most of the techniques, clients imagine a specific behavior and positive or negative consequences to develop or to suppress behaviors. The rehearsal of various behaviors in imagery has been shown to influence actual behavior in a number of circumstances (Cautela & Kearney, 1986, 1993). A few examples of covert conditioning techniques convey how they are used.

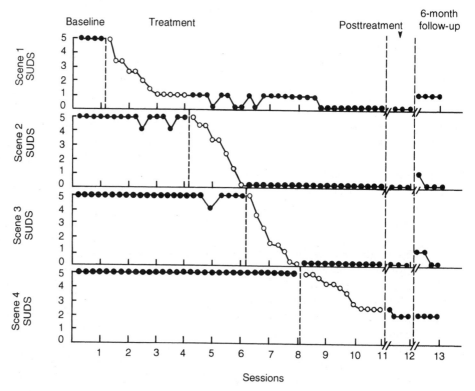

FIGURE 11-4 Joseph's ratings of discomfort, referred to as Subjective
Units of Disturbance (SUDS), in which 5 = maximum discomfort and
0 = no discomfort. Assessment was conducted to measure the discomfort caused by each scene during the treatment sessions. Treatment
reflects the period in which imagery-based exposure (flooding) focused on the specific scene.

(Source: Saigh, 1986)

One procedure based on imagery is referred to as *covert sensitization*. The procedure consists of having clients imagine themselves engaging in an undesirable
behavior (e.g., overeating, excessive alcohol consumption). When this image is
vivid, the clients imagine an aversive consequence associated with the behavior
(e.g., nausea). The purpose is to build an aversion toward stimuli that previously
served as a source of attraction or positive stimulus. The clients do not have to engage in overt behaviors related to the problem but only imagine the behavior and
its association with aversive consequences. The effects of treatment, however, carry
over to actual behavior in everyday life.

A classic illustration focused on sexual deviation of an adult male who was in
a psychiatric hospital (Hayes, Brownell, & Barlow, 1978). His history included attempted rape, multiple fantasies involving sadistic sexual acts (e.g., forced sexual

Table 11-3 Major Covert Conditioning Techniques

Technique	Procedure
Covert sensitization	The client is instructed to image engaging in the target behavior to be eliminated (e.g., consuming alcohol) and then to imagine an aversive consequence.
Covert extinction	The client imagines the target behavior to be reduced (e.g., acting obnoxiously) and then imagines that the reinforcer maintaining behavior (attention from others) is not forthcoming.
Covert response cost	The client imagines the target behavior to be decreased and then imagines loss of a reinforcer (e.g., money, valuable item).
Covert positive reinforcement	The client imagines the target behavior (e.g., approaching an employer) and then is asked to imagine a pleasant scene (e.g., listening to music) that is assumed to be reinforcing.
Covert negative reinforcement	The client imagines an aversive stimulus (e.g., nagging from a peer) and then is asked to terminate the aversive scene and to imagine the response that is to be increased (e.g., responding assertively to the peer).
Covert modeling	The client imagines a model (another person) who performs the behavior. Reinforcing (positive or negative) can be added to the scenes but strictly speaking is not central to the defining procedure.

acts with bound women, the use of pins and whips during intercourse), and exhibitionism. He had been arrested for both attempted rape and exhibitionism. Treatment consisted of having him imagine aversive consequences associated with situations in which exhibitionistic and sadistic acts were performed. A sample exhibitionistic scene with aversive consequences illustrates these situations (Hayes et al., 1978, p. 286):

> "I call her over to the car. She doesn't see what I'm doing. I say, 'Can you please help me with this?' She looks down and sees my dick. It's hard, and she's really shocked. Her face looks all kinds of distorted. I quickly drive away. As I drive away, I see her look back. I think, 'Oh, shit, she's seen my license plate!' I begin to worry that she might call the police. . . I get home and I'm still worried. My wife keeps saying, 'What's wrong?' . . . As we all sit down to dinner I hear a knock on the door. I go open it, and there are four pigs. They come charging in and throw me up against the wall and say, 'You're under arrest for indecent exposure!' My wife starts to cry and says 'This is it! This is the last straw.' "

After several days of treatment, similar scenes were developed to associate imagined aversive consequences with sadistic acts. Over the course of treatment, sexual arousal was directly measured by the degree of the client's erection (penile blood volume) as the client viewed slides of exhibitionistic, sadistic, and heterosexual scenes. For example, heterosexual slides displayed pictures of nude females and sadistic slides displayed nude females tied or chained down in a number of provocative positions. The client also reported his degree of arousal to cards describing various sexual situations.

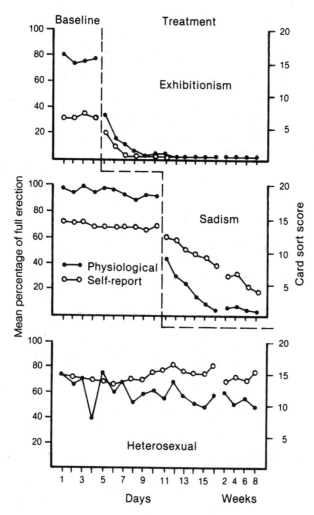

FIGURE 11-5 Percentage of full erection and self-reported arousal in response to exhibitionistic, sadistic, and heterosexual stimuli during baseline, treatment, and follow-up phases. Card sort data are daily averages in the baseline and treatment phases and weekly averages in the follow-up phase.

(Source: Hayes, Brownell, & Barlow, 1978)

    The effects of covert sensitization were evaluated in a multiple-baseline design across the two different types of scenes (exhibitionist and sadistic). As shown in Figure 11-5, both physiological arousal and self-reported attraction to deviant sexual stimuli decreased as a function of treatment. On the other hand, arousal to heterosexual stimuli was never focused on and did not change. Moreover, these effects were maintained up to eight weeks after treatment.

As another illustration, *covert positive reinforcement* was used with a developmentally disabled 29-year-old male (moderate level) with limited language ability, including both comprehension and speech (Groden, 1993). The client lived in a community-based group home and came for treatment at an institution during the day. He had an extended history of violence and aggression and was often restrained (e.g., with handcuffs) because of his aggressive behavior. The facility included a number of programs for vocational and academic training, including reinforcement programs such as contingency contracts. Of interest here is the use of covert positive reinforcement to develop nonviolent behavior. Situations were developed in which appropriate behavior could be imagined followed by a pleasant (presumably reinforcing) scene. Over the course of treatment, situations were presented in different forms including tape-recorded vignettes and pictures that would instruct him to carry out the procedure. Here are two sample scenes that illustrate covert positive reinforcement.

Change in the schedule: Imagine that it's time to work at the food bank. The food bank has just called and said there is no work today. You feel disappointed, but you take a deep breath, relax your whole body, and say to yourself, "I can go next time, and today, I will do some contract work. You feel relaxed and comfortable. Now imagine listening to your radio. You enjoy the music, and you have a nice smile on your face.

Feeling tense: Imagine yourself starting to get tense. You feel yourself beginning to rock, and you feel yourself getting angry. You tell yourself to relax, to take a deep breath, and to keep your hands at your sides. You feel yourself getting very comfortable and relaxed. You continue what you are doing, feeling very cool and comfortable. When you can imagine that, signal to me. Now imagine being up in the gym, shooting baskets, sinking the baskets. You feel great; you have a smile on your face—you feel happy (Groden, 1993, p. 147).

After a year, aggression was markedly reduced and indeed, in one of the settings, decreased to zero over the next five years. In another setting, aggression was still a problem but was decreased with further treatment. The case is useful in illustrating covert positive reinforcement scenes. Without a formal evaluation of the treatment and of any other treatments operative in the setting, one cannot be assured that the changes that occurred were due to covert positive reinforcement.

Covert conditioning techniques have been applied to a variety of problems, such as anxiety, sexual deviation, social withdrawal, obsessions, and alcohol consumption, to mention a few (Cautela & Kearney, 1993). Nevertheless, evidence on the effectiveness of these procedures with clinical samples is limited to a small number of problems. The procedures are usually conducted in treatment sessions in the presence of a therapist. Yet the treatments can also be viewed as self-control techniques because clients can imagine various scenes in their everyday life to handle problems that arise long after contact with the therapist has been terminated. By rehearsing (in imagination) behaviors that may be difficult to perform or by imagining rewarding or aversive consequences to facilitate or inhibit a response, clients can control their own behavior.

MODELING

Modeling, or observational learning, refers to learning by observing the performance of someone who engages in the behaviors that one wishes to develop. The use of modeling has been discussed previously in other contexts. For example, providing a model of how to do a particular behavior can be a useful antecedent (prompt) when developing behavior through reinforcement. Modeling has been used on its own as a form of treatment. Through observation, clients acquire desired responses without performing these responses. Whether one includes modeling as a cognitively based technique has much to do with the interpretation of how modeling leads to therapeutic change. The dominant view is that modeling achieves its effects by altering cognitive processes (Bandura, 1977). The observer sees the model perform but does not engage in the behavior. An assumption is that the modeled behaviors are acquired by altering cognitive mental processes that code the observed events. These processes may include images and verbal strategies such as self-statements that code the behaviors, their sequence or meaning, and their relations to each other. Whether the observed behaviors are performed may depend on a variety of circumstances such as incentives to perform them. However, the coding of these behaviors (their storage in memory) is often viewed as the basis for modeling effects.

There are several variations of modeling as a form of treatment. In the usual method, live or film models are used to convey the desired target behaviors. For example, in live modeling, a therapist demonstrates (models) the desired behaviors. Live modeling has the advantage of flexibility in modeling the specific behaviors that need to be developed in the client and in repeating the modeling situations based on how well the client is doing.

The use of live modeling is nicely illustrated in the treatment of a 3-year-old girl with a debilitating fear of animals (Matson, 1983). The girl would not go places where she thought an animal would be present. On seeing a dog or cat, she would freeze, shake visibly, go into a fetal position, and report fear of harm. Assessment was conducted to measure these signs of fear when the girl was in the presence of a dog and a cat. Treatment was carried out by the girl's mother in the backyard of their home. Before the treatment sessions, the mother was coached by a therapist on how to conduct the modeling sessions. Each day, treatment began with the mother and child spending a few minutes playing with a stuffed dog and cat. The mother modeled petting and holding the stuffed animal. The child was encouraged also to pet and hold the animal and was praised for doing so. After time with the stuffed animals, a live dog and cat were then introduced in each session. The child was told that she would not be required to move toward or to touch the live animal. The mother modeled approach behavior and petting. The child then was encouraged to walk over and to engage in these behaviors as well. The mother encouraged the child to try the behaviors. Gradually, the child engaged in increased approach behaviors modeled by the mother.

Assessment of the child's fear was completed (approximately 11 minutes) during baseline and each day before the treatment sessions, once treatment began. For this assessment, a live dog and cat were introduced, but the arrangement of the

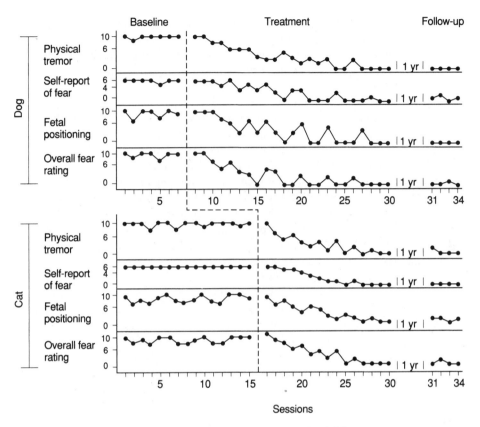

FIGURE 11-6 Ratings of fear behavior observed each day as the child was exposed to a tame dog (upper portion) and cat (lower portion) during baseline, treatment (modeling), and follow-up.

(Source: Matson, 1983)

fences in the yard precluded the possibility of physical contact with the animals. The data for the different measures of fear in the presence of the live dog and cat are shown in Figure 11-6. As indicated by the figure, training was first completed to develop approaching a dog and then a cat. The results show that introduction of treatment led to reductions in fear. The impact of treatment is suggested by the pattern of effects during the multiple-baseline portion of the design. Importantly, the benefits of the intervention were maintained after a one-year follow-up.

Modeling can also be carried out using imagery. One of the covert conditioning techniques noted previously (Table 11-3) is referred to as *covert modeling* (Cautela & Kearney, 1986). In covert modeling, clients *imagine* rather than observe models. Covert modeling has been used in outpatient treatment to train withdrawn and shy adults to act more assertively in a variety of social situations

(Kazdin, 1984). In treatment, these clients imagine a person similar to themselves behaving assertively in such situations as returning merchandise at a store, asking an apartment landlord to make needed repairs, responding to high-pressure salespersons, and asking one's employer for a raise. This enabled the clients to effect changes in their overt behavior.

In applied settings such as the home and school, modeling has been used more frequently as a component of a larger intervention package rather than as a behavior-change procedure by itself. Modeling in this context is particularly useful to demonstrate the behavior or task requirements. Once the behavior is demonstrated, the individual then performs the behavior and consequences can be applied directly to reinforce performance. For example, modeling is often used to develop social skills in children and adults. The skills may focus on speaking with another person, making requests, and responding to requests of others, and may entail both verbal and nonverbal behaviors (e.g., facing others, standing upright). Modeling would consist of the therapist's or trainer's showing a socially appropriate response by actually doing it with the client. Modeling is only the beginning of teaching the desired behaviors. After the behaviors are modeled, the client then rehearses or practices the behaviors (role-playing) that were modeled. Feedback, social reinforcement, and further modeling are then provided by the trainer to shape behavior. As the client role-plays, prompts (instructions, brief interruptions and quick modeling of the behavioral component) are used to carve the final behavior one wishes. Thus modeling, prompting, shaping, practice, and reinforcement are combined to develop behavior.

Although live modeling is the most frequent use in the context of treatment, film modeling has also been used. Films are made that show, for example, individuals engaging in prosocial behavior, such as interacting with others or approaching a feared stimulus. Film models permit standardization of presenting modeling situations to ensure that the situations are constant. The potential of film modeling as an intervention deserves special comment. The use of films and videotapes would permit large-scale dissemination of effective interventions. Also, videotapes can be standardized so that optimally effective variations can be placed on tape and delivered in diverse settings, including videos or a CD-ROM for home use or over such media as television, the Internet, and presumably movie theaters. In fact, videotaped models have been used in training in behavioral research. For example, in one program, videotaped models are used to train parents how to manage their oppositional and aggressive children. Videotaped models of parents using behavioral techniques has been shown to improve child performance at home and at school (Webster-Stratton, 1996).

COMBINED TECHNIQUES

The discussion of cognitively based treatments has emphasized relatively "pure" versions of treatment, that is, instances in which the clinical investigator applied a particular technique to achieve behavior change. The discussion is useful as a way to underscore key elements of the procedures. In clinical practice, different cognitive procedures are often combined.

As an example, cognitively based treatment has been applied to individuals who are pathological gamblers. Pathological gambling is included in current psychiatric diagnosis as a condition that reflects a persistent pattern that clearly interferes with and disrupts personal relations, family life, and work. Gambling is likely to seem uncontrollable and dominates the individual's activity and daily life. Cognitive factors have been shown to play a key role in development and continuation of gambling. Among the cognitions are beliefs that winning is not random (in games where it is), that success is much more likely than it is, and that one can predict and control the outcomes (e.g., slot machines, roulette wheel). As an example, one program used a cognitively based intervention that combined several procedures to alter erroneous perceptions and cognitions (Bujold, Ladouceur, Sylvain, & Boisvert, 1994). Three adult males with pathological gambling participated in individual outpatient treatment (one session per week) in which they received a combination of cognitive correction (understanding and challenging irrational beliefs), problem-solving training (to handle financial difficulties and identify new social activities), and relapse prevention (e.g., preparing the individual for what to do if gambling returned). Throughout, the three men self-monitored the perception of control over gambling (i.e., the key maladaptive cognition), perceptions of severity of gambling as a problem, and frequency of gambling. Maladaptive cognitions were challenged by first videotaping each individual as he played several hands of poker and spoke his thoughts aloud. These tapes were played back to the individual during treatment to identify, correct, and replace the maladaptive cognitions.

The treatment was provided on an outpatient basis and was introduced in a multiple-baseline design across individuals. As shown in Figure 11-7, the perceptions of control of gambling improved as treatment was introduced for each individual. Other measures showed similar effects. Moreover, the effects of treatment were maintained when checked three, six, and nine months after treatment had ended. Subsequent studies using similar procedures have confirmed the effectiveness of cognitively based procedures in the treatment of pathological gambling (e.g., Ladouceur, Sylvain, Letarte, Giroux, & Jacques, 1998; Sylvain, Ladouceur, & Boisvert, 1997).

The previous example conveys how cognitively based strategies are combined with each other. Many cognitively based procedures are combined with reinforcement, punishment, and extinction, that is, direct efforts to change behavior by altering the contingencies of reinforcement. For example, cognitive treatment, self-control, and reinforcement were combined in a study to treat two girls, named Mary and Lucy (ages 8 and 10) who experienced separation anxiety (Ollendick, Hagopian, & Huntzinger, 1991). Separation anxiety in children refers to their concern about time away from their parents, worry about the welfare of their parents, and interest in constant reassurance about their parents. The concern becomes worthy of treatment when it interferes with daily functioning. In the case of Mary and Lucy, the two girls treated in this program, refusal to sleep in their own beds because of their fears and concerns were problems for their

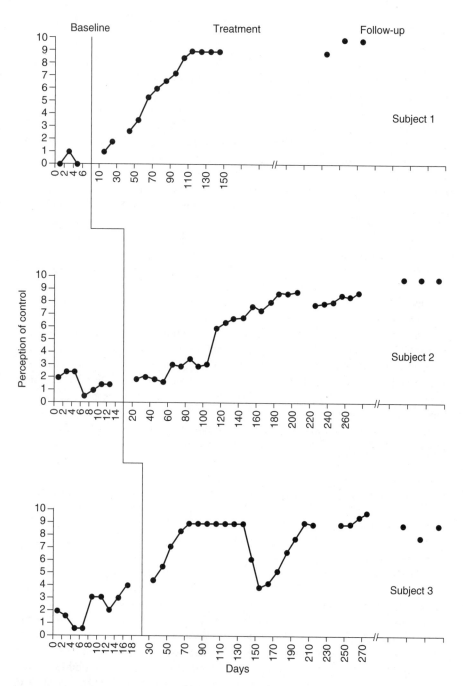

FIGURE 11-7 Perception of control of gambling behavior during baseline, treatment, and follow-ups.

(Source: Bujold et al., 1994)

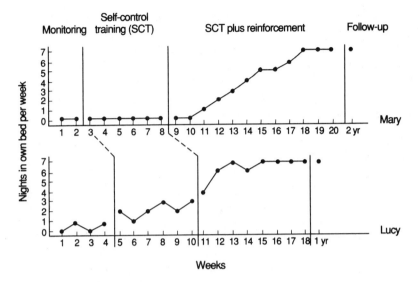

FIGURE 11-8 Number of nights each girl slept in her own bed during each week. During baseline, the children and parents observed their sleep behavior. In the self-control training phase, self-instruction training, relaxation, and self-praise were used. Parent praise was also provided for using the self-control techniques (but not for going to bed). In the final phase, self-control plus reinforcement, each girl received reinforcing consequences for sleeping in her own bed. Follow-up assessment one or two years after treatment showed that program effects were maintained.

(Source: Ollendick, Hagopian, & Huntzinger, 1991)

families. For baseline assessment, each girl, along with their mother, recorded when the child went to bed, whether she slept in her own bed through the night, and other related behaviors. After several days of observation, cognitively based and self-control procedures were implemented. Each girl was trained to use self-statements to help her manage and cope with anxiety, to apply relaxation exercises to help reduce anxiety, and to administer self-praise for using these approaches to control anxiety. Parents also provided praise when the girls used these strategies in treatment sessions and at home. After this phase of self-control training, reinforcement was added when the girls actually slept in their own beds. Reinforcement was provided in the morning (verbal praise; earning earrings or video rentals) based on whether the child slept in her own bed at night. A graduated approach (shaping) was used as needed to increase the number of nights each girl slept in her bed.

The effectiveness of the program was evaluated in a multiple-baseline design across the two children. Figure 11-8 shows the number of nights each girl spent in her own bed (out of seven nights for each week). For example, during baseline, Mary never slept in her bed in a two-week period; Lucy slept in her own bed two times in a four-week period. Self-control training (cognitive self-instructions and self-control training) led to weak and inconsistent effects. When positive reinforcement was added to the procedure, both girls increased the number of nights in their own beds. Essentially, the problem ended because both girls slept seven nights in their own beds during each week. These effects were maintained in follow-up assessment two years and one year later for Mary and Lucy, respectively. The program shows that sleeping in one's bed could be increased, but did the program also reduce anxiety? Several standardized measures indicated that treatment was associated with reductions in anxiety. Moreover, before treatment both girls met diagnostic criteria for separation anxiety, as delineated as a psychiatric disorder of childhood, based on the number and severity of their symptoms. Neither met criteria for the disorder after treatment. Thus the combined treatment seemed to have had a significant effect on their daily functioning.

Scores of other studies have shown that various cognitive techniques combined with each other or combined with various reinforcement techniques are effective. Very little research has examined whether combined treatments are more effective than individual treatments when presented by themselves (e.g., reinforcement procedures without cognitive procedures or vice versa) or whether combined treatments are needed or better for some types of problems or individuals rather than others. Yet the availability of effective treatments and treatment combinations is important in its own right even in advance of resolving these important questions.

CURRENT STATUS AND ISSUES

Advances in Research

Cognitively based techniques include a wide range of interventions, only some of which were sampled here. The techniques have been applied to a wide array of clinical problems (e.g., anxiety, depression, aggression, headaches, chronic pain, eating disorders, or substance use) and populations (e.g., children through adults, persons with clinical problems, or persons at risk for problems). Scores of controlled treatment outcome studies have supported several cognitively based treatments as a form of therapy (Durlak et al., 1991; Hollon & Beck, 1994; Kendall, 1991).

The advances in various types of therapy have stemmed in part from research on the cognitive features of various clinical problems. As mentioned in the discussion of several techniques, specific cognitive distortions or deficiencies are associated with many types of clinical dysfunction in children, adolescents, and adults (Kendall, 1991; Stein & Young, 1992). This does not necessarily mean that maladaptive cognitions cause the dysfunctions with which they are correlated. After all, there could be some other event (e.g., family processes, genetic influences, a combination of multiple factors) that lead to the clinical dysfunction and the cognitive distortions or deficiencies. At the same time, several studies have identified specific cognitive patterns associated with a particular clinical problem and then have intervened to alter these patterns. For example, for depression and gambling, noted in prior illustrations, specific cognitive patterns were identified to be associated with the problem, and then treatment altered these patterns. The effects were reflected in changes in the target focus. These results strongly support the critical role of cognitive processes as a basis of therapeutic change. Stronger evidence would be provided if changes in the hypothesized cognitive processes were shown to occur, then immediately followed by changes in the problem. There is little evidence of this kind, but that does not detract from the importance of the findings.

Why "Cognitive-Behavior Modification"?

Cognitively based techniques are often referred to as *cognitively based treatment, cognitive therapy, cognitive-behavior modification,* or *cognitive behavior therapy.* The terms are not used in a consistent fashion among book titles, journal articles, and professional conferences. The issues and evolution of the varied terms are not critical for us, but after reviewing several treatments, the term *cognitive-behavior modification* (or therapy) warrants special comment.

When cognitively based treatments first emerged, it was useful to distinguish them from behaviorally based procedures, that is, interventions that focused exclusively on overt behavior. This is in keeping with comments made earlier about S-R (stimulus-response) and S-O-R (stimulus-organism-response) views of learning. Cognitions emphasize the O (i.e., what is inside the organism or individual). Techniques are considered to be cognitive if they rely on cognitive processes in the theory underlying the emergence of problem behavior, the theory explaining how treatment works, or in the target focus of treatment, that is, attempts to alter such processes as beliefs, attributions, and self-statements. At a technique or procedural level, many of the cognitively based treatments rely heavily on direct overt behavior-change methods. This is not an inconsistency. Indeed, some authors have maintained that one of the best ways to change cognitions is to have individuals behave differently (i.e., act in different ways, practice new activities, engage in role-playing) (e.g., Bandura, 1977).

The use of many procedures that rely on direct attempts to alter behavior (i.e., noncognitive interventions) is obvious. Role-playing, practice, prompts, shaping, feedback, positive reinforcement, extinction, and techniques covered in prior chapters are often used. For example, problem-solving skills training with aggressive children teaches them to apply various problem-solving steps to interpersonal situations. An 8-year-old boy argues when his teacher asks him to do something. In the treatment session, a vignette (situation) individualized to address this problem area might be presented to the boy. He will be asked to apply the problem-solving steps to identify an appropriate (e.g., nonaggressive) solution to the problem, that is, to select an appropriate way to interact with the teacher. After this is identified while both therapist and child are sitting and talking in the session, the therapist might then say, "OK, let's get up and act out [role-play] this situation." At this point, the therapist pretends to be the teacher and makes a request of the boy. The boy goes through the problem-solving steps, selects an appropriate solution, and then acts it out. During this process, the therapist will use prompts (instructions, reminders, gestures) to encourage use of the steps and selection of an appropriate solution. Any prosocial solution is likely to be reinforced (nonverbal looks of approval, flashing an "OK" sign with one's hand to approve nonverbally without interrupting the child, verbal praise, and maybe even tokens at the end of the scene). Then, the therapist may provide feedback and the situation would be practiced again. Prompts might be provided immediately before the scene started to promote improved performance (e.g., "Remember this time, when you respond, try an even *better* solution . . . "OK, let's start."). At this point, the situation would be practiced again and better performance would be reinforced (shaping). It is possible that the boy and therapist will reverse roles; that is, the therapist pretends to be the boy to model good problem solving in this situation. The child will use prompts, reinforcement, and shaping with the therapist.

Without getting lost in the example, the overriding point is clear. Cognitively based techniques often rely heavily on noncognitive (behavioral) procedures. This is not a problem in understanding or describing the techniques. As noted in the example, antecedents, behaviors, and consequences play a critical role in developing the desired behaviors. Similarly, in other cognitively based interventions, such as cognitive therapy for depression, there is a focus on overt behavior and what individuals do as part of the treatment. Homework assignments are given to individuals to practice new behaviors (positive cognitions or self-statements) and during the sessions themselves, of course, the therapist directly reinforces statements that reflect adaptive and rational beliefs and unwittingly punishes statements that reflect maladaptive beliefs. The reinforcement is usually in the form of agreement and expressions of enthusiasm; the punishment is usually in the form of challenging, disagreeing, and questioning the veracity of the maladaptive assumptions of the client.

The purpose in noting the focus on overt behavior in many cognitive techniques is to provide the central basis for use of the term *cognitive-behavior modification*. The term captures the fact that many cognitively based techniques encompass behavioral procedures as well. The distinction between cognitive (e.g., how we think, perceive, anticipate, expect) and behavior (e.g., what we do, overt actions) is a meaningful one, and basic research in psychology often can tease apart influences by limiting or controlling one aspect to evaluate another. However, in therapy and everyday situations, cognitive processes and overt behavior often are intertwined in interactive and reciprocally influential ways.

Cognitive processes do not necessarily come before behavior, or vice versa, in explaining a psychological or interpersonal problem. Rather, they may emerge together and mutually influence each other. This is obvious when one jumps into the middle of a sequence. For example, we may see someone who looks sad to us. Actually they may not be sad, but they may appear that way even if only because the shape of their mouth (slightly downward as if slightly frowning) or because of our own perceptual and cognitive predilections. Our perception influences how we respond, whether the individual is or is not sad. These behaviors on our part may include whether we seek out, avoid, and comment in a friendly and upbeat way. Our cognition influenced our behavior. No doubt our behavior then will influence the other individual's behavior in response. That response, in turn, influences our cognitions, next behaviors, and so on. Looking for a simple order, namely, that cognition precedes and is *the* cause of behavior or behavior precedes and causes cognition, is somewhat simplistic, although each of these orders can be demonstrated in well-controlled laboratory research. From the standpoint of treatment, the fact that cognition and contingencies of reinforcement influence behavior is important and fortunate. There are different places one can intervene to affect cognition and behavior.

A critical feature that unites cognitively based treatments and behavioral treatments, making that distinction for a moment, continues to be a strong interest in evaluating the effects of treatment and whether functioning is altered in everyday life. Thus cognitively based therapy does not merely try to alter cognition so that a person thinks about things differently (e.g., has insight as to why he or she is anxious). The goal is to improve functioning in everyday life by reducing subjective, behavioral, and physiological measures of anxiety or arousal and improving functioning in situations that were impeded by anxiety. The end goal of cognitively based treatment is to have individuals change their cognitive processes so they can behave more adaptively.

Researchers who study cognitively based treatment have been quite interested in demonstrating that changes in overt behavior result from therapy. In contrast, researchers who study overt behavioral procedures such as reinforcement, punishment, extinction, and the many combinations elaborated in prior chapters have been less interested in studying or demonstrating changes in cognitive processes. This is unfortunate in many ways. It is very likely that changes in overt behavior have significant impact on cognitive processes. For example, improving academic competence among children, social skills among withdrawn adolescents, and marital communication among adults are likely to have broader effects than the specific behaviors that are altered. There is no doubt cognitive processes including self-perception (self-esteem), self-statements, and attributions are altered as well. Not evaluating the broad changes likely to occur with treatment hides the scope of the benefits that may result. More generally, there are important scientific questions about how to change emotions, behaviors, and cognitions and how a focus on any one of these might have effects that spread to the others.

General Comments

The effectiveness of several cognitively based treatments has been well demonstrated. There remain a number of questions to explain the effects, that is, why the treatment works and through what processes. Also, more needs to be learned about how to optimize the effects of treatment. Recall that in prior chapters, characteristics for effective implementation of a technique were discussed. For example, a great deal is known about the application of positive reinforcement and about many of the conditions that contribute to its effectiveness. Delay, magnitude, type, and schedule of reinforcement contribute to the extent of behavior change. If favorable conditions are not carefully implemented, as when reinforcement is very delayed, intermittent, or noncontingent, the intervention is not likely to change behavior. Indeed, there is a vast literature, including laboratory animal studies, showing the effects of violating or optimizing the conditions on which positive reinforcement depends. Cognitively based interventions have been less well studied than positive reinforcement in applied settings. Parallel information about the factors that must be in place to maximize therapeutic effects is not yet available. Within psychology, the study of cognitive process is an enormously rich area of experimental research. Much of this research has not filtered to clinical applications in ways that might understand how cognitively based treatments work or the ways in which they can be administered to achieve optimal effects. This is not necessarily a criticism of cognitively based treatment, but rather alerts us to the need to learn more about how they operate and what can be done to optimize their impact.

SUMMARY AND CONCLUSIONS

Cognitively based techniques include a broad range of interventions. Their common feature is the view that cognitive processes (perceptions, self-statements, attributions, expectations, beliefs, and images) relate in significant ways to behavior and that change in these processes leads to behavior change. Many of the cognitively based techniques are applied in the context of psychotherapy where the client is seen by a therapist in individual or group treatment sessions. A number of techniques have been extended to applied settings as well.

Several cognitively based treatments were highlighted and illustrated. In rational-emotive therapy, irrational cognitions are assumed to underlie maladaptive patterns of functioning. Treatment alters these cognitive processes as a way to develop prosocial behavior. Cognitive therapy for depression, one of the more well investigated cognitively based treatments, focuses on specific cognitive processes that are associated with depression. The cognitive processes (e.g., negative views about oneself, the world, and the future) are challenged and more adaptive cognitions are substituted.

Problem-solving skills training develops cognitive problem-solving processes that underlie interpersonal behavior. The individual uses a specific type of self-statement to identify effective solutions and approaches to interpersonal situations. Stress inoculation training focuses on developing cognitive and self-control skills to reduce the impact of stress. Individuals are trained to monitor events and their evaluations of them, use coping strategies such as relaxation, imagery, and positive self-statements, and apply coping skills in everyday life.

Imagery-based exposure treatments were discussed in the context of treatment of anxiety disorders. Systematic desensitization and flooding, in which anxiety-provoking stimuli are presented in imagery, are prime examples of the treatments. Covert conditioning refers to a family of intervention techniques in which various principles of learning (reinforcement, punishment, and extinction) were used as a basis to develop imagery-based treatments.

Modeling was discussed in part because a prominent interpretation of the procedure in behavior modification has been based on cognitive processes assumed to underlie behavior. Modeling is used often as part of behavioral interventions that combine a number of other procedures. Typically, these procedures consist of having individuals imagine various behaviors and consequences that are designed to alter the behaviors.

Although relatively pure forms of cognitively based interventions were presented, the treatments are often combined with each other or with other procedures (e.g., reinforcement, punishment) that are not considered to be cognitively based. The term *cognitive-behavior modification* has emerged to encompass cognitively based and behavioral techniques. The reason is that cognitively based treatments often use reinforcement and related procedures derived from altering antecedents, behaviors, and consequences, as discussed in prior chapters.

KEY TERMS

Cognitive-behavior modification

Cognitive processes

Cognitive therapy for depression

Covert conditioning

Exposure treatments

Modeling

Problem-solving skills training

Rational-emotive psychotherapy

Stress inoculation training

APPLYING PRINCIPLES AND TECHNIQUES TO EVERYDAY LIFE

1. Cognitive-behavioral interventions include many techniques, some of which were sampled in this chapter. Choose one technique and describe in what way(s) it is cognitive and in what way(s) is it behavioral.

2. Problem-solving skills training focuses on how individuals think and approach interpersonal situations. One of the critical processes is generating solutions to problems. Think of the following two situations: (1) there is a new person in a large lecture class that you would like to meet and (2) a friend has accused you of taking something of his. For each situation, identify three socially appropriate solutions or different ways of solving the problem.

3. Make up two situations that could be described and imagined by a person who is to receive covert sensitization to eliminate stealing. The person constantly steals items from department stores.

4. Give two reasons why combined treatments are used. Also give two reasons why one might be cautious in combining treatments.

FOR FURTHER READING

Cautela, J.R., & Kearney, A.J. (Eds.). (1993). *Covert conditioning casebook.* Pacific Grove, CA: Brooks/Cole.

Clark, D.A., Beck, A., & Alford, B.A. (1999). *Cognitive theory and therapy of depression.* New York: John Wiley & Sons.

Ellis, A. (1999). *Reason and emotion in psychotherapy: A comprehensive method of treating human disturbances.* Secaucus, NJ: Citadel.

Kendall, P.C. (Ed.). (1991). *Child and adolescent therapy: Cognitive-behavioral procedures.* New York: Guilford.

Shure, M.B. (1996). *Raising a thinking child: Help your young child to resolve everyday conflicts and get along with others.* New York: Pocket Books.

Stein, D.J., & Young, J.E. (Eds.). (1992). *Cognitive science and clinical disorders.* San Diego: Academic Press.

NOTES

1. Research on cognitively based treatments is published in several journals in clinical psychology, psychiatry, and social work. A few journals are devoted exclusively or primarily to such treatments (e.g., *Cognitive Therapy and Research* and *Cognitive and Behavioral Practice*.)

2. A cliché of everyday life is that, "Seeing is believing," a phrase to convey that a person will believe something or take as proof actual (visual) evidence. This is true of course, but it is also sometimes false and otherwise incomplete. The reason is that we do not see in a way that is free from bias, frame of reference, or preconceptions. Psychology has long demonstrated the converse of the phrase, namely, that "Believing is seeing." Once an individual has a belief, expectation, or perception, even if this is not derived from direct experience, this will greatly influence how one sees and interprets environmental events. These statements convey how cognition can interplay with everyday life but represent much broader issues in philosophy including how we experience the world and how we come to know.

3. The psychology of learning is a major topic of theory and research. Key issues that are highlighted here convey the underpinnings of interest in cognitive processes. Further information about the emergence of cognitive psychology and cognitive processes in learning and how these influenced behavior modification can be obtained from other sources (Kazdin, 1978; Wann, 1964).

4. The term *cognitive therapy* has been used in behavior modification in different ways. Occasionally, the term is used as a generic category and synonymous with cognitively based treatment (e.g., the journal, *Cognitive Therapy and Research*). Thus there are many different treatments that form cognitive therapy, as that term is used in this general sense. Cognitive therapy as a term also has been used to a specific treatment that has been applied to depression (Clark et al., 1999).

CHAPTER 12

Response Maintenance and Transfer of Training

T he techniques discussed in previous chapters have altered many behaviors among a wide range of clients. The changes are often dramatic. The ability to achieve changes in many behaviors is particularly significant in historical context. We take for granted that much can be done about a range of behaviors (self-injury, social interaction, promotion of health, etc.). Just a few decades ago, there was very limited evidence that changes in these and other domains could be achieved at all.

Although the accomplishments in changing behavior have been enormous, by itself this is not cause to begin the party and start celebrating. Dramatic changes in behavior are obviously impressive, but do those changes last? What happens when behavioral programs are discontinued or when clients leave the special settings in which the programs have been conducted? The issues raised by these questions, often referred to as generalization, constitute the topic of the present chapter.

The term *generalization* has been used very loosely to signify that behavior changes carry over (or generalize) to conditions other than those included in training. However, generalization can include many phenomena, among them behavior changes that carry over to situations, periods, or settings other than those in which the behavioral program was implemented (Allen, Tarnowski, Simonian, Elliott, & Drabman, 1991; Stokes & Baer, 1977). It is worthwhile to make distinctions to reflect key concerns that emerge in changing behavior.

The extension of behavior changes over time is usually referred to as *response maintenance*. The question addressed by response maintenance is whether behavior change is maintained after the program has been terminated. The extension of behavior changes to new situations, settings, and circumstances is usually referred to as *transfer of training*. The question addressed by transfer of training is whether behavior change extends to new or different stimulus conditions (e.g., situations, settings, the presence of other persons) not included in the program (e.g., to the home when the program is conducted in the classroom).[1]

Response maintenance and transfer of training are of great interest in behavior modification for obvious reasons—we not only want to show that we have the capacity to change behavior but also that the changes last and help individuals as they negotiate different and new aspects of their life (interactions with others, work, school). It is worth noting that response maintenance and transfer of training are not uniquely relevant to behavior modification. They apply to any enterprise or activity in which behavior change is a goal. Thus they represent critical issues for child rearing, education, religion, government, and psychotherapy.

For example, in education, a major hope is that after completing formal education, people will continue to read, educate themselves, and utilize critical thinking skills in the future (response maintenance) well beyond the college classroom (transfer). Similarly, governments are interested in having citizens maintain their law-abiding behaviors (e.g., traveling within the speed limit) and transfer these behaviors to situations when the contingencies (e.g., surveillance by police officers) are not in effect. Of course in psychotherapy, we do not want clients to be adjusted, less anxious, and free from serious problems (severe anxiety, drug abuse) merely in the therapy sessions while under the influence of a mental health professional. We want any changes to be maintained and to extend well outside of the session. Of course, it is one thing to hope for or want maintenance and transfer and quite another to figure out how they can be achieved.

Response maintenance and transfer of training have received special attention in behavior modification for three reasons. First, an obvious priority for treatment is developing ways of changing behavior. Only after effective procedures for changing behavior have been developed is it meaningful to raise questions about response maintenance and transfer of behavior. For many behaviors, changes can be achieved as illustrated throughout previous chapters. Although research continues to develop procedures to effect change, maintenance and transfer obviously require increased priority.

Second, evaluations of behavioral techniques have often suggested that maintenance and transfer do not automatically occur after treatment. For example, many studies have used an ABAB (or reversal) design in which treatment is temporarily withdrawn in a return-to-baseline phase. When this is done, behavior often reverts to or near baseline levels. Such loss of behavior during a reversal phase may provide a preview of coming attractions, namely, loss of the acquired behavior once the behavior-change program has been terminated. Similarly, in multiple-baseline designs, contingencies are often introduced, one situation at a time, into different situations, such as the home, classroom, and playground. Behavior change in one situation usually occurs without behavior changes in other situations until the program (e.g., reinforcement) has been introduced into those situations. This suggests that newly developed behaviors are not likely to transfer to new situations without special contingencies. In short, demonstrations of program effects often suggest that something special is needed to ensure maintenance and transfer.

Third, behavior modification programs consist of interventions that depart from the contingencies of reinforcement present in everyday life. For example, children who have behavioral and academic problems at school or who engage in bizarre self-injurious behaviors may participate in a classroom token economy to develop the desired behaviors. In most cases, the program is intended to be a temporary tool for developing behavior so that it is performed consistently. The assumption is that the person will return to a setting or situation in which the specific contingencies are not present. This raises the obvious question of what will happen when ordinary classroom practices are reinstated (e.g., no token economy) and when the individual enters new classes where the contingencies are not programmed to promote desirable behaviors.

In some situations, response maintenance is not an issue because the program is intended to remain in effect. For example, employees are often provided with incentives such as bonuses for exceeding a sales quota or using exercise facilities (because improved fitness reduces employee absenteeism). The reinforcement contingencies may remain in effect permanently and special procedures for maintaining behavior are not required.

Response maintenance and transfer of training can readily be distinguished in the abstract, but in practice they often go together. For example, if a special education student attends a special classroom where a token reinforcement system is in effect and then returns to a regular classroom, both response maintenance and transfer of training are important. Conditions of the special education classroom, such as frequent reinforcement of specific target behaviors, may no longer be used in the regular classroom (i.e., extinction of those behaviors). Understandably, such behaviors may not be maintained. At the same time, the setting is different, so the acquired behaviors may not transfer to the regular classroom. Response maintenance and transfer need not always go together. For example, in classroom situations, reinforcement programs are often implemented at one time of day (e.g., morning). Transfer of training can refer to whether behavior also changes during times of day (e.g., afternoon) or in situations (e.g., the playground) in which the reinforcement program has not been implemented. Response maintenance is not relevant here because the target behaviors are still reinforced in the morning. The issue is whether the reinforced behaviors transfer or generalize to other situations while the program is in effect. The present chapter examines the evidence bearing on both response maintenance and transfer of training and techniques to increase the likelihood that behaviors will be maintained and will carry over to new situations.

RESPONSE MAINTENANCE

At the outset, it is important to note that behaviors do not always revert to preprogram or baseline levels when the contingencies are withdrawn. Behaviors occasionally are maintained after a program has been terminated. Thus loss of behavior is by no means inevitable. For example, token reinforcement and response cost were used to alter behavior (using abusive language, not attending activities such as therapy sessions, and neglecting personal grooming) of hospitalized schizophrenic patients (Peniston, 1988). The program lasted 12 weeks. The marked improvements evident during treatment were maintained 6 and 12 months later, when performance was again assessed. Thus the gains were clearly sustained long after treatment ended.

When responses are maintained after reinforcing or other consequences have been withdrawn, the reason is usually unclear. One would expect behaviors to reflect the contingencies that currently operate in the environment. When the contingencies are withdrawn, one can only speculate why the behaviors are maintained. Various explanations have been offered. First, it is possible that behaviors developed through a reinforcement program may come under the control of other stimuli in the setting. For example, in a classroom, withdrawal of a token economy may not lead to the loss of appropriate behaviors. Because the teacher has been consistently paired with the delivery of token reinforcement, he or she may serve as a stimulus for appropriate behavior, even after reinforcement is withdrawn. Behavior might be maintained at least for a brief period until the students learn that reinforcement is no longer forthcoming.

Second, behaviors may be maintained because of reinforcement resulting directly from the behaviors themselves. Many behaviors result in their own reinforcement. For example, reading and social interaction may be maintained once they have been developed. These behaviors may be reinforced by the consequences that naturally follow their execution.

Finally, behavior may be maintained after the reinforcers have been withdrawn because the behavior of the persons who administered the program (parents, teachers, peers, hospital staff) has changed in some permanent fashion. For example, if a contingency contract system in the home is withdrawn, a child's desirable behavior may still be maintained at a high level because the parents may then provide reinforcement (allowance and praise) and punishment (loss of privileges) more systematically than they did before the contract system.

Each of the above explanations of response maintenance is usually offered after the fact. After behavior fails to revert to baseline levels when a program is withdrawn, an investigator may speculate why this occurred. Any of the explanations may be correct in a given instance. However, maintenance of behavior is more clearly understood when it is predicted in advance on the basis of the special procedures used to sustain performance after withdrawal of the program.

Despite the above examples and explanations of response maintenance, removal of the contingencies usually results in a decline of performance to or near baseline levels. This has led authors to state that if response maintenance is the goal of the behavior modification program, it has to be programmed systematically into the contingencies rather than merely hoped for as a desirable side effect (Baer, Wolf, & Risley, 1987)

TRANSFER OF TRAINING

Transfer of training can refer to different phenomena, depending on whether one is speaking of transfer across situations, settings, or the persons who implement the contingencies. In most programs, changes of behavior in one situation do not result in a transfer of those changes to other situations or settings, either while the program is in effect or after it has been withdrawn. Indeed, the stimulus conditions controlling behavior are often quite narrow, so that behavior changes are restricted to the specific setting in which training has taken place and even to the persons who administered the program. As we shall see in this chapter, techniques to change behavior differ from the techniques used to develop maintenance and transfer of training.

There are several occasions in which transfer of behavior to new situations and settings has been reported during treatment, even without special procedures to foster transfer. For example, in one program, parents were trained to use reinforcement and mild punishment (time out) to control disruptive behavior of their children (ages 2 to 7) (McNeil, Eyberg, Eisenstadt, Newcomb, & Funderburk, 1991). The behaviors (noncompliance, overactivity, and physical aggression) were selected because they were a problem at home. Treatment was carried out for 14 weeks. Youths who received the treatment, compared with control youths who did not, showed marked improvements. The gains were evident at home, which was expected because parents were trained to implement procedures to alter behaviors that were problematic at home. Interestingly, observations revealed that noncompliance and disruptive behavior decreased at school for these youths, even though performance at school was not included in the program. Thus the gains transferred to the school setting.

Other examples might be mounted where gains obtained in one setting carried over to other settings. Yet it would be important not to misrepresent the weight of the evidence. In general, transfer of behavior across situations and settings is unlikely to occur unless specific efforts are made to program generalization across the situations of interest. Without special procedures, transfer may occur—perhaps for some individuals in a program or across some situations of interest. Yet to obtain reliable (consistent, predictable) changes in behavior and extension of these changes across settings and situations, transfer of training usually has to be programmed directly.

PROGRAMMING RESPONSE
MAINTENANCE AND TRANSFER

The initial priority for behavior modification in applied settings has been to develop techniques that reliably alter behavior. Consequently, the technology for changing behavior has received much greater attention than the technology for developing maintenance and transfer of behavior. However, considerable progress has been made in assessing, evaluating, and ensuring generalization (see For Further Readings). The present section reviews major techniques for achieving response maintenance and transfer of training. Techniques to achieve maintenance and transfer will be treated together because they are often focused on simultaneously in a given program and also because the techniques that accomplish one often affect the other. Procedures that are more suited to maintenance than to transfer, or vice versa, will be noted as such.

Bringing Behavior Under Control
of the Natural Contingencies

Perhaps the most obvious procedure for ensuring that behavior will be maintained and will transfer to new situations is to bring it under the control of the consequences that naturally (i.e., ordinarily) occur in the environment. Reinforcing and punishing consequences that ordinarily follow behavior in everyday life may be sufficient to maintain behavior once it has been well established. Also, if behavior comes under the control of the natural contingencies, transfer of training will not be a problem because the consequences in the new situations may sustain the behavior. For example, praise and attention from others as well as the consequences that follow from the behavior itself, as in the case of exercising or reading, may sustain performance.

The notion of *behavioral traps* was introduced several years ago to convey how the natural contingencies might support response maintenance and transfer (Baer, Rowbury, & Goetz, 1976). Perhaps once a client's behavior has been developed, it will be "trapped" into the system of reinforcers available in the natural environment. The purpose of behavioral interventions should be to bring the client's behavior up to the level sustained by the natural consequences. Initially, his or her behavior may be developed by extraneous reinforcers (e.g., tokens, food and other consumables, praise) that the environment normally would not provide. After that behavior has been developed, other reinforcers (e.g., contact with peers) may sustain performance.

Occasionally very clear examples can be found where behavior appears to have become "trapped" in this fashion by naturally occurring reinforcers. For example, a program in a preschool classroom was designed to increase social interaction in a boy who was withdrawn (Baer et al., 1976). The teacher provided social reinforcement (attention, expressions of interest) whenever he socialized with his peers. In several phases of an extended ABAB design, teacher praise was alternately delivered and withdrawn. Two results emerged from the program. First, the teacher's praise was responsible for the boy's increased interaction. Second, over time, the boy's social interaction was maintained even when the teacher did not deliver praise. That is, each time a return-to-baseline phase was introduced, the behavior remained more at the levels achieved during the intervention. Apparently, over time, other factors were controlling the behavior than those that were responsible for change. Perhaps the reinforcement resulting from peer interaction maintained his social behavior after it had been well developed. That behavior was, as it were, "trapped" into the network of peer interactions and thus no longer required the behavior modification program. Other research has shown that training such social behaviors as smiling, sharing, and positive interactions fosters changes in the social behaviors of one's peers. Thus behaviors may be maintained by mutual social reinforcement among peers and target subjects even when the contingencies administered by the persons who initiated the program have been withdrawn.

Ideally, behavioral programs would just develop positive, prosocial behavior and then these behaviors would be "trapped" and maintained. Years of research have taught us that this hope is infrequently fulfilled. Behaviors that appear to be of the kind that the natural environment will maintain very often are not maintained at all. Part of the problem is that in everyday life, delivery of positive reinforcement is often delayed, intermittent, or not present at all. Thus working at one's job, working on an assignment, and giving to charity may have little or no contingent consequences that can exert control behavior. Indeed, each is associated with some effort or cost and hence may have influences that deter performance. Moreover, it is not just appropriate and prosocial behaviors that are likely to be maintained by the natural environment. Many deviant behaviors are reinforced and these too can be "trapped" by the natural environment. For example, among antisocial children and adolescents, peers reinforce talking about engaging in deviant behavior and breaking rules and tend to ignore talking about prosocial and more normative (nondeviant) activities (Dishion & Patterson, 1997). That is, deviant behavior is reinforced directly by peer attention and clearly is "trapped" into a naturally occurring network of reinforcement and behavior.

Parents, teachers, peers, and hospital staff often attend to and reinforce inappropriate behavior as a matter of course. It seems rather natural (i.e., requires little or no training) for parents and teachers to attend to interruptions, arguing among children, blurting out, and complaining. Thus the natural contingencies often seem to operate against the maintenance and transfer of prosocial behavior. Stated another way, the natural environment can support counterproductive behavior. Clearly, we would like to have all adaptive behaviors maintained because the natural environment supports them. Unfortunately, at present, one cannot identify in advance which behaviors will be maintained by naturally occurring events or how to make behaviors such that they do not depend on external events very much at all.

For individuals functioning normally in society, many adaptive behaviors *are* maintained by the natural environment. Yet most individuals have received extensive social training and respond to a variety of subtle external and self-imposed influences. In contrast, individuals in treatment, rehabilitation, and educational settings (for whom most behavior modification programs are conducted) are trained to respond to external consequences in carefully programmed situations to develop some behavior that is not otherwise present. It is no surprise, therefore, that their behaviors are not maintained when the consequences are withdrawn and the individuals are placed in social situations for which they have not been prepared. What often happens is that when a behavior modification program has been withdrawn, behaviors are maintained for a few persons but not for others. If behaviors continue, perhaps they are being maintained by the naturally occurring reinforcers. If behaviors are not maintained, specific procedures can be implemented to achieve response maintenance and transfer of training. Because unplanned and unprogrammed maintenance and transfer of behavior are exceptions rather than the rule, it is usually advisable to implement one or more of the procedures discussed next.

Programming Naturally Occurring Reinforcers

Waiting and hoping for behavior to be "trapped" by consequences in the natural environment is too unreliable to achieve maintenance and transfer of the behavior. If there are normally available reinforcers in the setting, perhaps these can be systematically programmed so that they are more likely to follow behavior once a program is ended that relied on external consequences (e.g., tokens). By programming, I refer to introducing them into training in a systematic way and making sure they are in fact connected to the desired behavior before the program is ended. In this way, consequences that are normally available can replace the extraneous events that were used to alter behavior initially.

The programming of naturally occurring reinforcers has been used successfully in many programs that were concerned with both response maintenance and transfer of training. For example, in one program, a male complained that he could not walk (Kallman, Hersen, & O'Toole, 1975). No physical problem could be identified to explain the problem. Yet the patient was hospitalized and confined to a wheelchair. A behavioral program was implemented in an effort to see if this could have impact on walking. Social reinforcement was used to develop his standing and walking in the hospital. Eventually, he walked by himself. He returned home, where the treatment effects were maintained for about a month. Then he again said that he could not walk, and he returned to the hospital. His walking was again developed with social reinforcement, and he again returned home. This was sort of a naturalistic ABAB design in which social attention in the hospital was shown to control behavior but behavior returned to baseline levels once the patient left the hospital. Videotaped interactions of the patient and his family revealed that his family had previously attended to his disability and had ignored his attempts to walk. Hence, to maintain walking, the patient's family was trained to reinforce walking and to ignore (extinguish) complaints of being unable to walk. After the family was trained, follow-up indicated that the behavior was maintained up to 12 weeks after treatment. In this program, social consequences in the natural environment were used to sustain the gains that had been achieved in treatment. In this case, natural consequences that were supporting, promoting, and reinforcing the deviant behavior were altered.

Similar effects have been evident in seminal programs early in the development of behavior modification in applied settings. For example, the importance of training relatives to ensure response maintenance and transfer has been emphasized in the treatment of autistic children (Lovaas, Koegel, Simmons, & Long, 1973). Follow-up assessment of the behavior of autistic children one to four years after treatment showed that children whose parents had been trained to carry out the behavioral procedures maintained their gains outside the treatment facility and indeed improved slightly. On the other hand, children who had been institutionalized where the contingencies were not continued lost the gains that they had achieved in treatment.

Also, in the classroom, changing naturally occurring reinforcers to promote transfer has been shown to be essential. In one program, teachers in regular classrooms were trained to continue the contingencies initiated in a special setting to achieve both transfer and maintenance (Walker, Hops, & Johnson, 1975). Highly disruptive children participated in a token economy in a special education classroom to develop appropriate classroom behavior. After improvements had been achieved, the children were returned to their regular classrooms. In some of these classrooms, the teachers conducted a behavioral program to sustain the gains that had been achieved in the special education classroom. The children who returned to a classroom where some of the contingencies were continued maintained their behavior in the new settings to a much greater extent than did the children who returned to a classroom where no program was in effect. When the special contingencies in the regular classrooms had been terminated, the behavioral gains were maintained among the children who had continued the program in their regular classrooms. Thus the substitution of one program for another helped maintain behavior and helped transfer it to a new setting, even though the program was eventually discontinued.

In classroom settings, programming of naturally occurring reinforcers has used the students themselves to foster contingent praise. Specifically, students are trained to prompt the teacher to evaluate their work and to deliver feedback and praise. Sometimes this is referred to as training students to *recruit* teacher praise. As an illustration, one program focused on fourth-grade students from two special education classrooms in a public elementary school (Craft, Alber, & Heward, 1998). The goal of the program was to develop academic behavior in each of the students by way of contingent praise. Observations were made of teacher praise, the number of times students recruited teacher praise, and accuracy and completion of spelling assignments. After baseline observations, students were individually trained to engage in recruiting behavior. Specifically, through instruction, role playing, prompts, and reinforcement, students were trained to go up to the teacher or raise one's hand, to wait quietly to be recognized, and to make a statement or question about work (e.g., "How am I doing?" "Is this right?" "Could you help me?"). Training of each student was completely individually. After training, students received rewards (selecting a small prize such as a sticker or a pencil) when at least two recruitment responses were completed that day. The program greatly improved academic performance of the children.

Figure 12-1 shows two behaviors of interest, namely, the number of times teachers praised the children (the bars in figure) and the number of times students carried out a recruitment response to solicit praise. Teacher praise obviously was almost completely absent during baseline and increased after training. The investigators wished to maintain student recruiting behavior but eliminate the reinforcement system for these behaviors. Consequently, they faded the reinforcement at the end of the day. Early in the program, students received rewards at the end of each day if they engaged in recruiting responses that day (phase marked as continuous reinforcement) but this was shifted to intermittent reinforcement. During this latter phase, students selected a card at the end of the day and the card determined whether they received a reward. They were praised each day but did not get a special reward. During the final phase, no rewards were administered but teacher praise continued. As shown in the figure, teacher praise was maintained by the student prompting, and student prompting (recruiting) was maintained as well. This is an example of programming the natural reinforcement and removing the special rewards.

In general, behaviors may need to be developed with special contingencies to achieve high and consistent levels of performance. After behavior has been developed, contingencies using sources of influence available in the natural environment can be substituted. The natural contingencies may not automatically sustain appropriate behavior, as has been noted in the discussion of behavioral traps. Yet, if naturally occurring consequences are altered to support behavior, they provide a useful transition between highly programmed contingencies and the haphazard and often counterproductive contingencies of the natural environment.

Gradually Removing or Fading the Contingencies

Losses of behavioral gains following a behavior modification program may result from abruptly withdrawing the reinforcing and punishing consequences.

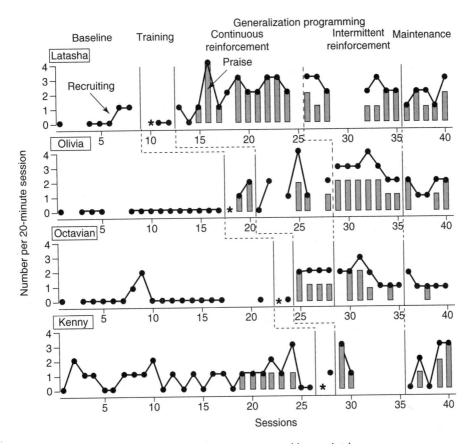

FIGURE 12-1 Frequency of student recruiting responses (data points) and teacher praise statements (bars) during 20-min seat-work sessions. Target recruiting rate was two to three responses per session. Asterisks show when each student received training in the special education resource room.

(Source: Craft, Alber, & Heward, 1998)

Gradually removing or fading the program is likely to be less discriminable to the client than is the abrupt withdrawal of consequences. Also, by gradually removing the program, behavior may become less dependent on the immediate controlling contingencies. Eventually, the consequences can be eliminated entirely without a return of behavior to its baseline rate. Fading of the contingencies can be accomplished in many ways. For purposes of illustration, different ways of gradually fading the contingencies are distinguished. In practice, they are often used together.

Making the Consequences Increasingly Intermittent. One component of fading the contingencies is to make the reinforcement more intermittent. As mentioned earlier, resistance to extinction can be enhanced by using intermittent

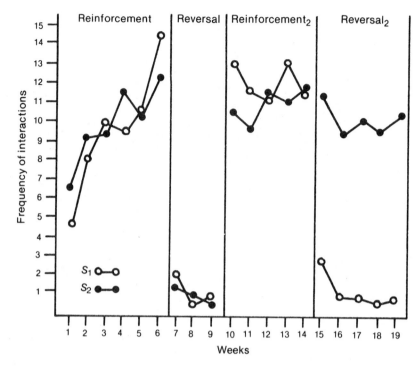

FIGURE 12-2 Mean frequency of interactions per day during reinforcement, reversal, reinforcement₂, and reversal₂ for Subject 1 (S₁) and for Subject 2 (S₂).

(Source: Kazdin & Polster, 1973)

reinforcement. After behavior has been well established with continuous reinforcement, reinforcing consequences can be delivered intermittently. The intermittence of the reinforcement can be increased so that very little reinforcement is provided for behavior. Eventually, very little or no reinforcement can be provided and high levels of the behavior may be maintained.

In a simple illustration of this, positive reinforcement was used to develop social behavior of two adults with developmental disabilities who attended a sheltered workshop (Kazdin & Polster, 1973). These men had engaged in little social interaction. They were informed that they would receive tokens for interacting with peers socially during three work breaks during the day. Each client received a token for each of the peers with whom he had spoken during each break. Thus every interaction was reinforced.

Figure 12-2 shows that during the first phase in which reinforcement was given, the daily average number of both clients' interactions gradually increased. Then, during a reversal phase in which tokens were withdrawn, their interactions decreased. When reinforcement was reinstated, one of the clients (S₁) received tokens as he had before (i.e., continuous reinforcement). The other client (S₂) was told that he would receive tokens only once in a while (i.e., intermittent reinforcement). Initially, the second client received tokens during two of the work breaks. Eventually, all of his token reinforcement was withdrawn.

As Figure 12-2 shows, during a second reversal phase, the client whose behavior had been continuously reinforced showed an immediate decline in social interaction. However, the client whose behavior had been intermittently reinforced maintained a high rate of social interaction. Thus intermittent reinforcement appeared to help maintain behavior. This is of course an effect only demonstrated with one client and there is no certainty that the behavior for that client would be maintained over time. Yet, the program shows fading of reinforcement along one dimension, namely, proportion of times in which the reinforcer is delivered for the target behavior. As mentioned previously, intermittent reinforcement does not develop behavior as well as continuous reinforcement, and hence one must be sure the behavior is well established or at a high rate before fading consequences in this way.

Intermittent reinforcement was also shown to enhance maintenance in a project designed to increase the selection of nutritious snacks among three children (ages 4 to 5) enrolled in a day-care center (Baer, Blount, Detrick, & Stokes, 1987). Each day, the children were offered a choice of snacks that were considered nutritious (fruit, vegetable) or relatively nonnutritious (cookie, cracker). The children were trained to identify the nutritious snacks, to state that they would choose such snacks, and then to select such a snack afterward. If the children completed this sequence, they were allowed to draw from a grab bag that included cards listing consequences (reinforcers) that they would receive (e.g., hugs, tickles, and stickers). After the behavior had been developed, the opportunities to select from the grab bag were made increasingly intermittent. At first, consequences were given every day (100% of the days). This was faded over periods of 5 to 10 days so that the consequences were delivered only 67% and then 33% of the days. Eventually, no consequences were provided. The results indicated that behavior was maintained up to seven weeks after the reinforcement had been terminated.

Intermittent reinforcement can be readily incorporated into most programs. It is important to make the schedule of reinforcement increasingly intermittent to increase resistance to extinction. It is unclear whether highly intermittent reinforcement forestalls extinction only temporarily or can virtually eliminate extinction even after a long extinction period. Behaviors reinforced intermittently have been maintained up to several months or a year after the intervention has been terminated (Hall, Cooper, Burmaster, & Polk, 1977; Morin, Ladouceur, & Cloutier, 1982).

Delaying Reinforcement. Another way to fade the contingencies is to increase the delay between reinforcement and the target behavior. When behavior is initially developed, immediate reinforcement is usually essential to ensure a high rate of responding. As behavior stabilizes and becomes well established, the delay between behavior and the reinforcing consequences can be increased without a loss in performance.

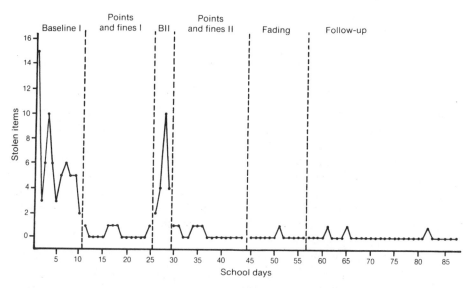

FIGURE 12-3 Number of items stolen each day during baseline and intervention (points and fines) phases. During the fading phase, consequences were provided less frequently for behavior. In the follow-up phase, the program was discontinued.

(Source: Rosen & Rosen, 1983).

An illustration of how delays can be used was provided in three classrooms where reinforcement was contingent on the appropriate behavior of the group (Greenwood, Hops, Delquadri, & Guild, 1974). After behavior had achieved a relatively high level, a delay was introduced in earning the group consequences. The classes were required to perform high levels of behavior for an increasing number of consecutive sessions before the reinforcer was delivered. A maximum delay of 10 sessions was attained before earning the reinforcer. Follow-up data three weeks after the program ended revealed that appropriate classroom behaviors were maintained.

In another example, delayed consequences were used to fade a combined token reinforcement and response cost program designed to reduce stealing in a 7-year-old boy who frequently took things from his classmates (Rosen & Rosen, 1983). Points (exchangeable for extra recess and other reinforcers) were provided if he did not have other children's possessions; fines were invoked if he did. The boy was checked every 15 minutes and received or lost points accordingly. This procedure effectively reduced his stealing. The program was then faded by checking and providing consequences only once every two hours. As shown in Figure 12-3, when the program was faded, virtually no stealing occurred. During the follow-up phase, checking, points, and fines were discontinued. The effects of the program were maintained over the 31-day follow-up period.

Delaying consequences is illustrated here as a way to fade contingencies. The shift from immediate to delayed reinforcement may be important in behavior-change programs because most of the reinforcers ordinarily available in the social environment are delayed. Hence, it is important to wean a client from immediate reinforcement. Behaviors should be well established before long delays are invoked. When delayed reinforcement is introduced, performance should be observed closely to ensure that there is no loss of behavioral gains. Eventually, reinforcement may be withdrawn entirely or delivered only after long delays without a loss in performance.

Often when parents and teachers develop a reinforcement program, they convey to the children that they can earn some consequence at the end of the week for performance of some target behavior (completion of homework for the week, cleaning one's room). It is important to convey again that such programs may *not* work very well in part because too much behavior is being required (an entire week of performance) and the single reinforcer is too delayed. It is much better to shape behavior (reinforce smaller units and build up to the desired target behavior) and to ensure that reinforcement is immediate and continuous. Thus moving to delayed reinforcement (e.g., consequences at the end of the week) is fine only after the behavior is well developed.

Using Levels to Promote Advancement through the Program. Another way to fade the contingencies is delineate levels or steps and to have individuals progress through these various levels based on their performance. As a client progresses through the levels, the consequences for behavior are more delayed, intermittent, or exert less direct and immediate control over behavior. For example, with psychiatric patients in hospital settings, token economies are often divided into levels. As patients perform the target behaviors consistently, they move to higher levels in the system, in which more or better reinforcers may be available (to encourage further progress). At the highest level, few or no contingencies may be in effect, so that the patients can function without direct and immediate consequences and have access to the available reinforcers without using tokens. In one such program for chronic psychiatric patients, the first level required patients to perform only minimal levels of behavior (such as attending activities) to earn tokens (Paul & Lentz, 1977). As they moved to higher levels, they could earn more tokens, and they had access to a larger range of backup reinforcers. At the highest level, they could buy themselves off the system. They used a credit card instead of tokens, and they had access to all of the available reinforcers as long as they continued to perform adequately.

The purpose of using levels is to develop higher levels of performance over time and to reduce dependence of behavior on highly structured contingencies. Ideally, the highest level in the program will resemble the contingencies that one is likely to encounter outside the setting. To ensure that performance is maintained at a high level, clients can be given the privilege of earning themselves off the highly structured contingencies (as in a token economy) only if their performance meets a particular criterion (Kazdin & Mascitelli, 1980). If a client's performance continues at a high level with few or no contingencies, behavior is more likely to be maintained when the client leaves the setting.

Gradually withdrawing contingencies may be very useful because it prepares clients for the conditions under which they must normally function. In everyday living, contingencies are often unsystematic, and consequences for performance, if any, may be delayed. The gradual withdrawal of contingencies provides a transition between a highly programmed environment and the ordinary conditions of everyday life. At present, several other studies have shown that fading the consequences leads to maintenance of behavior (e.g., Friman & Hove, 1987; Sullivan & O'Leary, 1990). Thus fading represents a maintenance strategy that should probably be routinely incorporated into behavioral programs.

Expanding Stimulus Control

One reason that behaviors may not be maintained and may not transfer to new settings is that clients readily form a discrimination between the conditions in which reinforcement (or punishment) is (S^D) and is not delivered (S^Δ). Behavior becomes associated with a narrow range of cues that may include specific behavior-change agents (e.g., parents, teachers) who administer the program, the times during the day in which the program is in effect, and the specific setting in which the contingencies are implemented (e.g., the classroom rather than the playground or home). This becomes obvious in school programs where a child may engage in deviant behavior throughout the day. For many children, a school day is divided into several periods, each associated with a different subject matter and teacher. If a behavioral program is implemented in one of the periods, it is likely that child performance would improve markedly in that period, but not in the other periods throughout the day. The child makes a clear discrimination and performs well under the conditions in which the contingencies of reinforcement support prosocial and adaptive behavior. Of course, changing behavior in one classroom is an initial step and an important one at that, but we wish the behavior to extend throughout the school day. Also, if the program were suspended (e.g., substitute teacher or simply withdrawing the program), the desirable behaviors may drop out as the child discriminates that the desirable behavior is no longer associated with certain consequences. Thus responses are not maintained and do not transfer to new situations. Maintenance and transfer can be developed by expanding the breadth of the stimuli that exert control over behavior. This can be accomplished in different and complementary ways.

Training the General Case. Usually, we want behavior to transfer across several dimensions, including who is present (parents, peers, teachers) and a range of activities, situations, and settings. The key question is how to do this? A systematic strategy for developing behavior across several conditions (e.g., settings, people, periods) is referred to as *training the general case* (Horner, Eberhard, & Sheehan, 1986). The term *general case* is used to refer to the goal, namely, to ensure the individual is trained to engage in the desired behavior beyond the very specific conditions in which training may have been initiated. Training the

Table 12-1   Requirements for Training the General Case

Step	What to Do	Example
1	Specify the set of stimulus situations across which a behavior is to be performed after training has been completed.	We would like the child to engage in the behavior during recess, at lunch, and during free time in class.
2	Define the range of relevant dimensions or characteristics across which they vary.	The different situations vary in the number of children present, in daily activities, and in the amounts of structure provided in the situations.
3	Define the range of response variations or the different behaviors required across the set of stimulus situations.	The responses we wish to include are initiating conversation, approaching others, responding to initiations of others, joining a group that is already engaged in an activity, and starting an activity with another person.
4	Select and teach examples that sample from the range of the stimulus and response domains (as specified in Steps 2 and 3).	Training will be carried out in different social situations, with different persons present, and with different social cues.

(Source: Adapted from Horner, Eberhard, & Sheehan, 1986)

general case helps the investigator develop behavior that is maintained and transferred.

There are several steps to training individuals so that they will respond across multiple situations. These steps, listed in Table 12-1, are considered at the beginning of the program. That is, the investigator asks, "Under what conditions do we want the target behavior(s) to be performed?" The steps are designed to provide critical answers and a concrete strategy to achieve the goals.

Consider the steps with a hypothetical program designed to teach a shy, withdrawn child to socialize with peers at school. The target behavior consists of speaking with other children. As listed in the table, in Step 1, we note the specific situations in which we wish the behavior to occur. In our example, we decide that we would like the child to engage in the behavior during recess, at lunch, and free time in class.

In Step 2, we identify the salient stimulus characteristics that vary among these conditions. Among such characteristics are differences in the number of children present, daily activities, in settings, and the amount of structure (e.g., rules, task assignments) provided in the situations. In this step, an indefinite number of characteristics might be identified, but the success of the strategy does not depend on identifying every conceivable characteristic on which the situations vary. The task is merely to identify some of the salient characteristics that differentiate the situations.

In Step 3, we specify the variations of the target behaviors that are required in these situations. The behaviors might include initiating conversation, approaching others, responding to initiations of others, joining a group that is already engaged in an activity, and starting an activity with another person. Finally, in Step 4, we select for training exemplary situations that represent the stimulus and response domains of interest. Thus training might be carried out in different social situations, with different persons present, and with different social cues. Using the overall approach, training systematically develops behaviors in diverse situations.

Several studies have evaluated training in the general case as a means of ensuring transfer of behaviors across stimulus conditions. One such study was designed to teach the simple skill of putting on a shirt to developmentally disabled persons (8 to 23 years old) who lived in community group homes (Day & Horner, 1986). Two training methods were used. The first method consisted of single-instance training, in which individuals were trained (prompts, praise) to put on a single type of shirt (T-shirt). The second method consisted of general-case training, in which additional types of shirts were presented in training (T-shirt, tank top, turtleneck). These shirts sampled a broader range of stimulus conditions (e.g., type of collar, sleeve length, fit, fabric), and as a consequence, they also required the broader range of responses entailed in "putting on a shirt." At different points in training, individuals were tested (without prompts or reinforcement) to see the extent to which they could put on a wide range of shirts, including types that had not been part of training. General-case training led to performance across a greater range of new stimulus conditions than did single-instance training. Other studies have used training the general case to develop self-care and community-relevant skills among people with developmental disabilities, as well as to train institutional staff working with special populations to use behavioral techniques with their clients (Ducharme & Feldman, 1992; Horner, Albin, & Ralph, 1986; Neef, Lensbower, Hockersmith, DePalma, & Gray, 1990). The results have shown that behavior transfers to a broader range of stimulus conditions with general-case training than from the usual single-case training.

Training in the general case focuses on enhancing transfer of training across situations, settings, and trainers. The most common use of the strategy is ensuring that training generalizes from the setting in which it is conducted to everyday life and more naturalistic situations. This emerges often because in many programs, training is conducted in highly controlled conditions such as individual laboratory sessions in a room with a trainer. Often it is quite useful to begin training in special laboratory sessions where the behaviors can be developed and simulated under controlled conditions. With control over the situations, sessions with an individual trainer, and careful shaping and reinforcement, behavior change is more easily achieved. Once the desired behaviors are developed, general-case training provides a way to foster transfer of behavior to everyday situations.

As an illustration in one program, adult mentally retarded women were trained in sexual abuse prevention (Miltenberger, Roberts, Ellingson, & Galensky, 1999). Sexual abuse of individuals with mental retardation is a significant problem rarely discussed in the media or more generally, in the context of sexual abuse. In this project, the investigators trained women to refuse sexual overtures from others, say no, leave the situation, and tell the incident to others when inappropriate approach responses were made to them. Training was conducted with pairs of women in which they practiced the target behaviors (what they would say and do) in a set of hypothetical situations. Training developed the desired behaviors using role-play, practice, feedback, and praise. Then tests were provided in a realistic situation in which an unknown male made approach responses. The results revealed that the behaviors occurred in the training sessions but did not transfer very well to ordinary situations. Training was then conducted in more everyday situations with confederates (research assistants working for the study) who made approach responses. As the behaviors developed, training ceased and assessments were made unobtrusively. The results indicated that the behaviors now carried over to everyday situations. In addition, assessment in everyday situations one month after the program ended indicated that the behaviors were maintained. The study conveys the importance of introducing into training the situations to which one wants the behavior to generalize.

At this point, the strength of the evidence for training the general case is in relation to transfer of training. Studies often report that behaviors developed through general case training are maintained months after treatment ends (Ducharme & Feldman, 1992, Ducharme & Holborn, 1992). The extent to which general case training develops maintenance is less well studied. Even so, general-case training is an important strategy to ensure that behaviors are not restricted to features of the training setting. The strategy is also valuable because it encourages one to consider at the outset of the program the range of conditions in which performance is ultimately desired.

In some cases, practical obstacles may prevent introducing diverse stimulus conditions into training. For example, many behavioral programs focus on developing community-related skills among various populations. Training is often conducted in the community to help train the general case. It may be difficult to make diverse settings available for training purposes. One alternative may be to use videotaped vignettes illustrating the diverse settings in which the behaviors are to be performed, a procedure that also facilitates generalization across settings (Haring et al., 1987).

Peer Facilitators. Parents, teachers, and staff are usually in charge of implementing behavior-change programs. Stimulus control can develop quickly as the client learns that consequences are likely to be provided in the presence of these other persons but not in their absence. One way in which stimulus control has been expanded is to involve peers in administering the program. Because peers have contact with the client across a variety of situations, their presence may provide the client with cues to continue the target behavior across these situations. After the specific contingencies have been terminated, peers may still influence the client's behavior.

Many programs using peers as behavior-change agents have been conducted in classroom settings. For example, in one program, fourth-grade children functioning well in their classes were trained to serve as tutors to help socially withdrawn children with developmental disabilities engage in cooperative play, activities, and self-help skills (Lancioni, 1982). The tutors were trained to model the target behaviors and to provide prompts and social reinforcement. For their assistance, the tutors received tokens. They worked with these children in activities in special sessions outside the classroom, which increased the social behavior of the developmentally disabled children. Moreover, the changes in the behavior of the developmentally disabled children transferred to social interaction with other children and to a play situation in which training had not been conducted. After training had been terminated, performance was maintained over a two-week follow-up period. These results suggest that the use of peers may facilitate both transfer of training and response maintenance.

Similarly, in another program, three junior high school students were trained to serve as tutors for children in need of remedial reading instruction (Greer & Polirstok, 1982). The tutors were trained to administer approval for on-task behavior and to ignore disruptive behavior. They received token reinforcement for their delivery of approval. The results indicated that the target children improved in their performance in reading assignments. After the tutors no longer received token reinforcement for helping the target children, they continued to provide approval and the target children maintained their improvements in reading. These results illustrate a potential advantage of peer-based reinforcement. Once peers have been trained, they may continue to provide reinforcement to persons under their charge. Alternatively, they may serve as discriminative stimuli and through stimulus control, help promote the target behaviors altered in training.

Other investigations have shown that peer-administered contingencies sometimes lead to maintenance and transfer of behavior to situations other than those in which training has been conducted (Peck, Cooke, & Apolloni, 1981). However, the use of peers as facilitators of transfer and maintenance remains to be exploited. In many of the situations in which behavioral programs are conducted, peers, siblings, or other inmates or residents might be involved in monitoring the behavior of a target subject and may help expand the stimulus control over behavior.

Self-Control Procedures. The situations, settings, and activities in which the behavior is performed can be greatly expanded by shifting the focus from other-administered reinforcement (e.g., parents, teachers, peers) to self-reinforcement. Perhaps, training clients to control their own behavior would prevent behavior changes from being lost when a program is withdrawn. Obviously, transfer of training could be less of a problem as well because self-administered programs presumably can go everywhere.

Few programs have carefully tested the effects of self-control strategies as a means of maintaining long-term gains or ensuring transfer of training. In one demonstration, self-control techniques were used with parents of preschool children who had been referred for treatment (Sanders & Glynn, 1981). The children were noncompliant, demanding, and difficult to manage at home. The parents were trained to provide prompts and praise for appropriate behavior, deliver feedback, and use reprimands and withdrawal of reinforcers for inappropriate behavior. Initially, training was conducted by a therapist who visited the home. After the parents' skills had been developed, a self-management training procedure was provided to help the parents maintain their skills. They were trained to monitor their own behavior, structure the situation to foster appropriate child behavior, identify target behaviors, and monitor their children's progress. The initial training increased the parents' skills (e.g., use of social reinforcement), which decreased disruptive child behavior in the home. With self-management training, the parents' skills were maintained in the home and generalized to community settings (shopping trips, visits to relatives), where disruptive child behavior also decreased. Moreover, a three-month follow-up assessment indicated that the parents' skills and low rates of disruptive child behavior were maintained.

Self-control strategies have been used to achieve transfer of training across situations (Ninness, Fuerst, Rutherford, & Glenn, 1991). In this program, three emotionally disturbed adolescents in a special education classroom were trained to engage in on-task behavior and to reduce socially inappropriate behavior (fighting, throwing objects, cursing). Modeling, reinforcement, role-playing, and self-control training (self-monitoring, self-reinforcement, matching self-assessment to the assessment of the teacher) led to reduction of inappropriate behavior. Socially inappropriate behavior did not change during periods between classes as students walked to other classes, which was assessed by means of a hidden camera. When students were instructed to apply self-control and self-evaluation to the between-classes period, socially inappropriate behavior decreased, as it had in the classroom. The effects were evaluated for only a few days; consequently, whether the gains would have been sustained in the classroom or between classes without additional contingencies is not known. Yet the results suggest that self-control can be used to enhance transfer.

In general, self-control strategies may be useful to enhance maintenance and transfer, but few demonstrations are available showing that they can exert long-term impact. Evidence, mostly from classroom settings with elementary school students, indicates that self-monitoring and self-reinforcement have short-lived effects unless external contingencies (e.g., those by the teacher) are applied to sustain behavior. The value of self-control techniques does not depend on whether they maintain behavior or lead to transfer when used by themselves. The techniques may serve as a useful adjunct to expand stimulus control across settings or to fade contingencies from other-administered to self-administered consequences.

Duration of the Intervention

Many behavioral programs have been implemented in settings such as the classroom, home, or community for relatively brief periods (e.g., several days or a few weeks). Marked changes in behavior can be achieved even in such brief periods. However, maintenance and transfer may be especially unlikely in programs implemented for relatively brief treatment periods. If one wishes to develop durable behaviors that are performed in many different situations, an extended period of training may be necessary.

The duration of the program appears to be related to response maintenance and transfer of training, although the effects of duration on maintenance and transfer have not been carefully tested. This is not a satisfactory statement because merely saying that programs in place for a while often lead to maintenance does not describe the process of how or why this is achieved. We know from everyday experience that behaviors initially developed or maintained by external contingencies (e.g., an initial exercise regimen, pattern of eating, or practice of a musical instrument) often become a part of a repertoire that seems to continue quite apart from those initial contingencies. This is not well understood. In a seeming parallel way, keeping programs in effect for a while also appears to foster continuation of the behavior after the program is withdrawn.

A number of programs that have become "classics" for the field have been carried out for protracted periods (from several months to a few years). In some instances, the results have suggested that the responses are maintained and transfer to new situations. An example already mentioned was one of the most comprehensive treatment programs for hospitalized psychiatric patients (Paul & Lentz, 1977). The program consisted of a token economy that was implemented for a period spanning several months. The patients continued to show gains $1\frac{1}{2}$ to 5 years after the program had ended. Moreover, the gains were reflected in community adjustment after patients had left the hospital. Thus both maintenance and transfer appeared to have been achieved.

As another example, a behavior modification program was implemented in elementary school grades over a period of several years and grade levels (Bushell, 1978). The program included more than 7,000 children in approximately 300 classrooms (from kindergarten through third grade) in 15 cities throughout the United States. The program relied heavily on token reinforcement to promote academic performance and several other practices such as instructing children in small groups within the class, using academic curricula that permitted evaluation of student progress, specifying performance criteria for teachers and students, and providing special training and feedback to teachers regarding their performance and the progress of their students. The gains in academic performance of students who participated in the program were markedly greater than were the gains of students in traditional classrooms. Moreover, those gains were still evident two years after the program had been terminated and the children in the program had entered classrooms where token reinforcement was not in effect.

Programs in place for extended periods often provide intensive treatment efforts. That is, the program is comprehensive in terms of the number of behaviors that are focused on and number of persons such as parents, teachers, and others who administer the program. It could well be the scope of the treatment rather than duration of the program that leads to long-term maintenance. For example, in a program for autistic children (under age 4), a behavioral intervention was provided in the home, school, and community (Lovaas, 1987, 1993). Treatment focused on eliminating maladaptive behavior (e.g., self-stimulation, aggression) and developing a variety of prosocial skills (e.g., play) and cognitive–academic skills (e.g., language, reading, writing). The program involved parents, teachers, and trained undergraduates so that almost all of each child's waking hours were devoted to developing adaptive behaviors. Treatment was provided for 40 hours a week, 365 days a year, for two to six years. The results indicated that 47% of the children were eventually placed in normal first-grade classes and improved markedly on standardized intelligence tests. These gains were not evident in control children who were not involved in the training program. The gains of the program appeared to transfer to regular public school functioning.

Follow-up was conducted for both treatment and control groups (McEachin, Smith, & Lovaas, 1993). At the time of follow-up, intervention youths had been out of treatment for a mean of five years (range zero to 12 years); control subjects were out of treatment for a mean of three years (range zero to nine years). The results indicated that the benefits of treatment were maintained. More youths in the intervention group remained in a regular class placement, mean IQ scores were higher, and adaptive behavior scores were superior to the control group. The original treatment and follow-up results represent critically important findings suggesting the impact of an intensive and long-term intervention.

The programs highlighted here do not show unequivocally that the longer a program is in effect, the more likely it is that behaviors will be maintained and will transfer to new settings. To obtain this information, research would need to compare the effects of a program applied to different clients for different durations. Yet some evidence has suggested that programs in effect for brief periods show little maintenance and that maintenance increases as treatment is continued. For example, in one program, peer interaction was developed among withdrawn elementary school children (Paine et al., 1982). The children received token reinforcement at recess and in-class training for social behavior. Behaviors improved, but the gains were lost in return-to-baseline phases. Treatment was introduced and withdrawn repeatedly in separate phases over time. With each successive treatment phase, less of the desired social behavior was lost when baseline conditions were reintroduced. By the end of the program, behaviors were maintained, and the children remained within the normal range of social interaction without continuing treatment. The reasons that behaviors were maintained are unclear. It is possible that as a behavior is performed for an extended period, reinforcers that naturally occur in the environment or are provided by the behavior itself begin to control the behavior (Baer et al., 1976).

As mentioned previously, maintenance and transfer of behavior are often evident in everyday life after an extended period of performing that behavior. Engaging in exercise or eating special foods may initially require some special incentive program. However, once the behaviors have been performed for an extended period, they often seem to be maintained "on their own." Similarly, in behavioral programs, repeated opportunities to perform a behavior over time appear to enhance maintenance (Greenwood, Delquadri, & Hall, 1984; Horner, Williams, & Knobbe, 1985). The process of developing behavior so that it becomes fixed in one's repertoire and relatively impervious to moment-to-moment contingency changes is not well understood. Additional research is needed in the context of behavioral programs to examine whether, in fact, programs in effect for longer periods are related to maintenance of behavior change once the programs have been terminated.

Combined Procedures

The previously discussed procedures for promoting response maintenance and transfer of training are not mutually exclusive. In fact, many of the procedures I have distinguished for purposes of presentation can be viewed as variations of a broader strategy, namely, making the circumstances in which training is conducted similar to the circumstances in which behavior will be performed once the program is terminated. The procedures reflect multiple ways in which this can be accomplished. For example, fading the contingencies and expanding stimulus control provide different ways in which one can develop behavior so that it is not connected to or performed exclusively in the presence of a narrow range of conditions.

To maximize the likelihood that responses will be maintained and will transfer to new situations, investigators often combine the various procedures. For example, in one study, adolescents in an institutional setting (nonspecified) received training in various social skills (responding politely, reacting prosocially to criticism or to confrontation from others) (Foxx, Faw, & Weber, 1991). Each youth had been identified with emotional and behavioral dysfunction. The skills were learned in special sessions in a novel part of the facility, although the goal was to develop skills that would generalize widely across others and to the youths' regular classroom. To achieve generalization and maintenance, several strategies discussed previously were combined. To begin, the responses (social skills) were considered to be important for natural interaction in the situation and hence were likely to be supported by the natural contingencies; the contingencies were gradually faded from token (monetary) reinforcement to praise for the desired behaviors; stimulus control was expanded by including training people who would be present in the nontraining setting after training; prompting and reinforcement by the trainers were gradually decreased as social skills improved; and youths assumed a larger role over their own training by self-monitoring (self-control) their progress on a score card and administering self-instructions covertly to guide behavior. The results indicated that training effects generally were maintained up to the three-month follow-up assessment and generalized to the regular classroom.

Many other programs have combined various techniques to promote response maintenance and transfer, such as substituting naturally occurring reinforcers for more contrived reinforcers and expanding stimulus control so that the training situation resembles natural stimulus conditions (Ducharme & Holborn, 1997); training in multiple settings to expand stimulus control and shifting to more intermittent reinforcement (Rasing & Duker, 1992); using delayed and intermittent reinforcement and fading the presence of the trainer (Dunlap, Koegel, Johnson, & O'Neill, 1987); and using peers, shifting from edible to social and from continuous to intermittent reinforcement, and increasing the delay of reinforcement (Lancioni, 1982).

The use of several strategies to achieve maintenance and transfer means that it is difficult to know which strategy or combination of strategies was responsible for the favorable effect. In applied settings, the primary goal has been to demonstrate that maintenance and transfer can be achieved. This is a priority to ensure that clinically important changes are made to help the people who participated in the program. Consequently a combination of several procedures is often used. This work has indicated that behaviors can be maintained after the program is terminated. Additional research is needed to analyze carefully what strategies lead to maintenance and transfer and how the effects of these strategies can be maximized. Despite the remarkable progress, it is still the case that we understand more about developing behavior than ensuring behavior is retained over the long run.

SUMMARY AND CONCLUSIONS

The remarkable effects of behavioral techniques in changing behavior raise two critical questions: (1) Once the behaviors are developed or altered, will they be maintained when the program has been withdrawn? and (2) Will the changes transfer to other settings in which the program has not been administered? These questions are about response maintenance and transfer of training, respectively. Maintenance and transfer are not automatic by-products of a behavior modification program. They usually have to be programmed directly by including specific procedures in the program.

Advances have been made in developing techniques that maintain behavior and ensure its transfer. Major techniques include (1) bringing behavior under the control of the natural contingencies, (2) programming naturally occurring reinforcers, (3) gradually removing or fading the contingencies, (4) expanding stimulus control over behavior, (5) continuing the program for an extended period, and (6) using combined procedures. Variations of these techniques were also discussed. These techniques vary in the extent to which they have been evaluated and to which they achieve maintenance, transfer, or both. In many programs several maintenance strategies are combined to maximize the likelihood that durable and broad changes in performance will be attained. Hence the effectiveness of individual techniques is often difficult to determine. Nevertheless, present work suggests that several of the techniques can be implemented to maintain high levels of performance and to extend these levels to the new situations in which the client will function.

KEY TERMS

Behavioral trap	Response maintenance	Transfer of training
Naturally occurring reinforcers	Training the general case	

APPLYING PRINCIPLES AND TECHNIQUES TO EVERYDAY LIFE

1. Behavior modification is not unique in its concern with response maintenance and transfer of training. Give an example from education (values, practices, and habits taught in school) of behaviors one would like to have maintained and to transfer to new settings.

2. Gradually removing or fading the contingencies is one way to ensure maintenance of behavior after a program is terminated. Briefly describe a behavior-change program. Then after behavior is developed, describe in more detail two ways in which you could gradually fade the contingencies.

3. Training the general case is an excellent way to ensure that behaviors are maintained and transfer to new situations and conditions. Give the steps involved in training the general case and describe specifically what you would do to ensure broad generality of the behavior. Use as your focus an adult who is socially withdrawn and does not socialize at all with others. Make up other details as you need them for the example.

4. Explain why the following is untrue or not quite accurate: "Intermittent reinforcement should never be used to develop maintenance of behavior. We know that intermittent behavior leads to much less behavior than does continuous reinforcement, so a program based on intermittent reinforcement is destined to produce mediocre effects."

FOR FURTHER READING

Albin, R.W., Horner, R.H., Koegel, R.L., & Dunlap, G. (Eds.). (1987). *Extending competent performance: Applied research on generalization and maintenance.* Eugene, OR: University of Oregon.

Allen, J.S., Jr., Tarnowski, K.J., Simonian, S.J., Elliott, D.S., & Drabman, R.S. (1991). The generalization map revisited: Assessment of generalized treatment effects in child and adolescent behavior therapy. *Behavior Therapy, 23,* 393–405.

Craft, M. A., Alber, S. R., & Heward, W. L. (1998). Teaching elementary students with developmental disabilities to recruit teacher attention in a general education classroom: Effects on teacher praise and academic productivity. *Journal of Applied Behavior Analysis, 31,*

399–415.

Esveldt-Dawson, K., & Kazdin, A.E. (1998). *How to maintain behavior* (2nd ed.). Austin, TX: Pro-Ed.

Horner, R.H., Dunlap, G., & Koegel, R.L. (Eds.). (1988). *Generalization and maintenance: Life-style changes in applied settings.* Baltimore: Paul Brookes.

Lovaas, O. I. (1993). The development of a treatment-research project for developmentally disabled and autistic children. *Journal of Applied Behavior Analysis, 26,* 617–630.

Stokes, T.F., & Osnes, P.G. (1989). An operant pursuit of generalization. *Behavior Therapy, 20,* 337–355.

NOTES

1. The reader will discern that transfer of training and maintenance at the level of the definition overlap. If transfer of training refers to performing the behavior under new situations and circumstances, does this not encompass maintenance? After all, response maintenance reflects whether performance continues in a "new situation," that is, one in which reinforcement is no longer present. Maybe response maintenance could just be a special case of transfer. (Actually, I am very impressed that the reader raised this. I would have never thought about this!) The point is well taken, but the distinction between response maintenance and transfer ought to be retained. The terms provide a different emphasis and concern. Maintenance emphasizes whether behavior continues over time (maintenance), and this is clearly future oriented as a concern. Transfer usually emphasizes changes while the program is in effect but in those settings or circumstances where the program is not in effect. If the program changes behavior in the classroom, does behavior change at home (transfer)? If the program is ended in the classroom, will behavior continue into the future (maintenance)?

CHAPTER 13

Social, Ethical, and Legal Contexts

Previous chapters have presented different principles and techniques of behavior change and have illustrated a wide range of applications. It should be evident that behavioral techniques have been effectively applied to many areas of the functioning of children, adolescents, and adults. Behavioral techniques have been extended to more areas of human functioning than have techniques of any other approaches to therapy, education, or rehabilitation. However, behavioral techniques are not just a matter of applying techniques to behavior. Several considerations relate to how the behavioral approach is carried out and to the social, ethical, and legal contexts in which the programs are conducted. This chapter considers the social, ethical, and legal contexts in which behavioral techniques are administered. Although the issues are discussed in the context of behavioral interventions, they are not unique to these interventions. Yet now that there are techniques to alter behaviors that are clearly demonstrated, issues regarding how these techniques are applied become more salient.

THE SOCIAL CONTEXT OF TREATMENT

The goal of clinical and applied research is not only to develop effective procedures but also to ensure that those procedures take into account the concerns of society and the concerns of the consumers of treatment (parents, teachers, clients). Consider advances in another area of research to convey the issues. With technological advances, new organisms (e.g., hybrid vegetables or animals that combine characteristics of different species and cloning) or indeed parts of organisms in the laboratory (e.g., use of stem cells to create organs) can be created. These advances in science and technology raise all sorts of value issues and questions. Should we control life in this fashion? Now that we can alter and control life in primitive ways, to what ends should the advances be applied? Of course, there are no simple answers but there will be emerging guidelines, constraints, and recommendations that convey the boundary conditions and the context in which emergent biological technologies can be applied.

In behavior modification, concern for the social context emerged several years ago. Wolf (1978), a pioneer of applied behavior analysis, introduced the notion of *social validation,* which drew attention to key questions that ought to guide intervention research. When designing and implementing an intervention, three questions ought to be raised:

- Are the goals of the intervention relevant to everyday life?
- Are the intervention procedures acceptable to consumers and to the community at large?
- Are the outcomes of the intervention important, that is, do the changes make a difference in the everyday lives of individuals?

These questions are critically important to any intervention research, regardless of whether behavioral procedures are used. They can be highlighted by examining the focus of treatment, acceptability of the procedures that are used to alter behavior, and importance of the changes or whether the changes make a difference to the individual or the community at large.

Focus of Treatment

Considerable agreement exists regarding the goals of most therapeutic programs, regardless of whether they are behavioral programs. Thus there is reasonable consensus that behavior-change techniques should be applied to improve the academic behaviors of children who are doing poorly in school, decrease the symptoms of severely depressed adolescents and adults, eliminate the self-destructive behavior of autistic or mentally retarded children, decrease antisocial behavior among delinquents, and develop behaviors that prevent disease. It would not be difficult to extend this list based on the overriding consideration that some behaviors reflect significant concurrent problems (e.g., fighting at school) or are likely to lead to significant problems later in life (e.g., cigarette smoking). It is important to mention that in most instances, the focus of treatment does not raise major questions both because of broad consensus of the goals of treatment and because people actively seek out treatment on their own. However, situations occasionally arise that pose fundamental questions about the focus and social implications of treatment.

Social and moral questions about the focus of treatment (target behaviors) have been actively discussed. Two examples from the 1970s are historically interesting because the foci are relevant to contemporary discussions of stereotypes and acceptable behavior. The first example pertains to the application of behavioral techniques to a boy named Kraig, almost 5 years old, who engaged in cross-gender (traditionally female-typed) behaviors (Rekers & Lovaas, 1974). These behaviors included dressing in women's clothes, playing with dolls and cosmetics, and mimicking feminine gestures and mannerisms. He avoided all male-typed activities. Treatment was implemented because of the social isolation and ridicule to which Kraig was exposed due to the cross-gender behavior. Also, such behaviors are sometimes precursors to later sexual deviance, such as transvestitism (cross-dressing) and transsexualism (role identity with the opposite sex). Consequently, the need to intervene seems obvious. In any case, Kraig's parents sought treatment.

Using reinforcement and extinction in sessions carried out by the mother, more male-typed behaviors were developed, including playing with toys typical of little boys (soldiers, guns, airplanes), engaging in aggressive behaviors (playing cowboys and Indians, playing with a dart gun and a rubber knife), and dressing in masculine-typed clothes (army shirt, football helmet). Such behaviors as dressing in girls' clothes, playing with dolls, taking the role of the girl in games, and showing feminine gestures were decreased. In therapy sessions, Kraig's mother attended to his masculine behaviors and ignored his feminine behaviors; at home, his parents used token reinforcement to develop gender behaviors that were considered more gender appropriate. The program was very effective in altering Kraig's cross-gender behaviors, and 26 months after treatment, his sex-typed behaviors were considered to have become "normalized." Indeed, follow-up revealed not only the absence of pretreatment feminine behaviors but also expanded sex-role activities characteristic of boys (e.g., more rough-and-tumble play and interest in camping out).

Fundamental questions were raised about the focus of this study (Nordyke, Baer, Etzel, & LeBlanc, 1977; Winkler, 1977). Developing masculine behaviors explicitly adheres to social stereotypes about how boys and girls, and later, men and women, ought to behave. Yet, traditional gender-role behaviors may be questioned; they are not necessarily psychologically "healthy" or natural. Indeed, the authors who raised the concerns cited studies noting that more highly gender-typed individuals (females who are high in femininity and males who are high in masculinity) often show such characteristics as high anxiety, low self-esteem, low social acceptance, and lower intelligence compared with less–gender-typed individuals. The important point here is that fostering sex-typed behavior reflects a value stance and the adjustment of the individual or the welfare of society may not necessarily be enhanced by stronger gender-typed behaviors. This point could be raised at any time but becomes more obvious in the 25 years since the original report. Gender roles, behaviors, and related stereotypes these reflect have been actively challenged in contemporary society in part because of the many consequences they foster (e.g., discrimination). Moreover, there is greater recognition now of more sex-role alternatives—not just male and female—as part of everyday life. That is, it is not just two categories and one's biological "assignment" that can differ from the gender role one assumes.

However, the investigators noted that the severity of Kraig's cross-gender behavior, the possibility of his sexual deviance in adulthood, and his parents' concern over his social adjustment prompted the focus of treatment and the need to intervene (Rekers, 1977; Rekers & Lovaas, 1974). The issue extends beyond any particular case and raises questions about areas of treatment that are controversial and value laden. Scientific research cannot resolve the many questions that arise. For example, it is not known that many or most children with cross-gender behaviors later become deviant or that Kraig would have been one of the individuals with an untoward outcome. If this were known, additional questions might be raised about whether the deviance (e.g., transvestism) would necessarily harm the individual or society. Obtaining informed consent from the persons involved in treatment does not resolve the problem because neither the therapist nor the client (or the parents) can be truly informed. Insufficient information exists about the consequences of treating or failing to treat the behavior, so the long-term risks and benefits of treatment cannot be known.

Concerns over the social value of target behaviors that are elected in behavioral and other forms of treatment also arise with behaviors that may evoke fewer emotional responses than are evoked by gender-role stereotypes. For example, classroom applications of behavioral techniques frequently focus on making children well behaved so that they remain in their seats, do not speak without permission, and attend to their lessons (Winett & Winkler, 1972). Most of these applications have not included especially deviant children who engaged in severely disruptive or dangerous behavior (e.g., hyperactivity, aggression). Yet for many years, the focus on having mildly disruptive or inattentive children pay attention went unchallenged. Many subsequent investigations have since shown that improving attentiveness among students in the classroom does not necessarily improve academic performance (Sulzer-Azaroff et al., 1988). Perhaps proponents of behavior modification have been too hasty to embrace goals selected by others. Is it good to have well-behaved and quiet children or to give such a high priority to docile behavior, while neglecting major goals of education, such as improved academic performance? A shift in the research focus in educational settings has shown that improving academic performance frequently has, as a side effect, improved classroom attentiveness and reduced disruptive behavior. Thus concerns that many teachers have about discipline can be remedied by improving academic behaviors. Unless severe behaviors are apparent, the focus on classroom deportment might be appropriately redirected to academic accomplishment.

Concerns over the focus of treatment have been raised in studies where there might seem to be little reason to do so. Consider contemporary examples where the focus is on behavior related to risk of acquired immune deficiency syndrome (AIDS). Mentioned earlier was a study with emergency room nurses (DeVries et al., 1991). The purpose of the study was to increase the frequency of wearing rubber gloves as a means of decreasing the risk of human immunodeficiency virus (HIV) exposure (through contact with bodily fluids). Feedback was shown to reliably increase glove wearing. What possible question could one raise about the goals of this intervention? Actually, two questions were raised (Finney, 1991).

To begin, glove wearing is only one of the behaviors that is likely to decrease the risk of HIV exposure for health-care workers. In fact, in the United States, several practices (target behaviors) are mandated for health-care workers (by the Occupational Safety and Health Administration [OSHA]), including using safe methods in disposing sharp objects (e.g., needles, scalpel blades), managing wastes (e.g., products that may include blood or other bodily fluids), and wearing diverse protective barriers (e.g., gloves, eye protection, and face masks). Glove wearing is only one of the behaviors that protect health-care workers. Hence the case might be made that the target focus was insufficient to decrease risk, the original goal of the program. Indeed, if there was any chance that glove wearing might give nurses a false sense of security or provide additional confidence that they were well protected, then the program could actually *increase* risk for HIV and AIDS. That is, the workers might be a little more lax in handling materials for which the gloves would not be protective.

One might reply that at least the study increased the frequency of one safe practice, and hence the target focus should not be challenged. However, wearing gloves does not prevent accidental needle sticks, one way that HIV is transmitted to health-care workers. Moreover, wearing gloves might even increase the likelihood of needle sticks if the gloves are worn too often (Finney, 1991). (Handling needles is more cumbersome while wearing gloves and may increase the risk of a needle stick.) In short, to reduce risk of exposure to HIV, a more comprehensive focus may be needed than increasing glove wearing alone. Perhaps a complete task analysis ought to be done by experts to identify the full range of behaviors nurses ought to perform and then to ensure that any training program encompassed all of the behaviors.

As another example, this program was designed to encourage patrons in three "gay" bars to take free condoms from a container available in the area adjacent to where individuals purchased their drinks (Honnen & Kleinke, 1990). Carefully executed and evaluated prompting procedures (e.g., signs noting that condoms were available, the number of persons who died of AIDS in the state, and reminders of safe sex practices) were shown in an ABAB design to increase the number of condoms that were taken in each of the bars. The target behavior can be easily defended as important, because possession of a condom is a precondition for its use. At the same time, taking free condoms is not the same as engaging in safe sex or using the condoms. Indeed, another study has shown that making condoms readily available among high school students does not increase use of condoms (Kirby et al., 1999). Dissemination of condoms may be important as part of an intervention. As a goal or end in its own right, this is questionable. Further assessment is needed to ensure that development of the target behavior, as operationally defined, has impact on the original focus of interest, namely, protective sexual practices. (Incidentally, in the previously cited study, increasing the availability of condoms did not lead to increases in sexual activity, a concern of parents and teachers.)

The purpose of the prior examples is not to derogate in any way the programs that were highlighted but rather to raise the larger questions. The target focus of an intervention—any intervention, whether from a behavioral or other perspective—can raise significant issues. These issues may reflect values (e.g., how one ought to behave) and social perspectives (e.g., what is deviant). Selection of the target focus may also make assumptions or rely on incomplete data (e.g., whether leaving behavior alone will have dire consequences, whether a particular amount of behavior change will actually improve an individual's functioning in everyday life or aid society overall). These issues are not easily resolved.

Mentioned previously (see Chapter 3) were guidelines for selecting target behaviors. One of the guidelines was selecting behaviors that people in everyday life regard as important. People in everyday life include the client, persons in contact with the client, or society at large who might be affected by the outcome of treatment (Schwartz & Baer, 1991). Opinions from others regarding the appropriate target focus are a useful guide. Yet, opinions, whether from lay persons or professionals, are not always informed and at best provide an imperfect guide to what behaviors will be adaptive, appropriate, and of benefit in the short and long run. Moreover, "people" is not a homogeneous category and many different segments argue for different and often diametrically opposed behaviors. For example, many argue for no smoking in public places (to avoid secondary smoke) and no peanuts as snacks on airplanes (because of a few allergic reactions) but each cause has a vocal group of individuals arguing the other side.

The investigator considering behavior-change interventions ought to make the goals explicit with all interested parties and raise questions for discussion regarding what is and what is not known and the potential benefits and risks associated with the intervention. When the intervention focuses on treatment of self-injurious behavior, physically abusive child-rearing practices, or severe anxiety, for example, the questions of whether to intervene and the appropriateness of the focus are less likely to emerge. Even so, the comprehensiveness of the focus is worth discussing to ensure that the behaviors to be changed will address the central concern or goal.

Treatment Acceptability

The selection of target behaviors raises issues about the focus and *goals* of treatment. The treatment techniques of course concern the *means* to obtain them. The social context is obviously relevant to the selection of the treatments. The techniques that can be used to alter behavior must consider people's opinions about what is appropriate and reasonable to do. It may be of little use to develop effective treatments if the procedures are highly objectionable to the people who need them (e.g., parents, teachers, clients) or to the people for whom they will be used (e.g., children, patients).

Attention has been given to the public reaction to treatment procedures and whether treatments are viewed as acceptable ways of changing behavior. The notion of *treatment acceptability* refers to judgments by laypersons, clients, and others of whether treatment procedures are appropriate, fair, and reasonable for the problem that is to be treated. Persons in a position to evaluate treatment, including review committees at institutions (e.g., hospital, university clinic), lay people, and clients themselves evaluate whether proposed treatment procedures are acceptable and reasonable for the client's problem. Treatment should be designed that is not only effective but also desirable or preferred among alternative treatments that might produce change.

The extent to which treatment is acceptable can influence several facets of the treatment process. For example, professionals who refer children to psychological treatment (e.g., pediatricians) are likely to recommend those procedures they consider to be more acceptable (Arndorfer, Allen, & Alijazireh, 1999). Also, how carefully professionals carry out treatment is a function of the extent to which they view the intervention as acceptable (Allinder & Oats, 1997). Among clients, treatments that are acceptable are more likely to be sought and adhered to once they have entered into treatment (Reimers et al., 1992). It is likely that acceptability also influences the decision to remain in treatment. In child and adolescent therapy, 40% to 60% of families who begin treatment drop out prematurely and against the advice of the clinician (Kazdin, 1996b; Wierzbicki & Pekarik, 1993). Dissatisfaction with the treatment and views that treatment may be demanding or irrelevant to the children contribute directly to dropping out (Kazdin, Holland, & Crowley, 1997). Clearly, professional and client views of the acceptability contribute to multiple aspects of treatment use and adherence.

Research has examined how people evaluate treatment and whether treatment procedures are acceptable. For example, in one project, young psychiatric inpatients, their parents, and hospital staff were asked to evaluate several procedures that were applied to children (hypothetical cases) for highly deviant and disruptive behavior at home and at school (Kazdin et al., 1981). The procedures were described in detail, and the subjects rated the extent to which the different treatments were consistent with commonly held notions of what treatment should be, whether the treatments were fair or cruel, and whether the treatments were appropriate for clients who could not give consent. Marked differences among the treatments were shown in a measure that assessed the overall acceptability of treatment. The children, parents, and staff agreed in their ordering of treatments. A reinforcement technique (in which appropriate behavior was reinforced as a way of reducing inappropriate behavior) was evaluated as much more acceptable than the alternative treatments. Time out (involving 10 minutes of isolation) was rated as the least acceptable treatment. Positive practice and medication to control disruptive behavior were intermediate in overall acceptability.

Evaluations of treatment acceptability have focused on several questions (see Elliott, 1988; O'Brien & Karsh, 1990). The most frequent focus has been to examine different procedures and their relative acceptability. Another line of research has been to examine differences in acceptability among different types of clients or consumers of treatment (e.g., children, parents, teachers, or the community at large) (e.g., Blampied & Kahan, 1992). Different perspectives are likely to lead to different views about acceptable treatment. Characteristics of the treatments themselves can influence acceptability, and efforts have been made to isolate a number of these. For example, whether the individual client plays a role in planning the treatment and whether treatment has adverse side effects are two of the many factors that can influence acceptability ratings (e.g., Kazdin, 1981).

People's views of treatment acceptability probably depend on many factors such as how treatment is applied, who applies it, the severity of the problem, and the number of alternative treatments that have been previously tried. It is important to understand these influences so that factors that may help to make treatment acceptable can be incorporated into effective interventions. Apart from effectiveness, it is important to develop treatments that are sensitive to the interests, values, and lifestyles of those who are consumers of treatment. For example, there are cultural and ethnic differences in seeking treatment, using clinical services, and treatment preferences (Tharp, 1991). Understanding factors that influence acceptability of treatment services may be helpful in fostering increased use of treatment by diverse groups.

The other side of making treatments more acceptable is educating individuals about existing treatments that are effective but less familiar, such as response cost, time out, and positive practice. The acceptability of treatments known to be effective can be enhanced by clarifying the rationale underlying their use and describing the procedures in some detail (see Foxx et al., 1996; O'Brien & Karsh, 1990). Thus views of acceptability of treatment can be influenced by variations in the procedures themselves, as well as by efforts to educate potential consumers more about the procedures.

Traditionally, treatment techniques have been evaluated by looking at how effective they are in changing an individual's performance on various measures of personality and behavior. Obviously, the effectiveness of a treatment is extremely important. However, treatments, whether behavioral or nonbehavioral in orientation, need to be evaluated along many dimensions. Acceptability is one of these dimensions and, as already noted, has direct implications for seeking and remaining in a given treatment. It is essential that effectiveness and acceptability be viewed together. In contemporary society there are many procedures that individuals find quite acceptable because they are quick and require little or no effort. Common examples are the unlimited array of exercise equipment, herbs, potions, teas, and nutritional supplements. For many of these, wonderful outcomes are promised even though there is no or questionable evidence of effectiveness. A good example is getting a suntan (an acceptable procedure for nondermatologists) that promises many benefits. For example, on bottles of lotion we are told that by using the product, "You'll love the way you look and feel. . ." Moreover, with a suntan, you will feel "vibrant, healthy, and confident," and in general, "look and feel your best" (Coppertone™, Schering-Plough, 1996). The procedures are *acceptable* to many people, but evidence of any of the benefits remains to be seen. Insofar as risk for cancer increases, promoting suntans may even foster health problems rather than or in addition to health benefits.[2] Overall, acceptability is very pertinent in selecting treatments, but is not an end in itself. The acceptability of treatment assumes here that there is evidence that treatment is effective, that is, it has controlled studies showing that it leads to therapeutic change.

Treatment Outcomes

The social context of behavioral treatment also arises in evaluating changes in performance. Although dramatic changes often result from behavioral interventions, it is still appropriate to ask whether the changes are really important and if they make a difference in the lives of the clients. The social context in which the clients perform is an important consideration in answering these questions. The social context refers to evaluation of change in relation to other persons and in the context of everyday life.

In the past 20 years, advances have been made in elaborating and using alternative criteria to evaluate the importance of changes. The term *clinical significance* is used to reflect the practical or applied value or importance of the effect of the intervention, that is, whether the intervention makes a real (genuine, palpable, practical, and noticeable) difference in everyday life to the client or to others with whom the client interacts. There may be changes in the target behavior and an effect that is clearly reliable, based on careful assessment and evaluation in one of the single-case designs highlighted previously. However, such a demonstration does not by itself answer the questions raised by clinical significance: Are the changes important? Do they make a difference in the client's functioning in everyday life? Several ways of measuring the importance of change in the client are illustrated below (Kazdin, 1998; Kendall, 1999).

Comparison Methods Comparison methods, as the name suggests, examine the clinical significance of the change by directly comparing clients with others. The most commonly used method is to evaluate the functioning of clients relative to the "normal" functioning of others in everyday life. Before the intervention is applied, presumably, the behavior of the client departs from others functioning well in everyday life. For example, individuals referred for a particular problem (e.g., anxiety, depression, or aggressive behavior) are likely to depart from normative functioning in the respective problem area. One measure of the extent to which treatment produces clinically important change is evidence at the end of treatment that the client falls within the normative range of a well-functioning sample on the measures of interest. That is, the level of anxiety, depression, or aggression falls within the levels of individuals who are functioning well and experience no particular problems in these areas.

Evaluating the extent to which individuals perform at or are within the normative range is the most commonly used method of evaluating clinical significance. To invoke this criterion, a comparison is made between treated clients and peers who are functioning well or without significant problems in everyday life. For example, in a study mentioned earlier, alternative treatments were applied to help aggressive and antisocial children (Kazdin et al., 1992). The effectiveness of three conditions was examined: problem-solving skills training (PSST), parent management training (PMT), and both combined (PSST + PMT). Treatment was provided to children (PSST) and/or their parents (PMT) based on one of the three conditions to which families were assigned. Among the outcome measures were standardized scales (Child Behavior Checklist) completed by parents and teachers that focus on child symptoms, deviance, and prosocial behavior. Development of the scales has included extensive normative data of boys and girls of different ages (Achenbach, 1991). Analyses indicated that among the normative sample, the 90th percentile is the cutoff point that best delineates clinic from community (nonreferred) samples. (The 90th percentile means that 90 percent of the individuals are below that score.) Stated another way, above the 90th percentile is clearly an extreme level of behavior and one likely to be associated with individuals not functioning well in everyday life; anything below that percentile appears more within the normative range and closer to behavior of individuals functioning well within everyday life. In this treatment study, scores at this percentile were used to define the upper limit of the "normal range" of emotional and behavioral problem behavior. If children began treatment above the cutoff (in the severe or deviant range) and after treatment fell below the cutoff (in the normative range), this was considered to reflect a clinically significant change.

Figure 13-1 shows the means at pretreatment, posttreatment, and a one-year follow-up for antisocial children in the different treatment conditions. Both parent (upper panel) and teacher evaluations (lower panel) are presented and show some improvement of groups toward the normative range. The results in the figure provide group means (average performance of each group). However, clinically significant change is of equal if not greater interest in relation to individuals. One can compute how many individuals fall within the normative range at the end of treatment. In the present example, for the parent-based measure referred to in the figure, results at posttreatment indicated that 33%, 39%, and 64% of youths from PSST, PMT, and combined treatment, respectively, fell within the normal range. The percentage of youths returned to "normative" levels of functioning reflect one way to examine the clinical importance of the change.

In a very different context, the normative range was used as a way to evaluate the impact of treatment of insomnia (Jacobs, Benson, & Friedman, 1993). Behavioral treatment, based on relaxation training and stimulus control (e.g., associating

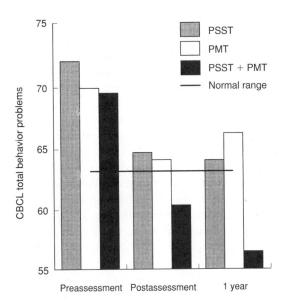

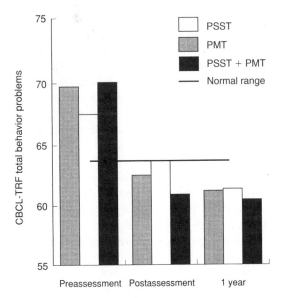

FIGURE 13-1 Mean scores for Problem-Solving Skills Training (PSST), Parent Management Training (PMT), and both combined (PSST + PMT) for the total behavior problem scales of the parent-completed Child Behavior Checklist (CBCL, upper panel) and the Child Behavior Checklist-Teacher Report Form (CBCL-TRF, lower panel). The horizontal line reflects the *upper* limit of the nonclinical ("normal") range of children of the same age and gender. Scores *below* this line fall within the normal range.

(Source: Kazdin, Siegel, & Bass, 1992)

going to bed with drowsiness and relaxation rather than restlessness and worrying), was provided to adults (ages 18 to 52) who could not get to sleep. A sample of individuals without sleep problems was assessed on several sleep-related measures to provide a normative range to evaluate the effectiveness of treatment. After treatment, individuals who were treated fell within the range of the normative sample in terms of such measures as time required to get to sleep (sleep onset latency).

Several other reports have evaluated whether behaviors of deviant, socially disruptive, or withdrawn children; the behaviors of anxious, depressed, or socially withdrawn adults; speech patterns of psychiatric patients; and many other domains of functioning have achieved normative levels after behavioral treatment (e.g., Kazdin, 1977b; Kendall & Grove, 1982). In each case, the study depends on identifying nondeviant peers who can serve as a basis for comparison. The performance of these peers is assessed to identify normative functioning. The mean and some interval about that mean are used to provide a window of functioning that is considered to represent persons in the normal range.

Another comparison method that has been devised is a comparison of clients after treatment with a *dysfunctional sample* that has not received the intervention. The notion is that at the end of treatment, clients who have made a clinically significant change will depart markedly from the original sample of dysfunctional cases. A statistical criterion has been suggested. Specifically, for an individual to be considered to be improved in a clinically important way, he or she should have a score on the measure that is two standard deviations from the mean (average) of the dysfunctional sample (Jacobson & Revenstorf, 1988). Thus at posttreatment, individuals whose scores depart at least two standard deviations from the mean of the dysfunctional group (untreated cases with demonstrated dysfunction) would be regarded as having undergone an important change. To be considered as clinically significant, the changes of course must reflect a departure from the deviant sample in the direction of a decrease of symptoms or increase in prosocial functioning.

For example, a study for the treatment of depression among adults compared two variations of cognitive problem-solving therapy (Nezu & Perri, 1989). To evaluate the clinical significance of change, the investigators examined the proportion of cases in each group whose score on measures of depression fell two or more standard deviations below (i.e., less depressed) the mean of the untreated sample. For example, on one measure of depression commonly used in treatment research (the Beck Depression Inventory), 85.7% of the cases who received the full problem-solving therapy regimen achieved this level of change. In contrast, only 50% of the cases that received the abbreviated problem-solving condition achieved this level of change. The more effective treatment led to a clinically significant change for most subjects; clearly, one treatment was better in this regard.

For many measures used in intervention research, normative data are available and can serve as a criterion for evaluating clinical significance. However, when normative data are not available or do not apply as an appropriate comparison (because of differences in culture, age), one can evaluate the extent to which the individuals have changed from their pre-intervention scores. In either case, the comparisons add important information about the impact of treatment.

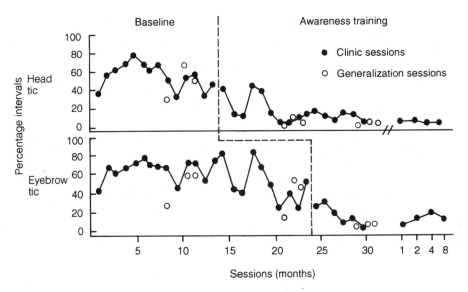

FIGURE 13-2 Percentage of intervals observed of two tics in the clinic sessions in which Steven sat and read for 25-minute periods and in generalization sessions (various places in the college library). Observers recorded the tics in these sessions across baseline and treatment phases.

(Source: Wright & Miltenberger, 1987)

Subjective Evaluation. Another method for evaluating whether the behavior changes achieved are important is to ask people in contact with the client or in a position of expertise whether the changes have made a difference. For example, in one program treatment was provided to a college student named Steven who wished to eliminate two muscle tics (uncontrolled movements) (Wright & Miltenberger, 1987). The tics involved head movements and excessive eyebrow raising. Individual treatment sessions were conducted in which Steven was trained to monitor and identify when the tics occurred and to be more aware of their occurrence. In addition, he self-monitored the tics throughout the day. Assessment sessions were conducted in which he read at the clinic or the college library and observers recorded the tics. The impact of self-monitoring and awareness training procedures was evaluated in a multiple-baseline design in which the two muscle tics were focused on in sequence. As shown in Figure 13-2, both of the tics declined in frequency when treatment was applied.

A central question is whether the reduction was very important or made a difference to either Steven or others. At the end of treatment, Steven's responses to a questionnaire indicated that he was no longer distressed by the tics and that he felt that they were no longer very noticeable to others. In addition, four observers rated randomly selected pretreatment and posttreatment videotapes. These were videotapes of assessment periods in which direct observations had been made of

Steven's tics. The observers rated the tics from the posttreatment tapes as not at all distracting, normal to very normal in appearance, and small to very small in magnitude. In contrast, they rated the tics from the pretreatment tapes as much more severe on these dimensions. The observers were then told which videotapes were the posttreatment tapes and were asked to report how satisfied they would have been if they had achieved the same results. All of the observers reported that they would have been satisfied with the treatment results. The evaluations from Steven and independent observers help attest to the importance of the changes achieved and provide information that cannot readily be discerned from the reductions graphed from direct observations.

Subjective evaluation has been used to assess whether improvements in writing skills of children are reflected in ratings of creativity or interest value of the compositions; whether individuals who are trained in public speaking skills are evaluated more positively by the audience, and whether people in contact with deviant children see their behaviors differently after treatment (Kazdin, 1977b). In many cases, the opinions of persons with special expertise is relevant. For example, in one project, young children were trained in how to escape from emergency fires in their home (Jones, Kazdin, & Haney, 1981). Escape includes a complex set of behaviors that vary depending on how far along the fire is, the location of the fire, and other factors (e.g., whether smoke is pouring under the door). The behaviors include crawling to the floor to avoid smoke inhalation, touching the door, checking the heat of the door, crawling out of the room, covering the crack in the door to stop the smoke from entering, and others). The behaviors were identified through task analysis and divided into trainable steps that encompassed several different scenarios of fires in the home. The children were successfully trained in the many different behaviors in simulated bedrooms. The question then became whether the training was likely to make a difference. One cannot make comparisons with a normative comparison group—most children (and adults) do not know how to respond to emergency fires and are likely to perform behaviors that place them at risk for injury and death. In this study, firefighters were asked whether the skills developed in escaping from emergency fire situations in the home would make a difference. Evaluations indicated that youths would be much less likely to be fatally burned in emergency situations after than before treatment. This suggests that the changes might in fact be important to the children's lives.

In most cases, the opinions of persons in everyday life and in contact with the client (parents, teachers, peers) serve as the basis for obtaining measures of subjective evaluations. Subjective evaluation is obviously important. If treatment is working and has an important impact, the effects ought to make a perceptible difference to clients themselves and to those with whom they interact. The opinions of others in contact with the client are important as a criterion in their own right because they often serve as a basis for seeking treatment in the first place and because they reflect the evaluations the client will encounter after leaving treatment.

Social Impact Measures. Another type of measure to evaluate the clinical or applied importance of treatment outcomes is to see whether measures of social impact are altered. Social impact measures refer to outcomes assessed in everyday life that are important to parents, teachers, and society at large. Rates of arrest, truancy, driving while intoxicated, cost, illness, hospitalization, and death are prime examples of social impact measures. Social impact measures can be added to other measures used in a study. For example, measures for programs designed to improve academic functioning, decrease aggressive behavior, and prevent coronary illness might include grades in school, arrest records, and mortality rates, respectively, in addition to the target behavior measures that might be assessed on a day-to-day basis. Consumers (e.g., clients who seek treatment, insurance agencies and health-care plans that pay for treatment) often regard indices such as these as the bottom line. Also, to the public at large such measures are often more meaningful and interpretable than psychological measures and even direct behavioral observations. For example, a behavior modification program may lead a child to pay better attention and do more and better work in class but final grades and whether the student passes and graduates are seen as more relevant by the public.

Social impact measures are often integrated into behavioral programs. For example, in one program, parent management training was used to treat adolescent delinquents (16 years of age or less) who had a history of offenses (Bank, Marlowe, Reid, Patterson, & Weinrott, 1991). Parents were trained to monitor delinquent behavior better and to use more age-appropriate incentives and punishment (e.g., work details, reporting law violations to authorities). Outcome measures included official offense reports, direct observation of home behavior, and parent report of problem behaviors. Parent training was compared with another group that received court-provided family treatment that included family therapy, group therapy, and drug counseling. The major results indicated that offense rates for both groups declined significantly after the onset of treatment. The decline was more rapid for the parent training group, as evident in lower offense rates for the adolescents during treatment and at the one-year follow-up assessment. Parent training cases spent significantly fewer days of incarceration during the first two follow-up years, which the authors note represented a significant cost saving favoring parent training. The measures of cost and offense rates through juvenile court records represent important social impact measures.

Social impact measures in business and industry provide another example. In studies that improve safety practices in business and industry, the benefits are often reflected in the number of injuries and accidents (Fox et al., 1987). Similarly, efforts to alter the habits of drivers not only have reduced speeding, the target behavior of interest, but also have been reflected in reductions in car accidents (Van Houten et al., 1985). In these studies, injuries and accidents are measures of obvious social importance.

General Comments. The use of comparative data, subject evaluation, and social impact measures represents an important step toward quantifying the extent to which outcomes produced with treatment really have made a difference in the clients' everyday lives. The measures address somewhat different questions about the importance of change and hence provide different conclusions about the impact of treatment. Each of the methods raises a number of issues that are far from resolved (Kazdin, 1999). Consider a few of these briefly.

The use of normative comparisons, perhaps the most commonly used method to evaluate the clinical or applied significance of change, raises many questions. An initial question is, Who should serve as the normative group? With whom should the developmentally disabled, chronic psychiatric patients, or prisoners be compared to evaluate the impact of an intervention? Developing a normative level of performance might be an unrealistic ideal in treatment, if that level is based on individuals functioning normally or well in the community.

Also, how does one define a normative population? We know, for example, that in a normative sample (i.e., children, adolescents, and adults from the community not involved in treatment), "normals" recruited for research can have high rates (e.g., 20%) of psychiatric disorder (Regier et al., 1984; U.S. Congress, 1991). That is, approximately one in five individuals in everyday life has a diagnosable psychiatric disorder. Clearly, there is a lot of social, emotional, and behavioral problems among people who might serve as a basis for comparison. In addition, rates of dysfunction and symptom patterns vary as a function of social class, ethnicity, and culture. In short, a normative sample and a simple comparison against which to judge treatment effects are not straightforward.

Even if a normative group can be identified, exactly what range of members' behaviors would be defined as within the normative level? Among individuals whose behaviors are not identified as problematic, there will be a range of acceptable behaviors. It is relatively simple to identify deviant behavior that departs markedly from the behavior of "normal" peers. However, as behavior becomes slightly less deviant, it is difficult to identify the point at which behavior is within the normative range. Is the normative range within some measure of variability of the average (mean) behavior of the normal peers, say, plus or minus one standard deviation? A subjective judgment is required to assess the point at which the individual has entered into the normal range of performance.

Another issue has to do with the criterion for normative functioning. For many behaviors and measures of interest, bringing individuals into the normative range is a questionable goal. Consider, for example, reading skills of elementary school children. A clinically significant change might well be to move children with reading dysfunction so that they fall within the normal range. However, perhaps the normal range itself should not be viewed as an unquestioned goal. The reading of most children might be accelerated from current normative levels. Thus normative data themselves need to be critically evaluated. As a more general statement, what one's peers do in a given culture or context (e.g., use drugs or weapons) is not necessarily a target at which treatment should aim.

There are interpretive issues regarding subjective evaluation as well. The greatest potential concern is the problem of relying on the opinions of others for determining whether treatment effects are important. Subjective evaluations and the global ratings on which they depend appear to be more readily susceptible to biases on the part of raters than are overt behavioral measures. Thus one must treat subjective evaluations cautiously; it is possible that subjective evaluations will reflect change when other measures of change do not. Indeed, in the context of therapy, many studies have shown little or no relation between how satisfied clients are with their treatment and the extent to which they improve in therapy (e.g., changes in symptoms or the problems that brought them to treatment) (Lambert, Salzer, & Bickman, 1998; Pekarik & Guidry, 1999).

When the client or person associated with a client is satisfied with treatment or asserts that a difference in behavior is noted as a function of the client's treatment, it does not mean that the extent of the client's change is clinically important. People in contact with the client may perceive a small change and report this in their ratings. However, this says nothing about whether treatment has accomplished enough to alleviate the problem for which it was sought or to bring the client within normative levels of behaving.

Finally, measures of social impact raise special problems. They are often relatively insensitive as measures of intervention effects. They are gross measures (e.g., grades, school attendance) and subject to a variety of influences (e.g., family stress, illness, school district) other than those associated with the intervention. Social impact measures are more likely to be recorded and scored somewhat haphazardly over time which introduces noise (error) into the results. Changes in funding (usually budget cuts), policy, procedures, and people responsible for recording all may operate in a systematic way to influence the reliability and validity of the data. For example, truancy is not scored consistently among different schools and even can be scored quite inconsistently over time as a function of the persons responsible for tracking student attendance in a given school.

Interpretive and assessment obstacles can plague social impact measures. Consider crime rate as an example because it is of interest for psychological as well as social interventions. First, what does the "crime rate" really assess, as evaluated in official reports (Uniform Crime Reports)? For one, crime is usually recorded in a hierarchical fashion, which means that any time there is a given crime incident, only the worst crime is counted (DiLulio, 1997). For example, on a given day, a criminal may rape someone, steal a getaway car, and assault the person from whom the car was taken. This is counted as one crime; the worst crime is counted (rape, in this case). Similarly, if two cars are stolen on the same night and two people are beaten up in the process but the same criminal did this, this is counted as one crime. In general, the most serious crime is counted, only that crime is counted in a given episode, and counted only once. That is fine, but crime rate does not necessarily reflect number of crimes completed nor number of victims. Still, showing a change in crime rate might be important, but the meaning of the measure is not obvious to most of us. More generally, social impact measures can supplement other psychological measures or observations of concrete behaviors that may reflect highly specific intervention targets. When social impact measures show a change, they convey important evidence that the impact of the intervention can be seen in ways that consumers are likely to appreciate.

ETHICAL AND LEGAL CONTEXTS

Several ethical and legal issues must also be taken into account in designing and implementing interventions. Most of the ethical and legal issues associated with treatment apply broadly across disciplines including psychology, psychiatry, social work, counseling, and nursing, all of which are involved in providing interventions for social, emotional, and behavioral problems. The issues also apply broadly across treatment approaches, including cognitive-behavioral, family-based, psychodynamic, humanistic, and other therapies. A few such issues have been raised in relation to behavioral techniques.

Behavior Control and Individual Freedom

The behavioral approach represents explicit attempts to alter specific behaviors in the context of education, treatment, rehabilitation, or everyday life. The focus on behavior and behavior change may raise special concerns about efforts to "control" people. The very term *behavior modification* may imply efforts to control, manipulate, or otherwise tinker with other people's lives. Indeed, the term, rather than the procedures it describes, is what seems to evoke negative reactions (Kazdin & Cole, 1981; Woolfolk, Woolfolk, & Wilson, 1977).

No inherent or unique control issues are raised by behavioral techniques that are not also raised by other approaches to treatment. Behavioral techniques do not necessarily embrace particular goals or an agenda for society. The issue relevant to behavioral interventions is not "control" or the dictating of objectives but bringing to bear behavioral interventions to the many goals of individuals, families, and society at large. Obvious examples of such goals are the education of young people, the minimization of crime, and the prevention of disease. The issue is whether behavioral or other forms of intervention can facilitate the achievement of these goals.

For example, in classroom settings, many of the attempts of teachers to control student behavior are based on corporal and verbal punishment. The issue here is not whether child behavior should be controlled to achieve certain goals. The goals of improved academic performance, appropriate classroom behavior, and increased enjoyment of specific activities such as reading are widely agreed on. Behavioral interventions can greatly improve reaching these goals. Indeed, it is still the case that routine techniques in the classroom (excessive reprimands, extra academic assignments as a form of punishment, and missed opportunities to praise and shape academic progress) compete directly with and undermine the stated aims of education. Techniques discussed in previous chapters, especially those based on positive reinforcement, offer means that can greatly improve on many of the techniques ordinarily used in everyday life. Ethical issues are not raised by the goals or the means (behavioral techniques) to achieve them. Indeed, one might ponder the ethics of using interventions that are known not to work or of not training teachers to promote prosocial and academic behavior in effective ways.

Behavioral principles and techniques do not argue for a particular way of life or particular goals. Indeed, the same principles and techniques have been applied to quite different styles of living. For example, behavioral principles and techniques have been applied to communal living. Small communities (such as Twin Oaks in Virginia and Los Horcones in Sonora, Mexico [see www.

loshorcones.org.mx]) have been developed on the basis of operant condit[]
principles (Skinner, 1948). For example, Twin Oaks, begun in 1967, is org[]
on the basis of a token economy in which credits are earned for perform[]
work and activities that the community requires to function. The lifestyl[]
community embraces such values as sharing of assets, individual autono[]
self-government in a way different from that of mainstream commu[]
(Kinkade, 1973).

The same behavioral principles and techniques used to support community
life can also be used by individuals as part of self-control techniques for advancing personal rather than communal goals. In general, the goals of professionals
concerned with the welfare of individuals are to increase effective living, personal
choices, and freedom from behaviors that may restrict functioning in everyday
life. The goals of behavior modification do not differ from the goals of other approaches to the welfare of individuals. Rather, they represent a means of obtaining consensually agreed on goals and reducing untoward side effects of commonly
used methods (e.g., punishment in the home and at school).

Misuse of Reinforcement and Aversive Techniques

Behavior-change practices need to be used responsibly and ethically. One can
readily conceive of ways of misusing techniques under the guise of laudatory purposes. In fact, outside the realm of behavior modification, there are many examples from everyday life where unacceptable practices (e.g., physical abuse of
children) are designed to achieve reasonable goals (e.g., improve child behavior).
Indeed, corporal punishment is used extensively in everyday life even though
there is considerable evidence that physical punishment used excessively can increase aggressive and antisocial child behavior (Wolfe, 1999). In recognition of
this, several countries such as Austria, Denmark, Finland, Norway, and Sweden
have banned corporal punishment as a means of child discipline at home and in
school (Greven, 1992). As shown in prior chapters, there are positive reinforcement alternatives to punishment for decreasing behavior and mild punishment alternatives (e.g., time out, response cost) when aversive techniques are used. Misuse
of well-intended interventions may be present in much of the status quo because
more effective and acceptable treatments are not being used.

Contingent Consequences and Environmental Restraint. A basic feature
of behavior modification programs is the contingent delivery of reinforcing
events to alter behavior. The potential for abuse in withholding reinforcers (e.g.,
food, activities) is readily conceivable. There are multiple sources for the protection of clients with whom such abuses might be practiced. Within the helping
professions (e.g., psychology, psychiatry, social work, counseling, and nursing),
various ethical codes are designed to protect the rights of clients. In addition,
legal decisions have helped clarify the rights of the clients who are most vulner-
able to abusive conditions.

Separate legal decisions have held that involuntarily confined populations
such as psychiatric patients, people with developmental disabilities, and

institutionalized delinquents, have the right to a variety of events and activities. For example, in the United States such populations have the right to receive nutritionally balanced meals, receive visitors, sleep in a comfortable bed, be given a place for their clothes, engage in regular exercise, and watch television. As a rule, these basic events and activities cannot be used as reinforcers or made contingent on behavior. Reinforcement programs for involuntarily confined individuals can provide backup events beyond those to which these individuals are entitled by right and which the setting normally provides. In such instances, use is generally made of token economies in which a large number of backup events are provided, including *extra* privileges and activities, as well as access to a store where tokens can purchase diverse items (e.g., Paul & Lentz, 1977).

In the vast majority of instances, behavioral techniques are applied in circumstances in which legal issues do not emerge. For example, adults in their own behalf and their children's behalf often seek treatment and agree to and help design the program that will be used in treatment, and they reserve the right to change their minds. In such cases, the participants provide their consent to engage in treatment. Other protections of the client, noted later, are aimed at ensuring that the program will not misuse contingent events.

Use of Aversive Techniques. Behavior modification relies much more heavily on positive reinforcement than on negative reinforcement and punishment. Yet the punishment techniques of behavior modification occasionally are used, especially variations of time out and response cost, as described previously. The courts have a history of evaluating punishment long before the development of behavior modification. Historically, physical restraint, corporal punishment, and inhumane conditions were often used under the guise of treatment or rehabilitation. The courts seek to protect individuals from "cruel and unusual" punishment, as specified by the Eighth Amendment of the U.S. Constitution.

Most of the judicial rulings on punishment do not apply to the procedures used in behavior modification because the more dramatic and intrusive forms of punishment such as chaining individuals or beating them, have never been part of behavioral techniques. It is instructive to consider the judicial rulings on punishment procedures that may be a part of behavior modification. Court decisions reached about punishment, of course, depend heavily on the specific procedures that are used. Obviously, the considerations governing a few minutes of isolation (one form of time out) differ from those governing electric shock or very long periods of isolation. Indeed, the courts have ruled that extended periods of isolation are not permissible and that during brief periods of isolation, the clients must have adequate access to food, lighting, and sanitation facilities (*Hancock* v. *Avery,* 1969).

Electric shock is rarely used as a punishing event, but the courts have delineated rather clear restrictions governing its use. For example, in one decision (*Wyatt* v. *Stickney,* 1972), shock was restricted to extraordinary circumstances, such as when a client is engaging in self-destructive behavior that is likely to inflict physical damage. Moreover, shock should be applied only when another procedure has been used unsuccessfully, when a committee on human rights within the institution has approved of the treatment, and when the client or a close relative has consented to its use. The fact that the courts permit the use of mild shock under any circumstances probably reflects their recognition that the procedure can permanently eliminate a behavior (e.g., self-injurious acts) after only a few applications. However, in behavior modification, there is rarely a need to use shock, as discussed previously.

In general, the courts have not addressed most forms of punishment that are currently used in behavior modification. A few of the court rulings have focused on punishments that bear a resemblance to behavioral techniques. Isolation or seclusion, for example, resembles time out from reinforcement. However, several characteristics of time out make it different from the punishments that the courts consider. In particular, the brevity of time out (one minute to a few minutes), the multiple variations of the time out procedures (e.g., with and without isolation, time-out ribbon), the procedures used during the "time in" period (e.g., reinforcement of positive behaviors), and the settings in which time out is usually applied (e.g., as the classroom or home) make time out from reinforcement quite different from the isolation and seclusion considered by the courts. In general, behavioral procedures, such as time out, response cost, and positive practice are not considered by the courts, but one still must be alert to their overuse and abuse.

There has been extensive debate within the profession regarding the use of aversive events (Repp & Singh, 1990). Many of the discussions have focused on self-injurious (e.g., head banging, face slapping) and aggressive behavior (e.g., fighting). Behaviors that are dangerous warrant immediate attention and require complete elimination if at all possible. Early in the development of behavior modification, electric shock was used (brief, mild, and delivered on few occasions) and was shown to be effective in eliminating self-injurious behavior. This was significant because in a number of instances, the behavior was long-standing and had not responded to other treatments. Over the past several years, significant advances have been made in devising alternative procedures to reduce and eliminate dangerous behaviors.

In general in behavior modification, when punishment is used, it is mild (e.g., brief intervals of time out or small fines from one's earnings of token reinforcement). In fact, relative to punishment commonly used in everyday life (e.g., spanking, slaps, expulsions from school), the actual events in behavior modification are tame. As important, in behavior modification, punishment is invariably connected to a positive reinforcement program to develop prosocial behaviors. The use of a reinforcement program means that the overall environment is more positive for the client, that punishment occasions can be relatively less frequent (than if no reinforcement program were in place), that mild forms of punishment can be effective, that fewer side effects (e.g., client tantrums) are likely to result, and that further punishment (for such tantrums) is less likely. Punishment is used in behavioral programs, and issues regarding its use are considered next.

LEAST-RESTRICTIVE-ALTERNATIVE DOCTRINE

Guideline for Use of Aversive Procedures

The use of aversive events and the varying degrees of restraint that they may pose for clients raises a broader issue. The use of aversive procedures has prompted many organizations and legislative bodies to adopt the *least-restrictive-alternative* doctrine of providing treatment.[3] The doctrine states that the least restrictive procedure is to be used to achieve therapeutic change. Least restrictive might refer to the least drastic or least aversive procedure.

Table 13-1 illustrates several procedures that vary in degree of restrictiveness and how the treatments might be applied to a child who engages in self-injurious behavior (Singh, Lloyd, & Kendall, 1990). The table lists procedures that move in ascending order from the least (reinforcement) to the most (restraint) restrictive procedure. Understandably, if a less aversive or drastic procedure can be effective, there is no justification for a more drastic procedure. There are two facets of the least-restrictive-alternative guideline. First, treatment ought to begin with a less restrictive (less aversive, drastic) procedure. Second and obviously related, more drastic procedures should be sought if evidence shows that the less restrictive procedure was ineffective.

The least-restrictive-alternative guideline has received greatest attention in the context of using aversive events, such as time out, physical restraint, and shock, for individuals who may not be able to consent to procedures, including individuals with developmental disabilities, young children, and severely impaired psychiatric patients (Repp & Singh, 1990). In this context, ethical issues, humane treatment, and abridging individual rights are most salient. For example, of considerable concern has been the treatment of individuals with developmental disabilities who engage in dangerous self-injurious behavior. A number of procedures might be used for this behavior. As mentioned previously, one candidate, rarely used, is electric shock, which can eliminate self-injury in a relatively brief period. The question in relation to the least-restrictive guideline is whether a less aversive, nonpainful, and indeed non–punishment-based procedure would be effective. If so, it ought to be tried first.

The doctrine is part of a larger social context that reflects a general view that freedom and lack of restraint are rights to which individuals are automatically entitled. Exceptions to these rights are made when the freedom of one individual impinges on the rights of others (e.g., dangerous criminal behavior that jeopardizes the freedom or safety of others). That individual's freedom is then restricted (e.g., by going to prison). For many years, treatment of special populations (e.g., psychiatric patients, individuals with developmental disabilities) relied heavily on hospitalization and institutionalization. Hospitalization of many individuals has decreased in part because less restrictive procedures could be used. People who can function in the community all or part of the time often do so because these are less restrictive living conditions.[4]

Table 13-1 Definitions and Examples of Some Procedures Commonly Used to Influence Maladaptive Behavior

Procedure	Definition	Example
Reinforcement[1]	The delivery of a consequence that increases the chances of the behavior recurring.	After every minute when Amy has kept her hands at her sides, the teacher stands near her, talks pleasantly to her, and gives her a token that she may use to buy special treats.
Punishment	The delivery of a consequence that decreases the changes of the behavior recurring. (Often these consequences are called aversives.)	When Amy pokes her finger into her eye socket, the teacher says, "No," and holds smelling salts under Amy's nose.
Extinction	The discontinuation of an environmental event that has served as a reinforcer for behavior.[2] Extinction decreases the chances of the behavior recurring.	When Amy pokes her finger into her eye socket, the teacher turns away and stops talking.[3]
Response cost	The removal of a reinforcer contingent upon the behavior occurring. This decreases the chances of the behavior recurring.	When Amy pokes her finger into her eye socket, the teacher takes away the tokens that Amy has accumulated.
Time out	The imposition of a brief time period when reinforcement is not available.	When Amy pokes her finger into her eye socket, the teacher stops awarding her tokens for three minutes.
Overcorrection	The institution of a more appropriate response and repeated practice of it contingent upon the behavior occurring. This decreases the chances of the behavior recurring.	When Amy pokes her finger into her eye socket, the teacher pulls Amy's hand away from her face, tells her to keep her hands down, and requires her to practice flexing and relaxing her hands repeatedly.
Visual or facial screening	The blocking of an individual's field of vision contingent upon the performance of a behavior. This decreases the chances of the behavior recurring.	When Amy pokes her finger into her eye socket, the teacher removes the poking finger and covers Amy's eyes with her hand (visual screening) or a terry-cloth bib (facial screening) for five seconds.
Restraint	The physical restriction of parts of the body involved in a behavior in order to make performance of the behavior impossible.	When Amy has been poking her finger into her eye frequently, the staff may decide to restrain her by wrapping a soft cloth around her wrists and running it behind her back. This "soft-tie" makes it impossible for Amy to raise her hands as high as her face.

[1] Reinforcement may be either positive or negative. In both cases, reinforcement increases behavior. Negative reinforcement is not the same as punishment.

[2] Technically, extinction also may include the discontinuation of a negative reinforcement contingency. The definition and example given here do not reflect this.

[3] This example assumes that eye-gouging is maintained by social attention. The details of extinction procedures vary, depending upon what feature of the environment maintains the behavior.

(Source: Singh, Lloyd, & Kendall, 1990)

Considerations

The least-restrictive-alternative guideline would seem to be a reasonable way to proceed in relation to the use of aversive events. At the same time, the view has raised considerable controversy. To begin, the view implies that for behaviors that are dangerous or extreme, more restrictive techniques are likely to be more effective. Yet the view that more restrictive interventions (e.g., using electric shock, restraining someone from actually engaging in the behavior) are more effective than less restrictive procedures (e.g., ignoring the behavior, giving attention for incompatible behaviors) is not supported by the data (Lennox, Miltenberger, Spengler, & Erfanian, 1988). In fact, some authors have argued and provided data to show that a variety of procedures that do not rely on aversive events can be effective in suppressing dangerous behavior such as self-injury (Donnellan & LaVigna, 1990). Thus aversive procedures in general may be avoidable in treatment. Although the least-restrictive-alternative guideline seems reasonable, one should be cautioned against the assumption that more restrictive is "better" or even needed at all.

A second consideration with the doctrine has to do with the notion of restrictiveness. Clearly, some treatments are more drastic, extreme, and restrictive than others. Yet how does one rate the restrictiveness of variations of response cost, time out, and positive practice? Presumably, restrictiveness might be measured by evaluating acceptability of treatment by consumers of treatment and the amount and speed of change that is likely to be produced. In short, the continuum of the restrictiveness of procedures is not entirely clear.

A final consideration rejects the doctrine as not particularly helpful in selecting treatment options (Pyles & Bailey, 1990). The causes of an individual's dangerous behaviors often can be identified through functional analysis. These causes, once identified, can then be used to identify effective treatment. The concern with the least restrictive alternative is that it suggests a continuum of selecting interventions that has little to do with identifying *effective* treatments. We do not wish to proceed from one procedure to the next based on the level of restrictiveness, particularly because more restrictive treatments are not more effective. The task is to understand the conditions that maintain behavior, test these, and then reduce behavior based on that understanding. In most instances in which this has been accomplished, as illustrated previously, aversive procedures that raise concerns about restrictiveness or individual rights are not even used (Pelios et al., 1999). Functional analysis often reveals that a negative reinforcement contingency is maintaining behavior and can be used to alter the behavior. Restrictiveness is not the issue; understanding the factors that maintain behavior is the issue. Once these factors are understood in a given case, they can be used to treat effectively.

Additional Guidelines

The least-restrictive doctrine raises an important issue about one characteristic of treatment but by itself does not guide treatment selection to help individual clients. This has led to alternative procedures to guide treatment (Green, 1990). For example, one alternative has been the Behavioral Diagnostic model (Pyles &

Table 13-2 Behavioral Diagnostic Model of Developing Effective Treatment

Step 1: Diagnose the Problem

Directly observe the behavior and assess possible causes (stimulus conditions, antecedents, and consequences) that might be maintaining the behavior.

Step 2: Develop a Plan Based on the Diagnosis

Consider alternative interventions. Some of these may require merely altering the antecedent conditions, i.e., how instructions, requests, or task demands are made to the individual. Others may require the more usual programs in which consequences (e.g., reinforcement, punishment) are applied.

Step 3: Test the Plan Under Controlled Conditions

Arrange to run special (perhaps very brief) sessions in which changes in the plan are tested. Two or more different conditions or procedures might be tried for brief periods that are varied in laboratory (off the ward, out of the classroom) sessions.

Step 4: Evaluate the Results

Measure the target behavior over the course of different conditions. Any related behaviors that might be of interest (e.g., side effects, prosocial behavior) might be assessed as well. From this evaluation, the more or most effective intervention can be identified or the steps can be initiated again (beginning with Step 1).

Step 5: Put the Program into Place

Train staff or persons who are to conduct the program in how to implement the procedures. Ensure that they can and do carry out the requisite behaviors to implement the program. Implement the contingency or program into the settings where needed. Continue to assess and monitor.

(Source: Adapted from Pyles & Bailey, 1990)

Bailey, 1990), which specifies a general strategy for identifying effective treatments. Table 13-2 presents the five steps for identifying effective treatments and a brief description of what they entail. The initial step consists of identifying the problem (direct observation) and proposing hypotheses about maintaining conditions. The second step consists of developing a treatment plan. Some of the plans may require manipulation of antecedent conditions rather than implementation of any consequences (aversive or otherwise) to change behavior, as illustrated through functional analysis. The third step tests the plan about what is maintaining behavior and then makes environmental changes as needed to implement the plan. The fourth step evaluates the results. The fifth step then puts the program into place where needed (e.g., in the home or institution) with continued observation and staff training.

Three key issues are raised by this model. One is the central role of functional analysis. The second is the importance of ongoing assessment of program effects. Both functional analysis and assessment have already been discussed. The third component has to do with staff (parent, teacher, institutional staff) training. The most effective and least restrictive procedure is not relevant if it is not implemented correctly. Consequently, procedures to ensure that those who administer the program implement it properly are critical.

General Comments

The general view embraced by the least-restrictive-alternative doctrine has obvious merit. We would not want to select an extreme procedure if a mild procedure would accomplish the same end. The critical feature of the guideline may be different from its primary emphasis. The primary emphasis is on procedures and how drastic, extreme, or restrictive they are. Yet implicit in the doctrine is the importance of monitoring and evaluating the intervention and its effects. A more restrictive intervention is justified only if another alternative has not achieved change.

The notions of monitoring and evaluating the intervention in relation to change are critically important. In society at large, the impact of many, if not the vast majority, of the interventions used or promoted (programs for delinquency, special education, hospitalized patients) are not monitored or evaluated. For example, over 550 forms of psychotherapy are in use for children and adolescents (Kazdin, 2000). Most of these have never been evaluated. Moreover, when therapy is conducted in clinical work with individual patients, systematic evaluation of patient progress is rare. Whether or not a given treatment is restrictive, the absence of assessment and evaluation raises ethical issues in its own right. The concern of the least-restrictive-alternative view is with client rights, including rights to effective interventions if they are available. Intervention without evaluation raises serious ethical issues. An intervention that places any restriction on a client, including seemingly innocuous interventions, might be unjustified if they are not shown to have some positive effect on behavior. Also, interventions may have untoward side effects so that absence of evaluation may increase risk for harming the individual in some way. The least-restrictive-alternative doctrine sensitizes us to procedures, as well as to their impact, and hence has relevance beyond the use of aversive events.

ETHICAL GUIDELINES AND PROTECTION
OF CLIENT RIGHTS

The ethical issues that can emerge in providing professional services and conducting research extend well beyond the use of aversive techniques. Delivery of services requires weighing alternatives that balance the individual rights of the clients and potential for untoward consequences, harm, and effects of withholding treatments that may be of benefit. A number of safeguards have emerged to guide the behavior of professionals and to protect the clients whom they serve. These safeguards include international codes and national guidelines to cover treatment and intervention research. In addition, organizations and professions involved in delivery of services have provided guidelines designed to protect clients and establish standards of professional conduct. The full range of regulations, codes, and guidelines that govern professional behavior and interactions with the public is too extensive to review here. However, a few are illustrated.

Table 13-3 Principles of Psychologists

Principle A: Competence

Psychologists strive to maintain high standards of competence in their work. They recognize the boundaries of their particular competencies and the limitations of their expertise. They provide only those services and use only those techniques for which they are qualified by education, training, or experience.

Principle B: Integrity

Psychologists seek to promote integrity in the science, teaching, and practice of psychology. In these activities psychologists are honest, fair, and respective of others. In describing or reporting their qualifications, services, products, fees, research, or teaching, they do not make statements that are false, misleading, or deceptive.

Principle C: Professional and Scientific Responsibility

Psychologists uphold professional standards of conduct, clarify their professional roles and obligations, accept appropriate responsibility for their behavior, and adapt their methods to the needs of different populations. Psychologists consult with, refer to, or cooperate with other professionals and institutions to the extent needed to serve the best interests of their patients, clients, or other recipients of their services.

Principle D: Respect for People's Rights and Dignity

Psychologists accord appropriate respect to the fundamental rights, dignity, and worth of all people. They respect the rights of individuals to privacy, confidentiality, self-determination, and autonomy, mindful that legal and other obligations may lead to inconsistency and conflict with the exercise of these rights.

Principle E: Concern for Others' Welfare

Psychologists seek to contribute to the welfare of those with whom they interact professionally. In their professional actions, psychologists weigh the welfare and rights of their patients and clients, students, supervisees, human research participants, and other affected persons, and the welfare of animal subjects of research.

Principle F: Social Responsibility

Psychologists are aware of their professional and scientific responsibilities to the community and the society in which they work and live. They apply and make public their knowledge of psychology in order to contribute to human welfare. Psychologists are concerned about and work to mitigate the causes of human suffering.

(Source: Adapted from American Psychological Association, 1992)

At the most general level, professional organizations provide guidelines to cover a variety of responsibilities of the profession. For example, the American Psychological Association (APA) has provided a set of principles and guidelines that delineate professional responsibilities in relation to a variety of activities and situations, including assessment, therapy, research, contacts with the media, and others. Central principles cover obligations in relation to standards of professional competence, integrity, professional and scientific responsibility, respect for the rights and dignity of others, concern for others' welfare, and social responsibilities. Principles from the most recent revision of the codes (APA, 1992) appear in Table 13-3 to convey the type of statements that are provided. These broad guidelines are designed to identify considerations, obligations, priorities, and potential conflicts of interest in relation to the people with whom professionals interact. More specific ethical standards are also provided to address many situations in which psycholo-

**Table 13-4   Ethical Issues for Human Services: Selected Questions
to Guide Professional Practice**

The questions related to each issue have deliberately been cast in a general manner that
applies to all types of interventions and not solely or specifically to the practice of behavior therapy. Issues directed specifically to behavior therapists might imply erroneously
that behavior therapy was in some way more in need of ethical concern than non-
behaviorally oriented therapies.

   In the list of issues the term *client* is used to describe the person whose behavior is to
be changed, and *therapist* is used to describe the professional in charge of the intervention; *treatment* and *problem,* although used in the singular, refer to any and all treatments and problems being formulated with this checklist. The issues are formulated so as
to be relevant across as many settings and populations as possible. Thus, they need to be
qualified when someone other than the person whose behavior is to be changed is paying the therapist, or when that person's competence or the voluntary nature of that person's consent is questioned. For example, if the therapist has found that the client does
not understand the goals or methods being considered, the therapist should substitute
the client's guardian or other responsible person for "client," when reviewing the issues
below.

A. Have the goals of treatment been adequately considered?
B. Has the choice of treatment methods been adequately considered?
C. Is the client's participation voluntary?
D. When another person or an agency is empowered to arrange for therapy, have the
     interests of the client been sufficiently considered?
E. Has the adequacy of treatment been evaluated?
F. Has the confidentiality of the treatment relationship been protected?
G. Does the therapist refer the clients to other therapists when necessary?
H. Is the therapist qualified to provide treatment?

(Source: Adapted from American Psychological Association, 1992)

gists are placed, such as interpreting psychological tests, providing psychotherapy,
or testifying before the courts. Apart from professional guidelines, universities and
many other institutions where research is conducted rely on review committees to
evaluate the extent to which research projects provide safeguards for subjects.

   Professional ethical codes and review-committee evaluation serve as a point of
departure for intervention research. That is, they are the basic standards for meeting professional responsibilities and providing care. Additional codes have been
provided to further guide the use of interventions in clinical and applied settings.
These do not replace professional codes but, rather, add other issues. One set of
guidelines that directs attention specifically to intervention issues has been provided by the Association for Advancement of Behavior Therapy (AABT), and
poses a number of questions that therapists (or persons who design and implement a program) should adequately address before implementing therapy. The
questions, which appear in Table 13-4, are intended to ensure that the procedures
are appropriate and that the client (or guardian) is fully aware of the intervention.
These guidelines are not directed specifically toward behavior modification procedures. The questions are intended to guide those who implement any form of
psychological treatment.

   The guidelines listed to this point emphasize very broad professional responsibilities (APA, 1992) and treatment in the context of therapist–client settings

(AABT, 1977). Applied settings such as the community at large, schools, homes in which behavioral interventions are implemented raise special considerations. Another set of guidelines has been proposed to be sensitive to issues that emerge when interventions are implemented in applied settings (Fawcett, 1991). The guidelines, presented in Table 13-5, are provided as values to guide research in applied settings. The three columns of the table convey what applied research ought to do, the perspective of the researcher or investigator who is conducting the research, and the community or consumer perspective. The different perspectives of the researcher and consumer (e.g., school district, community, clients) are important to identify to make explicit the interests, goals, and potential responsibilities of the different parties involved in applied settings. The guidelines emphasize many issues discussed earlier in the chapter, such as seeking intervention effects that maximize behavior change (e.g., clinically significant effects) and generalization.

The diverse guidelines highlighted here differ in their focus and in the domains and issues to which they alert professionals. However, the guidelines share broader values such as open communication between the professional (e.g., the researcher or therapist) and the person who is served, adherence to ethical standards and the public interest, and integration of scientific tenets (measurement, replication of research findings) with socially important ends. Clearly, the challenges of treatment extend beyond identifying and developing procedures that change behavior.

In most interventions in research and applied settings, clients or individuals acting in their behalf (such as parents) must provide informed consent. *Informed consent* refers to agreement to the intervention and conditions under which the intervention is provided. For consent to be informed, three elements are required, namely, competence, knowledge, and volition. These mean, respectively, that the individual must be competent to make rational decisions, understand the intervention and the available options, and act without duress. The issues of consent have been raised most often with involuntarily confined persons (e.g., hospitalized psychiatric patients). The purpose of informed consent is to ensure understanding of and agreement with the procedures. Individuals in treatment can revoke their consent at any time.

In addition to requiring consent, institutions that provide treatment or rehabilitation services have institutional review boards that consider the proposed treatment procedures. These boards may include experts in the area of treatment, as well as lawyers and laypeople who provide different perspectives regarding controversial applications of treatment. Many, if not most, behavior modification procedures (e.g., token reinforcement programs, brief time out) are considered standard and need not undergo special review. Special procedures (e.g., restraint of someone who presents a danger to others) or applications involving special populations that cannot act on their own behalf are reviewed routinely to ensure that individual rights are protected.

Another means of protecting individual rights is the use of a contractual arrangement between the therapist and the client. A contingency contract is used whenever possible to involve all of the parties that are included in the program. The contract can make explicit the goals of treatment, the procedures that will be

Table 13-5 Some Values Guiding Community Research and Actions

Values of Community Research and Action	Research Perspective	Community Perspective
1. Researchers should form collaborative relationships with participants.	Research should be grounded in the local context.	Communities should exert some control over research that affects them.
2. Descriptive research should provide information about the variety of behavior-environmental relationships of importance to communities.	Research should contribute knowledge about naturally occurring events.	Research should contribute to understanding about strengths (as well as deficits) and the variety of ways that individual and community goals can be met.
3. Experimental research should provide information about the effects of environmental events on behaviors and outcomes of importance.	The effects of research interventions should be replicable, durable, and generalizable to other people and situations.	Research should help identify goals, procedures, and effects that are important and acceptable to clients.
4. The chosen setting, participants, and research measures should be appropriate to the community problem under investigation.	Applied research should use valid measures to examine real-world problems in the natural context of people actually experiencing the concerns.	Research should target all those who contribute to the problem and should leave improved valued aspects of the community.
5. The measurement system must be replicable, and measures should capture the dynamic or transactional nature of behavior-environmental relationships.	Measurement systems should be replicable by typically trained researchers.	Research findings should tell the complete story, including the role that participants play in changing their environments.
6. Community interventions should be replicable and sustainable with local resources.	Interventions should be replicable by those available to implement them.	Community interventions should be sustainable with local resources and should build on local capacities for addressing community concerns.
7. Community action should occur at the level of change and timing likely to optimize beneficial outcomes.	Interventions should produce the maximum desired impact.	Interventions should be targeted to optimize benefits for the community and its members.
8. Researchers should develop a capacity to disseminate effective interventions and provide support for change agents.	Interventions should be disseminated cautiously so that their continued effectiveness is assured.	Interventions should be adapted to local conditions and their use should enhance local capacities for change.
9. Results should be communicated to clients, decision makers, and the broader public.	Research findings should be submitted for peer review and, if judged acceptable, disseminated to the broader scientific community.	Research findings should be communicated to participants and decision makers in understandable and maximally influential ways and these audiences should help assess what was valuable about the research.
10. Community research and action projects should contribute to fundamental change as well as understanding.	Community research should contribute to understanding of environmental events that affect behavior.	Community research should contribute to prevention of problems in living, capacity building, and empowerment of people of marginal status.

(Source: Fawcett, 1991)

used, and the likely risks and benefits. A useful feature of a contract is that it enables the client and his or her guardians to negotiate the final goals of treatment. Active client participation in the design of treatment is likely to make treatment fairer than it would be if treatment were unilaterally imposed on the client. Including the client in the development of the contract may have manifold benefits such as making the treatment more acceptable and fostering communication (negotiation) between the parties involved (e.g., parent and child, spouses).

SUMMARY AND CONCLUSIONS

Prior chapters have focused on the application of interventions in diverse settings and have covered multiple techniques, how they can be applied to achieve changes, and how they can be evaluated. Focusing on interventions and their effects omits critical aspects of research, treatment, and delivery of services. Intervening to help individuals, groups, or systems occurs in multiple contexts and these contexts reflect values and priorities that cannot be neglected.

The social context of intervention research was captured by the notion of social validation. This refers to whether the goals of the intervention program are relevant to everyday life, whether the interventions are acceptable to consumers and the community at large, and whether the outcomes of the intervention make a genuine difference to the individual in everyday life. Interventions to be useful and relevant ought to make a difference that is evident to others and ought to be seen as desirable and worthwhile.

Ethical and legal contexts also raise multiple considerations to guide interventions. Among the key issues are ensuring that the rights and privileges of clients are protected, that individuals provide consent, and that procedures that might in any way restrict the individual undergo review (e.g., by an institutional review board). The court involvement in aversive events has focused mainly on cruel and unusual punishment and extreme procedures that are not used in behavior modification. This was highlighted to convey society's concern with aversive events and to provide the context for guidelines in intervention research.

The least-restrictive-alternative doctrine guides the use of interventions that might be aversive. That guideline pertains to situations in which some restrictions may be required (e.g., to protect children from seriously injuring themselves). Among treatment alternatives, those that are less restrictive (e.g., reinforcement of positive opposites) ought to be tried before those that are more constraining (e.g., physical restraint). This is a reasonable guideline. However, restrictive procedures often are not needed at all. In circumstances in which restrictive procedures might seem necessary, functional analysis can be used to identify the factors that maintain the problem behavior. These factors can then be altered to produce change. Usually this has entailed altering the naturally occurring reinforcement contingencies that are supporting deviant behavior and new or restrictive interventions are not necessary.

Professional guidelines and ethical codes were presented to guide the research, practice, and application of interventions. These apply broadly well beyond behavioral interventions or the use of aversive techniques. The guidelines include principles and questions to which the investigator and practitioner should be sensitive. The principles and questions are usually presented in general form to permit their applicability to a wide range of circumstances. These guidelines underscore open communication between the professional (e.g., the researcher or therapist) and the client who is served, adherence to ethical standards and the public interest, and integration of scientific tenets (measurement, replication of research findings) with socially important ends.

KEY TERMS

Clinical significance   Least restrictive alternative   Treatment acceptability
Informed consent   Social validity

APPLYING PRINCIPLES AND TECHNIQUES TO EVERYDAY LIFE

1. In developing a treatment, whether medical or psychological, one would like the intervention to be effective and acceptable. From any type of intervention for any disorder or problem that you know of, identify: (1) a treatment that is both effective and acceptable, (2) that is effective but not acceptable, and (3) that is acceptable but probably not effective or not known to be effective. I did not mention treatments that are neither effective nor acceptable because these tend not to be brought to our attention. (As it turns out, we have discussed "interventions" such a child abuse, which tend not to be effective and are not acceptable.)

2. The goals of treatment and the means to obtain them can raise all sorts of issues related to acceptability and infringements of individual rights. Develop a program to address the following significant social problem. Very few people agree to donate organs on their death, although the procedures for agreeing to this in advance of death are easy. Each day 10 people die because of the paucity of available organs including kidneys, livers, hearts, and others (Wheelan, 1998). Ideas have been proposed to increase the supply of available organs. One idea is to provide money to families of organ donors; another is to have people register when they are too young to commit to donating organs. Those who commit early in life to donate their organs would have as an incentive top priority in receiving organs if they were in need. Consider developing a program that might encourage people to agree to donate organs. Can you do this in such a way that few would object, that this would be voluntary, that those who did not participate were not punished or otherwise discriminated against? What are some of the issues/questions of values that emerge in such a program?

3. What is the least-restrictive-alternative guideline? Why use this as a guide to selecting treatments? The guideline also assumes that a restrictive treatment

will be needed at all? This assumption is not always correct. Give an example where a nonrestrictive intervention might be used instead of a restrictive one (e.g., think DRA, DRI).

4. What are some of the ways and procedures that can be used to protect client rights? Describe how you would do this in a real situation in which rights might be jeopardized.

FOR FURTHER READING

American Psychological Association. (1992). Ethical principles of psychologists and code of conduct. *American Psychologist, 47,* 1597–1611.

Fawcett, S.B. (1991). Some values guiding community research and action. *Journal of Applied Behavior Analysis, 24,* 621–636.

Kazdin, A.E. (1999). The meanings and measurement of clinical significance. *Journal of Consulting and Clinical Psychology, 67,* 332–339.

Repp, A.C., & Singh, N.N. (Eds.). (1990). *Perspectives on the use of nonaversive and aversive interventions for persons with developmental disabilities.* Sycamore, IL: Sycamore.

Weller, E.S. (Ed.). (1990). Special section: Social validity: Multiple perspectives. *Journal of Applied Behavior Analysis, 24,* 179–249.

NOTES

1. Standard deviation reflects a measure of variation or spread of scores. The measure is used to provide a standard way of referring to how far away (in standard deviation units) a person's score is from the mean (average) of the group. A departure of two standard deviation units is arbitrary but reflects a rather large departure. For example, a person whose IQ score is two standard deviations above the mean would have an IQ higher than approximately 98% of other people. For the present discussion, the critical point is not the standard deviation units but rather the comparison of the scores of different groups.

2. Although getting a suntan as an intervention might be dismissed as silly, there are reasons to withhold strong statements about this. After all, treatment research has demonstrated that exposure to light (sunlight) improves some kinds of mood disorders (seasonal affective disorder; Lee et al., 1998).

3. Several of the guidelines devised by professional organizations that include the least-restrictive-alternative doctrine and guidelines for use of aversive events are presented elsewhere (Singh et al., 1990).

4. The issue is more complex than selecting the less restrictive alternative. The use of medication on an outpatient basis to control symptoms and interests in reducing costs of treatment have greatly reduced the use of institutions as a way of housing and treating various populations (e.g., zpsychiatric patients, individuals with mild mental retardation). Living in the community usually costs less per patient than does hospital care. At the same time, relying less on institutional and "restrictive" settings has increased the rates of homeless individuals and individuals wandering the street who cannot care for themselves or who have serious mental disorder. The least restrictive alternative for effective intervention is complex because trade offs sometimes are required about how little restriction can work (be effective) and with what consequences to the person and society at large.

CHAPTER 14

Current Issues and Future Directions

Prior chapters have discussed a range of behavior-change techniques, the principles from which they are drawn, and the conditions that influence their effective application. Two broad facets of behavior modification in applied settings were distinguished and then blurred whenever possible. These include the interventions or techniques themselves (e.g., positive reinforcement, punishment, group contingencies) and the methods to evaluate their impact on functioning (e.g., assessment, functional analysis, experimental design). Invariably, the techniques themselves are more fascinating because there is always an engaging case study to report where critical behavior has been changed. Examples from prior chapters included the elimination of uncontrollable and life-threatening vomiting in infants, reduction of accidents (on the road and industry), improvements in complying with medical regimens, and many others. The evaluation methods play a key role in the success of behavioral interventions by providing the means through which factors that control behavior can be identified, careful assessment of behavior over time, and analysis of whether the intervention rather than some other influence causes the changes. I have tried to underscore the importance of evaluation in behavior modification by stating that the successes of behavior modification are due in part to the ability to identify failures, that is, instances in which programs are not working or interventions effects are weak. Good (reliable) data provide the best way of helping clients and behavior modification has placed a premium on collecting such information.

This closing chapter places the accomplishments in perspective by highlighting the scope of applications, challenges in applying behavioral procedures, and current directions in intervention research. There are constraints on behavior-change methods and their application. These stem from our limited understanding of human behavior and difficulty in implementing interventions, but also from more general issues such as questions about what ought to be altered in a free society. This chapter addresses key issues and constraints on interventions.

SCOPE OF APPLICATIONS

Perhaps one of the most striking features of behavior modification is the scope of applications. This book has been devoted primarily to applied behavior analysis, the area of behavior modification that draws on principles of operant conditioning. Interventions most often carried out in applied settings such as the home, at school, and in the community, usually draw on these principles. In early applications beginning almost 50 years ago, behavioral techniques in applied settings were directed primarily to special populations such as psychiatric patients, mentally retarded children, autistic children, and delinquents. Applications with these populations have continued, but the scope of applications has expanded considerably. Currently, behavior modification techniques are applied to many domains and are used to do the following:

- Prevent illness and disease
- Alter dieting and exercise habits

- Help individuals cope with and manage pain
- Increase adherence to and compliance with medical regimens
- Enhance academic performance from preschool through college students
- Engage in safe behaviors in the community, at home, and in business settings
- Improve parenting and parent–child interactions
- Address clinical problems (e.g., eating disorders, tics) and diverse concerns in everyday life (e.g., energy conservation, waste recycling)

Many applications of behavior modification are in the context of psychotherapy and draw on a broad range of learning models and treatments (e.g., cognitive behavior therapy, systematic desensitization, graduated exposure), only a few of which were sampled in the present book. These techniques are applied to the full range of clinical problems that people bring to psychotherapy, including psychiatric disorders (e.g., anxiety disorders, mood disorders, eating disorders, conduct disorders, tics, sexual dysfunction and disorders, and others) and problems of everyday life (e.g., marital discord, bereavement, stress). The scope of applications of behavior modification including interventions in applied settings and psychotherapy is not even approximated by other approaches to treatment. As importantly, the evidence that interventions can produce change in many domains is also without peer.

Extrapolation from present work in behavior modification suggests that the focus of treatments will continue to expand. There are numerous places where individuals (parents, teachers) and society at large wish behavior change would occur. We would, for example, like to encourage people to have their young children vaccinated, engage in health-promoting behavior, seek treatment when needed, and not to smoke cigarettes. Can behavioral techniques help promote improvements of such goals on a large scale?

Many interventions in place for such goals rely on relatively weak interventions. For example, appeals by television and newspapers to consume less fat in one's diet, seek treatment for depression, and quit smoking rely on relatively weak techniques. The techniques focus on prompts, instructions, and models (exemplars) of the appropriate behavior. The effects that are produced tend to be weak and inconsistent and affect a small number of people. Of course, it is not just that the focus on antecedents alone is relatively weak. There are often strong "interventions" from one segment of society that promote those very behaviors (e.g., violence, smoking) that another segment of society wishes to decrease. Although media appeals to promote prosocial and positive behaviors often have weak effects, such appeals are relatively inexpensive and can reach a large number of people. Consequently even if only a small percentage of people change, this can be quite worthwhile. Yet given what is known about antecedents, behaviors, and consequences, better interventions could be designed. Better analyses of the contingencies that control behavior and use of consequences for positive, prosocial behavior are likely to have more widespread and enduring effects.

CHALLENGES AND CONTEXTS

Program Failures

Behavioral techniques bring to bear important influences to change behavior. Yet the techniques do not always achieve the desired outcomes. Over the years, there have been many instances in which behavioral programs failed to achieve the desired changes. No change may have occurred or the change may be too small to make an important difference in the lives of the clients or those with whom they interact. When behavioral programs initially fail to achieve the desired changes in behavior, one may conclude that behavior modification "does not work" or that the person who carried out the procedures (parent, teacher) did not administer the program properly.

The most common reason for program failures pertains to poor, mediocre, and inconsistent implementation of the contingencies. Part of the difficulty with implementation stems from the fact that behavioral procedures are in many ways familiar to people and this unwittingly leads to casual implementation of the procedures. For example, parents who are learning behavioral techniques for managing their children invariably note that these techniques are not new and that they have been using the techniques all along. They often assert that their use of reinforcement (praise or allowance) or time out (sending the child to his or her room) has not worked. Parents are usually correct in this assertion. Yet careful inquiry or direct observation of their behavior in the home reveals that the procedures they have tried are faint approximations of the ways in which reinforcing and punishing consequences are applied in behavioral programs. For example, parents often say that they have used reinforcement to alter behavior, but it has not helped. However, positive reinforcers need to be administered immediately after behavior, on a continuous or close to continuous schedule, and contingent on performance, especially at the beginning of the program. As important are the target behaviors, which need to be carefully specified so that reinforcement can be applied consistently and the results can be measured to see whether the program is having impact. More generally, behavioral programs consider antecedents, behaviors, and consequences, as well as quite specific ways of implementing the contingencies. Once these and related conditions (e.g., use of prompts, shaping) are faithfully rendered, one may be in a better position to say that the procedures have not worked.

Interestingly, several studies have shown that slight modifications in the program when clients have failed to respond often produce the desired behaviors (Kazdin, 1983). In some cases, the changes occur from implementing the program in ways more conducive to producing change (e.g., more immediate reinforcement). In other cases, procedures are changed. For example, defiant and aggressive child behavior in the home or at school may not be altered by simply having parents praise appropriate child behavior (Wahler & Fox, 1980; Walker et al., 1981). The undesired behaviors may not decrease until mild punishment (response cost, time-out) is added to the contingencies.

Similarly, one program focused on encopresis (lack of control of bowels) in young children (Reimers, 1996) and encouraged parents to praise and provide tangible reinforcers when the child sat on the toilet, attempted to have a bowel movement, or produced any stool at all in the toilet. The program did not work, and no successful bowel movements resulted. A mild punishment contingency (effort based/overcorrection type activity) was added and required the child to remove soiled clothing, assist parents in washing the clothing and cleaning herself, and dressing in new clothing. This was done matter-of-factly without the parents engaging in reprimands or other punishment. This led to marked changes and no further toileting accidents, effects maintained when checked up to a year later.

These examples and others that can be cited suggest that program changes can enhance outcomes. The critical facet of behavior modification in applied settings is the evaluation of behavior change over time. The evaluation permits one to identify mediocre intervention effects and then to make changes in the intervention or how the intervention is implemented to see if the desired outcomes can be achieved.

Programs may fail because of a misunderstanding of the current factors maintaining behavior. This explanation has been greatly supported in recent years with the more frequent use of functional analyses of behavior. As mentioned previously, functional analysis isolates factors that control behavior by assessing behavior directly under different conditions. Patterns frequently emerge to show how behavior is influenced by one particular condition or set of conditions rather or more than another. For example, a functional analysis might be completed to examine factors that contribute to a child's tantrum in the home. The analysis may reveal that the tantrums are primarily on the weekends and come after parents ask the child to do chores or homework. After a request or comment about the task from the parents, the child becomes "moody," retreats to his or her room, and begins a tantrum. During the tantrum, the parents may attend to the child, nag a bit, threaten some punishment, and make further demands. A behavioral program based on the functional analysis might suggest that the antecedent conditions, rather than the attention and other consequences, play a central role. A program designed to address antecedents might include devising a contingency contract with the child each Friday (before the weekend), deciding how much time or work will be done, when during the weekend the work will be completed, what positive consequences will be provided, and so on. In this case, tantrums were largely precipitated by antecedents. A number of other factors might well be involved and different approaches or models of human behavior (e.g., family therapy) might focus on such factors. However, the functional analysis identifies specific influences, obtains data to show their impact, and then alters these factors to obtain change. No other model or approach to treatment really tries to accomplish this and evaluate the effects empirically. In any case, identifying the precipitating influence and altering it in the home are likely to have potent and immediate effects on behavior.

Consider an alternative approach to the tantrum. This alternative approach is one that still is the most common use of behavior modification. The general recommendation to alter the tantrum is to suggest that the tantrum is probably maintained by social reinforcement. The parents ought to ignore tantrums (extinction) and perhaps provide reinforcement for nontantrum behavior (differential reinforcement of alternative or other behavior). A program might be developed in which demands of and requests to the child are not altered, but incentives are provided for not having a tantrum. This program is designed without a functional analysis. Actually, this program is likely to work if the contingency is implemented consistently. Indeed, for many years before functional analyses emerged, such programs had been quite effective. Functional analysis is a very useful place to begin before developing an intervention program. However, it is also useful when an intervention program is not working, and a better diagnosis of the situation is needed.

The principles of reinforcement, punishment, and extinction and the techniques derived from those principles are relatively simple. However, considerable skill is required to implement the techniques so as to attain the desired outcomes. The techniques need to be implemented systematically and consistently and with knowledge of the factors that influence their effects. Many successful programs have devoted considerable attention to ensuring that behavior-change agents (parents, teachers, hospital staff) are well trained. Once these change agents have been trained, their behaviors are often monitored carefully to ensure that the contingencies are carried out correctly (e.g., Bushell, 1978; Patterson, 1982; Paul & Lentz, 1977). Without careful training and monitoring, the care with which behavior-change programs are implemented may deteriorate over time (e.g., Harchik, Sherman, Sheldon, & Strouse, 1992). It is likely that assessment and monitoring of staff or others who implement the behavior-change procedures need to become a permanent part of the setting (e.g., school, hospital). There are examples where training staff and monitoring of staff and students are part of the ongoing program. Large-scale applications of behavioral programs in the school often include assessment and monitoring of teacher and student behavior to ensure that the techniques are implemented correctly and that children are learning (e.g., Selinske, Greer, & Lodhi, 1991). The assessment and supervision practices are central to the effectiveness of the procedures, and hence their incorporation as part of the program is critically important. In short, quality of program implementation is obviously important. In fact, what distinguishes behavior modification techniques from everyday uses of reward and punishment is *how* the techniques are applied and evaluated. The successful applications illustrated throughout this book depend on very careful implementation and evaluation of behavioral techniques.

In general, behavioral techniques have been quite effective in altering a number of behaviors in the context of treatment, education, child-rearing, health, and everyday life. Research continues to elaborate how problems emerge, the factors that currently influence and maintain these problems, and the interventions that can be used to alter them. Interventions that are based on knowing what is causing or maintaining behavior can be especially effective, as demonstrated in examples of functional analysis in prior chapters. Interestingly, change can be achieved even when the causes and maintaining factors are not known. As noted earlier, there are several effective treatments for anxiety disorders even though research has yet to understand how people develop these disorders to begin with. Behavioral techniques have made enormous gains by providing learning experiences and developing new behaviors even in the many applications where the onset of the problem is not understood.

Complexities of Behaviors and Environments

A significant challenge for any intervention approach pertains to the complexity of the task. For many behaviors we wish to change, there are multiple causes that are not well understood. Antecedent events (e.g., prompts) or consequences (e.g., reinforcers) in the ways outlined in prior chapters do not exhaust the range of the factors that influence normal and maladaptive behavior. The expansion of behavioral techniques to include cognitive events (self-statements, imagery) enhances the potential of treatment by increasing the range of the influences that can be brought to bear to produce therapeutic change. However, even the addition of cognitive and environmental influences does not exhaust the range of the factors that control behavior. Biological predisposition (e.g., temperament), genetic endowment, and environmental factors that usually cannot be controlled in treatment (e.g., family living conditions, maladjustment of parents) may limit the effects that any treatment can achieve.

For example, consider antisocial behavior in children. Severe antisocial behaviors in children (aggression, stealing, tantrums, destructiveness, lying, setting fires, and other related violent and rule-breaking behaviors) is referred to as conduct disorder in current psychiatric diagnosis and represents a problem that emerges in childhood. The emergence of conduct disorder is influenced by scores of factors, including child temperament, family history of conduct disorder, academic deficiencies of the child, harsh child-rearing practices, psychological dysfunction (depression, antisocial behavior, alcoholism) and criminality in the parent(s), marital discord of the family, teen marriage and pregnancy (of the child's mother), and many other factors (see Kazdin, 1995; Stoff, Brieling, & Maser, 1997). These and other influences do not invariably *determine* that a child will become antisocial, but they increase the risk that serious antisocial behavior will develop.

Training parents in behavioral techniques (parent management training) has been one of the most effective interventions for treating antisocial children (Brestan & Eyberg, 1998; Kazdin, 1997). Yet, it would be quite understandable if changing parent-child interaction and altering the contingencies of reinforcement in the home did not totally eliminate the problems of such children, because so many other factors than the reinforcement contingencies in the home may promote such behavior. Indeed, parent management training has been very effective in some applications but has produced mixed effects in others. The complexity of child antisocial behavior and the number of factors that influence such behavior will probably continue to present obstacles to any treatment approach.

The problem is not only that there are multiple factors that influence the onset of the problem but also that there are different paths leading to a problem. Different paths means that two (or more) individuals can experience the same problem for quite different reasons. This is true of many diseases as well as social, emotional, or behavioral problems. For example, two individuals can have the same outcome (lung cancer, hyperactivity) due to different causes. Thus no single set of interventions can be expected to solve the clinical and other problems to which it is applied and to do so for everyone. In short, many domains of function we wish to change in the context of therapy or society at large are multideter-mined and having impact on the determinants will be difficult. The benefit of a behavioral approach is that it suggests a place to intervene (current environment) and provides concrete procedures and guidelines (alter antecedents, behaviors, and consequences) to achieve change. This approach has worked extremely well in many areas of human functioning. Yet it would be a mistake to imply that a few environmental causes account for behavior or that their alteration invariably will be effective.

Behavior Change, Goals, and Individual Rights

There are limits to the range of problems to which behavioral interventions are likely to be applied. This may seem odd to say because early in the chapter, the scope of behavioral interventions was highlighted and shown to be vast. Indeed, it is difficult to identify a population, clinical problem, or mental and physical health goal toward which behavioral techniques have not been applied. Because applications have been extended widely, the implication might be that it is just a matter of time before all facets of society are encompassed by the approach or that there is no social problem too great for a behavioral intervention. The predomi-nant focus in the book has been on whether behavior *can* be changed. A broader issue that influences extension of behavior modification is whether behavior *ought* to be changed.

Whether a particular behavior should be changed in society reflects a value decision about the goals of an intervention. Consider a focus that is seemingly straightforward. Many dietary habits of individuals in society actively promote ill-ness, disease, and early death. The consumption of "junk food" (e.g., fast food, snacks, and beverages that are characterized by low nutritional value, low fiber, high sugar, high fat) in particular is suspected to play a major role in the high rates of obesity in the United States (Battle & Brownell, 1996). Persuasive evidence is available indicating that eating more fruits and vegetables can reduce weight and greatly reduce the incidence (rates of onset) of many serious physical disorders (e.g., heart disease, cancers). Dietary habits could be changed to reduce con-sumption of junk food and to increase consumption of fruits and vegetables. Small-scale demonstrations with individuals who seek treatment routinely show that eating patterns can be changed. Larger-scale demonstrations might be achieved by changing incentives in society at large as well to control diet and nu-trition. However, should we tinker with eating habits of people who do not refer themselves for treatment? In a free society, should we provide such interventions and, if so, to what extent?

One suggestion to address dietary habits and the health problems toward which they lead has been to increase the price of snack and junk foods and greatly reduce the price of healthful foods (fruits and vegetables) (Brownell, 1994). This is a viable suggestion and one that would be likely to have significant impact on a large number of individuals—not everyone of course because of the complexity of the problem—but many people. Indeed, there have been several demonstrations, especially in the context of alcohol consumption and cigarette smoking, that increasing the prices can significantly reduce consumption (Horgen & Brownell, 1998). Taxing junk food and providing incentives (very low cost) for fruits and vegetables would be quite likely to have significant social impact. However, there is remarkable resistance to the idea in part because of the value that such an intervention reflects. Control through government and taxation is viewed by many as an abridgment of individual freedom and violation of rights. It is unlikely that such program would be implemented because legislators and interest groups would be mobilized to argue against social oversight and control of eating. No doubt many citizens and interest groups would worry about a "slippery slope," that is, government control (local, state, or federal) over food consumption may be just the beginning of control over other behaviors. In the United States of course there is a historical reminder that tax over tea was one small puzzle piece (Boston Tea Party) leading to rebellion as the country was formed.

The key challenge, especially in a democratic society, is mobilizing interest or consensus on the goals of an intervention. Also, in a free society, multiple influences operate freely and can foster many of the problems one wishes to change. Violence in the media (e.g., movies, television, video games), availability of weapons, and use of harsh (but not quite legally abusive) child-rearing practices contribute to aggressive and antisocial behavior. The right to engage in each of these practices is protected to some extent and interventions might infringe on these rights. Privileges, rights, and social institutions provide a context in which all interventions must be provided. In some cases, the context may entail influences that seem to operate in ways that promote problems for which we design interventions. Also the freedom to pursue individual rights has implications for implementing changes that might have one benefit (e.g., improve health) but may be considered to jeopardize other aspects of living (e.g., individual rights).

Third and related, it is not merely the goals that limit application and extension of behavioral techniques. The means of obtaining these goals also can be viewed as interfering with rights. For example, a key to success in behavior modification has been careful assessment of behavior over time. The assessment permits identifying the extent of the problem and the extent to which an intervention is having impact. Indeed, if a program is producing little or mediocre effects, these become evident from the data and one can make changes to achieve the desired outcomes.

Assessment is not neutral and itself can infringe on the perceived or real rights of others. For example, from a technological standpoint, it is not difficult to monitor what people buy at stores or online and then to target them for interventions based on their buying preferences. This is already done for advertising so that one's credit card purchases and online (computer) shopping are tracked and used for mail lists. A minor shift could be used to identify people for behavior-change interventions. Those individuals who purchase substances that might be abused (e.g., alcohol, cigarettes) could be targeted for special mailings and interventions to correct their ways; those families with children who did not purchase enough books (or especially those who did not purchase this book) might be targeted for special interventions; and families who did (or perhaps did not) give to charity might be so informed and targeted for donations, and so on. In these hypothetical examples, the interventions to change behavior are not the issue, but of course these would raise their own problems. Rather, the assessment and accumulation of detailed information itself raises the prospect of abuse and infringement of individual rights. The collection of data is problematic because once the information is available it can be used, and the distinction between use and abuse is sometimes in the eye of the beholder.

Consider a more concrete example. Airline safety is a goal toward which multiple parties (manufacturers, pilots, maintenance crews, passengers, government agencies, and legislators) are committed. Most plane accidents are due to pilot error. One way to address pilot error is to monitor all pilot interactions in the cockpit for all flights. This is done in some way now, and the information is analyzed after a plane crash. Another way would be to monitor interactions by video taping all activity in the cockpit and use the information to provide feedback to pilots for every flight, that is, to not wait for a crash (Carley, 2000). The technology to monitor more of the interactions of pilots and to see precisely how they took off, landed, and made other maneuvers is available. Such information would permit tracking of performance and perhaps early identification of variable or checkered pilot performance. Pilots have objected to this level of oversight and scrutiny. Although citizens might object because of the importance of safety, the pilot reaction would be like that of the rest of us. Careful monitoring of how we work or study on a daily basis would usually be viewed an infringement of our rights.

Consider parallels in other facets of life. Parents who pay tuition and board for their children's college education might want to see what they are buying and how the money is being used by their children. For a small extra fee, consider giving parents the option of a special "monitoring charge" on their tuition bill. Let us suppose that this option provided assessment of a student in school with data that were given to the parents. Suppose a tiny camera could be in a student's room to monitor studying. Not high-tech enough? How about installing one of those devices placed in cars so that their location can be identified if the car is stolen. To our poor college student, such an assessment device might provide location and time and be installed in shoes or implanted under the skin. "Great data" would be provided to the parents regarding where and how time was spent. In long-distance phone calls, parents would not need to ask the plaintive, nagging question, "Did you study for your biology exam?" With the data, they might be able to say outright, "Why were you in the library for only 10 minutes on Tuesday afternoon and then left with two of your friends for coffee? Sweetie, this is not what we are paying for."

The hypothetical example with students is horrible enough, but I can imagine another that is even worse! What if a similar collection of data were conducted with faculty. How many hours do faculty *really* spend teaching, providing office hours, and so on? At state-funded, more than private universities, state legislators are often interested in the data for these questions and ask faculty to complete a form at the end of the academic term to collect information. Yet that is a low-tech and weak assessment. A monitoring device might be worn to record behavior and movements of all faculty, and then these could be decoded by computer. One actually could have a record of all that the faculty member did on each workday. Time at the gym, long lunches, getting to work at 11 AM on one day, letting class out early, attending a talk, and schmoozing with students in the middle of campus all might be graphed on a daily basis. The technology for all of this is not that difficult, but in each case the population (students, faculty) would view assessment as an abridgment of rights. No doubt from these examples, students and faculty would pull the cameras from the wall or pour syrup in the recording devices. (Monitoring would be aversive, and recall from Chapter 7, that aversive events often lead to undesirable side effects such as aggressive and escape behavior, destroying the assessment device would be an example of both.) In short, assessment raises issues and constraints. We would not want all behaviors of interest to some parties to be assessed and the very acts of assessment might be objectionable.

Values and Broader Social Goals

A final challenge of intervening to improve individuals and society shifts the focus a bit. There are many problems toward which behavioral interventions have been directed, and these involve more than just specific concrete behaviors. For example, interventions that focus on safety, driving habits, and adherence to medical regimens reduce accidents and save or extend lives. Stated another way, behavior modification does much more than the modification of behavior. There are many domains of social interest that are not addressed and these warrant mention. Concerns of each generation with the prior generation often involves nebulous notions of "values." These entail broad characteristics, principles that guide individual and social functioning, morals, ethics, and other such nebulous but meaningful and important terms. Examples include altruism, reverence for life, ties to family, and concern for disadvantaged and underprivileged people, to mention a few. We would like these values in our children but also in fellow citizens so that change at the individual and group level are needed.

How does one impart or change values? Certainly, the very question raises the concerns about the goals and means noted a few moments ago—what values, whose values, and so on. Even so, there is keen interest among parents, teachers, and government to foster prosocial values and morals. Are these too amorphous to address, or are there simply too many counter influences or diverse views that make this focus impossible? At the level of parents and their children, there would be a receptive interest group. How can parents impart values to their children? The usual sage advice (model the virtues you wish to instill, prompt, shape, and reinforce in your children) certainly would be helpful. Yet there is no clear body of data that support interventions to enhance or augment social values. Changing values might be approached by operationally defining the constructs (e.g., altruism) into discrete behaviors and then developing these. This is a quite reasonable approach, especially if multiple behaviors were used to operationally define the construct so that a trivial and very narrow definition was not used. Still, how to move from concrete behaviors to larger constructs of interest has not been systematically addressed.

A remarkable contribution of behavioral interventions has been to take complex behaviors and to break them down into steps that can be trained and developed (e.g., task analysis) and also to examine the complex array of influences that impinge on an individual to identify what is controlling behavior (e.g., functional analysis). Converting the complex to the simple has afforded major advances of behavioral interventions. Perhaps this is one reason why application of behavioral techniques is called applied behavior *analysis.* The return conversion is no less important, namely, ensuring that the broader goals are somehow addressed as well. Broad concepts such as values may seem too fuzzy and amorphous, but they also guide human actions and group large segments of behavior. Values are also of social concern and hence raise new challenges for intervention. Perhaps these broad goals might be approached by emergence of a new area of research, applied behavior *synthesis,* namely, addressing broad goals and changes in the more amorphous facets of life or those larger concepts that many concrete behaviors may comprise.

CURRENT DIRECTIONS IN INTERVENTION RESEARCH

The focus of the book has been on behavioral interventions, but it is useful to place these into a larger context in which interventions are implemented and evaluated. Two trends in particular are noteworthy, namely, the focus on evidence-based treatments and interest in combining treatments.

Evidence-Based Treatments

There has been a movement in treatment research to identify those interventions that have empirical evidence in their behalf. This focus has emerged primarily in the context of psychotherapy for children, adolescents, and adults who are seen in outpatient treatment. There are scores of treatments that are in use. Mentioned already is the fact that more than 550 therapy techniques are used for problems that children and adolescents present (Kazdin, 2000). Most of these have never been studied or shown to lead to change. This is a deplorable situation because it means that treatments provided in clinical practice may be ones that do not work or, even worse, that actually do some harm. Also, for many problems seen in treatment, there are effective treatments. It is possible and indeed likely that a therapist is using a treatment that has not been evaluated instead of one that has been evaluated and shown to be effective.

There are several reasons why there currently is an emphasis on identifying evidence-based treatment. A main interest is the spiraling and seemingly uncontrollable costs of health care. These concerns have stimulated major changes in mental and physical health services. Third-party payers (e.g., businesses, insurance companies, federal and state governments) cover the costs of diagnostic and treatment services for many individuals under their charge (e.g., employees and their

Table 14-1 Major Criteria for Identifying Evidence-Based Treatment

Treatment is studied in a carefully controlled investigation that includes random assignment of clients to treatment or control conditions.

Treatment is compared with another treatment that is known to work or is standard practice, or to a no-treatment control group

Treatment is specified in a manual, or format that can be described or outlined explicitly so one can discern what was actually done in treatment

The effects are replicated (repeated) in at least one additional investigation, preferably by a different team of investigators

Characteristics of the sample and their clinical problems are carefully described

These criteria are drawn from many different efforts to identify evidence-based treatments. For further details, other sources can be consulted (Kendall & Chambless, 1998; Lonigan & Elbert, 1998; Nathan & Gorman, 1998).

families, veterans) and have tried to reduce costs of these services. These efforts have placed all health-care practices under the spotlight and have raised the question of whether a particular procedure (e.g., diagnostic test, treatment) should be provided at all, let alone be reimbursed.

Psychotherapy is used to treat all sorts of problems, and traditional forms of treatment have gone largely without scrutiny by the health-care system. A goal of identifying evidence-based treatments is to discern what can be justified for use in clinical work. Health-care agencies make decisions about what to reimburse and, in this sense, control what treatments are provided. Professional efforts to identify evidence-based treatments are not only designed to inform practitioners but also to inform those who make decisions about what treatments ought to be reimbursed for what problems.

Within the past 10 years, various professional organizations and committees spanning different countries have delineated treatments that have scientific evidence in their behalf (*Evidence-Based Mental Health,* 1998; Nathan & Gorman, 1998; Roth & Fonagy, 1996; Task Force on Promotion and Dissemination of Psychological Procedures [TFPP], 1995). These efforts have used different terminology to delineate treatments that have evidence in their behalf. Among the terms that have been used are empirically validated treatments, empirically supported treatments, evidence-based treatments, evidence-based practice, and treatments that work. The criteria for identifying such treatments have varied but generally include those listed in Table 14-1. Essentially, the criteria call for carefully conducted studies that show therapeutic change. More than one study is required because of the importance of replication in science, that is, repetition of a finding provides greater confidence that the results are not unique to the conditions of the first experiment or not just chance findings.[1]

Several reviews have identified evidence-based treatments for clinical problems that children, adolescents, and adults bring to treatment. Table 14-2 lists major treatments that have emerged in the various reviews. There are two striking features of the table that relate to the present discussion. First, although hundreds

Table 14-2 Psychotherapeutic Treatments Identified as Evidenced Based

Problem Domain	Treatment
Anxiety, Fear, Phobias	Cognitive therapy Exposure therapy Modeling Reinforced practice Relaxation Systematic desensitization
Posttraumatic Stress Disorder	Exposure therapy Stress inoculation therapy
Depression	Behavior therapy Cognitive therapy Coping with depression course Interpersonal psychotherapy Problem-solving therapy
Oppositional and Conduct Disorder	Parent management training Problem-solving skills training Multisystemic therapy
Attention-Deficit/Hyperactivity	Classroom contingency management Parent management training

The techniques noted here draw primarily from several sources (DeRubeis & Crits-Christoph, 1998; Kazdin & Weisz, 1998; Lonigan & Elbert, 1998; Nathan & Gorman, 1998). Even though each of these techniques has evidence in its behalf, this does not convey the strength of the evidence among effective treatments. These sources can be consulted to convey the strength of the evidence among the techniques.

of treatments are available, a relatively small number of treatments have been de-lineated as having a strong basis in research. As mentioned before, most treatments have never been studied. Identifying treatments with evidence may encourage more research for those that are in use but not yet known to work, or to not use those techniques if more well-established treatments have been identified already. Second, there is a conspicuous heavy representation of behavioral and cognitive-behavioral treatments. There are all sorts of reasons for this. One is the fact that behavioral and cognitive-behavioral interventions began with a strong commit-ment to evidence. More traditional therapy approaches (e.g., psychoanalysis, psy-chodynamic therapy) have been studied less well in general.

Insistence on evidence as the criterion for evaluating interventions represents a relatively new thrust. This is in keeping with a major theme of the book, namely, evaluation is central to effective treatment whether the treatment is behavioral or not and whether the intervention focuses on physical disease, psychological func-tioning, education, rehabilitation, and other domains. The criterion for using and promoting treatment is not the conceptual view or theoretical approach to which one ascribes but whether in fact scientific evidence can be brought to bear to sup-port the interventions. Behavioral and cognitive interventions have fared well by these criteria.

Combined Treatments

In previous chapters, many behavioral procedures and their variations were de-scribed. It was important to focus on individual procedures such as token reinforcement, time out from reinforcement, and others to illustrate their variations and the manner in which they are applied to maximize behavior change, as well as to identify their individual effects. Often, several behavior-change procedures are combined into a single program. Indeed, in behavioral interactions, it is common to combine such components as feedback, social and token reinforcement, and response cost into a treatment "package." In many cases, entirely different treatments have combined such reinforcement techniques and cognitively based treatments or reinforcement techniques and medication.

There are several reasons to combine multiple procedures in a given behavioral program (Kazdin, 1996a). First, individual treatments may be limited in the effects they achieve. Combining more than one treatment is a reasonable way to try to augment outcome effects. Second, individuals who come for treatment often have multiple problems. For example, individuals who come to treatment because of depression, anxiety, or another psychiatric disorder are likely to meet criteria for another disorder. There usually is not one or two target behaviors but multiple problems that are reflected in many domains of functioning (home, school, work, relationships). Combined treatments are reasonable efforts to address the scope of impairment and problems. Third and related, the factors that impinge on clinical problems often are quite broad. For example, parent, child, peer, and school influences may be influencing the problem and can be mobilized to achieve therapeutic change. Addressing multiple influences is more likely to be accomplished by a combination of treatments.

As an example of a case where combined treatments seem to be essential is in the treatment of juvenile delinquency. Adjudicated adolescents who engage in criminal behavior do not do so because of one or two undesirable influences. Several factors may be involved in a delinquent lifestyle and contribute to the problem such as delayed school functioning, substance abuse, association with deviant peers, parental stress, parents' aggressive acts against each other and the child, or poor peer relations. Combined interventions that address a range of factors may be essential to achieve change in delinquency (Henggeler, Schoenwald, Borduin, Rowland, & Cunningham, 1998). Not every aspect that may influence the problem probably needs to be addressed in treatment, but multiple domains ought to be addressed.

Combinations of behavioral and cognitively based procedures are relatively common. For example, in one of our own studies mentioned earlier, we evaluated alternative treatments for aggressive and antisocial children (ages 7 to 13) who were referred for outpatient treatment (Kazdin et al., 1992). The effectiveness of three conditions was examined: (1) cognitively based problem-solving skills training, (2) parent management training, and (3) the combination of both of these. Families were randomly assigned to receive one of the three treatments. Treatment was provided weekly to children and/or their parents individually for a period of six to eight months. Each of the treatments led to improvements in child functioning at home and at school, based on measures completed by parents, teachers, and the children themselves. However, the combined treatment (both problem-solving skills training and parent training) led to the largest reductions in child dysfunction and improvements in parent functioning (reduced parental stress and depression). These effects were evident immediately after treatment and at a one-year follow-up. In this case, the combined treatment apparently was useful for addressing different components of antisocial behavior among children and their families.

The importance of combining different components can be seen with interventions for the prevention of the spread of AIDS (Kelly & Murphy, 1992). Preventive efforts have focused on behaviors that place individuals at risk for contact with HIV. There are several facets of the problem that require multiple interventions. For example, in one study, gay men received a multicomponent behavioral intervention (Kelly, St. Lawrence, Hood, & Brasfield, 1989). Gay men were selected because they represented a high-risk group (i.e., they had a disproportionally higher rate of AIDS cases than the general public in the United States). Treatment consisted of several components:

- An educational component (to teach information about behaviors that place individuals at risk for AIDS)
- Self-management techniques (self-monitoring of antecedent events leading to at-risk sexual behavior, use of self-statements to prompt nonrisk behavior)
- Assertiveness training (to discuss with partners the importance of protected sexual behavior, to respond assertively in coercive sexual situations)
- Problem-solving skills training (to foster steady relations and to handle potentially high-risk sexual encounters).

Individuals were randomly assigned either to the treatment condition where they received each of the above components or to a waiting-list control group that received treatment after it ended for the other group. The impact of treatment can be seen in Figure 14-1, which shows three behaviors that place individuals at risk for contracting HIV. As evident in the figure, sexual practices changed markedly with the treatment program.

Many studies combine different components of treatment along the lines of the above examples. One of the objections that is raised is that once a combined treatment is shown to be effective, one has no clear idea which component of the intervention was responsible for change or whether all were necessary. With complex and multifaceted problems, often multiple treatments are combined in an effort to exert initial impact. Obviously, in clinical and applied work, investigators are interested in developing interventions that lead to large and durable changes in behavior. There has been less interest in dissecting intervention packages by looking at the effect a program exerts with or without a particular component. Nonetheless, investigation of the individual treatments that are to be combined is very important.

Using a combined treatment is not merely a matter of adding everything that might help into a treatment program. Mentioned earlier was the regrettable finding that many treatments have not been studied at all and therefore are not known to be effective. Adding such treatments together may not be very sound because individually there is no evidence that they help. Indeed, often combined treatment does not produce greater changes than the individual components of treatment

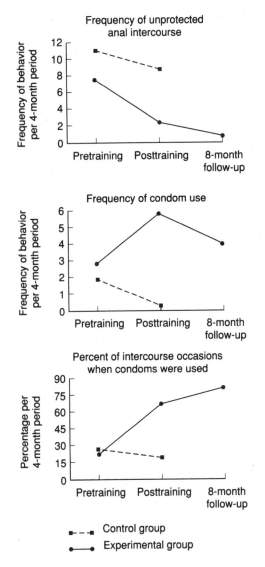

FIGURE 14-1 Frequency of unprotected anal intercourse, frequency of condom use during intercourse, and proportion of intercourse occasions protected by condoms among experimental and control (waiting-list) groups. After the intervention period (four months) the waiting-list group was then provided with treatment.

(Source: Kelly, St. Lawrence, Hood, & Brasfield, 1989)

administered by themselves; occasionally the combined treatment produces effects that are *worse* than the individual components (see Kazdin, 1996a). Consequently, merely piling on more treatments is not to be done casually. It is desirable to combine components of treatment to alter different facets of a problem but also to know that the components themselves can have impact. Research on individual treatments and their contribution to behavior change is often a prior step before combinations of treatments are studied.

CLOSING COMMENTS

Several challenges were raised, and these could be easily construed as outright limitations of behavioral interventions. However, more of the points pertain to interventions in general. They are raised in a book of behavior modification in applied settings only because behavioral interventions have pushed the frontier of effective intervention relatively far. Behavioral interventions have achieved beneficial changes in the home, school, hospitals, and nursing homes; with infants through the elderly; and for an enormous range of mental and physical health problems. The applications and extensions continue to prosper. There has been no approach to emerge from psychology, psychiatry, or other disciplines that has such strong evidence in its behalf as a basis for achieving behavior change and across such a wide range of populations, settings, and domains of functioning. Although this is a book on behavior modification in applied settings, the final message to impart is one that extends beyond behavior modification. From a scientific standpoint, the key questions for intervention are quite separate from any particular approach or conceptual view. Those questions are as follows:

- What evidence is available to support the notion that change can be achieved?

- What evidence indicates that the change is due to the intervention rather than to some other influence?

These are the questions always to be asked. The significance of behavior modification is that the techniques discussed in this book frequently emerge when these questions are asked. However, the priority is on the evidence rather than promulgating a particular set of techniques or intervention approach.

KEY TERMS

Combined treatments   Evidence-based treatment   Program failures

APPLYING PRINCIPLES AND TECHNIQUES
TO EVERYDAY LIFE

1. You have helped an elementary school teacher improve student behavior in class. The teacher notes that the program is producing mediocre effects. You expect that the program (tokens and praise for completing assignments) is not being implemented well. To check on this, you ask the teacher questions

about how reinforcers are administered. What questions would you ask the teacher? Hint: What conditions are required to maximize effective delivery? (see Chapter 6).

2. Assume the program was being implemented well, that is, the teacher was administering consequences as one would hope. What might you add to the program to improve effectiveness? Hint: Special contingency additions such as group or peer-administered contingencies (Chapter 9) or mild punishment (Chapter 7) might be added. Describe what you might do—develop details of the situation as needed.

3. Consider a significant social behavior that you believe ought to be promoted on a large-scale (e.g., society at large, worldwide). Examples might be vaccinating children, consuming healthful foods, donating to charity, improving the care of children, the elderly, animals, or any focus of your choice. Design an intervention based on the use of material from this book to produce a change. Describe the program in a paragraph or two. Remember, it is important to specify:

   - The target behavior(s)
   - How it will be measured
   - The intervention(s)
   - The means to evaluate your program (design)
   - How you will decide whether the impact is important or significant

4. It is often the case that reinforcement programs could be very effective, but getting control of the situation or administering consequences contingently can be difficult. Consider this significant health problem. Scientists in industry (drug companies) and academic settings work very hard to develop effective medicines. Ironically, this is only one facet of effective treatment. There is a problem that does not receive sufficient attention once effective medications are available. Approximately one half of the adults do not take their medication either on time or for the full duration that the medication has been prescribed (Kranhold, 1999). Experts have estimated that between 14% and 15% of patients never even fill their prescriptions. It is likely that the interventions selected to improve this situation will focus on advertising campaigns (e.g., prompts). Can you think of any way to improve compliance with medication to address this situation? What are obstacles to developing programs for this behavior? These obstacles are likely to apply to other social problems.

FOR FURTHER READING

Kazdin, A.E. (1996). Combined and multi-modal treatments in child and adolescent psychotherapy: Issues, challenges, and research directions. *Clinical Psychology: Science and Practice, 3,* 69–100.

Kendall, P.C., & Chambless, D.L. (Eds.) (1998). Special section: Empirically supported psychological therapies. *Journal of Consulting and Clinical Psychology, 66,* 3–167.

Lonigan, C.J., & Elbert, J.C. (Eds.) (1998). Special issue on empirically supported psychosocial interventions for children. *Journal of Clinical Child Psychology, 27,* 138–226.

NOTES

1. The identification of evidence-based treatment, the context in which this emerged, and the criteria of the different efforts to identify such treatments are important topics but beyond the scope of this discussion. The reader is referred to other sources (Kazdin, 2000; Kendall & Chambless, 1998; Lonigan & Elbert, 1998).

✳

Glossary

ABAB design: An experimental design in which the target behavior of a subject or a group of subjects is assessed to determine baseline performance. The experimental condition is then introduced and remains in effect until the target behavior changes. A reversal phase follows in which the experimental condition is withdrawn. Finally, the experimental condition is reintroduced. A functional relationship is demonstrated if the target behavior changes during each of the phases in which the experimental condition is presented and if it reverts to baseline or near baseline levels when the experimental condition is withdrawn. It is also called a reversal design because during the design the conditions often are "reversed" (baseline is reinstated).

Alternate response training: A technique used in therapy (e.g., desensitization) and as a self-control strategy in which the individual is trained to engage in a response (e.g., relaxation) that interferes with or replaces another response that is to be controlled or eliminated.

Analogue testing: Assessment of performance in a contrived, laboratory situation to permit careful control over the conditions presented to the client. This is often used in functional assessment so that the investigator can test changes in performance as various antecedents and consequences are altered. The antecedents or consequences (e.g., social attention for the behavior, making demands to complete a task) are varied in brief periods. Once the factors that control behavior are identified, an intervention can be planned and implemented in everyday situations.

Automatic reinforcement: The consequences that result from performing the behavior. The term has been used most frequently in the context of self-stimulatory behavior (e.g., rocking, hitting oneself) in which the stimulation resulting from the behavior (e.g., tactile, sensory) seems to serve as the reinforcer for the behavior.

Aversive event: A stimulus that suppresses a behavior that it follows or increases a behavior that results in its termination.

Avoidance: Performance of a behavior that postpones or averts the presentation of an aversive event.

B

Backup reinforcer: An object, activity, or event (primary or secondary reinforcer) that can be purchased with tokens. A reinforcer that "backs up" the value of tokens.

Backward chaining: Consists of developing behaviors in the opposite order in which they are to be performed. In a sequence of behaviors (e.g., getting dressed), the last or final behavior is performed (e.g., buttoning up a shirt that was placed on the individual) and reinforced. Additional behaviors (e.g., putting on that shirt by oneself) are added one at a time until the entire sequence (e.g., selecting clothes and putting all of them on) is performed. Compare with Forward chaining.

Baseline: The frequency with which behavior is performed before initiating a behavior modification program. The performance rate used to evaluate the effect of a behavior modification program. Operant rate of behavior. The initial phase of ABAB, multiple-baseline, and changing-criterion designs.

Behavior: Any observable or measurable response or act. (The terms *behavior* and *response* are used synonymously.) Behavior is occasionally broadly defined to include cognition, psychophysiological reactions, and feelings, which may not be directly observable but are defined in terms that can be measured by means of various assessment strategies.

Behavioral control: Exerting power or influence over others by altering the environmental contingencies to achieve a definite end.

Behavioral trap: Refers to the notion that once a client's behavior has been developed, it may become entrenched in and maintained (i.e., trapped) by the social system of available reinforcers in the client's everyday environment. That is, behaviors initially developed through special contingency arrangements may be maintained by ordinary, naturally occurring contingencies after the program has been withdrawn.

Bibliotherapy: *See* Self-help manuals.

Biofeedback: Procedures that provide information to the client about his or her ongoing physiological processes. The information enables the client to monitor moment-to-moment changes in these processes.

C

Chain: A sequence of behaviors that occurs in a fixed order. Each behavior in the sequence serves as a discriminative stimulus (S^D) for the next response. Each behavior in the sequence (except the first behavior) also serves as a conditioned reinforcer that reinforces the previous response.

Chaining: Developing a sequence of responses. The responses can be developed in a forward or backward direction in which one response is added to the other until the entire sequence is learned. See Backward chaining and Forward chaining.

Changing-criterion design: An experimental design in which the effect of the program is evaluated by repeatedly altering the criterion for reinforcement or punishment. If the target behavior matches the criterion as the criterion is repeatedly altered, this suggests that the contingency is responsible for behavior change.

Classical (or respondent) conditioning: A type of learning in which a neutral (conditioned) stimulus is paired with an unconditioned stimulus that elicits a reflex response. After the conditioned stimulus is repeatedly followed by the unconditioned stimulus, the association between the two stimuli is learned. The conditioned stimulus alone will then elicit a reflex response. In classical conditioning, new stimuli gain the power to elicit respondent behavior.

Client: The person for whom the behavior modification program has been designed and implemented. Used in the present text as a generic term to include the patient, student, subject, child, or other person for whom the intervention has been planned.

Clinical significance: Refers to the practical or applied value or importance of the effect of the intervention. The effects produced by the intervention should be large enough to be of practical value or have impact on the everyday lives of those who receive the intervention, as well as those in contact with them.

Cognitive heuristics: Mental processes that serve as aids to learning and help us negotiate many aspects of everyday experience by grouping people and experiences, categorizing, and solving problems in the environment. These processes are considered biases when human judgment is used to draw conclusions about relations among variables or characteristics of ourselves, others, and the environment. The heuristics are particularly important to acknowledge in the context of assessment because they underscore the need for using measures that can more accurately characterize the relations among antecedents, behaviors, and consequences and changes in performance over time.

Cognitive processes: Internal events such as attributions, thoughts, beliefs, self-statements, perceptions, and images.

Cognitively based treatment: An approach that considers cognitive processes such as thoughts, beliefs, and perceptions to play a major role in the conceptualization and treatment of clinical problems.

Conditioned aversive stimulus: An initially neutral event that acquires aversive properties by virtue of being paired with other aversive events or with a signal that no reinforcement will be forthcoming.

Conditioned reinforcer: *See* Secondary reinforcer.

Conditioned response: A reflex response elicited by a conditioned stimulus in the absence of the unconditioned stimulus. This response resembles, but is not identical to, the unconditioned response. *See* Classical conditioning.

Conditioned stimulus: A previously neutral stimulus that, through repeated associations with an unconditioned stimulus, elicits a reflex response. *See* Classical conditioning.

Consequence sharing: A contingency arrangement in which the consequences earned by one person are provided to both that person and his or her peers.

Contingency: The relationship among antecedents (e.g., prompts, setting events), a behavior (the response to be changed), and consequences (e.g., reinforcers).

Contingency contract: A behavior modification program in which an agreement or contract is made between a person who wishes behavior to change (e.g., a parent) and the person whose behavior is to be changed (e.g., a child). The contract specifies the relationship between behavior and its consequences.

Contingent delivery of a reinforcer: The delivery of a reinforcer only when a specified behavior has been performed. Contrast with Noncontingent delivery of a reinforcer.

Contingent on behavior: An event (e.g., praise, tokens, time out) is contingent on behavior when the event is delivered only if that behavior is performed.

Continuous reinforcement: A schedule of reinforcement in which a response is reinforced each time it is performed.

Control-group design: An experimental design in which the effect of the intervention is evaluated by comparing (at least) two groups, a group that receives the intervention and a group that does not.

Coverant: A private event such as a thought, a fantasy, or an image that is not "observable" to anyone other than the individual who is experiencing it. Private events can be viewed as responses that can be altered by varying the consequences that follow them. The term *coverant* is a contraction of the terms *covert* and *operant*.

Covert conditioning: Imagery-based procedures that require a client to imagine target behaviors and consequences. They are referred to as conditioning because they draw on learning, including classical conditioning, operant conditioning, and observational learning. The techniques assume that there is an interaction between overt and covert (imagined) behaviors and that changes in one are likely to influence the other.

Covert event: A private event such as a thought, a fantasy, or an image. *See* Coverant.

Covert sensitization: An imagery-based treatment in which clients imagine themselves engaging in an undesired behavior (e.g., overeating) and then imagine an aversive event or state (e.g., vomiting). The treatment is designed to decrease the undesired behavior.

Cue: *See* Discriminative stimulus (S^D).

D

Delay of reinforcement: The time interval between a response and delivery of the reinforcer.

Deprivation: Reducing the availability of, or access to, a reinforcer.

Differential reinforcement: Reinforcing a response in the presence of one stimulus (S^D) and extinguishing the response in the presence of other stimuli (S^Δ). Eventually, the response is consistently performed in the presence of the S^D but not in the presence of the S^Δ.

Differential reinforcement of alternative behavior (DRA): Delivery of a reinforcer after a response that is an alternative to the behavior one wishes to decrease. The alternative behavior is not necessarily physically incompatible with the undesired behavior. However, if the alternative behavior is performed, the net effect is to decrease the likelihood of the undesired behavior. If the alternative behavior is incompatible with the behavior, this is a special case of DRA and is referred to as differential reinforcement of incompatible behavior.

Differential reinforcement of incompatible behavior (DRI): Delivery of a reinforcer after a response that is incompatible or competes with a target response that is to be suppressed. The effect is to increase the frequency of the incompatible response (e.g., cooperative play) and to decrease the frequency of the undesirable target response (e.g., fighting).

Differential reinforcement of low rates (DRL): Delivery of a reinforcer for reductions in performance of the target behavior. Reinforcers may be delivered for reduction in the overall frequency of a response within a particular period or for an increase in the amount of time that elapses between responses. A DRL schedule can reduce the frequency of a target response.

Differential reinforcement of other behavior (DRO): Delivery of a reinforcer after any response except the target response. The reinforcer is delivered if the individual is not engaging in the undesired target response. The effect of reinforcing only behaviors other than the target response is to decrease the target (unreinforced) response.

Discrete categorization: A method of assessing behavior in which behaviors are dichotomously scored as having occurred or not occurred. This method is very useful when several different behaviors are to be scored.

Discrimination: Responding differently in the presence of different cues or antecedent events. Control of behavior by discriminative stimuli. *See* Stimulus control.

Discriminative stimulus (S^D): An antecedent event or stimulus that signals that a certain response will be reinforced. A response is reinforced in the presence of an S^D. After an event becomes an S^D by being paired with reinforcement, its presence can increase the probability that the response will occur.

Duration: A method of recording behavior that measures the amount of time in which a behavior is performed.

E

Elicit: To bring about a response automatically. Respondent or reflex behaviors are elicited by unconditioned stimuli. Contrast with Emit and Operant behavior. *See* Classical conditioning.

Emit: To perform a response spontaneously. Operant behaviors are emitted. They are controlled primarily by the consequences that follow them. Contrast with Elicit and Respondent. *See* Operant conditioning.

Empirically Supported or Validated Treatments: *See* Evidence-based treatments.

Escape: Performance of a behavior that terminates an aversive event.

Escape extinction: Extinction of a response that was maintained (reinforced) by escape from the situation. Extinction of a negatively reinforced behavior when it no longer leads to escape from the situation.

Establishing operation: An antecedent variable or factor that temporarily alters the effectiveness of some other event or consequence. Motivational states, emotions, and environmental events are establishing operations because they momentarily alter the effectiveness of the consequences that may follow behavior and influence the frequency of some behavior.

Evidence-based treatments: Treatments that have empirical evidence in their behalf. Most treatments used in the context of psychotherapy have not been evaluated in research. The delineation of treatments with evidence is a relatively recent movement in an effort to identify those that have been shown to be effective in rigorous studies. Other terms are also used including empirically validated treatments, empirically supported treatments, evidence-based practice, and treatments that work.

Experimental design: The plan for evaluating whether the behavior modification program, rather than various extraneous factors, was responsible for behavior change. An arrangement of conditions so that conclusions can be reached about the factors (e.g., intervention) responsible for change.

Extinction: A procedure in which the reinforcer is no longer delivered for a previously reinforced response that results in a decrease in the probability or likelihood of the response.

Extinction burst: An increase in the frequency and intensity of responding at the beginning of extinction.

F

Fading: The gradual removal of discriminative stimuli (S^D), including such prompts as instructions or physical guidance. Initially, developing behavior is often facilitated by prompts. However, in most situations, it is important to fade the prompt. Fading can also refer to the gradual removal of reinforcement, as in the progressive thinning of a reinforcement schedule.

Feedback: Knowledge of results of one's performance. Information is conveyed regarding how the person has performed.

Fixed-interval schedule: A schedule of administering reinforcement. In an FI schedule, reinforcement is given for the first occurrence of the target response after a fixed time interval elapses.

Fixed-ratio schedule: A schedule of administering reinforcement. In an FR schedule, an unvarying number of occurrences of the target response is required for reinforcement.

Flooding: A behavior therapy technique used for the treatment of anxiety-based disorders in which the individual is exposed in real life (*in vivo*) or in imagery to situations that provoke anxiety. Exposure is to situations that elicit relatively high levels of anxiety usually for prolonged periods until there is adaptation to the situation, as reflected in reductions in anxiety. Repeated exposure leads to diminished reactions and attenuation of anxiety.

Forward chaining: Consists of developing a sequence of behaviors in the order in which they are to be performed. In a sequence of behaviors (e.g., getting dressed), the first behavior is performed (e.g., selecting one's clothes) and reinforced and additional behaviors (e.g., putting on the first item) are added one at a time until the entire sequence is performed. Compare with Backward chaining.

Frequency: The number of times that a response occurs. *See* Rate of responding.

Functional analysis: Evaluation of the behavior and of antecedent and consequences associated with the behavior. A functional analysis identifies the "causes" of behavior, that is, current conditions that are maintaining the behavior by directly assessing behavior, proposing hypotheses about likely factors that are controlling behavior, and testing these hypotheses to demonstrate the conditions that cause the behavior. The information from functional analysis is then used to guide the intervention by direct alteration of conditions so that the desired behaviors are developed.

Functional communication training: Developing communication in the client to obtain the consequences that can support or maintain behavior. Functional communication training trains the client to request assistance with a difficult task (e.g., say, "help me," or "I do not understand.") or to prompt attention (e.g., "Am I doing good work?") from others.

Functional relation: A relationship between behavior and the experimental condition or contingency. A functional relationship is demonstrated if behavior systematically changes when the contingency is applied, withdrawn, and reapplied.

Functionally equivalent responses: *See* Reinforcement of functionally equivalent behavior.

G

Generalized conditioned reinforcer: A conditioned reinforcer that has acquired reinforcing value by being associated or paired with a variety of other reinforcers. Money is a generalized conditioned reinforcer.

Group contingencies: Contingencies in which the group participates. There are two major variations: (1) An individual's behavior can determine the consequences delivered to the group, and (2) the behavior of a group as a whole determines the consequences that each member of the group receives. Occasionally, for this latter variation, the group is divided into teams to add an element of competition. *See* Team-based contingencies.

H

High-probability behavior: A response that is performed with a relatively high frequency when the individual is given the opportunity to select among alternative behaviors. *See* Premack principle.

High-probability requests: The likelihood that an individual will comply with a request varies by the specific requests. Some requests are much more likely to achieve compliance. Those that are likely to attain compliance for a given individual are referred to as high-probability requests. This is an interesting category to delineate because research has shown that low-probability requests (e.g., clean up your room, wash up for dinner) are much more likely to occur if they are preceded by a few high-probability requests (e.g., give mommy a kiss, keep me company in the study while I am working).

I

Imagery-based techniques: Cognitively based behavior modification procedures that rely on the presentation of events in imagination.

Incompatible behavior: A behavior that interferes with, or cannot be performed at the same time as, another behavior.

Informed consent: Agreeing to participate in a program with full knowledge about the nature of the treatment and about the program's risks, benefits, expected outcomes, and alternatives. Three elements are required for truly informed consent—competence, knowledge, and volition.

Intensity: Intensity refers to the magnitude, strength, amplitude, force, or effort of the response. Examples include volume of one's voice, noise level, and magnitude of a tantrum (e.g., ranging from shouting only to shouting, throwing things, and hitting others).

Intermittent reinforcement: A schedule of reinforcement in which only some occurrences of a response are reinforced.

Interval recording: An assessment strategy in which behavior is observed as having occurred or not occurred. Observations are usually made in a single period (e.g., 30 minutes) that is divided into small intervals (e.g., 15 seconds). Behavior is scored as having occurred or not occurred during each of the small intervals.

Interval schedule of reinforcement: A schedule in which reinforcement is delivered on the basis of the amount of time that elapses before a response can be reinforced. Contrast with Ratio schedule of reinforcement.

L

Latency: The time between the presentation or onset of a stimulus and the occurrence of behavior.

Least restrictive alternative: A guideline for selecting interventions, especially among aversive (punishment) techniques that might be applied for therapeutic ends. The guideline states that the procedure to be used is the one that is the least restrictive necessary to achieve change. The least restrictive may include the least aversive, painful, or restrictive of freedom. Less restrictive procedures are to be tried first; more restrictive procedures are used only if the less restrictive procedures have not been effective.

Low-probability requests: The likelihood that an individual will comply with a request varies by the specific requests. Some requests are much more likely to achieve compliance. Those that are unlikely to attain compliance for a given individual are referred to as low-probability requests. *See* High-probability requests.

M

Model: The person whose behavior is observed or imitated in observational learning.

Modeling: Learning by observing another individual (a model) engage in behavior. To learn from a model, the observer need not perform the behavior nor receive direct consequences for his or her performance.

Multiple-baseline design: An experimental design that demonstrates the effect of a contingency by introducing the contingency across different behaviors, individuals, or situations at different points in time. A causal relationship between the experimental contingency and behavior is demonstrated if each of the behaviors changes only when the contingency is introduced.

N

Naturally occurring reinforcers: Uncontrived reinforcing events that are usually available as part of the environment. Such events include attention, praise, completion of an activity, and mastery of a task.

Negative reinforcement: An increase in the probability or likelihood of a response that is followed by the termination or removal of a negative reinforcer. *See* Negative reinforcer.

Negative reinforcer: An aversive event or stimulus whose termination increases the probability of the preceding response. The increase in frequency of the response that terminates or removes the aversive event is called negative reinforcement.

Noncontingent delivery of a reinforcer: The delivery of a reinforcer independent of behavior. The reinforcer is delivered without reference to how the individual is behaving. Contrast with Contingent delivery of a reinforcer.

O

Observational learning: *See* Modeling.

Observer drift: The gradual departure of observers from the definitions that they are supposed to use when they record behavior. If this happens, recorded changes in the target behavior may reflect changes in how responses are being scored rather than actual changes in behavior or the effectiveness of the intervention.

Obtrusive assessment: Measurement procedures in which the client or person being observed is aware of the assessment procedures, that is, that his or her behavior is being measured. There is the possibility that this awareness will influence behavior, at least temporarily, and distort the level of performance that would otherwise be evident. See Reactive assessment.

Occasion: Presenting an S^D and thus increasing the likelihood that a response will be performed. Certain cues in the environment (e.g., music) occasion certain responses (e.g., singing).

Operant behavior: Behavior that is emitted rather than elicited. Emitted behavior operates on the environment and responds to consequences (e.g., reinforcement, punishment), as well as antecedents (e.g., setting events, stimuli). Contrast with Respondent.

Operant conditioning: A type of learning in which behaviors are influenced primarily by the consequences that follow them. The probability of operant behaviors is altered by the consequences that they produce. Antecedents too are involved in learning as cues (S^D, S^Δ) become associated with different consequences and can influence the likelihood of the behavior.

Operant rate: *See* Baseline.

Operational definitions: Defining a concept (e.g., aggression, social skills) by referring to the specific operations that are to be used for assessment. The "operations" or methods of measuring the construct constitute the operational definition. The definitions represent the construct but usually do not measure all facets of the construct that may be of interest.

Overcorrection: A punishment procedure that consists of two components. The first component is called *restitution* and refers to correcting the environmental consequences of the undesirable behavior (e.g., cleaning up a mess). The second component is called *positive practice* and consists of having the individual repeatedly rehearse or practice the correct or desirable behavior (e.g., cleaning up messes made by several other people).

Overt behavior: Behavior that is publicly observable and measurable. Contrast with Covert event.

P

Paraprofessional: A person, such as a parent, teacher, or peer, who works with the mental health professional to implement a treatment program.

Positive opposite: A behavior that is an alternative to and preferably incompatible with the undesired behavior. Suppression or elimination of an undesirable behavior can be achieved or accelerated by reinforcing a positive opposite. This is not a technical term but rather a useful way to approach the task of developing behavioral interventions. When the goal is to reduce or eliminate behavior, it is helpful to consider the positive opposite behaviors that are to be developed in their stead. *See also* Differential reinforcement of alternative behavior.

Positive practice: Repeatedly practicing appropriate responses or responses incompatible with an undesirable response that is to be suppressed. This is a component of overcorrection, but it is often used alone as a punishment technique when the response that is to be suppressed (e.g., a self-stimulatory behavior such as rocking) has no clear environmental consequences that can be corrected.

Positive reinforcement: An increase in the probability or likelihood of a response that is followed by a positive reinforcer. *See* Positive reinforcer.

Positive reinforcer: An event whose presentation increases the probability of a response that it follows.

Premack principle: Of any pair of responses or activities in which an individual freely engages, the more frequent one will reinforce the less frequent one.

Primary reinforcer: A reinforcing event that does not depend on learning to achieve its reinforcing properties. Food, water, and sex are primary reinforcers. Contrast with Secondary reinforcer.

Problem-solving skills training: Cognitively based treatment in which individuals are trained to approach interpersonal situations. Training focuses on the requirements of a particular task or problem, the behaviors that need to be performed, the alternative courses of action that are available, the consequences of these actions, and then selection of a particular solution. Individuals engage in self-instruction to guide them through the problem-solving approach.

Prompt: An antecedent event that helps initiate a response. A discriminative stimulus that occasions a response. Instructions, gestures, physical guidance, and modeling cues serve as prompts.

Punishment: Presentation of an aversive event or removal of a positive event contingent on a response that decreases the probability or likelihood of the response.

R

Rate of responding: The frequency of responding is often expressed in relation to the amount of time that a behavior has been observed. The rate of responding equals frequency (number of occurrences of the behavior) divided by time (seconds or minutes).

Ratio schedule of reinforcement: A schedule in which reinforcement is delivered on the basis of the number of responses that are performed. *See also* Interval schedule of reinforcement.

Rational–emotive psychotherapy: Cognitively based treatment that considers psychological problems to arise from faulty or irrational thought patterns. These patterns are reflected in assumptions and self-verbalizations people make that lead to emotions and behaviors that are maladaptive. Treatment challenges these assumptions and verbalizations and substitutes more adaptive cognitions.

Reactive assessment: If the client is aware that his or her behavior is being observed or assessed, this may influence performance. Awareness of measurement does not invariably influence performance. When performance is influenced by awareness, this means that the assessment is reactive. *See* Obtrusive assessment.

Reinforcement: An increase in the probability or likelihood of a response when the response is immediately followed by a particular consequence. The consequence can be either the presentation of a positive reinforcer or the removal of a negative reinforcer.

Reinforcement of functionally equivalent behavior: Reinforcement of a prosocial, acceptable behavior that attains the same goals and consequences as the problem behavior. The behaviors that are developed are functionally equivalent if they achieve the same environmental consequences as the original behavior.

Reinforcer sampling: Providing the client with a sample or small portion of a reinforcer. The sample increases the likelihood that the entire event will be earned, used, or purchased. Reinforcer sampling occasionally is used to increase use of available reinforcers and hence the behaviors required to earn reinforcers. Reinforcer sampling is a special case of response priming in which the purpose is to develop or increase the use of an event as a reinforcer. *See* Response priming.

Reliability of assessment: In behavioral research, this term usually refers to interobserver agreement or the consistency with which different observers working independently score a target response. The method used to calculate agreement depends on the method used to assess behavior (e.g., frequency, interval, or duration). The calculation usually yields a percentage of agreement between observers.

Resistance to extinction: The extent to which a response is maintained once reinforcement is no longer provided.

Respondent: Behavior that is elicited. Reflexes are respondents because their performance automatically follows certain stimuli. The connection between such unconditioned respondents and the antecedent events that control them is unlearned. Through classical conditioning, responses may come under the control of otherwise neutral stimuli. Contrast with Operant behavior.

Response: *See* Behavior.

Response cost: A punishment procedure in which a positive reinforcer is lost contingent on behavior. With this procedure, unlike time out from reinforcement, no time limit to the withdrawal of the reinforcer is specified. Fines and loss of tokens are common forms of response cost.

Response covariation: The tendency of several responses to change together, even when only one of the responses serves as the focus for change. In a person's repertoire, many behaviors may be correlated. Changing one of those behaviors often changes behaviors with which it is correlated.

Response generalization: Reinforcement of one response increases the probability of other responses that are similar to that response. Contrast with Stimulus generalization.

Response priming: Any procedure that initiates early steps in a sequence or chain of responses. By initiating early steps, response priming increases the likelihood that the terminal response in the sequence will be performed.

Restitution: A component of overcorrection that consists of correcting the environmental effects of the undesired or inappropriate behavior. *See* Overcorrection.

Reversal design: *See* ABAB design.

Reversal phase: A phase in the ABAB design in which the program is withdrawn or altered to determine whether the target behavior reverts to baseline or near baseline levels.

S

Satiation: Providing an excessive amount of the reinforcer. A loss of effectiveness that occurs after a large amount of the reinforcer has been delivered.

Schedule of reinforcement: The rule denoting how many or which responses will be reinforced.

S^D: *See* Discriminative stimulus.

S$^\Delta$: An antecedent event or stimulus that signals that a certain response will not be reinforced.

Secondary (or conditioned) reinforcer: An event that becomes reinforcing through learning. An event becomes a secondary reinforcer by being paired with other events (primary or conditioned) that are already reinforcing. Praise and attention are examples of secondary reinforcers. Contrast with Primary reinforcer.

Self-administered reinforcement: Refers to the client's delivery of the reinforcer to himself or herself.

Self-control: Refers to those behaviors that an individual deliberately undertakes to achieve self-selected outcomes by manipulating antecedent and consequent events.

Self-determined reinforcement: Refers to the client's specification of the criteria for reinforcement.

Self-help manuals: Books, manuals, or brochures that are designed to teach clients how to implement treatments for themselves. Usually little or no therapist contact is required. The client merely applies the specified techniques in a step-by-step fashion.

Self-help resources: Information in the form of manuals, books, pamphlets, or available from the Internet that can be used to control one's own behavior, usually through help in identifying a problem or providing methods to carry out an intervention. *See also* Self-help manuals.

Self-instructions: *See* Self-statements.

Self-monitoring: Assessing or recording one's own behavior. Sometimes used as a self-control technique.

Self-punishment: Providing oneself with punishing consequences contingent on behavior.

Self-reinforcement: Providing oneself with reinforcing consequences contingent on behavior. For a procedure to qualify as self-reinforcement, the client must be free to partake of the reinforcer at any time, regardless of whether a particular response has been performed.

Self-statements: The statements that people make to themselves either aloud or privately (covertly). Self-statements are often used as part of cognitively based and self-control treatments.

Setting events: Antecedent events that refer to context, conditions, or situational influences that affect the contingencies that follow. Such events set the stage for behavior–consequence sequences that are likely to occur. *See also* Establishing operation.

Shaping: Developing a new behavior by reinforcing successive approximations toward the terminal response. *See* Successive approximations.

Social learning theory: A conceptual framework within behavioral research that integrates the influence of different types of learning (classical, operant, and observational learning) in explaining how behavior develops, is maintained, and is altered. Social learning theory emphasizes the significance of cognitive processes in mediating the influence of environmental events and performance.

Social reinforcers: Reinforcers that result from interpersonal interaction, such as attention, praise and approval, smiling, and physical contact.

Social validation: Refers to the evaluation of the social importance of target behaviors and the changes achieved in treatment. The applied or clinical significance of behavioral programs is often evaluated after treatment by comparing the behavior of the target subject with that of persons who perform adaptively or by soliciting the opinions of persons in the community with whom the client interacts.

Spontaneous recovery: The temporary recurrence of a behavior during extinction. A response that has not been reinforced may reappear temporarily during the course of extinction. The magnitude of such a response is usually lower than its magnitude before extinction began.

Stimulus: A measurable event that may have an effect on a behavior.

Stimulus control: The presence of a particular stimulus serves as an occasion for a particular response. The response is performed only when it is in the presence of a particular stimulus. *See* Discriminative stimulus.

Stimulus generalization: Transfer of a trained response to situations or stimulus conditions other than those in which training has taken place. The behavior generalizes to other situations. Contrast with Response generalization.

Stress inoculation training: A cognitively based treatment that focuses on developing cognitive and self-control skills to reduce the impact of stress. Individuals are trained to monitor events and their evaluations of them; to use coping strategies such as relaxation, imagery, and positive self-statements; and to apply coping skills in everyday life.

Subjective evaluation: A method used to evaluate whether the changes achieved by a behavioral program make an important difference to various consumers of·treatment, including the clients themselves, persons in contact with them, and persons who are in a position to evaluate the behaviors of interest. This method solicits the opinions and subjective evaluations of potential consumers to help decide whether these changes are important or make a difference in everyday situations.

Successive approximations: Responses that more closely resemble the terminal behavior that is being shaped. *See* Shaping.

Systematic desensitization: A behavior therapy technique used for the treatment of anxiety-based disorders in which the client is exposed in real life (*in vivo*) or in imagery to situations that provoke anxiety. A central feature of the procedure is exposure to the anxiety-provoking situations in a gradual fashion while the individual engages in a response such as relaxation. Exposure to the stimuli in a gradual fashion (beginning with situations that evoke only small amounts of anxiety) while the client is relaxed leads to attenuation of anxiety.

T

Target behavior: The behavior to be altered or focused on during a behavior modification program. The behavior that has been assessed and is to be changed.

Task analysis: An initial stage in developing a program, which consists of identifying the precise behaviors that need to be developed, dividing those behaviors into concrete steps that can be trained, and setting the sequence (or order) in which the training will take place.

Team-based contingency: A group contingency in which the members of a group earn reinforcers on the basis of the group's performance. Subgroups or teams are delineated that compete to earn reinforcers.

Terminal response: The final goal of shaping or the behavior that is achieved at the end of training. *See* Shaping.

Time in: The situation from which a person is removed when time out from reinforcement is used and access to available reinforcers is thus withdrawn for a brief period. The effectiveness of time out depends in part on how reinforcing that situation is.

Time out from reinforcement: A punishment procedure in which access to positive reinforcement is withdrawn for a brief period contingent upon behavior. Isolation from a group exemplifies time out from reinforcement but many variations do not require removing the client from the situation.

Token: A tangible object that serves as a generalized conditioned reinforcer. Poker chips, coins, tickets, stars, points, and check marks are commonly used as tokens. Tokens derive their value from being exchangeable for backup reinforcers. *See* Backup reinforcer and Token economy.

Token economy: A reinforcement system in which tokens are earned for a variety of behaviors and are used to purchase a variety of backup reinforcers. A token economy is analogous to a national economy, in which money serves as a medium of exchange and can be earned and spent in numerous ways.

Training the general case: A strategy designed to ensure that behaviors are performed across a variety of stimulus conditions (e.g., in different situations, in the presence of different persons) in which the behaviors will be required. The strategy requires that variations of different stimulus conditions be included during training.

Transfer of training: The extent to which responses trained in one setting transfer to settings other than the one in which training took place. *See* Stimulus generalization.

U

Unconditioned response: A reflex response elicited by an unconditioned stimulus. *See* Classical conditioning and Respondent.

Unconditioned stimulus: An event that elicits a reflex response. The connection between the stimulus (e.g., loud noise) and the response (e.g., startle) is unlearned. *See* Classical conditioning and Respondent.

V

Variable-interval schedule: A schedule of administering reinforcement. In a VI schedule, the first occurrence of the target response after a given interval has elapsed is reinforced. However, the time interval changes each time that reinforcement is delivered; the interval is variable. The schedule is denoted by the average time that must elapse before a response can be reinforced.

Variable-ratio schedule: A schedule of administering reinforcement. In a VR schedule, a number of occurrences of the target response are required for reinforcement. The number of required responses varies each time that reinforcement is delivered. The schedule is denoted by the average number of times that the response must occur before reinforcement is delivered.

Vicarious punishment: Punishment of one individual sometimes decreases performance of the punished behavior in individuals who have not been directly punished. A spread of punishment effects to individuals whose behaviors have not been directly punished.

Vicarious reinforcement: Reinforcement of one individual sometimes increases performance of the reinforced behavior in individuals who have not been directly reinforced. A spread of reinforcement effects to individuals whose behaviors have not been directly reinforced.

References

Achenbach, T.M. (1991). *Manual for the Child Behavior Checklist/4-18 and 1991 Profile.* Burlington, VT: University of Vermont, Department of Psychiatry.

Achenbach, T.M., McConaughy, S.H., & Howell, C.T. (1987). Child/adolescent behavioral and emotional problems: Implications of cross-informant correlations for situational specificity. *Psychological Bulletin, 101,* 213–232.

Adams, R. (1998). *The abuses of punishment.* New York: St. Martins Press.

Albin, R.W., Horner, R.H., Koegel, R.L., & Dunlap, G. (Eds.). (1987, September). *Extending competent performance: Applied research on generalization and maintenance.* Eugene, OR: University of Oregon.

Allen, J.S., Jr., Tarnowski, K.J., Simonian, S.J., Elliott, D.S., & Drabman, R.S. (1991). The generalization map revisited: Assessment of generalized treatment effects in child and adolescent behavior therapy. *Behavior Therapy, 22,* 393–405.

Allen, K.D., Loiben, T., Allen, S.J., & Stanley, R.T. (1992). Dentist-implemented contingent escape for management of disruptive child behavior. *Journal of Applied Behavior Analysis, 25,* 629–636.

Allen, K.D., & Stokes, T.F. (1987). Use of escape and reward in the management of young children during dental treatment. *Journal of Applied Behavior Analysis, 20,* 381–390.

Allen, L.D., & Iwata, B.A. (1980). Reinforcing exercise maintenance: Using existing high-rate activities. *Behavior Modification, 4,* 337–354.

Allinder, R.M., & Oats, R.G. (1997). Effects of acceptability on teacher's implementation of curriculum-based measurement and student achievement in mathematics computation. *Rase: Remedial and Special Education, 18,* 113–120.

Allport, G.W. (1937). *Personality: A psychological interpretation.* New York: Holt.

Altman, K., Haavik, S., & Cook, J.W. (1978). Punishment of self-injurious behavior in natural settings, using contingent aromatic ammonia. *Behaviour Research and Therapy, 16,* 85–96.

American Psychiatric Association. (1994). *Diagnostic and statistical manual of mental disorders* (4th ed.). Washington, DC: Author.

American Psychological Association. (1992). Ethical principles of psychologists and code of conduct. *American Psychologist, 47,* 1597–1611.

Ardoin, S.P., Martens, B.K., & Wolfe, L.A. (1999). Using high-probability instruction sequences with fading to increase student compliance during transitions. *Journal of Applied Behavior Analysis, 32,* 339–351.

Arndorfer, R.E., Allen, K.D., & Aljazireh, L. (1999). Behavioral health needs in pediatric medicine and the acceptability of behavioral solutions: Implications for behavioral psychologists. *Behavior Therapy, 30,* 137–148.

Association for Advancement of Behavior Therapy. (1977). Ethical issues for human services. *Behavior Therapy, 8, v–vi.*

Axelrod, S. (1998) *How to use group contingencies.* Austin, TX: Pro-Ed.

Ayllon, T., & Azrin, N.H. (1968a). Reinforcer sampling: A technique for increasing the behavior of mental patients. *Journal of Applied Behavior Analysis, 1,* 13–20.

Ayllon, T., & Azrin, N.H. (1968b). *The token economy: A motivational system for therapy and rehabilitation.* New York: Appleton-Century-Crofts.

Ayllon, T., & Haughton, E. (1964). Modification of symptomatic verbal behaviour of mental patients. *Behaviour Research and Therapy, 2,* 87–97.

Allyon, T., & Michael, J. (1959). The psychiatric nurse as a behavior engineer. *Journal of the Experimental Analysis of Behavior, 2,* 323–334.

Azrin, N.H., & Foxx, R.M. (1971). A rapid method of toilet training the institutionalized retarded. *Journal of Applied Behavior Analysis, 4,* 89–99.

Azrin, N.H., & Foxx, R.M. (1974). *Toilet training in less than a day.* New York: Simon & Schuster.

Azrin, N.H., Gottlieb, L., Hughart, L., Wesolowski, M.D., & Rahn, T. (1975). Eliminating self-injurious behavior by educative procedures. *Behaviour Research and Therapy, 13,* 101–111.

Azrin, N.H., & Holz, W.C. (1966). Punishment. In W.K. Honig (Ed.), *Operant behavior: Areas of research and application* (pp. 380–447). New York: Appleton-Century-Crofts.

Azrin, N.H., & Peterson, A.L. (1990). Treatment of Tourette's syndrome by habit reversal: A waiting-list control group. *Behavior Therapy, 21,* 305–318.

Azrin, N.H., & Powers, M.A. (1975). Eliminating classroom disturbances of emotionally disturbed children by positive practice procedures. *Behavior Therapy, 6,* 525–534.

Azrin, N.H., & Wesolowski, M.D. (1974). Theft reversal: An overcorrection procedure for eliminating stealing by retarded persons. *Journal of Applied Behavior Analysis, 7,* 577–581.

Barnett, A. (1998, September 9). Flying? No point in trying to beat the odds. *Wall Street Journal,* Vol. CCXXXII, No. 49, A22.

Baer, D.M., Rowbury, T.G., & Goetz, E.M. (1976). Behavioral traps in the preschool: A proposal for research. *Minnesota Symposia on Child Psychology, 10,* 3–27.

Baer, D.M., & Wolf, M.M. (1970). The entry into natural communities of reinforcement. In R. Ulrich, T. Stachnik, & J. Mabry (Eds.), *Control of human behavior* (Vol. 2, pp. 319–324). Glenview, IL: Scott, Foresman.

Baer, D.M., Wolf, M.M., & Risley, T.R. (1968). Some current dimensions of applied behavior analysis. *Journal of Applied Behavior Analysis, 1,* 91–97.

Baer, D.M., Wolf, M.M., & Risley, T.R. (1987). Some still–current dimensions of applied behavior analysis. *Journal of Applied Behavior Analysis, 20,* 313–328.

Baer, R.A., Blount, R.L., Detrick, R., & Stokes, T.F. (1987). Using intermittent reinforcement to program maintenance of verbal/nonverbal correspondence. *Journal of Applied Behavior Analysis, 20,* 179–184.

Ballard, K.D., & Glynn, T. (1975). Behavioral self-management in story writing with elementary school children. *Journal of Applied Behavior Analysis, 8,* 387–398.

Bandura, A. (1965). Influence of models' reinforcement contingencies on the acquisition of imitative responses. *Journal of Personality and Social Psychology, 1,* 589–595.

Bandura, A. (1977). *Social learning theory.* Englewood Cliffs, NJ: Prentice-Hall.

Bandura, A. (1986). *Social foundations of thought and action: A social cognitive perspective.* Englewood Cliffs, NJ: Prentice-Hall.

Bank, L., Marlowe, J.H., Reid, J.B., Patterson, G.R., & Weinrott, M.R. (1991). A comparative evaluation of parent-training interventions for families of chronic delinquents. *Journal of Abnormal Child Psychology, 19,* 15–33.

Barlow, D.H., & Hersen, M. (1984). *Single–case experimental designs. Strategies for studying behavior change* (2nd ed.). New York: Pergamon Press.

Barton, E.J., & Osborne, J.G. (1978). The development of classroom sharing by a teacher using positive practice. *Behavior Modification, 2,* 231–250.

Battle, E.K., & Brownell, K.D. (1996) Confronting a rising tide of eating disorders and obesity: Treatment vs. prevention and policy. *Addictive Behaviors, 21,* 755–765.

Beck, A.T. (1967). *Depression: Clinical, experimental, and theoretical aspects.* New York: Harper & Row.

Beck, A.T., Kovacs, M., & Weissman, A. (1975). Hopelessness and suicidal behavior: An overview. *Journal of the American Medical Association, 234,* 1146–1149.

Beck, A.T., Rush, A.J., Shaw, B.F., & Emery, G. (1979). *Cognitive therapy of depression.* New York: Guilford.

Bell, K.E., Young, K.R., Salzberg, C.L., & West, R.P. (1991). High school driver education using peer tutors, direct instruction, and precision teaching. *Journal of Applied Behavior Analysis, 24,* 45–51.

Bellack, A.S., & Hersen, M. (Eds.). (1988). *Behavioral assessment: A practical handbook.* Needham Heights, MA: Allyn & Bacon.

Belles, D., & Bradlyn, A.S. (1987). The use of the changing criterion design in achieving controlled smoking in a heavy smoker: A controlled study. *Journal of Behavior Therapy and Experimental Psychiatry, 18,* 77–82.

Bensen, M.D., & Klipper, M.Z. (1990). *The relaxation response.* New York: Avon.

Bernard, M.E., Kratochwill, T.R., & Keefauver, L.W. (1983). The effects of rational-emotive therapy and self-instructional training on chronic hair–pulling. *Cognitive Therapy and Research, 7,* 273–280.

Bierman, K.L., Miller, C.L., & Stabb, S.D. (1987). Improving the social behavior and peer acceptance of rejected boys: Effects of social skill training with instructions and prohibitions. *Journal of Consulting and Clinical Psychology, 55,* 194–200.

Bigelow, G.E., Liebson, I., & Griffiths, R. (1974). Alcoholic drinking: Suppression by a brief time–out procedure. *Behaviour Research and Therapy, 12,* 107–115.

Blampied, N.M., & Kahan, E. (1992). Acceptability of alternative punishments: A community survey. *Behavior Modification, 16,* 400–413.

Bootzin, R.R. (1972). Stimulus control treatment for insomnia. *Proceedings of the 80th Annual Convention of the American Psychological Association, 7,* 395–396.

Bootzin, R.R., Epstein, D., & Wood, J.M. (1991). Stimulus control instructions. In P.J. Hauri (Ed.), *Case studies in insomnia* (pp. 19–28). New York: Plenum.

Bootzin, R.R., & Rider, S.P. (1997). Behavioral techniques and biofeedback for insomnia. In M.R. Pressman & W.C. Orr (Eds.). *Understanding sleep: The evaluation and treatment of sleep disorders* (pp. 315–338). Washington, DC: American Psychological Association.

Brestan, E.V., & Eyberg, S.M. (1998). Effective psychosocial treatment of conduct-disordered children and adolescents: 29 years, 82 studies, and 5275 kids. *Journal of Clinical Child Psychology, 27,* 180–189.

Brownell, K.D. (1994, December 15). Get slim with higher taxes. *The New York Times,* A29.

Budd, K.S., & Stokes, T.F. (1977, August). *Cue properties of praise in vicarious reinforcement with preschoolers.* Paper presented at meeting of the American Psychological Association, San Francisco.

Budney, A.J., Higgins, S.T., Delaney, D.D., Kent, L., & Bickel, W.K. (1991). Contingent reinforcement of abstinence with individuals abusing cocaine and marijuana. *Journal of Applied Behavior Analysis, 24,* 657–665.

Bujold, A., Ladouceur, R., Sylvain, C., & Boisvert. J.M. (1994). Treatment of pathological gamblers: An experimental study. *Journal of Behavior Therapy and Experimental Psychiatry, 25,* 275–282.

Burling, T.A., Bigelow, G.E., Robinson, J.C., & Mead, A.M. (1991). Smoking during pregnancy: Reduction via objective assessment and directive advice. *Behavior Therapy, 22,* 31–40.

Bushell, D., Jr. (1978). An engineering approach to the elementary classroom: The Behavior Analysis Follow Through project. In A.C. Catania & T.A. Brigham (Eds.), *Handbook of applied behavior analysis: Social and instructional processes* (pp. 525–563). New York: Irvington.

Calhoun, K.S., & Lima, P.P. (1977). Effects of varying schedules of time out on high- and low-rate behaviors. *Journal of Behavior Therapy and Experimental Psychiatry, 8,* 189–194.

Carey, R.G., & Bucher, B.B. (1981). Identifying the educative and suppressive effects of positive practice and restitutional overcorrection. *Journal of Applied Behavior Analysis, 14,* 71–80.

Carey, R.G., & Bucher, B.B. (1986). Positive practice overcorrection: Effects of reinforcing correct performance. *Behavior Modification, 10,* 73–92.

Carley, W.M. (2000). Talk of video cameras in jet cockpits makes pilots fly into a rage. *Wall Street Journal,* Vol. CCXXXV, No. 70, A1, A8.

Carr, E.G., & Durand, V.M. (1985). Reducing behavior problems through functional communication training. *Journal of Applied Behavior Analysis, 18,* 111–126.

Carr, E.G., Taylor, J.C., & Robinson, S. (1991). The effects of severe behavior problems in children on the teaching behavior of adults. *Journal of Applied Behavior Analysis, 24,* 523–535.

Catania, A.C. (1997). *Learning* (4th ed.). Englewood Cliffs, NJ: Prentice-Hall.

Cautela, J.R., & Kearney, A.J. (Eds.). (1986). *The covert conditioning handbook.* New York: Springer.

Cautela, J.R., & Kearney, A.J. (Eds.). (1993). *Covert conditioning casebook.* Pacific Grove, CA: Brooks/Cole.

Chadwick, P., & Trower, P. (1996). Cognitive therapy for punishment paranoia: A single-case experiment. *Journal of Behavior Therapy and Experimental Psychiatry, 34,* 351–356.

Charlop, M.H., Burgio, L.D., Iwata, B.A., & Ivancic, M.T. (1988). Stimulus variation as a means of enhancing punishment effects. *Journal of Applied Behavior Analysis, 21,* 89–95.

Chase, M. (1999, November 19). Diagnosing depression by computer may spur more to get treatment. *Wall Street Journal,* Vol. CCXXXIV, No. 100, B1.

Clark, D.A., Beck, A., & Alford, B.A. (1999). *Cognitive theory and therapy of depression.* New York: John Wiley & Sons.

Clark, H.B., Greene, B.F., Macrae, J.W., McNees, M.P., Davis, J.L., & Risley, T.R. (1977). A parent advice package for family shopping trips: Development and evaluation. *Journal of Applied Behavior Analysis, 10,* 605–624.

Clark, H.B., Rowbury, T.G., Baer, A.M., & Baer, D.M. (1973). Time out as a punishing stimulus in continuous and intermittent schedules. *Journal of Applied Behavior Analysis, 6,* 443–455.

Cone, J.D. (Ed.). (1999). Special section: Clinical assessment applications of self-monitoring. *Psychological Assessment, 11,* 411–497.

Cook, J.W., Altman, K., Shaw, J., & Blaylock, M. (1978). Use of contingent lemon juice to eliminate public masturbation by a severely retarded boy. *Behaviour Research and Therapy, 16,* 131–134.

Craft, M.A., Alber, S.R., & Heward, W.L. (1998). Teaching elementary students with developmental disabilities to recruit teacher attention in a general education classroom: Effects on teacher praise and academic productivity. *Journal of Applied Behavior Analysis, 31,* 399–415.

Creer, T.L., Chai, H., & Hoffman, A. (1977). A single application of an aversive stimulus to eliminate chronic cough. *Journal of Behavior Therapy and Experimental Psychiatry, 8,* 107–109.

Cuijpers, P. (1997). Bibliotherapy in unipolar depression: A meta-analysis. *Journal of Behavior Therapy and Experimental Psychiatry, 28,* 139–147.

Cushing, L.S., & Kennedy, C.H. (1997). Academic effects of providing peer support in general education classrooms on students without disabilities. *Journal of Applied Behavior Analysis, 30,* 139–151.

Dawson, B., deArmas, A., McGrath, M.L., & Kelly, J.A. (1986). Cognitive problem solving training to improve the child-care judgment of child neglectful parents. *Journal of Family Violence, 1,* 209–221.

Day, H.M., & Horner, R.H. (1986). Response variation and the generalization of a dressing skill: Comparison of single instance and general case instruction. *Applied Research in Mental Retardation, 7,* 189–202.

Deitz, S.M. (1977). An analysis of programming DRL schedules in educational settings. *Behaviour Research and Therapy, 15,* 103–111.

Deitz, S.M., Repp, A.C., & Deitz, D.E.D. (1976). Reducing inappropriate classroom behavior of retarded students through three procedures of differential reinforcement. *Journal of Mental Deficiency Research, 20,* 155–170.

DeLuca, R.V., & Holborn, S.W. (1992). Effects of a variable–ratio reinforcement schedule with changing criteria on exercise in obese and nonobese boys. *Journal of Applied Behavior Analysis, 25,* 671–679.

DeRubeis, R.J., & Crits-Cristoph, P. (1998). Empirically supported individual and group psychological treatments for adult mental disorders. *Journal of Consulting and Clinical Psychology, 66,* 37–52.

DeVries, J.E., Burnette, M.M., & Redmon, W.K. (1991). AIDS prevention: Improving nurses' compliance with glove wearing through performance feedback. *Journal of Applied Behavior Analysis, 24,* 705–711.

DiLulio, J.J. (1997, January 8). What the crime statistics don't tell you. *Wall Street Journal,* Vol. CCXXIX, No. 5, A22.

Dishion, T.J., McCord, J., & Poulin, F. (1999). When interventions harm: Peer groups and problem behavior. *American Psychologist, 54,* 755–764.

Dishion, T.J., & Patterson, G.R. (1997). The timing and severity of antisocial behavior: Three hypotheses within an ecological framework. In D.M. Stoff, J. Breiling, & J.D. Maser (Eds.), *Handbook of antisocial behavior* (pp. 205–217). New York: John Wiley & Sons.

Dodge, K.A., & Schwartz, D. (1997). Social information processing mechanisms in aggressive behavior. In D.M. Stoff, J. Breiling, & J.D. Maser (Eds.), *Handbook of antisocial behavior.* (pp. 171–180). New York: John Wiley & Sons.

Doleys, D.M., Wells, K.C., Hobbs, S.A., Roberts, M.W., & Cartelli, L.M. (1976). The effects of social punishment on noncompliance: A comparison with time out and positive practice. *Journal of Applied Behavior Analysis, 9,* 471–482.

Donnellan, A.M., & LaVigna, G.W. (1990). Myths about punishment. In A.C. Repp & N.N. Singh (Eds.), *Perspectives on the use of nonaversive and aversive interventions for persons with developmental disabilities* (pp. 33–57). Sycamore, IL: Sycamore.

Donnelly, D.R., & Olczak, P.V. (1990). The effect of differential reinforcement of incompatible behaviors (DRI) on pica for cigarettes in persons with intellectual disability. *Behavior Modification, 14,* 81–96.

Dorsey, M.F., Iwata, B.A., Ong, P., & McSween, T.E. (1980). Treatment of self-injurious behavior using a water mist: Initial response suppression and generalization. *Journal of Applied Behavior Analysis, 13,* 343–353.

Ducharme, D.E., & Holborn, S.W. (1997). Programming generalization of social skills in preschool children with hearing impairments. *Journal of Applied Behavior Analysis, 30,* 639–651.

Ducharme, J.M., & Feldman, M.A. (1992). Comparison of staff training strategies to promote generalized teaching skills. *Journal of Applied Behavior Analysis, 25,* 165–179.

Dumont, F. (1993). Inferential heuristics in clinical problem formulation: Selective review of their strengths and weaknesses. *Professional Psychology: Research and Practice, 24,* 196–205.

Dunlap, G., Koegel, R.L., Johnson, J., & O'Neill, R.E. (1987). Maintaining performance of autistic clients in community settings with delayed contingencies. *Journal of Applied Behavior Analysis, 20,* 179–184.

Durand, V.M. (1990). *Severe behavior problems: A functional communication training approach.* New York: Guilford.

Durand, V.M., & Carr, E.G. (1991). Functional communication training to reduce challenging behavior: Maintenance and application in new settings. *Journal of Applied Behavior Analysis, 24,* 251–264.

Durlak, J.A., Fuhrman, T., & Lampman, C. (1991). Effectiveness of cognitive-behavioral therapy for maladapting children: A meta-analysis. *Psychological Bulletin, 110,* 204–214.

Eisen, A.R., & Silverman, W.K. (1991). Treatment of an adolescent with bowel movement phobia using self-control therapy. *Journal of Behavior Therapy and Experimental Psychiatry, 22,* 45–51.

Elliott, D.S., Dunford, F.W., & Huizinga, D. (1987). The identification and prediction of career offenders utilizing self-reported and official data. In J.D. Burchard & S.N. Burchard (Eds.), *Preventing delinquent behavior* (pp. 90–121). Newbury Park, CA: Sage.

Elliott, S.N. (1988). Acceptability of behavioral treatments: Review of variables that influence treatment selection. *Professional Psychology: Research and Practice, 19,* 68–80.

Ellis, A. (1979). *New developments in rational-emotive therapy.* Pacific Grove, CA: Brooks/Cole.

Ellis, A. (1999). *Reason and emotion in psychotherapy: A comprehensive method for treating human disturbances* (revised edition). Secaucus, NJ: Citadel.

Ellis, A., & Dryden, W. (1998). *The practice of rational emotive behaviour therapy.* New York: Free Association.

Emmelkamp, P.M.G. (1994). Behavior therapy with adults. In A.E. Bergin & S.L. Garfield (Eds.), *Handbook of psychotherapy and behavior change: An empirical analysis* (4th ed., pp. 379–427). New York: John Wiley & Sons.

Erhardt, D., & Baker, B.L. (1990). The effects of behavioral parent training on families with young hyperactive children. *Journal of Behavior Therapy and Experimental Psychiatry, 21,* 121–132.

Esveldt–Dawson, K., & Kazdin, A.E. (1998). *How to maintain behavior* (2nd ed.). Austin, TX: Pro-Ed.

Evidence–Based Mental Health (1998). (A journal devoted to evidence based treatments and linking research to practice.) Vol. 1, No. 1.

Fantuzzo, J.W., & Clement, P.W. (1981). Generalization of the effects of teacher- and self-administered token reinforcers to nontreated students. *Journal of Applied Behavior Analysis, 14,* 435–447.

Fawcett, S.B. (1991). Some values guiding community research and action. *Journal of Applied Behavior Analysis, 24,* 621–636.

Feingold, L., & Migler, B. (1972). The use of experimental dependency relationships as a motivating procedure on a token-economy ward. In R.D. Rubin, H. Fensterheim, J.D. Henderson, & L.P. Ullmann (Eds.), *Advances in behavior therapy* (pp. 121–127). New York: Academic Press.

Finney, J.W. (1991). Selection of target behaviors and interventions: A case of necessary but insufficient choices. *Journal of Applied Behavior Analysis, 24,* 713–715.

Fischer, J., & Nehs, R. (1978). Use of a commonly available chore to reduce a boy's rate of swearing. *Journal of Behavior Therapy and Experimental Psychiatry, 9,* 81–83.

Fishman, D.B., Rotgers, F., & Franks, C.M. (Eds.). (1988). *Paradigms in behavior therapy.* New York: Springer.

Fixsen, D.L., Phillips, E.L., Phillips, E.A., & Wolf, M.M. (1976). The teaching-family model of group home treatment. In W.E. Craighead, A.E. Kazdin, & M.J. Mahoney (Eds.), *Behavior modification: Principles, issues, and applications.* (pp. 310–320). Boston: Houghton Mifflin.

Fletcher, D. (1995). A five-year study of effects of fines, gender, race, and age on illegal parking in spaces reserved for people with disabilities. *Rehabilitation Psychology, 40,* 203–210.

Foley, F.W., Bedell, J.R., LaRocca, N.G., Scheinberg, L.C., & Reznikoff, M. (1987). Efficacy of stress-inoculation training in coping with multiple sclerosis. *Journal of Consulting and Clinical Psychology, 55,* 919–922.

Foot, H., Morgan, M., & Shute, R. (Eds.). (1990). *Children helping children.* Chichester, England: John Wiley & Sons.

Foster, S.L., Bell-Dolan, D.J., & Burge, D.A. (1988). Behavioral observation. In A.S. Bellack & M. Hersen (Eds.), *Behavioral assessment: A practical handbook* (119–160). Needham Heights, MA: Allyn & Bacon.

Fox, D.K., Hopkins, B.L., & Anger, W.K. (1987). The long-term effects of a token economy on safety performance in open-pit mining. *Journal of Applied Behavior Analysis, 20,* 215–224.

Fox, L. (1962). Effecting the use of efficient study habits. *Journal of Mathematics, 1,* 75–86.

Foxx, R.M., & Azrin, N.H. (1972). Restitution: A method of eliminating aggressive disruptive behavior of retarded and brain damaged patients. *Behaviour Research and Therapy, 10,* 15–27.

Foxx, R.M., & Bechtel, D.R. (1983). Overcorrection: A review and analysis. In S. Axelrod & J. Apsche (Eds.), *The effects of punishment on human behavior* (pp. 133–220). New York: Academic Press.

Foxx, R.M., Bremer, B.A., Schutz, C., Valdez, J., & Johndrow, C. (1996). Increasing treatment acceptability through video. *Behavioral Interventions, 11,* 171–180.

Foxx, R.M., Faw, G.D., & Weber, G. (1991). Producing generalization of inpatient adolescents' social skills with significant adults in a natural environment. *Behavior Therapy, 22,* 85–99.

Foxx, R.M., & Shapiro, S.T. (1978). The time out ribbon: A nonexclusionary time out procedure. *Journal of Applied Behavior Analysis, 11,* 125–136.

France, K.G., & Hudson, S.M. (1990). Behavior management of infant sleep disturbance. *Journal of Applied Behavior Analysis, 23,* 91–98.

Frederiksen, L.W. (1975). Treatment of ruminative thinking by self-monitoring. *Journal of Behavior Therapy and Experimental Psychiatry, 6,* 258–259.

Freud, S. (1936). *The problem of anxiety* (H.A. Bunker, Trans.). New York: Norton.

Friman, P.C., Finney, J.W., Glasscock, S.T., Weigel, J.W., & Christophersen, E.R. (1986). Testicular self-examination: Validation of a training strategy for early cancer detection. *Journal of Applied Behavior Analysis, 19,* 87–92.

Friman, P.C., & Hove, G. (1987). Apparent covariation between child habit disorders: Effects of successful treatment for thumb sucking on untargeted chronic hairpulling. *Journal of Applied Behavior Analysis, 20,* 421–426.

Geller, E.S., Bruff, C.D., & Nimmer, J.G. (1985). "Flash for life": Community-based prompting for safety belt promotion. *Journal of Applied Behavior Analysis, 18,* 309–314.

Geller, E.S., Winett, R.A., & Everett, P.B. (1982). *Preserving the environment: New strategies for behavior change.* New York: Pergamon Press.

Gentry, W.D. (1999). *Anger-free. Ten basic steps to managing your anger.* New York: William Morrow.

Glasgow, R.E., & Rosen, G.M. (1984). Self-help behavior therapy manuals: Recent developments and clinical usage. In C.M. Franks (Ed.), *New developments in behavior therapy: From research to clinical application* (pp. 525–570). New York: Haworth Press.

Glynn, E.L. (1970). Classroom applications of self-determined reinforcement. *Journal of Applied Behavior Analysis, 3,* 123–132.

Glynn, S.M. (1990). Token economy approaches for psychiatric patients. *Behavior Modification, 14,* 383–407.

Goldiamond, I. (1965). Self-control procedures in personal behavior problems. *Psychological Reports, 17,* 851–868.

Green, C.W., Reid, D.H., Canipe, V.S., & Gardner, S.M. (1991). A comprehensive evaluation of reinforcer identification processes for persons with profound multiple handicaps. *Journal of Applied Behavior Analysis 24,* 537–552.

Green, G. (1990). Least restrictive use of reductive procedures: Guidelines and competencies. In A.C. Repp & N.N. Singh (Eds.), *Perspectives on the use of nonaversive and aversive interventions for persons with developmental disabilities* (pp. 479–493). Sycamore, IL: Sycamore.

Greenberger, D., & Padesky, C.A. (1995). *Mind over mood: A cognitive therapy manual for clients.* New York: Guilford.

Greenwood, C.R., Delquadri, J.C., & Hall, R.V. (1984). Opportunity to respond and student academic performance. In W.L. Heward, T.E. Heron, D.S. Hill, & J. Trap-Porter (Eds.), *Focus on behavior analysis in education* (pp. 58–88). Columbus, OH: Merrill.

Greenwood, C.R., & Hops, H. (1981). Group-oriented contingencies and peer behavior change. In P.S. Strain (Ed.), *The utilization of classroom peers as behavior change agents.* New York: Plenum.

Greenwood, C.R., Hops, H., Delquadri, J., & Guild, J.J. (1974). Group contingencies for group consequences in classroom management: A further analysis. *Journal of Applied Behavior Analysis, 7,* 413–425.

Greenwood, D.R., Carta, J.J., & Kamps, D.M. (1990). Teacher versus peer-mediated instruction. In H. Foot, M. Morgan, & R. Schute (Eds.), *Children helping children* (pp. 177–205). New York: John Wiley & Sons.

Greer, R.D., & Polirstok, S.R. (1982). Collateral gains and short-term maintenance in reading and on-task responses by inner-city adolescents as a function of their use of social reinforcement while tutoring. *Journal of Applied Behavior Analysis, 15,* 123–139.

Greven, P. (1992). Exploring the effects of corporal punishment. *Child, Youth, and Family Services Quarterly, 15* (4), 4–5.

Griffen, A.K., Wolery, M., & Schuster, J.W. (1992). Triadic instruction of chained food preparation responses: Acquisition of observational learning. *Journal of Applied Behavior Analysis, 25,* 193–204.

Groden, J. (1993). The use of covert procedures to reduce severe aggression in a person with retardation and behavioral disorders. In J.R. Cautela & A.J. Kearney (Eds.), *Covert conditioning casebook* (pp. 144–152). Pacific Grove, CA: Brooks/Cole.

Gross, A.M., & Drabman, R.S. (1982). Teaching self-recording, self-evaluation, and self-reward to nonclinic children and adolescents. In P. Karoly & F.H. Kanfer (Eds.), *Self-management and behavior change: From theory to practice.* (pp. 285–314). New York: Pergamon Press.

Gumpel, T.P., & Frank, R. (1999). An expansion of the peer-tutoring paradigm: Cross-age peer tutoring of social skills among socially rejected boys. *Journal of Applied Behavior Analysis, 32,* 115–118

Gutkin, A.J., Holborn, S.W., Walker, J.R., & Anderson, B.A. (1992). Treatment integrity of relaxation training for tension headaches. *Journal of Behavior Therapy and Experimental Psychiatry, 23,* 191–198.

Hall, R.V., Axelrod, S., Foundopoulos, M., Sherman, J., Campbell, R.A., & Cranston, S. (1971). The effective use of punishment to modify behavior in the classroom. *Educational Technology, 11,* 24–26.

Hall, R.V., & Hall, M.L. (1998). *How to negotiate a behavioral contract* (2nd ed.). Austin, TX: Pro-Ed.

Hall, R.V., & Hall, M.L (1998). *How to select reinforcers* (2nd ed). Austin, TX: Pro-Ed.

Hall, R.V., & Hall, M.L. (1998). *How to use planned ignoring (extinction)* (2nd ed.). Austin, TX: Pro-Ed.

Hall, R.V., & Hall, M.L (1998). *How to use systematic attention and approval* (2nd ed). Austin, TX: Pro-Ed.

Hall, R.V., & Hall, M.L (1998). *How to use time out* (2nd ed). Austin, TX: Pro-Ed.

Hall, S.M., Cooper, J.L., Burmaster, S., & Polk, A. (1977). Contingency contracting as a therapeutic tool with methadone maintenance clients: Six single-subject studies. *Behaviour Research and Therapy, 15,* 438–441.

Hancock v. Avery, 301 F. Supp. (M.D. Tenn. 1969).

Harchik, A.E., Sherman, J.A., Sheldon, J.B., & Strouse, M.C. (1992). Ongoing consultation as a method of improving performance of staff members in a group home. *Journal of Applied Behavior Analysis, 25,* 599–610.

Haring, T.G., Kennedy, C.H., Adams, M.J., & Pitts-Conway, V. (1987). Teaching generalization of purchasing skills across community settings to autistic youth using videotape modeling. *Journal of Applied Behavior Analysis, 20,* 89–96.

Harris, K.R. (1986). Self-monitoring of attentional behavior versus self-monitoring of productivity: Effects on on-task behavior and academic response rate among learning disabled children. *Journal of Applied Behavior Analysis, 19,* 417–424.

Harris, V.W., & Sherman, J.A. (1973). Use and analysis of the "good-behavior game" to reduce disruptive classroom behavior. *Journal of Applied Behavior Analysis, 6,* 405–417.

Hartmann, D.P. (Ed.). (1985). Mini-series: Target behavior selection. *Behavioral Assessment, 7,* 1–78.

Hawkins, R.P. (1986). Selection of target behaviors. In R.O. Nelson & S.C. Hayes (Eds.), *Conceptual foundations of behavioral assessment* (pp. 331–385). New York: Guilford.

Hawkins, R.P., & Dobes, R.W. (1975). Behavioral definitions in applied behavior analysis: Explicit or implicit. In B.C. Etzel, J.M. LeBlanc, & D.M. Baer (Eds.), *New developments in behavioral research: Theory, methods, and applications: In honor of Sidney W. Bijou.* (pp. 167–188). Hillsdale, NJ: Erlbaum.

Hayes, S.C., Brownell, K.D., & Barlow, D.H. (1978). The use of self-administered covert sensitization in the treatment of exhibitionism and sadism. *Behavior Therapy, 9,* 283–289.

Haynes, S.N. (1992). *Models of causality in psychopathology: Toward dynamic, synthetic, and nonlinear models of behavior disorders.* Needham Heights, MA: Allyn & Bacon.

Haynes, S.N., & Horn, W.F. (1982). Reactivity in behavioral observation: A methodological and conceptual critique. *Behavioral Assessment, 4,* 369–385.

Haynes, S.N., & O'Brien, W.H. (1990). Functional analysis in behavior therapy. *Clinical Psychology Review, 10,* 649–668.

Henggeler, S.W., Schoenwald, S.K., Borduin, C.M., Rowland, M.D., &. Cunningham, P.B. (1998). *Multisystemic treatment of antisocial behavior in children and adolescents.* New York: Guilford.

Herbert, E.W., Pinkston, E.M., Hayden, M., Sajwaj, T.E., Pinkston, S., Cordua, G., & Jackson, C. (1973). Adverse effects of differential parental attention. *Journal of Applied Behavior Analysis, 6,* 15–30.

Hobbs, S.A., & Forehand, R. (1977). Important parameters in the use of time out with children: A reexamination. *Journal of Behavior Therapy and Experimental Psychiatry, 8,* 365–370.

Hobbs, S.A., Forehand, R., & Murray, R.G. (1978). Effects of various durations of time out on the noncompliant behavior of children. *Behavior Therapy, 9,* 652–656.

Hollon, S.D., & Beck, A.T. (1994). Cognitive and cognitive-behavioral therapies. In A.E. Bergin & S.L. Garfield (Eds.), *Handbook of psychotherapy and behavior change: An empirical analysis* (4th ed., pp. 428–466). New York: John Wiley & Sons.

Homme, L.E. (1965). Perspectives in psychology: XXIV. Control of coverants, the operants of the mind. *Psychological Record, 15,* 501–511.

Honnen, T.J., & Kleinke, C.L. (1990). Prompting bar patrons with signs to take free condoms. *Journal of Applied Behavior Analysis, 23,* 215–217.

Horgen, K.B., & Brownell, K.D. (1998). Policy change as a means for reducing the prevalence and impact of alcoholism, smoking, and obesity. In W.R. Miller & N. Heather (Eds.), *Treating addictive behaviors* (2nd ed., pp. 105–118). New York: Plenum Press.

Horner, R.H., Albin, R.W., & Ralph, G. (1986). Generalization with precision: The role of negative teaching examples in the instruction of generalized grocery item selection. *Journal of the Association for Persons with Severe Handicaps, 11,* 300–308.

Horner, R.H., Dunlap, G., & Koegel, R.L. (Eds.). (1988). *Generalization and maintenance: Life-style changes in applied settings.* Baltimore: Paul H. Brookes.

Horner, R.H., Eberhard, J.M., & Sheehan, M.R. (1986). Teaching generalized table bussing: The importance of negative teaching examples. *Behavior Modification, 10,* 457–471.

Horner, R.H., & Keilitz, L. (1975). Training mentally retarded adolescents to brush their teeth. *Journal of Applied Behavior Analysis, 8,* 301–309.

Horner, R.H., Williams, J.A., & Knobbe, C.A. (1985). The effects of "opportunity to perform" on the maintenance of skills learned by high school students with severe handicaps. *Journal of the Association for Persons with Severe Handicaps, 10,* 172–175.

Hutchinson, R.R. (1977). By-products of aversive control. In W.K. Honig & J.E.R. Staddon (Eds.), *Handbook of operant behavior* (pp. 415–431). Englewood Cliffs, NJ: Prentice-Hall.

Iwata, B.A. (1987). Negative reinforcement in applied behavior analysis: An emerging technology. *Journal of Applied Behavior Analysis, 20,* 361–378.

Iwata, B.A., Bailey, J.S., Fuqua, R.W., Neef, N.A., Mae, T.J., & Reid, D.H. (Eds.). (1989). *Methodological and conceptual issues in applied behavior analysis.* Lawrence, KS: Society of the Experimental Analysis of Behavior.

Iwata, B.A., Dorsey, M.F., Slifer, K.J., Bauman, K.E., & Richman, G.S. (1994). Toward a functional analysis of self-injury. *Journal of Applied Behavior Analysis, 27,* 197–209. (Reprinted from *Analysis and Intervention in Developmental Disabilities, 1982, 2,* 3–20.)

Iwata, B.A., Pace, G.M., Kalsher, M.J., Cowdery, G.E., & Cataldo, M.F. (1990). Experimental analysis and extinction of self-injurious escape behavior. *Journal of Applied Behavior Analysis, 23,* 11–27.

Iwata, B.A., Vollmer, T.R., & Zarcone, J.R. (1990). The experimental (functional) analysis of behavior disorders: Methodology, applications, and limitations. In A.C. Repp & N.N. Singh (Eds.), *Perspectives on the use of nonaversive and aversive interventions for persons with developmental disabilities* (pp. 301–330). Sycamore, IL: Sycamore.

Jacobs, G.D., Benson, H., & Friedman, R. (1993). Home-based central nervous system assessment of a multifactor behavioral intervention for chronic sleep onset insomnia. *Behavior Therapy, 24,* 159–174.

Jacobson, N.S., & Revenstorf, D. (1988). Statistics for assessing the clinical significance of psychotherapy techniques: Issues, problems, and new developments. *Behavioral Assessment, 10,* 133–145.

James, S.D., & Egel, A.L. (1986). A direct prompting strategy for increasing reciprocal interactions between handicapped and nonhandicapped siblings. *Journal of Applied Behavior Analysis, 19,* 173–186.

Jay, S.M., Elliot, C.H., Katz, E., & Siegel, S.E. (1987). Cognitive-behavioral and pharmacologic interventions for children's distress during painful medical procedures. *Journal of Consulting and Clinical Psychology, 55,* 860–865.

Jones, M.C. (1924). A laboratory study of fear: The case of Peter. *Pedagogical Seminary, 31*, 308–315.

Jones, R.T., Kazdin, A.E., & Haney, J.I. (1981). Social validation and training of emergency fire safety skills for potential injury prevention and life-saving. *Journal of Applied Behavior Analysis, 14*, 249–260.

Kallman, W.H., Hersen, M., & O'Toole, D.H. (1975). The use of social reinforcement in a case of conversion reaction. *Behavior Therapy, 6*, 411–413.

Kamps, D.M., Barbetta, P.M., Leonard, B.R., & Delquadri, J. (1994). Classwide peer tutoring: An investigation strategy to improve reading skills and promote peer interactions among students with autism and general education peers. *Journal of Applied Behavior Analysis, 27*, 49–61.

Kanfer, F.H. (1977). The many faces of self-control, or behavior modification changes its focus. In R.B. Stuart (Ed.), *Behavioral self-management: Strategies, techniques, and outcomes* (pp. 1–48). New York: Brunner Mazel.

Karoly, P., & Kanfer, F.H. (Eds.). (1982). *Self-management and behavior change: From theory to practice.* Elmsford, NY: Pergamon Press.

Kazdin, A.E. (1972). Response cost: The removal of conditioned reinforcers for therapeutic change. *Behavior Therapy, 3*, 533–546.

Kazdin, A.E. (1973). Role of instructions and reinforcement in behavior changes in token reinforcement programs. *Journal of Educational Psychology, 64*, 63–71.

Kazdin, A.E. (1977a). Artifact, bias, and complexity of assessment: The ABC's of reliability. *Journal of Applied Behavior Analysis, 10*, 141–150.

Kazdin, A.E. (1977b). Assessing the clinical or applied importance of behavior change through social validation. *Behavior Modification, 1*, 427–452.

Kazdin, A.E. (1977c). *The token economy: A review and evaluation.* New York: Plenum.

Kazdin, A.E. (1977d). Vicarious reinforcement and direction of behavior change in the classroom. *Behavior Therapy, 8*, 57–63.

Kazdin, A.E. (1978). *History of behavior modification: Experimental foundations of contemporary research.* Baltimore: University Park Press.

Kazdin, A.E. (1979). Vicarious reinforcement and punishment in operant programs for children. *Child Behavior Therapy, 1*, 13–36.

Kazdin, A.E. (1980a). Acceptability of alternative treatments for deviant child behavior. *Journal of Applied Behavior Analysis, 13*, 259–273.

Kazdin, A.E. (1980b). Acceptability of time out from reinforcement procedures for disruptive child behavior. *Behavior Therapy, 11*, 329–344.

Kazdin, A.E. (1981). Acceptability of child treatment techniques: The influence of treatment efficacy and adverse side effects. *Behavior Therapy, 12*, 493–506.

Kazdin, A.E. (1982a). Observer effects: Reactivity of direct observation. *New Directions for Methodology of Social and Behavioral Science, 14*, 5–19.

Kazdin, A.E. (1982b). *Single–case research designs: Methods for clinical and applied settings.* New York: Oxford University Press.

Kazdin, A.E. (1982c). The token economy: A decade later. *Journal of Applied Behavior Analysis, 15*, 431–445.

Kazdin, A.E. (1983). Failure of persons to respond to the token economy. In E.B. Foa & P.M.G. Emmelkamp (Eds.), *Failures in behavior therapy* (pp. 335–354). New York: John Wiley & Sons.

Kazdin, A.E. (1984). Covert modeling. In P.C. Kendall (Ed.), *Advances in cognitive behavioral research and therapy* (Vol. 3, 103–129). New York: Academic Press.

Kazdin, A.E. (1993). Evaluation in clinical practice: Clinically sensitive and systematic methods of treatment delivery. *Behavior Therapy, 24*, 11–45.

Kazdin, A.E. (1994). Informant variability in the assessment of childhood depression. In W.M. Reynolds & H. Johnston (Eds.), *Handbook of depression in children and adolescents* (pp. 249–271). New York: Plenum.

Kazdin, A.E. (1995). *Conduct disorder in childhood and adolescence* (2nd ed.). Thousand Oaks, CA: Sage.

Kazdin, A.E. (1996a). Combined and multi-modal treatments in child and adolescent psychotherapy: Issues, challenges, and research directions. *Clinical Psychology: Science and Practice, 3,* 69–100.

Kazdin, A.E. (1996b). Dropping out of child therapy: Issues for research and implications for practice. *Clinical Child Psychology and Psychiatry, 1,* 133–156.

Kazdin, A.E. (1996c). Problem solving and parent management in treating aggressive and antisocial behavior. In E.D. Hibbs & P.S. Jensen (Eds.), *Psychosocial treatments for child and adolescent disorders: Empirically based strategies for clinical practice.* (377–408). Washington, DC: American Psychological Association.

Kazdin, A.E. (1997). Parent management training: Evidence, outcomes, and issues. *Journal of the American Academy of Child and Adolescent Psychiatry, 36,* 1349–1356.

Kazdin, A.E. (1998). *Research design in clinical psychology* (3rd ed.). Needham Heights, MA: Allyn & Bacon.

Kazdin, A.E. (1999). The meanings and measurement of clinical significance. *Journal of Consulting and Clinical Psychology, 67,* 332–339.

Kazdin, A.E. (2000). *Psychotherapy for children and adolescents: Directions for research and practice.* New York: Oxford University Press.

Kazdin, A.E., & Cole, P.M. (1981). Attitudes and labeling biases toward behavior modification: The effects of labels, content, and jargon. *Behavior Therapy, 12,* 56–68.

Kazdin, A.E., French, N.H., & Sherick, R.B. (1981). Acceptability of alternative treatments for children: Evaluations by inpatient children, parents, and staff. *Journal of Consulting and Clinical Psychology, 49,* 900–907.

Kazdin, A.E., French, N.H., Unis, A.S., Esveldt–Dawson, K., & Sherick, R.B. (1983). Hopelessness, depression, and suicidal intent among psychiatrically disturbed inpatient children. *Journal of Consulting and Clinical Psychology, 51,* 504–510.

Kazdin, A.E., & Geesey, S. (1977). Simultaneous-treatment design comparisons of the effects of earning reinforcers for one's peers versus for oneself. *Behavior Therapy, 8,* 682–693.

Kazdin, A.E., Holland, L., & Crowley, M. (1997). Family experience of barriers to treatment and premature termination from child therapy. *Journal of Consulting and Clinical Psychology, 65,* 453–463.

Kazdin, A.E., & Mascitelli, S. (1980). The opportunity to earn oneself off a token system as a reinforcer for attentive behavior. *Behavior Therapy, 11,* 68–78.

Kazdin, A.E., & Polster, R. (1973). Intermittent token reinforcement and response maintenance in extinction. *Behavior Therapy, 4,* 386–391.

Kazdin, A.E., Siegel, T., & Bass, D. (1992). Cognitive problem-solving skills training and parent management training in the treatment of antisocial behavior in children. *Journal of Consulting and Clinical Psychology, 60,* 733–747.

Kazdin, A.E., Silverman, N.A., & Sittler, J.L. (1975). The use of prompts to enhance vicarious effects of nonverbal approval. *Journal of Applied Behavior Analysis, 8,* 279–286.

Kazdin, A.E., & Weisz, J.R. (1998). Identifying and developing empirically supported child and adolescent treatments. *Journal of Consulting and Clinical Psychology, 66,* 19–36.

Kelley, M.L., & McCain, A.P. (1995). Promoting academic performance in inattentive children: The relative efficacy of school-home notes with and without response cost. *Behavior Modification, 19,* 357–375.

Kelly, J.A., & Drabman, R.S. (1977). Overcorrection: An effective procedure that failed. *Journal of Clinical Child Psychology, 6,* 38–40.

Kelly, J.A., & Murphy, D.A. (1992). Psychological interventions with AIDS and HIV: Prevention and treatment. *Journal of Consulting and Clinical Psychology, 60,* 576–585.

Kelly, J.A., St. Lawrence, J.S., Hood, H.V., & Brasfield, T.L. (1989). Behavioral intervention to reduce AIDS risk activities. *Journal of Consulting and Clinical Psychology, 57,* 60–67.

Kendall, P.C. (Ed.). (1991). *Child and adolescent therapy: Cognitive-behavioral procedures.* New York: Guilford.

Kendall, P.C. (Ed.) (1999). Special series: Clinical significance. *Journal of Consulting and Clinical Psychology, 67,* 283–339.

Kendall, P.C., & Braswell, L. (1993). *Cognitive behavioral therapy for impulsive children* (2nd ed.). New York: Guilford.

Kendall, P.C., & Chambless, D.L. (Eds.) (1998). Special section: Empirically supported psychological therapies. *Journal of Consulting and Clinical Psychology, 66,* 3–167.

Kendall, P.C., & Grove, W.M. (1988). Normative comparisons in therapy outcome. *Behavioral Assessment, 10,* 147–158.

Kendall, P.C., & Treadwell, K.R.H. (1996). Cognitive-behavioral group treatment for socially anxious youth. In E.D. Hibbs & P. Jensen (Eds.), *Psychosocial treatment research of child and adolescent disorders: Empirically based strategies for clinical practice* (pp. 23–41). Washington, DC: American Psychological Association.

Ketterlinus, R.D., & Lamb, M.E. (Eds.), (1994). *Adolescent problem behaviors: Issues and research.* Hillsdale, NJ: Erlbaum.

Kiecolt–Glaser, J.K., & Glaser, R. (1992). Psychoneuroimmunology: Can psychological interventions modulate immunity? *Journal of Consulting and Clinical Psychology, 60,* 569–575.

King, G.F., Armitage, S.G., & Tilton, J.R. (1960). A therapeutic approach to schizophrenics of extreme pathology: An operant-interpersonal method. *Journal of Abnormal and Social Psychology, 61,* 276–286.

Kinkade, K. (1973). *A Walden Two experiment: The first five years of Twin Oaks Community.* New York: Morrow.

Kirby, D., Brener, N.D., Brown, N.L., Peterfreund, N., Hillard, P., & Harrist, R. (1999). The impact of condom distribution in Seattle schools on sexual behavior and condom use. *American Journal of Public Health, 89,* 182–187.

Kirby, F.D., & Shields, F. (1972). Modification of arithmetic response rate and attending behavior in a seventh–grade student. *Journal of Applied Behavior Analysis, 5,* 79–84.

Kirigin, K.A., Braukmann, C.J., Atwater, J.D., & Wolf, M.M. (1982). An evaluation of teaching–family (Achievement Place) group homes for juvenile offenders. *Journal of Applied Behavior Analysis, 15,* 1–16.

Kirigin, K.A., Wolf, M.M., Braukmann, C.J., Fixsen, D.L., & Phillips, E.L. (1979). Achievement Place: A preliminary outcome evaluation. In J.S. Stumphauzer (Ed.), *Progress in behavior therapy with delinquents.* (pp. 118–145). Springfield, IL: Charles C. Thomas.

Kohler, F.W., & Greenwood, C.R. (1990). Effects of collateral peer supportive behaviors within the classwide peer tutoring program. *Journal of Applied Behavior Analysis, 23,* 307–322.

Kohler, F.W., & Strain, P.S. (1990). Peer–assisted interventions: Early promises, notable achievements, and future aspirations. *Clinical Psychology Review, 10,* 441–452.

Korotitsch, W.J., & Nelson–Gray, R.O. (1999). An overview of self-monitoring research in assessment and treatment. *Psychological Assessment, 11,* 415–425.

Kranhold, K. (1999, December 16). Drug makers prescribed direct-mail pitch. *Wall Street Journal,* Vol. CCXXXIV, No. 118, B16.

Kratochwill, T.R., & Levin, J.R. (Eds.) (1992). *Single-case research design and analysis: New directions for psychology and education.* Mahwah, NJ: Lawrence Erlbaum.

Ladouceur, R., Freeston, M.H., Gagnon, F., Thibodeau, N., & Dumont, J. (1993). Idiographic considerations in the behavioral treatment of obsessional thoughts. *Journal of Behavior Therapy and Experimental Psychiatry, 24,* 301–310.

Ladouceur, R., Sylvain, C., Letarte, H., Giroux, I., & Jacques, C. (1998). Cognitive treatment of pathological gamblers. *Behaviour Research and Therapy, 36,* 1111–1119.

Lambert, W., Salzer, M.S., & Bickman, L. (1998). Clinical outcome, consumer satisfaction, and ad hoc ratings of improvement in children's mental health. *Journal of Consulting and Clinical Psychology, 66,* 270–279.

Lancioni, G.E. (1982). Normal children as tutors to teach social responses to withdrawn mentally retarded schoolmates: Training, maintenance, and generalization. *Journal of Applied Behavior Analysis, 15,* 17–40.

Lattal, K.A. (1969). Contingency management of toothbrushing behavior in a summer camp for children. *Journal of Applied Behavior Analysis, 2,* 195–198.

Lattal, K.A. (Guest Ed.). (1992). Special issue: Reflections on B.F. Skinner and psychology. *American Psychologist, 47,* 1269–1533.

LaVigna, G.W., & Donnellan, A.M. (1986). *Alternatives to punishment: Solving behavior problems with non-aversive strategies.* New York: Irvington.

Lazarus, A.A., & Abramovitz, A. (1962). The use of "emotive imagery" in the treatment of children's phobias. *Journal of Mental Science, 108,* 191–195.

Lee, C.D., Blair, S.N., & Jackson, A.S. (1999) Cardiorespiratory fitness, body composition, and all-cause and cardiovascular disease mortality in men. *American Journal of Clinical Nutrition, 69,* 373–380.

Lee, T.M., Chen, E.Y.H., Chan, C.C.H., Paterson, J.G., Janzen, H.L., & Blashko, C.A. (1998). Seasonal affective disorder. *Clinical Psychology: Science and Practice, 5,* 275–290.

Lennox, D.B., Miltenberger, R.G., & Donnelly, D.R. (1987). Response interruption and DRL for the reduction of rapid eating. *Journal of Applied Behavior Analysis, 20,* 279–284.

Lennox, D.B., Miltenberger, R.G., Spengler, P., & Erfanian, N. (1988). Decelerative treatment practices with persons who have mental retardation: A review of five years of the literature. *American Journal on Mental Retardation, 92,* 492–501.

Lepper, M.R., Sethi, S., Dialdin, D., & Drake, M. (1997). Intrinsic and extrinsic motivation: A developmental perspective. In S.S. Luthar, J.A. Burack, D. Cicchetti, & J. Weisz (Eds.), *Developmental psychopathology: Perspectives on adjustment, risk and disorder* (pp. 23–50). New York: Cambridge University Press.

Lerman, D.C., & Iwata, B.A. (1996). Developing a technology for the use of operant extinction in clinical settings: An examination of basic and applied research. *Journal of Applied Behavior Analysis, 29,* 345–382.

Lerman, D.C., Iwata, B.A., Shore, B.A., & Kahng, S. (1996). Responding maintained by intermittent reinforcement: Implications for the use of extinction with problem behavior in clinical settings. *Journal of Applied Behavior Analysis, 29,* 153–171.

Lerman, D.C., Iwata, B.A., & Wallace, M.D. (1999). Side effects of extinction: Prevalence of bursting and aggression during the treatment of self-injurious behavior. *Journal of Applied Behavior Analysis, 32,* 1–8.

Lerman, D.C., Kelley, M.E., Van Camp, C.M., & Roane, H. (1999). Effects of reinforcement magnitude on spontaneous recovery. *Journal of Applied Behavior Analysis, 32,* 197–200.

Liberman, R.P., Teigen, J., Patterson, R., & Baker, V. (1973). Reducing delusional speech in chronic, paranoid schizophrenics. *Journal of Applied Behavior Analysis, 6,* 57–64.

Lindsley, O.R. (1956). Operant conditioning methods applied to research in chronic schizophrenia. *Psychiatric Research Reports, 24,* 289–291.

Lindsley, O.R. (1960). Characteristics of the behavior of chronic psychotics as revealed by free–operant conditioning methods. *Diseases of the Nervous System* (Monograph Supplement), *21,* 66–78.

Linscheid, T.R., & Cunningham, C.E. (1977). A controlled demonstration of the effectiveness of electric shock in the elimination of chronic infant rumination. *Journal of Applied Behavior Analysis, 10,* 500.

Linscheid, T.R., Iwata, B.A., Ricketts, R.W., Williams, D.E., & Griffin, J.C. (1990). Clinical evaluation of the self-injurious behavior inhibiting system (SIBIS). *Journal of Applied Behavior Analysis, 23,* 53–78.

Linscheid, T.R., & Meinhold, P. (1990). The controversy over aversives: Basic operant research and the side effects of punishment. In A.C. Repp & N.N. Singh (Eds.), *Perspectives on the use of nonaversive and aversive interventions for persons with developmental disabilities* (pp. 435–450). Sycamore, IL: Sycamore.

Lombard, D., Neubauer, T.E., Canfield, D., & Winett, R.A. (1991). Behavioral community intervention to reduce the risk of skin cancer. *Journal of Applied Behavior Analysis, 24,* 677–686.

Lonigan, C.J., & Elbert, J.C. (Eds.) (1998). Special issue on empirically supported psychosocial interventions for children. *Journal of Clinical Child Psychology, 27,* 138–226.

Lovaas, O.I. (1987). Behavioral treatment and normal educational/intellectual functioning in young autistic children. *Journal of Consulting and Clinical Psychology, 55,* 3–9.

Lovaas, O.I. (1993). The development of a treatment-research project for developmentally disabled and autistic children. *Journal of Applied Behavior Analysis, 26,* 617–630.

Lovaas, O.I., Koegel, R.L., Simmons, J.Q., & Long, J.S. (1973). Some generalization and follow-up measures on autistic children in behavior therapy. *Journal of Applied Behavior Analysis, 6,* 131–166.

Lovaas, O.I., & Simmons, J.Q. (1969). Manipulation of self-destruction in three retarded children. *Journal of Applied Behavior Analysis, 2,* 143–157.

Luce, S.C., Delquadri, J., & Hall, R.V. (1980). Contingent exercise: A mild but powerful procedure for suppressing inappropriate verbal and aggressive behavior. *Journal of Applied Behavior Analysis, 13,* 583–594.

Luce, S.C., & Hall, R.V. (1981). Contingent exercise: A procedure used with differential reinforcement to reduce bizarre verbal behavior. *Education and Treatment of Children, 4,* 309–327.

Lueck, S. (1999, December 14). Bringing back those books. *Wall Street Journal,* Vol. CCXXXIV, No. 116, B2, B4.

Luiselli, J.K. (1996). Functional assessment and treatment of aggressive and destructive behaviors in a child victim of physical abuse. *Journal of Behavior Therapy and Experimental Psychiatry, 27,* 41–49.

Lyons, L.C., & Woods, P.J. (1991). The efficacy of rational-emotive therapy: A quantitative review of the outcome research. *Clinical Psychology Review, 11,* 357–369.

Mace, F.C., & Belfiore, P. (1990). Behavioral momentum in the treatment of escape-motivated stereotype. *Journal of Applied Behavior Analysis, 23,* 507–514.

MacPherson, E.M., Candee, B.L., & Hohman, R.J. (1974). A comparison of three methods for eliminating disruptive lunchroom behavior. *Journal of Applied Behavior Analysis, 7,* 287–297.

Madsen, C.H., Becker, W.C., & Thomas, D.R. (1968). Rules, praise, and ignoring: Elements of elementary classroom control. *Journal of Applied Behavior Analysis, 1,* 139–150.

Madsen, C.H., Becker, W.C., Thomas, D.R., Koser, L., & Plager, E. (1970). An analysis of the reinforcing function of "sit down" commands. In R.K. Parker (Ed.), *Readings in educational psychology* (pp. 265–278). Boston: Allyn & Bacon.

Mahoney, K., VanWagenen, R.K., & Meyerson, L. (1971). Toilet training of normal and retarded children. *Journal of Applied Behavior Analysis, 4,* 173–181.

Maloney, K.B., & Hopkins, B.L. (1973). The modification of sentence structure and its relationship to subjective judgments of creativity in writing. *Journal of Applied Behavior Analysis, 6,* 425–433.

Mansdorf, I.J. (1977). Reinforcer isolation: An alternative to subject isolation in time out from positive reinforcement. *Journal of Behavior Therapy and Experimental Psychiatry, 8,* 391–393.

Marchand-Martella, N.E., Martella, R.C., Agran, M., Salzberg, C.L., Young, K.R., & Morgan, D. (1992). Generalized effects of a peer-delivered first aid program for students with moderate intellectual disabilities. *Journal of Applied Behavior Analysis, 25,* 841–851.

Marholin, D., II, & Gray, D. (1976). Effects of group response cost procedures on cash shortages in a small business. *Journal of Applied Behavior Analysis, 9,* 25–30.

Marholin, D., II, & Townsend, N.M. (1978). An experimental analysis of side effects and response maintenance of a modified overcorrection procedure: The case of a persistent twiddler. *Behavior Therapy, 9,* 383–390.

Marlow, A.G., Tingstrom, D.H., Olmi, D.J., & Edwards, R.P. (1997). The effects of classroom–based time in/time–out on compliance rates in children with speech and language disabilities. *Child and Family Behavior Therapy, 19* (2), 1–15.

Marshall, W.L., Presse, L., & Andrews, W.R. (1976). A self-administered program for public speaking anxiety. *Behaviour Research and Therapy, 14,* 33–40.

Mash, E.J., & Terdal, L.G. (Eds.) (1997). *Assessment of childhood disorders* (3rd ed.). New York: Guilford

Masia, C.L., & Chase, P.N. (1997). Vicarious learning revisited: A contemporary behavior analytic interpretation. *Journal of Behavior Therapy and Experimental Psychiatry, 28,* 41–51.

Mathews, R.M., & Dix, M. (1992). Behavior change in the funny papers: Feedback to cartoonists on safety belt use. *Journal of Applied Behavior Analysis, 25,* 769–775.

Matson, J.L. (1983). Exploration of phobic behavior in a small child. *Journal of Behavior Therapy and Experimental Psychiatry, 14,* 257–259.

Matson, J.L., Manikam, R., & Ladatto, J. (1992). A long-term follow-up of a recreate the scene, DRO, overcorrection, and lemon juice therapy program for severe aggressive biting. *Scandinavian Journal of Behaviour Therapy, 19,* 33–38.

Matson, J.L., & Ollendick, T.H. (1977). Issues in toilet training normal children. *Behavior Therapy, 8,* 549–553.

Matson, J.L., & Taras, M.E. (1989). A 20-year review of punishment and alternative methods to treat problem behaviors in developmentally disabled persons. *Research in Developmental Disabilities, 10,* 85–104.

Mayhew, G.L., & Harris, F.C. (1978). Some negative side effects of a punishment procedure for stereotyped behavior. *Journal of Behavior Therapy and Experimental Psychiatry, 9,* 245–251.

McClannahan, L.E., McGee, G.G., MacDuff, G.S., & Krantz, P.J. (1990). Assessing and improving child care: A personal appearance index for children with autism. *Journal of Applied Behavior Analysis, 23,* 469–482.

McClannahan, L.E., & Risley, T.R. (1975). Design of living environments for nursing-home residents: Increasing participation in recreation activities. *Journal of Applied Behavior Analysis, 8,* 261–268.

McComas, J.J., Wacker, D.P., & Cooper, L.J. (1998). Increasing compliance with medical procedures: Application of the high-probability behavior request procedure to a toddler. *Journal of Applied Behavior Analysis, 31,* 287–290.

McConaghy, N. (1990). Sexual deviation. In A.S. Bellack, M. Hersen, & A.E. Kazdin (Eds.), *International handbook of behavior modification and therapy* (2nd ed., pp. 565–580). New York: Plenum.

McCord, J. (Ed.). (1998). *Coercion and punishment in long-term perspectives.* Cambridge: Cambridge University Press.

McEachin, J.J., Smith, T., & Lovaas, O.I. (1993). Outcome in adolescence of autistic children receiving early intensive behavior treatment. *American Journal of Mental Retardation, 97,* 359–372.

McGee, G.G., Almeida, M.C., Sulzer-Azaroff, B., & Feldman, R.S. (1992). Prompting reciprocal interactions via peer incidental teaching. *Journal of Applied Behavior Analysis, 25,* 117–126.

McGill, P. (1999). Establishing operations: Implications for the assessment, treatment, and prevention of problem behavior. *Journal of Applied Behavior Analysis, 32,* 393–418.

McGrady, A., & Gerstenmaier, L. (1990). Effect of biofeedback assisted relaxation training on blood glucose levels in a Type I insulin dependent diabetic: A case report. *Journal of Behavior Therapy and Experimental Psychiatry, 21,* 69–75.

McMahon, R.J., & Forehand, R. (1978). Nonprescription behavior therapy: Effectiveness of a brochure in teaching mothers to correct their children's inappropriate mealtime behaviors. *Behavior Therapy, 9,* 814–820.

McNeil, C.B., Eyberg, S., Eisenstadt, T.H., Newcomb, K., & Funderburk, B. (1991). Parent–child interaction therapy with behavior problem children: Generalization of treatment effects to the school setting. *Journal of Clinical Child Psychology, 20,* 140–151.

McReynolds, W.T., & Church, A. (1973). Self-control study skills development and counseling approaches to the improvement of study behavior. *Behaviour Research and Therapy, 11,* 233–235.

Meichenbaum, D.H. (1985). *Stress inoculation training.* Elmsford, NY: Pergamon Press.

Michael, J. (1993). Establishing operations. *The Behavior Analyst, 16,* 191–206.

Miller, D.L., & Kelley, M.L. (1994). The use of goal-setting and contingency contracting for improving children's homework performance. *Journal of Applied Behavior Analysis, 27,* 73–84.

Miller, W.R. (1977). Behavioral self-control training in the treatment of problem drinkers. In R.B. Stuart (Ed.), *Behavioral self-management: Strategies, techniques, and outcomes* (pp. 154–175). New York: Brunner Mazel.

Miltenberger, R.G., Roberts, J.A., Ellingson, S., & Galensky, T. (1999). Training and generalization of sexual abuse prevention skills for women with mental retardation. *Journal of Applied Behavior Analysis, 32,* 385–388.

Morin, C., Ladouceur, R., & Cloutier, R. (1982). Reinforcement procedure in the treatment of reluctant speech. *Journal of Behavior Therapy and Experimental Psychiatry, 13,* 145–147.

Morris, E.K., & Redd, W.H. (1975). Children's performance and social preference for positive, negative, and mixed adult-child interactions. *Child Development, 46,* 525–531.

Moss, M. (1996, September 18). Does annual survey of U.S. drug use give straight dope? *Wall Street Journal,* Vol. CCXXVIII, No. 56, A1, A10.

Mudde, A.N., de Vries, H., & Strecher, V.J. (1997). Cost-effectiveness of smoking cessation modalities: Comparing apples with oranges? *Preventive Medicine, 25,* 708–716,

Mundell, E.J. (1999, June 16). Failure to follow medical advice an "enormous problem," Reuters Health Information.

Murphy, H.A., Hutchison, J.M., & Bailey, J.S. (1983). Behavioral school psychology goes outdoors: The effect of organized games on playground aggression. *Journal of Applied Behavior Analysis, 16,* 29–36.

Nakano, K. (1990). Operant self-control procedure in modifying Type A behavior. *Journal of Behavior Therapy and Experimental Psychiatry, 21,* 249–255.

Nathan, P.E., &. Gorman, J.M. (Eds.) (1998). *Treatments that work.* New York: Oxford University Press.

Neef, N.A., Lensbower, J., Hockersmith, I., DePalma, V., & Gray, K. (1990). In vivo versus simulation training: An interactional analysis of range and type of training exemplars. *Journal of Applied Behavior Analysis, 23,* 447–458.

Neef, N.A., Mace, F.C., Shea, M.C., & Shade, D. (1992). Effects of reinforcer rate and reinforcer quality on time allocation: Extensions of matching theory to educational settings. *Journal of Applied Behavior Analysis, 25,* 691–699.

Neisworth, J.T., & Moore, F. (1972). Operant treatment of asthmatic responding with the parent as therapist. *Behavior Therapy, 3,* 95–99.

Nelson, R.O., & Hayes, S.C. (Eds.). (1986). *Conceptual foundations of behavioral assessment.* New York: Guilford.

Nevin, J.A. (1996). The momentum of compliance. *Journal of Applied Behavior Analysis, 29,* 535–547.

Nezu, A.M., & Nezu, C.M. (Eds.). (1989). *Clinical decision making in behavior therapy: A problem–solving perspective.* Champaign, IL: Research Press.

Nezu, A.M., & Perri, M.G. (1989). Social problem-solving therapy for unipolar depression: An initial dismantling investigation. *Journal of Consulting and Clinical Psychology, 57,* 408–413.

Ninness, H.A.C., Fuerst, J., Rutherford, R.D., & Glenn, S.S. (1991). Effects of self-management training and reinforcement on the transfer of improved conduct in the absence of supervision. *Journal of Applied Behavior Analysis, 24,* 499–508.

Nordyke, N.S., Baer, D.M., Etzel, B.C., & LeBlanc, J.M. (1977). Implications of the stereotyping and modification of sex role. *Journal of Applied Behavior Analysis, 10,* 553–557.

Novaco, R.W. (1979). The cognitive regulation of anger and stress. In P.C. Kendall & S.D. Hollon (Eds.), *Cognitive–behavioral interventions: Theory, research, and procedures* (pp. 241–285). New York: Academic Press.

O'Brien, S., & Karsh, K.G. (1990). Treatment acceptability: Consumer, therapist, and society. In A.C. Repp & N.N. Singh (Eds.), *Perspectives on the use of nonaversive and aversive interventions for persons with developmental disabilities* (pp. 503–516). Sycamore, IL: Sycamore.

O'Brien, S., & Repp, A.C. (1990). Reinforcement–based reductive procedures: A review of 20 years of their use with persons with severe or profound retardation. *Journal of the Association for Persons with Severe Handicaps, 15,* 148–159.

Odom, S.L., McConnell, S.R., & McEvoy, M.A. (1992). *Social competence of young children with disabilities: Issues and strategies for intervention.* Baltimore: Paul H. Brookes.

Ollendick, T.H., Hagopian, L.P., & Huntzinger, R.M. (1991). Cognitive–behavior therapy with nighttime fearful children. *Journal of Behavior Therapy and Experimental Psychiatry, 22,* 113–121.

O'Neill, R.E., Horner, R.H., Albin, R.W., Storey, K., & Sprague, J.R. (1990). *Functional analysis of problem behavior: A practical assessment guide.* Sycamore, IL: Sycamore.

O'Reilly, M.F., Green, G., & Braunling-McMorrow, D. (1990). Self-administered written prompts to teach home accident prevention skills to adults with brain injuries. *Journal of Applied Behavior Analysis, 23,* 431–446.

Pace, G.M., Iwata, B.A., Edwards, G.L., & McCosh, K.C. (1986). Stimulus fading and transfer in the treatment of self-restraint and self-injurious behavior. *Journal of Applied Behavior Analysis, 19,* 381–389.

Paine, S.C., Hops, H., Walker, H.M., Greenwood, C.R., Fleischman, D.H., & Guild, J.J. (1982). Repeated treatment effects: A study of maintaining behavior change in socially withdrawn children. *Behavior Modification, 6,* 171–199.

Pardeck, J.T. (1993). *Using bibliotherapy in clinical practice.* Westport, CT: Greenwood.

Parrish, J.M., Cataldo, M.F., Kolko, D.J., Neef, N.A., & Egel, A.L. (1986). Experimental analysis of response covariation among compliant and inappropriate behaviors. *Journal of Applied Behavior Analysis, 19,* 241–254.

Patterson, G.R. (1982). *Coercive family process.* Eugene, OR: Castalia.

Patterson, G.R., Reid, J.B., & Dishion, T.J. (1992). *Antisocial boys.* Eugene, OR: Castalia.

Paul, G.L., & Lentz, R.J. (1977). *Psychosocial treatment of chronic mental patients: Milieu versus social learning program.* Cambridge: Harvard University Press.

Pavlov, I.P. (1903, April). Experimental psychology and psychopathology in animals. Speech presented to the International Medical Congress, Madrid. (Also, reprinted in I.P. Pavlov [1955], *Selected works.* Moscow: Foreign Languages Publishing House.)

Peacock, R., Lyman, R.D., & Rickard, H.C. (1978). Correspondence between self-report and observer–report as a function of task difficulty. *Behavior Therapy, 9,* 578–583.

Peck, C.A., Cooke, T.P., & Apolloni, T. (1981). Utilization of peer imitation in therapeutic and instructional contexts. In P.S. Strain (Ed.), *The utilization of classroom peers as behavior change agents* (pp. 69–99). New York: Plenum.

Pedalino, E., & Gamboa, V.U. (1974). Behavior modification and absenteeism: Intervention in one industrial setting. *Journal of Applied Psychology, 59,* 694–698.

Pekarik, G., & Guidry, L.L. (1999). Relationship of satisfaction to symptom change, follow–up assessment, and clinical significance in private practice. *Professional Psychology: Research and Practice, 30,* 474–478.

Pelios, L., Morren, J., Tesch, D., & Axelrod, S. (1999). The impact of functional analysis methodology on treatment choice for self-injurious and aggressive behavior. *Journal of Applied Behavior Analysis, 32,* 185–195.

Peniston, E.G., (1988). Evaluation of long-term therapeutic efficacy of behavior modification program with chronic male psychiatric patients. *Journal of Behavior Therapy and Experimental Psychiatry, 19,* 95–101.

Pfiffner, L.J., & O'Leary, S.G. (1987). The efficacy of all-positive management as a function of the prior use of negative consequences. *Journal of Applied Behavior Analysis, 20,* 265–271.

Phillips, E.L., Phillips, E.A., Fixsen, D.L., & Wolf, M.M. (1971). Achievement Place: Modification of the behaviors of pre-delinquent boys within a token economy. *Journal of Applied Behavior Analysis, 4,* 45–59.

Phillips, E.L., Phillips, E.A., Wolf, M.M., & Fixsen, D.L. (1973). Achievement Place: Development of the elected-manager system. *Journal of Applied Behavior Analysis, 6,* 541–561.

Pinkston, E.M., Reese, N.M., LeBlanc, J.M., & Baer, D.M. (1973). Independent control of a preschool child's aggression and peer interaction by contingent teacher attention. *Journal of Applied Behavior Analysis, 6,* 115–124.

Pizacani, B., Mosbaek, C., Hedberg, K., Bley, L., Stark, M., Moore, J., & Fleming, D. (1999). Decline in cigarette consumption following implementation of a comprehensive tobacco prevention and education program—Oregon, 1996–1998. *Morbidity and Mortality Weekly, 48,* 140–143.

Plummer, S., Baer, D.M., & LeBlanc, J.M. (1977). Functional considerations in the use of procedural time out and an effective alternative. *Journal of Applied Behavior Analysis, 10,* 689–705.

Porterfield, J.K., Herbert–Jackson, E., & Risley, T.R. (1976). Contingent observation: An effective and acceptable procedure for reducing disruptive behavior of young children in a group setting. *Journal of Applied Behavior Analysis, 9,* 55–64.

Premack, D. (1965). Reinforcement theory. In D. Levine (Ed.), *Nebraska symposium on motivation* (pp. 123–180). Lincoln: University of Nebraska Press.

Puder, R., Lacks, P., Bertelson, A.D., & Storandt, M. (1983). Short-term stimulus control treatment of insomnia in older adults. *Behavior Therapy, 14,* 424–429.

Pyles, D.A.M., & Bailey, J.S. (1990). Diagnosing severe behavior problems. In A.C. Repp & N.N. Singh (Eds.), *Perspectives on the use of nonaversive interventions for persons with developmental disabilities* (pp. 381–401). Sycamore, IL: Sycamore.

Ragnarsson, R.S., & Bjorgvinsson, T. (1991). Effects of public posting on driving speed in Icelandic traffic. *Journal of Applied Behavior Analysis, 24,* 53–58.

Rasing, E.J., & Duker, P.C. (1992). Effects of a multifaceted training procedure on acquisition and generalization of social behaviors in language-disabled deaf children. *Journal of Applied Behavior Analysis, 25,* 723–734.

Redd, W.H., & Birnbrauer, J.S. (1969). Adults as discriminative stimuli for different reinforcement contingencies with retarded children. *Journal of Experimental Child Psychology, 7,* 440–447.

Redd, W.H., Morris, E.K., & Martin, J.A. (1975). Effects of positive and negative adult-child interactions on children's social preference. *Journal of Experimental Child Psychology, 19,* 153–164.

Regier, D.A., Myers, J.K., Kramer, M., Robins, L.N., Blazer, D.G., Hough, R.L., Eaton, W.W., & Locke, B.Z. (1984). The NIMH Epidemiologic Catchment Area program: Historical context, major objectives, and study population characteristics. *Archives of General Psychiatry, 41,* 934–941.

Reimers, T.M. (1996). A biobehavioral approach toward managing encopresis. *Behavior Modification, 20,* 469–479.

Reimers, T.M., Wacker, D.P., Cooper, L.J., & DeRaad, A.O. (1992). Clinical evaluation of the variables associated with treatment acceptability and their relation to compliance. *Behavioral Disorders, 18,* 67–76.

Reiss, S. (Ed.). (1991). Special issue: Applied learning theory: Research issues for the 1990s. *Clinical Psychology Review, 11,* 123–203.

Rekers, G.A. (1977). Atypical gender development and psychosocial adjustment. *Journal of Applied Behavior Analysis, 10,* 559–571.

Rekers, G.A., & Lovaas, O.I. (1974). Behavioral treatment of deviant sex role behaviors in a male child. *Journal of Applied Behavior Analysis, 7,* 173–190.

Repp, A.C., Felce, D., & Barton, L.E. (1988). Basing the treatment of stereotypic and self-injurious behaviors on hypotheses of their causes. *Journal of Applied Behavior Analysis, 21,* 281–289.

Repp, A.C., & Singh, N.N. (Eds.). (1990). *Perspectives on the use of nonaversive and aversive interventions for persons with developmental disabilities.* Sycamore, IL: Sycamore.

Rescorla, R.A. (1988). Pavlovian conditioning: It's not what you think it is. *American Psychologist, 43,* 151–160.

Resick, P.A., Forehand, R., & McWhorter, A.Q. (1976). The effect of parental treatment with one child on an untreated sibling. *Behavior Therapy, 7,* 544–548.

Reynolds, L.K., & Kelley, M.L. (1997). The efficacy of a response cost treatment package for managing aggressive behavior in preschoolers. *Behavior Modification, 21,* 216–230.

Richman, D.M., Wacker, D.P., Asmus, J.M., & Casey, S.D. (1998). Functional analysis and extinction of different behavior problems exhibited by the same individual. *Journal of Applied Behavior Analysis, 31,* 475–478.

Riordan, M.M., Iwata, B.A., Finney, J.W., Wohl, M.K., & Stanley, A.E. (1984). Behavioral assessment and treatment of chronic food refusal in handicapped children. *Journal of Applied Behavior Analysis, 17,* 327–342.

Robins, L.N., & Regier, D.A. (1991). *Psychiatric disorders in America: The Epidemiologic Catchment Area Study.* New York: Free Press.

Rolider, A., Cummings, A., & Van Houten, R. (1991). Side effects of therapeutic punishment on academic performance and eye contact. *Journal of Applied Behavior Analysis, 24,* 763–773.

Rollings, J.P., Baumeister, A.A., & Baumeister, A.A. (1977). The use of overcorrection procedures to eliminate the stereotyped behaviors of retarded individuals: An analysis of collateral behaviors and generalization of suppressive effects. *Behavior Modification, 1,* 29–46.

Ronen, T. (1991). Intervention package for treating sleep disorders in a four-year-old girl. *Journal of Behavior Therapy and Experimental Psychiatry, 22,* 141–148.

Rortvedt, A.K., & Miltenberger, R.G. (1994). Analysis of a high-probability instructional sequence and time-out in the treatment of child noncompliance. *Journal of Applied Behavior Analysis, 27,* 327–330.

Rosen, G.M. (1987). Self-help treatment books and the commercialization of psychotherapy. *American Psychologist, 42,* 46–51.

Rosen, G.M., Glasgow, R.E., & Barrera, M., Jr. (1976). A controlled study to assess the clinical efficacy of totally self-administered systematic desensitization. *Journal of Consulting and Clinical Psychology, 44,* 208–217.

Rosen, H.S., & Rosen, L.A. (1983). Eliminating stealing: Use of stimulus control with an elementary student. *Behavior Modification, 7,* 56–63.

Roth, A., & Fonagy, P. (1996*). What works for whom: A critical review of psychotherapy research.* New York: Guilford.

Saigh, P.A. (1986). In vitro flooding in the treatment of a 6-year-old boy's post-traumatic stress disorder. *Behaviour Research and Therapy, 24,* 685–688.

Salter, A. (1949). *Conditioned reflex therapy: The direct approach to the reconstruction of personality.* New York: Creative Age Press.

Sanders, M.R., & Glynn, T.L. (1981). Training parents in behavioral self-management: An analysis of generalization and maintenance. *Journal of Applied Behavior Analysis, 14,* 223–237.

Sasso, G.M., Reimers, T.M., Cooper, L.J., Wacker, D.P., Berg, W.K., Steege, M., Kelly, L., & Allaire, A. (1992). Use of descriptive and experimental analyses to identify the functional properties of aberrant behavior in school settings. *Journal of Applied Behavior Analysis, 25,* 809–821.

Schepis, M.M., Reid, D.H., & Fitzgerald, J.R. (1987). Group instruction with profoundly retarded persons: Acquisition, generalization, and maintenance of a remunerative work skill. *Journal of Applied Behavior Analysis, 20,* 97–108.

Schering–Plough, Inc. (1996, copyright). Coppertone™ Gold (SPF 4)—Dark tanning oil. Product description from the back of the 8-oz. bottle.

Schnelle, J.F. (1974). A brief report on invalidity of parent evaluations of behavior change. *Journal of Applied Behavior Analysis, 7,* 341–343.

Schreibman, L. (1988). *Autism.* Newbury Park, CA: Sage.

Schwartz, L.S., & Baer, D.M. (1991). Social validity assessments: Is current practice state of the art? *Journal of Applied Behavior Analysis, 24,* 189–204.

Schwartz, M.S., & Andrasik, F. (1998). *Biofeedback: A practitioner's guide.* New York: Guilford.

Seaman, J.E., Greene, B.F., & Watson-Pertzel, M. (1986). A behavioral system for assessing and training cardiopulmonary resuscitation skills among emergency medical technicians. *Journal of Applied Behavior Analysis, 19,* 125–136.

Selinske, J.E., Greer, R.D., & Lodhi, S. (1991). A functional analysis of the comprehensive application of behavior analysis to schooling. *Journal of Applied Behavior Analysis, 24,* 107–117.

Shriver, M.D., & Allen, K.D. (1996). The time-out grid: A guide to effective discipline. *School Psychology Quarterly, 11,* 67–75.

Shure, M.B. (1996). *Raising a thinking child: Help your young child to resolve everyday conflicts and get along with others.* New York: Pocket Books.

Shure, M.B. (1997). Interpersonal cognitive problem solving: Primary prevention of early high-risk behaviors in the preschool and primary years. In G.W. Albee & T.P. Gulotta (Eds.), *Primary prevention works* (pp. 167–188). Thousand Oaks, CA: Sage.

Shure, M.B. (1999). Preventing violence the problem-solving way. *Juvenile Justice Bulletin,* April, 1–11. Publication of the US Department of Justice, Office of Juvenile Justice and Delinquency Prevention, Washington, DC.

Singh, N.N., Dawson, M.J., & Manning, P. (1981). Effects of spaced responding DRL on the stereotyped behavior of profoundly retarded persons. *Journal of Applied Behavior Analysis, 14,* 521–526.

Singh, N.N., Lloyd, J.W., & Kendall, K.A. (1990). Nonaversive and aversive interventions: Issues. In A.C. Repp & N.N. Singh (Eds.), *Perspectives on the use of nonaversive and aversive interventions for persons with developmental disabilities* (pp. 3–16). Sycamore, IL: Sycamore.

Singh, N.N., Watson, J.E., & Winton, A.S.W. (1986). Treating self-injury: Water mist spray versus facial screening or forced arm exercise. *Journal of Applied Behavior Analysis, 19,* 403–410.

Skinner, B.F. (1938). *The behavior of organisms: An experimental analysis.* New York: Appleton–Century.

Skinner, B.F. (1948). *Walden Two.* New York: Macmillan.

Skinner, B.F. (1953). *Science and human behavior.* New York: Free Press.

Smith, B.M., Schumaker, J.B., Schaeffer, J., & Sherman, J.A. (1982). Increasing participation and improving the quality of discussions in seventh-grade social studies classes. *Journal of Applied Behavior Analysis, 15,* 97–110.

Smith, D., & Dumont, F. (1997). Eliminating overconfidence in psychodiagnosis: Strategies for training and practice. *Clinical Psychology: Science and Practice, 4,* 335–345.

Smith, L.K.C., & Fowler, S.A. (1984). Positive peer pressure: The effects of peer monitoring on children's disruptive behavior. *Journal of Applied Behavior Analysis, 17,* 213–227.

Smith, R.G., & Iwata, B. (1997). Antecedent influences on behavior disorders. *Journal of Applied Behavior Analysis, 30,* 343–375.

Solomon, R.L., Kamin, L.J., & Wynne, L.C. (1953). Traumatic avoidance learning: The outcomes of several extinction procedures with dogs. *Journal of Abnormal and Social Psychology, 48,* 291–302.

Soroka, G.E. (1996). *Biofeedback without machines: A strategy for living.* Demarest, NJ: Ariel Starr Productions.

Sowers–Hoag, K.M., Thyer, B.A., & Bailey, J.S. (1987). Promoting automobile safety belt use by young children. *Journal of Applied Behavioral Analysis, 20,* 133–138.

Spivack, G., Platt, J.J., & Shure, M.B. (1976). *The problem–solving approach to adjustment.* San Francisco: Jossey-Bass.

Spivack, G., & Shure, M.B. (1982). The cognition of social adjustment: Interpersonal cognitive problem–solving thinking. In B.B. Lahey & A.E. Kazdin (Eds.), *Advances in clinical child psychology* (Vol. 5, pp. 323–372). New York: Plenum.

Sprague, R.L., & Newell, K.M. (Eds.) (1996). *Stereotyped movements: Brain and behavior relationships.* Washington, DC: American Psychological Association

Steege, M.W., Wacker, D.P., Cigrand, K.C., Berg, W.K., Novak, C.G., Reimers, T.M., Sasso, G.M., & DeRaad, A. (1990). Use of negative reinforcement in the treatment of self-injurious behavior. *Journal of Applied Behavior Analysis, 23,* 459–467.

Stein, D.J., & Young, J.E. (Eds.). (1992). *Cognitive science and clinical disorders.* San Diego: Academic Press.

Stoff, D.M., Breiling, J., & Maser, J.D. (Eds.) (1997). *Handbook of antisocial behavior.* New York: John Wiley & Sons.

Stokes, T.F., & Baer, D.M. (1977). An implicit technology of generalization. *Journal of Applied Behavior Analysis, 10,* 349–367.

Stokes, T.F., & Osnes, P.G. (1989). An operant pursuit of generalization. *Behavior Therapy, 20,* 337–355.

Strain, P.S., Shores, R.E., & Kerr, M.M. (1976). An experimental analysis of "spillover" effects on the social interaction of behaviorally handicapped preschool children. *Journal of Applied Behavior Analysis, 9,* 31–40.

Striefel, S. (1998). *How to teach through modeling and imitation* (2nd ed.). Austin, TX: Pro–Ed.

Sturmey, P. (1994). Assessing the functions of self-injurious behavior: A case of assessment failure. *Journal of Behavior Therapy and Experimental Psychiatry, 25,* 331–336.

Sturmey, P. (1996). *Functional analysis in clinical psychology.* Chichester, England: John Wiley & Sons.

Sullivan, M.A., & O'Leary, S.G. (1990). Maintenance following reward and cost token programs. *Behavior Therapy, 21,* 139–149.

Sulzer–Azaroff, B., Drabman, R.M., Greer, R.D., Hall, R.V., Iwata, B.A., & O'Leary, S.G. (1988). *Behavior analysis in education 1968–1987.* Lawrence, KS: Society for the Experimental Analysis of Behavior.

Sulzer–Azaroff, B., & Mayer, G.R. (1991). *Behavior analysis for lasting change* (2nd ed.). Fort Worth: Holt, Rinehart & Winston.

Swain, J.J., Allard, G.B., & Holborn, S.W. (1982). The good toothbrushing game: A school-based dental hygiene program for increasing the toothbrushing effectiveness of children. *Journal of Applied Behavior Analysis, 15,* 171–176.

Switzer, E.B., Deal, T.E., & Bailey, J.S. (1977). The reduction of stealing in second graders using a group contingency. *Journal of Applied Behavior Analysis, 10,* 267–272.

Sylvain, C., Ladouceur, R., & Boisvert, J.M. (1997). Cognitive and behavioral treatment of pathological gambling. *Journal of Consulting and Clinical Psychology, 65,* 727–732.

Task Force on Promotion and Dissemination of Psychological Procedures (1995). Training in and dissemination of empirically validated psychological treatments: Report and recommendations. *The Clinical Psychologist, 48 (1),* 3–23.

Tharp, R.G. (1991). Cultural diversity and treatment of children. *Journal of Consulting and Clinical Psychology, 59,* 799–812.

Thibadeau, S.F. (1998). *How to use response cost.* Austin, TX: Pro-Ed.

Thomas, J.D., Presland, I.E., Grant, M.D., & Glynn, T.L. (1978). Natural rates of teacher approval and disapproval in grade-seven classrooms. *Journal of Applied Behavior Analysis, 11,* 91–94.

Timberlake, E.M. (1981). Child abuse and externalized aggression: Preventing a delinquent lifestyle. In R.J. Hunner & Y.E. Walker (Eds.), *Exploring the relationship between child abuse and delinquency.* (pp. 43–51). Montclair, NJ: Allanheld, Osmun.

Tkachuk, G.A., & Martin, G.L. (1999) Exercise therapy for patients with psychiatric disorders: Research and clinical implications. *Professional Psychology: Research and Practice, 30,* 275–282.

Tolman, E.C. (1948). Cognitive maps in rats and men. *Psychological Review, 55,* 189–208.

United States Congress, Office of Technology Assessment. (1991). *Adolescent health.* (OTA-H-468). Washington, DC: US Government Printing Office.

Upper, D. (1973). A "ticket" system for reducing ward rule violations on a token economy program. *Journal of Behavior Therapy and Experimental Psychiatry, 4,* 137–140.

Van Houten, R. (1998). *How to motivate others through feedback* (2nd ed.). Austin, TX: Pro-Ed.

Van Houten, R. (1998). *How to use prompts to initiate behavior.* Austin, TX: Pro-Ed.

Van Houten, R., Malenfant, L., & Rolider, A. (1985). Increasing driver yielding and pedestrian signaling with prompting, feedback, and enforcement. *Journal of Applied Behavior Analysis, 18,* 103–110.

Van Houten, R., Nau, P.A., MacKenzie-Keating, S.E., Sameoto, D., & Colavecchia, B. (1982). An analysis of some variables influencing the effectiveness of reprimands. *Journal of Applied Behavior Analysis, 15,* 65–83.

Van Houten, R., Nau, P.A., & Marini, Z. (1980). An analysis of public posting in reducing speeding behavior on an urban highway. *Journal of Applied Behavior Analysis, 13,* 383–395.

Van Houten, R., & Rolider, A. (1989, May). *The side effects of punishment: Does it matter how well punishment is applied? You bet it does!* Paper presented at the 15th annual convention of the Association for Behavior Analysis, Milwaukee.

Van Houten, R., Rolider, A., Nau, P.A., Friedman, R., Becker, M., Chalodovsky, l., & Scherer, M. (1985). Large-scale reductions in speeding and accidents in Canada and Israel: A behavioral ecological perspective. *Journal of Applied Behavior Analysis, 18,* 87–93.

Varni, J.W. (1981). Self-regulation techniques in the management of chronic arthritic pain in hemophilia. *Behavior Therapy, 12,* 185–194.

Vollmer, T.R., & Iwata, B.A. (1991). Establishing operations and reinforcement. *Journal of Applied Behavior Analysis, 24,* 279–291.

Vollmer, T.R., Marcus, B.A., & LeBlanc, L. (1994). Treatment of self-injury and hand mouthing following inconclusive functional analysis. *Journal of Applied Behavior Analysis, 27,* 331–344.

Wacker, D.P., McMahon, C., Steege, M., Berg, W.K., Sasso, G., & Melloy, K. (1990). Applications of a sequential alternating treatments design. *Journal of Applied Behavior Analysis, 23,* 333–339.

Wacker, D.P., Steege, M., Northup, J., Reimers, T., Berg, W. K., & Sasso, G. (1990). Use of functional analysis and acceptability measures to assess and treat severe behavior problems: An outpatient clinic model. In A.C. Repp & N.N. Singh (Eds.), *Perspectives on the use of nonaversive and aversive interventions for persons with developmental disabilities* (pp. 349–359). Sycamore, IL: Sycamore Publishing Company.

Wahler, R.G. (1975). Some structural aspects of deviant child behavior. *Journal of Applied Behavior Analysis, 8,* 27–42.

Wahler, R.G. (1980). The insular mother: Her problems in a parent-child treatment. *Journal of Applied Behavior Analysis, 13,* 207–219.

Wahler, R.G., & Fox, J.J. (1980). Solitary toy play and time out: A family treatment package for children with aggressive and oppositional behavior. *Journal of Applied Behavior Analysis, 13,* 23–29.

Wahler, R.G., & Fox, J.J. (1981). Setting events in applied behavior analysis: Toward a conceptual and methodological expansion. *Journal of Applied Behavior Analysis, 14,* 327–338.

Walker, H.M., Hops, H., & Greenwood, C.R. (1981). RECESS: Research and development of a behavior management package for remediating social aggression in the school setting. In P.S. Strain (Ed.), *The utilization of classroom peers as behavior change agents* (pp. 261–303). New York: Plenum.

Walker, H.M., Hops, H., & Johnson, S.M. (1975). Generalization and maintenance of classroom treatment effects. *Behavior Therapy, 6,* 188–200.

Wann, T.W. (Ed.). (1964). *Behaviorism and phenomenology: Contrasting bases for modern psychology.* Chicago: University of Chicago Press.

Watson, D.L., & Tharp, R.G. (1992). *Self-directed behavior: Self-modification for personal adjustment* (6th ed.). Pacific Grove, CA: Brooks/Cole.

Watson, J.B. (1919). *Psychology, from the standpoint of a behaviorist.* Philadelphia: Lippincott.

Watson, J.B. (1924). *Behaviorism.* Chicago: The People's Institute.

Watson, J.B., & Rayner, R. (1920). Conditioned emotional reactions. *Journal of Experimental Psychology, 3,* 1–14.

Watson, T.S. (1993). Effectiveness of arousal and arousal plus overcorrection to reduce nocturnal bruxism. *Journal of Behavior Therapy and Experimental Psychiatry, 24,* 181–185.

Watson, T.S., & Sterling, H.E. (1998). Brief functional analysis and treatment of a vocal tic. *Journal of Applied Behavior Analysis, 31,* 471–474.

Webster-Stratton, C. (1996). Early intervention with videotape modeling: Programs for families of children with oppositional defiant disorder or conduct disorder. In E.D. Hibbs & P. Jensen (Eds.), *Psychosocial treatment research of child and adolescent disorders: Empirically based strategies for clinical practice* (pp. 435–474). Washington, DC: American Psychological Association.

Weist, M.D., Ollendick, T.H., & Finney, J.W. (1991). Toward the empirical validation of treatment targets in children. *Clinical Psychology Review, 11,* 515–538.

Weller, E.S. (Ed.). (1990). Special section: Social validity: Multiple perspectives. *Journal of Applied Behavior Analysis, 24,* 179–249.

Wells, J.K., Howard, G.S., Nowlin, W.F., & Vargas, M.J. (1986). Presurgical anxiety and postsurgical pain and adjustment: Effects of a stress inoculation procedure. *Journal of Consulting and Clinical Psychology, 54,* 831–835.

Wheelan, C.J. (1998, December 20). To get an organ, offer to give one. *Wall Street Journal,* Vol. CCXXXII, No. 126, A12.

White, M.A. (1975). Natural rates of teacher approval and disapproval in the classroom. *Journal of Applied Behavior Analysis, 8,* 367–372.

Wierzbicki, M., & Pekarik, G. (1993). A meta-analysis of psychotherapy dropout. *Professional Psychology: Research and Practice, 24,* 190–195.

Williams, C.D. (1959). The elimination of tantrum behaviors by extinction procedures. *Journal of Abnormal and Social Psychology, 59,* 269.

Williamson, D.A., Williamson, S.A., Watkins, P.C., & Hughes, H.H. (1992). Increasing cooperation among children using dependent group-oriented reinforcement contingencies. *Behavior Modification, 16,* 414–425.

Wilson, D.D., Robertson, S.J., Herlong, L.H., & Haynes, S.N. (1979). Vicarious effects of time out in the modification of aggression in the classroom. *Behavior Modification, 3,* 97–111.

Winett, R.A., & Winkler, R.C. (1972). Current behavior modification in the classroom: Be still, be quiet, be docile. *Journal of Applied Behavior Analysis, 5,* 499–504.

Winkler, R.C. (1977). What types of sex role behavior should behavior modifiers promote? *Journal of Applied Behavior Analysis, 10,* 549–552.

Wolf, M.M. (1978). Social validity: The case for subjective measurement, or how applied behavior analysis is finding its heart. *Journal of Applied Behavior Analysis, 11,* 203–214.

Wolfe, D.A. (1999). *Child abuse* (2nd ed.). Newbury Park, CA: Sage.

Wolpe, J. (1958). *Psychotherapy by reciprocal inhibition.* Stanford: Stanford University Press.

Wong, S.E., Terranova, M.D., Bowen, L., Zarate, R., Massey H.K., & Liberman, R.P. (1987). Providing independent recreational activities to reduce stereotypic vocalizations in chronic schizophrenics. *Journal of Applied Behavior Analysis, 20,* 77–82.

Woolfolk, A.E., Woolfolk, R.L., & Wilson, G.T. (1977). A rose by another name...: Labeling bias and attitudes toward behavior modification. *Journal of Consulting and Clinical Psychology, 45,* 184–191.

Wright, D.G., Brown, R.A., & Andrews, M.E. (1978). Remission of chronic ruminative vomiting through a reversal of social contingencies. *Behaviour Research and Therapy, 16,* 134–136.

Wright, K.M., & Miltenberger, R.G. (1987). Awareness training in the treatment of head and facial tics. *Journal of Behavior Therapy and Experimental Psychiatry, 18,* 269–274.

Wyatt v. Stickney, 344 F. Supp. 373, 344 F. Supp. 387 (M.D.AlA.1972); affirmed sub nom. *Wyatt v. Aderholt,* 503 F.2d 1305 (5th Cir. 1974).

Zanolli, K., Daggett, J., & Adams, T. (1996). Teaching preschool age autistic children to make spontaneous initiations to peers using priming. *Journal of Autism and Developmental Disabilities, 26,* 407–422.

Zeiss, R.A. (1978). Self-directed treatment for premature ejaculation. *Journal of Consulting and Clinical Psychology, 46,* 1234–1241.

Author Index

Subject Index

Credits

Chapter One: Figure 1–1: From Ayllon, T., & Haughton, E., Modification of symptomatic verbal behaviour of mental patients, *Behaviour Research and Therapy, 2,* 87–97, Copyright 1964. Reprinted with permission from Elsevier Science and the author.

Chapter Three: Table 3–3: From O'Reilly, M. R., Green, G., & Braunling-McMorrow, D. (1990). Self-administered written prompts to teach home accident prevention skills to adults with brain injuries. *Journal of Applied Behavior Analysis, 23,* 431–446. Copyright 1990 by the Society for the Experimental Analysis of Behavior, Inc. Reprinted with permission; **Table 3–4:** From Friman, P. C., Finney, J. W., Glasscock, S. G., Weigel, J. W., & Christophersen, E. R. (1986). Testicular self-examination: Validation of a training strategy for early cancer detection. *Journal of Applied Behavior Analysis, 19,* 87–92. Copyright 1986 by the Society for the Experimental Analysis of Behavior, Inc. Reprinted with permission.

Chapter Four: Figure 4–1: From R. E. O'Neill, R. H. Horner, R. W. Albin, K. Storey, & J. R. Sprague, *Functional Analysis of Problem Behavior: A Practical Assessment Guide,* p. 33. Copyright 1990 by Sycamore Publishing Company. Reprinted by permission of Wadsworth/Thompson Learning; **Figure 4–2:** From Repp, A. C., Felce, D., Barton, L. E. (1988). Basing the treatment of stereotypic and self-injurious behaviors on hypotheses of their causes. *Journal of Applied Behavior Analysis, 21,* 281–289. Copyright 1988 by the Society for the Experimental Analysis of Behavior. Reprinted with permission; **Figure 4–3:** From Watson, T. S., & Sterling, H. E. (1998). Brief functional analysis and treatment of a vocal tic. *Journal of Applied Behavior Analysis, 31,* 471–474. Copyright 1998 by the Society for the Experimental Analysis of Behavior, Inc. Reprinted with permission.

Chapter Five: Figure 5–5: From Murphy, H. A., Hutchinson, J. M., & Bailey, J. S. (1983). Behavioral school psychology goes outdoors: The effect of organized games on playground aggression. *Journal of Applied Behavior Analysis, 16,* 29–35. Copyright 1983 by the Society for the Experimental Analysis of Behavior, Inc. Reprinted with permission; **Figure 5–6:** From Ronen, T., Intervention package for treating sleep disorders in a four-year old girl, *Journal of Behavior Therapy and Experimental Psychiatry, 22,* 141–148, Copyright 1991. Reprinted with permission from Elsevier Science and the author; **Figure 5–7:** From De Vries, J. E.,

Burnette, M. M., & Redmon, W. K. (1991). AIDS prevention: Improving nurses' compliance with glove wearing through performance feedback. *Journal of Applied Analysis, 24,* 705–711. Copyright 1991 by the Society for the Experimental Analysis of Behavior, Inc. Reprinted with permission; **Figure 5–8:** From DeLuca, R. V., & Holborn, S. W. (1992). Effects of a variable-ratio reinforcement schedule with changing criteria on exercise in obese and non-obese boys. *Journal of Applied Behavior Analysis, 25,* 671–679. Copyright 1992 by the Society for the Experimental Analysis of Behavior, Inc. Reprinted with permission; **Figure 5–9:** From Ladouceur, R., Freeston, M. H., Gagnon, F., Thibodeau, N., & Dumont, J. (1993). Idiographic considerations in the behavioral treatment of obsessional thoughts. *Journal of Behavior Therapy and Experimental Psychiatry, 24,* 301–310. Copyright 1993. Reprinted with permission of Elsevier Science and the author; **Figure 5–10:** From Burling, T. A., Bigelow, G. E., Robinson, J. C., and Mead, A. M. (1991). Smoking during pregnancy: Reduction via objective assessment and directive advice. *Behavior Therapy, 22,* 31–40. Copyright 1991 by the Association for Advancement of Behavior Therapy. Reprinted by permission; **Figure 5–11:** From Azrin, N. H., and Peterson, A. L. (1990). Treatment of Tourette Syndrome by habit reversal. *Behavior Therapy, 21,* 305–318. Copyright 1990 by the Association for Advancement of Behavior Therapy. Reprinted with permission.

Chapter Six: Figure 6–1: From Kirby, F. D., & Shields, F. (1972). Modification of arithmetic response rate and attending behavior in a seventh-grade student. *Journal of Applied Behavior Analysis, 5,* 79–84. Copyright 1972 by the Society for the Experimental Analysis of Behavior, Inc. Reprinted with permission; **Figure 6–2:** From Lombard, D., Neubauer, T. E., Canfield, D., & Winett, R. A. (1991). Behavioral community intervention to reduce the risk of skin cancer. *Journal of Applied Behavior Analysis, 24,* 677–686. Copyright 1991 by the Society for the Experimental Analysis of Behavior, Inc. Reprinted with permission; **Figure 6–3:** From Budney, A. J., Higgins, S. T., Delaney, D. D., Kent, L., & Bickel, W. K. (1991). Contingent reinforcement of abstinence with individuals abusing cocaine and marijuana. *Journal of Applied Behavior Analysis, 24,* 657–665. Copyright 1991 by the Society for the Experimental Analysis of Behavior, Inc. Reprinted with permission; **Figure 6–4:** From Fox D. K., Hopkins, B. L., & Anger, W. K. (1987). The long-term effects of a token economy on safety performance in open-pit mining. *Journal of Applied Behavior Analysis, 20,* 215–224. Copyright 1987 by the Society for the Experimental Analysis of Behavior, Inc. Reprinted with permission; **Figure 6–6:** From Donnelly, D. R., & Olczak, P. V. (1990). The effect of differential reinforcement of incompatible behaviors (DRI) on pica for cigarettes in persons with intellectual disability. *Behavior Modification, 14,* 81–96. Copyright 1990. Reprinted by permission of Sage Publication; **Figure 6–7:** From Deitz, S. M., An analysis of programming DRL schedules in educational settings, *Behaviour Research and Therapy, 15,* 103–111, Copyright 1977. Reprinted with permission from Elsevier Science; **Figure 6–8:** From Allen, K. D., Loiben, T., Allen, S. J., & Stanley, R. T. (1992). Dentist-implemented contingent escape for management of disruptive child behavior. *Journal of Applied Behavior Analysis, 25,* 629–636. Copyright 1992 by the Society for the Experimental Analysis of Behavior, Inc. Reprinted with permission.

Chapter Seven: Figure 7–1: From Mansdorf, I. J., Reinforcer isolation: An alternative to subject isolation in time out from positive reinforcement, *Journal of Behavior Therapy and Experimental Psychiatry, 8,* 391–393, Copyright 1977. Reprinted with permission from Elsevier Science; **Figure 7–2:** From Reynolds, L. K., & Kelley, M. L. (1997). The efficacy of a response cost treatment package for managing aggressive behavior in preschoolers. *Behavior Modification, 21,* 216–230. Copyright 1997. Reprinted with permission from Sage Publications; **Figure 7–3:** From Azrin, N. H., & Wesolowski, M. D. (1974). Theft reversal: An overcorrection procedure for eliminating stealing by retarded persons. *Journal of Applied Behavior Analysis, 7,* 577–581. Copyright 1974 by the Society for the Experimental Analysis of Behavior, Inc. Reprinted with permission; **Figure 7–4:** From Luce, S. C., Delquadri, J., & Hall, R. V. (1980). Contingent exercise: A mild but powerful procedure for suppressing inappropriate verbal and aggressive behavior. *Journal of Applied Behavior Analysis, 13,* 583–594. Copyright 1980 by the Society for the Experimental Analysis of Behavior, Inc. Reprinted with permission.

Chapter Eight: Figure 8–1: From Neisworth, J. T., & Moore, F. (1972). Operant treatment of asthmatic responding with the parent as therapist. *Behavior Therapy, 3,* 95–99. Copyright 1972 by Academic Press, reproduced by permission of the publisher; **Figure 8–2:** From France, K. G., & Hudson, S. M. (1990). Behavior management of infant sleep disturbance. *Journal of Applied Behavior Analysis, 23,* 91–98. Copyright

1990 by the Society for the Experimental Analysis of Behavior, Inc. Reprinted with permission; **Figure 8–3:** From Pinkston, E. M., Reese, N. M., LeBlanc, J. M., & Baer, D. M. (1973). Independent control of a preschool child's aggression and peer interaction by contingent teacher attention. *Journal of Applied Behavior Analysis, 6,* 115–124. Copyright 1973 by the Society for the Experimental Analysis of Behavior, Inc. Reprinted with permission; **Figure 8–4:** From Liberman, R. P., Teigen, J., Patterson, R., & Baker, V. (1973). Reducing delusional speech in chronic, paranoid schizophrenics. *Journal of Applied Behavior Analysis, 6,* 57–64. Copyright 1973 by the Society for the Experimental Analysis of Behavior, Inc. Reprinted with permission.

Chapter Nine: Figure 9–1: From Mathews, R. M., & Dix, M. (1992). Behavior change in the funny papers: Feedback to cartoonists on safety belt use. *Journal of Applied Behavior Analysis, 25,* 769–775. Copyright 1992 by the Society for the Experimental Analysis of Behavior, Inc. Reprinted with permission; **Figure 9–2:** From Miller, D. L., & Kelley, M. L. (1994). The use of goal-setting and contingency contracting for improving children's homework behavior. *Journal of Applied Behavior Analysis, 27,* 73–84. Copyright 1994 by the Society for the Experimental Analysis of Behavior, Inc. Reprinted with permission; **Figure 9–3:** From Miller, D. L., & Kelley, M. L. (1994). The use of goal-setting and contingency contracting for improving children's homework behavior. *Journal of Applied Behavior Analysis, 27,* 73–84. Copyright 1994 by the Society for the Experimental Analysis of Behavior, Inc. Reprinted with permission; **Figure 9–4:** From Switzer, E. B., Deal, T. E., & Bailey, J. S. (1977). The reduction of stealing in second graders using a group contingency. *Journal of Applied Behavior Analysis, 10,* 267–272. Copyright 1994 by the Society for the Experimental Analysis of Behavior. Reprinted with permission; **Figure 9–5:** From Swain, J. J., Allard, G. B., & Holborn, S. W. (1982). The good toothbrushing game: A school-based dental hygiene program for increasing the toothbrushing effectiveness of children. *Journal of Applied Behavior Analysis, 15,* 171–176. Copyright 1982 by the Society for the Experimental Behavior Analysis, inc. Reprinted with permission; **Figure 9–6:** From Feingold, L., & Migler, B. (1972). The use of experimental dependency relationships as a motivating procedure on a token–economy ward. In R. D. Rubin, H. Fensterheim, J. D. Henderson, & L. P. Ullmann (Eds.), *Advances in behavior therapy.* Copyright 1972 by Academic Press, reproduced by permission of the publisher; **Figure 9–7:** From James, S. D., & Egel, A. L. (1986). A direct prompting strategy for increasing reciprocal interactions between handicapped and nonhandicapped siblings. *Journal of Applied Behavior Analysis, 19,* 173–186. Copyright 1986 by the Society for the Experimental Analysis of Behavior, Inc. Reprinted with permission.

Chapter Ten: Table 10–1: From Bootzin, R. R., Epstein, D., & Wood, J. M. (1991). Stimulus control instructions. In P. J. Hauri (Ed.). *Case studies in insomnia.* Copyright 1991. Reprinted with permission from Plenum; **Figure 10–1:** From *Journal of Behavior Therapy and Experimental Psychiatry, 21,* Nakano, K., Operant self-control procedure in modifying Type A behavior, 249–255, Copyright 1990. Reprinted with permission from Elsevier Science; **Figure 10–2:** From Belles, D., & Bradlyn, A. S., The use of the changing criterion design in achieving controlled smoking in a heavy smoker: A controlled case study, *Journal of Behavior Therapy and Experimental Psychiatry, 18,* 77–82, Copyright 1987. Reprinted with permission from Elsevier Science; **Figure 10–3:** From Gutkin, A. J., Holborn, S. W., Walker, J. R., & Anderson, B. A., Treatment integrity of relaxation training for tension headaches, *Journal of Behavior Therapy and Experimental Psychiatry, 23,* 191–198, Copyright 1992. Reprinted with permission from Elsevier Science; **Figure 10–4:** From Varni, J. W. (1981). Self-regulation techniques in the management of chronic arthritic pain in hemophilia. *Behavior Therapy, 12,* 185–194. Copyright 1987 by the Association for Advancement of Behavior Therapy. Reprinted with permission; **Figure 10–5:** From McMahon, R. J., & Forehand, R. (1978). Nonprescription behavior therapy: Effectiveness of a brochure in teaching mothers to correct their children's inappropriate mealtime behaviors. *Behavior Therapy, 9,* 814–820. Copyright 1978 by Academic Press, reproduced by permission of the publisher; **Table 10–3:** From the University of Illinois at Urbana-Champaign and from the Web site (www.odos.uiuc.edu/Counseling_Center). Used with permission.

Chapter Eleven: Figure 11–1: From Bernard, M. E., Kratochwill, T. R., & Keefauver, L. W. (1983). The effects of rational-emotive-therapy and self-instruction training on chronic hair-pulling. *Cognitive Therapy and Research, 7,* 273–280. Copyright 1983. Reprinted with permission from Plenum; **Figure 11–2:** From Chadwick, P., & Trower, P. (1996). Cognitive therapy for punishment paranoia: A single-case experiment. *Journal of Behavior Therapy and Experimental Psychiatry, 34,* 351–356. Copyright 1996. Reprinted with

TO THE OWNER OF THIS BOOK:

I hope that you have found *Behavior Modification in Applied Settings, Sixth Edition,* useful. So that this book can be improved in a future edition, would you take the time to complete this sheet and return it? Thank you.

School and address: _____

_____

Department: _____

Instructor's name: _____

1. What I like most about this book is:_____

_____

_____

2. What I like least about this book is: _____

_____

_____

3. My general reaction to this book is: _____

_____

_____

4. The name of the course in which I used this book is: _____

_____

5. Were all of the chapters of the book assigned for you to read? _____

    If not, which ones weren't? _____

6. In the space below, or on a separate sheet of paper, please write specific suggestions for improving this book and anything else you'd care to share about your experience in using this book.

_____

_____

OPTIONAL:

Your name: _____ Date: _____

May Wadsworth quote you, either in promotion for *Behavior Modification in Applied Settings, Sixth Edition,* or in future publishing ventures?

Yes: _____ No: _____

Sincerely yours,

Alan E. Kazdin

'011

7

FOLD HERE

- -

NO POSTAGE
NECESSARY
IF MAILED
IN THE
UNITED STATES

BUSINESS REPLY MAIL
FIRST CLASS   PERMIT NO. 34   BELMONT, CA

POSTAGE WILL BE PAID BY ADDRESSEE

ATTN: *Alan E. Kazdin*

WADSWORTH/THOMSON LEARNING
10 DAVIS DRIVE
BELMONT, CA   94002-9801

FOLD HERE